Reassessing the Aztatlán World

Reassessing the Aztatlán World

Ethnogenesis and Cultural Continuity in Northwest Mesoamerica

Edited by
Michael D. Mathiowetz and John M. D. Pohl

THE UNIVERSITY OF UTAH PRESS
Salt Lake City

Copyright © 2025 by The University of Utah Press. All rights reserved.

 The Defiance House Man colophon is a registered trademark of the University of Utah Press. It is based on a four-foot-tall Ancient Puebloan pictograph (late PIII) near Glen Canyon, Utah.

LIBRARY OF CONGRESS CATALOGING-IN-PUBLICATION DATA

Names: Mathiowetz, Michael D., editor. | Pohl, John M. D., editor.
Title: Reassessing the Aztatlán world : ethnogenesis and cultural continuity in Northwest Mesoamerica / edited by Michael D. Mathiowetz and John M. D. Pohl.
Description: Salt Lake City : The University of Utah Press, [2025] | Includes bibliographical references and index.
Identifiers: LCCN 2023049016 | ISBN 9781647691493 (cloth) | ISBN 9781647691509 (ebook)
Subjects: LCSH: Ethnology—Mexico. | Ethnology—Central America. | Indians of Mexico—Antiquities. | Indians of Central America—Antiquities. | Excavations (Archaeology)—Mexico. | Excavations (Archaeology)—Central America. | Interdisciplinary research—Case studies. | Mexico—Antiquities. | Central America—Antiquities.
Classification: LCC F1219 .R298 2024 | DDC 305.897/072—dc23/eng/20231213
LC record available at https://lccn.loc.gov/2023049016

Cover credits:
Group of Wixárika (Huichol) *jicareros* or "gourd-people" from Keuruwit+a on their pilgrimage to Wirikuta. Photograph taken by Johannes Neurath in 2008 during a protest against the destruction of one of the sacred sites on the route from Keuruwit+a to Wirikuta.

Iguanas Polychrome (AD 1100–1350+) jar from coastal southern Sinaloa or northern Nayarit with narrative codex-style scenes of high-status individuals or deities engaged in political-religious activities. Catalog number M.2000.86, Los Angeles County Museum of Art. Public domain.

This volume is dedicated to the Indigenous people
of the Gran Nayar region and broader northwest Mesoamerica

In memory of David R. Wilcox (1944–2022),
a consummate scholar of the U.S. Southwest and northwest Mexico.

David R. Wilcox, standing in a ballcourt in Arizona at the Hohokam
site of Tres Alamos in 1997, demonstrates the use of stone paddles
possibly used during the ballgame. Photo by Henry D. Wallace.

Editors' Note: As this volume went to press, we learned of the unfortunate passing
of John P. Carpenter (1957–2024), a contributor to our volume. Carpenter was a giant of
Northwest/Southwest and west Mexican archaeology. Like Wilcox, John conducted
multidisciplinary research at grand scales of time and space, weaving together data from
archaeology, ethnohistory, ethnology, linguistics, and other fields.
In this volume, we honor his friendship, his vision, his work, and his legacy.

Contents

List of Figures ... ix
List of Tables ... xi
Preface ... xiii

Introduction. Integrated Approaches to the Aztatlán Tradition: History, Scale, and New Directions ... 1
JOHN M. D. POHL and MICHAEL D. MATHIOWETZ

Part I. What is Aztatlán? A Historical Perspective

1. The Current Status of the Aztatlán Phenomenon in Far Western Mexico: What? Where? and When? ... 41
JOSEPH B. MOUNTJOY

Part II. Local and Regional Viewpoints: Aztatlán Sociopolitical Organization and Complexity from Continental to Local Scales

2. Coast-to-Coast: Evidence for Aztatlán Articulation in Supraregional Interaction Networks ... 61
LAURA SOLAR VALVERDE
3. Ritual Objects as Cultural Capital: A Comparison between the Mixtec-Zapotec, Aztatlán, and Casas Grandes Cultural Co-traditions ... 71
JOHN M. D. POHL
4. Social Organization in the Aztatlán Tradition (AD 850–1350): The Sayula and Chapala Basins (Jalisco), a Case Study ... 83
SUSANA RAMÍREZ URREA
5. San Felipe Aztatán: An Aztatlán Political and Ceremonial Center in the Lower Basin of the Río Acaponeta, Nayarit ... 97
MAURICIO GARDUÑO AMBRIZ
6. Not All that Glitters Is Aztatlán Ceramics: The Development of Complex Societies in Southern Sinaloa ... 111
LUIS ALFONSO GRAVE TIRADO
7. Was There a Coastal Colony in the Western Valleys of Durango? Notes on Aztatlán-Chalchihuites Interaction ... 124
CINTHYA ISABEL VIDAL ALDANA
8. Interaction and Integration on the Northern Aztatlán Frontier in Sinaloa ... 139
JOHN P. CARPENTER and GUADALUPE SÁNCHEZ
9. Selective Influence of West Mexico Cultural Traditions in the Ónavas Valley, Sonora, Mexico ... 152
CRISTINA GARCÍA MORENO, JAMES T. WATSON, and DANIELLE PHELPS

Part III. Technologies, Economies, and Trade in the Aztatlán Region and Beyond

10. Obsidian Usage and Trade in Postclassic West Mexico ... 167
DANIEL E. PIERCE
11. A Spatial and Temporal Comparative Analysis of Metal Objects from Michoacán to the Greater Southwest ... 180
JOSÉ LUIS PUNZO DÍAZ and LISSANDRA GONZÁLEZ

Part IV. Aztatlán Religion, Ritual Practice, and Worldview: The Archaeological Past and Continuities in the Ethnographic Present

12. Funerary Practices during the Epiclassic and Postclassic: La Pitayera, Nayarit — 193
    José Carlos Beltrán Medina, María de Lourdes González Barajas, Jorge Arturo Talavera González, *and* Juan Jorge Morales Monroy

13. A World within the World: Portraiture Effigy Bowls and Cargo Systems in Mitote Cycles of the Aztatlán Tradition — 207
    Michael D. Mathiowetz

14. The Flowering World of the Gran Nayar: An Ethnographic Approach for Conceptualizing Political Legitimacy in the Aztatlán World — 227
    Philip E. Coyle

Part V. Concluding Thoughts and New Directions

15. Discussion: The Three Transitions of Aztatlán — 241
    Christopher S. Beekman

References — 253
Contributors — 293
Index — 295

Supplemental digital material is available online at the University of Utah's J. Willard Marriott Digital Library: https://collections.lib.utah.edu/ark:/87278/s6kb9osf.

Figures

I.1. Map of archaeological sites in Mesoamerica, northern Mexico, and the Greater U.S. Southwest. 2
I.2. Map of the Aztatlán coastal core zone and adjoining highlands. 3
I.3. Maps of hypothesized ethnolinguistic subregions around major Aztatlán centers and a regional system organized around Ixtlán del Río, Nayarit. 10
I.4. Highland and lowland Aztatlán architecture and political centers in Nayarit. 11
I.5. Local architecture and terrain along the Pacific coast of west-central Nayarit. 12
I.6. Highland Aztatlán architecture and political centers in Zacatecas and Durango. 13
I.7. Iguanas Polychrome jar with narrative codex-style scene from southern Sinaloa or northern Nayarit. 16
I.8. *Estampa* from 1673 report by Fray Antonio Arias de Saavedra depicting Cora rites and ceremonies at the "House of the Nayarit" at the Mesa del Nayar. 22
I.9. Map of social networks in the Postclassic Mesoamerican world, AD 1150–1450. 26
I.10. Map of social networks of the Aztatlán region and the U.S. Southwest/Northwest Mexico, AD 850/900–1350+. 30
1.1. Regional map of Aztatlán sites. 40
1.2. Pottery stamp and jar with depictions of Xiuhcoatl. 44
1.3. Aztatlán Red-on-buff sherds from the Nahuapa II site, Tomatlán valley, Jalisco. 47
1.4. Incense burners from Ixtapa, Jalisco. 48
1.5. Mazapan figurines from coastal Nayarit and Jalisco. 49
1.6. Codex-style ceramics from Arroyo Piedras Azules, Jalisco, Nayarit. 52
2.1. The Aztatlán Network at the time of its maximum expansion (ca. AD 950–1350). 62
2.2. The Peripheral Coastal Lowlands network. 64
2.3. Items shared by the Eastern and Western Lowlands. 66
2.4. Items shared by the Eastern and Western Lowlands. 68
3.1. Political titles, gift-giving, and alliance rituals in Mixtec codices. 72
3.2. Back shield-mirrors in Mesoamerica and northwest Mexico. 74
3.3. Use of shield-mirrors in Mixtec political rituals. 75
3.4. Nose-piercing rituals and awarding of the *tecuhtli* political title. 78
3.5. Nose and ear ornaments of a Sinagua noble, Ridge Ruin, northern Arizona. 80
3.6. Elite exchange in ritualism and their role in political-economic systems. 82
4.1. Map of western Mexico. 84
4.2. Settlement patterns in the Sayula Basin, Jalisco, during the Late Sayula phase (AD 850–1000/1100). 87
4.3. The site of La Peña, Jalisco. 88
4.4. Scenes from the West Plaza, La Peña, Jalisco. 89
4.5. Aztatlán material culture in Jalisco. 92
4.6. Aztatlán material culture from La Peña, Jalisco. 93
4.7. Proposed polities of the Aztatlán tradition during the Middle Postclassic period. 94
5.1. Location of San Felipe Aztatán and hydrological networks of the Nayarit lowlands. 98
5.2. Location of San Felipe Aztatán and hydrological networks along the Nayarit coast. 98
5.3. Topographic site map of mounds at San Felipe Aztatán, Nayarit. 100
5.4. Central architectural complex at San Felipe Aztatán, Nayarit. 101
5.5. Pre-Aztatlán material culture at San Felipe Aztatán and the Nayarit coastal plain. 102
5.6. Material culture located above the *empedrada adosada* of Mound 6, San Felipe Aztatán, Nayarit. 104
5.7. Stratigraphic profile of Basurero 1 at San Felipe Aztatán, Nayarit. 105
5.8. Aztatlán material culture from San Felipe Aztatán and coastal Nayarit. 106
6.1. Microgeographic zones and archaeological sites in southern Sinaloa and the lower basin of the Río Baluarte. 112
6.2. Distribution of archaeological sites and historic-period Indigenous political provinces in southern Sinaloa. 114
6.3. Sketch maps of archaeological sites in southern Sinaloa. 116

6.4. Archaeological sites in the Escuinapa marshlands in southern Sinaloa. 118
6.5. Ceramics of southern Sinaloa. 120
6.6. Petroglyphs of southern Sinaloa. 121
6.7. Petroglyphs near the Río Baluarte, southern Sinaloa. 122
7.1. Archaeological sites in Durango with presence of Pacific-coastal material culture. 126
7.2. Aztatlán pyriform tripod vessels from Sinaloa and Durango. 127
7.3. Foreign ceramics recovered between 1952–1958 by J. Charles Kelley at La Ferrería, Durango. 128
7.4. Coastal ceramics registered in 1954 by J. Charles Kelly in the Guadiana Valley at Navacoyán, Durango. 129
7.5. Ceramics analyzed by Thin Section Petrography in the Guadiana Valley, Durango, and southern Sinaloa. 130
7.6. Local and coastal ceramic vessels recovered in situ at La Ferrería, Durango. 135
8.1. The Cahita and their neighbors in northwest Mexico. 140
8.2. Archaeological sites in northern Sinaloa and southern Sonora. 144
8.3. Aztatlán polychrome plates from Mochicahui, Sinaloa. 146
8.4. Distribution of funerary mounds in southern Sonora and northern Sinaloa. 147
8.5. Foreign ceramics in Buyubampo and La Viuda, Sinaloa. 148
8.6. Objects from Buyubampo and La Viuda, Sinaloa. 149
9.1. Map of the site of El Cementerio, Sonora. 153
9.2. Material culture from El Cementerio, Sonora. 154
9.3. Burial intrusion and superposition within the burial mound at El Cementerio. 156
9.4. Bar graph of the age and sex distribution of the El Cementerio skeletal sample. 157
9.5. Tabular oblique cranial modification from El Cementerio, Sonora. 158
9.6. Forms of dental modification observed in the El Cementerio skeletal sample. 159
9.7. Cluster and outlier analysis (Local Moran's I) for the inhumations at El Cementerio, Sonora. 161
10.1. Map of Aztatlán sites and regional obsidian sources. 168
10.2. Site map of Zone II at Coamiles, Nayarit. 171
10.3. Spatial distribution of Coamiles obsidian by source. 172
10.4. Site map and four zones at Chacalilla, Nayarit. 174
10.5. Distribution of obsidian sources by site. 176
10.6. Obsidian source at Volcán las Navajas, Nayarit. 177
11.1. Bell distribution in Tarascan and southeastern Aztatlán regions. 181
11.2. Map of archaeological sites in the Tarascan and southeastern Aztatlán regions. 182
11.3. Copper ornaments and sprue from Paquimé, Chihuahua. 184
11.4. Tlaloc bell types in west Mexico. 185
11.5. Diverse metal objects in west Mexico. 186
12.1. Overview of cemetery and cists at La Pitayera, Nayarit. 194
12.2. Plan view of cist groups in the cemetery at La Pitayera, Nayarit. 197
12.3. Set of cists in the cemetery at La Pitayera, Nayarit. 198
12.4. Exposed architectural components of main structure at Mound 7, La Pitayera, Nayarit. 199
12.5. Mazapan figurines in situ at La Pitayera, Nayarit. 202
12.6. Burials in flexed position on the ground adjacent to cist at La Pitayera, Nayarit. 204
13.1. Map of the U.S. Southwest, northwest Mexico, and west Mexico with the distribution of Aztatlán portraiture vessels. 208
13.2. Solar symbolism in the Aztatlán region. 210
13.3. Venus as Morning Star and god bowls. 211
13.4. The feathered serpent, wind god Ehecatl, and god bowls. 213
13.5. Site map of Amapa, Nayarit. 216
13.6. Aztatlán portraiture vessels. 217
13.7. Aztatlán cargo-system material culture and Wixárika "god house" (*xiriki*). 222
13.8. Aztatlán carved-stone *teparite* probably used in god houses. 223
14.1. Regional map of the Gran Nayar region in relation to archaeological sites. 228
14.2. Undecorated *tepextle* altar at Santa Teresa, Nayarit. 229
14.3. Undecorated *cháanaka* pole in church at Santa Teresa, Nayarit. 230
14.4. The *cháanaka* wheel at Santa Teresa, Nayarit. 231
14.5. Cora *watsiku* ceremonial offering. 232
14.6. Gourd bowl used in Cicada Ceremony near Santa Teresa, Nayarit. 234
15.1. Aztatlán material culture reported in 1845 near Santiago Ixcuintla, Nayarit. 242

Tables

I.1. Chronological sequences of cultural traditions and archaeological sites in Mesoamerica, northwest Mexico, and the U.S. Southwest.   4
1.1. Radiocarbon dates for Aztatlán deposits.   55
7.1. Provenance of Aztatlán ceramics in southern Sinaloa and Durango.   132
7.2. Manufacturing technologies of Aztatlán ceramics.   134
8.1. Ceramic types at La Viuda and Buyubampo, Sinaloa.   149
9.1. Frequency of associated funerary objects in sample, El Cementerio, Sonora.   156
9.2. Distribution of cranial and dental modification in sample, El Cementerio, Sonora.   158
9.3. Results of spatial analyses, El Cementerio, Sonora.   161
12.1. Burial and offering data from cemetery at La Pitayera, Nayarit.   200

Preface

Reassessing the Aztatlán World: Ethnogenesis and Cultural Continuity in Northwest Mesoamerica has its origin in a session organized by the editors in 2014 at the 79th Annual Meeting of the Society for American Archaeology held in Austin, Texas. Most of the volume's authors presented the work that became their chapters with the exception of Joseph Mountjoy and Christopher Beekman who were invited to join the volume after the session. Two participants, Paul Liffman and Peter Jiménez, ultimately did not contribute their presentations to the volume, but we thank them for their role in making the session a success. The contributing authors comprise many of the main Aztatlán scholars—both senior and junior—working across the region today. However, we extend gratitude and recognition to others—past and present—whose work in the region has contributed knowledge of Aztatlán, pre-Aztatlán, and broader west Mexican archaeology.

This volume honors the memory of David R. Wilcox, a scholar whose far-ranging research on the archaeology of the U.S. Southwest and northwest Mexico has left a lasting imprint on the field (Doyel 2022). Readers of this volume should recognize that many avenues of research that Wilcox pursued echo throughout the chapters, including topics as diverse as the Mesoamerican ballgame, Indigenous ethnogenesis, language distribution and corridors of interaction, and the nature of connectivity between Mesoamerican, U.S. Southwestern, and northwest Mexican societies, among many other themes that crosscut the Chacoan, Hohokam, Puebloan, and Mogollon worlds (Gregory and Wilcox 2007; Scarborough and Wilcox 1991; Wilcox 1986a, 1986b, 1991, 2000; Wilcox and Sternberg 1983; Wilcox et al. 2008). Wilcox was the original discussant for the 2014 Society for American Archaeology session that served as the basis for this volume. While Dave ultimately did not contribute a chapter, his comments were insightful and, recognizing the importance of the session, he quickly encouraged the editors and authors to further develop the papers and publish them as an edited volume.

We sincerely thank Reba Rauch, the Utah Press acquisitions editor whose enduring patience, guidance, and encouragement during the editorial process helped to keep the volume on track. Justin Bracken, the current acquisitions editor, provided helpful assistance in the final stages of the volume's completion. Special thank you to Will Russell for composing the maps in the Introduction chapter and Daniel Pierce for redrawing site maps. We also would like to thank Amy Davidhizar for copyediting the volume. We are grateful to the authors for their patience during the long editorial process and back-and-forth dialogue that was necessary to ensure that the text, bibliography, and figures were fine-tuned for accuracy and clarity. Finally, two reviewers offered helpful critiques that improved the volume.

Broader Themes of the Volume

This volume follows on the heels of a few key works recently published on the Aztatlán tradition both in English (Foster, ed. 2017; Jiménez 2020) and in Spanish (Solar Valverde and Nelson 2019). The present tome is distinguished as the first English-language edited volume to synthesize the most current viewpoints on the nature and variability of populations who contributed to the Aztatlán phenomenon in Nayarit, Sinaloa, Jalisco, Sonora, Durango, Zacatecas, and Michoacán, their relation with cultures in adjoining regions, and their integration into continental-scale social networks of more far-flung locales. Unfortunately, until the last two decades or so, the Aztatlán tradition had received comparatively little attention than the more well-studied Puebloan, Hohokam, and Mogollon cultures to the north and the highland and southern Mesoamerican cultures to the southeast partly because of misperceptions of west Mexico as being peripheral to—or betwixt and between—these more well-known cultural traditions and areas (Englehardt et al. 2020; Hers 2013; Williams 2020). A significant portion of research on the Aztatlán region over the past few decades is found in "gray literature," primarily in Spanish-language *informes* derived from salvage projects sponsored by the Instituto Nacional de Antropología e Historia. This situation has further led to a paucity of accessible literature, particularly for scholars north of the border who often are reliant on English-language publications for insights on the regional archaeology. As such, this volume provides data and interpretations that will fill some of the large gaps in knowledge of this critical region.

Apart from each chapter's consideration of local dynamics, cultural formations, regional interaction networks, and change in areas that formed part of the Aztatlán tradition, the volume as a whole relates to two broad concerns. First, we examine the development of Aztatlán societies within current conceptions of "Big Picture" dynamics at the continental-scale ranging from the U.S. Southwest and northern Mexico and to the south and east in highland central and southern Mesoamerica, Lower Central America, and the Gulf Coast. Second, we focus on how Aztatlán relates to historical processes of ethnogenesis and cultural continuities among Indigenous people of the Gran Nayar region of west Mexico who exist amidst an ongoing struggle for autonomy, self-determination, and cultural preservation.

In addressing these themes, we hope that this volume clarifies the character of local dynamics among the various ethnic groups that comprised the Aztatlán tradition, the nature of its extensive continental-scale networks, the critical role Aztatlán plays in the Mesoamerica-U.S. Southwest interaction debate, and the importance of Aztatlán in historical processes of ethnogenesis and identity formation for Indigenous people of the Gran Nayar region and broader northwest Mesoamerica. One of our goals with this volume is to lay a solid foundation for the study of Aztatlán in the immediate future including the multiple avenues of research that branch outward at great distances to the north, east, and south to include other societies with whom Aztatlán people interacted. By emphasizing the point that there is clear historical continuity between late-prehispanic Aztatlán people and their descendants in the Gran Nayar region and broader northwest Mesoamerica including the Wixárika (Huichol), Náayeri (Cora), O'dam (Tepehuan), Náhuat (Mexicanero), and Caxcans (Caz' Ahmo), we see great potential for this volume to contribute towards more collaborative agendas in the future in which archaeologists work together with and for the benefit of Indigenous people of these regions. Native people today continue to make meaningful the sacred landscape of the former Aztatlán region through ritual action, pilgrimage, and ritual deposition in order to recreate the world anew, much as did their ancestors before them. Much work remains to be accomplished in Aztatlán studies, and we heed the encouragement of David Wilcox (personal communication, 2011) who was so fond of saying: "Onward!"

INTRODUCTION

Integrated Approaches to the Aztatlán Tradition

History, Scale, and New Directions

John M. D. Pohl and Michael D. Mathiowetz

SECTION I. THE AZTATLÁN PHENOMENON IN NORTHWEST MESOAMERICA

This volume presents a spectrum of interdisciplinary research on the Aztatlán tradition of west Mexico (Figures I.1, I.2). It combines innovations in archaeological methods together with historical and ethnographic studies that are leading to significant revelations about west Mexico's critical role in over a millennium of cultural interaction between societies in northwest and northeast Mexico, the Greater U.S. Southwest, Mesoamerica, Lower Central America, and beyond. We divide our work into five parts starting in Part I with Joseph Mountjoy's historiography of past research to define Aztatlán as a cultural phenomenon together with a set of chapters in Parts II and III examining its geographical extent and evidence for the systems of exchange that functioned within it. We follow in Part IV with more focused studies of social, political, and religious ideology reflected in funerary patterns together with associated painted or engraved artifacts emblematizing a system of shared ideological values. Chapters in Part IV conclude with insights into the fundamental meaning of those values as they continue to be preserved in the ritual practices of the Indigenous descendants of the Aztatlán tradition today. Finally, we invited Christopher Beekman to comment on the chapters in Part V from the perspective of a specialist in historiography and archaeological materialism with his unique appreciation for evaluating Aztatlán cultural developments in light of over three millennia of civilizational development across west Mexico.

Part I. What is Aztatlán?
A Historical Perspective

Joseph Mountjoy (Chapter 1) poses a set of questions that have been perennial to identifying Aztatlán as a cultural co-tradition (Levine 1958): what, where, and when? He presents a concise historiography of how Aztatlán has been defined and redefined through successive generations of investigators whose research has been largely directed by these same questions and yet differs in ways that reflect successive developments in North American archaeological methodologies from typological to processual (Willey and Phillips 2001; Willey and Sabloff 1993). His chapter explores the diverse range of architecture, material culture, economies, and available natural resources at sites in various types of terrain along the coastal plain and highlands that—at least in the southern Aztatlán region—appears to have been organized around multiple provinces, as well as broader ethnolinguistic regions documented in the historic period revolving around the major center of Ixtlán del Río, Nayarit (Figures I.3–I.6). For Mountjoy, the essential identification of Aztatlán is still classificatory. In other words, it was and continues to be identified on the ground archaeologically by the presence of specific ceramic forms—especially polychrome or incised wares—together with an associated symbol set that shares much with the Nahua-Mixteca-based international art style and communication system of southern Mexico. Nevertheless, it is clear that despite the introduction of a unifying ritual ideology inherent in this art style, there is a remarkable amount of local variability in methods of manufacture, vessel forms, and preference for ornamentation that have their roots in traditions of artifactual diversity across west Mexico since the Preclassic. There is still much to define before we can determine what the implications are, but it is notable that comparable phenomena are found in other major traditions such as the Moche fineline versus three-dimensional representation in ceramic forms, for example. This was originally thought to be a chronological issue but has since been determined to be social.

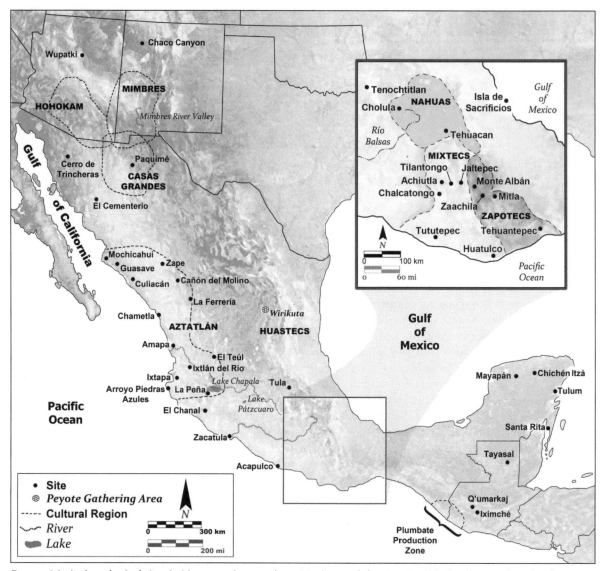

FIGURE I.1. Archaeological sites in Mesoamerica, northern Mexico, and the Greater U.S. Southwest. Drawing by Will Russell.

Part II. Local and Regional Viewpoints: Aztatlán Sociopolitical Organization and Complexity from Continental to Local Scales

In contrast to Mountjoy's focus on Aztatlán as a regional phenomenon, Laura Solar Valverde (Chapter 2) examines how transcultural influences characterizing this cultural co-tradition were transmitted and who transmitted them. The answers are rooted in a reevaluation of the sociopolitical and economic dynamics of greater Mesoamerica emblematic of the Early and Middle Postclassic periods prior to the rise of the Aztec empire. Solar Valverde proposes that much in Aztatlán has more in common with other peripheral areas of Mesoamerica than the "big" societies of the central highlands. She believes the effectiveness of peripheral polity networks is apparent in the shared demand for products but their quality as agents of communication is even more pronounced in conveying ideological principles. Exchanges in goods formed an indivisible set of tools for Indigenous ceremonialism and these were associated with the institutionalization of cult ritualism. John Pohl (Chapter 3) advances Solar Valverde's proposals by demonstrating a close relationship between the Aztatlán *señoríos* and the Nahua, Mixtec, and Zapotec-dominated confederacy of southern Mexico. Calling themselves the Children of Quetzalcoatl, they advocated that the Tolteca-Chichimeca hero or one of his followers had founded their kingdoms following the twelfth-century collapse of Tula. We know that this confederacy was responsible for introducing the Late Postclassic International Style and symbol set. Indeed, there is explicit evidence that ritualism portrayed on

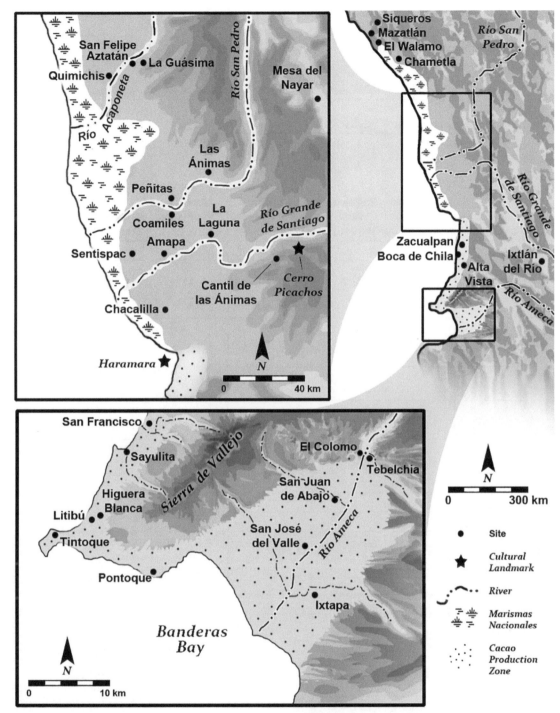

FIGURE I.2. The Aztatlán coastal core zone and adjoining highlands between Mazatlán, Sinaloa, and the Nayarit/Jalisco border at Puerto Vallarta, Jalisco. Archaeological sites indicated in proximity to the Marismas Nacionales and the primary cacao-cultivation zone. Drawing by Will Russell.

some Aztatlán polychrome ceramics is specifically connected with the Mixtec codices. This suggests that interaction between the two cultural co-traditions was conveyed along a Pacific-coastal route in what amounts to the kind of peripheral network that Solar Valverde proposes.

While archaeologists and art historians have tended to look at finely crafted artifacts in precious metals, stones, and shell as prestige goods or artistic masterpieces, Pohl examines how such objects were manipulated in highly ritualized exchanges between political actors in the codices who engage in marriages

TABLE I.1. Chronological sequences in Mesoamerica, northwest Mexico, and the U.S. Southwest. Periods are marked in bold with phases italicized. Less well-defined date ranges or overlaps are indicated in parentheses. Chichén Itzá is defined by its ceramic complexes. Table by Daniel Pierce and Michael Mathiowetz.

Date	Durango	Sinaloa			Nayarit	Jalisco
	Guadiana Valley	Chametla	Culiacán	Guasave	Amapa	Sayula Basin
	(Punzo Díaz 2019)	(Kelley and Winters 1960)	(Kelley and Winters 1960)	(Álvarez 1990; Carpenter 1996)	(Garduño Ambriz and Pierce 2022)	(Ramírez and Cárdenas 2016; Ramírez Urrea 2019)
1600						
1550						
	Bajikam					
1500			*La Quinta*	**Guasave**	*Santiago*	*Late Amacueca*
1450						
			Yebalito			
1400						
1350						
	Calera				*Ixcuintla/ Taste-Mazatlán*	*Early Amacueca (AD 1000/ 1100–1350)*
1300						
1250						
		El Taste	*La Divisa*			
1200						
1150						
	Tunal	*Acaponeta*	*Acaponeta*			

TABLE I.1. (cont'd.) Chronological sequences in Mesoamerica, northwest Mexico, and the U.S. Southwest.

U.S. Southwest/Northwest Mexico (SW/NW)				San Luis Potosí	Puebla	Oaxaca	Hidalgo	Yucatán
Chaco Canyon	Southwest New Mexico	Northwest Chihuahua	Hohokam	Tamtoc	Cholula	Mixteca Alta	Tula	Chichén Itzá
(Gruner 2019)	(Anyon et al. 2017)	(Minnis and Whalen 2015)	(Wright 2021)	Alarcón and Ahuja (2015)	(Lind 1994; Plunket Nagoda and Uruñuela Ladrón de Guevara 2018)	(Spores 1972)	(Healan et al. 2021)	(Pérez de Heredia Puente 2010)
					Convento		Tesoro	
						Convento		
					Mártir			Chenku/Tases (AD 1250/1300–1550)
						Natividad		
					Tamuín		Palacio	
	Late Post-classic	Cliff	Late Medio	Classic				
						Tecama	Fuego	
Mesa Verde	Early Post-classic	Black Mountain	Early Medio					Kulun/Hocaba (AD 1150/1200–1250/1300)
McElmo				Tamul				
		Late Viejo	Sedentary		Aquiáhuac		Late Tollan	Sotuta-Sotuta (AD 900/920–1100/1150)
Late Bonito	**Mimbres Classic**	Terminal Mimbres						

TABLE I.1. (cont'd.) Chronological sequences in Mesoamerica, northwest Mexico, and the U.S. Southwest.

Date	Durango	Sinaloa			Nayarit	Jalisco
	Guadiana Valley	Chametla	Culiacán	Guasave	Amapa	Sayula Basin
	(Punzo Díaz 2019)	(Kelley and Winters 1960)	(Kelley and Winters 1960)	(Álvarez 1990; Carpenter 1996)	(Garduño Ambriz and Pierce 2022)	(Ramírez and Cárdenas 2016; Ramírez Urrea 2019)
1100					Cerritos (AD 850/900–1100)	
1050						Late Sayula (AD 800/850–1000/1100)
1000	Las Joyas			Huatabampo		
950						
900						
		Lolandis				
850	Ayala					
800						Middle Sayula (AD 600–800/850)
		Baluarte				
750						
					Amapa	
700						
650						
600						

TABLE I.1. (cont'd.) Chronological sequences in Mesoamerica, northwest Mexico, and the U.S. Southwest.

U.S. Southwest/Northwest Mexico (SW/NW)				San Luis Potosí	Puebla	Oaxaca	Hidalgo	Yucatán
Chaco Canyon	Southwest New Mexico	Northwest Chihuahua	Hohokam	Tamtoc	Cholula	Mixteca Alta	Tula	Chichén Itzá
(Gruner 2019)	(Anyon et al. 2017)	(Minnis and Whalen 2015)	(Wright 2021)	(Alarcón and Ahuja 2015)	(Lind 1994; Plunket Nagoda and Uruñuela Ladrón de Guevara 2018)	(Spores 1972)	(Healan et al. 2021)	(Pérez de Heredia Puente 2010)
Classic Bonito								
							Early Tollan	
Early Bonito								
	Late Pithouse	Transitional Mimbres	Early Viejo			Las Flores		
			Colonial					
								Huuntun/Cehpech (AD 830/850–930/950)
	Three Circle			Tanquil	Nextli		Terminal Corral	
White Mound							Late Corral	
								Yabnal/Motul (AD 600(?)–800/830)
	San Francisco		Pioneer					
	Georgetown			Coy				
							Early Corral (AD 400–600/650)	

TABLE I.1. (cont'd.) Chronological sequences in Mesoamerica, northwest Mexico, and the U.S. Southwest.

Date	Durango	Sinaloa			Nayarit	Jalisco
	Guadiana Valley	Chametla	Culiacán	Guasave	Amapa	Sayula Basin
	(Punzo Díaz 2019)	(Kelley and Winters 1960)	(Kelley and Winters 1960)	(Álvarez 1990; Carpenter 1996)	(Garduño Ambriz and Pierce 2022)	(Ramírez and Cárdenas 2016; Ramírez Urrea 2019)
		Tierra del Padre				*Early Sayula (AD 400/450–600)*
550						
500						
					Gavilán	
450						
400						
350						
300						
250						
					Chinesco	
200						
150						
100						
50						
0						
50 BC						
100 BC						
150 BC						
200 BC						

TABLE I.1. (cont'd.) Chronological sequences in Mesoamerica, northwest Mexico, and the U.S. Southwest.

U.S. Southwest/Northwest Mexico (SW/NW)				San Luis Potosí	Puebla	Oaxaca	Hidalgo	Yucatán
Chaco Canyon	Southwest New Mexico	Northwest Chihuahua	Hohokam	Tamtoc	Cholula	Mixteca Alta	Tula	Chichén Itzá
(Gruner 2019)	(Anyon et al. 2017)	(Minnis and Whalen 2015)	(Wright 2021)	Alarcón and Ahuja (2015)	(Lind 1994; Plunket Nagoda and Uruñuela Ladrón de Guevara 2018)	(Spores 1972)	(Healan et al. 2021)	(Pérez de Heredia Puente 2010)
								Cochuah
	Early Pithouse	Plainware						
			Early Ceramic					
								Chingú
							Ramos	
				Tantuán III			Tepeji	
			Early Agricultural					
								Tihosuco

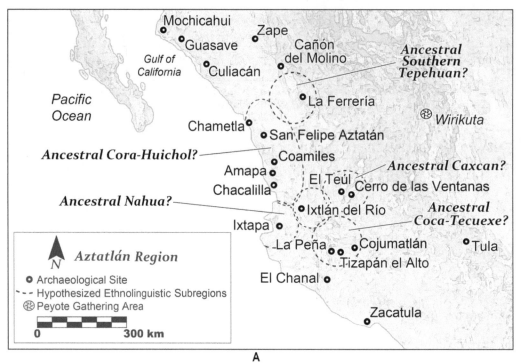

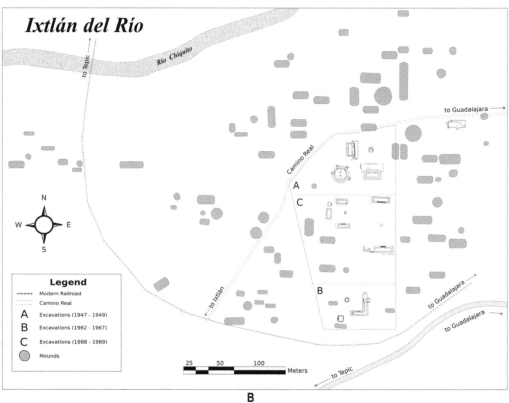

FIGURE 1.3. Maps of hypothesized ethnolinguistic subregions around major Aztatlán centers and/or site clusters and a regional system organized around Ixtlán del Río (Los Toriles). (a) Based upon early-historic data on the distribution of O'dam (southern Tepehuan), Náayeri (Cora), Wixárika (Huichol), Caz' Ahmo (Caxcan), Nahua, Coca, and Tecuexe communities, Mathiowetz (2023a:Figure 5.19) proposes that the southern Aztatlán region was generally structured around these four broad ancestral ethnolinguistic subregions with Ixtlán del Río situated at the intersection. Another undefined sphere may be present in the Autlán-Tuxcacuesco region south of Ixtlán del Río. Drawing by Will Russell. (b) Site map of Ixtlán del Río, Nayarit, with excavated areas at center surrounded by large area of unexcavated structures. Ixtlán del Río may have been a multiethnic coordinating center and neutral gathering place for elites from adjoining subregions (Pohl and Mathiowetz 2022). Individual palace structures and palace groups are oriented around courtyards with round "Temple of Quetzalcoatl" at center of section "A." Drawing by Daniel Pierce after map on file at the Instituto Nacional de Antropología e Historia, Nayarit, that was produced by Gabriela Zepeda in 2000.

FIGURE 1.4. Highland and lowland Aztatlán architecture and political centers in Nayarit. (*a*) Ixtlán del Río, Nayarit. Note masonry palace structures oriented around courtyards and the round "Temple of Quetzalcoatl" (*center right*). View to the south. Photo by Scott Ure. (*b*) Large earthen-mound pyramid at San Juan de Abajo, Nayarit, near modern Puerto Vallarta. View to the southeast. Photo by Michael Mathiowetz.

FIGURE I.5. Local architecture and terrain along the Pacific coast of west-central Nayarit. (*a*) Traditional palm thatch-roofed house with walls comprised of sapling poles (wicker-work style) often plastered with mud. Located in the community of La Palma, Nayarit, around 12 km southeast of San Blas. Note rock alignments that serve as the structure platform or foundation (*cimiento*). (b) Broad and tranquil bay and shore along the southern part of Matanchen Bay, Nayarit. View to the northwest from Aticama. Photos taken in the late 1960s by Joseph Mountjoy.

FIGURE I.6. Highland Aztatlán architecture and political centers in Zacatecas and Durango. (*a*) El Teúl, Zacatecas. Note masonry structures, plaza, stairs, and causeways. View to the southeast toward the Presa del Teúl. Photo by Laura Solar Valverde. (*b*) La Ferrería (Schroeder), Durango. Structure 1 (La Casa de los Dirigentes). View to the west. Photo by Michael Mathiowetz.

and other forms of partnership. In so doing, he shows that ear flares, nose ornaments, and divining mirrors among other objects were associated with ritual titles and appointments to political positions. Therefore, they constitute a form of social capital bonding elites into systems of mutual reciprocity through gift-giving networks. The fact that such objects were manufactured of the same materials in directly comparable forms and share the same iconographic programs testifies to how social-political, economic, and ritual values could be exchanged not only between people in Oaxaca and west Mexico but northern Mexico and the Greater U.S. Southwest as well in the ways that Solar Valverde proposes as an international system.

Solar Valverde is struck by the comparable geographical settings of the peripheral systems she examines and observes that for the most part they each constitute coastal environments of successive alluvial plains bounded by the spurs of the Sierra Madre Occidental and Sierra Madre Oriental. Populations in these regions doubtless faced similar needs, challenges, and opportunities for adaptation and exploitation of the surrounding environment perhaps extending back millennia, and she proposes that certain shared characteristics are consequential. For example, both Oaxaca and west Mexico largely have been treated as anomalies in Mesoamerican studies, yet anthropologists and archaeologists have long noted many basic similarities in belief systems, social organization, and the widespread distribution of Uto-Aztecan languages, particularly with the shared employment of Nahuatl as a *lingua franca*.

The problem is that we are dealing with peer polities, which can be difficult to study because their archaeological remains tend to be more or less equal in size and are found broadly distributed over wide geographical regions (Renfrew and Cherry 1986). In some cases, ethnohistorical sources such as the *relaciones geográficas* may lend some insights into ritual hierarchy, but for the most part these accounts lack the detail that we have for other parts of New Spain while deep archival research of the kind developed for central and southern Mexico is still in its infancy for west Mexico.

Historical sources inform us that during the Postclassic, people in west Mexico and Oaxaca were organized in directly comparable ways and dominated by segmentary noble lineages who invested in the same forms of wealth finance upon which they mutually depended for their staple and ritual economies. Susana Ramírez Urrea has worked extensively both in the Valley of Oaxaca and the Mixteca where the methodology for mapping peer polities was first introduced by deploying full coverage surveys to document all sites within a region together with controlled excavations for the development of a chronology. Originally used to measure population densities through time to document processes of political centralization with the rise of Classic urban centers like Monte Albán from Formative village antecedents, the survey maps reveal just as much about the breakup of these capital centers and the redistribution of authority among the succeeding *señorío* organizations after AD 1000 across southern Mexico.

For Ramírez Urrea (Chapter 4), past studies of the Aztatlán tradition focused on either macroregional perspectives or basic site-level analyses while far less attention has been given to how *señoríos* were structured at the intraregional level. To address questions regarding regional sociopolitical organization, Ramírez Urrea chose the Sayula Basin and adjacent regions of the Chapala Basin of Jalisco to carry out a full-coverage survey because the area had not been heavily impacted by subsequent human occupation as it had in the west, especially in coastal areas. It also features an Early Postclassic component to the sequence that could shed insight into the dynamics of expansion of the Aztatlán phenomenon in west Mexico. Ramírez Urrea's survey determined that the Sayula-Chapala region experienced a burst of population growth at the outset of the Postclassic that reflected external influence on an existing network. One site, La Peña, eventually emerged as the *cabecera* of the region where political, religious, and socioeconomic power was concentrated. Even more significant was the identification of a number of sites presumed to be occupied by a class of secondary elite functionaries. These sites appear to have specialized in certain aspects of regional control through extraction, production, and distribution of prestige goods and commodities ranging from metallurgy to salt processing.

If the settlement pattern Ramírez Urrea identified is reflective of the kind of sociopolitical organization documented for southern Mexico at this time, then we could envision a widely distributed system of ranked elites—at least some are identified in historical sources as *tetecuhtin* or lineage heads—who intermarry to form monopolies over production and exchange. They then invest in a shared religious ideology expressed through the Aztatlán pictographic communication system and symbol set transcending local differences in language and ethnicity. Creation stories and hero cults, portrayed on Aztatlán ceramics, would have played a significant ideological role when these peer polities incorporated themselves into larger reciprocal entities. The goal of sharing myth and heroic history was to elevate the ideology of an elite group to a point above and beyond the petty disputes of individuals that would divide others from the mutual benefits of coalition.

Contrasting with Ramírez Urrea's full-coverage survey, Mauricio Garduño Ambriz (Chapter 5) reports on an urban archaeological *rescate* (salvage project) at

San Felipe Aztatán in northwest Nayarit. Here, Sauer and Brand first identified the unique polychrome tradition that has proven so fundamental to identifying the Aztatlán horizon. Although coastal areas have been severely impacted by urban development connected with infrastructure projects and international tourism among other factors, a precolumbian substrate can be detected. By working in and around developed areas, Garduño Ambriz confirmed that over 100 ha of the Aztatlán occupation composed a dense network of residential complexes, plazas, temples, workshops, and storage areas of the paramount elite governing center extending back to the Early Postclassic period. He also confirmed that the Aztatlán polychrome tradition was introduced into the region around this same time. This is significant because we tend to equate the introduction of the Late Postclassic International Style with a developmental sequence for polychrome ceramics at Cholula. It appears therefore that the introduction of polychrome in west Mexico was a separate phenomenon (Smith and Heath-Smith 1980). Both the vessel forms and the intricate linework that compose the abstract ornamentation typical of this early manifestation suggest closer affiliations with Central America than central Mexico. Considering that metallurgy was introduced into west Mexico from the same region around AD 850/900, it appears that we have more than simply evidence for trade but rather the introduction of a package of traits specifically adapted to facilitate social integration as a political-ideological strategy among the paramount chiefdoms of Lower Central America (Pohl and Mathiowetz 2022).

The presence of Plumbate, on the other hand, suggests that San Felipe Aztatán (and other Aztatlán sites where these ceramics are present) was not only engaged with the Pacific coast of Guatemala and Chiapas—a primary cacao producing region—but probably Tula as well where this ceramic type is widespread (Jadot et al. 2019). This is confirmed at other Aztatlán sites where Mazapan figurines indicative of more specifically Toltec forms of ritualism are pervasive (Diehl 1993; Forest et al. 2020; Solar Valverde et al. 2011). Archaeological survey around Puerto Vallarta suggests that sudden population growth documented in the Aztatlán region may be partly attributable to a Toltec-affiliated colonization (Mountjoy et al. 2020). This may help explain the rationale behind the establishment of Tula at a strategic location of the frontier zone linking the Valley of Mexico to western and northern Mexico (Pohl and Mathiowetz 2022). Aztatlán constitutes a distinct but directly engaged co-tradition during the Early Postclassic that could be characterized as Western Toltec.

The fall of Tula by AD 1150 signaled the end of a major polity dominating central Mexico, but it also fostered the rise of the Tolteca-Chichimeca, who subsequently migrated into the Valley of Puebla and the Tehuacan Valley to establish a confederacy of Nahua-dominated city-states and great houses. By AD 1250, Nahua nobles had intermarried with ranking Mixtec royal families and established a constellation of alliances integrating much of southern Mexico from Cholula to Tututepec. At this time, the Late Postclassic international communication system and symbol set was then absorbed into the existing Aztatlán polychrome tradition with a particularly intensive manifestation appearing at San Felipe Aztatán; this is evidenced both through the recovery of ceramic fragments by Garduño Ambriz and one whole vessel depicting an elaborate codex-style ritual scene comparable to vessels in the Los Angeles County Museum of Art and the Metropolitan Museum of Art (Figure I.7).

Luis Alfonso Grave Tirado (Chapter 6) reports on archaeological sites that demonstrate a cultural extension of the Aztatlán tradition from Nayarit north to the Río Piaxtla of Sinaloa. By mapping architectural remains and correlating some of these sites with historical descriptions of them as independent polities, he demonstrates a remarkable continuity in site size and distribution of peer-polity organization. He proposes that the coastal area of southern Sinaloa was divided into eight principal centers, each of which represented a defined territorial polity ruled by an autonomous ruler. The tendency was for these centers to juxtapose themselves in areas linking differing environmental zones ranging from the estuaries south of Mazatlán, where the exploitation of shellfish was a primary industry, to an upland coastal plain crossed by river drainages, by which access to the sierra of Zacatecas and Durango was gained. In this way, each polity controlled production, the movement of goods, and the extraction of tribute along parallel and probably competing corridors. Grave Tirado surmises that we need to reconsider the nature of "power" in a segmentary and factional system of this kind. He questions what kinds of authority these independent Aztatlán noble families wielded. How was power inherited and how did they recognize legitimacy among each other?

We know that historically some of the rulers of these polities possessed the title of *tecuhtli*. Gods and heroes on some vessels are portrayed wearing turquoise nose ornaments characteristic of *tetecuhtin* (Figure I.7a; Pohl 2012a, 2012b). Comparison to the cultural co-traditions of southern Mexico with whom Aztatlán nobles were intensively engaged could provide some insights on political organization. Centered on the Plain of Puebla and the Tehuacan Valley, the Eastern Nahuas recognized the authority of the *tecuhtli* as head of a *teccalli* (lineage estate) over that of the *calpulli* and *tecpan*. The title *tecuhtli* basically functioned as a fictive kinship term, but it is comparable in many ways as the direct

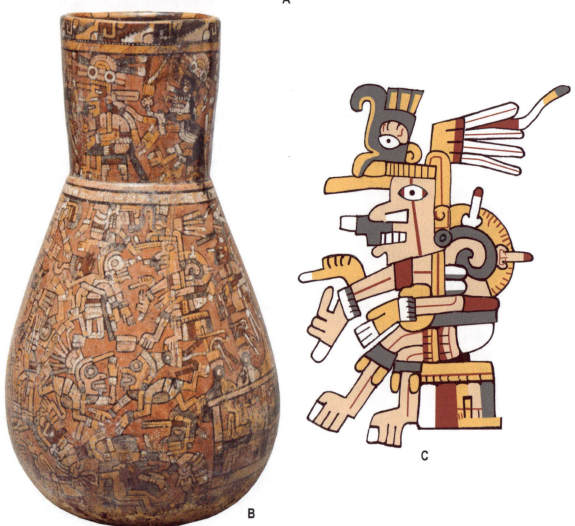

FIGURE I.7. Iguanas Polychrome (AD 1100–1350+) jar with narrative codex-style scene from coastal southern Sinaloa or northern Nayarit. (*a*) High-status individuals and/or deities wear elaborate headdresses and regalia while seated on chairs or stools and flanked by two standing or dancing figures. Detail of scene on neck of Iguanas Polychrome jar. Catalog number M.2000.86, Los Angeles County Museum of Art. Drawing by John M. D. Pohl. (*b*) Iguanas Polychrome jar, Catalog number M.2000.86, Los Angeles County Museum of Art. Public domain. (*c*) Seated yellow-haired male (possibly Piltzintli-Xochipilli) with butterfly brow piece and large solar disk on back. Figures with yellow hair in highland Mexican codices and art are typically associated with the sun. Detail of Iguanas Polychrome jar, Catalog number M.2000.86, Los Angeles County Museum of Art. Drawing by John M. D. Pohl.

equivalent of the Mixtec *Yya* or the Zapotec *Coqui* with whom Eastern Nahuas allied themselves. However, *tetecuhtin* were cremated at death and so there is little to suggest that they were attributed any sense of divinity as was attributed to their Mixtec and Zapotec counterparts whose divine remains were consulted as oracles.

Mixtec paramount kings and queens were endowed with the title *Yya*, which means both "high lord" and "god." At death, these nobles were preserved as religious objects in sacred caves in surrounding mountains. There the spirits of the dead could communicate with their descendants through priestly intermediaries who served as powerful oracles consulted on affairs of marriage and warfare. These funerary cults ensured social stability among various members of otherwise rival kin groups. In this regard, we are reminded of historical accounts of the mummified remains of Cora nobles who were consulted as oracles in comparable fashion. Perhaps syncretic systems characterize the Aztatlán tradition just as they did in southern Mexico. Mixtec nobles could affect the title of a *tecuhtli* if it served their purposes when they intermarried with Nahua noble families. It was just a question of participating in rituals of confirmation after which one was awarded elements of facial jewelry. A marriage between Nahua and Mixtec families would then satisfy Mixtec requirements of real kinship.

Archaeologists tend to focus on the remains of communities while ethnohistorical and ethnographic studies indicate that significant landscape features including mountains, rivers, springs, and caves were correspondingly regarded as places of significant social intercourse and economic exchange through systems of boundary reciprocity. Recognizing the potential for the interpretive limitations that may result from these different subfields of inquiry, Cinthya Vidal Aldana (Chapter 7) applies a provocative interdisciplinary methodology while investigating routes of exchange between the Pacific coast, the Sierra Madre Occidental, and the *altiplano* of Durango. Focusing on the Guadiana Valley, Vidal Aldana examined ceramics and developed typological classifications to define temporal and spatial limits for a coastal presence together with a petrographic analysis of decorated ceramics from Durango and Sinaloa to reveal the mineralogical origin of clays. While she acknowledges the existence of the Aztatlán Mercantile System proposed by J. Charles Kelley, she suggests that it was far more dynamic and complex with cultural influences moving both ways through the Sierra Madre along specific corridors of exchange. When test results lead Vidal Aldana to question why forms of raw material might be imported even though local sources were more accessible, she wonders whether spiritual properties might augment value in production by examining ethnographic examples of such concepts among the Cora. She concludes that in addition to being a function of commercial exchange, defined routes between the coast and the highlands were also perceived cosmogonically as extending along the pathway of the sun from east to west to bring warmth to the coast, which in turn generates the rains that move west to east to fertilize the desert of the *altiplano*. From this perspective, both raw and finished products would be considered as much in terms of their potential for the ritual transfer of their metaphysical properties as their commercial potential.

John Carpenter and Guadalupe Sánchez (Chapter 8) examine the extension of the Aztatlán complex into the northern frontier of Sinaloa. Their research indicates that northwest Mexico was integrally linked to the Greater U.S. Southwest with sedentary farmers occupying the North Mexican Coastal Plain and adjacent foothills to form a continuous link from southern Sinaloa to the Arizona border by AD 250. Cultural continuity in the material record suggests that these settlements represent an early establishment of Cahitan-speaking populations encountered by the Spanish in the first half of the sixteenth century, including the Tahue, Comanito, Mocorito, Mayo, Yaqui, and Opata. At the southern end of the spectrum, the Tahue are identified as the contact-period descendants of Aztatlán populations while the Opata of the north have been identified with both the Río Sonora and Casas Grandes traditions. The remarkably diverse sources of artifacts indicate that the Opata were actively engaged in both long-distance and regional exchange extending from the Gulf of California to Chihuahua. From this perspective, Culiacán and Paquimé would have been situated at opposite ends of a single, attenuated linguistic and cultural spectrum of integrated heterogeneous social and economic strategies.

Cristina García Moreno, James Watson, and Danielle Phelps (Chapter 9) summarize archaeological work at the burial mound of El Cementerio in the Ónavas Valley of southeast Sonora, Mexico. The site dates between AD 1000–1521 and is comprised of a low earthen platform encompassing nearly 9 ha situated above the floodplain of the Río Yaqui. Over 100 human burials were investigated together with an array of mortuary artifacts. For many archaeologists, the Río Yaqui would seem to constitute a natural corridor for the movement of prestige goods between the Gulf of California and Paquimé. However, when analysis of the ceramics at El Cementerio revealed that over 90 percent were of local manufacture together with much of the lithic material, García Moreno and her associates questioned what role this population may have played in any regional and macroregional interactions. On the other hand, they do attribute ceramic material to contacts with both Guasave and the eastern Sonoran manifestation of the Casas Grandes tradition. The presence of Pacific-coastal marine shell and turquoise sourced in the Greater U.S. Southwest and northern Mexico, as well the incorporation of unique forms of cranial and dental modification, clearly link the populations to the Aztatlán tradition along the west Mexican coast from northern Sinaloa to Nayarit. García and colleagues therefore consider the site to represent an example of the broader sociocultural changes associated with the Aztatlán horizon in west Mexico. However, they propose that this population actively managed their identity in response to these macroregional influences by selectively adopting limited aspects of the Aztatlán tradition along with traces of Casas Grandes material culture.

The differential engagement of prehispanic Sonoran communities with regard to the core Aztatlán tradition of coastal Jalisco, Nayarit, and southern Sinaloa led Carpenter and Sánchez to propose that while some polities may have held a vested interest in the acquisition of goods, the actual exchange mechanism can be explained without relying upon core-periphery models of political-economic exploitation. Rather, Carpenter and Sánchez suggest that interaction and integration was largely predicated on a flow of information and materials among peoples engaged in a number of parallel organizational, production, and transportation strategies. Instead of concentrating on the distribution of a few isolated traits to define the presence or absence of cultural interaction, they advocate a consideration of a range of social, political, economic, and ideological behaviors represented in the archaeological record.

The Postclassic burial mound at Guasave is a good case in point. Located in northern Sinaloa within a region that might otherwise be regarded as marginal to the Aztatlán core area, the archaeological materials from this cemetery nonetheless reveal an extraordinary investment in the Aztatlán material complex (Ekholm 1942). It suggests that we are looking at interlinked systems rooted in varying mutualistic strategies perhaps exhibiting some sense of territoriality within certain regions together with factional rivalries extending along parallel corridors of exchange that differentially integrated populations like those in the Ónavas and other local valley systems.

Carpenter and Sánchez have subsequently discussed a "gap-and-corridor" framework that has been proposed to extend across northern Sinaloa and southern Sonora (Carpenter et al. 2023:1–3). In so doing they critique what they perceive to be the "leap-frogging" agency that is implied in the evidence for intensive cultural engagement extending between west Mexico and the U.S. Southwest/Mexican Northwest presented by us among other scholars whom they lump together. We cannot speak for arguments for hypothesized Maya hero twins among the Mimbres (Gilman et al. 2014, 2019), Casas Grandes tobacco shamans (VanPool and VanPool 2007), or Chaco Canyon "kings" (Lekson 1999, 2008, 2015). Rather, in this volume as well as our other publications (Pohl, this volume; Pohl and Mathiowetz 2022), we examine many distinct lines of evidence that extend beyond discussions of simply iconographic traits reflective of religious beliefs or foreign ceramic styles. These include the incorporation of both genetic and chemical osteological studies that suggest long-distance engagement through marriage alliances between groups (e.g., Shafer 2012; Snow et al. 2011; Tuross 2017). This could only be achieved by carefully negotiating with local groups the corridors of exchange that extend through their borderlands, which is why the contributions to Borderlands studies by Carpenter, Sánchez, and colleagues are so critical. Furthermore, we interpret the existence of exotic materials such as shell, copper, and turquoise together with Casas Grandes and Aztatlán ceramics—spartan as they might be in the Borderlands—as material evidence of not only marriage alliances but related forms of fictive kinship rather than some measure of greater or lesser trade in commodities. Given the high level of volatility that Carpenter, Sánchez and their colleagues postulate for the Sinaloa-Sonora borderlands, assurances for secure passage alone would certainly warrant the careful negotiation and long-term maintenance of close intergroup relationships.

Part III. Technologies, Economies, and Trade in the Aztatlán Region and Beyond

The heterogeneity in cultural behavior extending between Sonora, Nayarit, Jalisco, Sinaloa, and Durango (discussed by Carpenter and Sánchez and García and colleagues in Chapters 8 and 9) was documented historically by Bernardino de Sahagún (1950–1982, Book 10:171–176) in describing the peoples of these regions as being engaged in a spectrum of integrated subsistence strategies ranging from sedentary agriculture to hunting and foraging while also engaging in the location and extraction of specialized resources that they traded, including obsidian, flint, animal hides, feathers, turquoise, and peyote. The first European to observe such a macrosystem in operation was Alvar Núñez Cabeza de Vaca (1993). Shipwrecked off the coast of Texas in 1528, Cabeza de Vaca spent years living among various tribes as a slave until he gained his freedom by becoming a merchant and curer. He described most of the people with whom he lived as being subsistence specialists. It seems that tribes even distinguished themselves from one another by what they collected or hunted—from grains, cactus fruits, and roots, to oysters, fish, deer, and rabbit. Eventually, he became a shell and mesquite-bean trader, taking the products he collected to inland tribes in exchange for red ochre, canes, flint, sinew, cement, and deer hair. After several years, his knowledge of trails enabled him to set out across the northern Mexican frontier with three companions. Soon the group found that they were being credited with the ability to cure illness and, as their reputation spread, they were traded from one tribe to another as a kind of valued commodity themselves. By the time Cabeza de Vaca reached the Opata and Pima of Sonora, he had learned much of the voluminous trade in subsistence goods and commodities crossing northern deserts—later writing that turquoise was a priceless gem that was traded for the dazzling plumage of parrots. Shell and coral were obtained from the Pacific coast to the west and copper was mined in the south (Cabeza de Vaca 1993:110, 119).

Obsidian has always been essential to evaluating the nature of internal distribution and hierarchical relationships as well as long-distance exchange across Mesoamerica. Contrasting and comparing collections from the archaeological sites of San Felipe Aztatán, Coamiles, Chacalilla, and Amapa, Daniel Pierce (Chapter 10) examines the interconnection between sources and distribution of obsidian artifacts within the Aztatlán core region along the coastal plain providing significant insights into coastal-highland interaction. West Mexico features one of the largest and most diverse concentrations of obsidian in the world, so it is not surprising that up to 99 percent of all lithic artifacts recovered at sites like Chacalilla consist of obsidian. Pierce found that no single obsidian source was utilized exclusively although, curiously, some were more intensively exploited while others were neglected almost entirely. For example, seven distinct sources were identified for the nearly 1,500 obsidian artifacts recovered from San Felipe Aztatán, yet the largest percentage of the material came from only three. Proximity to sources was not necessarily a significant factor in consumption as the closest source at Volcán las Navajas contributed 29 percent of the assemblage while a more distant source at La Joya comprised 34 percent of the total.

A more restrictive group at the site were importing prismatic blades from the Sierra de las Navajas (Pachuca) source in Hidalgo that comprised 12 percent of the assemblage. This is entirely unique, and it suggests some particularistic ritual investment in the original source employed by the Toltecs of central Mexico despite the existence of an equally unique green obsidian source in west Mexico at Volcán las Navajas. Pierce proposes that with so many quality sources available, the trade of obsidian may not have focused solely upon proximity and quality. It may have been the intention of Aztatlán nobles to create trade networks for the acquisition of reciprocal items or establishing cooperative relationships between both local and distant polities, an observation that Vidal Aldana also makes with regard to ceramic production. Pierce asserts that superfluous economic exchange can develop as an expression of socioeconomic superiority by vaunting interpersonal relationships with powerful trading partners. Thus, as one's status increases, the access to more diverse and rare resources may also increase. Yet just as important as the material items being exchanged were the interpersonal relationships created through these economic and social negotiations. Furthermore, such relationships extended beyond mercantile interaction alone and could also be exploited for the ritual display of stratification within the society as dictated and perpetuated by differential access to resources and exotic goods.

Although rare copper objects appear in Jalisco and Nayarit perhaps as early as AD 600, the adoption of metallurgy only becomes a regional phenomenon around AD 800–900 at the outset of the Aztatlán expansion. Far more than simply ornaments, we have seen that copper artifacts were part of an entire package of traits associated with the paramount chiefdoms of Lower Central America including Nicoya, Guanacaste, and Diquís, among other traditions that also included the production of a highly sophisticated polychrome tradition and, more rarely, peg-based basalt effigies. José Luis Punzo Díaz and Lissandra González (Chapter 11) propose two distinct phases in the production and distribution of metal work (Hosler 1994b). Period 1, extending between AD 900–1200, is limited almost exclusively to the mining and smelting of copper. Specific sources are debated but several mining areas have been identified across Jalisco and Michoacán as well as Guerrero. What is especially notable is the distribution of copper bells (or crotals) among the Ancestral Puebloan populations to the north, which constitutes irrefutable evidence of cultural interaction between the emerging Aztatlán system and those social networks of the Greater U.S. Southwest and northwest Mexico at this time.

Punzo Díaz and González propose that Period 2, which extends between AD 1200–1550, is characterized by the introduction of technological advances in manufacturing techniques for casting, hammering, and embossing together with the invention of an array of metallic alloys that includes copper-tin bronze and copper-arsenic bronze, copper-silver, and copper-gold throughout Jalisco, Colima, northwest Guerrero, Michoacán, and the southern state of Mexico. The diversity of objects produced is extraordinary. In addition to bells or crotals, they include tweezers, awls, discs, plates, masks, chains, ear spools, nose ornaments, pectorals, and zoomorphs. Many works are unique and suggest that elites were sponsoring production according to their own designs for their own particular uses with selective aesthetic choices being made for color and sound as well. Other objects, especially bells, appear to travel through remarkably complex corridors of interchange. A number of distinctive types are shared between the Aztatlán and Casas Grandes traditions but also appear among the Purépecha (Tarascan). Nevertheless, Aztatlán metallurgical material culture is decidedly distinct, which reflects a considerable degree of rivalry between the two systems.

Metallurgy also appears in Oaxaca during Period 2, the primary location for the gold that would have been imported into west Mexico and Michoacán from sources extending between the Mixteca Alta to the Pacific Coast. The development of gold alloys therefore represents a second unique elite cultural characteristic linking Oaxaca to Aztatlán paralleling the shared investment in the Nahua-Mixteca Late Postclassic International Style manifested in the polychrome ceramics. We know that Mixtec expansionism from the Mixteca Alta to the coast by AD 1200 led to the establishment of the coastal kingdom of Tututepec with its port at Huatulco.

Part IV. Aztatlán Religion, Ritual Practice, and Worldview: The Archaeological Past and Continuities in the Ethnographic Present

Death not only constitutes the ultimate life crisis for an individual but it dramatically affects the social wellbeing of the entire group to which the deceased had belonged. The disposal of the dead through funerary rituals enables the living to express their emotional loss, but they commonly do so through the manipulation of objects, signs, and symbols in special performances that can reveal much about the Aztatlán worldview. As valuable a source of data as they can be, however, burials can also be extraordinarily difficult to identify, excavate, and conserve. Furthermore, they contain the physical remains of people whose direct descendants we look to for the extension of meaning beyond simply cultural materialism—including production, exchange, and feasting—to the cognitive and emotional qualities embedded within artifacts.

José Carlos Beltrán Medina, Lourdes González Barajas, Jorge Talavera González, and Juan Jorge Morales Monroy (Chapter 12) report on the Jala-Vallarta archaeological project located below the southern slope of the Ceboruco volcano some 15 km west of Ixtlán del Río. Their discovery of a cemetery zone was remarkable for the diversity of burial types being used including vault tombs, stone cists, direct burials, cremations, and ceramic urns. Of 22 excavated interments in the La Pitayera cemetery, the majority of the remains were of individuals who had been cremated with the ashes placed in urns. Comparisons with previous excavations elsewhere confirm that this had been a common practice across the region up through the Terminal Classic. However, the placement of the urns within cists together with the deposit of hundreds of artifacts of shell, copper, obsidian, polished stone, ceramic vessels, figurines, spindle whorls, and even a fragment of woven cloth indicate dramatic changes reflecting an unprecedented engagement with a broader international culture at the outset of the Postclassic.

The recovery of copper bells indicates a major innovation in technology with the initial introduction of metal embossing, hammering, smelting, and casting techniques into Mesoamerica through west Mexico during what Punzo and González identify as Period 1. Other objects make it apparent that, while people in west Mexico were investing in the social strategies deployed by segmentary chiefdoms of Central America, they were simultaneously engaging with the Toltec social, political, and religious ideology centralized at Tula, Hidalgo. The discovery of Mazapan figurines at the La Pitayera cemetery is most notable. Mazapan figurines are a hallmark of the Early Postclassic horizon throughout Mesoamerica even as far south as El Salvador. They are relatively simple, low-relief, flat human effigies cast from one piece "cookie" molds and low fired (Acosta 1940; Linné 1934; Scott 1993). The figurines are most often found in household contexts and burials. They have been found stacked in deposits suggesting some kind of repetitive or even numerical counting in their manipulation as offerings. Over 50 were found at Amapa in central-coastal Nayarit, for example.

Although the medium is clay rather than *amate* paper, the figurines could be compared to the effigies used by contemporary Nahua healers. They attribute disease to anthropomorphic beings associated with the surrounding natural environment and diagnosis is performed by maize casting and scrying (Sandstrom 1992:235–237). Many are responsible for drought, rain, thunder, lightning, and other atmospheric phenomena. Ritualism is rooted in a sacrificial metaphor in which food together with beverages of Coca-Cola or aguardiente in bowls and cups, as well as cigarettes, are offered to the appropriate spirit forces. Chicken blood is spread over the sacrificial offerings during the course of the rituals to consecrate them for spiritual "consumption."

In this regard, it is notable that green obsidian prismatic blades that may have been used for bloodletting rituals were found at La Pitayera. The Toltec custom was to use a variety from a single source at Sierra las Navajas in Pachuca, Hidalgo; it is found in archaeological sites extending from central through southern Mexico as a Postclassic temporal marker. The fact that

Daniel Pierce identified it at San Felipe Aztatán suggests a display of prestige by nobles in their ability to import material from the original Tula-controlled source itself. Those buried at La Pitayera were using green obsidian from the Volcán las Navajas source—located just outside of Tepic, Nayarit—for the same type of artifact, which testifies to an Aztatlán familiarity with standard Toltec ritual practice on the one hand while taking advantage of a local resource carrying similar symbolic connotations on the other.

The ceramic serving wares excavated at La Pitayera as well as other burial sites are evidence of ancestor veneration through offerings of food for the dead as well as a consideration of the feast as a fundamental social contrivance among the living in Aztatlán culture. This is particularly evident in the sophisticated polychrome tradition with which Aztatlán was originally identified as a cultural co-tradition by Sauer and Brand (1932). As we have seen, both the emulation of vessel forms and the use of abstract design work point to Central American influences in polychrome traditions during the Early Postclassic. Then, and perhaps most remarkably, we begin to see the production of ceramics in the Late Postclassic International or Nahua-Mixteca Style with representational images of people, places, and things together with an associated symbol set that had evolved at Cholula on the Plain of Puebla and spread south into Oaxaca after AD 1250 (Boone and Smith 2003; Pohl 2003c).

Pictographic narratives like those found on some Aztatlán vases are clearly connected to the precolumbian codices of southern Mexico where considerable advancements have been made not only in the decipherment of directly comparable creation stories but the association of the ritual feasts they record with known archaeological sites and sacred landscape features (Pohl 2003c, 2007). The problem, however, is that southern Mexico was very quickly evangelized by the Dominican and Franciscan orders, which caused Indigenous intellectuals to adopt a European worldview rooted in Christian belief that contrasted dramatically with precolumbian ontologies.

West Mexico presents us with an entirely different study situation. Pioneering scholars like Carl Lumholtz, Konrad Theodor Preuss, Eduard Seler, and Robert Zingg, among others, were quick to recognize that much in Cora, Huichol, and Tepehuan ritualism was far more prehispanic in nature than anyone had encountered elsewhere in Mesoamerica. Michael Mathiowetz (Chapter 13) was struck by the existence of an extraordinary social dimension that might otherwise go undetected by examining the complex performative use of *jícaras* or gourd bowls that attend contemporary *mitote* ritualism among the Cora, Huichol, and Tepehuan peoples as documented in recent ethnographic studies (Kindl 2000; Neurath 2000). *Mitotes* are festivals timed to the maize-agricultural cycle throughout the year but are equally associated with status roles as well. What is fascinating is how something as basic as a *jícara*, whether in gourd or ceramic form, could be promoted to such a sublime level of social currency. Mathiowetz proposes that key religious-ritual tenets, symbolism, and sociopolitical organization might very well be sourced in Aztatlán ceramics.

Mathiowetz makes it very clear that the manufacture and application of religion-based symbolism endows both the contemporary *jícaras* and the ancient vessels with elevated values of social currency. He has identified three principal religious themes: the veneration of the solar deity named Piltzintli (Xochipilli), a deity associated with the planet Venus (linked to Tlahuizcalpantecuhtli), and the feathered serpent—the principal avatar of Quetzalcoatl. Continuities in ritual performances can then be detected in the portrayal of *mitote* rituals appearing in the full-figure narratives of these same themes painted on other polychrome ceramic forms as well (Pohl 2012a, 2012b). By establishing the antiquity of the Huichol cargo system as evident in Aztatlán "god bowls" and associated landscape ritualism, Mathiowetz identifies the route to Wirikuta as a mechanism to bundle resource acquisition—such as scarlet macaws via the Gulf Coast Huasteca—into pilgrimage routes for subsequent incorporation into long-distance economic networks that led into the U.S. Southwest and northern Mexico.

As Joseph Mountjoy (Chapter 1) asserted, west Mexico has languished from a lack of any holistic approach to its cultural history. For example, scholars attempting to fill gaps in what they perceive to be an understanding of the esotericism of shamanic behavior have tended to use the Huichol selectively by comparing certain objects, beliefs, or ritual practices to discoveries made with the Olmec, Maya, Aztec, or other cultures in Mesoamerica across all time and space. This came to a head with the work of Barbara Myerhoff and Peter Furst who were instilled by Walter Goldschmidt at the University of California, Los Angeles, with the goal of elevating the appreciation for Native American intellectual erudition among anthropologists. Their emphasis on shamanic practices in many ways succeeded (Furst 1972; Myerhoff 1974). However, we have been left with a stereotype of the Huichol as a facile culture of desert wisdom seekers that remains pervasive due to the subsequent incorporation of their work into the novelization of Don Juan Matus, recast as a Yaqui sorcerer, by fellow graduate student Carlos Castañeda (Fikes 1993). The fact is that these misconceptions of the Huichol as well as the Cora and the Tepehuanes are due more

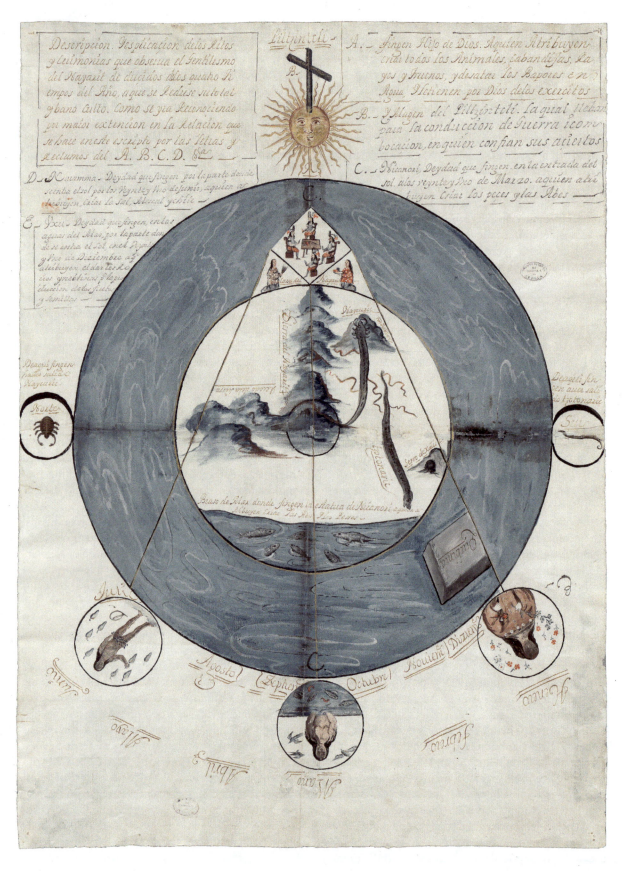

FIGURE I.8. Depiction of the rites, ceremonies, and deity worship of Cora-Nayarit Indians at the "House of the Nayarit" at the Mesa del Nayar. *Estampa* from 1673 report of Antonio Arias de Saavedra, Archivo General de las Indias, Seville, Spain.

to their resistance strategy in dealing with the Spanish Viceregal and Mexican governments over the past 500 years than to any passion for high-plateau asceticism.

Historical connections between the coastal Aztatlán area and the Gran Nayar have long been recognized. Ethnohistoric sources show that the Cora are descendants of societies governed by palace-based elites destroyed by Nuño de Guzmán. The Huichol, on the other hand, extend their territorial narratives into the upland deserts as far as San Luis Potosí where they acquire dream-inducing peyote for redistribution among peoples of the highlands and coast. Historical sources indicate that the Huichol had been engaged in the acquisition of many other materials including shell and the feathers of exotic birds (Weigand 1975). Their invocation of the deer hunt has its cognates in the highland Mexican *Historia Tolteca-Chichimeca* and the *Mapas de Cuauhtinchan*, in which the establishment of kingdoms and the routes connecting them are portrayed as ritualized hunting expeditions. The trails were even invoked metaphorically as the "Road to Tollan" in prayer, indicating that the origin of this ritualism lay in exchange strategies that originally linked Tula with the Gran Chichimeca in ways directly comparable to Huichol customs today (Pohl 1994). Consequently, the cultural distinctions between the Cora and Huichol are now recognized more as a result of mutualistic socioeconomic strategies than ethnic or linguistic differences. Philip Coyle (Chapter 14) therefore argues that direct "upstreaming" from the contemporary to prehispanic period is methodologically sound. Like Mathiowetz, he proposes that major patterns of culture—such as worship of the solar deity Piltzintli (Xochipilli)—have remained stable over long periods, producing a uniformity in behavior that makes west Mexico unique as a study area (Figure I.8).

Coyle's ethnographic research in the Gran Nayar region, which is encompassed within the former Aztatlán interaction sphere, focuses on themes of sacrifice through a hunting metaphor that positions political authorities as mediators between the living and their ancestors through whom regenerative power flows. In so doing, he offers new insights into a complex interplay of cosmology, visionary shamanism, and ritual that he proposes has long been associated with the legitimization of Indigenous political leaders in the region. He emphasizes the fundamental role of elders in maintaining balance between the world of a disease-prone living and that of the immortal dead by appealing to a hierarchy of dynamic vital forces in the natural environment. Among these, the deer has primacy, for it was the creature that first gave freely of itself to provide sustenance to the original hunters so that they could thrive on earth. Consequently, the deer are believed to serve as mediators between the realm of the hunter and the flower world paradise of their ancestors who negotiated the original contract of mutual reciprocity. Cora elders today offer sacrifice through fasting and sleep deprivation in order to project meditative thought into the deer so that the spirit being will pity humankind through their petitions and continue to give of itself.

Section II. The Big Picture: Broader Themes in Aztatlán Research

Joseph Mountjoy's summary of 90 years of investigation into the Aztatlán phenomenon exposes the point that its constitution and significance have been elusive to scholars who defined it as everything from a geographical region, a ceramic horizon, a cultural complex, a time period, and a commercial system. Consequently, John Carpenter and Guadalupe Sánchez wonder whether the use of the term "Aztatlán Complex" should be discontinued. If not, they propose redefinition to move forward with a more holistic perception of how it unified west Mexico socially, politically, economically, and religiously. For the most part, the contributors to this volume advocate for the efficacy of an interdisciplinary approach to the prehispanic past. Such an approach should apply the same questions to the varying data sets, followed by a comparison of perspectives through processes of inductive and deductive reasoning. Ethnohistorical, ethnographical, and archaeological research has demonstrated cultural continuity throughout west Mexico over the last millennium, meaning that those responsible for the Aztatlán Complex were the direct ancestors of the Indigenous peoples who continue to reside across the region today. What is emerging is a recognition of the Aztatlán Complex as a set of cultural strategies more than anything else. But whose strategies were they and how were they directed?

Garduño Ambriz's research at San Felipe Aztatán represents one area where ethnohistorical sources together with architectural and artifactual evidence confirm that the site represented the elite residential area of an autonomous paramount lord. The prevalence of high-quality polychrome ceramics supports the elite status, but the fact that the site is a primary source for a complex representational style of human figures organized into codex-style narratives indicates that the paramount lord (a *cacique* or *cacica*) was also invested in the invocation of a cycle of creation stories and heroic sagas by which they most likely claimed ancestral ritual and probably hereditary authority.

Since some of the polychrome vases display scenes specifically relating to *mitote* rituals, we can deduce that the feasting system over which the San Felipe Aztatán lord presided was directly related to forms of ritualism as they continue to be performed by Indigenous communities today (Pohl 2012a, 2012b). Full-coverage surveys of the kind Ramírez Urrea performed reveal the existence of at least a two-tiered hierarchy of nobles with a class of secondary administrators living in smaller residential complexes located at strategic points across a territorial landscape. These nobles engaged in specialized forms of production and resource acquisition as well as the coordination of agricultural production by a widely distributed farming population. Ethnohistorical evidence for the titles born by some Aztatlán lords suggest the use of a Nahua-based system of *tetecuhtin* (ranked lineage heads) who represent their own estates within the greater polity ruled, in turn, by a *tlatoani* (great speaker), but this would not preclude local ethnically based titles of authority (Rounds 1978). Situating the development of Aztatlán political-religious and economic systems in relation to interregional connections is a key concern.

Tula, Cholula, and Lower Central American Connections

Toltec engagement with west Mexico has long been debated, but the coincidence of the distribution of a complex of archaeological material culture, survey evidence for a dramatic population increase, and ethnohistorical accounts relating the founding of communities by Toltec ancestors clearly point to a Phase 1 establishment of the Aztatlán Complex through close relations with Tula, Hidalgo (see Diehl 1993; Jiménez 2020:133–187; Pohl and Mathiowetz 2022:188–193). J. Charles Kelley (1986) proposed that Phase 2 was characterized by the introduction of the Nahua-Mixteca-associated Late Postclassic International art style and pictographic communication system expressed in the Aztatlán polychrome tradition that emerged through a special relationship with Cholula. This may have been the case as the origin of the style is documented stratigraphically at Cholula (Lind 1994; Lind et al. 2002; McCafferty 1994; Plunket Nagoda and Uruñuela Ladrón de Guevara 2018; Smith and Heath-Smith 1980). However, the question is whether Cholula was directly engaged with west Mexico as Kelley proposed or whether its influence was expressed through the intermediate area dominated by a confederacy of city-states extending from southern Puebla to coastal Oaxaca (Pohl 2001:Figure 65, 2003c).

Noting certain pictographic signs and symbols in the polychrome traditions of Lower Central America, some investigators proposed that the Nahua-Mixteca style originated in that region and was conveyed to Cholula and west Mexico through cultural and commercial interchange during the Early Postclassic (Amaroli and Bruhns 2013; McCafferty 2019; Smith and Heath-Smith 1980). They emphasize *grecas* and plumed serpents, for example, together with abstract representations of human beings and animals that directly anticipate the characteristics that become standardized during the Late Postclassic to constitute a visual language. Christopher Beekman (Chapter 15) finds these proposals compelling and discusses them at length in his concluding chapter of this volume. Incredibly, none of the "Central America-first" advocates consider the role played by the predominant Mesoamerican culture that anteceded both the Central American and Cholulteca cultural co-traditions; that is, the Classic Maya who had developed a complex visual vocabulary dating at least to the fifth century in a wide variety of styles ranging from abstract to naturalistic.

Studies of representational imagery on early Cholula polychrome led to the identification of iconography associated with Classic Maya deities including the Maize God, Akhan, God M, and God N, anticipating the Late Postclassic "cults" of the Nahua gods Xochipilli, Maquilxochitl, Ixtlilton, and Tezcatlipoca in the Cholula developmental sequence (Coltman 2020; Coltman et al. 2020; Pohl 2003c, 2021; Pohl and Lind 2024; Rojas Martínez Gracida 2008a; Rojas Martínez Gracida and Hernández Sánchez 2019). This should hardly be surprising given the cultural connections linking Cholula's direct antecedent Cacaxtla with the Late Classic upper Usumacinta Maya city-states followed by the subsequent transfer of Cacaxtla's political power to Early Postclassic Cholula by the end of the ninth century (Plunket Nagoda and Uruñuela Ladrón de Guevara 2018; Pohl 2021; Pohl and Lind 2024; Turner 2019).

Consequently, we can identify two distinct areas in which polychrome and its associated symbol systems developed during the Early Postclassic. Cholula was one locale; however we must consider its development in response to the mutualistic relationships and exchange systems that had already developed between both the Classic Maya city-states and Central American paramount chiefdoms during the Late Classic (Doyle et al. 2021). Following the Maya collapse, a new Cholula merchant elite rose to power to fill the void by investing in, if not sponsoring, the Chorultega-Nicarao-Pipil phenomenon expanding across Central America. This fostered the subsequent cultural and economic exchanges between highland Mexico and Central America that characterized the Late Postclassic. By that time, who is transferring whose *grecas* and plumed serpents to whom becomes irrelevant as influences moved equally in both directions. The second area is west Mexico. Archaeological survey and excavation over the past 50 years demonstrated that west Mexico probably was directly affected by immigration into the region by peoples possessing a decidedly Toltec material culture (Pohl and Mathiowetz 2022:189–190). Plumbate ceramics imported from Guatemala, likely by way of the Pacific coast, may even indicate that west Mexico was a primary source for the widespread distribution of these ceramics east into Tula. The fact that Plumbate has not been identified in substantial quantities in west Mexico, a point emphasized by Beekman (Chapter 15) in his critique of this proposal, is hardly unique. It is equally difficult to detect in any substantial quantities in any other major region of the Mexican highlands across which it must have been transported. On the other hand, the production of basalt peg-based, full-figured human effigies of Lower Central American form, along with the introduction of metallurgy and the development of a polychrome tradition that emulates ceramic manufacturing techniques, forms, and designs, clearly connects west Mexico to Lower Central America. While Aztatlán nobles invested in the Toltec social, political, and religious ideology centralized at Tula, they simultaneously adapted a package of traits utilized by Central American segmentary chiefdoms—an integrative strategy that afforded local autonomy while facilitating the integration of multicultural societies over vast distances (Figure I.9).

The Nahua-Mixteca Connection

While polychrome ceramics in Nayarit such as Gavilán Polychrome predate the Aztatlán era (Grosscup 1976: Plates 4–7), they do not bear the symbol set that characterizes later Aztatlán ceramics. Rather, what we see during the Late Postclassic is the development of a west Mexican expression of the Late Postclassic International Style and communication system. However, it is notable that it rarely, if ever, exhibits the symbolic sorcery formulas associated with the ritualism across the Plain of Puebla south through the Tehuacan Valley, indicating Cholula was not contributing in any significant way to its development as Kelley had proposed (see Lind 1994; Pohl 2003c, 2007 for discussion of ritualism and culturally associated symbolic formulas). Examination of the iconographic themes portrayed on Aztatlán vessels more precisely connects them to the Mixtec tradition. This not only includes the emphasis on representational narrative, a particular characteristic of Mixtec codices and associated polychrome ceramics, but also specific forms of iconography for deities and culture heroes that are uniquely Mixtec, such as the earth lord (*ñuhu*) or the dog-headed twins Sahuaco Turquoise "Xolotl" and Sahuaco Golden "Xolotl" among others (Pohl 2012a, 2012b).

Considering how polychrome ceramics were deployed in Mixtec feasts as the symbolic documents of royal marriage and confederacy building, it seems likely that Aztatlán codex-style vases were intended to advertise distinctive kinship connections both among their own noble lineages as well as those of Oaxaca. In some cases, Aztatlán deities appearing on the vases may be connected to particular landscape features that might associate creation stories and heroic sagas with periodic boundary markets in much the same way as those maintained by Mixtec kingdoms. These were marked with a sophisticated system of pictographs like those appearing on a monumental scale at Coamiles, for example (Pohl and Mathiowetz 2022). The designs are known from spindle whorls and ceramics, which suggests an association with textile and ceramic production in particular. The standardized swirl and *greca* compositions reflect an ideological system of broad social and regional integration.

A deity complex with a significant role, particularly in the core zone along the Pacific coast, was that associated with Piltzintli (Mathiowetz 2011). Venerated as the personification of the sun, Piltzintli is represented as an Aztatlán avatar of a god more widely known as Xochipilli, the Flower Prince. Patron of royal marriages and palace feasts, Xochipilli was particularly associated throughout southern Puebla and Oaxaca with the "cults" of deceased royal ancestors. In contrast to the Eastern Nahuas who preferred to dispose of the royal dead by cremation, mummies could function as oracular intermediaries by which the descendants of the royal dead could petition Xochipilli for curing disease, for example (Pohl 2003c:206). Such ritualistic behavior is so similar to Cora ethnohistorical accounts of the mummified remains of El Rey Nayar, a deceased noble who was worshipped as Piltzintli, as to suggest a synchronous investment in this form of veneration that was shared exclusively between west Mexico and Oaxaca. The fact that El Rey Nayar was attributed a paramount status over other rulers suggests a system of ranking within lineages, perhaps in ways that would be comparable to systems in both Oaxaca as well as highland Guatemala (Pohl 2009; Van Akkeren 2000).

The connections between west Mexico and Oaxaca extend to artifactual materials of wealth finance. Punzo Díaz and González (Chapter 11) note the appearance of a high degree of sophistication in Aztatlán metallurgy during Period 2, especially with regard to the use of gold and gold alloys. The principal source of gold was Oaxaca and the discovery of gold-casting molds at the Mixtec coastal capital of Tututepec may be indicative of the source of the alloy technologies (Levine 2019, 2020). The mutual investment by both cultural co-traditions in such a rare and sophisticated technology is strong evidence of direct engagement between their artisans who regarded Xochipilli as the patron of their skills in gold production (see Mathiowetz 2023a). His image appears frequently in ornaments as diverse as pectorals, rings, pendants, and ear flares.

What would the Mixtecs be interested in for a return on the Aztatlán investment in their gold resources?

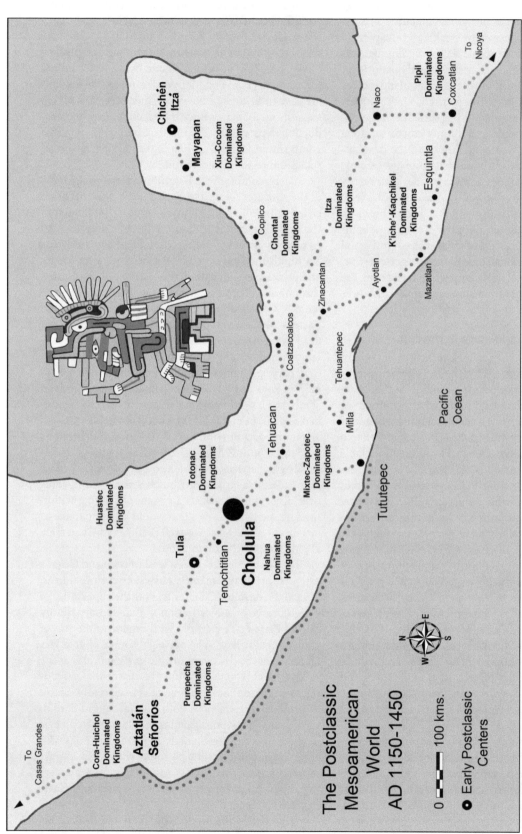

FIGURE I.9. Social networks of the Postclassic Mesoamerican world, AD 1150–1450. The collapse of the Classic Maya kingdoms precipitated a dramatic restructuring of sociopolitical and economic organization across Mesoamerica after AD 850. West Mexico emerged as a cultural and economic crossroads where Aztatlán centers engaged with Tula on the one hand and Central American paramount chiefdoms on the other to introduce a remarkably diverse complex of Tolteca-Chichimeca cultural and economic innovations. The Olmeca-Xicalanca of Veracruz on the other hand established a new pilgrimage and commercial center at Cholula and expanded their exchange corridors through Chiapas into Central America. Following Tula's collapse around AD 1150, Tolteca-Chichimeca populations migrated to the Plain of Puebla where they joined with the Olmeca-Xicalanca at Cholula. By AD 1300, Nahuatl, together with the introduction of the Late Postclassic International Style and communication system, essentially constituted a *lingua franca* among confederacies of states that extended from the Huasteca region to the north, the Maya region to the east, Oaxaca to the south, and the Aztatlán region to the west. Drawing by John M. D. Pohl and Michael Mathiowetz.

Tututepec was the primary source for the importation of turquoise and copper into highland Mexico. It has long been assumed that the turquoise was imported from sources in the southwest United States (Harbottle and Weigand 1992; King et al. 2012; Mendoza 2022). These sources were used by Casas Grandes artisans, for example (Hull et al. 2008; Hull et al. 2013; but see Thibodeau et al. 2015). Chemical analysis of turquoise tesserae from a Mixtec funerary mask indicates that the raw material from which they were manufactured was acquired from sources as far north as Nevada (Gyarmati et al. 2022:7). Comparison with chemical signatures derived from west Mexican copper deposits, on the other hand, might point to some hypothetical but now "lost" turquoise source within the Aztatlán system itself (Thibodeau et al. 2018). Could Aztatlán nobles be operating as either middle men or source procurers for the distribution of copper and turquoise into Oaxaca? Chemical sourcing of turquoise from Aztatlán sites has yet to be performed, but the results will no doubt contribute a significant dimension to our understanding of the emergence of the Aztatlán Complex in regard to its special relationship with Oaxaca after AD 1250.

World-Systems versus Decentralized Complexity

Perhaps the most compelling evidence for direct engagement between the *señoríos* of west Mexico and Oaxaca is in the studies of settlement size and distribution presented in this volume. Like Oaxaca during the Late Postclassic, the Aztatlán tradition has been characterized as a peripheral phenomenon by archaeologists and ethnohistorians. Core-periphery models have been a cornerstone of World-Systems approaches in Mesoamerican studies for many years (Smith and Berdan, eds. 2003). However, the models are largely predicated on the assumption that core societies support large urban centers with monumental-scale ceremonial complexes and complex sociopolitical structures. The Aztecs of the Basin of Mexico constitute the prime example. Peripheral societies, on the other hand, are seen as functioning outside of core societies, largely as decentralized small polities with relatively simple levels of social complexity while serving as subordinate tributary states. This premise presumes that decentralization is to be equated with marginalization. However, we can see in the discussions of the complexities of the Aztatlán phenomenon presented in this volume that this is not the case for either Postclassic west Mexico, or Oaxaca for that matter.

Solar Valverde (Chapter 2) recognizes the drawbacks in a core-periphery model for Aztatlán while Carpenter and Sánchez (Chapter 8) think it is time to reevaluate the entire paradigm. Since there was no single centralized Aztatlán state, it is probably inappropriate to characterize Aztatlán political organization in the first place. Rather, the Aztatlán tradition appears to have supported some aspects of state-like institutions but distributed them among the *señoríos*, their dependents, and their distant associates differentially in what might be better characterized as a strategy of decentralized complexity that integrated settled agricultural communities with migratory foraging tribes (Earle 2002; Jiménez 2018, 2020; Kristiansen 2010; Malkin 2011; Powell et al. 2022).

From this perspective, decentralization emerges not in response to the stimulus of a core system but rather in response to environments where productive resources are widespread across highly variable topographies making them extraordinarily difficult to control from a single center. Such strategies share a number of fundamental principles in that they foster ideological and material exchanges uniting leaders and their constituents into networks of mutual support. Support is, in turn, expressed through the production of wealth finance in small portable objects to be distributed and redistributed through gift-giving networks of the kind examined by John Pohl (Chapter 3). In this way, the unifying social-political ideology binding these networks is made tangible both through the value in the rarity of the materials used to manufacture them—precious metals, minerals, shell, and textiles—but also by endowing them with meaningful signs and symbols. More specifically, these signs and symbols invoke the religious stories by which the gods and ancestors first established the systems of reciprocity and mutual obligations through rituals of contractual agreement to be reenacted and performed at palace feasts or boundary markets.

"Glocalization" and Decentralized Organization

A contemporary correlate to our proposal that the Aztatlán tradition constituted a decentralized social-political and economic strategy can be found in what sociologists call "glocalization" (Robertson 1992; Roudometof 2016). A conflation of the terms "global" and "local," glocalization results from the effects of the contemporary global economy on local markets. Sociologists first began to apply it to studies of companies that needed to succeed in foreign countries by creating new products, such as the development and marketing of rice-based meals for India and China by global corporations like McDonalds. Since McDonalds could not develop the product itself, the brand was leased to local companies that could assure production together with the high quality expected of the brand globally. Therefore, glocalization works best for decentralized organizations as they can assure that quality locally at a far lower cost than if McDonalds had tried to produce the product themselves through their own US corporate infrastructure. Glocalization therefore presents a competitive strategy to businesses dependent on maintaining high-cost core administrative operations exclusively and succeeds by intensifying social relations and transmitting ideas, meanings, and values around the world through both universalizing and particularizing tendencies through franchisees.

Tolteca-Chichimeca ritualism such as the Xochipilli complex composes what could be seen as the brand originating with a corporate headquarters at Cholula, but franchisees have the ability and independence to conduct operations according to the resources that are locally available. This would explain all of the "McTulas" that emerge across Mesoamerica during the Late Postclassic and the localization of the awarding of *tecuhtli* titles to franchisees even though the local sociopolitical systems all have their own ways of defining rank and social status as well (Pohl, this volume). The benefit for Cholula is the assurance that the return from local investment will be in a form that can be reinvested into the economic systems of the Plain of Puebla over which they predominate. A decentralized complex strategy, like that of the western Tolteca-Chichimeca Aztatlán tradition, may not be entirely incompatible with a core-periphery model either if we consider that a core could represent simply a zone of greatest integration with various areas within the periphery representing zones of progressively decreasing integration. From this perspective, north-coastal Jalisco, Nayarit, and southern Sinaloa would constitute a core region of decentralized complexity functioning as primary nodes of administrative activity within what Alfonso Grave (Chapter 6) proposed as at least eight territorial polities in southern Sinaloa. However, there is considerable variation in architectural complexity between sites. Consequently, each great house (or political-religious center) together with its subject communities may be contributing to the system in ways that reflect differing levels of ethnicity, rank, ritual responsibilities, and specializations in acquisition and production.

It is clear that the use of the Nahua-Mixteca variant of the Late Postclassic International Style and symbol set appears in highly variable forms in the Aztatlán core zone. The investment in polychrome ceramics together with the emphasis on the portrayal of creation stories and heroic narratives is suggestive of an internal ranking within the elite, perhaps with some sense of paramountcy invested in a *señorío* like San Felipe Aztatán that probably is identified with a prehispanic domain or *provincia* known as Aztatlán. Following proposals by Michael Mathiowetz (Chapter 13), the paramount lord of this and other *señoríos* in the coastal core zone may have administrated a system of rotating positions of authority and responsibilities among a secondary class of nobles through the manipulation of polychrome ceramic bowls and vases used in cargos. The emphasis on heroic narratives and creation stories also suggests a shared investment in the strategies of lineage hierarchies between the Aztatlán core region and those of Oaxaca, such as the Nochixtlán Valley and the Valley of Oaxaca (Marcus 1983:358–362). One cannot discuss the politics of Mixtec kinship hierarchies, for example, without also discussing the way in which kinship segments defined by genealogies had distributed themselves over the landscape. Like the elite kinship structure, the division of the land was justified by mythohistorical events involving founding ancestors of the various kin-group segments described in colonial sources as *linajes*, or lineages (Pohl 2009).

The system of alliance corridors controlled by these lineages was seen as the solution to the management of extreme variability in the environment. Decentralization, it seems, became the more stable long-term adaptation for the region as a whole following the circa AD 1000 collapse of the highly nucleated polities of the Classic period. Stability lay in the fact that these multiple small units were simply more buffered against potential volatility within neighboring *señoríos* and hence more resilient to stress than a more highly integrated centralized system focusing on an urban center. These lineage organizations empowered nobles with unlimited authority to control and direct human labor not only to intensify agricultural production anywhere it was needed but even relocate entire farming communities from one region to another. They could draft whole populations to serve as troops during military campaigns, enforce rule over communities that spoke as many as 10 different languages, or demand tribute from remote regions as if they were participating in some giant monopoly game (Marcus 1983:358–360).

Nevertheless, shared kinship ideology alone would not support such a level of decentralized complexity without the use of some physical manifestation. Integrating mechanisms were therefore sponsored by embedding the religious ideology of lineage networks into the landscape through the establishment of a system of pilgrimage shrines. The shrines consisted of sacred mountains, caves, or cliffs marked with pictographs among other remote locations that were established along major routes of interaction. Many served as boundary markers while some were major devotional shrines despite their remote setting. For example, members of the highest-ranked Mixtec lineage of Tilantongo were preserved as mummies in a cave presided over by an oracular priestess named Lady Nine Grass located over 96.5 km (60 mi) south of the kingdom on a route leading to the Pacific coast and Tututepec along the Río

Verde. In comparable fashion, other Mixtec and Zapotec lineages were united across the Valley of Oaxaca and maintained at an oracular center at Mitla where the remains of the highest-ranking Zapotec lineage of Zaachila were preserved and consulted through a priest of Bezelao (Lord Thirteen Flower), an avatar of Xochipilli.

Ixtlán del Río: An Aztatlán Regional Coordinating Center

Like Mitla, the site of Ixtlán del Río is anomalous in size and sophistication in masonry construction, and yet it does not appear to have functioned as a dominant center of rule over a political system. Instead, it is located in an intermediate zone of cooperative dynamics between the coast, the sierra, and Lake Chapala (Figures I.3, I.4a). The fact that most of the ruins surrounding the central ceremonial precinct are replicas of the kinds of residential structures found at ranking Aztatlán sites in the immediate surrounding region suggests that it was maintained as a ceremonial center for the performance of ritualism essential to the ideology of noble-class cohesion, such as the awarding of lineage titles, decisions over the conduct of military campaigns, the resolution of political disputes, or arrangements of royal marriages. By means of comparison, the then-contemporaneous (post-AD 1250/1280) paramount Casas Grandes center at Paquimé in northern Chihuahua also shares much in terms of comparable size together with the use of specific forms of ceremonial construction with Ixtlán del Río, such as stone-faced platform architecture. It therefore seems plausible to consider that it too functioned as a ritual center with its concentration of otherwise discrete occupational units more typical of residential architecture at secondary centers maintained across the Casas Grandes region by Paquime's outlying constituents. We see that many of the characteristics discussed for the lineage-based hierarchies that dominated Oaxaca have been identified and discussed as major features of the Aztatlán tradition by the contributors to this volume. If Aztatlán nobles maintained a level of state-like integration but deployed it through systems of decentralized complexity, it seems likely that we are dealing with co-traditions that—in league with Oaxaca and Puebla—constituted a parallel sociopolitical system of both competitors and agents to the Aztec and Purépecha empires. This western Tolteca-Chichimeca system—with Ixtlán del Río situated at a strategic intersection of various ethnolinguistic-group subregions in the southern Aztatlán region (Figure I.3a; see Mathiowetz 2019a, 2023a)—established connectivity with social networks in northern Mexico and the Greater U.S. Southwest via links and hubs that incorporated the local systems of production through and around which it expanded while promoting its integrating identity and civilizational content to facilitate coordination and exclusivity. As a result, the distinction between center and periphery became less meaningful as organization became more dependent on local custom, culture, and environment than the dominance of a political center.

Aztatlán and the Debate on Mesoamerica-U.S. Southwest/Mexican Northwest Interaction

It is clear from the preceding discussion that the Aztatlán tradition has been almost entirely absent from the dialogue on social changes in broader Mesoamerica during the Postclassic period. The recognition that Aztatlán societies developed vast social networks to the south and east opens new avenues of research for scholars of the Toltec (Kowalski and Kristan-Graham 2011; Stanton, Taube, Coltman, and Marengo 2023; Wren et al. 2017), Nahua-Mixteca and Zapotec (Blomster 2008; Zborover and Kroefges 2015), Huastec (Faust and Richter 2015), and Tarascan cultures (Pollard 2000), not to mention Lower Central American societies and beyond (Beekman and McEwan 2022; McEwan and Hoopes 2021; Steinbrenner et al. 2021). Until recently, the details of Aztatlán dynamics rarely have been factored into models of social change in the U.S. Southwest and Northwest Mexico (SW/NW), a subject to which we now turn.

In our view, the Aztatlán tradition is situated at the crux of the more than century-long debate on the nature and degree of Mesoamerica and SW/NW interaction (Figure I.10). The literature on this debate is voluminous, and here we provide examples of some key publications from recent decades on the archaeology of northwest Mesoamerica and northern Mexico including syntheses on the subject of Mesoamerica and SW/NW interaction for readers to consult (Hers et al. 2000; Bonfiglioli et al. 2006; Caseldine 2020; Foster and Weigand 1985; Lekson 1999, 2008, 2015; Mathien and McGuire 1986; Mathiowetz 2011, 2018; McGuire 1980, 1987, 2011; McGuire and Villalpando 2007; Nelson 2004; Nelson and Minnis 2018; Nelson et al. 2015; Phillips Jr. 2002; Pohl 2016a; Pohl and Mathiowetz 2022; Punzo Díaz and Villalpando 2015; Reyman, ed. 1995; Riley 2005; Wilcox 1986a; Wilcox et al. 2008; Woosley and Ravesloot 1993; Wright 2022). The push for an "archaeology without borders" that considers the intertwined histories of the U.S. Southwest and Mexican Northwest has led to a series of publications looking beyond the national boundaries established over a century and a half ago with the Treaty of Guadalupe Hidalgo (Hays-Gilpin et al. 2021; Hegmon 2000; Villalpando and McGuire 2014; Webster and McBrinn 2008). A florescence in research in the Borderlands region also has provided insights on a key

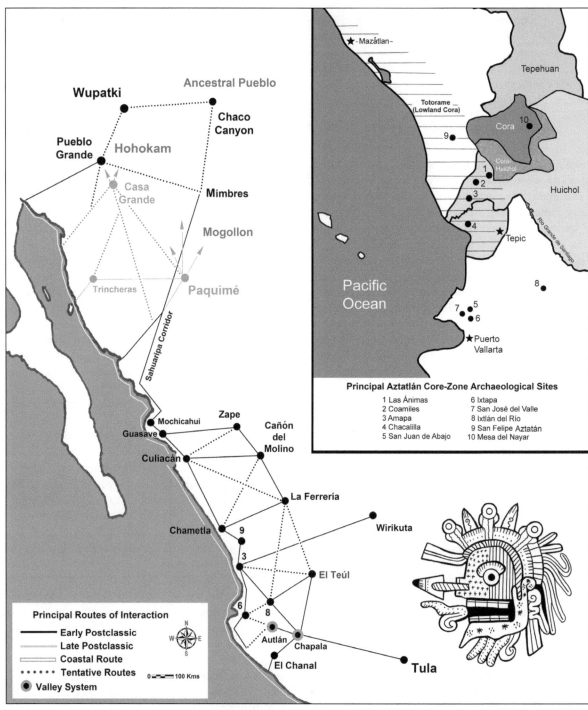

FIGURE I.10. Social networks of the Aztatlán region and the U.S. Southwest/Northwest Mexico, AD 850/900–1350+. Aztatlán social networks developed and expanded across and beyond west Mexico after AD 850/900 in response to economic interchange and ritual behaviors that crisscrossed the coast and highlands. In some instances, they may have been based on earlier Epiclassic interaction corridors. The northward expansion of these networks included Chaco Canyon, Mimbres, and Hohokam to the north in different ways and probably by multiple routes after AD 850. These routes would have changed through time as indicated in the schematic networks presented here. Coastal routes from the Gulf of California led up various drainages into the interior (see more detailed maps in Vokes and Gregory 2007:Figures 17.1, 17.3, 17.4, 17.6, 17.7, 17.8, 17.9). By AD 1200, the Sahuaripa corridor led from the coast to Casas Grandes sites. It may have been based on an earlier route utilized by Mimbres people. After AD 1200, Paquimé developed extensive networks of connectivity ranging from Cerro de Trincheras, Casa Grande, and northward to Puebloan and Mogollon societies—each of which devised their own interaction and distribution networks. Drawing by Michael Mathiowetz and John M.D. Pohl.

area that lies between the northern extent of the Aztatlán tradition and the southern Southwest (Carpenter and Pailes 2022; Carpenter et al. 2023; Carpenter and Sánchez, eds. 1997; Pailes 2017). Given the proposal that Aztatlán core-zone material culture, ideas, and practices reshaped the lives of U.S. Southwestern and northern Mexican people (Mathiowetz 2011, 2018, 2019a), it is imperative to continue research on the dynamics of this intervening region. Additional work is needed at sites along routes of interchange, such as the proposed Sahuaripa corridor leading from the Pacific coast to the Chihuahuan interior (Carpenter and Sánchez 2022; Carpenter et al. 2021).

We hope that the data presented in this volume serve as a catalyst for reexamining (that is, contribute towards revising) current conceptions of social dynamics, social change, and historical processes of ethnogenesis among various cultural traditions of the U.S. Southwest and Mexican Northwest so as to better contextualize local cultural transformations within "Big Picture" supraregional dynamics. Our knowledge of Aztatlán political, religious, economic, and social organization and interaction networks has increased exponentially over the past two decades since Kelley's (2000) final publication on the northward orientation of Aztatlán networks and Di Peso's (1974; Di Peso et al. 1974) earlier postulations of Casas Grandes connections to the Pacific coast. As such, we are in a better position to revisit current conceptions of U.S. Southwest and northern Mexican dynamics with a series of overarching culture-specific questions in relation to the Aztatlán tradition's role in the Mesoamerica-U.S. Southwest interaction debate:

1. How did Aztatlán polities, religion, and dynamics impact the development and nature of the Chaco Canyon Great House system, regional interaction, ritualism and ritual economies linked to political-religious hierarchies, and the explosive period of construction that occurred around AD 1040 (see Gruner 2019; Heitman and Plog 2015; Kennett et al. 2017; Lekson 1999, 2008, 2015; Lekson, ed. 2006; Nelson 2006; Van Dyke and Heitman 2021)?
2. What role did Aztatlán developments have in the pithouse-to-pueblo transition during the AD 900s in the Mimbres region and the social, political, and religious transformations that coincided with the florescence of the Classic Mimbres figurative bowl tradition (see Anyon and LeBlanc 1984; Brody 2004; Gilman and LeBlanc 2017; Gilman et al. 2014, 2019; Nelson and Hegmon 2010; Powell-Martí and Gilman 2006; Roth et al. 2018; Schafer 2003; Seltzer-Rogers 2021; Snow et al. 2011)?
3. In what ways did pre-Aztatlán dynamics (i.e., pre-AD 850/900) in west Mexico impact the Hohokam world? How did that influence change after AD 850/900 and through time during the Aztatlán era, particularly with the emergence of the Salado phenomenon after AD 1300 that coincided with the rise of the Casas Grandes culture (see Borck and Clark 2021; Caseldine 2020; Crown 1994; Dean 2000; Fish and Fish 2007; Haury 1976; Hill 2018; Kelly 1944; McGuire and Villalpando 2007; Nelson et al. 2017; Wallace 2014; Wallace, ed. 2014; Wright 2014, 2021)?
4. How did societies in the Aztatlán region influence Medio-period (AD 1200–1450) dynamics in the Casas Grandes region and Paquimé, the most "Mesoamerican" of all sites in the U.S. Southwest and Mexican Northwest (see Cruz Antillón and Maxwell 2018; Kelley and Phillips Jr. 2017; Mathiowetz 2011; Minnis and Whalen 2015; Pailes and Searcy 2022; Schaafsma and Riley 1999; VanPool and VanPool 2007; Whalen and Minnis 2001, 2009)?
5. In what ways did Jornada Mogollon communities, interacting at the time with Classic Mimbres societies after AD 1000 and with Paquimé and Casas Grandes sites by AD 1300, adapt or incorporate ideas or practices that stem from participation in social networks that extended to the Aztatlán region (see Miller 2018; Rocek and Kenmotsu 2018; Wiseman 2019)?
6. How did Aztatlán networks (either directly or indirectly through interaction with the Casas Grandes region) play a role in the Trincheras tradition (see McGuire and Villalpando 2012; McGuire et al. 1999; Villalpando and McGuire 2017) and broader Sonoran and Sierra Madre Occidental dynamics (see Carpenter and Pailes 2022; Pailes 2017; Pailes and Searcy 2022)?
7. How did Aztatlán interaction and intellectual networks that led into the U.S. Southwest through various avenues influence the late thirteenth-century depopulation of the Four Corners region and the subsequent social, political, religious, economic, and demographic transformation of Pueblo IV villages by AD 1300 (see Adams and Duff 2004; Bernardini et al. 2021; Duff 2002; Duwe 2020; Duwe and Preucel 2019; Gregory and Wilcox 2007; Ortman 2012; Peeples 2018; Ware 2014; Whiteley 2018)?

Given the vast interconnectedness of social networks across the U.S. Southwest and northern Mexico (Mills et al. 2013), it is difficult to overlook the fact that many of these major transformations coincided with the Aztatlán era (AD 850/900–1350+) when there is evidence of an increasingly heightened northward interchange of material culture and religious beliefs and practices. These interactions in no way were unidirectional, and it is equally compelling to ask how social changes in the U.S. Southwest and Mexican Northwest shaped Aztatlán dynamics—a topic that has received much less attention.

Social and demographic changes in these far northern regions—such as the depopulation of the Four Corners region in the northern U.S. Southwest in the mid to late AD 1200s—often are characterized by archaeologists as adaptative responses to a fluctuating environment (Kohler et al. 2010; Scheffer et al. 2021), although religious factors certainly played a pivotal role (Crown 1994; Fowles 2013; Glowacki 2015; Glowacki and Van Keuren 2011; Hays-Gilpin and Hill 1999; Hays-Gilpin and Schaafsma 2010; Mathiowetz 2011, 2021a; Mathiowetz and Turner 2021; McGuire 2011; Schaafsma 1999, 2000, 2001; Schaafsma, ed. 2000; Schaafsma and Taube 2006; Taube 2001; Wright 2014). In the Aztatlán region, by comparison, the sudden florescence of new ideologies and ritual practices coincided with, if not precipitated, major changes in political and economic organization and the expansion of social networks after AD 850/900. It is possible that newly adopted religious tenets and ideologies were a driving force in Aztatlán sociopolitical and economic transformations. While ecological change surely played a role in the north, perhaps the decision by people in the U.S. Southwest and northern Mexico to adopt and adapt (to varying degrees) religious beliefs and ritual practices deriving from the Aztatlán region shaped periods of social reorganization in the far north. Chapters in this volume illustrate the point that Aztatlán societies flourished during an era of extraordinary internationalism and connectivity, yet this conclusion draws a striking contrast when juxtaposed with the historical conceptions of societies to the far north as being largely isolated and insular such that they are suitable for study as relatively isolated cultural evolutionary developments.

The Control of Relevant Data: A Key Issue

From our perspective, the foremost obstacle to the resolution of questions on Mesoamerican-U.S. Southwestern interaction is the varying degrees of control of relevant data by scholars involved in this debate. We agree with Stephen Lekson's (2011; Lekson and Peregrine 2004) conclusion that what is needed in North American archaeology is a dramatic amplification in the scale and scope of analyses towards writing "Big Histories" (see Beekman et al. 2025). It is clear to us that developments in the Aztatlán region cannot be understood without contextualizing them within continental-scale social dynamics of the era ranging from Chaco Canyon in the north to Lower Central America in the southeast.

Jane Kelley (2017:183–184), the late senior scholar of Chihuahuan archaeology, expressed concerns on the control of relevant data and shared her view on the state of the field:

> One of the chronic challenges in assessing archaeological propositions is the control of relevant bodies of data [...]. In other words, there is no scholar (or even team of scholars) working today that controls the data needed to understand long-distance contacts and their consequences in the greater region. Until there is an entire cohort of archaeologists who share such a broad body of comparative information, the debate about long-distance influences cannot move into the mainstream, but the challenge is enormous given the sheer quantity of data.

Kelley (2017:184–185) extended her concerns to Casas Grandes studies in terms of this culture's relation to societies of Pacific-coastal Mexico (i.e., the Aztatlán region):

> In contrast to their US counterparts, Mexican archaeologists working in Chihuahua and Sonora have no problem hearing echoes of Mesoamerican cultures (especially those of Mexico's west coast), but they were trained in Mesoamerican archaeology and understand its internal variations and many examples of population movements and interregional contacts. Moreover, their theoretical foundations differ from those of the gringos who for years tried to understand prehistoric cultures as shaped only by local natural environments.

Kelley's concerns about lack of control of data are not unique. Scholars over the past few decades have noted that the lack of control of relevant literature and data spanning multiple regions from Mesoamerica to the U.S. Southwest has hindered the resolution of questions of mutual interest on long-distance interaction (Kelley 1986:81; Plog 1993:291), a problem that surely contributed to the polemics surrounding this debate. Twenty-five years ago, Randall McGuire (1996:433) shared his view on the problem: "The reality is, however, that the vast majority of Southwestern archaeologists remain relatively uninformed and unconcerned about the archaeology of northern Mesoamerica." Plog and colleagues (2022:4–6) note that a renewed focus on determining the geographical origins of Mesoamerican influence and objects has been shaped by two prevailing factors: (1) the increasing recognition that U.S. Southwestern and northern Mexican social networks were vastly larger than previously accepted, and (2) a suite of publications over the past two decades that has focused on narrow topics including ballcourts (Wilcox 1991), copper bells (Boyce 2015; Vargas 1994, 1995, 2001), human skeletal remains and ancient DNA (Morales-Arce et al. 2017; Snow et al. 2011), scarlet macaws (Crown 2016; George et al. 2018; Schwartz et al.

eds., 2022; Watson et al. 2015), cacao (Crown 2020; Crown and Hurst 2009; Mathiowetz 2011, 2019a; Washburn et al. 2011), religious parallels (Mathiowetz 2011, 2018; Schaafsma 1999, 2001; Schaafsma and Taube 2006; Taube 2000, 2001), and others. While we applaud recent collaborations in the study of connectivity, there remain many underdeveloped avenues of research that are worthy of pursuit.

West Mexican scholars today widely recognize the foundational model of the Aztatlán tradition and its links to U.S. Southwestern and northwest Mexican dynamics that J. Charles Kelley (1986, 1995, 2000; see Jiménez 2020) devised based on his decades of field research (along with elaborations on this model by Michael Foster [1986a, 1999]). It is curious to note, however, that engagement with this body of work (not to mention even recently published Aztatlán literature) is scarcely evident in the current dialogue on social change and dynamics of the southwestern United States and northern Mexico except when noted in passing. Scholars in these northern regions who advocate against Aztatlán (or any Mesoamerican) influence often have very little, if any, base of knowledge in the specific details and current understandings of Mesoamerican religion, iconography, deity complexes, or the social, political, economic, and demographic dynamics that characterized the Postclassic period during the era when Mesoamerica-U.S. Southwest connectivity was heightened. The problem we see is that this variability in data control can only lead to complications when it comes time to assess or critique models of interaction proposed by colleagues in the south who possess a broader base of knowledge on Mesoamerican dynamics. To be fair, only a handful of Aztatlán and northwest Mesoamerican scholars working today possess the requisite knowledge of U.S. Southwest/Mexican Northwest archaeology and dynamics. In order to adequately address issues of connectivity, it is imperative that scholars in both regions operate at the same scales, have control of the same datasets, and work from a common base of knowledge. Perhaps as a result of the general omission of Mesoamerican dynamics from consideration, it is generally concluded by some that societies in these northern regions had little to no significant interaction or integration with their neighbors to the south in Mesoamerica (including west Mexico) that contributed in any meaningful way to social changes. Societies in the north often are simply characterized as distant consumers of intermittently acquired esoteric Mesoamerican prestige goods (e.g., scarlet macaws, cacao, and copper) that may have lost their meaning along the way while traveling to their destination locale.

The scale of most projects conducted today trends toward favoring the perception of endogenous forces (Pailes 2017). This view of cultural insularity is perhaps most notable in current conceptions of the major center of Paquimé in the Casas Grandes region—a site with the most unequivocal Mesoamerican-style material and visual culture, ritualism, political organization, and architectural forms. Critical responses were antagonistic to Charles Di Peso's (1974; Di Peso et al. 1974) continental-scale approach to Casas Grandes, his historical methods, and his vision of an interconnected prehispanic world. Rather than engage J. Charles Kelley's insights on Aztatlán that better fit the revised chronology of the Medio-period Casas Grandes tradition as a post-AD 1200 phenomenon (see Dean and Ravesloot 1993), subsequent models of Casas Grandes instead pivoted inward to focus almost exclusively on local cultural-evolutionary processes that are largely predicated on the decision to simply not factor in Mesoamerican dynamics (Whalen and Minnis 2001, 2009). While this approach has greatly enriched our knowledge of the local archaeology, the sole focus on such a narrow region surrounding Paquimé consequently has isolated these developments from the broader historical contexts that make Paquimé and its clearly Mesoamerican and Aztatlán components so compelling. Such models sharply contrast with more holistic assessments of Casas Grandes developments that have adapted to the revised chronology and include local, regional, and macroregional data along with data from adjoining regions in the Aztatlán world, broader Mesoamerica, and Lower Central America to place Paquimé in its supraregional context (Pohl and Mathiowetz 2022). This approach supports the views of Charles Di Peso and J. Charles Kelley on the proper scale at which we should examine precolumbian historical dynamics and further aligns with the recent "historical turn" in U.S. Southwestern archaeology (Fowles and Mills 2017). Local-origin models do acknowledge probable west Mexican influence in Casas Grandes dynamics and recognize that "distant contacts were clearly of critical importance" to the Casas Grandes world (Whalen and Minnis 2003:310). However, the specific details of these critical distant dynamics in Mesoamerica and west Mexico almost never factor into local-origin models to any significant degree. Peer-polity models and down-the-line exchange have become the general explanatory frameworks for interaction. In our estimation, the inclusion of only local or immediate regional data in the formulation of more insular models of the Casas Grandes polity highlights an inherent weakness in these approaches. Excluding the dynamics of then-contemporaneous societies in Mesoamerica that supplied the clearly foreign elements of "critical importance" to Casas Grandes political and religious legitimization strategies inhibits an accurate characterization of the nature of Paquimé, its regional system, and its influence on U.S. Southwestern social change. One lingering issue not addressed in these sorts of models pertains to the social processes involved in long-distance interaction (Lekson 2018:99). How, by what mechanism, and for what reason, did Casas Grandes, Mimbres, Chacoan, and Hohokam people come to establish, negotiate, and maintain social relations for centuries with people in the Mesoamerican source region/s in order to acquire scarlet macaws, copper, and cacao from hundreds and thousands of kilometers away? This question can only be answered by factoring in social dynamics of the source region/s and the intervening areas through which these items and associated ideas passed.

While scholars trained in Mesoamerican art, archaeology, ethnohistory, and ethnology more regularly venture to publish a "view from the south" with insights on U.S. Southwest and Mexican Northwest cultural developments, there are exceedingly few scholars trained in the archaeology, ethnohistory, and ethnology of these northern regions who publish insights on developments in the Aztatlán region. Thus, few archaeologists who specialize in the archaeology of the U.S. Southwest or northern Mexico have proposed a "view from the north" to examine how these northern regions relate to or influenced Aztatlán societies or, more generally, west Mexico and beyond (Hopkins 2012; Mathiowetz 2011; Punzo Díaz and Villalpando 2015; Wright 2022). VanPool and colleagues (2008), who work in the Casas Grandes region, concluded that the Aztatlán region played a significant role in the Medio-period development of Paquimé, particularly in relation to their more generalized model of tobacco shamanism as a central organizing principle of this society. Issues emerge with their model, however, partly due to lack of control of relevant Aztatlán data. First, their interpretation of Aztatlán religion and its relation to descendant Indigenous practices glosses over the complexities of Gran Nayar ethnology and largely relies on Peter Furst and Barbara Myerhoff's publications on Wixárika (Huichol) that have been critiqued by some ethnologists working in the region for lack of intensive fieldwork (e.g., Fikes 1993; Neurath 2021:54–55). Second, while Van Pool and colleagues adequately summarize J. Charles Kelley's then-current model of Aztatlán as a mercantile system, their analysis of Aztatlán religion does not focus on objects or iconography from this tradition. Instead, they draw sweeping conclusions on the nature of Aztatlán religion by extrapolating from a few objects of the much earlier Comala culture of Colima. By and large, west Mexican archaeologists do not consider Aztatlán societies to be direct inheritors of Comala traditions. To be fair, this study preceded more intensive studies of Aztatlán religion, symbolism, and ritualism published over the past decade (see below). In sum, longstanding patterns exist wherein models of U.S. Southwestern and northern Mexican social change largely have excluded Aztatlán and Mesoamerican dynamics. Misperceptions persist on the nature of Aztatlán societies and their role in this debate while the lack of control of relevant data has inhibited open dialogue rooted in a common base of knowledge.

Aztatlán Religion and "Flower Worlds"

Since the 1940s, Aztatlán scholars have periodically assessed the religious, ritual, and iconographic content in ceramics, sculpture, and rock art. Deities (and associated symbols) in Aztatlán art found in the highland Mexican pantheon include the feathered serpent Quetzalcoatl (and his wind aspect Ehecatl-Quetzalcoatl), a skeletal deity variously identified as the Venus war god Tlahuizcalpantecuhtli or the god of death Mictlantecuhtli, the god of spring and regeneration Xipe Totec, and the storm/rain god Tlaloc (see Ekholm 1942; Meighan 1976; Mountjoy 1974a, 1987b; Nicholson 1989; Schöndube 1974; Von Winning 1977). The solar deity Xochipilli-Piltzintli was added to the Aztatlán pantheon more recently (Mathiowetz 2011, 2019b). During the past two decades or so, more intensive focus on Aztatlán religion, ritual practice, and symbolism has emerged in conference presentations and recent publications (Bojórquez Diego 2009; Forest et al. 2020; Garduño Ambriz 2013b, 2013c; Jiménez 2018, 2020; Mathiowetz 2011, 2018, 2019a, 2019b, 2020a, 2021a, 2023a, 2025b; Mathiowetz et al. 2015; Mountjoy 2001a, 2005; Pohl 2012a, 2012b; Pohl and Mathiowetz 2022; Solar Valverde 2019; Solar Valverde et al. 2011). These advances have facilitated cross-comparative studies with the religion and ritual of other Mesoamerican societies to the south and east as well as cultures of the broader U.S. Southwest and northern Mexico. While scholars have sometimes sought direct comparisons between Puebloan religion and that of Mesoamerican societies such as the Aztec and others (e.g., McGuire 2011; Schaafsma 1999, 2001; Young 2000), we find it to be most appropriate to compare Puebloan cosmology and ritualism first and foremost to that of societies in the Gran Nayar and Aztatlán regions of west Mexico. It is important to recognize, however, that Aztec and Aztatlán ideologies and deities share some common roots through their connections to the Toltec and Nahua-Mixteca cultures.

A schism exists among U.S. Southwestern and northwest Mexican scholars today as to the degree to which ideologically loaded items from Mesoamerica retained (or lost) their meaning as they were transferred from the source region/s to their arrival and incorporation into ritual programs at northern destination locales. For instance, Crown (2020; Crown and Hurst 2009) contends that cacao at Chaco Canyon was acquired from Mesoamerica (in her view the Maya region) perhaps with the culinary knowledge of its preparation and associated ritualism. On the other hand, while Schwartz and colleagues (2022:325) conclude that scarlet macaws from Mesoamerica are closely linked to the sun, rain, and agricultural fertility, they contend that no uniform complex of ideas associated with these birds and other Mesoamerican objects in the U.S. Southwest and northern Mexico was adopted from Mesoamerica. There is no evidence that northern Mexican and U.S. Southwestern people ever sought or acquired other Mesoamerican exotica including gold, silver, jade, copal incense, amber, jaguar pelts, obsidian mirrors, the feathers of other valued birds including the quetzal or lovely cotinga, or other goods esteemed in southern ritual economies such as those illustrated in highland Mexican tribute lists (e.g., the *Codex Mendoza*; see Berdan and Anawalt 1997). This begs the question, what common attributes of scarlet macaws, copper, and cacao were so important that U.S. Southwest and northern Mexican people sought these select items for inclusion in their ritual programs for centuries to the exclusion of other Mesoamerican goods?

It is noteworthy that the three main items obtained by U.S. Southwestern and northwest Mexican people from Mesoamerica (cacao, scarlet macaws, and copper) all are linked to Flower Worlds ritualism—a term devised by Jane Hill that has been adopted by a growing body of scholars to encompass a complex set of ideas across Mesoamerica and the SW/NW with culturally variable expressions revolving around the sun, rain, and agricultural fertility (e.g., Chinchilla Mazariegos 2023; Coltman 2021, 2023; Hays-Gilpin and Hill 1999; Hill 1992; Hosler 1994b; Jordan 2023; Mathiowetz 2011, 2018, 2019a, 2019b, 2021a, 2022; Mathiowetz and Turner 2021; Pohl 2021; Stanton, Taube, and Coltman 2023; Taube 2001, 2010; Turner 2016; Turner and Mathiowetz 2021; Weiner 2015). The materialization of flower world domains among various cultures may well relate to the complementary yet antagonistic interplay of both diurnal and nocturnal forces of fertility. Notably, the Chacoan, Mimbres, and Casas Grandes engagement with Aztatlán Flower World concepts appears to be different than that of the Hohokam who did not adopt cylinder jars (Chaco), cargo-bowl traditions (Mimbres), or Xochipilli (i.e., Sun Youth) ritualism (Casas Grandes). It may be no coincidence that the U.S. Southwestern and northern Mexican societies who acquired these items all have some identified material expression of Flower Worlds ritualism.

In the Aztatlán core region, Flower Worlds rites and symbolism appear to be a post-AD 850/900 phenomenon that is partly linked to a newly adopted narrative related to the creation of the sun and/or its diurnal and nocturnal aspects, which provides evidence against the hypothesis that there was a "hard nucleus" of Flower Worlds ritualism shared among populations as early as the Archaic period spanning the U.S. Southwest and Mesoamerica (see Boyd 2016; Wright 2022). Rather, the development of Flower Worlds ritualism among various societies at particular places and times appears to be a historical phenomenon traceable among interacting societies who share intellectual lineages (see Turner and Mathiowetz 2021). Given that copper and cacao in these northern regions likely derive from the Aztatlán region (particularly in the core zone) where they were used in Flower World contexts (Mathiowetz 2011, 2019a, 2023a, 2025b), it is reasonable to propose that Aztatlán people probably also played a role in the transmission of scarlet macaws to the north along with the solar ideologies invoked through these birds (Mathiowetz, this volume).

Indeed, nearly every object, idea, architectural form, political formation, and ritual practice typically characterized as being of Mesoamerican derivation in the U.S. Southwest and northwest Mexico can be found in the Aztatlán core zone, essentially in a region that triangulates between Mazatlán (Sinaloa), Puerto Vallarta (Jalisco), and Ixtlán del Río in Nayarit (Mathiowetz 2021b, 2021c). These practices include Flower Worlds ritualism, cylinder jars, cacao cultivation and consumption, *tezcacuitlapilli* (back mirrors), I-shaped ballcourts, platform-mound architecture, colonnades, feathered and horned serpent traditions, solar (Xochipilli-Piltzintli) worship, solstice and equinoctial ritualism, Venus-related warfare, Tlaloc and ancestral-rain rites, portraiture bowls, copper production, and others. Few of these characteristics appear to be present in the Cahitan-speaking region (see Carpenter and Sánchez, this volume), which points to a spatial discontinuity in the distribution (or acceptance) of these items and ideas that largely bypassed broad intervening regions, which may be indicative of a "voyaging" form of interaction (see Nelson 2004:294–295). This is not a matter of simple "leap-frogging" of items and ideas over the Borderlands region. Perhaps we might instead relate these patterns of distribution to selective engagements for corridor access that changed through time. It is clear that the Borderlands region through which goods, ideas, and people passed is a key area of interest where more fieldwork is needed (see Carpenter et al. 2023). It may be the case that different ethnic-group subregions participating in the Aztatlán tradition all possessed unique political-religious ideologies, but the expansion and selective adoption and adaptation of aspects of core-zone Flower Worlds ritualism was a malleable glue binding together different Aztatlán regions and polities and those in adjoining regions.

We recognize that not all contributors to this volume advocate models of Aztatlán socioreligious organization that include the identification of Flower World domains. For example, Laura Solar Valverde (2023:826) recently expressed doubts on the significance of the concept of "Flower Worlds" and its applicability for interpretations of the archaeological record in broader Mesoamerica, although she incorrectly characterizes studies on the expression of diverse floral realms among various cultures of different eras as a "generalizing explanation." It is worth noting that ethnologists who have worked directly with various Indigenous ethnic groups in west Mexico and the Gran Nayar (i.e., in the former Aztatlán region) in recent decades have reported significant insights on the critical role of flowers in contemporary Indigenous ontologies that complement Jane Hill's original cross-cultural analysis, including among Wixárika, Náayeri, and Caz' Ahmo (e.g., Benciolini 2014; Castillo Badillo and Coyle 2022; Coyle 2001, this volume; Neurath 2021; Ocampo 2019). In adjoining regions of northwest Mexico, Flower World domains are well-documented among the Yoreme, Yoeme, and Rarámuri cultures (e.g., Camacho Ibarra 2011; Evers and Molina 1987; Mathiowetz 2023c; Molina and Shorter 2021; Morrison 1992; Salmón 1999) that may be traceable in archaeological material culture and ritual behaviors. The proposition that flowers played a significant role in Indigenous worldviews, ethics, morality, and conceptions of culturally specific flowery world domains in the Aztatlán region (particularly in the coastal core zone) is well-grounded in the ethnographic realities of flower-centered ritual and symbolism among descendant Indigenous traditions in the Gran Nayar region and broader northern Mexico and Mesoamerica, a point that Solar Valverde neglects to consider in her critique.

Moving forward, additional studies of Aztatlán political-religious organization and social dynamics will help to clarify the role of Aztatlán societies in prehispanic Mesoamerican and U.S. Southwestern interactions that included the interchange of goods and ideas. A continental-scale approach to this issue may transform our views on the histories and dynamics of Indigenous societies in the U.S. Southwest and northwest Mexico in fundamental ways that will enable us to refine comparable supraregional models on the relation of U.S. Southwestern societies to Plains cultures (Hill and Ritterbush 2022; Montgomery 2015; Spielmann 1991) and Mississippian societies to the east (Peregrine and Lekson 2006), Fremont groups to the north (Searcy and Talbot 2015), and California societies to the west (Smith and Fauvelle 2015).

Ethnogenesis, Cultural Continuity, and Collaboration

Since the 1990s, archaeologists increasingly have focused on the historical forces shaping social identities and ethnogenesis (e.g., Hu 2013; Meskell 2002; Weik 2014). In the U.S. Southwest, examinations of ethnogenesis and identity formation, sometimes characterized as the process of "becoming," have contributed a more balanced approach that equally values Indigenous perspectives on their own histories. These studies indicate that identity is intimately connected to the landscape by repetitive visitations to sacred locales; through movement, migration, and pilgrimage; and in social memories that are attached to cultural or natural features on that landscape (Bernardini 2005; Bernardini et al. 2021; Duwe 2020; Duwe and Preucel 2019; Ferguson and Colwell-Chanthaphonh 2006; Fowles 2010; Gregory and Wilcox 2007; Kuwanwisiwma et al. 2018; Mills 2004; Nelson and Strawhacker 2011; Snead 2008), as is well documented in other parts of the world (Ashmore and Knapp 1999) including Mesoamerica.

Northwest Mexico and the broader Aztatlán region were occupied in antiquity by a vast array of ethnic and linguistic groups as evident in the extraordinary diversity of people encountered by the Spaniards in the early 1500s. Chapters in this volume draw connections between the ethnology, ethnohistory, and archaeology of some of these late prehispanic and early historic peoples, including Cahitan-speaking populations between southern Sinaloa and the Arizona border such as the Tahue, Comanito, Mocorito, Mayo, Yaqui, and Opata (Eudeve, Jova, and Teguima groups) in Sonora and Sinaloa (Chapter 8); Wixárika, Náayeri, O'dam, and Náhuat (Chapters 7, 13, 14) in the broader Gran Nayar; and Tarascan people of Michoacán (Chapter 11), for example. In addition, Caz' Ahmo (Caxcan) people today closely identify with archaeological centers in Zacatecas such as Cerro de las Ventanas and nearby sites (Mathiowetz 2025b; Ocampo 2019). While many of these societies became acculturated during the colonial period, rich Indigenous traditions persist in the Gran Nayar and adjoining regions that have been the intensive focus of ethnologists and ethnohistorians over the past few decades. In the Aztatlán coastal core zone, the identification of solar and maize-oriented Flower Worlds ritualism as a central tenet of the political and ritual dynamics of decentralized centers points to a nearly 1,200-year continuity that has been documented among the Náayeri (Cora) and Wixárika (Huichol) today (Benciolini 2014; Coyle 2001, this volume; Mathiowetz 2011, this volume; Neurath 2021) and is a testament to historical processes of ethnogenesis and identity formation. As such, Aztatlán archaeology has much to offer towards addressing questions on the histories of

Indigenous peoples of the region and their centuries-long engagement with and resistance to the Spanish and Mexican governments. Collaborative work with Native groups of the region surely will benefit them in their claims of land rights and historical territoriality amid continuing disputes with local ranchers and farmers, state and national governments, and multinational corporations (Liffman 2011; Morris 2020; Negrín da Silva 2018; Neurath 2022).

Moving Forward in Aztatlán Studies

We consider ourselves to be in the midst of a "Golden Age" of Aztatlán archaeology, emerging from a baseline of knowledge on regional archaeology established in the foundational works of earlier scholars. Ongoing fieldwork by a cohort of archaeologists in the multiple Aztatlán subregions across northwest Mesoamerica highlights the variability of societies that participated in this extensive interaction network and the political-religious programs and economies that bound together these diverse societies into a system of mutualistic interests and relations. We envision a continued florescence in Aztatlán studies in the coming decades in which northern Mexican, U.S. Southwestern, and broader Mesoamerican scholars work together in an open dialogue to devise more accurate models of local and "Big Picture" histories. Finally, we see great potential for connecting the ethnohistory, ethnology, and Indigenous oral histories in west Mexico to the Aztatlán archaeological record and sacred landscape through collaborative archaeologies with descendant communities and stakeholders, as characterizes the practice of archaeology in many areas of the world (Castañeda and Matthews 2008; Colwell-Chanthaphonh and Ferguson 2008; Dongoske et al. 2000; Swidler et al. 1997), including the U.S. Southwest (see above) and other parts of Mesoamerica (Byland and Pohl 1994; Pohl and Byland 1990). Additional opportunities exist for collaborations between Aztatlán archaeologists and Indigenous groups in the U.S. Southwest whose oral traditions relate details of distant southern connections and clan histories of migrations to and from the far south in Mexico, Mesoamerica, and sometimes as far as South America (see Bernardini 2005; Ferguson 2007; Hopkins et al. 2021; Mathiowetz 2011; Reyman 1995; Tosa et al. 2019). Such endeavors will contribute to the push for a more "collaborative synthesis" in archaeology (see Altschul et al. 2017) that at once benefits Indigenous people in their struggle for autonomy, moves toward protection of their cultural heritage that is at risk in a colonial context, and provides knowledge and data to the broader scientific community, policy makers, and the general public.

PART I

What is Aztatlán?

A Historical Perspective

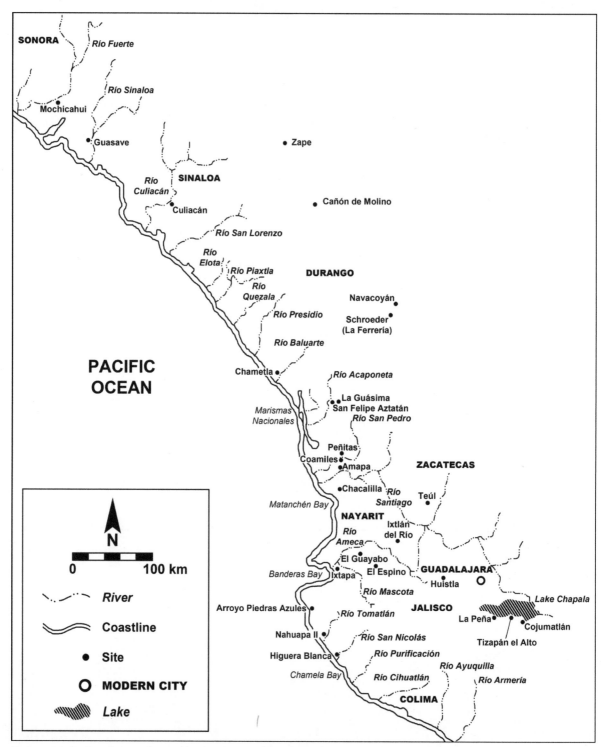

FIGURE 1.1. Regional map of Aztatlán sites in west Mexico. Drawing by Will Russell after original by author.

CHAPTER 1

The Current Status of the Aztatlán Phenomenon in Far Western Mexico

What? Where? and When?

Joseph B. Mountjoy

There are four basic questions regarding the Aztatlán phenomenon central to its investigation during the past eight decades, though each has received significantly different amounts of research emphasis. These questions are: What is Aztatlán? Where is Aztatlán? When is Aztatlán? And, finally, Why is Aztatlán? I will attempt to address the current status of the first three here, leaving my discussion of "Why is Aztatlán?" for some future date due to publication limits for this text. I will begin with the question of "What is Aztatlán?" and trace the historical development of the use of the term and the archaeological materials associated with it (Figure 1.1).

WHAT IS AZTATLÁN?

Fortunately, it is possible to cite a recent summary description of the "Aztatlán Complex" provided by Susan Toby Evans (2008:410) in her impressive, encyclopedic summary of the archaeology of ancient Mexico and Central America:

> This term [Aztatlán Complex] was applied in the Early Colonial period to the cultural complex found along the Pacific Coast of West Mexico and the Northwestern Frontier. Archaeological research has indicated that the sites in the Aztatlán complex emerged in the early Postclassic. The pottery that characterizes these sites is so similar to Mixtec codex style that some researchers once speculated that Aztatlán was the result of a colonization effort by Mixteca-Puebla peoples. These coastal and uplands regions were clearly part of the period's extensive trade networks, but Aztatlán sites were not just trading centers. They were the focal communities in river valleys along the coast, supported by local farming and by production of metal objects and obsidian as well as pottery.

The Historical Basis for the Aztatlán Concept

As for the historical basis for the Aztatlán concept, credit for the formulation of an Aztatlán archaeological phenomenon is usually given to Carl Sauer and Donald Brand who in 1932 published the results of a six-month archaeological and geographical survey they executed during the first half of 1929, inspecting 30 habitational sites and archaeological remains along the coastal plain of Sinaloa and the northern part of the coastal plain of Nayarit (Sauer and Brand 1932). Their stated purpose was to explore the possible existence of a cultural corridor through which contacts occurred between Native cultures of highland Mexico and the southwestern United States during prehispanic times. Sauer and Brand were surprised to find that in the entire coastal area between the Río Sinaloa in northwestern Sinaloa and San Blas, Nayarit, to the southeast, there was evidence of an unexpectedly novel and advanced archaeological culture, especially notable for ceramics they considered superior to modern Mexican wares (Figures I.1–I.2).

Sauer and Brand obtained the name Aztatlán from the 1570 *Teatrum Orbis Terrarum* map by Abraham Ortelius designating an area of northern Nayarit, seemingly just to the north of Culiacán, as having been a native province called Astatlán that was in existence when the Spanish first entered this area of northwestern Mexico. Ganot and Peschard (1995:151) noted inclusions of a province called Aztatlán on other maps, including that of the *Portulano de las Costas Occidentales* dated 1587 by Juan Martínez, H. Iaillot's map of 1694, and the *America Septentrional* map of 1715 by Sanson d'Abbeville.

However, prior to Sauer and Brand's research, M. Leon Diguet mentioned the similar term "Azatlan" as a place visited by Nuño de Guzmán where the "governor" of the town presented him with gifts that included necklaces of pearls (Diguet 1903:11), a gift I have not been able to verify in the Tello *Crónica* (Tello 1968:162). Diguet (1903:4) discusses the area between Culiacán, Sinaloa, and the Río Grande de Santiago in Nayarit as an area of developing Native civilization arising from Toltec roots which survived to the time of the conquest as evident in the tradition reported to the Spanish by the Native Francisco Pantecatl, which encompassed the area from Sentispac south to the Río Grande de Santiago on the central coastal plain of Nayarit.

The Pantecatl account was utilized by Fray Antonio Tello in a *Crónica* he wrote in 1652. In Tello's account, it is related that Pantecatl told his descendants that in ancient times his ancestors invaded the Nayarit coast from another land called Aztatlán, subjected the local inhabitants and founded a great town called Aztatlán near Acaponeta (Tello 1968:33). That town was known by the invading Spaniards to be the main settlement of a province by the same name. So, in brief, that is the ethnohistorical origin of the term Aztatlán, a term that has come to be utilized in the archaeology of west Mexico to designate distinctive preconquest archaeological materials. Such was the case even with Leon Diguet when in 1903 he included the Aztatlán province in the now thoroughly discounted idea of the existence of a Chimalhuacan Confederation. Diguet's description of that Confederation is curiously not much different from what has been attributed to the Aztatlán phenomenon.

Diguet states that besides being a Toltec-affiliated people who invaded northwestern Mexico from some other area of Mexico, subjugated the local populations over a large territory, and imposed their Nahuatl language, customs, and religion, the Chimalhuacan were great artisans and craftspersons. They were known for fabricating objects of different kinds of metals as well as jewelry of precious stones, items that were often important for them in a system of commerce or exchange they used to obtain nonlocal goods possessed by people living outside of the territory they controlled (Diguet 1903:4, 11).

Carl Sauer and Donald Brand's (1932) research provided a more specific inventory of cultural elements they proposed to characterize Aztatlán archaeological material, including pottery vessels with fine, nonlocal paste; decoration of pottery that included such varieties as red on buff, fine incised, and elaborate polychromes with red, white, brown, and black colors—sometimes with white, black or fine incisions used to delineate design patterns and the notable use of "fishhook," "eye," and "feather-like" decorative motifs; pottery *molcajetes* with rattle supports; pottery pipes; pottery spindle whorls; pottery stamps; pottery figurines of "gingerbread" form; stone axes with animal heads depicted on the butt end; abundant artifacts of clear gray obsidian, especially flakes and prismatic blades, but rarely projectile points; and burial of the dead in funerary urns. They also mentioned the construction of mounds, including one quite large example at what they seem to have considered the "type site" of Aztatlán culture, San Felipe de Aztatlán (San Felipe Aztatán) in the Acaponeta Valley. It was there that they reported having found the best representation of the ceramics they termed "Aztatlán" (Sauer and Brand 1932:33).

Culiacán and Chametla, Sinaloa

Sauer and Brand recognized some geographical variation in the Aztatlán phenomenon, with a northern expression in Sinaloa and a southern one in Nayarit. Isabel Kelly followed up on their work in the Sinaloan sector in 1931, first at Chametla in southern Sinaloa (1938) and then in 1935 and 1939 around Culiacán in central Sinaloa (1945a). At Chametla, she excavated at three sites and isolated Aztatlán Complex material in the next-to-final phase (Late Chametla II) of her stratigraphic excavations in all three. Here, the Aztatlán component was characterized by Red-rimmed Decorated and similarly decorated Black-on-buff pottery ware, pipes, and spindle whorls. Prismatic obsidian blades were found associated with Aztatlán pottery but not listed by Kelly as an Aztatlán trait. No figurines or copper objects were included in her Aztatlán Complex.

In Kelly's investigations in the Culiacán area, she both constricted and expanded on the previous definition of the Aztatlán phenomenon. She expanded the definition of Aztatlán ceramics to include vessel shapes, such as bowls with simple, rounded contour, tall, straight-necked jars, and some beakers. Red-rimmed Decorated was common, and she found that incisions were added to some of the red decoration. She noted that the similarly decorated Black-on-buff ware found at Chametla was lacking at Culiacán.

Kelly also expanded the definition of Aztatlán to include a suite of decorative elements found on the pottery vessels, including motifs she describes as: saw, hook, maze, hatch, circle-bar, scallop, wavy panel, bar panel, feather or flower, cursive monster, and face. And she noted that such elements are typically found organized in bands on either the exterior or interior of vessels. She also found a coarser version of polychrome incised Aztatlán ware, and included both plainware and redware *ollas* and jars in the Aztatlán Complex. Kelly's constriction of Aztatlán (in contrast to Sauer and Brand) came in confining its ceramic expression to one phase (Early Culiacán II) at the early end of her stratigraphically ordered sequence, although there is an obvious continuation of Aztatlán-type polychrome wares, albeit with some variation in decorative elements. Post-Aztatlán pottery was characterized primarily on the basis of the addition of "negative overpainting." In the

Culiacán study, pipes, spindle whorls, a pottery mask, prismatic obsidian blades, overhang mano grinding stones, and three-quarter grooved and slab axes were attributed to the Aztatlán complex, but copper objects were considered to be post-Aztatlán.

Guasave, Sinaloa

Kelly's (1942) research was followed by Gordon Ekholm in the Guasave area in the extreme northern part of Sinaloa, especially through excavations conducted at a cemetery in an earthen mound at the El Ombligo site. This gave a much different picture of the Aztatlán "culture" from that of previous surface studies by Sauer and Brand and the excavations by Kelly in trash middens. At El Ombligo (Guasave) there were over 182 human burials (Carpenter 2008:149), at least 102 of which are attributable to the Aztatlán Complex. Forty-eight of these were accompanied by mortuary offerings that (along with some pieces from other local sites) included many items or decorative motifs Ekholm traced to highland central Mexican sources, and especially to the Mixteca-Puebla area based on sophisticated religious iconography depicted on some pottery vessels. Ekholm (1942:124) proposed that the introduction of the Mixteca-Puebla traits into the west coast of Mexico was in part responsible for the formation of the Aztatlán Complex, perhaps in combination with some locally developed traits in the previous phase at Chametla.

Although it is not always possible to determine exactly which of the artifact types or pottery vessels pertained to the Aztatlán Complex at El Ombligo (as opposed to other sites in the vicinity of Guasave), the following is a list of characteristics that Ekholm's research added to the cultural inventory of the Aztatlán phenomenon: extended human burials in an artificially constructed earthen mound; frontal deformation of the head and both the filing and blackening of some teeth; trophy skulls; dusting of burials with red ochre powder; beads of iron pyrite, stone, baked clay, and shell; copper bells, tubular beads, buttons, one ring, one ear spool, and a rectangular sheet; beads and pendants of turquoise; shell beads, pendants, bracelets, tinklers, and plaques for mosaics; footless slab metates; stone vessels of alabaster and banded onyx; incised clay plaques; tall pottery jars with gadrooned bodies and gadrooned bowls; ceramic masks in the form of bird heads; cloisonné-decorated gourds; bone "daggers"; and mortuary cotton shrouds and cotton cords.

Ekholm took special note of the fact that there were no pottery figurines or stone carvings found in Aztatlán contexts and very few prismatic obsidian blades. He proposed that the Red-on-buff decorated ware might be a domestic Aztatlán ware that contrasted with the fancy ceremonial wares, and because of that, might represent a different process of diffusion. The elaborate funerary wares, however, contributed many new design elements to the list of Aztatlán iconic motifs, including: representations of gods from Mixtec codices, especially Mictlantecuhtli or Tlahuizcalpantecuhtli and perhaps Ehecatl or Quetzalcoatl as a wind god; feathered serpent; feathered ball; jaguar skin; tree; flint knife; blood symbols; heart; spider; tied element; stepped grecque; and the arc-through-circle motif.

Cojumatlán, Michoacán, and Ixtlán del Río, Nayarit

After Ekholm's investigations, the focus of Aztatlán studies shifted to areas peripheral to Sinaloa to the east, south, and southeast. In 1941, Robert Lister excavated at Cojumatlán, Michoacán, located just over 11 km (7 mi) southwest of the point where the Río Lerma empties into Lake Chapala (Lister 1949). His stratigraphic excavations revealed a two-phase ceramic sequence suggesting a possible two-phase division in the Aztatlán complex in the Lake Chapala basin. To the pottery inventory of the Aztatlán Complex, Lister added vessel supports of solid conical, animal and human effigies, and stepped-slab forms. Design elements included serpent motifs that we can now attribute to the Toltec fire serpent, or Xiuhcoatl (Figure 1.2). Along with that Toltec-related design motif, Lister recovered two items of pottery also usually associated with the Toltecs: Plumbate (alumina/iron glaze) ware and Mazapan-type mold-made slab figurines. Metal items were abundant; 93 metal artifacts were recovered. Some of the human remains were found buried in a seated position, something later recorded at Amapa in central Nayarit. Lister also found evidence of house floors associated with burned mud daub from wattle and daub wall construction.

In 1946, E. W. Gifford conducted a surface study in the area of Ixtlán del Río in the southeastern corner of Nayarit, in the course of which he located and studied 16 archaeological sites in the drainage of the Río Ahuacatlán, a few kilometers from Ixtlán del Río (Gifford 1950). He was able to isolate a "Middle Period" of occupation characterized primarily by Aztatlán pottery, Mazapan-type mold-made figurines, and both effigy and three-quarter grooved axes (Gifford 1950:225).

Between 1947 and 1953, José Corona Núñez investigated the Los Toriles site, sometimes referred to as the Ixtlán del Río site, continuing excavations there until 1953, which focused on the exploration of the circular temple near the center of the ceremonial precinct. Corona Núñez attributed this temple to the adoration of Ehecatl-Quetzalcoatl. His excavations recovered stone facing-slabs with petroglyphs, one of which is reported to be in the image of a Xiuhcoatl, as well as Mazapan

FIGURE 1.2. (*a*) Pottery stamp with the image of Xiuhcoatl from the Arroyo Piedras Azules site on the north coast of Jalisco. (*b*) Aztatlán Polychrome jar displaying the image of Xiuhcoatl from the area of San Blas, Nayarit. Museo Comunitario de Aticama, Nayarit.

mold-made figurines (Figures I.3, I.4a; Zepeda García-Moreno 1994:43).

Later explorations in 1961 and 1967 by Eduardo Contreras focused on clearing a pavement that connected the circular temple with a ceremonial precinct containing four rectangular buildings around a plaza located immediately to the northwest of the circular temple. Two of these temples were cleared and their platforms consolidated and somewhat reconstructed (Zepeda García-Moreno 1994:44). These investigations by Corona Núñez and Contreras appeared to reveal construction of the center and its more than 50 structures primarily if not wholly during the local Aztatlán phase, possibly with two major purposes in mind: to dominate the large local source of fine-quality gray obsidian, and to control a major route of communication between the central highlands of Jalisco and the coast of Nayarit.

La Ferrería (Schroeder), Durango

Next, archaeological investigations by J. Charles Kelley in Durango discovered presumed trade pottery and other artifacts attributed to the Aztatlán Complex in stratigraphic contexts within the Schroeder site (now called La Ferrería) in Sinaloa. This situation allowed J. Charles Kelley and Howard Winters (1960) to propose a two-part division of the Aztatlán Complex: Acaponeta (correlated with the Aztatlán materials found at Chametla and Culiacán) and Guasave (correlated with the Aztatlán materials recovered from the Guasave area).

The overwhelmingly abundant Aztatlán ware at La Ferrería (Schroeder) was Red-rimmed Decorated, appearing suddenly in the local sequence, without developmental precedent. Attributing Cocoyolitos hollow figurines to this early Aztatlán phase now appears definitely erroneous. Such figurines are surely of Classic-period date. The second Aztatlán phase is characterized by the appearance of certain Guasave and Culiacán-related Aztatlán fancy polychromes and copper artifacts, although Red-rimmed Decorated ware continued to occur.

Peñitas, Nayarit

The third area peripheral to Sinaloa was the coastal plain of northern Nayarit to the south. Here, large-scale and numerous excavations were conducted beginning in 1956, first at the Peñitas site near Tuxpan on the north bank of the Río San Pedro (Bordaz 1964), and then at the immense site of Amapa on the north side of the Río Grande de Santiago (Meighan, ed. 1976), both sites having major Aztatlán components.

Jacques Bordaz excavated at Peñitas in 1956 as part of a University of California, Los Angeles project initiated by George Brainerd and stimulated by the inspection of a looted collection from Peñitas that was donated to the Southwest Museum in Los Angeles and described in a publication by Hasso von Winning (Bordaz 1964:2; von Winning 1956). At Peñitas, Bordaz excavated three of the several pit kilns found at the site. The kilns, composed of a rectangular fire box and a circular chamber to hold the vessels, were the first prehispanic kiln structures to be discovered in the Americas (Bordaz 1964:11), and they were a product of the Aztatlán occupation of the site. The pottery recovered, according to Bordaz, was essentially the same as that reported for the sequence in Sinaloa, with marked similarities to ceramics from San Felipe Aztatán and Amapa in Nayarit. Importantly for Aztatlán studies, this was evidence indicating (to Bordaz at least) that at Peñitas there were pottery workshops where craftspersons worked under the direction of rulers associated with the temple mound found at the site. George Brainerd died in 1956 and Clement Meighan took over the direction of the University of California, Los Angeles project, focusing his attention on the site of Amapa in Nayarit, to the south of Peñitas.

Coamiles, Nayarit

There is also the matter of associating pecked petroglyphs and/or painted pictographs with the Aztatlán phenomenon (see Mountjoy 1974a, 1987a, 2018). One of the most probable associations of petroglyphs with Aztatlán material is the elaborate petroglyphs at the Coamiles site in Nayarit, located on a mountainside 6 km southwest of Peñitas (Bell 1971:703). Coamiles is a site with a heavy Aztatlán-phase occupation, similar to that of its neighbor Amapa, located a little farther down the Río Grande de Santiago toward the coast (Duverger 1998; Duverger et al. 1993; Garduño Ambriz 2006, 2008, 2009, 2019).

In 1979, Jacques Soustelle of the School of Advanced Studies in Social Sciences in Paris began a study of Coamiles. His work was followed in 1984 and 1988 by Christian Duverger and Daniel Levine of the same French school (Duverger et al. 1993). They made a map of the ceremonial center at the site that includes large rectangular platforms, two pyramidal mounds, and a ballgame court. They also excavated several stratigraphic pits in order to recover information on the sequence of habitation at the site. The deepest pit (#7) reached a depth of a little more than 6 m. They recovered 12 samples of carbon from different levels that indicated an occupation of the site between the Late Classic and the end of the Early Postclassic, and the decorated pottery they recovered were of the same types recovered at Amapa (Meighan, ed. 1976). Based on the stratigraphic sequence, the types of decorated pottery, and the radiocarbon dates, they distinguished two phases of the Aztatlán occupation at the site corresponding with the Cerritos and the Ixcuintla phases at Amapa (Meighan, ed. 1976).

In 2005, Mauricio Garduño Ambriz began further investigations at the Coamiles site on behalf of the Instituto Nacional de Antropología e Historia of Mexico, which continued until 2010 (Garduño Ambriz 2019). A major achievement of this work was the registration of 149 rocks with petroglyphs at different locations on the mountain. Also, nearly 5,000 obsidian artifacts from excavated contexts were chemically analyzed to determine the source of the material. Approximately 98.5% of them came from three sources: Volcán las Navajas, Nayarit (the most abundant at 71%), followed by La Joya, Jalisco, at 18%, and Ixtlán del Río, Nayarit, at 9% (Garduño Ambriz and Pierce 2022).

Amapa, Nayarit

At Amapa, Aztatlán material was intensively studied for the first time at a huge habitation and ceremonial center with large platform mounds constructed mainly of earth but with the use of some adobe and cut stone, often with an open plaza space bounded by four mounds, as well as a ballcourt and an associated cemetery for the burial of elite individuals. The core of the site was mapped and found to cover about 1 km². Construction of the 71 mounds in the nucleus of the site was commenced during the Cerritos phase (AD 900–1100) of Aztatlán development atop midden deposits pertaining to Classic- and Formative-period occupations.

The excavations at Amapa in 1959 were on a scale not before seen in an Aztatlán site, and have not been equaled since. Between 50 strata pits and one bulldozer trench, around 1,843 m³ of deposit were explored (Meighan 1976:13). They revealed that the mounds were constructed by building chambers with adobe block walls that were then infilled with dirt and refuse. Wattle and daub structures, some apparently temples and others residential, were built on top of the platforms. One ceramic temple model dating to the Ixcuintla phase (AD 1100–1350) of Aztatlán development at the site was recovered. It shows a beehive-like main structure with a white-painted stela or screen at the top of the steps and in front of the door. One small group of four mounds constituted an I-shaped ballcourt with cupped stone markers set in the floor. The elite cemetery, contained within an area measuring 16 m by 23 m, was primarily of the Ixcuintla phase.

Attribution of pottery sherds and other artifact types to the two phases of Aztatlán and the one phase of post-Aztatlán occupation was complicated at Amapa because many of the strata pits were excavated in mounds constructed using refuse dug up and redeposited as fill. The total pottery collection consisted of 154,000 sherds and over 660 whole or restorable vessels. Gordon Grosscup (1961) worked out a typology of the sherds and figurines, and Betty Bell (1960) wrote a doctoral dissertation on the whole vessels. There was evidence, including numerous "pot polishers," that Aztatlán pottery was made in workshops at Amapa, and some of these vessels were made specifically to be deposited with the deceased.

The commonly known Aztatlán decorative pottery types, including Plumbate, previously found in other sites were represented at Amapa, but with a decidedly greater similarity to the pottery at Cojumatlán in Jalisco than to the Aztatlán pottery in Sinaloa. One Red-on-buff bowl appears to have a representation of the number four in association with the depiction of a rabbit. The designs reproduced in Bell's (1960:108–142) dissertation include what I believe to be feathered serpents (including the fire serpent or Xiuhcoatl), turtles, cranes, parrots, and one strombus-shell snail. There are also several elaborately rendered figures of human beings.

At Amapa there were also frying-pan incense burners, a few vessels classified as *comales* that were more likely *cazuelas*, plus a lot of bowls and a few jars with annular bases. However, the research at Amapa added many traits to the known cultural inventory of Aztatlán, including: a Xipe Totec ceramic figure that was part of the lid of an incense burner; sandstone abraders used to work shell; "tool kits" for making bone awls and ornaments; side-notched projectile points and flaked blades of chalcedony; copper pins and fishhooks, although bells (some with Tlaloc faces) were the most common metal item (Meighan, ed. 1976; Pendergast 1962a); small laminates of gold; beads of *Spondylus* shell, as well as shell bracelets; bone awls, needles, and one bone tube; and pottery beads of tubular or biconical form. The presence of slag from smelting activities at Amapa indicates there were probably workshops for the production of metal objects.

Also found were clay plaques with designs suggesting they might have been models for textile patterns (Meighan 1976:87), and some stone slabs (Meighan, ed. 1976:Plates 17, 19) incised with what we can recognize as "abbreviated" *patolli* game board designs (Mountjoy 2005). Typically, Aztatlán figurines were made in molds, and often are recognizable as being of the well-known Mazapan type. Early Aztatlán spindle whorls were globular in shape, whereas some of the later Aztatlán ones at Amapa were sometimes in the shape of pots. Some stone "plummets" (casting net weights?) were reportedly found in Aztatlán contexts.

Huistla and Tizapán el Alto, Jalisco

In 1963–1964, Michael Glassow (1967) conducted excavations in Aztatlán remains at the Huistla site located west of Guadalajara, Jalisco, within the framework of a project grant by the National Science Foundation to Henry B. Nicholson. In 1964–1965, Clement Meighan focused his interest regarding the Aztatlán phenomenon on a large and complex site at Tizapán el Alto in Jalisco, on the shoreline of Lake Chapala only about 20 km to the west of the site of Cojumatlán, Michoacán (Meighan and Foote 1968). The excavations at Huistla did not add much to what was already known about the Aztatlán phenomenon, except perhaps to describe what appears to be a localized, and I believe late, variant of Aztatlán polychrome, even though this polychrome is associated with abundant, typical Aztatlán Banded Red-on-buff as well as some Band-incised-buff decorated pottery.

At Tizapán el Alto, Meighan and Foote were able to distinguish two phases of Aztatlán development, and human burials were often found placed in a seated position. The authors include a table in which they list 22 cultural traits present at Tizapán el Alto (14 of pottery, three of metal, four of stone, and one of iron pyrite) that have also been found in one or all of nine contemporaneous archaeological assemblages located between northern Sinaloa and southeastern Jalisco (Meighan and Foote 1968:160, Table 23). Other than these traits, they reported a bone pin and a bone needle associated with Aztatlán ceramics.

Marismas Nacionales of Nayarit and Sinaloa

From this point on, not many cultural traits were added to the Aztatlán list, although one can cite a few notable exceptions. From 1968 to 1978, Stuart Scott directed investigations in the Marismas Nacionales area on the border between northern Nayarit and southern Sinaloa (Foster, ed. 2017; Scott and Foster 2000). In this area, they found sites of the Aztatlán archaeological culture intimately related to the exploitation of the marine and estuary resources, especially oysters.

A full description of the ceramics from this project has only recently been published (Foster 2017b), and a description of the pottery obtained primarily from the 1968 field season was published by Rosemary Sweetman (1974). Sweetman relates the decorative elements on Marismas Nacionales pottery to Aztatlán pottery from other areas and she describes what she calls a "reptile eye" decorative motif that especially links the Marismas area to the Amapa site (Sweetman 1974:75).

Burials of humans and animals were found in 10 Aztatlán-affiliated sites in the Marismas Nacionales, in both habitation mound and burial mound contexts. The human remains were analyzed by George W. Gill (1974) and the animal remains by Elisabeth Wing (Gill 1974). Human burials included several variants: "flexed sitting," secondary mass inhumation, extended on the back, flexed on the side, face down, isolated skulls, and burial in urns. Wing's analysis indicated inten-

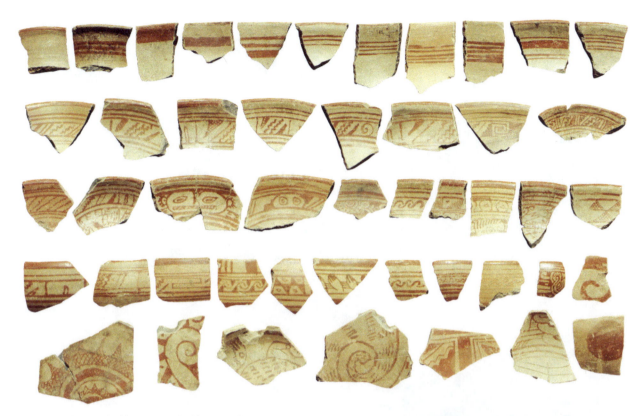

FIGURE 1.3. Aztatlán Red-on-buff sherds from the Nahuapa II site in the Tomatlán valley of central-coastal Jalisco.

tional interment of 42 dogs, and at least six raccoons (Gill 1974:96).

Tomatlán, Jalisco

By 1975, I was conducting research in the Tomatlán river basin as part of a salvage archaeology operation related to the construction of the Cajón de Peña dam. Aztatlán pottery wares were abundant in the Tomatlán Valley, a fact that Isabel Kelly had noted nearly 30 years before (Kelly 1948:62). In fact, we found Aztatlán pottery at 50 of the 165 sites we located in the valley (Mountjoy 1982, 1987a, 2019), and a trench excavated at the Nahuapa II site yielded 4,190 fragments of Aztatlán pottery, 66% of which was the Red-on-buff-type Aztatlán ware (Figure 1.3; Mountjoy 1990:548). A stone altar was excavated at the same site. Associated with it were four items of copper: a tiny bell, two thin strips and part of what might have been a needle, plus a sherd of Tohil Plumbate carved into the shape of a pendant (Mountjoy 1990:547). The carbon samples from this excavation were lost by the Instituto Nacional de Antropología e Historia, but fortunately much of the same Aztatlán ceramic material was recovered recently at the Arroyo Piedras Azules site on the northern coast of Jalisco and dated to beginning or slightly postdating AD 1215 ± 30 years (Mountjoy et al. 2020).

El Cañón del Molino, Durango

In 1983, Jaime Ganot and Alejandro Peschard began to report on sites with Aztatlán material in Durango (other than La Ferrería [Schroeder]), especially the site of El Cañón del Molino. By 1995, their list had grown to include a total of nine sites with Aztatlán material, located in four different regions of Durango, extending as far to the north as El Zape (Ganot and Peschard 1995:165–166). The sites are identified as pertaining to the "Aztatlán Culture" based primarily on ceramic types previously reported from Guasave and Culiacán in Sinaloa and Amapa in Nayarit. Unfortunately, the material described as being from the Cañón del Molino site came from looting activities, but it includes many metal items, including a breastplate, a pendant, a chain with a clasp attached to a ring, a turtle effigy, and many bells, one of which was decorated with a Tlaloc face (Ganot and Peschard 1995:163).

The Aztatlán cultural inventory at El Cañón del Molino also includes: pottery pipes similar to the ones found in Sinaloan sites; rectangular-worked and side-notched pottery sherds; stone discoidals; rings made of lava stone; stone *molcajetes*, one of which is decorated with the head of a serpent; pestles of both cylindrical and animal form; animal effigy and three-quarter grooved axes; stone palettes; small, Amapa-type,

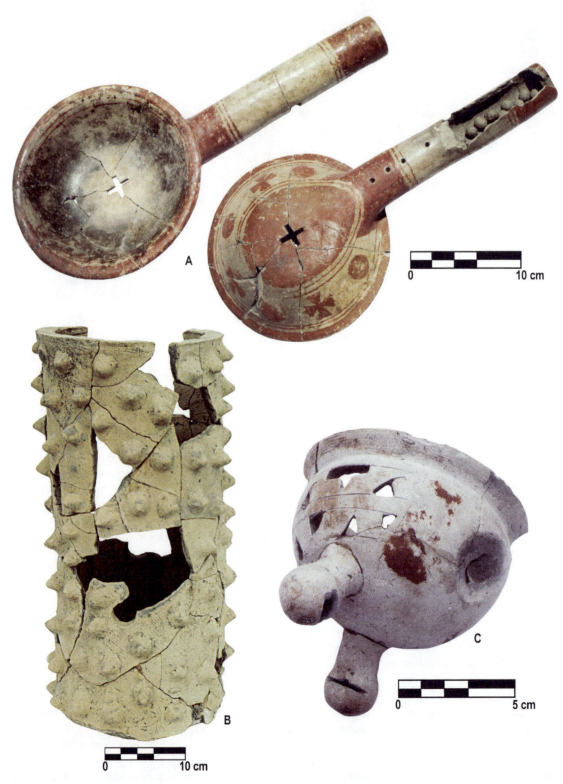

FIGURE 1.4. (*a*) "Frying pan," (*b*) spiked, and (*c*) *sahumador* incense burners from Ixtapa, municipality of Puerto Vallarta, Jalisco.

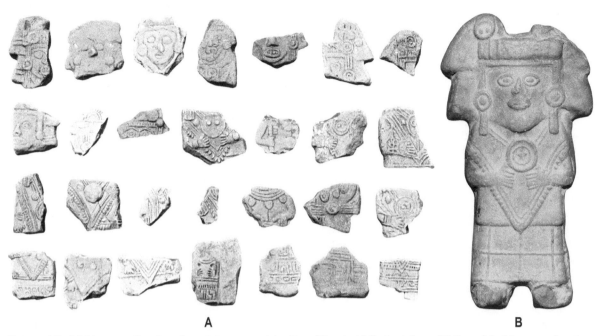

FIGURE 1.5. (*a*) Mazapan figurines from Ixtapa, municipality of Puerto Vallarta, Jalisco. (*b*) Complete Mazapan figurine from the area of San Blas, Nayarit.

basal- and side-notched arrow points; shell bracelets, pendants, incised pectorals, and beads; stone pendants in the shape of birds, mammals, and snakes; an effigy stone incense burner; one anthropomorphic stone sculpture; and bone awls. Thirty-seven skulls were found to have intentional frontal deformation, and one set of teeth had notches filed on both the upper and lower incisors (Ganot and Peschard 1995:159–167).

Ixtapa and La Majada del Espino, Jalisco

In 1986, I began investigations in the municipality of Puerto Vallarta, Jalisco, focused on the large site of Ixtapa which was found to have a long history of prehispanic occupation beginning in the Middle Formative and persisting for about 100 years after first contact with the Spanish (Mountjoy et al. 2003). The ceremonial center of Ixtapa once contained three large platform mounds of earth and cobblestones, a ballcourt, a special residential area, and a cemetery for the elite. Besides the usual Aztatlán Red-banded-on-buff ware and some incised polychrome ware, we recovered one rattle-handle "frying pan" incense burner and a large cylindrical incense burner covered with spikes, probably in imitation of the bark of the sacred ceiba tree (Figure 1.4). Mazapan-type mold-made figurines were common at Ixtapa (Figure 1.5; Mountjoy et al. 2003). Excavations in one of the smaller ceremonial mounds revealed Aztatlán-phase construction including use of a slab stela that had subsequently been broken up and reused in the construction of an altar by the local group that eventually expelled the Aztatlán foreigners (Mountjoy 1991; Mountjoy et al. 2003). Another small stela-like stone with a face and feather headdress was found at the PV-61 (Arroyo Seco) site, almost wholly attributable to the Aztatlán phase, and which also contained several ceremonial structures and remnants of a ballcourt (Mountjoy et al. 2003).

These investigations in the municipality of Puerto Vallarta continued into 1994, resulting in the registration of 111 archaeological sites, 44 (40%) of which had Aztatlán pottery (Mountjoy et al. 2003). This inventory of sites included remote sites such as Las Vegas (PV-103) where we even found Aztatlán-phase ceremonial mound construction (Mountjoy et al. 2003).

In 1997, I added a bit more to our knowledge of Aztatlán distribution and cultural traits by investigating a copper bell in the image of the deity Mictlantecuhtli that had been found during looting activities at the site of La Majada del Espino in a remote area of the western sierra of Jalisco in the municipality of San Sebastián del Oeste (Mountjoy 2001a). The Aztatlán ceramics at this site were basically the same as I had found at Ixtapa on the coast of Jalisco, including fragments of broken spiked cylindrical incense burners. The metal bell was found by looters in a burial dug into the side of a low hill upon which had been constructed a ceremonial center of design-painted daub plaster over a wattle framework.

La Peña, Jalisco

Much new information on the Aztatlán phenomenon has come from investigations by an archaeological team in the Sayula Basin of Jalisco, south of Guadalajara. Research in the Sayula Basin began in 1997, but especially noteworthy for the discussion here are the excavations in Aztatlán-phase deposits at the large site of La Peña that began in 2000 and continued there until 2004 (Liot et al., eds. 2006). The Aztatlán occupation of La Peña began after a period of abandonment of that location that lasted about 1,000 years (Liot, Ramírez, Reveles, and Schöndube 2006:417); the Aztatlán occupation represented a new social, political, economic and ideological regimen for the Sayula basin introduced by foreigners who "colonized" the existing local population (Liot, Ramírez, Reveles, and Schöndube 2006:426).

The associated Aztatlán cultural inventory at La Peña most closely resembles the Cojumatlán-phase material in the Lake Chapala area of Michoacán, although there appears to be some "hybridization" between this early Aztatlán material and the ceramics of the antecedent Sayula phase in the Sayula lake basin. Later Aztatlán material at La Peña more closely resembles the Aztatlán Complex at Tizapán el Alto in the Lake Chapala area of Jalisco. During the earliest phase, both ritual and domestic units were constructed at La Peña, and there is evidence of social stratification in the burials and their offerings, as well as residences attributable to local elites. Archaeological evidence of ceremonialism during the initial Aztatlán phase includes representations of Ehecatl-Quetzalcoatl, Mictlantecuhtli, and Xiuhcoatl, as well as a calendrical date commonly associated with Tezcatlipoca. Other motifs include many animals such as rabbits, opossums, birds, and deer reminiscent of animal signs used in the 260-day ritual *tonalpohualli* calendar of the central Mexican highlands (Liot, Ramírez, Reveles, and Schöndube 2006:421).

The second phase of the Early Postclassic, the one more similar to the expression of Aztatlán at Tizapán el Alto, seems related to the growth of population at La Peña and a coincidental expansion of agricultural and habitation terrace construction, including canals for irrigation and for controlling runoff patterns. Architectural features were now better made and more finely finished. Ritual activities involved the use of many incense burners, often with modeled Tlaloc faces. At this time there was an expansion of elite habitations and a cemetery especially for the elite population. Religious decorative motifs continue to include the previously mentioned Central Mexican gods, but with the possible addition of Xipe Totec and perhaps Tezcatlipoca as well. A list of cultural traits present at La Peña, most of which are commonly found at Aztatlán sites (e.g., prismatic obsidian blades, Mazapan figurines, and metal objects), is presented in their publication (Liot, Ramírez, Reveles, and Schöndube 2006:427, Table 29).

San Felipe Aztatán and La Guásima, Nayarit

Recent research on Aztatlán material has been conducted in northern Nayarit. Lorena Gámez (2004) carried out investigations at various archaeological sites in the Acaponeta Valley. This research included 15 Cerritos-phase (Amapa sequence) sites, and some 22 sites that included both Cerritos- and Ixcuintla-phase remains (Gámez 2004:206–207). Gámez arranged these sites in a hierarchy based on number of structures and size in hectares. The largest Cerritos-phase site was San Felipe Aztatán with 74 structures covering an area of 90 ha. The second largest site was La Guásima, which covered 49 ha and contained 49 structures. Eleven more Cerritos-phase sites contained from one to 12 structures.

More recently, Mauricio Garduño Ambriz (2015) conducted further studies in that area, including some excavations at San Felipe Aztatán where he found that all of the domestic and ritual structures explored there were built during the Cerritos phase and continued to be used during the subsequent Ixcuintla phase, albeit with some remodeling (see Garduño Ambriz, this volume). These excavations also revealed the rather common construction and use of cobblestone pavements in various parts of the site for the purpose of leveling the original surface and to provide work spaces. Another important discovery was an upright stone stela in the North Acropolis of the site that served as a calendrical marker for the solar equinoxes.

Trash deposits contained commonly known Aztatlán items, including the elaborately decorated polychrome ware, prismatic obsidian blades, fragments of pipes, and objects of copper. Also found were two green beads of nonlocal stone. One spectacular Tohil Plumbate crocodilian effigy jar was accidentally found during the excavation of a septic tank in the Huachotita neighborhood area of the site.

Among the new information about the Aztatlán phenomenon produced through this research, neutron activation analysis revealed that 30 fragments of prismatic obsidian blades were obtained from three sources: La Joya (Jalisco), Ixtlán del Río (Nayarit), and Sierra de las Navajas (Hidalgo). Importantly, therefore, the analysis revealed that this great Aztatlán center was directly linked to the major source of obsidian in the central Mexican highlands controlled in turn by Teotihuacan, then Tula, and finally by the Mexica (Garduño Ambriz 2015:13). Also novel was the discovery of the importance of coastal fish to the Cerritos-phase inhabitants of this inland site. The list of fish utilized includes marine catfish, porgy, two-banded sea bream, and guaviña. Charring of some of the fish bones may indicate they were smoked to preserve them for exportation inland from the coast to the interior (Garduño Ambriz 2015:13). Other bones recovered from trash deposits indicate the consumption of turkeys, dogs, white-tailed deer, rabbits, and land turtles (Garduño Ambriz 2015:14).

Punta de Mita, Nayarit

Another recent project in Nayarit was carried out at Punta de Mita at the extreme southern end of the Nayarit coast, on the northern edge of Banderas Bay (González Barajas and Beltrán Medina 2007). The discoveries of most note include a large number of metal artifacts, especially copper fishhooks, and abundant pottery sherds decorated with codex-type designs. Also recovered were large stone weights that the Aztatlán people used for deep-sea diving, presumably to recover shells such as *Spondylus*, and which are identical to stone weights used in prehispanic times by deep-sea divers along the coast of Ecuador (Beltrán Medina 2019).

Cerro del Teúl, Zacatecas

Since 2010, Laura Solar and Peter Jiménez have conducted research at the large ceremonial center of Cerro del Teúl (El Teúl), in southwestern Zacatecas (Solar Valverde et al. 2021). Their excavations have revealed an Aztatlán-period ballcourt with associated stone sculptures of what they interpret to be the "hero twins" of Maya mythology. Also present are temple-type mounds, one of which is associated with a large serpent carving of Toltec type that depicts the god Xiuhcoatl. In addition, they uncovered a system of water distribution and drainage similar to Aztatlán hydraulic systems found at Amapa, Tizapán el Alto, La Peña, and Cojumatlán, and clear evidence of a metalworking industry that includes two smelting pits.

Other cultural traits associated with Cerro del Teúl during the Aztatlán occupation include cranial deformation, dental alteration, turquoise jewelry, and many objects of metal that include: bells with Tlaloc faces; tweezers; buttons; sheets; and one finger ring with a face and headdress identical to finger rings found in the site of Guasave (El Ombligo), Sinaloa, and the Sayula basin of Jalisco. The pottery recovered includes polychrome and incised sherds with representations of Xiuhcoatl, musical instruments (especially whistles), and a few Mazapan figurines. Items of stone include lip plugs and cruciforms.

Arroyo Piedras Azules, Jalisco

In 2015, I began the investigation of Arroyo Piedras Azules, a small site on the northern coast of Jalisco which was occupied by Aztatlán colonists starting about AD 1215. In 2017 and 2018, we conducted extensive excavations in the site (Mountjoy et al. 2020; Mountjoy et al. 2022). Aztatlán colonists appear to have selected this spot as a base from which they could exploit beds of *Spondylus* and Mother of Pearl (*Pinctada mazatlanica*) shells found along a short stretch of rocky coastline in order to export these shells (or jewelry worked locally from them) both to major Aztatlán centers to the north and the Mixteca-Puebla area to the south. The initial Aztatlán occupants of Arroyo Piedras Azules used decorated pottery identical to that found in the nearby Tomatlán valley. But during the occupation of the site, the people began to acquire pottery decorated in a codex style traceable to the Mixteca-Puebla area (Figure 1.6).

So, What then is Aztatlán?

Garduño Ambriz's final comments in a recent article (2015:14–16) provide an excellent description of the Aztatlán phenomenon as manifested in the area of northern coastal and piedmont Nayarit, as well as most other areas in Sinaloa, Jalisco, and Michoacán where major Aztatlán occupations have been studied. I will try to summarize his comments (originally in Spanish) below.

The regional Aztatlán culture was marked by permanent settlements resting on an autochthonous demographic, social, and economic base. Its development was characterized by an increasing specialization and diversification in agricultural, technological, and socioeconomic affairs. There was a rise of central political authority of a lordship type residing in principal towns that served as provincial capitals. In such places, temples were built on astronomically oriented platforms where festivals took place related to a ritual calendar linked to the agricultural cycle, especially focused on sun worship. The iconography present on the sumptuary pottery commonly depicts the Central Mexican god Xiuhcoatl, thought responsible for guiding the sun on its path through the celestial dome of the daytime sky. The elites of Aztatlán society controlled the long-distance interchange of exotic materials or sumptuary goods like jadeite, turquoise, onyx, copper objects, and fine ceramics. They also organized the acquisition of strategic resources and raw materials (such as obsidian) as well as their transformation into finished products and their distribution.

To Mauricio's observations, I will add some of my own (see Mountjoy 2000). The Aztatlán phenomenon has always been primarily defined on the basis of its fine-quality decorated ceramics. The excellence of fabrication and decoration are superior to almost every type of ceramics that antecede Aztatlán in the areas where it is found. The most basic Aztatlán ware is of quite fine paste and well fired, although usually with

FIGURE 1.6. (*a–i*) Codex-style Aztatlán Polychrome pottery from the Arroyo Piedras Azules site on the northern coast of Jalisco. Possible representations of the Mixtec culture hero Lord Eight Deer as: (*b*) leader, (*c*) ballplayer, (*d*) hunter, and (*e*) the god of the hunt and the night, Mixcoatl. (*f–g*) Codex iconography of hands, bloody deer bone awls, and scorpions related to the nose-perforation ceremony. (*h–i*) Mixtec codex-like representations of human sacrifice by means of a defleshed skull and crossed femurs. Ceramics not to scale.

an unoxidized, darkened core. The pottery is decorated with a (sky) band design on the exterior or interior, primarily on bowls. This band design most commonly has geometric elements separated by sets of diagonal or vertical lines, but sometimes has designs that represent the fire serpent Xiuhcoatl or codex-like elements. Such band designs are overwhelmingly executed in red paint over a buff or natural-colored base, and less frequently are painted in black or are incised into the surface of the vessel.

This type of Aztatlán pottery can be found at extremely remote sites lacking any other items identifiable as Aztatlán. This indicates an extreme degree of control over the production and distribution of basic utilitarian pottery within the vast territory under the domination of Aztatlán elites. The centers of its production were nonlocal, probably at major sites like Peñitas on the coastal plain of northern Nayarit, an area where the technological sophistication of antecedent pottery is most similar to that of Aztatlán pottery found in more peripheral areas. But even the elaborate, fancy codex-style Aztatlán polychrome pottery can sometimes be found at relatively small, isolated habitation sites or at ritual centers lacking monumental architecture, yet such sites were apparently inhabited or used by people who were somehow privileged within the Aztatlán network of tightly controlled production and distribution of both basic and sumptuary goods (Figure 1.6).

During the second phase of Aztatlán development, beginning around AD 1200, much of the codex-style pottery found at the Arroyo Piedras Azules site on the northern coast of Jalisco appears related to the ceremonial perforation of the nasal septum of the Mixtec cultural hero Lord Eight Deer (Figures 1.6f–1.6g), as well as possible depictions of Eight Deer as a chiefly leader (Figure 1.6b), ballgame player (Figure 1.6c), hunter (Figure 1.6d), and as the god of the night and the hunt, Mixcoatl (Figure 1.6e) as he is depicted in the *Codex Borgia* (Mountjoy et al. 2020). Other sherds from this site depict the theme of human sacrifice in a manner nearly identical to its representation in the Mixtec codices (Figures 1.6h–1.6i).

Another basic Aztatlán-controlled utilitarian item found at small, remote sites is the prismatic obsidian blade made of high-quality material usually obtained from the La Joya source in Jalisco, the Ixtlán del Río source in Nayarit or the Sierra de las Navajas (Pachuca) source in Hidalgo (Pierce 2016). Other standardized items to which these small, remote Aztatlán sites had access include Mazapan-style figurines produced in molds, and even copper objects such as bells produced at Aztatlán-controlled metallurgical workshops capable of controlling the technologically sophisticated process of lost-wax metal casting.

WHERE IS AZTATLÁN?

There is an obvious difference between places where a few Aztatlán-type objects have been found and places where there is ample evidence of ritual or habitation sites created and used by the bearers of the Aztatlán archaeological culture. I want to focus my discussion on sites of the latter type (see Figure 1.1). The northernmost site of Aztatlán occupation thus found is at Mochicahui in the municipality of Fuerte in northernmost Sinaloa (Manzanilla and Talavera 1988) where Guasave-like Aztatlán pottery sherds were recovered. Two flat-bottomed bowls with codex-like polychrome-painted designs in the center also were reported, one of a human face below what appear to be feathered wands, and the other being a Xiuhcoatl-type design (Manzanilla and Talavera 1988:Photos 43–44). Southward along the coast, the farthest south that Aztatlán material has been reported is at the Higuera Blanca site near the mouth of the Río San Nicolás, Jalisco (Mountjoy 2019; Mountjoy and Schöndube 2014). Although there are purported to be Aztatlán occupations farther south along the Jalisco coast, such sites have not yet been substantiated by archaeologists.

The northeastern part of Aztatlán territory extends up the western side of the central Mexican highland plateau where there are three sites in the state of Durango with major Aztatlán occupations. These sites are, north to south, El Cañón del Molino, Navacoyán, and La Ferrería (or Schroeder; Ganot and Peschard 1995). However, Aztatlán material has been reported as far north in Durango as the site of Zape, although the nature of Aztatlán presence there and at several other Durango sites is not clear. The eastern side of the Aztatlán site distribution is marked by El Teúl in southern Zacatecas where, since 2010, Laura Solar and Peter Jiménez have conducted several field seasons of excavations (Figure I.6a; Solar Valverde et al. 2021).

The southeastern distribution of Aztatlán sites is focused on the area around Lake Chapala in Michoacán and Jalisco, especially the sites of Cojumatlán (Michoacán) and Tizapán el Alto (Jalisco), as well as a little further to the south in the Sayula lake basin area—especially the site of La Peña, Jalisco. There is some evidence of Aztatlán occupation in the municipality of Villa Purificación (Mountjoy 2008), and there is a not yet well-understood relationship between the Postclassic polychrome pottery of the Autlán Valley (Kelly 1945b) and the Aztatlán phenomenon. Both of these areas are in southern Jalisco not far north of the border with Colima.

The three states of Sinaloa, Jalisco, and Nayarit cover a total area of 165,371 km². While not all of this area has evidence of Aztatlán habitation, it is a fairly accurate calculation of the total area of Aztatlán site distribution given that Aztatlán sites are also found in a large part of western Durango and in some parts of southern Zacatecas, as well as the western fringe of Michoacán. By way of comparison, the Mexican states of Yucatán, Campeche, and Quintana Roo, which were dominated by the Maya, cover an area of 144,874 km². Perhaps more appropriate is a comparison with the area of the west Mexican state of Michoacán which approximates the area controlled by the Tarascan state. Michoacán covers an area of 58,599 km². So, whatever the archaeological remains of Aztatlán represent, they extend over an area two to three times as big as that dominated by the Tarascan state, and slightly larger than the area of the Yucatán Peninsula inhabited by the Maya.

When is Aztatlán?

We have available 65 radiocarbon dates associated with remains identifiable as pertaining to the Aztatlán archaeological culture that can be used to estimate the beginning and end dates of the Aztatlán phenomenon, and therefore also its duration. Darden Hood of Beta Analytic has kindly provided new calibrations for some dates from: Ixtapa, Jalisco; La Pedrera, Jalisco; El Ombligo, Sinaloa; Amapa, Nayarit; and Peñitas, Nayarit, and these recalibrations are registered in Table 1.1.

There are several ways one can evaluate these dates. Within the range calibrated against radiocarbon assays done on tree rings of known date, one can be 95% certain that the true date of the associated Aztatlán material lies within that range, along with a 5% probability that it does not. Therefore, any suggested dates on Aztatlán materials are only probable ones, never exact ones. If one uses the early end of the 95% probability range, the Aztatlán phenomenon would have begun in the late AD 700s or early 800s and lasted until around AD 1300, a total of 500 years. If one were to use the late end of the 95% probability range, the Aztatlán phenomenon would have begun around AD 1100 and have lasted until at least AD 1400, a total of 300 years (Table 1.1). Neither of these scenarios seems fully acceptable. Part of the problem of using the extremes of the 95% range lies in the fact that the less accurate the date, the wider the range. In this case the plus/minus factor varies from ± 30 years to ± 161 years. I believe the best way to resolve this problem is to use the central date of the 95 percent range. The results are presented in Table 1.1, arranged from the earliest central date to the latest.

This ordering of the dates indicates the beginning of Aztatlán at about AD 901 and has it ending around AD 1473, which seems a little late. This gives a total span of slightly over 500 years for the Aztatlán phenomenon, certainly plenty of time for Aztatlán material to have spread over such a large territory, for there to have developed a second phase after the initial one, and for there to have been a reasonable remnant of the Aztatlán phenomenon in northern Nayarit by the time the Spanish entered that area.

Without overly interpreting Table 1.1, this ordering also suggests that there is no clear center of Aztatlán development. There appears to have been a rapid development and expansion of this phenomenon within the area stretching between the environs of Lake Chapala and northern Sinaloa, including northern Nayarit in between, and perhaps up into southern Zacatecas. The most doubtful area of initial development from which Aztatlán might have spread would seem to have been far northern Sinaloa. But a development and spread from either northern Nayarit or the Lake Chapala area seem about equally probable given the radiocarbon dates. One thing does seem certain however: Aztatlán expansion and development along the coast of Jalisco was comparatively late, although it was contemporary with continued Aztatlán developments to the north in Nayarit and Sinaloa.

Apart from the radiocarbon dates, one might suggest southern Sinaloa as an area of origin based on the development of Aztatlán material out of a local Indigenous cultural base around Chametla. One possibility is for Middle Chametla Polychrome Engraved ware to have been a precursor to Aztatlán engraved polychromes. However, the local "Red-rimmed Utility" ware there seems an unlikely precursor for the much more technologically and decoratively sophisticated Red-on-buff decorated ware of the Aztatlán complex (Kelly 1938).

In northern Nayarit, Aztatlán materials appear suddenly and fully developed in the stratigraphic sequence at Amapa, enough so to have prompted the proposal of a "hypothetical" Tuxpan phase to account for a prior development of the Aztatlán Complex (Meighan, ed. 1976). However, the existence of such a phase has never been proven in northern Nayarit. In the Lake Chapala area, Chapala Red-on-brown and Zapotlán Engraved wares might have been precursors to the Aztatlán wares of the Cojumatlán Complex, but the Chapala Complex lacks a ceramic precursor to the Aztatlán polychromes of the Cojumatlán Complex (Lister 1949).

Other ceramic material that could be a possible precursor to the early phase of Aztatlán development is that of the Sayula phase found in the Sayula Basin area (Valdéz et al. 2005). This material includes: fine incised pottery ware; red, orange, and white polychrome wares; vessels with tripod foot or annular base supports; and slab-like mold-made figurines and pottery bells. However, the Sayula-phase pottery wares do not bear typical Aztatlán designs, and there is a significant overlap of the Sayula phase (thought to date in the

TABLE 1.1. Radiocarbon Dates for Aztatlán Deposits.

Date	Location	Description
AD 901	Arrinitas, Nayarit	AD 842 ± 62 years (NSTF-9) (charcoal). Calibrated to AD 775–1027 with 95% certainty (Foster and Scott 2017).
AD 910	El Teúl, Zacatecas	AD 830 ± 40 years (Beta-288049) (charcoal). Calibrated to AD 810–1010 (AD 910 central date) with 95% certainty (Laura Solar, personal communication, 2016).
AD 967	Coamiles, Nayarit	AD 860 ± 70 years (Groningen-16015) (charcoal). Calibrated to AD 772–1150 with 95% certainty (Duverger et al. 1993).
AD 985	La Peña, Jalisco	(INAH-1943) (charcoal). (Liot et al. 2006)
AD 1000	Tizapán el Alto, Jalisco	(UCLA-1073A) (charcoal). (5730 ± 40 years half-life). Calibrated to AD 920–1080 (Meighan and Foote 1968).
AD 1010	San Felipe Aztatán, Nayarit	AD 1048 ± 64 years (INAH-2108) (charcoal). Calibrated to AD 860–1160 with 95% certainty (Garduño Ambriz 2015).
AD 1013	Arrinitas, Nayarit	AD 935 ± 110 years (Isotopes-5530) (charcoal). Calibrated to AD 776–1251 with 95% certainty (Foster and Scott 2017).
AD 1022	El Ombligo (Guasave), Sinaloa	AD 550 ± 65 years (Arizona-17249) (shell). Corrected to AD 885–1160 with 95% certainty (Carpenter 2008).
AD 1025	La Peña, Jalisco	AD 1040 ± 60 years (BETA-179273) (charcoal). Calibrated to AD 890–1160 with 95% certainty (Liot et al. 2006).
AD 1055	La Peña, Jalisco (AD 825 calibration of same)	Calibrated to AD 860–1250 with 95% certainty (charcoal) (Susana Ramírez, personal communication, 2015). Same sample calibrated to AD 810–840 with 95% certainty (Liot et al. 2006).
AD 1055	Rincón de Panal, Sinaloa	AD 1055 ± 161 years (charcoal). Calibrated to AD 894–1216 with 95% certainty (Foster and Scott 2017).
AD 1060	El Teúl, Zacatecas	AD 940 ± 40 years (Beta-288050) (charcoal). Calibrated to AD 980–1140 (intersection AD 1020) with 95% certainty (Laura Solar, personal communication, 2016).
AD 1070	La Peña, Jalisco	AD 970 ± 90 years (BETA-196966) (charcoal). Calibrated to AD 890–1250 with 95% certainty (Liot et al. 2006).
AD 1075	El Ombligo (Guasave), Sinaloa	AD 595 ± 55 years (Arizona-17248) (shell). Corrected to AD 964–1187 with 95% certainty (Carpenter 2008).
AD 1090	La Peña, Jalisco	AD 980 ± 60 years (BETA-162044) (charcoal). Calibrated to AD 980–1200 with 95% certainty (Liot et al. 2006).
AD 1096	Tecualilla, Nayarit	AD 1096 ± 116 years (NSTF-7) (charcoal). Calibrated to AD 980–1213 with 95% certainty (Foster and Scott 2017).
AD 1105	La Peña, Jalisco	AD 1000 ±60 years (BETA-196963) (charcoal). Calibrated to AD 990–1220 with 95% certainty (Liot et al. 2006).
AD 1110	El Ombligo (Guasave), Sinaloa	AD 1095 ± 50 years (Arizona-1752) (gourd). Corrected to AD 1041–1280 with 95% certainty (Carpenter 2008).
AD 1112	Tizapán el Alto, Jalisco	AD 1112 (UCLA-1073G) (charcoal). (5730 ± 40 years half-life) Calibrated to AD 1025–1200 (Meighan and Foote 1968).
AD 1130	La Peña, Jalisco	AD 1040 ± 50 years (BETA-162042) (charcoal). Calibrated to AD 1020–1240 with 95% certainty (Liot et al. 2006).
AD 1136	Coamiles, Nayarit	AD 1050 ± 70 years (Groningen-16014) (charcoal). Calibrated to AD 1014–1257 with 95% certainty (Duverger et al. 1993).
AD 1138	Peñitas, Nayarit	AD 1080 ± 100 years (Norwegian Institute of Technology-219) (charcoal). Calibrated to AD 985–1290 with 95% certainty, AD 1280 intersection with the calibration curve (Bordaz 1964) (Beta 2016).
AD 1148	Tecualilla, Nayarit	AD 1080 ± 80 years (UCLA-1628a) (charcoal). Calibrated to AD 1023–1273 with 95% certainty (Foster and Scott 2017).

TABLE 1.1. (cont'd.) Radiocarbon Dates for Aztatlán Deposits.

Date	Location	Description
AD 1155	La Peña, Jalisco	AD 1100 ± 60 years (BETA-173333) (charcoal). Calibrated to AD 1030–1280 with 95% certainty (Liot et al. 2006).
AD 1158	El Ombligo (Guasave), Sinaloa	AD 1090 ± 50 years (Arizona-17253) (charcoal). Corrected to AD 1037–1280 with 95% certainty (Carpenter 2008).
AD 1159	Coamiles, Nayarit	AD 1130 ± 60 years (Groningen-16012) (charcoal). Calibrated to AD 1042–1276 with 95% certainty (Duverger et al. 1993).
AD 1165	Ixtapa, Jalisco	AD 1140 ± 70 years (BETA-62399) (charcoal). Calibrated to AD 1040–1290 with 95% certainty, AD 1225 intersection with the calibration curve (Mountjoy et al. 2003) (Beta 2016).
AD 1165	Coamiles, Nayarit	AD 1120 ± 60 years (Groningen-16011) (charcoal). Calibrated to AD 1040–1273 with 95% certainty (Duverger et al. 1993).
AD 1168 (or AD 1373)	Ixtapa, Jalisco	AD 1150 ± 90 years (BETA-62398) (charcoal). Calibrated to AD 1025–1310 or AD 1360–1385 with 95% certainty, AD 1250 intersection with the calibration curve (Mountjoy et al. 2003) (Beta 2016).
AD 1168 (or AD 1375)	Ixtapa, Jalisco	AD 1150 ± 80 years (BETA-031462) (charcoal). Calibrated to AD 1035–1300 or AD 1370–1380 with 95% certainty, AD 1250 intersection with the calibration curve (Mountjoy et al. 2003) (Beta 2016).
AD 1170	Tizapán el Alto, Jalisco	AD 1170 (UCLA-1073K) (charcoal) (5730 + 40 years half-life). Calibrated to AD 1120–1220 (Meighan and Foote 1968).
AD 1175	Ixtapa, Jalisco	AD 1145 ± 65 years (INAH-11/92) (charcoal). Calibrated to AD 1030–1320 with 95% certainty, AD 1250 intersection with the calibration curve (Mountjoy et al. 2003).
AD 1175	El Ombligo (Guasave), Sinaloa	AD 1150 ± 55 years (Arizona-17250) (cloth). Corrected to AD 1019–1260 with 95% certainty (Carpenter 2008).
AD 1213	El Teúl, Zacatecas	AD 1120 ± 30 years (Beta-417628) (dental collagen). Calibrated to AD 1160–1265 with 95% certainty (Laura Solar, personal communication, 2016).
AD 1218	Rincón de Panal, Sinaloa	AD 1175 ± 60 years (BGS-110) (charcoal). Calibrated to AD 1052–1385 with 95% certainty (Foster and Scott 2017).
AD 1220	Coamiles, Nayarit	AD 1190 ±110 years (Groningen-16013) (charcoal). Calibrated to AD 1040–1400 with 95% certainty (Duverger et al. 1993).
AD 1223	La Pedrera, Jalisco	AD 1160 ± 60 years (BETA-62396) (charcoal). Calibrated to AD 1155–1290 with 95% certainty, AD 1255 intersection with the calibration curve (Mountjoy et al. 2003) (Beta 2016).
AD 1225	Arroyo Piedras Azules, Jalisco	AD 1215 ± 30 years (BETA-419370) (charcoal). Calibrated to AD 1165–1265 with 95% certainty, AD 1220 intersection with the calibration curve (Mountjoy et al. 2020).
AD 1225	Arroyo Piedras Azules, Jalisco	AD 1215 ± 30 years (BETA-419371) (charcoal). Calibrated to AD 1165–1265 (AD 1225 central date) with 95% certainty, AD 1220 intersection with the calibration curve (Mountjoy et al. 2020).
AD 1230 (or AD 1338)	Amapa, Nayarit	AD 1305 ± 80 years (UCLA-956) (charcoal). Calibrated to AD 1225–1235 or AD 1245–1430 with 95% certainty. AD 1300, AD 1370, and AD 1380 intersection with the calibration curve. Corrected to AD 1230–1415 (Foster 1995) (Beta 2016).
AD 1238	El Ombligo (Guasave), Sinaloa	AD 1120 ± 130 years (UCLA-964) (charcoal and pitch). Calibrated to AD 975–1400 with 95% certainty. AD 1220 intersection with the calibration curve (Foster 1995) (Beta 2016).
AD 1248	Tecualilla, Nayarit	AD 1195 ± 90 years (Isotopes-5528) (charcoal). Calibrated to AD 1045–1401 with 95% certainty (Foster and Scott 2017).
AD 1230	La Peña, Jalisco	AD 1170 ± 60 years (BETA-162046) (charcoal). Calibrated to AD 1160–1300 with 95% certainty (Liot et al. 2006).

TABLE 1.1. (cont'd.) Radiocarbon Dates for Aztatlán Deposits.

Date	Location	Description
AD 1255	La Peña, Jalisco	AD 1210 ± 50 years (BETA-162043) (charcoal). Calibrated to AD 1210–1300 with 95% certainty (Liot et al. 2006).
AD 1260	La Peña, Jalisco	AD 1110 ± 50 years (BETA-173334) (charcoal). Calibrated to AD 1040–1280 with 95% certainty (Liot et al. 2006).
AD 1261	El Ombligo (Guasave), Sinaloa	AD 820 ± 45 years (Arizona-17246) (shell). Corrected to AD 1209–1333 with 95% certainty (Carpenter 2008).
AD 1270 (or AD 1373)	Amapa, Nayarit	AD 1240 ± 50 years (UCLA-1848) (charcoal). Calibrated to AD 1225–1315 or AD 1355–1390 with 95% certainty (Foster 1995) (Beta 2016).
AD 1275	La Peña, Jalisco	AD 1230 ± 40 years (BETA-196963) (charcoal). Calibrated to AD 1250–1300 with 95% certainty (Liot et al. 2006).
AD 1277	La Peña, Jalisco	AD 1230 ± 40 years (BETA-162047) (charcoal). Calibrated to AD 1250–1305 with 95% certainty (Liot et al. 2006).
AD 1291	Arrinitas, Nayarit	AD 1250 ± 90 years (Isotopes-5531) (charcoal). Calibrated to AD 1158–1425 with 95% certainty (Foster and Scott 2017).
AD 1295	Tecualilla, Nayarit	AD 1250 ± 80 years (UCLA-1298) (charcoal). Calibrated to AD 1178–1413 with 95% certainty (Foster and Scott 2017).
AD 1300	Peñitas A, Nayarit	AD 1270 ± 100 years (Norwegian Institute of Technology-218) (charcoal). Calibrated to AD 1165–1435 with 95% certainty, AD 1165 intersection with the calibration curve (Bordaz 1964) (Beta 2016).
AD 1302	Peñitas, Nayarit	AD 1255 (UCLA-974) (charcoal). Corrected to AD 1200–1405 with 95% certainty (Foster 1995).
AD 1306	Rincón de Panal, Sinaloa	AD 1267 ± 55 years (BGS-108) (charcoal). Calibrated to AD 1229–1403 with 95% certainty (Foster and Scott 2017).
AD 1309	Arrinitas, Nayarit	AD 1265 ± 56 years (NSTF-5) (charcoal). Calibrated to AD 1218–1401 (AD 1309 central date) with 95% certainty (Foster and Scott 2017).
AD 1310	La Peña, Jalisco	AD 1250 ± 70 years (BETA-162045) (charcoal). Calibrated to AD 1210–1410 with 95% certainty (Liot et al. 2006).
AD 1310	Amapa, Nayarit	AD 1250 ± 75 years (Michigan-1164) (charcoal). Calibrated to AD 1210–1410 with 95% certainty (Foster 1995) (Beta 2016).
AD 1331	La Guásima, Nayarit	AD 1288 ± 33 years (INAH-1955) (charcoal). Calibrated to AD 1272–1391 with 95% certainty (Gámez Eternod 2004).
AD 1335	Venadillo, Sinaloa	AD 1330 ± 60 years (S.I.-2727) (shell). Calibrated to AD 1265–1405 with 95% certainty. Corrected to AD 1322–1631 (Foster and Scott 2017).
AD 1349	Coamiles, Nayarit	AD 1330 ± 80 years (Groningen-16010) (charcoal). Calibrated to AD 1262–1436 with 95% certainty (Duverger et al. 1993).
AD 1350	Rincón de Panal, Sinaloa	AD 1341 ± 56 years (BGS-107) (charcoal). Calibrated to AD 1283–1418 with 95% certainty (Foster and Scott 2017).
AD 1362	Venadillo, Sinaloa	AD 1370 ± 85 years (S.I.-2723b) (shell). Calibrated to AD 1265–1460 with 95% certainty. Corrected to AD 1325–1656 (Foster and Scott 2017).
AD 1370	El Ombligo (Guasave), Sinaloa	AD 1095 ± 45 years (Arizona-17251) (cordage). Corrected to AD 1295–1445 with 95% certainty (Carpenter 2008).
AD 1392	Rincón de Panal, Sinaloa	AD 1310 ± 64 years (BGS-109) (charcoal). Calibrated to AD 1268–1417 with 95% certainty (Foster and Scott 2017).
AD 1473	Tecualilla, Nayarit	AD 1473 ± 169 years (Isotopes-5529) (charcoal). Calibrated to AD 1304–1642 with 95% certainty (Foster and Scott 2017).

range of AD 600–1100 [Valdéz et al. 2005:394]) with the local Cojumatlán-like Aztatlán phase (suggested to date within the range of AD 850/900–1100 [Ramírez, Liot, and Schöndube 2006:19]). Thus, there is a real possibility that the Indigenous inhabitants of the Sayula Basin were becoming acculturated to intrusive Aztatlán culture and imitating some Aztatlán features in their own local culture; for example, imitating, as they did, cast copper bells in pottery.

Thus far, there has not been any suggestion that the Aztatlán phenomenon developed in western Durango or Zacatecas and spread from there down the river drainages to the coastal plain of Sinaloa and Nayarit, and southward from there to the Lake Chapala area. I am not advocating that interpretation either. However, to be fair, of the areas of Aztatlán development under consideration here, it is the Zacatecas-Durango area of the Chalchihuites archaeological culture that has the most developed Mesoamerican-type architectural and iconographic tradition in the Late Classic of any of these areas prior to the arrival or the development of the Early Postclassic Aztatlán phenomenon (Kelley 1985).

This is most obvious at Alta Vista in Zacatecas where the epitome of local development, the Alta Vista phase, begins at AD 650 with the site abandoned shortly after AD 900. This chronology is based on the central dates of 10 radiocarbon assays (Kelley 1985:279). It seems significant that this important regional center in northwestern Zacatecas was abandoned about the time that evidence of the Aztatlán phenomenon begins to appear in Durango and in areas of Sinaloa, Nayarit, Michoacán, Jalisco, and southern Zacatecas.

Several sites in Durango show contact with developing archaeological cultures on the Sinaloan coast. Such contact begins with non-Aztatlán pottery of the Middle Chametla phase that appears in Ayala-phase deposits at La Ferrería (Schroeder) in southern Durango (Kelley and Winters 1960:554), dated there approximately AD 600–850 based on seven radiocarbon dates (Kelley 1985:273). During the subsequent Las Joyas phase at La Ferrería, coastal wares identified as Aztatlán-type Red-on-buff decorated, incised, engraved, and incised polychrome appear as intrusives into the local sequence.

There are no radiocarbon dates available for deposits in which Aztatlán materials are found, but based on the previous Ayala phase the Aztatlán intrusives cannot be earlier than AD 850 and could be as late as the end of the Las Joyas phase, or around AD 1050 (Kelley 1985: 273). During the subsequent Río Tunal phase at the La Ferrería site (Schroeder), copper objects appear along with Aztatlán polychromes of varieties known at Culiacán and Guasave and notched-edge spindle whorls known from Aztatlán deposits on the Sinaloan coast (Kelley and Winters 1960:555). Only one radiocarbon date is available for this phase: a central date of AD 1223 (Kelley 1985:273) that fits well with radiocarbon dates on Aztatlán in other areas; for example, the AD 1215 central date on similar Aztatlán material from Arroyo Piedras Azules on the northern coast of Jalisco (Table 1.1).

To conclude, there also is the matter of the dating of the disintegration of Aztatlán hegemony in far western Mexico. This is a process that seems to take place during the AD 1300s and, based on available radiocarbon dates, appears to involve a retraction from the Aztatlán periphery while Aztatlán occupation persists along the coast in southern Sinaloa and northern Nayarit. A major, if not the primary, factor responsible for this disintegration was likely climate change that took place over a large area of western North America about this time (Schwindt et al. 2016:83). This change in climate adversely affected maize production and therefore the ability to sustain high population densities that had been achieved in some areas during the more favorable previous climatic regime.

PART II

Local and Regional Viewpoints

Aztatlán Sociopolitical Organization and Complexity
from Continental to Local Scales

CHAPTER 2

Coast-to-Coast

Evidence for Aztatlán Articulation in Supraregional Interaction Networks

Laura Solar Valverde

In recent decades, interest has grown in the study of social developments in northwest Mexico within the fields of archaeology and ethnography. Advancements in these disciplines have contributed to filling voids in knowledge as well as to diversifying analytical perspectives, which motivates scholars to pose new questions concerning the cultural processes that articulated this region and fostered its interaction with others. Such a reappraisal also requires reflection on the archaeological indicators that constitute the material expression of those processes.

In studying the prehispanic history of the coastal plain of west Mexico, pioneering work carried out in the 1930s and 1940s laid the foundation (i.e., Ekholm 1942; Kelly 1938, 1945a; Sauer and Brand 1932). More recently, knowledge has been enhanced through subsequent analysis of material culture from sites dotting the Pacific coastal lowlands and the alluvial plains of its tributaries (e.g., Beltrán Medina 1997, 2019; Foster, ed. 2017; Garduño Ambriz 2015, 2019; Garduño Ambriz et al. 2000; Garduño Ambriz and Vázquez del Mercado 2005; Grave Tirado 2003, 2019a; Meighan, ed. 1976; Mountjoy 1983, 2000; Ohnersorgen 2019), which in preconquest times integrated a regional structure commonly known today as Aztatlán.[1] In parallel, this area is being continually reassessed in terms of its role in the development of other contemporary sites in northern Mexico, such as Casas Grandes (Foster 1999; Kelley 2000), as well as its function in relation to ties between prehispanic Mesoamerica and the US Southwest (see Figures I.1–I.2; Anawalt 1992; Foster 1999; Jiménez 2020; Kelley 1986, 2000; Mathiowetz 2019a, 2020a; Sauer and Brand 1932:1).

On a different scale and geographical direction, the objective of this chapter is to propose that this region of west Mexico simultaneously participated in a supraregional communication system that fostered the exchange of artifacts and cultural patterns with societies of the Gulf of Mexico and Central America.

THE AZTATLÁN NETWORK

The strip formed by the modern states of Sinaloa, Nayarit, and northwest Jalisco—the Aztatlán heartland—was the setting of a long-lasting cultural development whose roots and evolution can be analyzed from the standpoint of a tradition (i.e., a deep-time local development; see Beltrán Medina 2001a, 2019; Grave Tirado 2003; Sauer and Brand 1932:65). However, sometime around AD 950 and for roughly four centuries, the region experienced a cultural peak and consolidation as one of the most remarkable interaction networks in ancient Mexico. The heyday of this "Aztatlán Network" can be discerned on the basis of the incorporation of inland sites into its economic and ideological sphere, expanding its configuration to the east and south to include, at least, the central and southern portions of the modern state of Durango, southern Zacatecas, central and western Jalisco, and the northwest edge of Michoacán (Figure 2.1; see Beltrán Medina 2001a; Foster 1999; Ganot and Peschard 1997; Kelley 1986; Kelley and Winters 1960; Kelly 1941:205, 1948:62; Liot et al., eds. 2006; Lister 1949; Mathiowetz 2019a, 2020a; Meighan and Foote 1968; Mountjoy 1990, 2001b; Punzo Díaz et al. 2017; Ramírez Urrea 2006a; Solar Valverde and Jiménez Betts 2008:47–49; Solar Valverde et al. 2019:8–19).[2]

The appearance at inland sites of many features shared with the heartland of the Aztatlán Network can be considered archaeological evidence of that incorporation. Some of these items, such as certain ceramic types and styles, were imports or emulations of those produced on the coastal plain (see Kelley 1986; Punzo

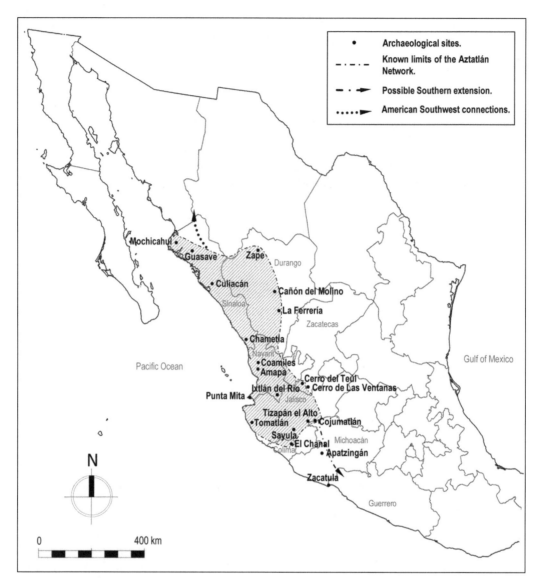

FIGURE 2.1. Approximate configuration of the Aztatlán Network at the time of its maximum expansion (ca. AD 950–1350). Dotted lines with arrows show possible extensions or connections with other networks. Sites depicted on the map were possible participants in this network.

Díaz et al. 2017; Ramírez Urrea 2006a; Vidal Aldana 2011). Nevertheless, beyond the presence of isolated objects, one significant pattern involving the main sites in both regions was the generalized adoption of an artifact complex composed of fancy pottery vessels—local or imported—(e.g., Aztatlán polychromes or Plumbate), musical instruments (rattles, whistles, *ocarinas*, flutes, drums, bell rattles, etc.), stone and ceramic smoking pipes, obsidian prismatic blades, copper and bronze tools (needles, hooks, tweezers, wire, buttons, etc.), Mazapan-style figurines of a particular variety, clay spindle whorls and stamps, ceramic masks, and ornaments or amulets made of diverse materials such as shell (bracelets, pendants, pectorals, etc.) and metal rings, bell rattles, ear ornaments, etc. (Beltrán Medina 2001a:53–61, 2019; Ekholm 1942:83–90; Foster 1999: 150; Garduño Ambriz 2015; Gifford 1950:231–237; Kelly 1938:45–54, 1941:200, 1945a:121–156; Liot et al., eds. 2006; Lister 1949:55–73; Meighan 1976:66–126; Meighan and Foote 1968:122–137; Mountjoy 2000:96–100, 2001b:58; Sauer and Brand 1932:31–36; Schöndube 1980a:215–253; Solar Valverde et al. 2019:4–8). These items likely were complemented by perishable materials such as feathers and textiles (Anawalt 1992; Mathiowetz 2020a; Mountjoy 2000:96) as well as ingestible substances such as tobacco, cacao, salt, dried foods, and entheogens (Kelley 2000:144; Mathiowetz 2019a; Mountjoy 2000:102) that have since disintegrated in the archaeological record but whose abundance and appreciation can be gleaned in historical sources.

A typological focus would favor the analysis and quantification of these items separately with each group containing multiple varieties. However, by observing them from the perspective of their function, and particularly the social context of their use, they seem to comprise an integral system.[3] In light of ethnographic analogy, it is sensible to propose that most of these objects comprise a set of tools for Indigenous ceremonialism involving music, chants, dance, the ingestion of tobacco and other psychotropic substances, auto sacrifice, votive offerings, certain outfits and ceremonial paraphernalia, and accoutrements of investiture, much as is reflected today in the Gran Nayar region (e.g., Gutiérrez 2002; Guzmán 2002; Jáuregui 1993, 2005; Jáuregui and Neurath 1998, 2003; Neurath 2002; Neurath et al. 2003). Close similarities between Aztatlán materials and the ritual implements in present ceremonialism allow us to discern deep cultural roots in this region extending at least into Early Postclassic times. Thus, ethnographic records appear to be a promising starting point for an intercontextual analysis of archaeological finds at various sites within the Aztatlán Network (Solar Valverde 2007, 2019).

Through time and space, prehispanic Indigenous ceremonies in Mesoamerica shared similar performative expressions, such as dance and music. However, an apparent innovation that stems from the time of the expansion of the Aztatlán Network is the standardization of the essential instruments for ritual practice and the uniformity of their tangible expression independently of the specific deities or celebrations involved on different occasions. This standardization could indicate the institutionalization of cult praxis in regions participating in the network, which, as already mentioned, is still materialized in similar ways among present Indigenous communities and is referred to in the more abstract notion of "*el costumbre*" (Solar Valverde 2007; Solar Valverde et al. 2019:22).

In the economic sphere, it has been posed that the expansion of the Aztatlán Network responded to a gradual integration of regions whose natural resources or cultural practices may have contributed to the production, consumption, and distribution of those ritual implements (Foster 2000; Jiménez 2014, 2020; Jiménez and Solar Valverde 2008, 2012; Kelley 2000; Mountjoy 2001b). Over time, these areas would have become interdependent regions for the acquisition and transformation of raw materials for the development and maintenance of technologies or industries—such as metalworking, obsidian work, or textile work—indispensable for the practice of the institutionalized cult (Jiménez and Solar Valverde 2008, 2012). In this way, the network would have provided key elements and situations for displaying symbols and performing actions of ideological and/or political legitimization (Earle 1997; Helms 1979, 1993).

Strategic access to specific resources was an outstanding aim for network expansion. Inland sites offered resources unavailable on the coast, such as obsidian from the highlands of Nayarit and Jalisco (see Mountjoy 2001b:58; Pierce 2015a), and perhaps tin from Zacatecas to make copper alloys (Solar Valverde 2011). Additionally, in some inland regions it was possible to extract or produce goods that were already available in the lowlands, but an increase in demand would have resulted in the need to augment and diversify the supply of these products. Industries already in operation, such as the intensive salt extraction in the Sayula Basin (see Liot 2000; Ramírez Urrea 2006a), would facilitate the inflow of those resources between the network participants.

In sum, the Aztatlán Network achieved its panregional configuration ranging from the Pacific coast to the eastern spurs of the Sierra Madre Occidental from the tenth to thirteenth century, perhaps articulated by a ritual economy derived from the institutionalization of religious cults. On a broader scale, by the end of this period (or perhaps earlier), the Aztatlán Network successfully converged with other networks that were already operating in more distant geographic regions, and this supraregional connection promoted long-distance cultural interchange.

Gulf of Mexico and the Southern Lowlands

One of the leading arteries in prehispanic Mesoamerica was dubbed the Peripheral Coastal Lowlands by Lee Parsons (1969, 1978, see Figure 2.2). Given Mexico's distinctive geography, this network meshed regional subspheres and distributional systems located at opposite ends of ancient Mexico and Central America. The extensive distribution of the Olmec style in the Preclassic period is only one example of the importance of this corridor and the riverine networks that connected it inland (Smith and Heath-Smith 1980:30; Webb 1978).

During the Classic period (ca. AD 300–600), activity in these coastal lowlands was eclipsed by the ideological prestige, political importance, and economic networks spearheaded by Teotihuacan. However, it is highly significant that the process of political decentralization characterizing the Epiclassic period (ca. AD 600–900) was accompanied by a revitalization of that coastal system and an increase in the macroregional prestige of those regions (e.g., Davies 1977; Parsons 1969; Pasztory 1978; Solar Valverde 2002; Zeitlin 1993). The efficiency of this network as a channel through which goods and ideas circulated from the Epiclassic to the time of the conquest must have facilitated the dispersal of cultural canons promoted by those regions.

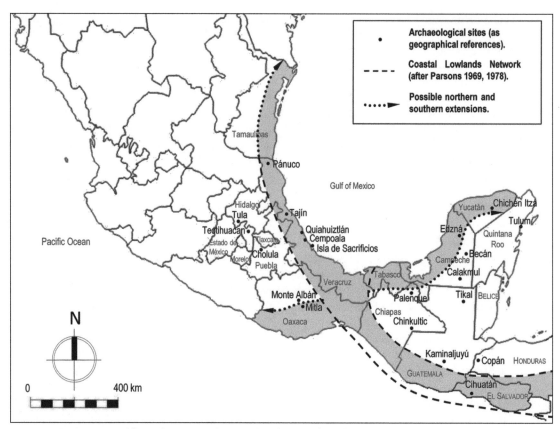

FIGURE 2.2. Segmented lines demarcate the Peripheral Coastal Lowlands network as proposed by Lee Parsons (1969, 1978). Dotted lines with arrows show possible extensions as can be discerned by subsequent investigations. Sites depicted on the map are geographical references.

Despite the compelling framework drawn by Smith and Heath-Smith (1980:25) over 40 years ago, the role played by these regions in the events of the Early and Middle Postclassic periods (ca. AD 900–1350) is rarely treated with the significance it deserves. Even so, the panregional distribution of some distinctive traits demonstrates that during those times prestige goods circulated throughout the strands of this network, which makes it necessary to reconsider its scope. The geographical boundaries originally assigned to the Lowlands Network coincided with voids in the archaeological record, but from subsequent research it is now evident that other regions were also participants.

In his seminal work, Parsons (1969, 1978) traced the extent of the network on the basis of features shared between Central America and the Gulf of Mexico, including sites in El Salvador, Guatemala, Chiapas, Tabasco, and Veracruz (see Thompson 1953). Since then, researchers have corroborated the similarities between all those regions, expanding the limits of the network to the east on the coast of the Yucatán Peninsula and the Northern Maya Lowlands (Ekholm 1944; Schmidt 1998; Sharp 1978) and to the southwest toward the coast of Oaxaca (Figure 2.2; Zeitlin 1993). To the north, the network extended into Huastec territory and possibly continued beyond.

Moreover, by the Early and Middle Postclassic periods this network articulated with the Aztatlán Network, as it becomes evident in the many cultural traits they share (see Smith and Heath-Smith 1980:26). It remains to be discerned, though, to what extent and through which places both networks connected.

A SET OF SIGNIFICANT FEATURES SHARED BY THE EASTERN AND WESTERN LOWLANDS

If one examines separately the ceramic and architectural complexes of the archaeological sites in eastern and western Mesoamerica, differences between those regions become apparent. However, various significant features appear within them with the same frequency. The traits to which I refer are mainly prestige goods, but also technological expertise, burial patterns, iconographic styles, and ceremonial implements that suggest close ties between the elites of both regions, probably denoting shared ritual praxis.

A representative expression of the Aztatlán Network is polychrome pottery. The most complex variety reproduces symbols and characters that follow conventions present in highland Mexican codices (especially those of the *Borgia* group and the *Codex Nuttall*). Some Aztatlán scholars have proposed that the presence of such images was the product of migration from central Mexico (Ekholm 1942) or the result of direct influence from the Mixtec region (Pohl 2012a). Nonetheless, there is sufficient evidence indicating that polychrome wares from Sinaloa, Nayarit, and Jalisco developed on the basis of local pottery traditions and their appearance antedates the Mixteca-Puebla ceramics to which they often are compared (Garduño Ambriz 2012a: 6–7; Grave Tirado 2012a:6; Kelly 1938, 1941; Smith and Heath-Smith 1980:22).

Despite its local development, these polychromes display noteworthy similarities with then-contemporaneous ceramics from the Gulf Coast and Central America (Figures 2.3a–2.3b). This similarity was perceived by Isabel Kelly several decades ago:

> There is, moreover, a surprising affinity between Early and Middle Culiacán [polychromes] and the Vera Cruz material excavated the past season by Stirling; and it is precisely this same east coast zone which produces incised wares similar to those of the Aztatlán complex. This unexpected ceramic parallel between east and west coasts is undoubtedly significant (1941:202).

Sometime later, Smith and Heath-Smith (1980:21–25) highlighted some correspondences between the iconographic content of all those wares and proposed the notion of a Postclassic Religious Style as an alternative to the centralist implications of the term "Mixteca-Puebla."

Another characteristic shared between the ceramics of both coasts—and that of Central America—is vessel shape (Smith and Heath-Smith 1980:22, 26–27; Sweetman 1974:78–79). Pear-shaped (pyriform) tripod or footless vessels and stylized vases or tall jars are distinctive of the Aztatlán Network (e.g., Ekholm 1942:61–62; Kelley and Winters 1960:550; Kelly 1945a:40, 207; Sauer and Brand 1932:33–34; Schöndube 1980a:215). These vessel shapes are found in common with ceramics from the Gulf Coast and among Central American polychromes (Figures 2.3f–2.3h; e.g., Ekholm 1942:61–62; Fahmel 1988:38–47; Lothrop 1979 [1926]:101–141; Medellín Zenil 1955:29; Nuttall 1910; Patel 2012).

The same shapes and some decorative designs on ceramics were also reproduced in travertine, onyx (*tecali*), or alabaster vessels, found in abundance in the same regions; handsome effigies were carved on some of these pieces (Figures 2.3c–2.3e; e.g., Ekholm 1942: 103,105; Kelly 1941:200, 205; Medellín Zenil 1955:86, 88; Nuttall 1910; Patel 2012; Schöndube 1980a:215, 221). Because of the material from which they were made, these containers might have been produced only in certain regions and exported to other areas, as well as in the case of Plumbate ware, which is also present in both coastal networks (e.g., Fahmel 1988; Lister 1949:51; Medellín Zenil 1955:49; Schöndube 1980a:215; Smith and Heath-Smith 1980:25–26).

At the same time, effigy vessels made of travertine or Plumbate inspired conceptually equivalent pieces in pottery, which understandably were much more abundant than the former. This phenomenon can be seen in collections from the Pacific, the Gulf of Mexico, and Central America (Figures 2.3i–2.3l; e.g., Lothrop 1979 [1926]:101–141; Medellín Zenil 1955:29–34, 42–49; Patel 2012; Schöndube 1980a:215, 224; Sweetman 1974: 76–77).

In addition to vessels—which are common elements in exchange networks—the concurrence of certain objects in the artifact complexes of both areas reflects cultural proximity between societies on the east and west coastal plains. With reference to the material complex already mentioned for the Aztatlán region, incised spindle whorls, cylindrical and rectangular clay stamps, clay and stone pipes, and musical instruments also are found in the Gulf Coast regions (Figures 2.4a–2.4j; e.g., Coe 1965:710–715; Medellín Zenil 1955:55, 64, 82, 89; Patel 2012; Wilkerson 2001:333).

As mentioned above, copper and bronze ornaments and tools were abundant in the Aztatlán Network during the Early and Middle Postclassic periods. Metal objects have been found as well at sites articulated by the Coastal Lowlands Network in the Gulf Coast and southern Mexico, where bell rattles, needles, hooks, and other objects made of the same metals are reported (Figures 2.4k–2.4p; e.g., Coe 1965:710–712, 715; Medellín Zenil 1955:90; Wilkerson 2001:333). In this regard, one significant discovery is evidence for the practice of metallurgy in the Huasteca during the Late Postclassic period (Hosler and Stresser-Péan 1992), which denotes the efficient dissemination of a specialized knowledge earlier dominated by societies in west Mexico. This fact drew the attention of Hosler and Stresser-Péan, who noted: "We do not know how metallurgy was introduced to the Huastec region from West Mexico." In their view, "the transfer of a complex technology, demands long-term face-to-face contacts" (Hosler and Stresser-Péan 1992:1219).

A distinctive variety of the so called Mazapan-style figurines is common at sites in the Aztatlán Network. It represents a female character rendered in a standardized position and attire (Figures 2.4q–2.4r; see Grosscup 1961), closely linking these western figurines to pieces from El Salvador (Solar et al. 2011) but setting them apart from the Mazapan-style terracottas common in central Mexico which reproduce both

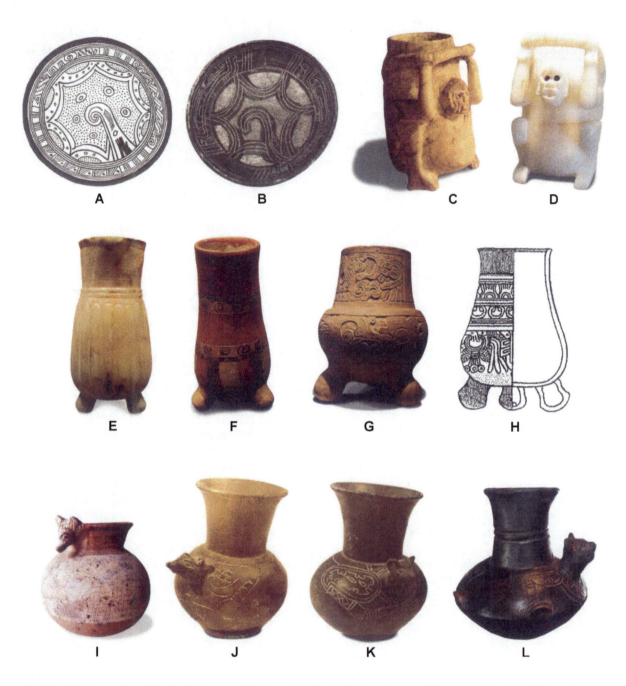

FIGURE 2.3. Items shared by the Eastern and Western Lowlands. (I) Ceramic vessel forms and motifs: (*a*) Guasave, Sinaloa (Ekholm 1942). (*b*) Isla de Sacrificios, Veracruz. Gobierno del Estado de Veracruz (Nuttall 1910; Medellín Zenil 1955). (II) Travertine, onyx, or alabaster effigy vases or jars: (*c*) Nayarit coast, Museo Regional de Guadalajara (Schöndube 1980a). (*d*) Isla de Sacrificios, Veracruz. Museo Nacional de Antropología (Nuttall 1910). (III) Tripod vases with pear-shaped body: (*e*) Travertine vase, Isla de Sacrificios, Veracruz, Museo Nacional de Antropología (Caso 1938; Nuttall 1910). (*f*) Polychrome ceramic vase from west Mexico, Museo Nacional de Antropología. (*g*) Engraved ceramic vase from the Gulf Coast, Museo Nacional de Antropología. (*h*) Incised ceramic vase from Guasave, Sinaloa (Ekholm 1942). (IV) Ceramic effigy vessels with incising (probably emulating the same concept as Plumbate pottery): (*i*) Nayarit coast, Museo Regional de Nayarit (Vladimir Cora collection). (*j*) Fine Orange type vessel and (*k*) "Metallic" type vessel, Isla de Sacrificios, Veracruz. Gobierno del Estado de Veracruz (Medellín Zenil 1955). (*l*) Plumbate-type vessel, Museo Nacional de Antropología. All figures are reproduced with legal permission of the National Institute of Anthropology and History (Secretaría de Cultura, INAH, Mex., Of. 401-3-2314), with the exception of Figures 2.3a and 2.3h which are courtesy of the Division of Anthropology, American Museum of Natural History.

genders with diverse headdresses and a variety of postures. For its part, on the Gulf Coast of Mexico there is an abundance of clay figurines displaying the same conventional traits as the Aztatlán examples—such as the emphasis on the female figure, the position of her hands, the bilobular headdress, and details of the attire—but manufactured in a different style and using different techniques (Figures 2.4s–2.4t). There are also some specimens from the Isla de Sacrificios, Veracruz (reproduced in Patel 2012:Figures 7.32–7.35), that can be ascribed to the variety of west Mexican terracottas (possibly imports from the Aztatlán region?).

Many of the artifacts listed above also appear at the main sites in the central highlands, which indicates that exchange ties indeed existed between all areas. However, these items appear with lesser frequency there than at lowland settlements and, more importantly, in general not all of the traits are found in a single highland site. This is significant when considering that access to the goods did exist; so, it might not be a matter of supply but, rather, of differential demand. This selective phenomenon was distinguished earlier in the specific case of ceramics, as Smith and Heath-Smith noted: "While some of this trade reached Central Mexico [...] ties were much stronger *within* the 'peripheral' regions of Mesoamerica than *between* these areas and the central highlands" (1980:26 [emphasis in original]).

The efficiency of a distribution network is perceptible through tangible imports and exports, or the manufacturing and demand for products throughout an extensive territory, but its quality as a communication agent is evident when it reflects the less visible movement of ideological principles over vast distances (e.g., Solar Valverde 2002). As Smith and Heath-Smith (1980) conclude, it seems to me that some related principles were assimilated and reproduced by societies residing in the eastern and western lowlands, with more points of coincidence between each other than with their neighbors in the central highlands. This perspective could help in understanding the joint adoption of the mentioned artifacts, but also the reproduction of cultural patterns that transcend material exchange. Some instances include the widespread practice of dental mutilation and cranial deformation among societies linked to both the eastern and western lowland networks (e.g., Ekholm 1942:119; Ganot and Peschard 1997:256–268; Kelly 1945a:193; Lister 1949:87; Medellín Zenil 1955:95; Romano 1965; Schöndube 1980a:249–250) and the human interments in ceramic urns reported for the Postclassic in both the Gulf Coast and Pacific networks (e.g., Ekholm 1942:39–41; Ganot and Peschard 1997:261; Kelly 1938:62–63, 1941:201, 205, 1945a:4–5, 192–193, 1948:62; Lister 1947:76; Medellín Zenil 1955:22–23, 60, 94; Sauer and Brand 1932:36; Schöndube 1980a:248).

Regardless of their interaction with other contemporary networks, would it be feasible that a greater "social proximity" or "cultural affiliation" existed among groups that shared similar geographical environments, despite the vast physical distance between them? This seems more likely if one takes into account that the geographical setting of both regions constituted a coastal environment of successive alluvial plains bounded by the spurs of the Sierra Madre Occidental and Sierra Madre Oriental, respectively. This situation implies that populations in these regions must have faced similar needs, challenges, and opportunities for adaptation and exploitation of the surrounding environment. Since cosmology is closely related to the inhabited landscape (see Kristiansen 2006:171), there might also have been a concurrence in the way people conceptualized and sacralized physical space and natural forces.

A disjointed acquisition of the same objects in the central highlands would make sense if these goods acted as an ensemble in relation to a ritual praxis shared by lowland societies, since the latter might have had a greater degree of cultural convergence. Going further, an interesting reflection emerges:

> By this the focus is shifted from tracing and discussing random similarities in material culture to studying the transmission and possible transformation of the structured material evidence of social institutions in time and space (Kristiansen and Larsson 2005:11).

In other words, underlying the coinciding distribution of the aforementioned artifacts could be the propagation of an institutionalized ritual protocol embraced by societies linked to the lowland networks. This would not exclude the individual worth of objects as luxury and prestige goods for societies in other regions, but it would cast them in a different light. Such an assessment does not intend to insinuate that the various sites involved were subjected to the same social structure, since it is possible to appropriate certain cultural patterns without having to adopt the political or economic framework of the sources of transmission of those patterns (Kristiansen and Larsson 2005:6).

Unlike the recurring scenario in the central highlands, the geographical setting of the coastal lowlands did not favor the consolidation of centralized political systems (Solar Valverde 2002). Instead, a more realistic perspective is a multicentric system articulated by prestige goods and information networks, following the nested networks model developed by Chase-Dunn and Hall (1997).[4] This viewpoint offers a better fit with descriptions of sites and subregions in these geographical "corridors" (e.g., Grave Tirado 2019a; Schöndube 1980a:246; Wilkerson 2001:328, 333), which seem to represent a series of equipollent settlements organized around a main site (Jiménez and Solar Valverde 2008).

FIGURE 2.4. Items shared by the Eastern and Western Lowlands. (I) Flat and cylindrical clay stamps: (*a–b*) Nayarit, Museo Regional de Nayarit. (*c*) Nayarit, Museo Local de Historia y Arqueología de Compostela. (*d*) Gulf Coast, Museo Nacional de Antropología. (*e–f*) Veracruz, Museo de Antropología de Xalapa. (II) Clay rattles: (*g*) Veracruz, Museo de Antropología de Xalapa. (*h*) Nayarit, Museo Regional de Nayarit. (III) Smoking pipes: (*i*) West Mexico, Museo Nacional de Antropología. (*j*) Gulf Coast, Museo Nacional de Antropología. (IV) Metal artifacts present in both regions: Fish hooks: (*k*) Veracruz, Museo de Antropología de Xalapa. (*l*) West Mexico, Museo Nacional de Antropología. Copper bells: (*m*) Veracruz, Museo de Antropología de Xalapa. (*n*) West Mexico, Museo Nacional de Antropología. Chisels: (*o*) Veracruz, Museo de Antropología de Xalapa. Needles: (*p*) Veracruz, Museo de Antropología de Xalapa. (V) Mazapan-style figurines, West Mexico variety: (*q–r*) Nayarit, Museo Local de Historia y Arqueología de Compostela. (*s–t*) Ceramic figurines similar to Mazapan style, Museo de Sitio de Cempoala, Veracruz. All figures are reproduced with legal permission of the National Institute of Anthropology and History (Secretaría de Cultura, INAH, Mex., Of. 401-3-2314), with the exception of Figures 2.4e–2.4g, 2.4k–2.4m, and 2.4o–2.4p, which are reproduced with the permission of the Museo de Antropología de Xalapa.

The Early Postclassic Scene

The analysis of the Early Postclassic period tends to be influenced by the preconception of a highly centralized system that brought together the principal exchange networks under a single political regime for almost three centuries (for a comprehensive discussion, see Gillespie 2011). In the 1940s, this perspective initially arose from extrapolations of sixteenth-century historical accounts concerning the place of origin of the principal artistic and ideological traits characterizing Mesoamerica at the time of the Spanish conquest (see Sociedad Mexicana de Antropología 1941). But the notion of an Early Postclassic "Toltec empire" entails serious obstacles for a horizontal analysis of the period (Davies 1977; Gillespie 2011). With that approach, the most valued sumptuary goods of the time are often taken as diagnostics of "the Toltec," although their place of origin and geographical distribution go beyond the feasible reach of a political configuration of that kind (i.e., an empire) in ancient Mesoamerica. Therefore, such an assumption blurs the possibility of reflecting on the differential roles played by diverse regions or sites in the global dynamics of that period.

In addition to surmising Toltec influence, for decades Aztatlán iconography was catalogued as a dissemination of Mixteca-Puebla "culture" resulting from a migration from central Mexico (e.g., Ekholm 1942: 125–132), even though, as stated above, it is known that Aztatlán ceramics evolved locally and prior to the development of its southern analogues. Today, as a result of the greater geographic coverage of archaeological research in Mexico, other interpretations are proving to be more prudent for explaining the generalized distribution of features during the Early and Middle Postclassic periods. It is no longer necessary to refer to a single focal point from which these traits spread. Notions like the Postclassic Religious Style coined by Smith and Heath-Smith (1980) in their classic work, or the International Styles and Symbol Sets (Boone and Smith 2003), are more convenient models for their efficacy in shaking off earlier prejudices. What remains to be accomplished are efforts to go beyond the definition of this phenomenon and begin to assess the underlying social processes.

With regard to the standardized representations of symbols on materials from this period characteristic of their Postclassic Religious Style, Smith and Heath-Smith commented:

> their widespread distribution indicate[s] a uniformity on at least the level of religious symbolism, and probably also point to similarities among regions in such matters as cosmology and ritual, though this has yet to be demonstrated (1980:30).

Similarly, I believe that the shared adoption of an ensemble of objects essential to materialize religious celebrations is significant. Beyond the fact that those instruments do not necessarily imply the adoption of the same pantheon or matching ceremonial cycles in all regions of the lowlands, they do indeed reveal similarities in aspects of cosmology and ritual.

On the other hand, despite the clarity with which Smith and Heath-Smith (1980) explain the relevance of the lowlands in the dispersion of symbols and features characterizing the Postclassic Religious Style, in making a generalizing designation of the period the term ends up encompassing all regions. In so doing, we again lose sight of the nuances that allow us to anticipate that these symbols and features might not have had the same meaning for all areas.

Finally, a number of questions arise: Is there enough evidence to advocate for a close interaction between the East and Northwest Lowlands Networks? Which could have been the transverse channels connecting these areas (Central America, the Isthmus of Tehuantepec, and/or the Mixteca-Puebla-Tlaxcala region)? Were there two parallel networks that occasionally shared the same commodities, or is it correct to speak of one lowlands network that included an eastern and western branch during the Early and Middle Postclassic periods? What were the social motivations and mechanisms facilitating ideological flow, and what were the political and economic implications?

To consider the Aztatlán Network's connection with the Gulf of Mexico-Central American networks, and to ponder an efficient cultural flow between those areas, opens up an interesting range of questions on the transactions of that period. All the more, it encourages us to discern the character of the goods and concepts that promoted the lowland elites' intertwinement at different times in prehispanic Mesoamerica.

Notes

1. The term was adopted by Diguet (1903) and Sauer and Brand (1932:5) from the first atlas of the world (*Teatrum Orbis Terrarum*) by Abraham Ortelius (1570), which documented the Indigenous provinces found by the Spaniards between modern northern Nayarit and central Sinaloa. Regarding the distribution of the most representative Aztatlán material culture, those boundaries have expanded out of a better understanding of prehispanic settlements in northwest Mexico (Solar Valverde and Nelson 2019).

2. Southern Jalisco and Colima are traditionally excluded from the area of distribution of the Aztatlán Complex (see Bell 1971:699, 751; Kelly 1945a:10–11; Mountjoy 1990). Nevertheless, excavations undertaken at the site of

El Chanal (Olay 2004) recovered many items characteristic of this network (i.e., metal, Plumbate ware, ceramic stamps). The absence of spindle whorls and pipes (that in the present work are regarded as indicative of the Aztatlán Network) could be illusory. Olay (2004) noted that more systematic excavation is needed to offset the years of deterioration and intensive looting that has assailed the ancient settlement. Likewise, in the western state of Guerrero, artifacts considered to be Aztatlán diagnostics have been reported (see Lister 1971).

3. While advising Bojórquez Diego (2009) on her thesis, I suggested that she could apply Kristiansen and Larsson's (2005) *intercontextualisation* framework to approach this set of artifacts since the typological classification she was attempting to carry out appeared to be inappropriate for the analysis of objects that were quite different in their form and style but were definitely affiliated in their function and meaning. I recommended that Bojórquez Diego refer to this set as a "ritual complex," not in the sense of a well-defined religious complex, but as an ensemble of objects essential to materialize religious celebrations. While she accomplished a laborious record of artifacts reported by other authors (Bojórquez Diego 2009), a full assessment of Aztatlán objects within an *intercontextualisation* framework remains to be completed.

4. This proposal coincides to a great extent with the nonnuclear approach employed by Smith and Heath-Smith (1980), but it differs subtly in the emphasis or the causality attributed in each case. They utilized this perspective to describe the behavior of a period. In other words, they considered it a temporal circumstance (Smith and Heath-Smith 1980:29, 38). The multicentric system proposed here—although it occurs in certain alternating periods in Mesoamerican history—underscores the geographical factor (Solar Valverde 2002:291).

CHAPTER 3

Ritual Objects as Cultural Capital

A Comparison between the Mixtec-Zapotec, Aztatlán, and Casas Grandes Cultural Co-traditions

John M. D. Pohl

One of the most remarkable features of the narrative scenes in the Mixtec codices is the extraordinary amount of gift giving between nobles that focuses on objects made from wealth-finance commodities. *Codex Vienna* 30 depicts the institution of ear piercing in which we see the culture hero Nine Wind "Quetzalcoatl" piercing the ear of the aged Lord Two Dog, while priests present gifts of tunics called *xicollis* (Furst 1978:175–176). The *xicollis* are part of a reciprocal exchange of honors, for directly afterwards Lord Two Dog pierces the ears of Nine Wind. The hero Nine Wind then intiates the naming rituals for an assembly of 44 Mixtec gods (Figure 3.1a). On *Codex Nuttall* 78, we see Lord Eight Deer together with his Tolteca-Chichimeca ally Lord Four Jaguar presenting themselves before the oracle of the sun god, Priest One Death, at Achiutla in the Mixteca Alta. Eight Deer offers the priest a golden bell while Four Jaguar presents a jeweled pendant. On the following page the oracle presents Eight Deer with a turquoise and gold necklace and thereby confirms his support for the usurper's claim to the kingdom of Tilantongo (Figure 3.1b).

Examples of jewelry art in precious stones and metals like those portrayed in the codices appear in major private and institutional collections around the world. They were meticulously created, especially works fashioned with thousands of turquoise tesserae or "tiles" in some cases (McEwan et al. 2006). For archaeologists, these objects therefore possess intrinsic value not only because of the geographically distant sources of the material, but also because of their labor intensive manufacture. Aesthetics must have played a role as well. The appealing blue color symbolized the brilliant sunlit sky and life-giving water, for example.

The use of precious material to fashion objects for facial jewelry, especially ear flares and labrets, was intended to not only convey superior status but also a sense of the superior qualities of intelligence and sensitivity (see Houston and Taube 2000). Nahua nobles were compared to turquoise and gold in early Indigenous colonial accounts while Mixtec nobles were pictographically named for these materials in precolumbian codices. Turquoise known as *teotlxihuitl* was attributed spiritual value. *Xihuitl* means turquoise in Nahuatl while *teotl* is used to invoke the divine as an intangible "force" that imbues people, places, and things with qualities of spiritual "life" (Weigand and Weigand 2001:188–189). A turquoise mosaic mask preserved in the British Museum was once fastened to the face of a Mixtec mummified noble. It was believed by its creators to be endowed with the supernatural power or "*ñuhu*" to communicate with the deceased ancestor on whose corpse it was displayed (Domenici and Laurencich Minelli 2014).

Given the diverse range of qualities attributed to these objects, the Late Postclassic exchange systems we are studying might be more broadly conceived as the transference of cultural capital as it was originally defined by Pierre Bourdieu (1986) rather than simply economic capital. Functioning within an objectified state of material objects used to define social class, systems of cultural capital emphasize ideological value. Furthermore, they have proven to be remarkably compelling among elite classes, particularly for fostering the replication of institutionalized states across the broad geographical networks upon which high status, together with the exclusive access to the wide variety of foreign and domestic commodities, was dependent.

Here I will focus on several categories of objects crafted in precious stones and metals that have been recovered archaeologically in southern Mexico. After presenting case studies that demonstrate how these ob-

FIGURE 3.1. (*a*) Mixtec *Codex Vienna* 30 portrays the rituals for awarding the titles of the gods instituted by the culture hero Nine Wind (Ehecatl-Quetzalcoatl) and his associate the priest-elder Two Dog who pierce one another's ears. Note the gifts of textiles that are exchanged. This naming ritual was recorded historically in the Greater Southwest. Anthropologist Frank Hamilton Cushing wrote of having his ears pierced by the Zuni when awarding him the kinship title Té-na-tsa-li after the name for a flowering medicinal plant (Cushing 1883:511). (*b*) *Codex Nuttall* 78 portrays Lord Eight Deer and Lord Four Jaguar presenting the Mixtec oracle-priest Lord One Death (Sun God) of Achiutla with golden jewels. In return, the priest confirms the alliance of Mixtec and Toltec warlords and supports Eight Deer's claim to the throne of Tilantongo. Author's illustrations.

jects functioned within a gift-wealth system of the cultural capital depicted in the highland Mexican codices, I will consider equivalent meanings for comparable objects found within archaeological contexts from Aztatlán elite societies of Jalisco and Nayarit to the Casas Grandes culture of Chihuahua. Finally I will propose that these objects have implications for studying Late Postclassic sociopolitical and economic organization shared throughout Mexico and the Greater Southwest between 1250–1600.

Networks

The Eastern Nahuas, Mixtecs, and Zapotecs, together with more than 15 other language groups across southern Mexico that they dominated, had composed a significant part of a Late Postclassic economic system extending from Central America up the Pacific coast to Oaxaca, Jalisco, Nayarit, Zacatecas, Chihuahua, New Mexico, Arizona, and California (see Figures I.1–I.2, I.9–I.10; Pohl 2003a, 2003b, 2003c, 2003d, 2016a; Pohl and Mathiowetz 2022). These populations maintained *barrios* within each others' kingdoms, intermarried to form exclusive monopolies over resources, and enriched themselves through trade in exotic commodities like textiles, dyes, turquoise, copper, gold, shell, and the feathers of exotic tropical birds.

The Eastern Nahuas of the Plain of Puebla and the Tehuacan Valley invested in Cholula as their new "Tula" to coordinate the social, political, and economic agendas of their constituent city-states, while the Mixtecs and Zapotecs endowed Mitla with many of these same organizational qualities (Pohl 1999). I have proposed that functionally equivalent centers were emerging at the same time among Ancestral Pueblo peoples in the north, first at Pueblo Bonito in New Mexico and subsequently at Paquimé in northern Chihuahua (Lekson 1999, 2015; Pohl and Mathiowetz 2022). By AD 1300, Paquimé had become a significant Mesoamerican trading center uniting many of the attributes of the Mogollon tradition with those of highland Mesoamerica (Di Peso 1974). Particularly notable was the construction of Late Postclassic Mesoamerican ballcourts together with artifacts of cast and hammered west Mexican copper and the remains of scarlet macaws whose natural habitat otherwise extended no further than the Isthmus of Tehuantepec. Some archaeologists have concluded that Paquimé originated as a late Mogollon response to dramatic population movements following the abandonment of Ancestral Pueblo and Mimbres communities to the north followed by a significant restructuring of social, political, and economic organization in Chihuahua to the south.

One of the principal characteristics of the new order was the construction of platform mounds surmounted by residential structures mirroring the scores of palaces identified archaeologically throughout southern Mexico at this same time with their networks of small courts and rooms. It is notable that such architectural innovations were accompanied by the production of polychrome ceramics and typical Mesoamerican jewelry forms like ear spools, nose ornaments, and pectorals suggesting a direct engagement with Mesoamerican peoples including reciprocal exchanges in kinship titles among nobles (Pohl 2016a).

Divining Mirrors

Charles Di Peso excavated over 650 copper artifacts at Paquimé, more than the total recovered from all other sites between northwest Mexico and the U.S. Southwest combined. Among these were hammered copper disks on which designs were engraved, reminding Di Peso of the back "shields" on the monumental Toltec warriors from Building B at Tula, Hidalgo (Figure 3.2). The imagery is directly comparable in depicting the four sacred cardinal world directions together with four Xiuhcoatl serpents. Xiuhcoatl means both "fire serpent" or "turquoise serpent" in Nahuatl. The fire serpent in Mixtec is Yahui, a term that is also used to identify a necromancer or priest who can miraculously speak with the dead. While the function of these artifacts is not clear at Paquimé from archaeological contexts alone, an examination of the use of comparable objects as they appear in the Mixtec codices is informative.

The Toltec "back-shield" is a specific artifact type that has been excavated both at Tula and Chichén Itzá. It consists of a wooden disk upon which an elaborate rendition of the sacred directional scheme has been applied using intricate turquoise mosaic. The fact that the center is composed of a reflective surface of pyrite indicates it functioned as a divining mirror for consulting supernatural entities, and it is notable that the face of an ancestor appears within the center of the back shields as they are on the Tula warriors.

Mirrors have a long tradition in Mesoamerican sorcery practices, extending back to the Formative period (Taube 2016). They continue to be used by Indigenous healers to determine the cause of diseases by visioning the spirit entity that a patient may have offended and evaluate what offerings are necessary to appease the being and negotiate a cure. Diviners use mirrors to see both past and future events and in so doing recommend a proper course of action for those who seek their advice in decision making. Mirrors appear frequently in Classic Maya vase painting, being consulted by paramount lords presumably engaged in divination of this kind. The mirror was considered to be such a powerful instrument that it was frequently invoked together with the reliquary contents of a paramount lord's sacred

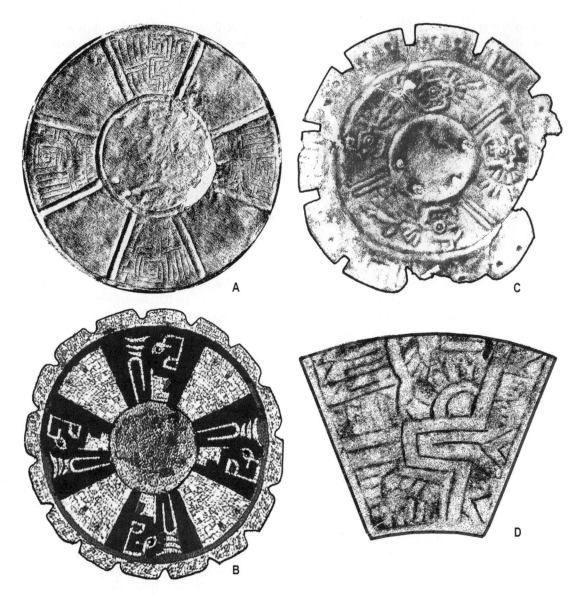

FIGURE 3.2. (*a*) Copper shield-mirror from Paquimé depicting the sacred four directions and associated fire serpents. (*b*) Turquoise and pyrite-mosaic back mirror from Chichén Itzá. (*c*) Copper mirror depicting the sacred four directions with associated fire serpents from west Mexico. (*d*) A section of a copper mirror in distinctive Aztatlán style depicting the head of a fire serpent. Drawings by author.

bundle upon accession to high office among the Classic Maya (Schele and Miller 1983).

In comparable fashion, the symbolism of the turquoise mosaic mirror by Late Postclassic nobles associates it directly with the polity itself, perhaps something comparable to a king's "orb" in Medieval Europe. The cruciform of the surface image invokes the four sacred directions that define a noble person's realm while the mosaic itself symbolizes the surface of the earth. It is notable in that regard how much the radial map appearing in the *Mapa de Teozacoalco* resembles a turquoise mosaic mirror with its fractures defined by roads, trails, mountain ranges, and rivers of the Teozacoalco landscape. *Codex Borgia* depicts a sun god drilling fire with a mirror mounted to the back of a fire serpent. Whether this refers to an actual mechanism for making fire and how this worked exactly is unknown. However fire drilling was an act associated with bringing the "first light" to a kingdom as part of the rituals involved in founding a realm by Mixtec culture heroes in *Codex Vienna* (Furst 1978).

Mirrors have been recovered from elite burials in Oaxaca as well and testify to the inheritance of Tolteca-Chichimeca ritualism among the Mixtec and Zapotec elite during the Late Postclassic. An example recovered from Tomb 1 at Zaachila is smaller and simpler

FIGURE 3.3. (*a*) The Mixtec oracle priest Lady Nine Grass awards a turquoise mosaic mirror to Lord Eight Deer. (*b*) The mirror is then taken by Eight Deer together with his sacred bundle to the kingdom of Tututepec where he claims rulership. (*c*) Actual mosaic mirrors like this example from Tomb 1 at Zaachila, Oaxaca, have been recovered from tombs together with the remains of sacred bundles. Drawings by author.

in design than its Toltec antecedent, but it is directly comparable to representations appearing in the Mixtec historical codices where it plays a very specific role as a ritual gift object. *Codex Colombino* portrays the legend of Lord Eight Deer, an eleventh-century Mixtec culture hero whose descendants founded the royal houses of Tilantongo, Teozacoalco, and Zaachila, the highest-ranked royal line at the time of the Spanish entrada into Oaxaca. On *Codex Colombino* 3–4, Lord Eight Deer is dressed in a jaguar suit seated before a series of gifts including a conch shell trumpet, a back-shield mirror, a spear ornamented with the head of an owl, and a golden fish, among other objects that he receives from the priestess Lady Nine Grass (Figure 3.3). Although the image of the priestess herself is damaged, it is clear from the depiction of her skull-ornamented temple that she had appeared prominently in the scene. Furthermore, *Codex Colombino* 3 is cognate with *Codex Nuttall* 42 where we see Lady Nine Grass very clearly meeting with both Eight Deer and his rival Lady Six Monkey.

In awarding Lord Eight Deer with the gifts Lady Nine Grass confers upon him, he is offered the rulership of Tututepec, the Mixtec city-state that emerged to dominate the Pacific coast during the Postclassic. On *Codex Colombino* 4, Eight Deer travels to his new kingdom with a retinue including his brothers, each of whom carries one of the gifts presented by Lady Nine Grass. The mirror appears slung from a tumpline and it is notable that it is carried along with Eight Deer's sacred bundle, the principal emblem of his accession to the throne of Tututepec. After performing the rituals for claiming his kingdom by venerating the trees that stand at the sacred directions, Eight Deer is depicted on *Codex Colombino* 5 as arriving at Tututepec where he places the emblems of rulership within the principal cult temple there.

Codex Bodley and *Codex Selden* depict the same meeting that took place in *Codex Colombino* 3–4. However, the emphasis is on the gifts Lady Nine Grass conferred on Lady Six Monkey, who aspires to the rulership of Jaltepec and will ultimately prove to be Eight Deer's principal rival for control over the Tilantongo lineage. Among the emblems of rulership given to Six Monkey are a number of richly embroidered textiles together with necklaces and jewelry pendants including a gold ballcourt like that from Monte Albán Tomb 7, and most importantly a mirror ornamented with a bird's head. Following this event Lady Six Monkey goes to war against two prominent kingdoms and sacrifices the lord of one before her sacred bundle at Jaltepec and the other at the home of her future husband. Lady Six Monkey then receives an additional award—a textile cape embroidered with a chevron band signifying her prowess as a warrioress—before she marries Eight Deer's principal rival.

The awarding of the mirrors to two prominent aspirants to Mixtec thrones is a significant event. Lady Nine Grass presided over a famous burial cave located at the kingdom of Chalcatongo (Pohl 1994:75). This cave was venerated by all of the Mixtec noble families as the mummified ancestors of the lords of Tilantongo, the highest-ranking royal lineage, were preserved there. The spirits of the dead were believed to reside in a royal paradise and Lady Nine Grass was credited with the oracular ability to contact them and interpret their wishes to their descendants with regard to the affairs of inheritance, marriage, and the resolution of conflicts. The Spaniards therefore compared oracles like Lady Nine Grass to their archbishops or even the pope in their powers.

Mummy bundles served as physical proof of the ranking lines of succession upon which Mixtec and Zapotec social order was defined. The maintenance of a funerary cult that focused on the grouping of the remains of the royal dead in central places like Chalcatongo was ingenious. In societies like the Mixtec and Zapotec, rank was traced through one's familial relationship with the oldest royal lineages. By controlling access to the divine dead and managing their cult, oracles like Nine Grass were actually manipulating the affairs of the living descendants as kings and queens were forced to use them as mediators in their lineage disputes. Funerary cults thereby provided a source of corporate identity insuring political stability among various members of the competitive royal kin groups in the absence of any single governmental capital in Postclassic Oaxaca (Pohl 1994:69–82).

The size, form, and iconography of Paquimé copper divining mirrors suggests that they very likely functioned in the same way as their Toltec turquoise mosaic counterparts. If so, their presence at this northern Mexican center could provide some insights into sociopolitical relationships within the greater Casas Grandes system. Charles Di Peso believed that the sheer quantity of copper objects at Paquimé proved that its artisans were smelting and fabricating the material as a trade commodity. Bells are found throughout the southwestern United States and northwest Mexico, for example. They have appeared in both Hohokam and Ancestral Pueblo sites dating to as early as AD 900, which indicates a long history of trade relationships with centers of copper bell production to the south. If Di Peso was correct, then Paquimé's artisans may have produced the mirrors for powerful priest-mediators who awarded the objects to constituent nobles. These nobles, in turn, displayed them as confirmation of their positions of authority over outlying polities. In fact, fragments of mirrors have been found at sites nearly 20 km north of Paquimé in the upper reaches of the Río Casas Grandes, which suggests a distributive network of just this kind (Di Peso 1974:2:498). Clearly Paquimé elites had a preference for the ritual value of embossed copper over turquoise mosaic, but why would the symbolism of the divining mirrors shared with paramount titles of rulership in Oaxaca be important to them?

A number of scholars have questioned the evidence for metallurgical processing at Paquimé itself and have proposed that the primary source for copper artifacts at the site lies to the south in west Mexico in the Aztatlán region where networks of ranked *señoríos* or city-states had emerged along the coastal plain of Jalisco extending north through Nayarit into Sinaloa (Rakita and Cruz 2015:76–78; Vargas 2001). It is here that metallurgical technology was first introduced from Lower Central America between AD 800–900 at a time when the region was experiencing a dramatic increase in population together with the construction of large-scale pyramid and plaza complexes typical of Central and Southern Mexico. Carl Sauer first proposed the term "Aztatlán" for this cultural tradition after the site of San Felipe Aztatlán (Sauer and Brand 1932), now known as San Felipe Aztatán (see Garduño Ambriz, this volume).

Artifact categories such as Mazapan figurines suggest that Aztatlán nobles were at first closely associated with Tula itself, which may have even sponsored settlement of the region (Pohl and Mathiowetz 2022). Then, by AD 1300 dramatic changes—particularly the adoption of the Nahua-Mixteca or Postclassic International Style manifested in polychrome ceramics and iconography—suggest a dramatic shift in orientation to southern Mexico. Systematic archaeological investigations have demonstrated the evolution of the Nahua-Mixteca style at Cholula beginning about AD 950. But it is only after AD 1250 that we see the spread of the style and its associated symbol set that composed its pictographic communication system into regions as diverse as the Basin of Mexico, Tlaxcala, Puebla, Oaxaca, Veracruz, west Mexico, and even northern Mexico and the U.S. Southwest. This distribution has led archaeologists to define it as a "horizon style," a term for artifacts combining narrow temporal distribution, broad spatial distribution, and stylistic complexity (Pohl 2012a, 2012b). Horizon styles therefore signify to archaeologists periods of panregional cultural integration. The question is, what mechanisms would explain its widespread distribution among peoples who were so otherwise culturally distinct in the previous Classic period and whose descendants continue to speak more than 15 different Indigenous languages today?

Lineage Organizations and Political Titles as Cultural Capital

At the time of the conquest, the principal seat of the cult of Quetzalcoatl was centered at Cholula (Pohl 2003a: 62–63). Ethnohistorical studies combined with an urban archaeological survey have confirmed the location of the great temple of Quetzalcoatl at what is today the Convento de San Gabriel in Cholula's main *zócalo*. Between AD 1200 and 1520, confederations of kingdoms throughout the central and southern highlands venerated Cholula as a major market and pilgrimage center and even submitted to the authority of its priests in matters of alliance and factional dispute. The foundation of this theocratic authority was a religious ceremony dedicated to Quetzalcoatl whereby a prince was required to journey to Cholula to meet with two high priests called the Tlalchiach and the Aquiach. After several days of prayer and penitence, the ears, nose, and lips of the initiate were pierced with sharpened eagle and jaguar bones, and an ornament was inserted according to the custom of the kingdom from which the petitioner came. The prince was then declared a *tecuhtli* or lineage head and granted, through Quetzalcoatl's divine authority, the rulership of a royal estate or *teccalli*. The appeal of the cult of Quetzalcoatl and the *tecuhtli* ceremony was that it transcended all local religious customs and bound ethnically diverse peoples together into similar social and political units, thereby facilitating elite alliance and economic exchange throughout the Central and Southern Mexican Highlands (Figures 3.4a–3.4b).

The *tecuhtli* ceremony was an essential part of the Mixtec Lord Eight Deer's rise to power. In AD 1100, the last male heir to the throne of Tilantongo, Lord Two Rain, committed suicide. Eight Deer returned from Tututepec to usurp, but being the son of the kingdom's high priest his bloodline was too distant to claim any legitimate right to the throne. He resolved the issue by seeking outside forms of legitimacy from the Eastern Nahua-dominated confederacies of Puebla and northern Oaxaca. *Codex Nuttall* 52, *Codex Colombino* 13, and *Codex Bodley* 9 all portray the event. Tolteca-Chichimeca ambassadors are dispatched from "Tula," in this case a local Mixtec cult center maintained at San Miguel Tulacingo and a subject of the powerful kingdom of Coixtlahuaca (Pohl 1994:96–97).

After meeting with the Tolteca-Chichimeca ambassadors, Eight Deer agreed to compete in a ballgame match, the outcome of which will be used to evaluate his qualifications for promotion in much the same way as it was first instituted at Cholula itself. Having succeeded, Eight Deer is dispatched to attack Yucu Yoo, Hill of the Moon, where he captures a lord and presents him for sacrifice to the Tolteca-Chichimeca priest Four Jaguar at Tulancingo. Eight Deer is then directed to lie over a jaguar skin while a priest pierces the septum of his nose and inserts the *yacaxihuitl*, or turquoise nose jewel. In return for this honor, Eight Deer apparently traded one form of political legitimacy for another, by sending his son and daughter to the Toltecs for marriage into the royal house of San Miguel Tulancingo.

Research over the past 20 years has forced us to reevaluate traditional evolutionary models for the Late Postclassic period. The shift toward political decentralization after the abandonment of Tula is often equated with notions of "collapse" or "fall" when in fact we know that many social institutions actually became more complex. The explanation for this may very well lie in the advantages in organizational principles upon which tribes and chiefdoms are predicated. If chiefdoms, for example, can adopt systems of social stratification to make them more effective producers of raw materials like turquoise that are consumed by states, then states might just as easily appropriate aspects of the segmentary systems of chiefdoms to reorganize themselves more effectively across wider geographical ranges than their Classic predecessors. One need look no further than the Chicomoztoc creation accounts in the *Historia Tolteca-Chichimeca* and the *Mapas de Cuauhtinchan* to see how careful the Tolteca-Chichimeca were to invoke "tribal" organizational principles in the formulation of their confederacies while seating a state ideology of centrality in the pilgrimage and market center of Cholula (Carrasco and Sessions 2007; Fargher et al. 2011; Kirchhoff 1961; Knab 1983; Pohl 2001, 2003a).

We know that turquoise was used as a high-status material among Aztatlán nobles (Beltrán Medina 2001a:53). Analysis of ritual dress depicted on polychrome vases proves that the Aztatlán nobles were also invested in the *tecuhtli* system. The *yacaxihuitl* ornament appears in the noses of culture heroes engaged in a number of foundation rituals along with other turquoise jewels adorning their heads, arms, legs, and torsos. We also know that the title of "*tecuhtli*" was used by west Mexican nobles at the time of the first Spanish entradas into west Mexico. For example, the Lord of Zapotitlan was named Xiuhtecuhtli while the Lord of Tuscacuesco was named Itztecuhtli (Figures 3.4c–3.4d; Acuña 1988:63, 73).

The extensive narratives on Aztatlán polychrome vases, the appearance of specific Mixtec gods and spirit

FIGURE 3.4. (*a*) *Codex Nuttall* 52 portrays a Toltec priest awarding the title of *tecuhtli* to the Mixtec Lord Eight Deer (see Pohl 1994:83–93). (*b*) Detail of Lord Eight Deer wearing nose ornament signifying the title of *tecuhtli*, *Codex Nuttall* 54. (*c–d*) Nose ornament forms are shared between nobles of Oaxaca (*left*) and Nayarit (*right*) suggesting an investment in ritualism that facilitated social, political, and economic exchange between these cultural systems. Drawings by author.

entities like the Ñuhu, and the rituals portrayed indicate that the Nahua-Mixteca influences in the Aztatlán tradition originated in Oaxaca. During the Postclassic period, coastal Oaxaca was inhabited by a multicultural society of no less than six different language groups (Joyce 2010). The Chatinos occupied much of the lower Río Verde valley to the west, the Chontal occupied the central coastal area, and the Huave occupied the Tehuantepec river valley to the east. A fourth population, occupying Pochutla, spoke Nahuatl and advocated a Tolteca-Chichimeca heritage by way of a trade corridor extending north to Acatlán in the Mixteca Baja of Puebla as well as a coastal connection with Jalisco (Bartholomew 1980; Boas 1917; Campbell and Langacker 1978; Knab 1980; Pohl 2003b:63–64).

By the twelfth century, a large population of Mixtecs migrated south from the Nochixtlan Valley region and established a powerful city-state at Tututepec (Joyce et al. 2004; Spores 1993). The Tututepec elite advocated both dynastic connections to the Mixteca Alta kingdoms and a Tolteca-Chichimeca heritage through their integration of local populations on the coast (Pohl 2003b:63–64). They spoke Nahuatl and even used Nahuatl names (Berlin 1947). Expanding eastward, they subsequently absorbed the Nahua, Chatino, and Chontal populations into their small empire, dominating the port at Huatulco, and engaged in the importation and distribution of turquoise and copper throughout the Mexican highlands (Pohl 2003c:176). The use of Nahuatl calendrical day names among some noble families such as Mazatl, Coatl, and Ocelotl, together with titles like *tecuhtli*, indicate that a Tolteca-Chichimeca organizational model was employed in much the same way as it was in areas of Oaxaca where Nahua influences were expressed more intensively such as at Coixtlahuaca and Tututepec regardless of the language of the populations they ruled (Acuña 1988:59, 63, 73, 321; Pohl 2017). This does not mean that the Aztatlán elite were Nahua; on the contrary, their veneration of the dead as mummy bundles would suggest more in common with the Mixtecs and Zapotecs, but it does imply that Nahuatl served as a *lingua franca* (McCarty and Matson 1975: 204). Aztatlán nobles, like the Mixtecs, were therefore probably investing in a local Tula for their source of *tecuhtli* ritualism. The *Relación de Poncitlán* identifies a "Tollan" in that province (Acuña 1988:197). Another possibility is Unión de Tula, a community in the present day Amula region where the lords Xiuhtecuhtli and Itztecuhtli discussed above had ruled.

Archaeologically, the ruins of Ixtlán del Río in Nayarit may be significant in this regard as well. The site is anomalous in its size and sophistication in masonry construction, reminding one of Mitla where ranking nobles otherwise engaged in factional rivalries maintained a ceremonial center with attendant quarters where they would reside together when they needed to meet with the Vuijatao, or "Great Seer." This oracular high priest would then supernaturally consult with the mummies of the highest-ranking royal lineage to arbitrate inheritance, arrange marriages, and resolve disputes among their descendants in much the same way as the Mixtec oracles at Achiutla and Chalcatongo (Pohl 1999, 2008). Ixtlán del Río may have served as a Tula, but given the multiethnic composition of west Mexico, Aztatlán nobles were probably deploying a number of ritual strategies for maintaining a centralized ideology for their regional system in much the same way as their Mixtec and Zapotec counterparts in southern Mexico.

Conclusion

Phil Weigand proposed that demand for turquoise as a rare gem stone had been fundamental to the establishment of an early Postclassic exchange system integrally linking the Toltecs of Tula with the Ancestral Pueblo peoples of Chaco Canyon (Harbottle and Weigand 1992). Subsequent research has shown that turquoise was actually being used as early as the ninth century as a form of ritual and social currency circulating around the entire U.S. Southwest (Hull et al. 2014). Elite burials like those found at Chaco Canyon are testament to the importance of conspicuous display of turquoise as a visual symbol of paramount rank at Pueblo Bonito (Akins 2003; Lekson 2008:126, 293).

In 1943, Museum of Northern Arizona archaeologist John McGregor published what continues to be one of the most important studies of the remains of a regional elite male personage of just the rank and authority we might envision for a person functioning within the broader Southwest exchange system (McGregor 1943). The burial was discovered beneath a Sinagua pueblo at Ridge Ruin located roughly 13 km (20 mi) east of Flagstaff, Arizona. The individual had been placed in a masonry tomb together with a remarkable collection of ritual paraphernalia. McGregor invited several Hopi tribal members to examine the remains, and they not only agreed that the person had held very high rank but that he may have been a sorcerer due to the presence of the staffs comparable to those ritually swallowed in demonstrations of feats of magic. Among the objects of personal adornment were a number of turquoise mosaic pendants, earrings, a large nose ornament, and a headdress (Figure 3.5).

The burial is associated with the Sinagua culture of northern Arizona, which emerged near the end of Chaco Canyon's influence over the area and may represent a shift in social interaction toward the newly emergent Classic Hohokam centers to the south. Wupatki, a principal ritual center, represents an early form of

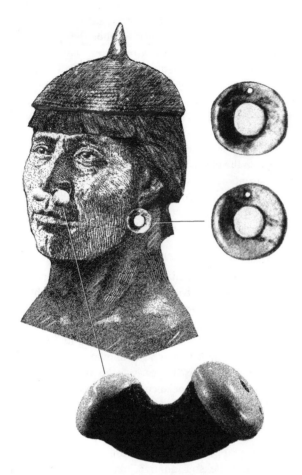

FIGURE 3.5. Nose and ear ornaments excavated from the tomb of a Sinagua noble dated to circa AD 1025. This individual participated in a turquoise exchange network extending between New Mexico, Arizona, and California that anticipated the gem's introduction into Mesoamerica among the Tolteca-Chichimeca during the Postclassic. The association of turquoise with "Chichimec" ritualism is confirmed by historical sources (Sahagún 1950–1982, Book 10:173). Drawings by author.

the platform mound complexes that would eventually characterize U.S. Southwestern and northern Mexican architecture in general after this time. Its largest structure contained over 100 rooms and functioned as a defensible great house. Even more remarkable is a kiva, suggesting that the center had an administrative function and an expansive masonry ballcourt. Such an architectural investment in ritualism was integrally related to the distribution of titles of elite authority manifested in the display of turquoise facial ornamentation throughout highland Mexico, as we have seen.

Given the evidence for such an extensive turquoise circulation network throughout the U.S. Southwest as early as the ninth century, it seems that much of the *tecuhtli* ritualism associated with the Late Postclassic in southern Mexico originated with the rise of ranked societies in the region where the gem stone originally served as a fundamental form of cultural capital. Elsewhere, I have discussed some of the social mechanisms of exchange in ritualism associated with wealth finance trading systems (Pohl 2001). Is it possible that the segmentary nature of the *teccalli* system over which the *tetecuhtin* ruled might be connected with the U.S. Southwest as well?

Surveys of the Valley of Mexico, the Plain of Puebla, the Tehuacan Valley, the Mixteca Alta, and the Valley of Oaxaca all document a period of reorganization between AD 850 and 1150 when large ceremonial centers that had dominated these regions during the Epiclassic had been largely abandoned. Oaxaca has been especially problematic as transitional sites between Early and Late Postclassic are very difficult to identify. However, by AD 1300, there is no question that Oaxaca was characterized by constellations of independent city-states ruled by a segmentary elite living in great houses. Kent Flannery and Joyce Marcus (1983:214–215) first summarized it best with their evaluation of the rise of secondary states in the Mixteca Alta:

> The great Classic centers of the Mixteca, obviously influenced by the Zapotec both in their architecture and their writing, declined with the rise of Tula. After the fall of Tula, they emerged with different settlement patterns, greca patterned architecture, with screenfold manuscripts and with a whole new set of vessel shapes.

I have proposed that these phenomena resulted from the emulation of new forms of political organization emerging on the Plain of Puebla after AD 1150 when a large Nahua population migrated from Tula after its collapse to establish a new market and pilgrimage center at Cholula. Founded by a class of merchants who promoted it to override the divisiveness of kinship-based clans while at the same time centralizing a cult at their major center of trade, Cholula provided state-like political and economic functions but still granted local autonomy among its constituent noble class, the *tetecuhtin*, in that it supplied the ideology of centralization without the dominance of a centralized government. In addition to the administration of the principal cult by the two priests of Quetzalcoatl, it also possessed a rotational system of government held in the hands of a number of families who competed with one another for the sponsorship of the annual feast dedicated to the patron deity and the rewards that sponsorship accrued (Knab and Pohl 2019; Pohl 2003a).

Some investigators have gone even further and proposed that one of Cholula's constituents, the city-state of Tlaxcala, was being governed as a "republic" (Fargher et al. 2010; Fargher et al. 2011). For them, Tlaxcala was a "*teccalli*-council state" in which political officials, called *tetecuhtin*, were equally ranked and decision making was achieved through consensus. A ruling council maintained sway over military matters and international diplomacy, as well as maintaining control over political officials and their recruitment to the governing council, the latter based primarily on merit but only to a limited degree. The resulting political structure would have exhibited only limited centralization of power in the hands of any single individual or even a limited group of powerful lineages.

Actually, Hernan Cortés (in Pagden 1986:68) was the first to compare Tlaxcala to several republics in Italy with which Spaniards had interacted during their military campaigns on the peninsula beginning in the early fifteenth century:

> The orderly manner in which [...] these people have been governed is almost like that of the states of Venice or Genoa or Pisa, for they have no overlord. There are many chiefs, all of whom reside in this city, and the country towns contain peasants who are vassals of these lords.

The roots of these republics were tied to the emergence of Visigoth and Lombard tribal systems of regional dominance by autonomous warlords called dukes (from *dux*, the title for a supreme Roman military commander). Eventually, permanent settlements began to emerge around the castle giving rise to city-states. By the fifteenth century, some of these states, especially those engaged in long-distance overseas trade, became "republics" when the commercial role of the most powerful merchant families superceded that of the dukes. In some cases, a republic might ally itself with a dukedom for protection while offering the duke a share in the profits from their commercial endeavors. Only Alfonso V of Aragon and his descendants functioned as hereditary kings on the Italian peninsula. All other noble and ecclesiastical titles were open to election, purchase, or outright seizure (Pohl 2015, 2016b).

Although we should be cautious in applying them, Cortés' comparison between Italian republics and Eastern Nahua *teccalli* was rooted in two factors within both societies, an increase in independent autonomy characterizing tribal systems of organization and a profound emphasis on commercialism in the economy—an attribute introduced with a package of social traits through a Tolteca-Chichimeca engagement with both the Greater U.S. Southwest and Lower Central America (Pohl 2016a). On the other hand, the field of anthropology's fascination with political diversity and shared power systems in American Indian tribal organizations goes back to Morgan and Bandelier. The problem has been how to identify diversified political organizations archaeologically. Archaeologists working throughout the Greater U.S. Southwest, for example, see the existence of kivas as indicative of the kinds of shared power systems characterizing Pueblo societies today. Platform mounds and high-status burials of individuals with extraordinary amounts of wealth objects, conversely, suggest the existence of paramount nobles—essentially kings and queens (Lekson 2008:169–171, 184).

The fact is that the Greater U.S. Southwest and northern Mexico have a history of investment in varying forms of political organization at different times, and the systems of egalitarianism that we admire in their societies today are only achieved with an extraordinary amount of bureaucratic effort in suppressing the ambitions of aggressive individuals or particular groups. The Pueblo Revolt, for example, demonstrated a remarkable ability on the part of a tribal regional system to coordinate military strategy over great distance inspired by the visions of a charismatic leader, but when that same leader began to exercise the powers of an institutionalized ruler, he was deposed (Pohl 2016a). The revolt accounts suggest that traditional Pueblo society was very familiar with autocratic systems of governance from past experience long before the Viceregal administration. In fact, the egalitarian qualities they value today are sourced in religious stories commemorating the rejection of such forms of governance. The legend of an autocrat known as the Great Gambler of Chaco Canyon is an outstanding example, as Stephen Lekson has emphasized (Lekson 2008:200).

Herein I have discussed how specific ritual objects might have been symbolic of political and social relationships above and beyond their existence as works of art or forms of wealth finance in trading systems among multicultural elites. No doubt some objects functioned as forms of wealth exchanged between social statuses such as Glycymeris shell bracelets manufactured within the Greater U.S. Southwest but traded as far south as Nayarit, or perhaps cacao (McGuire and Howard 1987; Mathiowetz 2019a). However, I believe that by the Late Postclassic period, Aztatlán polities were organized along many of the same lines as the Mixtec kingdoms with which they were integrally connected, with rule by despotic kings and queens. The shared usage of specific ritual objects, like mirrors and certain forms of facial jewelry, suggests that status and rank within the Casas Grandes system also was institutionalized but conveyed through specialized relationships with members of the Aztatlán system. This is particularly evident in the preferred usage of copper, the "red Chichimec" metal associated with the Aztatlán tradition where the smelting technology for it had been introduced as early as AD 900 (Figure 3.6).

In many ways the existence of these objects would therefore reflect the kinds of complex relationships that existed between the positions of the Eastern Nahua

82 John M. D. Pohl

FIGURE 3.6. Exchange in ritualism leads to innovations in political systems. There is little evidence that Paquimé was manufacturing copper. (*a*) This suggests that shield-mirrors were awarded to Casas Grandes system elites by Aztatlán patrons to confirm their status as political leaders within their own city-state level confederacies. (*b*) The effect of these elite exchanges then regulated trade at secondary elite and commoner levels through both wealth and staple finance material such as Glycymeris shell bracelets, turquoise, and cacao that is so essential to bridewealth and dowry systems underlying trade monopolies. Drawings by author.

tecuhtli, the Mixtec *yya*, and the Zapotec *coqui* in which individuals could hold differing statuses within each of these systems of cultural capital in ways shown to be critical to the success of comparable regional political and economic systems throughout other parts of the world (Friedman 1998; Leach 1973).

Acknowledgments

This work benefited greatly from discussions with a number of colleagues including Christian De Brer, Mauricio Garduño Ambriz, Stephen Lekson, Michael Mathiowetz, Juan Jorge Morales Monroy, Harry Schafer, Karl Taube, David Wilcox, and Danny Zborover.

CHAPTER 4

Social Organization in the Aztatlán Tradition (AD 850–1350)

The Sayula and Chapala Basins (Jalisco), a Case Study

Susana Ramírez Urrea

While little is known about social organization in the Aztatlán tradition, research conducted in several areas of western Mexico has provided some insight on how Aztatlán groups were politically, economically, and ideologically structured. Archaeological research in the Sayula Basin and in comparative regions such as the Chapala Basin has allowed us to determine that the Aztatlán network was organized into political units sharing different aspects of ritual activities, burial patterns, ceramic styles, specialization, and exchange, among other commonalities. It appears each of these units had a major site, or *cabecera*, where higher-status people who may have controlled the regional exchange systems and specialization of that political unit lived, as outlined below.[1]

Research conducted during the past three decades—much of it with a multidisciplinary approach supported by new technologies used to analyze materials and contexts—has brought about significant progress in understanding cultural developments in west and northwest Mexico, particularly after AD 400 when the Shaft Tomb tradition ended (Foster and Gorenstein 2000; Jiménez 2018, 2020; Liot et al., eds. 2006; Valdez et al., eds. 2005; Weigand et al. 2008; Williams et al., eds. 2005). As a result, the original vision once held regarding western and northwestern Mexico has changed. Far from these being marginal regions, it is becoming increasingly evident that the two regions were closely linked and were part of broader Mesoamerican cultural dynamics and processes, especially from the Middle Classic to the beginning of the Epiclassic (ca. AD 400–600).

Despite such advances, in west and northwest Mexico as in many other regions of Mesoamerica, the transition between the Epiclassic and Early Postclassic periods between AD 800 and 1000 is poorly documented, and therefore it remains difficult to draw conclusions regarding this period. In both regions, this was a turbulent period of time highlighted by profound cultural and social innovations and changes in power structures which brought about a transformation in social, political, religious, and economic organization (Liot, Ramírez, Reveles, and Schöndube 2006). The Aztatlán tradition is considered to be one of the major contributors to this adjustment in socioeconomic structures and political power. In his research on west Mexico, Schöndube (1980a:215–230) suggested that, by the Postclassic period, this region was unquestionably a part of the cultural framework of Mesoamerica. Furthermore, it is also at this time that a number of cultural expressions, which are strongly characteristic of Mesoamerica, likely emerged in northwestern and western Mexico (Otto Schöndube, personal communication).

The Aztatlán tradition has always been an enigma and, lately, has served as one of the most discussed topics in the study of western and northwest Mexico. The varied manner of referencing it as a phenomenon, tradition, culture, complex, horizon-style, or network, and the lack of a systematic approach to information and research, has resulted in very diverse approaches and assumptions. While these approaches have enriched the research process and dialogue, taken together these concepts have created confusion in our understanding of this period and in establishing a timeline for its development. This situation is reflected in the archaeological literature and in the viewpoints held by scholars within western Mexico and elsewhere in relation to this era. The term "Aztatlán tradition" is used in this chapter, not because—strictly speaking—it actually constitutes a tradition, but rather because it is the "generic" term or stock phrase coined for this cultural manifestation. It is firmly established that the Aztatlán tradition was part of broader developments in

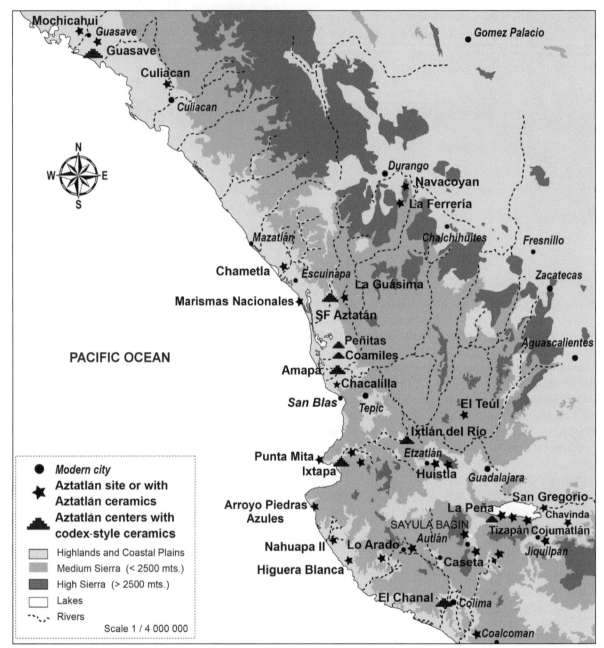

FIGURE 4.1. Western Mexico with sites mentioned in the text.

Mesoamerica during the Early and Middle Postclassic periods (Kelley 2000; Mountjoy, this volume; Ramírez Urrea 2003, 2005, 2016; Smith and Berdan 2003). In western and northwestern Mexico, this was a period of cultural and technological innovations, new economic and trade patterns, and shifting religious beliefs which allows us to assume that it was a period of important regional changes extending to social groups and power structures (Figures I.1, I.2, 1.1, 4.1; Ramírez Urrea 2005, 2016; Smith and Berdan 2003).

One of the most readily apparent characteristics, which has served as one of the factors in proposed connections with Central Mexico (Aztec I style) and Oaxaca (Mixtec-Puebla style), is that both regions share an iconography with strong ideological and ritual elements relating to religious themes. The imagery depicts deities or cosmic and earthly symbols that are fairly standardized and created in a range of bright colors in a geometric style in Central Mexico and the Mixteca region of Puebla and Oaxaca with a more curvilinear style in the west. This style (with regional variations) was incorporated into local ceramic-design repertoires and on other objects in each of the above-mentioned regions and more generally in broader Mesoamerica (Ekholm

1942; Jiménez 2020; Kelley 2000; Lister 1949; Meighan, ed. 1976; Meighan and Foote 1968; Nicholson 1982, 2001; Nicholson and Quiñones Keber 1994; Ramírez Urrea 2003; Ramírez and Cárdenas 2006; Smith and Berdan 2003).

Relevant Issues and Their Significance

Part of the problem in studying the Aztatlán tradition is that most of the research has focused on examining it either from a macroregional perspective, as part of a long-distance economic system, as a pan-Mesoamerican phenomenon, or at a local scale by concentrating analyses at the site level. However, little attention has been given to how this tradition was structured at the intraregional level within a social system. Therefore, it is relevant to address and analyze the political, social, economic, and ideological structure on a smaller scale by focusing on the regional structure and its social dynamics within a given geographic area.

The objective of this chapter then is to address and discuss some of the cultural patterns and social indicators related to the Aztatlán structure at a regional scale through evidence recovered at the La Peña site and within the Sayula Basin system inclusive of evidence from sites in the southern region of Lake Chapala in Jalisco and Michoacán. To this end, it is important to ask a series of interrelated questions: (1) How were Aztatlán groups organized at a panregional and intraregional level?, (2) How was the social system structured?, (3) Did the implicit ideology serve as an agent of power and cohesion among the different groups?, (4) What factors shaped the regional identity and how?, and (5) How were these factors extrapolated to a macroregional and panregional level?

In several cases it has been observed that Aztatlán features/culture (or groups?) were inserted into preestablished, complex local settlements such as in the Sayula Basin (Liot, Ramírez, Reveles, and Schöndube 2006; Liot et al., eds. 2006; Ramírez Urrea 2006a, 2016) or along the Jalisco coast (Mountjoy et al. 2020). For this reason, a host of additional questions have arisen: (6) What strategies could people have used and how did they manage to incorporate themselves into the regional system?, (7) How did they affect the regions where they were present?, (8) Were the groups ethnically diverse?, and (9) Did the iconography and symbols work as a control agent, as a means of communication between elites, as restricted codes associated with power, and/or were they part of a broader pan-Mesoamerican international style? These issues deserve deeper analysis and cannot be decisively determined herein, although these questions will comprise part of the discussion in future studies.

The Study Area

In order to determine the research approach, it was necessary to analyze the evidence from a given region—the Sayula area—and establish specific criteria. The criteria included recognizing several diagnostic features as a whole and identifying whether there were patterns in ritual, economics, social organization, architecture, burials, and politics in the given territory, which may or may not necessarily be part of the same geographic area. All of these factors are important because they enable us to determine whether the different groups that settled in these regions were part of the same cultural unit in which elites used certain ideological mechanisms by which they materialized or embodied the ideology through symbols, rituals, and burial practices. These factors presumably would have given elites legitimacy and provided a basis for their economy in having control over specialized activities and regional exchange networks. Furthermore, the analyses sought to establish if ideology played a major role as an element of cohesion and control between different groups.

To this end, it was necessary to analyze contemporaneous archaeological evidence of distinctive Aztatlán features recovered from excavations which have similar contexts within a given region. Reliable information derived from excavations in neighboring regions, including sites in the southern Lake Chapala region, helped to establish sound comparisons in order to determine if a cultural identity and cohesion existed in any territory beyond a given geographical region (Figures 4.1–4.2).

This study focuses on the time period between AD 1000–1350, primarily during the Middle Postclassic period. The area selected for research was the greater Sayula Basin region in the state of Jalisco inclusive of the sites of Tizapán el Alto in Jalisco and Cojumatlán and San Gregorio in Michoacán—the first two located south of Lake Chapala and the latter located to the east of the lake. This area is situated 60 km to the south of modern Guadalajara on the highway leading to Colima. Why was the Middle Postclassic period significant, and what was the role of the Sayula Basin and the southern Lake Chapala Basin in social dynamics? For one thing, there is a broader spectrum of information for this period, and in the Sayula region the archaeological features are more widespread and clearly evident for undertaking this sort of study. Systematic archaeological research has been conducted in the Sayula Basin over the past 33 years, thereby providing an ample perspective on the sociocultural dynamics of the region, particularly between AD 400–1532 (Schöndube et al. 1994; Schöndube et al. 1996). Furthermore, there is convincing material evidence associated with the Aztatlán tradition from two excavation sites in Sayula and two in the Chapala Basin—a neighboring area with very close cultural ties to the Sayula area—that enables a joint analysis with those sites included in the study area.

Thus, the Sayula Basin offers an excellent opportunity to study issues at the regional system level, including the impact on settlement patterns, the societal composition and social dynamics, and the effects on regional identities. First, we have identified the existence of an Aztatlán tradition site at La Peña (CS-171), a ceremonial, economic, and political civic center (Liot et al., eds. 2006). Second, the site of Caseta (CS-32), which was a contemporary of La Peña, constituted a regional variant of the Aztatlán tradition seemingly with particular functions within the regional hierarchy. Caseta has been classified as a "derivative Aztatlán site" because, although it has a number of cultural elements like luxury/prestige objects, tools, and typical iconography related to Aztatlán materials, it also has many other remains of the Amacueca phase characteristic of the Postclassic period in the basin (Ramírez Urrea 2016, 2019). However, ceramic styles such as those of La Peña and other Lake Chapala sites were absent. Instead, Caseta had different ceramics decorated with Aztatlán iconography—a regional variant or type named Autlán Polychrome.[2]

Moreover, in the Sayula Basin we identified a regional hierarchical system with complex social organization dating between AD 400/450–1000 that we term the Sayula Complex (Liot et al. 2007). This antecedent development does not have cultural and ideological links to the Aztatlán tradition but was contemporary with the Early Aztatlán period for about 200 years. The evidence recovered, together with progress in research on empirical data and comparative ethnological evidence (particularly in relation to data from the La Peña site), make it feasible to combine the analysis of the iconography (and its ritual themes and anthropomorphic representations) with the archaeological contexts. A study by the author sought to associate ritual patterns with the iconography observed in material culture in order to ascertain whether there is a correlation between these and the representations of associated deities or icons found in the Aztatlán iconography and to determine the connection between these elements and their significance among the social groups (Ramírez Urrea 2011).

Finally, in the Chapala Basin, adjacent to the proposed study region and near La Peña, two sites contemporary to La Peña—that is, Tizapán el Alto and Cojumatlán—have been reported and excavated (Lister 1949; Meighan and Foote 1968). Recently, another site near Tizapán el Alto called Tuxcueca, which is much larger in size than Cojumatlán and Tizapán el Alto, was located near the town of Tuxcueca. This site has several terraces that probably were used for agricultural or housing purposes. These three sites (four if we include San Gregorio) are contemporary and share similar, possibly identical, cultural features such as pottery types, funerary patterns, and food practices to those reported at La Peña and more generally within the basin in association with the Aztatlán tradition. Tizapán el Alto and Tuxcueca are located within a 30–40 km radius northeast of the La Peña settlement. In fact, they are only separated by the hills of the Sierra de la Difunta, near the natural passage or route known as Tuxcueca, which connects both basins (Figure 4.2). Finally, evidence of ceremonialism from the Sayula Basin excavations, which possess a well-established chronology and material collected from controlled contexts, was analyzed to determine if there were patterns that could be extrapolated to other sites within the basin itself, as well as to the Lake Chapala sites.

THE AZTATLÁN TRADITION AND THE SAYULA AND CHAPALA BASINS: A SYNTHESIS

In the Sayula Basin, the first evidence of the Aztatlán tradition is around AD 800/850, the period of the basin's greatest regional florescence in which a complex social structure was precisely organized with a deeply rooted common identity (Kelly c. 1944; Valdez et al., eds. 2005). During this stage, which is known locally as the Sayula phase (AD 500 to 1000), there is an evident hierarchy in the settlement pattern where five site categories have been identified.[3] These categories include: first-level sites, administrative centers, villages or small civic-ceremonial centers, small towns and villages devoted to agricultural activities, and multifunctional workshops (22 in total) for the large-scale production and extraction of salt and the production of stone tools and shell objects (Figure 4.2; Liot et al. 2007; Mas 2015).

The features of the Sayula phase are different from those of the basin's Postclassic period in general and, in particular, from those of the Aztatlán tradition. Recent work at La Picota[4]—the largest civic and ceremonial center during the Sayula phase—together with a review of the ceramic materials collected during this research, may indicate that only a few of the technological and stylistic features arising at the end of the Sayula phase were very common during the Postclassic period, including some characteristic of the Aztatlán tradition. In spite of this, the technological and stylistic schism in the settlement and funerary patterns between both periods is remarkable.

Data from the Sayula Basin suggest that the Aztatlán-related evidence in the area might indicate a response to the intrusion of at least one group in La Peña around AD 800/850 (Liot et al., eds. 2006; Ramírez Urrea 2016, 2019). However, ancient DNA studies will

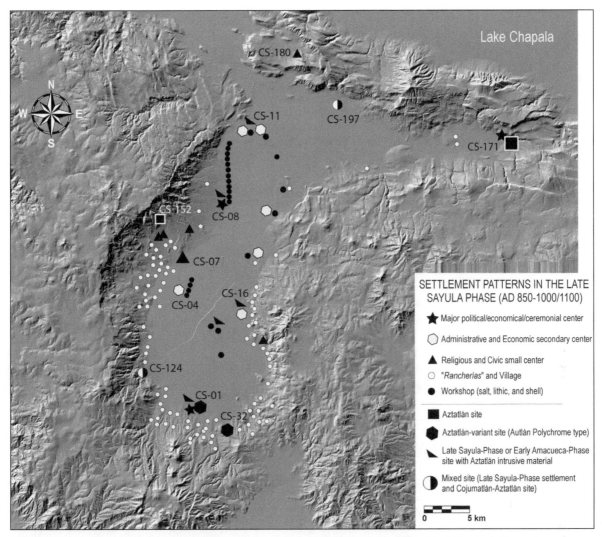

FIGURE 4.2. Settlement patterns during the Late Sayula phase (AD 850–1000/1100), Sayula Basin, Jalisco.

be necessary to clarify these relations with confidence. Materials affiliated with the Aztatlán tradition as well as those specific to the region (Amacueca complex) have been identified in other settlements, however the only "pure" Aztatlán site—so to speak—is La Peña (Figure 4.3). Likewise, during the era of the Aztatlán tradition both in the Sayula and Chapala Basins, only La Peña shows monumental features such as spatial planning, hydraulic systems, agricultural terraces, residential areas for elites and common people, and areas devoted to ritual activities and otherwise. It has been proposed that one of the factors strengthening La Pena's ideological and economic dominance was its strategic location, both controlling the Sayula Basin's eastern passage and linking the site to the ritual landscape (Ramírez Urrea 2016). It is important to point out that the Sayula Basin is a nodal center—a geographic corridor where several natural passages and routes from neighboring and more distant regions converged and connected. This has al-

lowed the area to serve as a hub during prehispanic times since at least AD 300 (Ramírez Urrea 2005).

La Peña is located in the eastern arm of the basin in the Citala subvalley, and the work undertaken here has found that it was a central and important place in the Aztatlán tradition. Evidence shows that the site had a key role in panregional developments during this time (Liot et al., eds. 2006; Ramírez Urrea 2005, 2006a, 2016). Located at an altitude between 1500 and 1700 m above sea level on steep topography, La Peña is strategic and defensive in nature and covers an area of over 100 ha. It was occupied during the Aztatlán era from AD 800/850 to about AD 1450 (Liot, Ramírez, Reveles, and Schöndube 2006; Ramírez Urrea 2016; Ramírez Urrea et al. 2005). The architectural pattern identified consists of architectural ensembles called terrace-square sets, some quite large in size. These are distributed throughout the site and built on artificial terraces, in some cases consisting of large platforms. The largest set

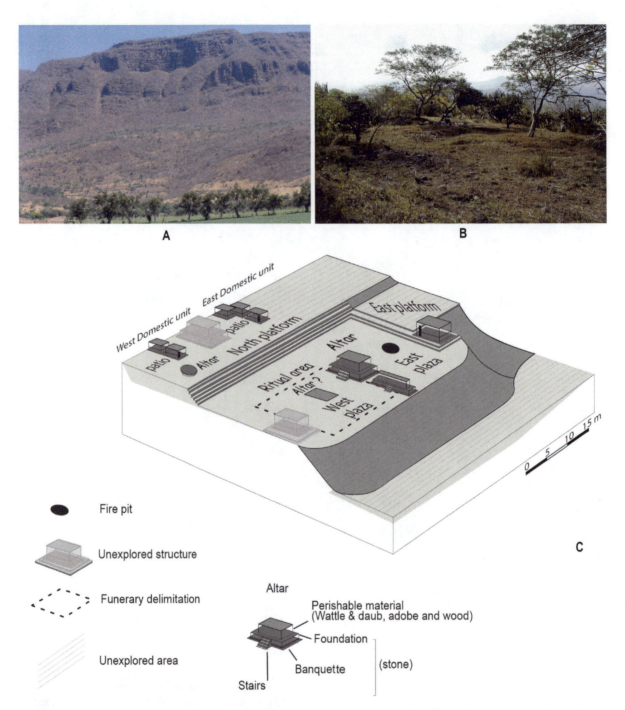

FIGURE 4.3. The site of La Peña, Jalisco. (a) View of the La Peña site in the Citala Valley, Jalisco. La Peña is located in the section above the foot of the mountain. (b) View of Group A, La Peña, Jalisco. (c) Reconstruction of Group A, La Peña, Jalisco (modified from Liot et al. 2006:Figure 83).

is designated as Group A where extensive excavations were conducted in 1997, 2000, and 2002 (Liot et al., eds. 2006; Ramírez Urrea et al. 2000.)

Group A consists of a platform that is 7 m in height and 70 m long by 30 m wide.[5] It has two plazas or squares, the West Plaza and East Plaza, divided by a central altar on the rectangular-shaped platform. On another terrace to the north that is part of the same set, the remains of two elite households were excavated—one located to the east and one to the west (Ramírez, Bojórquez, and Liot 2006). Certain contexts were identified that indicate evidence of specialized ritual and production activities, such as textile manufacturing (Ramírez Urrea 2006b). In one of the housing units

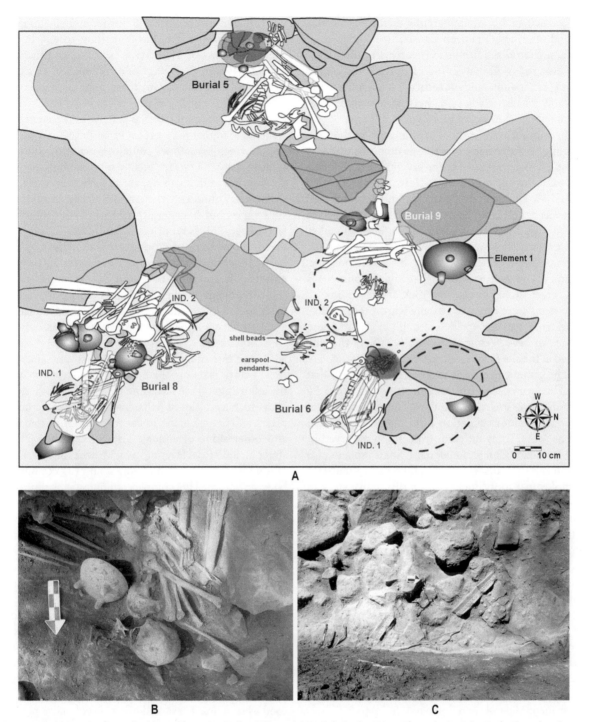

FIGURE 4.4. Scenes from the West Plaza, La Peña, Jalisco. (*a*) Burials in the West Plaza during the Early Tizapán phase (AD 1050/1100) (modified from Liot, Reveles, and Acosta 2006:Figure 56). (*b*) Burial 8 in the West Plaza. (*c*) Ritual area with "killed" braziers and incense burners found in the West Plaza at Group A. Photos from the Sayula Basin Archaeological Project.

(west) there was a circular altar in the patio. Between the two units, a rectangular structure was identified that appears to be a second altar. Remains of other household units were found on another terrace to the east, and a structure in one corner appears to be a temple.

The West Plaza was used for ritual activities and a cemetery, which was found under an intact stuccoed floor (Figure 4.4; Liot and Reveles 2006; Liot, Reveles, and Acosta 2006). In the central altar, several bones that appear to be part of burials were found in addition to disarticulated bones apparently deposited as ceremonial offerings (Ramírez Urrea 2016). In the East Plaza, a centralized fire pit or hearth was identified. However, paleosoil analysis indicates that some kind of plant (perhaps amaranth or tobacco) was grown there, probably for restricted use. Otherwise, it is difficult to explain why a crop would be grown in this area.

In another terrace-square set located to the west (Group D), the remains of a simple domestic unit was excavated along with one of the several water channels that exist throughout the site. Here, the burial of an animal—a young dog (*Canis*) around four months old—was deposited as an offering adjacent to a slab of carved stone.[6] As a result of the excavations, a number of diverse materials were recovered, including domestic objects, elegant pottery, prismatic blades, stone tools, ornaments made from shell, metal, and various stones (e.g., green stone, pyrite, and rock crystal). Some of these items were produced locally while other objects came from further afield, although many of these seemed to have been for the exclusive use of the elite settled at the site (Liot et al., eds. 2006).

The ceramic and stone analysis, and generally that of all recovered remains, demonstrated that the La Peña materials are related to those considered to be of Aztatlán-tradition affiliation from the Jalisco plateau and are completely different from those observed in the Late Sayula Complex materials.[7] Some remains also shared certain traits with those of the Early Amacueca Complex (AD 1000/1100–1350)—a distinctive stage of the Postclassic period in the basin. The remains are very similar if not identical in style, shape, and iconography to those reported at Tizapán el Alto (Jalisco), Cojumatlán, and San Gregorio (Michoacán). Both Lister (1949) and Meighan and Foote (1968) emphasized the similarity of Cojumatlán and Tizapán el Alto material to that from Aztatlán sites reported from Sinaloa and Nayarit; they further noted that some types resembled the Mixtec style (Lister 1949; Meighan and Foote 1968; Ramírez Urrea 2005; Ramírez and Cárdenas 2006). Thus, for the sake of simplicity, the same phase names for these sites are used at La Peña: the Cojumatlán Complex (AD 850–1100) and the Tizapán Complex (AD 1100–1350; see Lister 1949; Meighan and Foote 1968).

The excavation of the Chapala sites (Cojumatlán and Tizapán el Alto) demonstrated many similarities with the evidence found in the Sayula Basin, particularly at the La Peña site. At Tizapán el Alto, excavation of one of the largest platforms revealed a cemetery, remains of ritual activities, and other structures—all of which appear to be associated (Meighan and Foote 1968). Both the burial patterns and the ritual activities appear to share close similarities with those of the La Peña site. Among these commonalities are concentrations of ash with broken and burned remains of deer antlers, human long bones and some animal bones (deer), remains of Tlaloc-type braziers, and incense burners (Figure 4.4c). Part of a rectangular structure was found associated with these remains that could have served as an altar platform—as in La Peña's West Plaza. In addition, the burial pattern in the cemetery is identical to that found at La Peña: flexed and seated in pits which sometimes contain rocks at the bottom (Figure 4.4a). These are mostly multiple burials, and the interred individuals appear to have been wrapped as mortuary bundles. Orientation of the burials at these sites varies but is generally east/west with the head facing east. This is reported not only in the sites mentioned above, but is also present in sites in the Chapala Basin. In all cases, the offerings were placed by the feet and usually consisted of tripod bowls, fragments of shell ornaments, green stones, and occasionally knives (silex or flint knives and, in some cases, obsidian blades and/or bifaces) as well as other items—all associated with individuals.

In the case of La Peña, several layers were encountered before reaching the burial. These layers include the following: (1) ash layer, and (2) ash layer with metal items such as rattles or bells, traces of objects or sheet plates, and occasionally copper tweezers. Shell remains and other stone ornaments also were found. Other strata include (3) a layer of soil with ashes and vestiges of long human and animal bones, and (4) the buried body or bodies. This complex stratigraphy is repeated in all of the West Plaza burials at La Peña, suggesting that this pattern reflects a very elaborate ritual. Unfortunately, there is no detailed information regarding the layers prior to the burial layer at Cojumatlán and Tizapán el Alto, but there is evidence of a first layer of ash and surrounding ash stains with remains of certain objects as described above.

As for the ceramic material at these sites, tripod mortars were introduced for domestic use as were mortars; together they constitute part of the "elegant" dish sets usually used, among other purposes, as a burial offering (Figure 4.5). Likewise, we observed the introduction of other ceramic vessels apparently used as *comales*. These and other objects were part of a change in dietary practices that had not been previously recorded for the region (Ramírez Urrea 2018). With respect to the shell ornaments, several Caribbean and Pacific species have been identifed (Elodie Mas, personal communication). The conch ornaments are similar at the three sites while obsidian prismatic blades became very popular (Reveles 2006, 2021). Metal objects are equal in chemical composition (i.e., copper) and morphology and correspond to Period I (García Zaldúa 2007, 2016). In contrast, at the Caseta site, a contemporary of La Peña, the ornaments and objects were made of copper-tin, gold-tin, and silver alloys, which corresponds with Period 2 (Figures 4.5g–4.5h; García Zaldúa 2007, 2016).

It is worth mentioning that Caseta—located in the southern Sayula Basin—also demonstrates traits of the Aztatlán tradition but to a lesser degree than La Peña. The dates that have been established indicate that it was contemporary with La Peña as of AD 1050. A cemetery was found at the site as well as the remains of a large structure, the house of the local lord. Many of the recovered materials associated with burials are sumptuous, with several of them being of allochthonous origin. However, the ceramics are a stylistic variation of Aztatlán wares that are quite common in the southern part of the basin, but particularly in southern Jalisco and Colima (Ramírez Urrea 1996, 2016, 2019). This type is known as Autlán Polychrome, and its distribution suggests that it is part of a separate Aztatlán interaction sphere in southern Jalisco and Colima (Figures 4.5a–4.5b). Finally, it is significant that the recovered sherds at the Caseta site include Cerritos-phase types such as Botadero Incised, Cerritos Polychrome, and Tuxpan Engraved—all of which surely originate in Nayarit.

At La Peña, a hydraulic system was identified that served to divert water for domestic consumption and farming (Santoyo Alonso 2012). La Peña has numerous artificial terraces for farming while the Tuxcueca settlement in Chapala also has many terraces—many apparently used for crops. Thus far, no other site outside of La Peña has been found to possess hydraulic systems.

Sociopolitical Organization. The Case of the Sayula Basin and Neighboring Chapala Sites: Preliminary Findings

Taken together, data collected from the Sayula and Chapala sites enable us to make preliminary proposals. The sites share unequivocal similarities reflecting cohesion in their identity, which can be characterized as a closely interrelated sociopolitical and economic organization supported by a complex ideology controlled and shared among elite groups on a broader scale. It was observed that these sites have the same ceramic types, or at least share some of them, and many of the ornaments are alike. However, there are materials that only are found at La Peña, but this probably has more to do with issues of access restricted to only a certain group of the population: the elite. Second, these sites and Caseta have burials with the same funerary pattern, which are grouped in cemeteries. Except for Caseta, which is located on a hill in the piedmont region, the cemeteries are located on platforms.[8] Third, at La Peña, Tizapán el Alto, and Cojumatlán (Tuxcueca has not been excavated), evidence found in the cemetery areas suggests a ritual pattern probably associated with the gods of wind (Ehecatl-Quetzalcoatl) and water (Tlaloc) and, in general, to the Mesoamerican agricultural cycle (Ramírez Urrea 2011, 2016). Fourth, among the various excavated contexts, we observed the widespread use of materials (mainly ceramics) with representations of the fire serpent or Xiuhcoatl (which has been related to the sun god) and certain feathered serpent types which allude to the wind god Ehecatl-Quetzalcoatl, along with other icons.

The existence of material with this iconography suggests that the use of some emblems was standardized among the population settled in these sites. From this we can assume that there was a widespread and commonly shared "cult" among these groups. Other images or more complex iconography such as portrayals of death deities, cosmological symbols such as Venus, possible priestly figures, figures associated with the sun and the moon, and codex-style ceramics were found only at La Peña.[9] In addition, the use of engraved stones, and in some exceptional cases stones engraved with notations that may indicate a ritual use of the Mesoamerican 260-day calendar, could attest to the fact that the groups in power exerted control over certain ideological concepts (Figures 4.6a–4.6b).

Preliminary Findings

The foregoing discussion leads us to reflect on why certain shared patterns and elements are found in various sites and, in turn, why there are differences or style variations among elements in the same region. What have we observed and what does it reflect with respect to the political organization and structure of the Aztatlán tradition? The preliminary research results are very encouraging. The evidence analyzed at the Sayula Basin sites and the sites located on the southern margin of the Chapala Basin lead us to the idea that these sites constituted a political entity. This political entity was sustained by an interwoven ideology and economy that shared many cultural traits including ceramic types, technology, subsistence patterns, ritual, and burial patterns, among others that together formed a cultural unity. The political unit was part of structural frameworks constituting and sustaining the sociopolitical, religious, and economic structure of the Aztatlán tradition (Figure 4.7).

These results raise the possibility that the Aztatlán tradition may have been organized and structured into various polities, such as lordships or manors (*señoríos*) with characteristics of a city-state, that may or may not have had the same ethnic affiliation (Ramírez Urrea 2016).[10] Within these polities, the most complex sites among all—with forms of organization indicating social power, monumental architecture, engraved

FIGURE 4.5. Aztatlán material culture in Jalisco. (*a*) Autlán Polychrome vessel found as an offering in a burial from Caseta, Jalisco. (*b*) Autlán Polychrome ceramic vessel with codex-style iconography, southern Jalisco. (*c–d*) Vessels found as an offering in burials, Cojumatlán type, La Peña, Jalisco. (*e*) Tripod *cajete*, Tizapán Incised type, La Peña, Jalisco. (*f*) Tripod *cajete*, Citala Polychrome incised subtype, La Peña, Jalisco. (*g*) "L-shaped" gold plate found as an offering in a burial from Caseta (Amacueca Complex AD 1000/1100–1350) that is similar to engraved examples of (*h*) "L-shaped" gold plate from El Chanal, Colima (photo by Otto Schöndube). All photos from the Sayula Basin Archaeological Project and from Susana Ramírez Urrea (except where otherwise noted).

FIGURE 4.6. Aztatlán material culture from La Peña, Jalisco. (*a–b*) Engraved stone with possible representation of a death god. Note the *chalchihuites* depiction at bottom, which could suggest the number "one". (*c*) Worked bones probably used for textile manufacturing. (*d*) Copper axe. Photos and drawing from the Sayula Basin Archaeological Project.

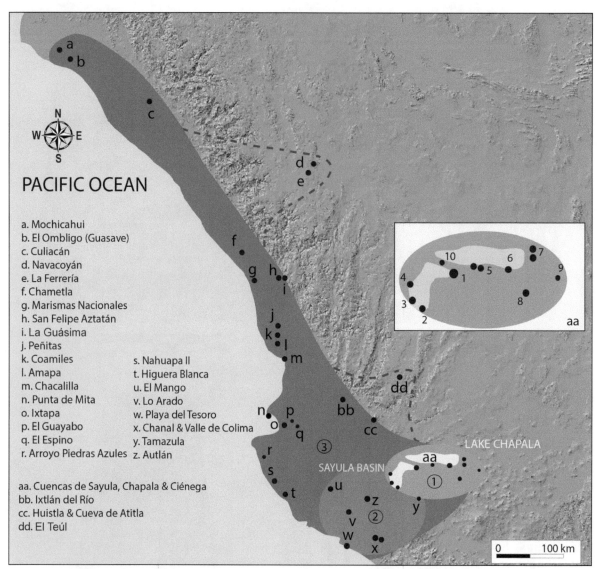

FIGURE 4.7. Proposed polities of the Aztatlán tradition during the Middle Postclassic period. Numbers in circles indicate: (1) Jalisco plateau, (2) Southern and coastal areas of Jalisco and Colima, and (3) Nayarit and southern Sinaloa with locations of political entities. Numbers in the inset indicate the following sites: (1) La Peña, (2) Caseta, (3) Santa Inés, (4) Mesa de los Indios, (5) Tuxcueca and Tizapán el Alto, (6) Cojumatlán, (7) San Gregorio, (8) Jiquilpan, (9) Chavinda, and (10) CS-80. Drawing by Kiyo Gutierrez.

stones, codex-style ceramics, and structured spatial organization linked to the ritual landscape—acted as the dominant center, maintaining control through ideology, alliances with other powerful groups, and trade networks. In general, these cultural traits testify to the presence of a ruling elite that clearly held power.

A political entity may or may not have a sphere of influence over a considerable area or, on the other hand, they may bind together several surrounding regions. Mountjoy (1990, 1993, 2000) suggests that social organization during the Aztatlán era in western Mexico could have been similar to that observed in the region of the Mixteca during the Late Postclassic in Oaxaca, that is, under a city-state model. These small political units or city-states seem to be viable in regions such as Jalisco and Colima, as well as in Nayarit, Sinaloa, and perhaps in Durango and Zacatecas (Ramírez Urrea 2016).

Based upon the evidence in the Sayula and Chapala regions, it is proposed that La Peña served as the major site (or *cabecera*) of the polity where political, religious, and socioeconomic power was concentrated. Smaller settlements in the area, perhaps less important in the regional hierarchy, had strong ties to their leading site or *cabecera* at La Peña. This kind of city-state in turn played a role at the panregional level, as they were like cogs in the structure of the Aztatlán network that shared an ideology similar to that of other centers like Amapa, San Felipe Aztatán, Ixtlán del Río, Coamiles, and others in Nayarit (see Garduño Ambriz 2007, 2012b, 2015) and El Chanal in Colima, which surely strengthened intersocietal alliances.

Each entity could have specialized in and/or controlled certain aspects of the economy, such as part of the production, manufacture, or distribution of strategic commodities, consumer goods, and/or luxury and prestige goods including salt, cotton, pigments, metal, green stones, prismatic blades, pyrite, quartz, shell ornaments, tobacco, codex-style ceramics, and other items. Some areas, such as the Sayula Basin, had regional specializations. Indeed, Aztatlán groups based in this region surely had close ties to salt production during the Middle Postclassic as well as some types of textile manufacturing and the control of products that passed through the area (Figure 4.6b; Liot et al., eds. 2006; Ramírez Urrea 2005, 2006a, 2016).

For instance, around AD 1000 there were changes in salt extraction techniques in the Sayula region (Liot 1998). Salt production was clearly no longer controlled by elites of the Late Sayula Complex (AD 800–1000). The number of workshops decreased, but not the amount of production. Liot (1998) interpreted this change as an innovation in techniques that achieved optimization and standardization in production. Several sherds of the Cojumatlán (Aztatlán) ceramic type were found in salt-production stations (Ramírez Urrea 2006b:190; 2016, 2019).

Groups in the basin who participated in the Aztatlán network had much to do with the changes in technology and the control over production, distribution, and trade. This is observed with respect to metal objects and ornaments found both in the basin and in southern Jalisco. It has been proposed that metallurgy in this region enjoyed a faster and more advanced development than in Nayarit and Sinaloa. That is, metal technologies and chemistry correspond with the Period 2 composition, but apparently are contemporary with Period 1 (García Zaldúa 2007, 2016; Hosler 2009). We also find the distribution of Autlán Polychrome (an Aztatlán ceramic variant), which may indicate close ideological ties between these regions (Figures 4.5a–4.5b, 4.5g–4.5h; Ramírez Urrea 2016, 2019).

Due to these and several other factors,[11] we may consider that within the area of southern Jalisco, Colima, and probably part of the Banderas Bay region in Jalisco and Nayarit, a different political entity could have existed that dominated and perhaps developed metallurgical technologies and controlled its distribution. It should be noted that most of the metal objects and ornaments (many of them gold) such as pendants and earrings are very elegant and sophisticated (Figures 4.5g–4.5h). Due to their iconographic content and religious themes, it might be assumed that they were for the exclusive use of the elite, particularly for the lords (Ramírez Urrea 2011, 2016).

Finally, the stylistic differences or variants of ceramic types as well as the styles themselves—which nevertheless share some of the emblematic icons and representations within the Aztatlán tradition—can be interpreted not only as an international style as Smith and Berdan (2003) have proposed, but they also reflect evidence of the existence of two interrelated political units in the same area and/or the presence of two or more ethnic groups linked by an ideology for mutual economic interests and exchange networks. For instance, Caseta is a small site and does not seem to be a major center. However, its location is strategic as it controls the passage to Zapotlán el Grande, San Gabriel, Autlán and, in general, routes to southern Jalisco, Colima, and the coast. The Autlán Polychrome type and the majority of the most elaborate metal objects manufactured with alloys have been reported in this region (García Zaldúa 2007, 2016; Kelly 1945b; Olay de Barrientos 2006:255–265; Ramírez Urrea 1996, 2016, 2019).

Further research and more detailed analyses of the evidence, as well as future regional studies, will enable us to better establish the structure of the Aztatlán tradition, the complexity of its dynamics, and its exchange networks. A comparative analysis of ceramics has revealed that there are at least three well-defined corpora of ceramic styles, including: (1) the Jalisco plateau, (2) the southern and coastal areas of Jalisco and Colima, and (3) the region of Nayarit and southern Sinaloa. These stylistic variants could reflect, at the least, the existence of political entities or spheres of influence that may have consisted of at least three lordships or city-states. It seems that the common thread or core themes that tied the regions together were (1) an ideological strategy by elites based upon similar iconography and religious beliefs that served to legitimize and expand their economic and political ties and control (see DeMarrais et al. 2002), (2) the use of and demand for luxury and prestige goods and emblems associated with power, and (3) an interrelated economy sustained by exchange networks. There is still much work to do and leads to investigate, but the analysis of data thus far collected is promising. This research will enable us to reach clearer conclusions—supported by data from increasingly systematic research work—on sociocultural dynamics and sociopolitical and economic organization of the Aztatlán tradition.

Acknowledgments

I would like to thank Kiyo Gutiérrez who helped me with the graphics presented in this work.

Notes

1. This chapter is drawn from part of the research that was conducted for a doctoral dissertation in anthropology.
2. The La Peña and Caseta sites have been the focus of at least two excavation seasons as part of the Sayula Basin Archeological Project in Jalisco (Liot, Ramírez, Reveles, and Schöndube 2006; Ramírez Urrea et al. 2005; Schöndube et al. 1994; Schöndube et al. 1996; Valdez et al. 2005).
3. For more information, see Liot and colleagues (2007).
4. Three field-excavation seasons have been conducted at the La Picota site (2004, 2008, 2009) led by Catherine Liot, Javier Reveles, and Susana Ramírez Urrea as part of the research program of the Sayula Basin Archaeological Project.
5. See Liot and colleagues (2006) for more information on the La Peña excavations.
6. Aurelie Manin (2015) made a preliminary analysis of the faunal remains from La Peña.
7. Archaeological work in the Sayula Basin (Liot et al., eds. 2006; Valdez et al., eds. 2005) determined the overlap of 150–200 years between the Late Sayula complex (local development) and the Cojumatlán complex, which is the early period associated with the Aztatlán tradition (Ramírez Urrea 2016, 2019).
8. As previously mentioned, ceramic types that are similar were not found. In contrast, a ceramic type variation named Autlán Polychrome was recorded in association with intrusive Aztatlán material that probably derives from Nayarit.
9. Codex-style ceramics, usually on pyriform vessel and vase forms, are characterized by scenes painted on the pottery that narrate events or stories, usually with ritual and/or cosmological themes. It should be noted that this ceramic style has been dated at La Peña and multiple sites in Nayarit to the Middle Postclassic Period (AD 1100–1350), or up to 250 years prior to the regions of Oaxaca and Puebla. It is pertinent to mention that there is a difference between codex-style ceramics and ceramics that show iconography which appears in the codices. The latter refers to pottery that has representations, images, or symbols displayed in the codices, but unlike the codex-style ceramics, there are no scenes or narratives of myths. Rather, it shows abstract representations of cosmological and religious codes and, in most cases, its meaning and use was restricted to the groups in power (Ramírez Urrea 2006a:437, 2016).
10. For more details about the city-state concept, see Hansen (2000), and as a possible model for Aztatlán sociopolitical organization, see Ramírez Urrea (2016).
11. For more information, see García Zaldúa (2007) and Ramírez Urrea (2016, 2019).

CHAPTER 5

San Felipe Aztatán

An Aztatlán Political and Ceremonial Center in the Lower Basin of the Río Acaponeta, Nayarit

Mauricio Garduño Ambriz

Within the scope of regional archaeology, the lower basin of the Río Acaponeta is an area that has received little attention from specialists in relation to systematic studies of archaeological prospection and testing, if we take as a comparison the scope of investigations carried out further north on the floodplain of the Río Baluarte in Sinaloa (Gámez Eternod and Garduño Ambriz 2001; Grave Tirado 2003; Kelly 1938; Sauer and Brand 1932) and the studies carried out in the river systems located towards the south along the deltas of the Río San Pedro Mezquital and Río Grande de Santiago (Bordaz 1964; Duverger and Levine 1993; Garduño Ambriz and Vázquez del Mercado 2005; Meighan, ed. 1976), located on the central coast of Nayarit (Figures I.1–I.2). Although pioneering surface reconnaissance and stratigraphic testing have provided valuable data advancing the reconstruction of the history of the Mesoamerican northern coastal region, various factors have hindered research in the northwestern lowlands of Nayarit in recent years. This situation is aggravated further when one considers that the landscape has been severely transformed by agricultural grading affecting various architectural complexes of the Postclassic period. The result has been the irreversible modification of the original layout of the settlements and their spatial distributions, activity areas, and construction volumes (Gámez Eternod and Garduño Ambriz 1997).

In this context, we implemented a short archaeological salvage season in 2002 in the town of San Felipe Aztatán in the coastal municipality of Tecuala (Nayarit) to address the complex problem related to the protection, registration, and investigation of the important prehispanic site underlying this modern town. To satisfactorily cover the objectives set forth in our work program, we conducted a topographical survey of the prehispanic foundations, platforms, and mounds within the urban area of San Felipe Aztatán, mainly concentrated in the Huachotita *barrio* located in the town's western end.

Most of these buildings show severe structural deterioration caused both by the introduction of public services (e.g., drinking water, drainage, lighting, etc.) and by various domestic activities (e.g., construction or expansion of houses, septic tanks, and water supply wells), factors which over time significantly and progressively altered numerous structures, deposits, and archaeological contexts.

Geography

The physiographic province of the *Llanura Costera del Pacífico* (Pacific Coastal Plain) in the state of Nayarit is a narrow and elongated strip of more than 100 km in length by approximately 50 km wide, mostly covered by alluvial sediments deposited in extensive floodplains adjacent to the Río Acaponeta, Río San Pedro, and Río Grande de Santiago, as well as by coastal lagoon, wetland, estuary, and mangrove systems. Geologically, the territory is formed by low mountainous areas and ridges of extrusive igneous rocks from the Tertiary that are directly associated with flat topographical plains formed by the accumulation of sediments from the Quaternary covering an altitudinal range between sea level and 200 m (Jardel 1994:18–20).

In Nayarit, the prevailing climate in the coastal plain is warm subhumid or tropical savanna (Aw), where average annual temperatures range between 26° and 28°C with the coldest month being over 18°C. The annual average rainfall fluctuates between 800 and 1,400 mm^3 primarily concentrated during the summer (from June to October), while winter rain comprises less than 10 percent of the total. From a climatic point of view, the characteristic vegetation of the coastal plain corresponds to the tropical savanna with the representative species of the lower deciduous forest prevailing. The vegetation observed along the main river channels and flat lands flooded with brackish tidal waters is basically comprised of mangroves,

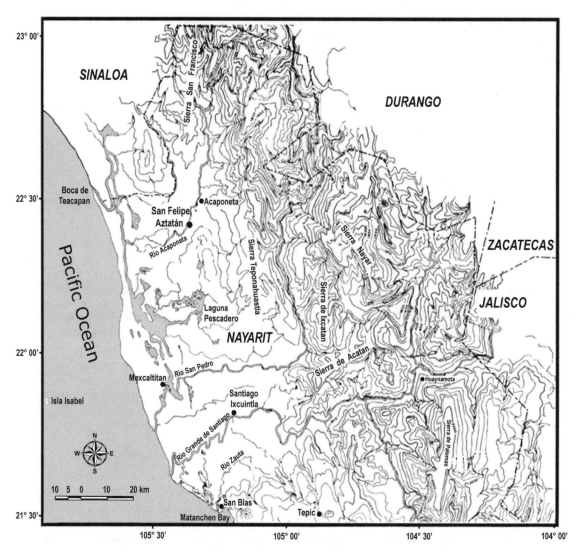

FIGURE 5.1. Location of the site of San Felipe Aztatán, Nayarit, with perspective of the complex hydrological networks of the northwestern lowlands of Nayarit. Drawing by author.

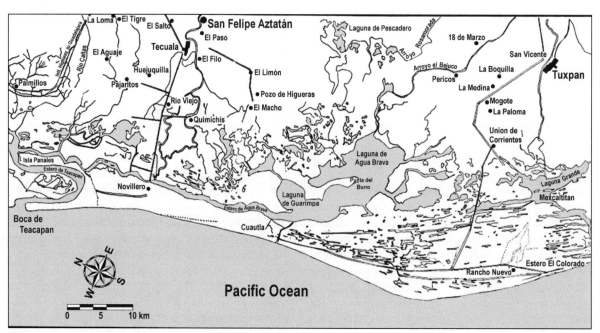

FIGURE 5.2. Location of the site of San Felipe Aztatán, Nayarit, with alternate perspective of the complex hydrological networks of the northwestern lowlands of Nayarit. Drawing by author.

while in the plains surrounding the lagoon systems it is possible to observe halophytic grasslands and thorny scrub communities associated with xerophytic plants (Secretaría de Programación y Presupuesto 1981). Currently, the landscape has been severely transformed by intense agricultural activity that takes place mainly in the deltaic plains where the highest yielding alluvial soils are located, as well as by the recent construction and expansion of aquaculture farms in the marsh area (Garduño Ambriz 2005) which has caused a progressive change in the various ecosystems that make up this province.

General Description of the Site

The prehispanic site of San Felipe Aztatán was officially registered in 1987 by the Dirección de Registro Público de Monumentos y Zonas Arqueológicos of the Instituto Nacional de Antropología e Historia (INAH) within the first stage of the Atlas Arqueológico Nacional project under the code F13A78-18-028 (Figures 5.1–5.2). The site is located at UTM East 456,000 and North 2' 475,300 (Acaponeta F13A78 topographic chart, scale 1:50,000/ Instituto Nacional de Estadística y Geografía [INEGI]).

The original site likely covered an area of at least 120 to 150 ha as we have verified via photointerpretation and subsequent field verification of the continuous dispersion of mounds and platforms with associated ceramics representative of the Aztatlán cultural complex (AD 850/900–1350). The available information indicates that the population nucleus was comprised of an extensive conglomerate of structures including elite housing units, temples, workshops, storage areas, and residential complexes that were part of the most important governing settlement of the lower basin of the Río Acaponeta during the Early Postclassic (Cerritos phase: AD 850/900–1100) and Middle Postclassic (Ixcuintla phase: AD 1100–1350) periods.

Documentary sources from the sixteenth century seem to support models of complex prehispanic social organization and a highly diversified mixed economy that involved the exploitation of diverse resources and varied ecosystems. These documents also mentioned the abundance of food provisions with up to three maize harvests per year, indicating that intensive agriculture was practiced. The cultivation of beans and squash was complemented by the raising of turkeys, ducks, and other birds. They hunted deer, hares, and rabbits and also were engaged in fishing and harvesting oysters, sole, and other fish (Anguiano 1992:Tables 4, 6–8). At the time of contact, the Aztatlán *señorío* apparently was the largest of those found on the coastal plain with various subject towns offering tribute. Its sphere of influence extended from the coast to the foothills of the mountains where other populations were subjects.

Objectives of the Project

Registration and Delimitation of Archaeological Monuments

Considering the severe and progressive destruction of platforms and mounds, as well as the frequent anthropic alteration of archaeological remains by the population residing in modern San Felipe Aztatán, we carried out a general surface survey within this locality to identify the main architectural features visible on the surface within the current settlement. Subsequently, a detailed topographic survey of all previously identified elements was carried out so that all information was georeferenced within the current urban layout.

Establishment of Local Occupation Sequence and Chronocultural Succession at the Site

The intensive excavation of 10 test units distributed in four general areas in different sectors of the site aimed to obtain stratified samples to establish a reliable chronological typology of the representative archaeological materials and contexts of each identified cultural level. Furthermore, the ordering and eventual reconstruction of the local stratigraphic sequence will establish specific correlations with other cultural entities and regions both on the coast and in the southern highlands of Nayarit. On the other hand, we were interested in obtaining a representative sample of the functional heterogeneity of occupied spaces within the site.

Regional Archaeological Problems

From our perspective, one of the main contributions of the pioneering works of archaeological prospection carried out by Carl Sauer and Donald Brand in the northwestern lowlands of Nayarit and Sinaloa was the recognition of regional cultural developments pertaining to the Aztatlán culture, a complex society built upon its own material bases which was on par with the "high" cultures of Mexico—the geographical scope of which was characterized in the oldest historical cartography (e.g., the *Teatrum Orbis Terrarum* produced by Abraham Ortelius in 1570). The recurring mention of favorable climatic conditions and the high productive potential of the immediate environment of the main archaeological sites referred to in their report, taken together with their explicit statements of the profuse evidence of material culture linked to the Aztatlán settlements visited by these authors, illustrates their position that these populations had complex forms of social organization, which is objectively demonstrated in the archaeological evidence of prehispanic societies in the northern coastal regions of Mesoamerica.

In this way, arguments in favor of the existence of important and permanent population centers organized in well-defined settlement patterns within the

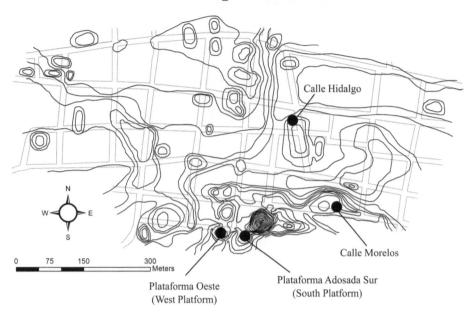

FIGURE 5.3. Topographic map of the mounds located within the urban zone of San Felipe Aztatán as documented in 2002. Drawing by Daniel Pierce after Garduño Ambriz and Gámez Eternod (2005:Figure 1).

regional geography find opposition with strong regional historiographical trends which accept as a proven truth the existence of Aztlán (the mythohistorical home of the Aztecs) as a geographically precise and historically objective point of reference located in the coastal area of Nayarit or Sinaloa rather than as a mythical archetype within Mesoamerican symbolism. In this conception, the archaeological settlements located in this coastal region were conceived *a priori* as places of temporary transit characterized by a relatively short period of residence since its inhabitants would have formed part of the Mexica (Aztec) contingent which migrated to highland central Mexico to found the Aztec capital of Tenochtitlán.

Subsequent archaeological prospection, survey, and excavation carried out on the coastal strip has satisfactorily corroborated Sauer and Brand's (1932) initial observations and has made it possible to document on a solid archaeological basis the existence of a long process of adaptation and transformation of the environment and of a continuous cultural development on the part of the Aztatlán coastal population. In relation to the problem of cultural succession, it is most notable that these authors—solely based on the volume, density, and quality of the archaeological remains observed during their reconnaissance—could infer a prolonged prehispanic occupation sequence in the region. Their observation gains greater relevance when we consider that at that time there were no stratigraphic studies for reference to reconstruct the history of the prehispanic population settlement of the northwestern lowlands.

Results and Discussion
Topographic Survey

One of the principal objectives of our project was to conduct a general surface reconnaissance and topographic survey of the prehispanic structures located in the urban area of San Felipe Aztatán, concentrated mainly within the locale of the present-day Huachotita *barrio*. The registration of the remaining architecture as well as the documentation of the general topographic plan of the site were priorities within our archaeological salvage program due to the progressive deterioration due to anthropic factors among the affected structures.

Surface reconnaissance and subsequent controlled topographic survey enabled the registration of a total of 33 structures of variable size and orientation within the urban area (Figure 5.3). These included small, isolated mounds and sets of platforms organized around plazas with a range of elevations from 0.40 m, in the case of the lowest platforms, up to a maximum of 9 m, which corresponds to the upper-level surface of the principal mound of the site (that is, of Loma de la Cruz). Testimony provided by local residents indicated that the current evidence does not represent the totality of the original buildings nor the real extension of the prehispanic settlement; around 15 years ago it was still possible to observe a greater number of mounds within the lots adjacent to the households.

On the other hand, from the registration and delimitation work carried out during the fifth stage of the *Proyecto INAH-Procede en Nayarit* (Zepeda and Fajardo 1999) it was possible to count and sketch a total

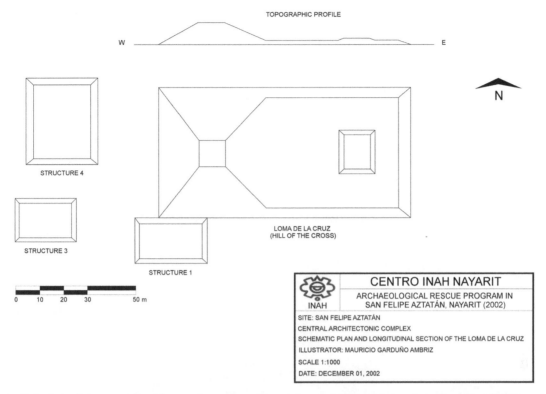

FIGURE 5.4. Plan of the central architectural complex of San Felipe Aztatán and Loma de la Cruz. Drawing by author.

of 59 mounds distributed on the parcels located to the south of San Felipe Aztatán (where the mechanized leveling of agricultural land constitutes the primary factor in the site's alteration), which would then bring the total to 92 archaeological structures.

Ceremonial Architecture

The Loma de la Cruz constitutes the main structure not only of the site but very likely of the entire lower basin of the Acaponeta River, corroborated from previous reconnaisance and archaeological survey carried out in 1998 in the deltaic plain of this important river system (Pérez et al. 2000). Loma de la Cruz was described by Sauer and Brand (1932:21–22, Plate 4a) in their pioneering report in the following terms:

> From a peón on the road we heard of a high loma, called La Cruz. We found it only a little to the west of San Felipe, really the most conspicuous land-mark in all this flat alluvial region. It stands about thirty-five feet high, is about fifty feet across at the top, and has a base little more than one hundred fifty feet through. The base is rudely quadrangular, making it a small earth pyramid with a truncated top. At this as well as at a number of the other mounds there was a well-marked depression to one side of the base. A number of small mounds are disposed about this high one [...] According to tradition, there has 'always' been a cross maintained on the hill, which has a somewhat mysterious reputation of sanctity [...] The pottery fragments on the hill were of unusually fine quality.
>
> This site was the best source of what we designate the Aztatlán ware.

Certainly the Loma de la Cruz represents the most notable structure and construction volume in this area, both for its location, size, and configuration, and for its orientation. It occupies a central position within the most important architectural ensemble of the site and is surrounded by several hierarchically subordinate structures (Figure 5.4).

The detailed topographic survey enables us to determine that the Loma de la Cruz is not an isolated mound situated directly on the coastal plain, but instead is a complex pyramidal structure comprised of at least three components. The lower part of this mound complex consists of a rectangular base averaging around 1.60 m in height and measuring approximately 100 m in length by 60 m in width. Its longitudinal axis is oriented on an east-west orientation in accordance with the daily transit of the sun through the celestial vault. Upon this base is situated the Loma de la Cruz, a mound of 9 m in height located at the western end of the earthen base whose main façade points towards the eastern horizon. At the opposite end, it is still possible to observe a low quadrangular platform—probably an altar—of around

FIGURE 5.5. Pre-Aztatlán material culture at San Felipe Aztatán and the Nayarit coastal plain. (*a*) Hollow anthropomorphic female figurines stylistically linked to the Chinesco cultural complex (100 BC–AD 200/250), recovered in San Felipe Aztatán. (*b*) Two Gavilán Polychrome bowls (Gavilán phase, AD 250–500), Nayarit coastal plain. (*c*) Possible Amapa White-on-red jar (Amapa phase, AD 500–800/850), Nayarit coastal plain. (*d*) Amapa Red-on-cream jar (Amapa phase, AD 500–800/850), Nayarit coastal plain. (*e*) Amapa Red-on-buff jar (Amapa phase, AD 500–800/850), Nayarit coastal plain. Photos by author.

0.40 m in height, also situated atop the earthen base. Between Loma de la Cruz and this platform there is a level topography that could have functioned as a ceremonial plaza for this complex.

It is notable that at the site of La Guásima, the second-most important Aztatlán population center in the region after San Felipe Aztatán, we carried out a topographic survey and controlled test units in a mound known locally as La Montosa (Pérez et al. 2000: 85–91, Plans 15–18, Photo 32)—a pyramidal structure that faithfully reproduces, although on a smaller scale, the same architectural pattern and orientation as that of Loma de la Cruz. Similarly, La Montosa—along with the aforementioned Complejo Sur—is also part of the architectural core of La Guásima and constitutes the construction of the greatest monumentality, hierarchy, and symbolism within the site.

Stratigraphy and Cultural Sequence

As in most of the settlements in the fertile alluvial lowlands of the humid floodplain of the Río Acaponeta (Garduño Ambriz et al. 2000), our test pits in San Felipe Aztatán allowed the identification of deep stratified deposits made up of a continuous succession of cultural layers with only some archaeologically sterile sandy alluvium interspersed within the local archaeological sequence. The stratigraphic superposition coincided in many cases with an evident chronotypological change in the diagnostic ceramics associated with each layer. From the seriation of this material, it is possible to affirm a long occupational sequence at the site directly exemplified by various representative materials of the Chinesco cultural complex (100 BC–AD 250) of the terminal Formative period (Figure 5.5a). Likewise, in several of the excavated units we identified levels of occupation of the Gavilán (AD 250–500) and Amapa (AD 500–800/850) phases of the Classic period with ceramic types commonly found on the Nayarit coastal plain (Figure 5.5b–5.5e). Furthermore, it was possible to explore contexts in which various archaeological materials were recovered and recorded (e.g., transitional ceramics, atypical anthropomorphic figurines, flutes, and an unusual concentration of green obsidian prismatic blades derived from the Cerro de Las Navajas source in Hidalgo). These items belong to a transitional interface tentatively located within the Epiclassic period between cultural strata of the Amapa (AD 500–800/850) and Cerritos (AD 850/900–1100) phases, a temporal period which is worthy of separate research.

In numerous units, we found a rich Aztatlán cultural substratum belonging to the Cerritos phase of the Early Postclassic period, and most of the explored primary contexts (e.g., refuse disposal areas, lithic pavement, hearths, burials, etc.) were associated with these levels of occupation. On the other hand, representative diagnostic ceramic types of the El Taste-Mazatlán complex (AD 1100–1350) of the Middle Postclassic period were concentrated in the upper layers of the deposit, although our preliminary measurements indicate their percentage of the total sample (23,249 sherds) is comparatively much lower in relation to the earlier Cerritos phase (AD 850/900–1100) material of the Aztatlán complex.

It is important to mention that materials commonly associated with the terminal phase of prehispanic occupation in the northwestern coastal plain of Nayarit—represented mainly by the Santiago White-on-red ceramic type and distinctive of the Santiago phase (ca. AD 1350–1530)—are not represented within the ceramic sample collected in the various test units at San Felipe Aztatán. This aspect is of great interest for regional archaeological research if we consider that the earliest documentary sources and historical cartographic records indicate that the head town of the Aztatlán *señorío* was located on the floodplain of the Río Acaponeta. From our point of view, it is essential to carry out systematic surface reconnaissance and controlled excavations to obtain contextual information and datable samples that can determine which elements of the material culture function as reliable chronocultural markers, that is, as indicators of the occupation corresponding to the terminal Santiago phase.

Excavated Contexts

Considering the fact that we continue to conduct morphological and functional analyses of the artifactual assemblages and of the archaeological elements (e.g., floors, hearths, refuse disposal areas, construction fill, etc.) associated with each cultural level of occupation identified within the local sequence, we tentatively propose that most of the excavated contexts comprise a portion of sets of domestic activities carried out within the scope of common housing units or elite residential complexes. These activity areas appear to correspond primarily to contexts related to the preparation, consumption, and disposal of food, from which originated the accumulation and formation of rich residual deposits with abundant associated organic and inorganic material. On the other hand, special attention should be paid to the lithic banquette explored in Unit "D" (located at Frente Calle Morelos), upon which artisanal activities apparently related to the application of postfired engraved decoration was carried out on certain Aztatlán ritual vessels located chronologically within the Cerritos phase of the Early Postclassic period.

FIGURE 5.6. Material culture located above the *empedrada adosada* attached to Mound 6, San Felipe Aztatán. Photo by author.

Pavement (Empedrados)

Empedrados are artificially constructed lithic conglomerates or pavement located in various sectors of the site. These are comprised of angular rocks of porous volcanic scoria similar in appearance to *tezontle*, which has crushed and rounded edges, cemented within a compact silt-clay matrix. This fill material is well characterized with size variances between 4 and 10 cm. Domestic ceramic sherds also were used selectively as construction material, mostly derived from monochrome *ollas* or *tecomates*.

It is important to note that these conglomerates served as a support to condition a horizontal occupation surface, upon which was dispersed a surficial scatter of abundant Aztatlán archaeological material from the Early Postclassic period (Figure 5.6). In some cases, this material also functioned as fill in embankments built for the purpose of leveling the uneven original ground surface. We hypothesize that these elements formed part of banquettes structurally and functionally attached to habitation platforms, probably in the case of roofed outdoor spaces upon which various activities were carried out.

The construction and utilization of these *empedrados* appears to have been a common practice among the population residing at San Felipe Aztatán during the Early Postclassic period, since at Loma Cecyten (a habitation platform located at a distance of approximately 1 km from Loma de la Cruz but which was part of the same settlement) we also explored an *empedrado* of this type with abundant associated material from the Cerritos phase of the Aztatlán complex (Gámez Eternod and Garduño Ambriz 2003:10–12, Figure 2). We estimate that to satisfy the demand for these conglomerates there must have been a relatively specialized industry in the selection, extraction, transfer, and processing (crushing) of the construction material, probably coordinated by a central authority. Subsequent fieldwork will enable us to evaluate with greater precision the volume of rock processed and used as construction fill material.

Refuse Disposal Areas (Basureros)

The primary waste context, referred to here as Basurero 1, constitutes one of the richest and best preserved archaeological elements explored in San Felipe Aztatán (Figure 5.7). The material recovered within the feature includes decorated Aztatlán ceramics with elaborate symbolism, monochrome utilitarian ceramics, prismatic blades, pipes and spindle whorls, axes, copper artifacts, clam shells and mother-of-pearl shell, burned animal bones, fish bones, charred maize cobs without seeds (*olotes*) and leguminous seeds, ash, and scattered charcoal residues.

Virtually all the ceramics discarded in Basurero 1 were located chronologically in the Cerritos phase (AD 850/900–1100), and for this reason the comprehensive analysis and interpretation of material associated with this context permits us to reconstruct paleodiet (at least partially), including cultural patterns of use and consumption of an extensive variety of resources by coastal Aztatlán populations during the Early Postclassic period. Considering the location of the waste disposal area in relation to the general architectural context of the site and the quality of the materials deposited at the site, the domestic waste in these residential contexts appears to be linked to elite households. This hypothesis eventually will be tested in relation to the corpus of information generated in subsequent analyses.

ARCHAEOLOGICAL MATERIALS

The recovery of two allochthonous green-stone beads in controlled excavation contexts, as well as the accidental discovery of a Toltec-affiliated Tohil Plumbate zoomorphic effigy vessel in a septic tank excavation in the Huachotita zone (Figure 5.8a), indicates that settled communities along the northwestern coastal strip of Nayarit were active participants in an extensive and

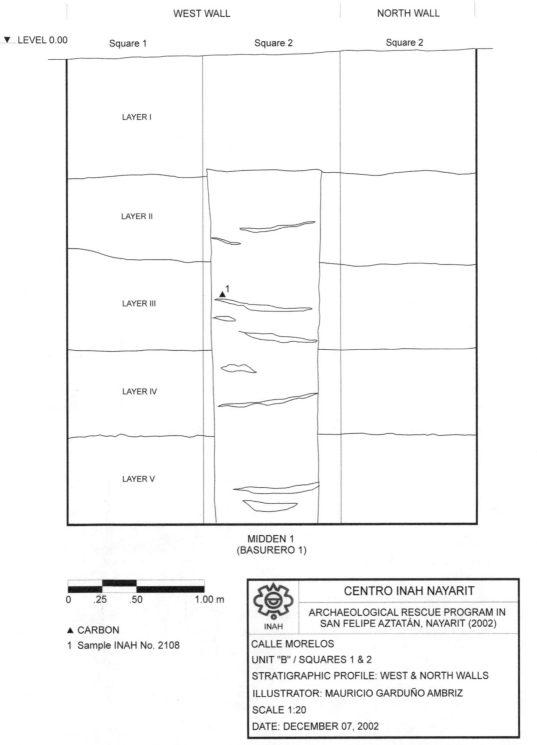

FIGURE 5.7. Stratigraphic profile of Basurero 1, Unidad "B" at Frente Calle Morelos in San Felipe Aztatán. Drawing by author.

complex network of luxury-goods exchange with societies in distant regions of Mesoamerica. Aztatlán decorated ceramics collected during the test excavations in San Felipe Aztatán are notable for complex iconography and a symbolic repertoire principally linked to solar worship and ritual sacrifice. Although mold-made and hollow-bodied Mazapan-style figurines are commonly found at Postclassic sites on the Nayarit coastal plain (Figure 5.8b), none were recovered in our excavations at the site.

FIGURE 5.8. Postclassic Aztatlán material culture from San Felipe Aztatán and coastal Nayarit. (*a*) Toltec-affiliated Tohil Plumbate (AD 850/900–1100) effigy vessel in the form of a crocodile recovered during the excavation of a septic tank in San Felipe Aztatán. (*b*) Mold-made and hollow-bodied Mazapan-style figurine, Nayarit coastal plain. Museo Regional de Nayarit and Instituto Nacional de Antropología e Historia. (*c*) Locally manufactured Iguanas Polychrome codex-style vessel from San Felipe Aztatán (Ixcuintla phase, AD 1100–1350). (*d*) El Taste Red-on-cream bichrome jar recovered in association with codex-style vessel from San Felipe Aztatán (Ixcuintla phase, AD 1100–1350+). Photos by Mauricio Garduño Ambriz.

An Aztatlán Codex-style Vessel

One locally manufactured Aztatlán-affiliated Iguanas Polychrome tripod jar from San Felipe Aztatán is profusely decorated in the Mixteca-Puebla style pictorial tradition, but it is typologically associated with the Ixcuintla cultural phase (AD 1100–1350) within the occupation sequence established for the northwestern coastal plain of Nayarit (Figure 5.8c). The vessel was located by chance in 1990 by a local resident of the Huachotita *barrio* on the upper-level surface of a platform located to the west of Loma de la Cruz, the main ceremonial building located within the architectural nucleus of San Felipe Aztatán. The significance of the location of the find on this platform, which is astronomically oriented on an east-west axis and ritually linked to the solar "cult," is explained below. In association with this codex-style vessel was a bichrome El Taste Red-on-cream vessel, a diagnostic ceramic type of the El Taste-Mazatlán complex (AD 1100–1350) which is distinctive of southern Sinaloa and northern Nayarit (Figure 5.8d; Garduño Ambriz 2014, 2016).

Grouped into two main scenes on the codex-style vessel, a total of 24 characters are depicted—five on the neck, 15 on the body, and four on the base—which are distributed practically over the entire external surface of the vessel including its base. In general terms, these representations are grouped into two main themes: a funerary rite of cremation (which involves an associated ritually decapitated individual) and the representation of the ritual sacrifice of a character by heart extraction. From the testimony of the person who removed the piece from its original context, it was learned that at the time it was cleaned there were ashes, crushed bones, and teeth inside—all of which suggests that the piece could have served as a mortuary urn.

Cremation Funerary Rites

An exceptional cremation scene on the vessel involves the participation of six characters. These include two priests who have facial masks in the form of emaciated jaws along with the distinctive headdress of the death god Mictlantecuhtli with sacrificial knives (*tecpatl*) alternating with blood streams topped by jewels (*chalchihuites*). One of these figures stands while playing a *huehuetl* drum while the other appears in a sitting position while holding two torches that he introduces into the funeral pyre. To their right is the cross section of a convex oven-like structure (*horno*) in which the mortuary bundle of a character appears in a sitting position on a bundle of firewood. In front of this figure, there is a container with broken arrows, a representation that within the Mesoamerican pictographic tradition symbolizes subjugation, expiration, or death.

Presiding over the cremation scene and situated in front of the mouth of the oven is Mictlantecuhtli, the ruling deity of the underworld. In addition, situated directly outside of the oven, a decapitated character stands with arms outstretched. The representation of this figure is highly significant in that ritual sacrifice by decapitation in relation to cremation funerary rites was an important element of the funerals of hierarchically important figures within Aztatlán society.

Ritual Sacrifice by Heart Extraction

The ritual sacrifice by heart extraction brings together the most characters on this vessel into a scene in which nine individuals participate. Presiding over the immolation is a character, standing richly attired, who wears a large, feathered headdress topped with a serpent's head in front. This male's arms extend forward, and his hands hold a ceremonial spear that could be analogous to batons—a hallmark of high-ranking figures. In this regard, it should be noted that this is the largest human figure relative to all other characters represented on the vessel, and they also wear the most elaborate attire and clothing, which reinforces their hierarchical position.

In front of this key figure are four priests who hold, by the limbs, an individual who is lying on his back, above a polychrome sacrificial stone sitting on a platform. Just above this character, another priest appears holding a knife (*tecpatl*) which he inserts into the chest of the sacrificed male figure. The spatial configuration of this scene—in which four priests appear holding the limbs of the sacrificial figure in the place occupying the four points of the *quincunx* with the fifth figure situated at the central vertical point (i.e., the axis mundi)—clearly refers to the Mesoamerican cosmic ideogram marking the four directions and center, which makes the ritual act all the more sacred.

Another character appears to be suspended in the air in direct association with the sacrifice who, in fact, points with their left hand to the precise place of the sacrificial victim's open chest. With their gaze directed in the opposite direction, this figure looks toward the high-ranking character who presides over the ritual. We propose that this figure could be the representation of a priest who fulfilled a function analogous to that of the *yahui* priests associated with ritual sacrifice who appear in some Mixtec codices descending from heaven to bring the hearts of those sacrificed to the sun god (see Hermann Lejarazu 2011:70, Figure 4).

In this regard, data from the regional archaeology indicate that during the Early and Middle Postclassic periods, cremation likely was a ritual act reserved only for elite segments of society and that its practice was part of an ideological discourse of legitimation related to rulers' identification with the solar deity who governed festivities linked to the agricultural cycle. Cremation and the associated ritual complex were acts that emulated the appearance of the solar disk and new fire (*xiuhmolpilli*) on the sacred mountain Coatepetl, a mythical archetype where the rebirth and rising of the sun in the east was periodically celebrated. It should be noted that the scenes represented on the body of the vessel take place precisely on the upper-level surface of a platform, much like where ceremonial precincts of Aztatlán temples were located.

It is highly significant that on the ceramic temple model recovered at Amapa (Meighan 1976:41–43; Meighan, ed. 1976:Plate 12)—which constitutes the only representation of a ceremonial building within the archaeology of the Aztatlán coastal nuclear zone—the oven (structure) and the sacrificial stone are depicted in both symbolic and functional association. These elements represent two of the basic constituent elements within the ceremonial complex linked to cremation rites and ritual sacrifice. Apparently, the complex iconographic configuration depicted on the codex-style vessel from San Felipe Aztatán corresponds to a narrative sequence of two ritual scenes linked to important events for high-ranking segments of Aztatlán society: (1) a funerary rite of cremation overseen by Mictlantecuhtli, and (2) a ritual sacrifice by heart extraction.

Metal Artifacts

A sample of four objects—a fish hook, a needle, a bell, and a generalized hook—were analyzed using Particle-Induced X-ray Emission (PIXE) at the Institute of Physics (Universidad Nacional Autónoma de México) with the objective of identifying their constituent metallic elements and the relative percentage of each. The results indicate that the four objects are copper (Cu), with other elements in very low quantities: nickel (Ni), arsenic (As), and silver (Ag). The only secondary element that appears in appreciable quantities is silver (Ag), in the case of the fish hook. Likewise, the fish hook also is distinguished from the other artifacts by the presence of nickel (Ni).

Although the copper is not 100 percent pure, it is likely that the identified trace elements were part of the ore to produce the objects. Comparatively, the fish hook shows significant quantities of silver (Ag), which could be explained by an intentional mixing of two or more minerals when melting the metal or producing the object. On the other hand, the similarity of the content of metallic elements among the other three objects suggests that they were made with material extracted from the same source (Barba et al. 2004).

Obsidian Artifacts

A total of 30 obsidian prismatic blade fragments recovered from San Felipe Aztatán were selected and sent (courtesy of Michael Ohnersorgen and Michael Glascock) to the University of Missouri Archeometry Laboratory (Missouri University Research Reactor, or MURR) with the objective of determining their chemical and mineralogical characterization. The preliminary results of Neutron Activation Analysis (NAA) identified three geological sources of extraction: La Joya, Jalisco; Ixtlán del Río, Nayarit; and the Sierra de las Navajas, Hidalgo (Glascock 2007). Daniel Pierce (2012, 2015a, 2017a) subsequently conducted a geochemical analysis (using X-Ray Fluorescence [XRF]) of a total of 1,492 obsidian artifacts from various excavation contexts with the intention of identifying their geological sources. The elemental composition analysis of these samples revealed that the best represented obsidian (in descending order) was from the La Joya source in Jalisco (34 percent), Volcán las Navajas (29 percent) and Ixtlán del Río (23 percent) in Nayarit, and the Cerro de las Navajas (12 percent) source in the Sierra de Pachuca (Hidalgo) located in the *altiplano* of central Mexico. Other sources located in western Mexico—namely Osotero, Boquillas, and San Juan de Los Arcos in the Jalisco highlands—together represented only 2 percent of the sample (see Pierce, this volume, Figures 10.1–10.6).

Archaeobotanical Material

Among the archaeological materials of organic origin recovered in Basurero 1, various charred fragments of maize (*Zea mays*) were contextually associated with three charred leguminous seeds, most likely *guaje* (Xelhuantzi 2003).

Archaeozoological Material

Malacology

The shell sample analyzed (682 valves) belongs taxonomically to the group of molluscs characterized by soft bodies that, in the case of gastropods (univalves) and pelecypods (bivalves), are protected with one or more calcareous pieces. Considering the biological characteristics of each of the seven species identified within the waste disposal area (*basurero*), we found that *Rangia mendica*, which represents 42 percent of the sample, *Tivela argentina* (26 percent), and *Donax panamensis* (12 percent) are pelecypods that still constitute a rich source of protein supply as a relatively abundant and easily obtainable resource in local mangroves, coastal lagoons, and sand bars. On the other hand, the genre *Unio* sp. also stands out, contributing 16 percent of the sample. This freshwater mussel was collected in the surrounding wetlands and surely represented a food in high demand by the resident population of the site (Villanueva 2004).

Ichthyofauna

The analysis of 942 fish remains discarded in Basurero 1 during the course of the Cerritos phase (AD 850/900–1100) occupation identified the use of 10 taxa that include at least eight species. Within these taxa there is evidence for the first use of some species in the area—*Cathorops* sp. (sea catfishes), *Lutjanus* cf. *L. argentiventris* (snappers), *Eugerres* sp. and *"Chichlasoma" beani* (mojarras), *Dormitator latifrons*, and *Gobiomorus* sp. (guavinas)—which broadens the spectrum of organisms consumed by the coastal Aztatlán population. Evidence indicates that their capture took place in the estuary systems and coastal lagoon adjacent to the alluvial floodplain within the Marismas Nacionales. The taxa best represented by the abundance of remains indicate that the relatively complete fish recovered in the waste disposal area were processed, consumed, and discarded at the site itself. Several bone segments exhibit evidence of exposure to fire, which could indicate that these fish were roasted for consumption or smoked for preservation and subsequent consumption. Since the archaeological ichthyofauna recovered is similar to those currently found in the sea, the estuaries, and the lower basin of rivers and streams adjacent to the prehispanic settlement (e.g., Las Cañas, Acaponeta, San Francisco, etc.), there does not appear to be any indication that, at the time of the use of Basurero 1, the area would have been affected by macroclimatic phenomena such as "El Niño" or that its effects would have had repercussions affecting the local climate, hydrology, or ecology (Guzmán 2004).

Reptiles, Birds, and Mammals

From the analyzed bone material derived from cultural strata and sealed primary contexts—as in the case of the aforementioned Basurero 1—it was possible to taxonomically identify at the genus and species level various bones of turkey (*Meleagris gallopavo*), dog (*Canis familiaris*), and white-tailed deer (*Odocoileus virginianus*). In addition, some leporid bones (hares and rabbits) and terrestrial turtles (*Kinosternon* sp.) also were recovered, although in these cases it was not possible to achieve a more precise biological determination based upon diagnostic elements. Most of these bones show traces of direct or indirect exposure to fire depending on the color gradient observed on their surface, which indicates that they were sometimes cooked (boiled, cremated, or incinerated) as part of the food preparation process (Manrique 2004). Together these examples constitute a significant portion of the organic waste materials recovered within habitational contexts at the site. The consumption of these species by the resident population surely constituted among the main sources of animal protein as a basic component of their diet.

Radiometric Dating (^{14}C)

Carbon samples obtained from the interior of Basurero 1—which contained an abundant sample of decorated Aztatlán ceramics from the Early Postclassic (Cerritos phase: AD 850/900–1100)—were processed in the Laboratorio de Fechamiento of the Instituto Nacional de Antropología e Historia (sample INAH-2108). These samples were dated to 1048 ± 64 years BP, corresponding to a temporal range from AD 860 to 1160, with a 95.4 percent reliability (de los Ríos 2004; see Mountjoy, this volume).

Conclusion

The archaeological data presented here corroborate the existence of complex social developments at least since the first century of our era. As in most of the sites studied on the Río Acaponeta delta plain, it appears that the colonization and initial settlement by sedentary farmers in San Felipe Aztatán occurred during the terminal Formative period (100 BC–AD 200/250). This occupation level is represented by archaeological materials with a clear stylistic affiliation with the Chinesco cultural complex, which was originally reported in the zone of the intermontane valleys of the Altiplano Meridional of Nayarit. It is worth recalling that the stratigraphy observed in the archaeological deposits revealed a continuous succession of levels of occupation, including strata from the Gavilán (AD 250–500) and Amapa (AD 500–800/850) phases underlying the construction and contexts of the Aztatlán cultural complex dated between AD 850/900–1350 (Garduño Ambriz and Gámez Eternod 2005).

The architectural structures explored at the site, including the residential platforms and the structures for ceremonial use (e.g., Loma de la Cruz), were built during the Cerritos phase (AD 850/900–1100) and permanently occupied during the subsequent Ixcuintla phase (AD 1100–1350). In some cases, the resident population conducted remodeling and expansion works of these platforms to refurbish their living spaces.

We have the necessary evidence to affirm that the Aztatlán regional culture developed upon its own demographic, social, and economic bases which enabled the establishment of complex permanent settlements. Increasing productive specialization—which took place with agricultural intensification and the intensive exploitation of estuaries—stimulated economic diversification and social divisions of labor that led to the development of new technologies (e.g., metallurgy) and artisanal labor in obsidian, ceramics, lapidary work, and others.

At the same time, the necessary coordination of public works, as well as the administration and redistribution of productive surpluses, stimulated the emergence of centralized political institutions within the capitals (*cabeceras*) of the *señoríos*. The construction of monumental temples with clear astronomical orientations—such as Loma de la Cruz and La Montosa—and the execution of complex ritual practices point to the existence of specialized social groups in the organization of festivals related to the ritual calendar and the agricultural cycle. The elites of Aztatlán societies controlled the long-distance exchange of sumptuary goods for ritual use or for use as distinctive markers of social rank, such as jadeite, turquoise, *tecali*, diverse copper objects (such as bells used in propitiatory rites), and fine ceramic vessels. These groups also organized the exploitation, transformation, and distribution of manufactured products and the strategic control of resources such as obsidian.

Currently we have diverse archaeological data that indicate a solar "cult" was widespread among coastal Aztatlán populations as inferred from the iconography, architecture, and the limited available data on burial patterns (see Mathiowetz, this volume). Symbolic representations of the fire serpent (Xiuhcoatl), which guided the sun on its daytime journey through the celestial vault, are frequent in decorated ritual vessels and sherds at San Felipe Aztatán. It should be recalled that both Loma de la Cruz and La Montosa are specifically oriented on an east-west axis, and these structures could be considered as true solar markers thereby reinforcing their function as temples and their connotation as sacred spaces for ritual use.

Similarly, recent investigations in the North Acropolis (Acrópolis Norte)—or Platform 5 of Zone II, according to Duverger (1998:624)—at the site of Coamiles on the central coast of Nayarit (see Garduño Ambriz 2008, 2009) enable us to corroborate that the strategic architectural plan of this important monumental center was designed based on the astronomical observation of the equinoxes. These findings represent a significant advance in understanding the symbolic connotations of Aztatlán ceremonial architecture along the Pacific coast of northern Mesoamerica.

At the top of Cerro de Coamiles, and aligned on an east-west axis with the principal structures of the North Acropolis, we located a smooth stone arranged vertically in the manner of a stela. This stela would have served as a solar calendrical marker signaling the appearance of the solar disk at the equinoxes in relation to a central point of observation at Mound 1 of the West Plaza complex (Conjunto Plaza Oeste), the façade of which points towards the eastern horizon. With the available information, it is possible to affirm that the two architectural spaces comprising the North Acropolis of Coamiles—the Conjunto Plaza Este and Conjunto Plaza Oeste—were planned based on the central zenith transit of the sun at the equinox and the symbolic interaction established between this trajectory and the principal structures (platforms, altars, stelas, etc.). The construction of the North Acropolis as a sacred space for ritual use occurred during the Cerritos (AD 850/900–1100) and Ixcuintla (AD 1100–1350) phases of the Aztatlán cultural tradition.

Moreover, the specialization and technical diversification of metallurgy are remarkable within the developments in Aztatlán technologies (see Punzo Díaz, this volume). The population not only had objects of ritual, sumptuary, or ornamental use, but people used metal objects in daily utilitarian activities. The results of the elemental composition analysis of the fish hook by the Institute of Physics at the Universidad Nacional Autónoma de México indicated that its manufacture is the product of the mixture or alloy of at least two metallic minerals: copper (Cu) and silver (Ag). In relation to the other objects analyzed, the relatively high proportion of silver in the fish hook indicates a specific technical manipulation on the part of craft persons to improve the functional demands of this artifact. The greater tenacity of this fish hook confirms a better response to the constant tensions to which it was sometimes exposed in its use as a fundamental part of fishing activities.

With regard to the abundant evidence of organic material discarded in the disposal area (Basurero 1), we can affirm that the population's diet included a wide spectrum of food resources, including cultivated plants such as maize and seeds collected from wild species such as *guaje*. On the other hand, hunting of smaller animals, fishing, and collecting molluscs were the primary sources of animal protein. This mixed economy involved the exploitation of the agricultural floodplain, rivers and wetlands, brackish lagoons and marshes of the estuarine zone, coastal sand bars, and the foothills adjacent to the lowlands. In addition, our data indicate that raising dogs for their eventual consumption as food was an important activity. It is also probable that the breeding and raising of birds such as turkey, as well as the domestication of certain animal species, was conducted within the habitation areas.

The data included here are a modest contribution to the complex history of the prehispanic Aztatlán populations settled along the northern Mesoamerican coast. The continual destruction of the remaining material evidence linked to these populations, as well as the progressive displacement of the cultural and natural landscape associated with these sites (e.g., endemic flora and fauna; ritual aspects of topography, hydrology, and orography; disruptions of cultural practices of contemporary Indigenous communities, etc.), demands the participation of all social sectors and institutions in order to guarantee their protection, conservation, and an appropriate public engagement as elements of local and regional cultural heritage.

CHAPTER 6

Not All that Glitters Is Aztatlán Ceramics

The Development of Complex Societies in Southern Sinaloa

Luis Alfonso Grave Tirado

The archaeology of western Mexico in general, and that of Sinaloa in particular, has focused almost exclusively on ritual-affiliated ceramics (Grave Tirado 2019b; Hernández Díaz 2013). Ceramic objects are undoubtedly some of the most attractive material manifestations of the societies who occupied this vast area, but their inhabitants were much more than just skilled potters. Thus far in the twenty-first century, scholars in southern Sinaloa have carried out various surface investigations and archaeological excavations in addition to engaging new approaches to the documentary sources of the sixteenth century. This work has allowed us to obtain a large body of data on settlement patterns, production activities, architectural complexity, the celebration of public ceremonies, and regional political organization, among other topics (Figures 6.1 and 6.2). This work has shown us that the people and societies who inhabited this region exhibited a high degree of political, economic, and religious development as evident in Aztatlán ceramics, which was only one of the ideological control mechanisms that elites used in one of the periods of their historical process. Before reviewing these works, I provide a brief presentation of the sources and mechanisms of power.

POWER AND ITS MECHANISMS

Power, according to Henri Claessen (1979:7), is nothing more than "the ability to impose one's own will on others." For his part, Max Weber characterized power in these terms: "In general, we understand by 'power' the chance of a man or of a number of men to realize their own will in a communal action even against the resistance of others who are participating in the same action" (Weber 1977:45). To achieve power, it is not only force that is used, but most of the time it is enough when threat, manipulation, influence, and authority are exerted. In fact, when exercising physical force, rather than demonstrating that one has power over another person or others, what it shows is that there is a scarcity or even a lack of power over them (Luhman 1995). Thus, power manifests itself in multiple ways, but all that matters is to be obeyed; to impose one's own will on others.

In reality, the use of the various tactics depends on the "degree of legitimacy" that the person exercising power retains. On the one hand, the less legitimate the power, the greater the use of force. On the other hand, if it is accepted that whoever exercises it has the authority to impose their will, the power is legitimate. It is obeyed because the superiority of the ruler is recognized.

There is certainly a great difference between being compelled through the use of force versus being induced without force, at times even unconsciously. However, it is clear that in both situations:

> [one is] able to cause me to behave in a way that I otherwise wouldn't [...] It accordingly seems sensible to say that the difference between the two cases is that it's a different kind of power attaching to your role rather than that the first is an exercise of power and the second an exercise of something else (Runciman 2000:65).

What is different is the way in which it is induced and/or sanctioned. According to W. G. Runciman, who in turn follows Max Weber, power can be exercised through three mechanisms: economic, ideological, and coercive. The first mechanism "enables you either to endow me with, or deprive me of, wealth or income in money, services or goods"; the second "enables you either to bestow on me, or take away from me, social esteem, honour or prestige"; and the third "enables you either to bring to bear on me, or protect me from, the exercise of physical force" (Runciman 2000:65–66). Although it is possible to distinguish these for their analysis, in practice they are always related. In fact, to fully exercise power it is necessary to apply the three mechanisms in combination, but, depending on historical circumstances, sometimes one of them has priority and

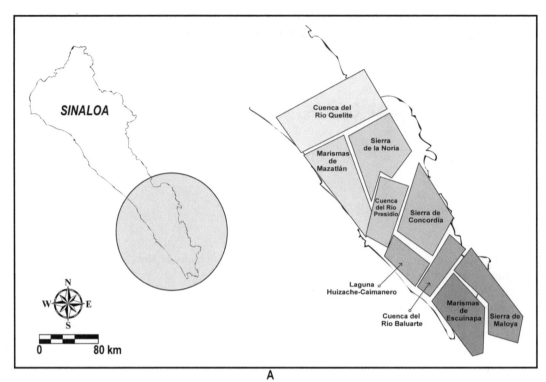

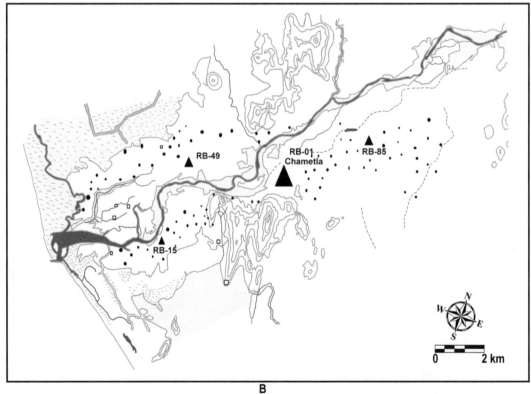

FIGURE 6.1. Maps of southern Sinaloa and the distribution of archaeological sites in southern Sinaloa. (*a*) Microgeographic zones of southern Sinaloa. Drawing by Gibrán de la Torre Vázquez. (*b*) The lower basin of the Río Baluarte with sites including Chametla (RB-01), El Bebelamo (RB-15), Coacoyolitos (RB-49), and Apoderado (RB-85). Drawing by author.

sometimes another. Therefore, as Runciman (2000:69) notes, "to grasp the institutional workings of the particular society, let alone to explain why it has evolved as it has, you will always need to analyse the relation between the three."

To explain the emergence of social complexity, this study has been approached from different perspectives. Strictly speaking, these can be reduced to only two basic positions: that of consensus and that of conflict. For the first, "stratification arises basically out of the needs of societies, not out of the needs or desires of individuals" (Lenski 1966:15); those who defend the second position consider that social inequality arises "out of the struggle for valued goods and services in short supply" (Lenski 1966:16).

If we observe behaviors of various societies both past and present—either with states or without states—there are situations in which cooperation and integration between members of society sometimes prevail, and it is clearly recognized that, whoever is in power, they have the full right to be there. However, there are also cases, very often if we pay attention to historical evolution, in which the conflicts between the governed and the rulers are accentuated. These confrontational situations end most of the time with the triumph of the rulers, who give themselves again to the task of creating consensus around them; sometimes, though, they end with the victory of the governed or an enemy group who take advantage of the crisis, and a new leader gains power.

It is from a position of power that the different mechanisms are put into practice, meaning it is necessary then to already have power to establish them. These mechanisms make it possible to maintain power and are not, as it might be thought, exclusive to state societies, but are also widely manifested in chiefly societies. According to Timothy Earle (1997:14), a chiefdom is defined as "a regional polity with institutional governance and some social stratification organizing a population of a few thousand to tens of thousands of people." In reality, the differences between a state society and a chiefdom are of only a degree since the ways in which power is exercised are basically the same (Earle 1997:14).

The three sources or mechanisms of power, as we have noted, are economic, ideological, and coercive (i.e., war). Economic power is manifested archaeologically through productive intensification in order to generate surpluses (Earle 1997). In other words, even though the environment is favorable, such as that in southern Sinaloa, surpluses are not produced for their own sake. Rather, producers are forced to do more (Claessen 1979). Control over the means of production is one of the most important mechanisms for exercising and maintaining power.

But how are people forced to produce surpluses? In principle, for control to be effective in the long term it is necessary to make use of ideological mechanisms. Ideology is "the set of ideas, beliefs, concepts and others" which are presented as common to all of society, but which are actually those used by the ruling group to legitimize their dominance over the rest of society (Žižek 2003). Ideology is materialized through public ceremonies, monuments, symbolic objects, and iconography (Earle 1997:151).

War itself, in conjunction with human sacrifice and collective festivals, is one of the most effective ideological mechanisms of political control, since through war the governed become a mass and therefore more easily manipulated and steerable (Canetti 1983; Grave Tirado 2018a). In other words, the military apparatus is not only a coercion mechanism, but is actually used more to unite society around the ruler since there is nothing that unites a society more than an enemy, whether real or figurative (Canetti 1983; Earle 1997; Grave Tirado 2018a).

Recent Archaeological Investigations in Southern Sinaloa

In general, southern Sinaloa is geographically homogeneous; however, it is possible to recognize up to nine microgeographic zones with characteristics that distinguish them from the rest. These zones include the following: (1) Cuenca del Río Quelite, (2) Sierra de La Noria, (3) Marismas de Mazatlán, (4) Cuenca del Río Presidio, (5) Sierra de Concordia, (6) Laguna Huizache-Caimanero, (7) Cuenca del Río Baluarte, (8) Sierra de Maloya, and (9) Marismas de Escuinapa (Figure 6.1a). Building upon work begun during the beginning of the present century, during the past two decades I have carried out several investigations in regions in which we have been able to confirm a high degree of social complexity achieved by the populations who settled here. In the following sections, we will go through the data, briefly by necessity, from north to south.

La Cuenca del Río Quelite and Las Marismas de Mazatlán

Seventy-one archaeological sites have been registered in the Quelite river basin, of which only El Gachupín seemed to function as a guiding center; 10 were villages, 24 hamlets, 16 dispersed hamlets, and 19 isolated houses (Grave Tirado 2021). The occupation spanned from AD 250 until the arrival of the Spanish. Between AD 250 and 500, there were only five inhabited sites; but for the following period (AD 500–750), there were already 18 settlements, with El Gachupín standing out at almost 15 ha in size.

During the Aztatlán horizon (AD 750–1100/1200), the population increased approximately threefold:

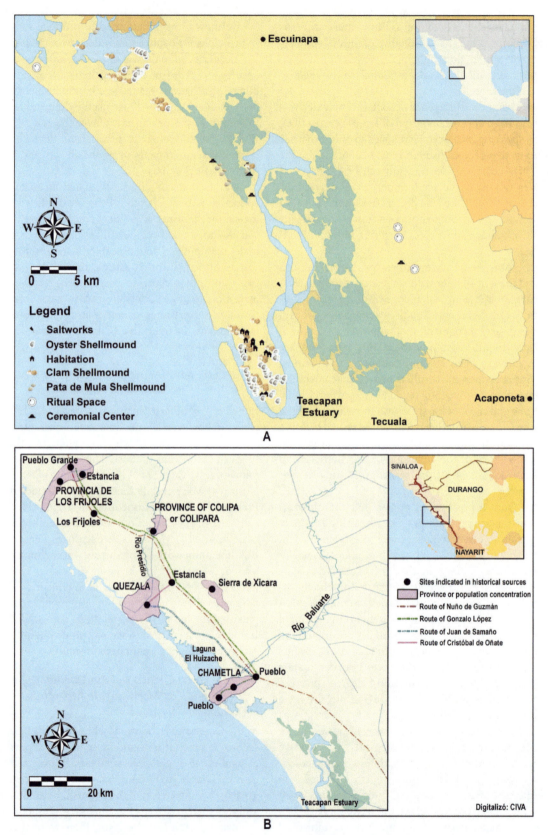

FIGURE 6.2. Distribution of archaeological sites and historic-period Indigenous political provinces in southern Sinaloa. (*a*) The Escuinapa marshlands (*marismas*). (*b*) Location of Indigenous political provinces on the arrival of the Spanish. Drawings by Cinthya I. Vidal Aldana.

45 settlements were distributed from the foothills to the vicinity of the coast, and El Gachupín reached almost 25 ha and contained a small mound and some low platforms. However, it was practically uninhabited during the following period, although the population of the basin remained more or less the same and no political community seemed to have political control. The Spanish encountered this scene in 1531. In the lower sierra, there are abundant petroglyphs associated with propitiatory ritual practices related to the fertility of the land (Grave Tirado and Samaniega Altamirano 2013).

Between the Río Quelite and the marshes near Mazatlán, just over 30 archaeological sites have been recorded (Grave Tirado 2000, 2020). Most are made up of the few remains of scattered houses located on one of the many mounds found on the landscape. However, we have also located shell mounds, which demonstrate an intense exploitation of estuarine resources at the end of the prehispanic occupation (AD 1200–1531).

La Cuenca del Río Presidio

In the Cuenca del Río Presidio, we detected 22 archaeological sites. Unfortunately, since the introduction of irrigation systems, the destruction of the archaeological remains has been intensive and the once abundant mounds there hardly remain (Gálvez 1967a, 1967b; Sauer and Brand 1932). However, archaeological materials are widespread for areas of up to 60 ha (Grave Tirado 2012b). Even one of the largest and most complex communities, El Walamo or Rancho La Loma, which is located on the lower part of the river, had several earthen mounds including what Sauer and Brand (1932:24) described as "an artificial pyramid about thirty feet high and flattened on top" when they visited the area in 1930, a site where Héctor Gálvez (1967b) later identified a ballgame court. All other architecture has since disappeared (Grave Tirado 2000).

One site still containing preserved parts of ceremonial structures is La Limonera. Located on the north bank of the river, almost in the foothills, it is possible to see an enormous platform of more than 100 m per side upon which sit three elongated mounds. The largest, located to the west, is topped at its southern end by a pyramidal structure over 6 m in height. To the east is the Río Zacanta where there is a series of petroglyphs with designs clearly alluding to the fertility of the land, including the repeated representation of female genitalia (Grave Tirado 2012b).

La Cuenca del Río Baluarte

The archaeological research conducted along the Río Baluarte has been more intensive. Thus far, 108 prehispanic settlements have been registered with 73 sites located along its southern margin and 35 others on its northern shore (Grave Tirado 2017). Practically all of the settlements are located along a strip of land measuring about 2 km wide between the river and the brackish waters of the estuaries and/or the slopes of the hills (Figure 6.1b). The agglomeration of archaeological remains is so dense and so little space separates one site from another that it gives the appearance that this is a single community with a dispersed settlement pattern. However, not all sites were occupied at the same time, and there are notable differences in the size and complexity of their components.

Most of the sites barely exceed 1 ha, and there is often only a slight elevation indicating a mound. But in other examples (e.g., La Loma del Guancho [RB-09], El Bebelamo [RB-15], La Loma de los Magueyes [RB-75], El Pozole [RB-88], La Loma de las Pilas [RB-92], to name a few), the mounds are still clearly visible—some of them measuring over 3 m in height. The sites of Apoderado (RB-85) on the south bank and Coacoyolitos (RB-49) on the other side of the river stand out from the rest of the settlements for the greater number of architectural structures, especially the size of some of these. Both sites contain protruding platforms, with the first measuring almost 200 m long in an east-west direction and almost 100 m wide with a mound over 5 m high situated at its eastern end. The platform at Coacoyolitos measures almost 400 m long by 160 m wide and has an approximate height of 3 m upon which are located five low mounds.

However, none of these are the main settlement of the lower basin of the Río Baluarte. Such a role has always been reserved for Chametla (Kelly 1938; Sauer and Brand 1932). The prehispanic settlement (RB-01) covers more than 90 ha and is comprised of more than 50 mounds (Figures 6.1b, 6.3a), among which are a ballcourt and two platform and pyramid complexes measuring over 8 m high with an architectural pattern similar to that described for Apoderado. On the other hand, nearly all the buildings of worship in the lower basin of the Río Baluarte were erected while taking into reference one or more of the main hills of the surrounding landscape. These geographical features include the San Isidro hill to the north, the Nanche hill to the south and west, and especially the Yauco hill to the east—the point at which the sun rises.

The occupation of the lower basin of the Río Baluarte began in the period between 100 BC and AD 200. By approximately AD 250, the population was stable and the construction of ritual structures had begun, in this case by adding clay earthen fill to a natural hill to give it a homogeneous shape, which we were able to determine with the excavation of the Loma de Ramírez at Chametla. The discovery of the remains of three funerary urns in Loma de Ramírez demonstrates that this

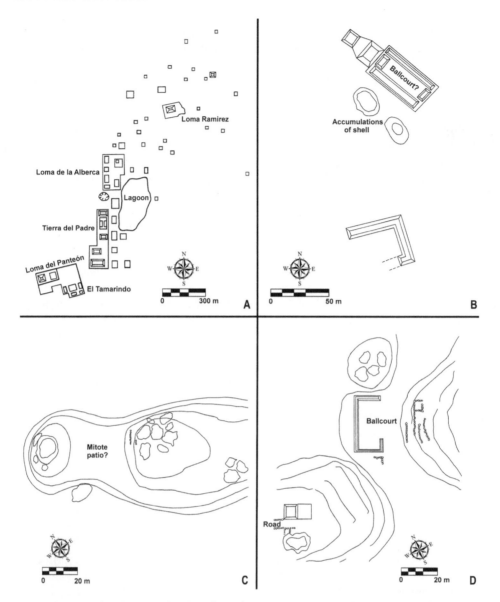

FIGURE 6.3. Sketch maps of archaeological sites in southern Sinaloa. (*a*) Chametla (RB-01). (*b*) Isla del Macho (MSS-95). (*c*) Palos Prietos (MSS-100). (d) La Loma de los Indios (MSS-102). Drawings by author.

mortuary practice, so widespread during the Aztatlán horizon throughout Sinaloa, began in the region during the Baluarte phase (AD 500–750).

Around AD 500, both the population and the erection of ceremonial structures notably increased, at least at the main site of Chametla. This process intensified during the Aztatlán horizon (AD 750–1200), corresponding with the construction of the main pyramid (Loma del Panteón) and the ballgame court. The population grew towards the end of the prehispanic occupation, and accounts of the Spanish conquest are unanimous in recognizing the Río Baluarte drainage as one of the most densely populated areas in northwestern Mexico with Chametla as the notable head town (Ortega León and Grave Tirado 2019).

The location of the settlements and the associated materials indicate that agriculture was not the only important economic activity, but to a large extent fishing and shellfish harvesting were as well. These activities intensified from at least AD 500, increasing even during the last stage of occupation both here and in the neighboring marshes (*marismas*) of Escuinapa (see below). The increased exploitation of estuary resources and the intensification in agricultural practices coincided with the gradual increase in population and a marked social differentiation that manifested itself with some clarity from the second half of the first millennium, but which seems to have begun a little earlier in time as is evident in Loma de Ramírez at Chametla.

The construction of monumental architectural

structures in only some of the settlements indicates to us that, in terms of political stratification, these sites were elevated above the others as were the drivers of their construction—these being priest-rulers. In this sense, it is worth noting that the main ceremonial buildings have a similar architectural design; that is, an elongated platform with a mound at one end. This design is shared in other areas of southern Sinaloa and northern Nayarit (Garduño Ambriz 2007), and it is one of the elements which allow us to establish this vast area as part of the same cultural region through time (Grave Tirado 2012c).

We do not yet know the specific meaning of this architectural pattern outside of the general idea that every pyramid serves as an image of a sacred mountain (e.g., Eliade 1994; López Austin and López Luján 2009). In fact, as we noted, the structures were built in reference to three of the main hills in the area: San Isidro hill to the north, the Yauco hill to the east, and the Nanche or Chametla hill to the west. Let us now highlight the meaning of these names. San Isidro is the patron saint of farmers. Yauco is a term of Nahuatl origin and can be translated as "the place of the *yauhtli*," or "the place of those who are from *yauhtli*," one of the formulas with which they refer to the *tlaloque* (rain gods) in the *Florentine Codex* (see López Austin and López Luján 2009:54). Therefore, the Yauco hill can be related to the eastern hill of Tlalocan. The name of Chametla, for its part, has always been derived from *chiametlan*, "the place of chia." However, the Franciscan friar Antonio Arias de Saavedra reported in 1673 that the name is derived from Ychamet "the place of maguey and mezcal" or from Ichamictla "the place of death" (Arias de Saavedra 1990 [1673]:300–303).

Las Marismas de Escuinapa

The site of Juana Gomez is located just 3 km away from the marshes (Figure 6.4a). In 1968, this site was still comprised of nine earthen mounds distributed around central plazas. The main mound measured over 5 m in height and the rest ranged between 2 and 3 m (Wolynec et al. 1968). The occupation of the site began between AD 250 and AD 500, although the construction of the buildings occurred between AD 500 and AD 750 (Grave Tirado and Nava Burgueño 2012; Wolynec et al. 1968). That is, as in the Río Baluarte basin, a certain degree of social complexity had already been reached during this time apparently related to the intensive exploitation of estuary resources.

In the early 2000s, I (Grave Tirado 2010a) conducted research at the site of El Calón, an enigmatic pyramidal shell mound discovered by a team led by Stuart Scott in 1968 and which for more than 30 years was attributed to the Middle Formative period in western Mexico (Foster, ed. 2017; Scott 1974, 1985, 1999; Scott and Foster 2000; Weigand 1993; Figure 6.4b). However, according to the investigations of the last 10 years both on the site itself and in southern Sinaloa in general, we were able to establish that this shell mound was built between AD 500–750, although in all likelihood it continued to function for much longer, at least during the Aztatlán horizon (Grave Tirado 2011). El Calón was the site of propitiatory ceremonies for abundant fishing harvests through much of the economic, population, and political development in southern Sinaloa during the prehispanic era (Grave Tirado 2010a). However, it was not the only shell mound in the region.

Within the framework of the *Proyecto Arqueológico Marismas del Sur de Sinaloa* (PAMSS), we have registered 182 archaeological sites (Grave Tirado 2018b). Of these, 145 are prehispanic, one is associated with the colonial period and two with the nineteenth century. Twenty-two sites correspond to the twentieth century, and 12 sites are modern. In the following discussion, we will focus attention on those sites of the prehispanic era.

Of the 145 sites from this time period, there are deposits of oyster shell ($n = 55$), clam shell ($n = 32$), deposits in which both species are mixed ($n = 3$), and *pata de mula* shell ($n = 3$), a type of clam (Figure 6.2a). There are 37 habitation sites, which is surprising if we consider the relatively unattractive conditions of the marsh to settle, although a good portion of these sites ($n = 14$) were inhabited by mollusk gatherers as evident in the shell accumulations—particularly clam-shell deposits. In general, the clam shells correspond to the Baluarte phase (AD 500–750) while the oysters are mostly from the last stage of prehispanic occupation. In addition, it was possible to determine that three remains of saltworks (*salinas*) are undoubtedly from the prehispanic era. Finally, we registered nine settlements that we can consider as sacred or ritual spaces. Two of them, like El Calón (see prior discussion), were built entirely with mollusk shells, including El Macho (MSS-96) and Isla del Macho (MSS-95). The first site is an elongated structure measuring almost 50 m long by 20 m wide with a height of more than 6 m, which makes it stand out with some clarity in the middle of the mangrove swamp.

Although the Isla del Macho site has been affected by intense looting of the shell, its components are still visible. To the east is situated a low and elongated platform upon which are located two mounds and a ballgame court, while to the west a U-shaped or horseshoe-shaped structure is present (Figure 6.3b). On the banks of the marsh there is another site named Panzacola (MSS-114) that we can also consider to be ceremonial in nature, and this site is comprised of seven earthen mounds situated around two plazas. All of these site layouts are oriented to 25° northeast.

The importance of these settlements, in addition to their intrinsic characteristics, is confirmed by their

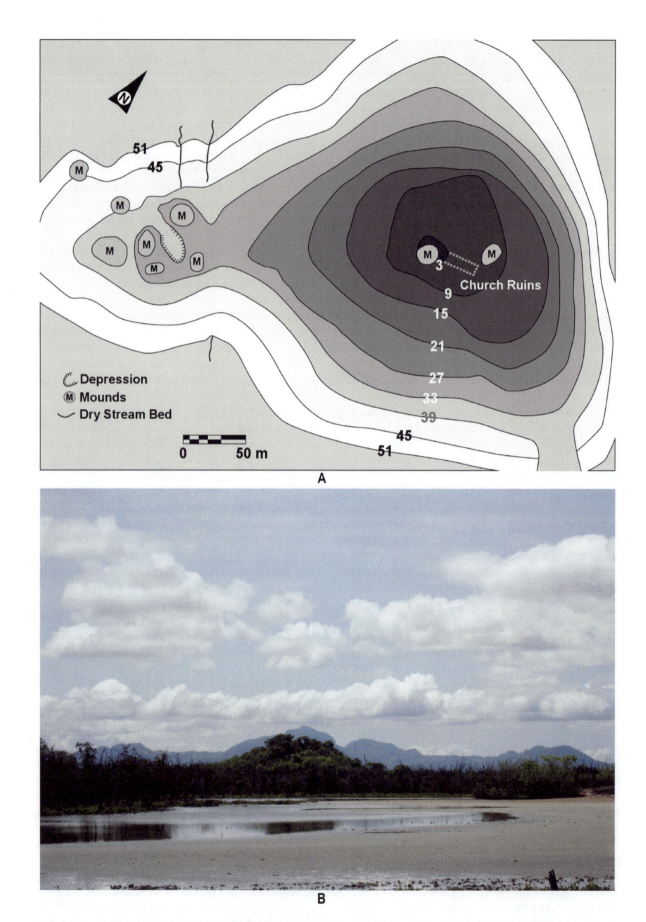

FIGURE 6.4. Archaeological sites in the Escuinapa marshlands (*marismas*), southern Sinaloa. (*a*) Juana Gómez. Drawing by Gibrán de la Torre Vázquez. (*b*) El Calón. Photo by author.

location almost exactly halfway between two of the most significant hills on the ritual landscape of southern Sinaloa where ritual practices evidently were carried out: Cerro del Muerto to the east and Cerro de las Cabras to the west. We have identified three sites on the west slope of Cerro del Muerto and one site on Cerro de las Cabras with evidence that they functioned as *mitote* courtyards in operation during the Aztatlán horizon (Figures 6.3c–6.3d2d; Grave Tirado and Samaniega Altamirano 2012).

Discussion and Conclusion

For over a millennium and a half, a society with complex economic, political, and religious organization developed in southern Sinaloa. The bases of its development were conceived within the region itself, and there is clearly a lineal connection uniting the communities that settled this area nearly 2,000 years ago with those societies inhabiting this landscape at the time of Spanish contact. The regional settlement patterns indicate that agricultural activities and the exploitation of the estuarine resources intensified at least from the period between AD 500–750 and expanded in scale around AD 900. A similar development is evident in the erection of ceremonial structures which also began around AD 500, including the construction of El Calón—the most conspicuous architectural monument in southern Sinaloa. These activities continued to develop over the next 750 years both in the river basins and in the marsh areas with the addition of new elements such as ballgame courts.

The ceremonial structures were oriented in reference to one of the prominent hills at the foot of nearby mountain ranges (Figure 6.4b). It is probable, then, that ceremonies were held within or at these edifices in relation to the rising and/or setting of the sun on certain special dates. These dates could include the beginning of planting and harvesting, the start and end of the fishing season, or the beginning and end of the salt-extraction season, which roughly coincide with the solstices and equinoxes. In these ceremonies, the role of the "singer" or orator in rites would be assumed by the ruler, who also would have been one of the main priests. In this role, imbued with divinity, the priest-rulers would be able to convince their subjects of almost anything.[1]

Ceremonial edifices and public festivals were important elements in imposing the ruling group's ideology, but there were more factors. Symbolic objects and iconography also had great significance in this regard. Ceramic vessels on the one hand and rock art on the other were two elements used to express the same ideological content (Grave Tirado and Samaniega Altamirano 2013). The iconography was already present in certain vessels by AD 500–750 during the Baluarte phase (Figure 6.5a), although it is accentuated during the so-called Aztatlán horizon when representations of gods and ritual scenes become evident (Figures 6.5c–6.5f).

It cannot be denied that some of these designs on ceramics are reminiscent of those of the Mixteca-Puebla tradition, a factor that undoubtedly indicates some kind of relationship. Most of those who have addressed the issue consider that Aztatlán ceramics were the result of a direct influence from central Mexico to the Aztatlán nuclear zone in Sinaloa and Nayarit, either through artisans who came from the central and southern highlands (Ekholm 1942; Hers 2013; Meighan 1976, ed.; Pohl 2012a, 2012b; Von Winning 1996) or as part of a commercial exchange in which traveling merchants, or *pochteca*, brought these materials (Braniff 1989; Kelley 1990, 2000; Publ 1985).

In fact, it seems clear that the Aztatlán ceramic vessels—including the codex vessels—were manufactured in each of the regions sharing this decorative tradition, including in northern, central, and southern Sinaloa; the Nayarit coast and *altiplano*; the Durango *altiplano*; southern Zacatecas; and the Sayula Basin of Jalisco (Carpenter 1996, 2008; Ekholm 1942; González Barajas and Beltrán Medina 2010; Kelly 1945a; Mountjoy 1990; Punzo Díaz et al. 2017; Solar Valverde 2011; Vidal Aldana 2011). These developments are considered to be the result of the political and economic processes and interactions of the populations who inhabited this vast area. In fact, these ceramics were part of the ideological mechanisms of the groups in power. This ideology was also shared by the mountain groups of Durango, Sinaloa, and Nayarit, and the rock art manifestations speak eloquently to these sensibilities (Figures 6.6a–6.6c, 6.7; Grave Tirado and Samaniega Altamirano 2013). It is worth noting that all of these regions were inhabited by groups belonging to the southern Uto-Aztecan language family, the same to which the Mixteca-Puebla ceramic producers belong. In other words, it appears that we are faced with a complex set of interrelations rather than a simple importation of goods or artisans.

Throughout the prehispanic era, social groups in southern Sinaloa retained an economic and ideological unity that transcended even its current political borders, since the extensive area that runs from the Río Piaxtla in Sinaloa to the Río Grande de Santiago in Nayarit formed the same cultural region (Grave Tirado 2012d). However, this region was fragmented into several political-territorial units. These provinces include three in northern Nayarit (Sentispac, Omitlán, and Aztatlán) and five (Chametla, Quezala, Colipa, Xicara, and Los Frijoles) in southern Sinaloa (Figure 6.2b; Grave Tirado and Ortega León 2020; Ortega León

FIGURE 6.5. (*a*) Middle Chametla polychrome bowl fragment (Baluarte phase, AD 500–750) recovered along Río Presidio drainage, La Chicura, Sinaloa. (*b*) White-filleted, painted vessel in the form of a prisoner (Baluarte phase, AD 500–750), Museo Comunitario de Chametla, Sinaloa. (*c*) El Taste Polychrome jar (AD 1100–1350), Aztatlán complex, southern Sinaloa. Museo Arqueológico de Mazatlán, Sinaloa. (*d*) Aztatlán alabaster effigy vessel in the form of the deity Piltzintli, Siqueros, Sinaloa. Museo Arqueológico de Mazatlán, Sinaloa (*e*) Aztatlán codex-style vessel, Iguanas Polychrome (AD 1100–1350), southern Sinaloa or northern Nayarit. Dr. Macias collection. Photo by Mauricio Garduño Ambriz. (*f*) Codex-style vessel with deity Xipe Totec (AD 1100–1350), Museo Arqueológico de Mazatlán, Sinaloa. Photos by author unless indicated otherwise.

and Grave Tirado 2019). Each of these provinces had their own political leader, and it is likely they were regularly involved in conflict, much as appears to be the case in accounts from the chronicles of the conquest and pacification of the area (Ortega León and Grave Tirado 2019). For example, in the collection of the Museo Comunitario in Chametla there is a ceramic figurine in the form of a naked prisoner with his hands tied, an object that we can place chronologically to the Baluarte phase between AD 500–750 (Figure 6.5b).

War, human sacrifice, and public festivals were used in prehispanic societies of Mexico as ideological

FIGURE 6.6. Petroglyphs of southern Sinaloa. (*a*) Petroglyphs at Cañón del Burro in the Juantillos tributary arroyo of the Río Presidio, Sinaloa. Probable Aztatlán affiliation. (*b*) Drawing of petroglyphs at Cañón del Burro, Sinaloa. Two of the faces strongly recall the image of Tlaloc. (*c*) Petroglyphs at Las Pintadas in the Río Quelite drainage, Sinaloa. Probable Aztatlán affiliation. Photos by author.

FIGURE 6.7. Human figure on north face of the Piedra del Danzante, near the Río Baluarte, Sinaloa. Baluarte phase (AD 500–750) or Aztatlán affiliation. Photo by author.

mechanisms by the group in power (Grave Tirado 2018a) and, apparently, the southern part of Sinaloa was no exception. The few available data indicate that, from at least AD 500 and 750, there were captives destined for sacrifice at the same time that the construction of the ceremonial buildings began, which presumably would be the venue for periodic festivals. These were the main mechanism to maintain power, especially if they were combined with war and sacrifice.

Public festivals legitimize disorder, a time when anything is allowed. The person in charge of restoring order is the ruler who appears at the moment of climax, that of the sacrifice of the war captives. In southern Sinaloa, several chiefly societies developed during the prehispanic era wherein leaders widely and effectively used the mechanisms of economic, ideological, and military control to retain power.

Notes

1. "An order to many people, therefore, has a very peculiar character. It seeks to make a mass of the majority and, to the extent that this is achieved, it does not arouse fear. The slogan of the orator who imposes a direction upon the gathered individuals has precisely this function and can be considered as an order to many. From the point of view of the mass, which would like to establish itself in a hurry and remain as a unit, such slogans are useful and indispensable. The orator's art is that everything they pursue is vigorously summarized and expressed in slogans that help in the constitution and maintenance of the mass. The orator generates the mass and keeps it alive by means of a higher order. If one has accomplished this, it is hardly significant what they later really demand. The speaker can insult and threaten an agglomeration of individuals in the most terrible way, yet they will love the orator if in this way they manage to form them as a mass"

(Canetti 1983:397). Writing in the mid-1600s, the Jesuit missionary Andrés Pérez de Ribas described political-ritual leaders in the Sinaloa province:

> One of the duties of the sorcerers of whom I have spoken was to preach and deliver extraordinary sermons and speeches [...] It was very common practice among all these nations to have such preachers. They were ordinarily their principales or caciques, especially if they were sorcerers. The role played by such individuals paralleled somewhat that of the priests of the gentiles' idols (Pérez de Ribas 1999:97).

These priests, he added, "truly had a great capacity to move people to do whatever they wished, be it good or evil" (Pérez de Ribas 1999:98).

CHAPTER 7

Was There a Coastal Colony in the Western Valleys of Durango?

Notes on Aztatlán-Chalchihuites Interaction

Cinthya Isabel Vidal Aldana

The end of the 1920s and the beginning of the 1930s marked a milestone in the archaeology of northwest Mexico, particularly in the states of Sinaloa and Durango—territory that until then remained unknown. In 1929, the exploration of the Pacific coastal plain began and, almost simultaneously, so too began studies in the Durango *altiplano* that sought to link prehispanic inhabitants of the coast and *altiplano* with the people and cultures of the southwestern United States (see Figures I.1, I.10; Kelley 1953; Mason 1971; Sauer and Brand 1932).

Since then and even today, at sites in the Durango *altiplano* we continue to find fragments of copper, shell, and ceramics with origins in the Aztatlán complex on the Pacific coast. Traditionally, the presence of these objects, especially ceramics, has been interpreted as being the result of commercial relationships or perhaps even colonization of inland regions by coastal people (Kelley 2000; Kelley and Kelley 1971; Kelley and Winters 1960). In response to this problem, the objective of the present work is to provide a balanced approach to the interpretation of Chalchihuites-Aztatlán links and, at the same time, to propose a new model of such interaction based upon recent studies of decorated ceramics (Gómez Ambríz 2013; Gómez Ambríz and Vidal Aldana 2014; Vidal Aldana 2011).

Coastal Material Culture on the Durango Plateau

The first incidence of foreign material culture in the state of Durango was recorded by J. Alden Mason in Hervideros during his investigation into the maximum scope of the Chalchihuites culture in the northern regions of Mexico. At this site, he found bells and copper earrings, biconical spindle whorls, as well as shell ornaments and beads (Mason 1971). During the same era as Mason's work, Donald Brand observed hemispherical, biconical, and punched spindle whorls in the Zape area that, in his opinion, were very similar to those found at sites on the coastal plain of Nayarit and Sinaloa during the survey he conducted with Carl Sauer (Brand 1971; Sauer and Brand 1932).

Later, during the writing of the Chametla report, Isabel Kelly (1938) reviewed the objects in Mason's study and maintained a correspondence with Brand, ultimately suggesting that the ceramics decorated with red rims found in Durango could well belong to the Aztatlán complex in Sinaloa.[1] Likewise, she pointed out that similarities between ceramics with red-rimmed decorations from the coast and the *altiplano* could account for a fundamental link between these regions (Kelly 1938).

However, the ideas of Isabel Kelly echoed into the 1960s when J. Charles Kelley and Howard Winters revised the Sinaloa sequences and proposed a new chronology with ^{14}C data from La Ferrería, Durango (Kelley and Winters 1960).[2] At La Ferrería, diverse material associated with the Pacific coast included bells, shell pendants, pipes, figurines, a Sinaloa polychrome tripod vessel associated with an Otinapa-type vessel, and at least two burials in funerary urns. Around 1952, Kelley excavated the Weicker site (Santa Bárbara) in the southern part of the Sierra de Durango, which he classified as characteristic of the Loma San Gabriel culture. Michael Foster (1986b) later published the results of the exploration and specified that in addition to finding evidence of the Chalchihuites culture, a conical spindle whorl recovered in the settlement was similar to those recorded by Gordon Ekholm at Guasave.

Another discovery of foreign pottery was found at the Las Ánimas ranch, located in the upper Río Piaxtla, where Michael Spence reported 30 archaeological sites. In La Cueva de los Muertos Chiquitos, Spence

(1978:168) located a series of burials along with a biconical spindle whorl fragment. Likewise, at a site associated with the Madroños complex, he recovered a biconical spindle whorl and a cylindrical ceramic stamp similar to those at Guasave (Spence 1978).[3] On the other hand, at El Cañón del Molino, located near the Laguna de Santiaguillo, Jaime Ganot Rodríguez and Alejandro Peschard Fernández (1997) bought archaeological pieces and recorded Chalchihuites items as well as materials with a coastal affinity. This included ceramics that appear to be a mix of Chalchihuites and Aztatlán ceramic traditions, which they called the Molino type (Ganot Rodríguez and Peschard Fernández 1997). Likewise, they reported funerary urns and human skulls with intentional deformation and dental mutilation, similar to those recorded at Guasave.

For her part, Marie-Areti Hers (1996) reported Chametla Polychrome ceramics at various archaeological sites, from the Laguna de Santiaguillo to Tepehuanes. In addition, she pointed out the discovery of copper objects in Chalchihuites-affiliated sites. Contrary to the proposal of Ganot Rodríguez and Peschard Fernández, Hers (1996) observed a very small Aztatlán presence in Cañón del Molino and stated that the looted pieces were part of funerary contexts.

In relation to the upper Río Ramos, Fernando Berrojalbiz (2012) recorded at least seven foreign ceramic types, all linked to the Pacific coast: one similar to the Amapa Red-on-buff, another similar to Botadero Incised (Aztatlán), one related to White and Red-on-cream Engraved,[4] another analogous to Tuxpan Engraved, one equivalent to Amapa Polychrome, and a fragment of Orange and Black-on-natural[5] and Brown-on-cream Engraved.

Finally, great advances have been made during the twenty-first century in understanding the Chalchihuites-Aztatlán link, mainly thanks to three projects: the *Proyecto de Investigaciones Arqueológicas del Área Centro Oeste de Durango* (PIACOD), the *Proyecto de Investigación y Conservación de las Casas en Acantilado de la Cueva del Maguey, Durango* (PROCUMA) and the *Proyecto Arqueológico Sextín* (PAS). The first of these projects, through several seasons of survey and excavations in addition to the analysis of the archaeological material housed at Southern Illinois University (repatriated to Mexico), studied the coastal presence in the Guadiana Valley through two approaches. On the one hand, José Luis Punzo Díaz and colleagues (2017) analyzed the incidence of foreign ceramics at La Ferrería and reviewed the chronological sequence of the Chalchihuites culture. On the other hand, Cinthya Vidal Aldana (2011) conducted a study on the provenance of vessels associated with the Pacific coastal plain.

Led by Bridget Zavala, the *Proyecto Arqueológico Sextín* undertook research in the little-studied region of northern Durango. A copper bell found at the Corral de Piedra site was attributed to type 11b of Dorothy Hosler's classification system, which corresponds to the time periods AD 800–1200/1300 or AD 1200–1300/1500 (Murguía Hernández 2011; Zavala and Murguía Hernández 2013). On the other hand, Jose Luis Punzo Díaz's (2013) study of cliff houses at Cueva del Maguey in the Sierra Madre Occidental recorded seashells and a crocodile tooth. Finally, coastal evidence was reported during an archaeological salvage project at the Las Humedades site (near La Ferrería) where two burials deposited in a seated position were excavated. One peculiar burial of the two had the remnants of a Lolandis vessel placed between the legs (Punzo Díaz et al. 2012).

From a panoramic viewpoint, it is apparent that the broad scope of materials from the coast extends into the entire area of the western Durango valleys, from south to north, following the course of the rivers that flow into the Pacific Ocean in addition to some points in the sierra—although it must be considered that the latter area has been studied to a lesser extent. The material evidence indicates a connection of great time depth between the inhabitants of both regions, which probably lasted throughout the chronological sequence of both cultural developments (Figure 7.1).

The Western Valleys of Durango: An Inland Aztatlán Colony?

Thus far I have focused on describing evidence that points to Chalchihuites-Aztatlán interactions, but what does it mean on an interpretive level to find such material inland? In general, the proposals on the problem can be grouped into three models: cultural historical, World-Systems, and contemporaneous. The first and second models are those that have endured for some time, while the third model—derived from approaches in other disciplines—is just beginning to be explored.[6]

According to Johnson (2000), the cultural-historical model positions ancient societies as static and quite conservative. Thus, when foreign artifacts are noted in an area of certain affiliation, the materials are interpreted as being derived from the incursion of other cultures by trade, diffusion, or migration. The proposals of both Kelley (Kelley and Kelley 1971; Kelley and Winters 1960) and Ganot Rodríguez and Peschard Fernández (1997) are part of this approach as they consider objects recovered inland, particularly ceramics, as evidence for the foundation of colonies from the Pacific-coastal plain.

The World-Systems model is a mechanism that explains the redistribution of resources of an empire, considering both the center and periphery where the peripheral groups are developing societies and the

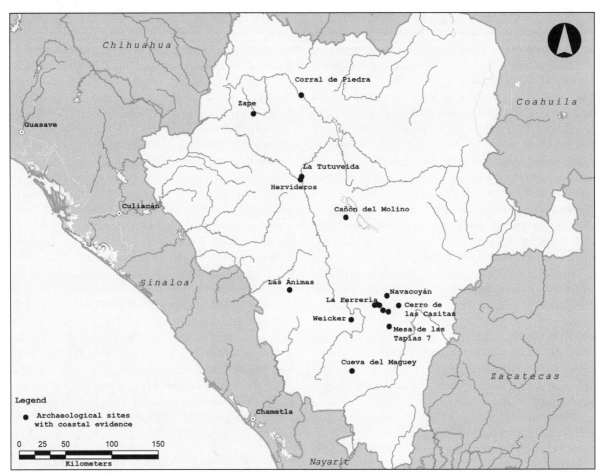

FIGURE 7.1. Archaeological sites in Durango with the presence of Pacific-coastal material culture. Drawing by author.

center is comprised of a developed society (Wallerstein 1974). Although this framework emerged from the analysis of the capitalist world economy, Kelley (2000) used this approach to explain the development of prehispanic societies of Mexico and, from this, proposed the Aztatlán Mercantile System. According to Kelley, this system was comprised of trade routes along various geographical corridors which were responsible for the dissemination of Aztatlán materials in north and west Mexico, mainly during the Postclassic-period horizon (Kelley 2000).[7]

Most recently, the third model emerged as a criticism of these traditional positions and is somewhat more heterogeneous. These are regional works that begin with an analysis of the evidence from the region itself, consider that prehispanic societies are part of dynamic social processes, and interpret the presence of foreign objects as indications of commercial relationships which also involved the exchange of ideas. Likewise, advocates of this approach—taken by the author in the present work—postulate that it is not necessary to consider migrations in order to explain the presence of foreign objects (Gómez Ambríz 2018; Gómez Ambríz and Vidal Aldana 2014; Grave Tirado 2003, 2012e; Vidal Aldana 2011).

TOWARD A NEW INTERPRETATION

Before proposing that ceramic materials in the *altiplano* are foreign, it is essential to know if, in fact, these objects indeed came from the coast (Figure 7.2). Likewise, it is necessary to consider these questions: (1) What were the mechanisms by which the artifacts reached the Durango *altiplano*?, (2) What were the social relations that allowed the movement of objects?, and (3) What was the nature of interaction between the inhabitants of the coast and the *altiplano*?

To address these questions, although limiting consideration only to the connections between the Pacific-coastal plain and the Guadiana Valley, I conducted a study of foreign ceramics through two approaches: macroscopic and microscopic analyses. The first approach consisted of a typological classification of the sherds to roughly delimit the temporal and spatial limits of the coastal presence in the Guadiana Valley. The second approach was based on petrographic analyses of decorated pottery from Durango and Sinaloa to reveal,

FIGURE 7.2. Aztatlán pyriform tripod vessels from Sinaloa and Durango. (*a*) Rollout image of Sinaloa Polychrome recovered by Gordon Ekholm at Guasave, Sinaloa (Ekholm 1942:58, Figure 7k). Courtesy of the Division of Anthropology, American Museum of Natural History. (*b*) Sinaloa Polychrome, Museo Regional de Sinaloa. Photo by Cristian Pérez Herrera. (*c*) Sinaloa polychrome recovered by J. Charles Kelley at La Ferrería, Durango. Archival photo, Instituto Nacional de Antropología e Historia-Durango. (*d*) Aztatlán or Botadero Incised, Museo Regional de Sinaloa. Photo by Cristian Pérez Herrera. (*e*) Iguanas Polychrome, Museo Arqueológico de Mazatlán, Sinaloa. Photo by Emmanuel Gómez Ambríz. Ceramics not to scale.

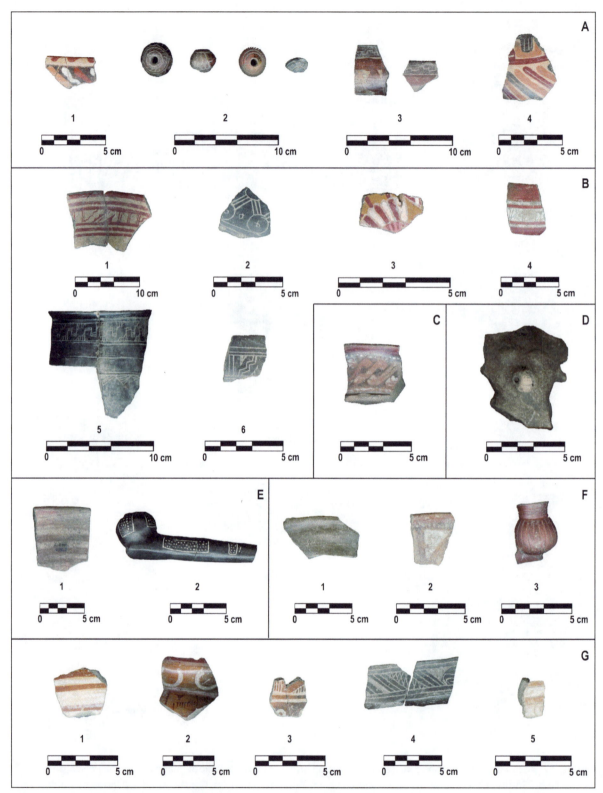

FIGURE 7.3. Foreign ceramics recovered by J. Charles Kelley's team at La Ferrería, Durango (1952–1958). (*A*) Material associated with the Baluarte/Amapa/Ayala phase (circa AD 600–750). (*a-1*) Middle Chametla Polychrome. (*a-2*) Small incised spindle whorls. (*a-3*) Black-banded Engraved. (*a-4*) Middle Chametla Polychrome Engraved. (*B*) Sherds from the Aztatlán complex (circa AD 750–1100). (*b-1*) Red-rimmed Decorated. (*b-2*) Tuxpan Engraved. (*b-3*) Cerro Izabal Engraved. (*b-4*) Aztatlán Ware. (*b-5*) Aguaruto Incised. (*b-6*) Tuxpan Engraved. (*C*) Iguanas Polychrome. (*D*) Smooth-faced figurine, possibly from southern Sinaloa. (*E*) Ceramics without particular temporal association appearing during all phases of the west-coast influence. (*e-1*) Red-rimmed Marbelized. (*e-2*) Punched pipe, Culiacán Valley. (*F*) Fragments of the El Taste/La Divisa phase AD 1100–1250 and La Quinta phase AD 1400–1530. (*f-1*) Dun. (*f-2*) Culiacán Polychrome. (*f-3*) Cocoyolitos pipe. (*G*) Ceramics associated with the Pacific coast. (*g-1* to *g-5*) No type identification. Instituto Nacional de Antropología e Historia, Durango. Photos by author.

FIGURE 7.4. Coastal ceramics registered in the Guadiana Valley at Navacoyán, Durango, by J. Charles Kelley in 1954. Archival photo, Agnes Howard collection, Instituto Nacional de Antropología e Historia, Durango.

as far as possible, the mineralogical origin of the vessels and, at the same time, identify methods and techniques used in the manufacture of the objects (Vidal Aldana 2011).

We know that ceramics from the coast were found in eight locales in the Guadiana Valley: La Ferrería, Navacoyán, Cerro de las Casitas, La Ferrería 6, Plan de Ayala, Puerta de la Cantera 1, Mesa de las Tapias 7, and Las Humedades, which, it is worth mentioning, are some of the most important settlements in the valley (Figure 7.1). La Ferrería contains the greatest diversity of ceramic materials,[8] including Middle Chametla Polychrome (with engraved variety), Black-banded Engraved, Aztatlán Ware, Red-rimmed Decorated, Tuxpan Engraved, Cerro Izábal, Aguaruto Exterior Incised, Iguanas Polychrome, Culiacán Polychrome, and Culiacán Dun. There also is a "Smooth Face" figurine, small, incised spindle whorls, a punched pipe, a Cocoyolitos pipe, sherds of Red-rimmed Utility ware (including "marbelized" variety), and various sherds that could not be classified (Figure 7.3; Vidal Aldana 2011). In Navacoyán, fragments of Middle Chametla Polychrome, Aztatlán Ware, Red-rimmed Decorated, Tuxpan Engraved, El Taste Satin, El Taste Polychrome, Sentispac Polychrome, and a fragment of an annular base (possibly of the Ixcuintla Polychrome type) were identified along with remains of Red-rimmed Utility (*Mano colorada* variety) (Figure 7.4).

During the study of the artifacts from the Plan de Ayala site, only two vessels of the Red-rimmed Decorated type were observed, one with a checkered exterior. At Cerro de las Casitas, a spindle whorl fragment of the Middle Culiacán style was recorded. Red-rimmed Decorated ceramics were reported at Puerta de la Cantera 1, Mesa de las Tapias 7, and Ferrería 6 (Vidal Aldana 2011), while a fragment of a red-rimmed vessel was found at Las Humedades (Punzo Díaz et al. 2011; Punzo Díaz and Sandoval Mora 2012).

Based upon the classification of these materials, preliminary conclusions indicate that two interpretations can be outlined concerning both temporal and spatial perspectives. In the temporal sense, if we begin from the chronological sequence of Kelley and Winters (1960) we see that the earliest evidence of the Chalchihuites-Aztatlán relationship corresponds to AD 600 (Ayala/Baluarte/Amapa phases) and extends until approximately AD 1300, suggesting long-term connections that span almost the entire chronology of both regions. However, most of the sherds are diagnostic of the period between AD 700–1100 at which time the coast-*altiplano* relationship apparently was strengthened along with the florescence of the Aztatlán horizon.

From a spatial perspective, when we consider the stylistic "origin" of the objects, it can be argued that the highland settlements had links with specific coastal regions. Thus, it seems that the Mesa de las Tapias 7, Puerta de la Cantera 1, and Navacoyán sites were only linked with southern Sinaloa and northern Nayarit; Cerro de las Casitas was connected to the Culiacán valley; Plan de Ayala and Ferrería 6 were linked with the Culiacán area or the Río Fuerte valley; and, finally, La Ferrería was related to all of the mentioned areas.

Taking the results of the macroscopic and microscopic analyses into consideration, we may preliminarily conclude that although the coast-*altiplano* link endured for centuries, interaction between both regions was heightened during the period AD 700–1100 as evident in the movement of decorated coastal pottery to these eight sites in the Guadiana Valley. Still, other aspects are important to consider. For example, these

FIGURE 7.5. Ceramics analyzed by Thin Section Petrography. (*a*) Sherds collected from projects by J. Charles Kelley at La Ferrería (Instituto Nacional de Antropología e Historia-Durango) and by José Luis Punzo Díaz in the Guadiana Valley, Durango. (*b*) Sherds recovered by Luis Alfonso Grave Tirado in southern Sinaloa. Photos by author.

settlements have not been studied equally, and only three of them have been excavated (La Ferrería, Plan de Ayala, and Navacoyán). Thus, it is necessary to expand investigations to other sites in the Guadiana Valley to acquire more data, which will enable us to detail further or even modify the interpretations.

After conducting first-hand analyses and with knowledge of Pacific-coastal ceramics from Escuinapa to Guasave, I have found the objects registered in Durango do not completely coincide with the stylistic characteristics of the ceramics of that region. Although it is true that the designs and polychromy are similar, differences in the application of the strokes, the consistency of the paint, the surface finishes, and the color of the slip are evident. An example of this variance is the tripod vessel recovered by Kelley at La Ferrería, which is attributed to the Sinaloa Polychrome type yet originated in the Río Fuerte Valley.

After careful analysis of this piece in comparison to various vessels, this vessel at La Ferrería has greater similarities in designs with the Cerro Izábal type from the Culiacán Valley. However, ultimately it does not fit well with other elements of that style, particularly in color and shape, or with those elements of any other polychrome vessels. In any case, the designs and color scheme close to the rim are reminiscent of Aztatlán or Botadero Incised ceramics, although the style of the three personages arranged around the central part of the vessel does not match graphics of the coastal plain. This vessel appears to include a local adaptation of coastal symbols (Figure 7.2c; Gómez Ambríz 2018).

FINGERPRINTS IN CLAY: FROM PROVENIENCE TO CERAMIC TECHNOLOGY

The results of petrographic studies of decorated sherds from the Guadiana Valley and southern Sinaloa provide insight into the origin of vessels and the technology used in their manufacture.[9] It should be emphasized that the study's sample size was small, and it is undoubtedly necessary to extend this type of analysis to more sherds. Six ceramic fragments from sites in Durango were analyzed: one Middle Chametla polychrome (engraved variety); one Aztatlán and one Iguanas Polychrome recovered at La Ferrería; one Tuxpan Engraved and one El Taste Polychrome collected in Navacoyán; and, finally, a Red-rimmed Decorated (similar to the Guasave Red-on-buff variety) recorded from Plan de Ayala. In relation to the question of origins, it was observed that the temper of five samples possibly comes from the Río Baluarte and Río Acaponeta while the Aztatlán-type minerals were related to the sands of the Río Tunal in Durango. Finally, the components of the Tuxpan Engraved fragment did not resemble any of the sands sampled (Figure 7.5, Table 7.1).

While these results could support the hypothesis of a coastal manufacture and subsequent transfer inland, after observing the stylistic differences between the ceramics of both regions, it is possible that the temper and the objects were manufactured by ceramicists from the Guadiana Valley, perhaps with local clay (Gómez Ambríz and Vidal Aldana 2014).[10] In this sense, the Aztatlán vessel made with temper of the Río Tunal supports the interpretation of a possible adaptation of certain related symbols and ideas between inhabitants of the coastal plain and the Guadiana Valley between AD 600–1300.

The microscopic study of four sherds from southern Sinaloa included the following: one Middle Chametla Polychrome came from the Coacoyolitos site while one Red-rimmed Decorated sherd and one El Taste Satin sherd were collected at La Chicura. In addition to the fourth example, a Red-rimmed Decorated sherd from Chametla, we observed that two of the above (Middle Chametla Polychrome and El Taste Satin) have their mineralogical origin in the Río Acaponeta. The Red-rimmed Decorated sherd from La Chicura is associated with the sands of the Río Baluarte while the elements of the Red-rimmed Decorated sherd from Chametla resemble those of the Río Tunal.

These results allow us to elaborate on two interpretations. First, the potters of the coastal plain did not necessarily use the material resources closest to their community, a factor that informs our understanding of the social relationships maintained within the region.[11] Second, the mineralogical origin of the Red-rimmed sherd from Chametla indicates that this type of pottery was made not only on the coast, which opens the possibility that the exchange of objects (and perhaps ideas) was manifest not just from the coast inland to the *altiplano* but from the *altiplano* to the Sinaloan lowlands.

The data also provide clues to aspects of pottery technology and the *chaîne opératoire* (Table 7.2). In most cases, the ceramicists used a proportion of 75–85 percent clay and 15–25 percent temper, with the exception of materials associated with the Río Acaponeta where the percentage of raw material does not have a specific pattern. In particular, several sherds possessed additional soil sediments in the structure of the clay mixture. The shape of the pores in the paste shows that, in general, the clay was well selected, mixed, and kneaded.

In relation to manufacturing techniques, two patterns were identified. Three of the sherds from southern Sinaloa made with temper from the coastal plain had oriented paste, while three sherds from the Guadiana Valley had no orientation whatsoever, the exception being the Aztatlán-type sherd. The paste from the Red-rimmed Decorated sherd from Chametla, whose mineralogical origin was associated with the Río Tunal, did not show any orientation either. In this regard, I consider three possible interpretations: (1) the vessel was completely manufactured in southern Sinaloa following Guadiana Valley traditions, (2) the paste was prepared in Durango and transported to the coastal plain where the piece was manufactured, or (3) the vessel was completely manufactured in the *altiplano* and then transported to Chametla. Whatever the case, this data broadens our perspective on interactions between populations of the coast and *altiplano*.

On the other hand, we observed a very fine base or slip on the surface of all analyzed sherds (except for the

TABLE 7.1. Provenance of Aztatlán ceramics in southern Sinaloa and Durango.

Sherd/Sand Sample	Quartz	Plagioclase	Potassium-Feldspar	Intergrowth of quartz-feldspar	Micas	Amphibole-pyroxene
Sherds collected in the Guadiana Valley, Durango						
Middle Chametla Polychrome Engraved	XXXX	XXX		XXX		XX
Tuxpan Engraved	XX	XXX			XX	XXXX
Aztatlán	XXXX	XXX		XXX		
Red-rimmed Decorated	XXXX	XX	XXX	XX		
Iguanas Polychrome	XXXX	XXX	XX	XXX	XX	X
El Taste Polychrome	XX	XXXX				XX
Sherds collected in Southern Sinaloa						
Middle Chametla Polychrome	XXX	XXX	XXX	XXX	XX	XXX
Red-rimmed Decorated (from Chametla)	XXXX	XXXX			XXX	X
Red-rimmed Decorated (from La Chicura)	XXXX		XXXX		XX	XX
El Taste Satin	XXXX	XXX			XX	XX
Samples of sand						
Río San Pedro, Nayarit	XXXX	XXX	XXX	XXXX	XXX	X
Río Acaponeta, Nayarit	XXXX				XXX	XX
Río Baluarte, Sinaloa	XXX	XXX	XXX		XX	XX
Río Presidio, Sinaloa	XXX	XXX	XXX	XXXX	XXX	XXX
Río Tunal, Durango	XXXX			XXX		XX

Legend: XXXX – Abundant; XXX – Present; XX – Few; Trace – X.

Middle Chametla Polychrome), comprised of the same sediment as the paste, upon which the decoration was drawn. In contrast, the Chametla samples had a thick slip made from a clay different from that of the paste to which a paint made with clay minerals and iron oxide was applied.

Finally, using a petrographic microscope, we observed that eight of the analyzed sherds were fired under a reduced atmosphere. Only the El Taste Satin and El Taste Polychrome sherds showed a partially oxidized environment, which confirms the use of open-air kilns (*hornos*) for firing the objects. However, it was noted that care was taken to reach a higher temperature for certain pieces, which resulted in an enhanced degree of hardness.

In sum, the results of the petrographic study indicate no temporal or typological differences regarding the manufacture of the analyzed ceramics. It seems that the production of the pieces is related to the raw material, that is, the method depended on the origin of the temper. In this sense, two manufacturing patterns were observed: one involved sherds with temper from the Río Tunal while the other involved temper associated with the Río Baluarte. In the case of the Río Acaponeta, the evidence does not present a clear trend. However, it is also feasible that after obtaining the raw material, the vessels were made in accordance with local pottery traditions. This perspective created a new question: Why did potters carry or bring temper from other regions if they had closer deposits? From my point of view, the regional historical and ethnographic data can shed light on this problem.

According to Arturo Gutiérrez del Ángel (2002), the Wixárika (Huichol) collect natural materials during their pilgrimages to Wirikuta in San Luis Potosí, including peyote, flowers, grass, and water, and bring them home to their communities. Later, during rituals, they transform them from a natural state to a cultural one. In the same way, Olivia Kindl (2003:79) noted that "the technical process of artisanal manufacturing is linked to ritualized collective actions, mainly in the case of ceremonial and votive bowls (my translation)." Theoretically, all Wixárika can and should make their bowls (*jícaras*), but only the *mara'akame* has the specific knowledge on how to make them, since through dreams "he receives messages and instructions from the ancestors regarding its elaboration (my translation)" (Kindl 2003:79). If we extrapolate from the ethnographic example for the prehispanic era, it is feasible to conclude that potters made their technical decisions in accor-

Table 7.1. (cont'd.) Provenance of Aztatlán ceramics in southern Sinaloa and Durango.

Volcanic Rocks	Glass	Iron Oxide	Shale	Garnet	Chalcedony	Grain with reaction halo	Minerals of the Epidote group
XXX	X		X				
XX		XX		X			X
XXXX		XX			X	X	
XXX	X	XX					
XXX		XX					
XXX	XXX						
XXX		XXXX					X
XXX		X			X		
XX		XXXX					
XX							X
XX	XX	XXX					
XX	X	XXX					X
XXXX		X					
XXXX	X						
		XX	XXX			XX	XX

From the Coast to the Valley... and Back?

Thus far we have focused our attention on archaeological objects independently, but we turn now to the real heart of the matter: people. If we begin from a traditional perspective (form/function), the purpose of ceramics was their use wherein the vessels are nothing more than containers. However, in accord with the characteristics observed under the microscope, these artifacts were not suitable for storing liquids or heating food on a daily basis. In addition, these types of activities would have damaged the decoration of the objects, and for this reason we might rule out their "profane" use.

Decorated pottery is regularly found in archaeological contexts at large settlements along the Pacific coast and is often associated with funerary contexts, for example in southern Sinaloa and the Culiacán Valley (Carballal et al. 1994; Gálvez 1968; Kelly 1938, 1945a; Vicente López 2004, 2005; Vidal Aldana 2018), Guasave (Carpenter 2008; Ekholm 1942), Amapa (Meighan, ed. 1976), and the Marismas Nacionales (Gill 1971; Grave Tirado 2000), to name a few examples. In the Guadiana Valley, these materials also have been found with burials, particularly at La Ferrería (Kelley 1954a, 1954b; 1956) and Las Humedades (Punzo Díaz et al. 2012). However, at the moment the only recorded context where a conjunction of Chalchihuites-Aztatlán artifacts is undoubtedly reflected is with the Sinaloa Polychrome vessel found alongside an Otinapa vessel at La Casa de los Dirigentes, which was excavated in 1954 during the Southern Illinois University project led by J. Charles Kelley (Figure 7.6a).

In light of these data, this discovery can be interpreted as the meeting of two complementary oppositions. On the one hand, the presence of the Aztatlán vessel indicates the physical (and possibly ritual) transfer of properties from the west coast to the highlands while the Chalchihuites vessel serves as a microcosm (Gómez Ambríz 2013) in which, contrary to the "foreign" coastal artifact, the basket-style handle emphasizes the importance of the pathway of the sun from east to west.

In the case of the physical properties of the west, it is possible that carrying (or bringing) an object from the

Commentary: The text mentions that Wixárika in the recent past still made clay bowls, or *jícaras* (Kindl 2003:64; see Mathiowetz, this volume).

TABLE 7.2. Manufacturing technologies of Aztatlán ceramics.

Provenance of the sample			Durango	Durango	Sinaloa	Durango	Sinaloa	Durango	Durango	Sinaloa	Sinaloa
		Sherds	Middle Chametla Polychrome Engraved (La Ferreria site)	Iguanas Polychrome (La Ferreria site)	Red-rimmed Decorated (La Chicura site)	Aztatlán (La Ferreria site)	Red-rimmed Decorated (Chametla site)	Red-rimmed Decorated, similar to Guasave (Plan de Ayala site)	El Taste Polychrome (Navacoyán site)	Middle Chametla Polychrome (Coacoyolitos site)	El Taste Satin (La Chicura site)
Mineralogical provenance		Río Acaponeta, Nayarit						X	X	X	X
		Río Baluarte, Sinaloa	X	X	X		X				
		Río Tunal, Durango				X					
Porosity		% Matrix	80	85	80–85	75–80	75	75	85	80–85	60–70
	Size	Medium to thick	X	X	X	X	X				X
		Thin to medium						X		X	
		Heterogeneous							X		
	Shape	Planar				X		X			
		Channel		X		X			X	X	X
		Vesicular	X	X	X		X		X	X	X
	Striations	Present	X	X	X	X	X	X	X	X	X
		Absent									
	Orientation	With orientation			X	X				X	X
		Grid structure		X							
		No orientation	X				X	X	X		
	Color	Homogeneous							X		X
		Transitional	X		X	X				X	
		Differential		X							
Slip		Evident	X		X		X	X		X	X
		Transitional		X		X	X	X	X		
Organic remains		Present	X	X	X		X	X	X		X
		Absent				X				X	

FIGURE 7.6. (*a*) Otinapa vessel with Sinaloa polychrome vessel. Structure 1 (Casa de los Dirigentes), La Ferrería, Durango. Archival photo, Southern Illinois University and Instituto Nacional de Antropología e Historia-Durango. (*b*) Nevería-type vessel with basket handle located near House 1, La Ferrería, Durango. Photo by author (see Punzo et al. 2011:167).

coast to the highlands in turn implied the transfer of humidity and rain, elements that were crucial for seasonal agriculture practiced by the residents of the Guadiana Valley (Punzo Díaz 2014). Observations made by Carl Lumholtz (1902) among the Wixárika at the beginning of the twentieth century support this perspective:

> When a temple is to be built, six stones, supposed to be male and female, are brought from the sea. Of these, one pair is buried under the fireplace, the second under the altar, and the third under the doorway. The Indians believe that, as these stones have been in the water, they will draw water after them (Lumholtz 1902:2:195).

On the other hand, the Sinaloa Polychrome vessel may refer to the west as a ritual geographic marker possibly associated with the place of the dead, whose path, like the sun, has a westward-facing direction (Oseguera et al. 2015; Rangel Guzmán 2008). The Otinapa pot reemphasizes this idea through its arching basket handle, thought to represent the pathway of the sun. In the Southern Illinois University archives there are no specific notes on the discovery of these vessels, and the photographs lack scale and a north arrow. However, the hypothesis that the handle of the Otinapa vessel represents the pathway of the sun is feasible because a piece (although of the Neveria type) with similar characteristics was recently found at La Ferrería in which the assemblage had an east-west orientation (Figure 7.6b; Punzo Díaz et al. 2011).

The association of the coast with the place of the dead is found in the earliest historical sources of the sierra, and these ideas remain part of the worldview of Indigenous groups of the Gran Nayar region. Their accounts of the road of the dead, the healing of the sick, funeral rituals, and ritual geographies present a cosmogonic and commercial route from east to west that ends in the Marismas Nacionales, the final destination of souls (Leal Carretero 1992; Oseguera et al. 2015; Preuss 1998a, 1998b; Rangel Guzmán 2008; Reyes Valdez 2013).[12] The route to the west is associated with death while the coastal plain is the place of "below" in the cosmos, which is linked to humidity, femininity, and unbridled fertility. However, it is also the place where the world originated and from where emerged the primeval fire (Jáuregui and Magriñá 2013; Preuss 1998a, 1998c; Sánchez Olmedo 1980; Zingg 2004). In contrast, the east is associated with the sunrise, the "above", and life (Gutiérrez del Ángel 2002; Neurath 2002; Neurath et al. 2003).

Archaeological evidence, such as ceramic iconography and the architectural arrangement of the pyramid at La Ferrería, indicate that prehispanic people in the Guadiana Valley viewed their world in a similar way to that of contemporary groups in the Gran Nayar, which is based on the summer-rain cycle and annual solar transit (Gómez Ambríz 2013; Punzo Díaz 2014). In this sense, I contend that the presence of coastal pottery in the highlands is an indication that groups on the Pacific coastal plain also shared these belief systems, which is also evident in other objects such as vessels and effigy pipes (Gómez Ambríz and Vidal Aldana 2014). From my perspective, support for these hypotheses can be found in historical records which mention that the Totorame (the inhabitants of the coastal plain at the time of contact) sent their first fruits to the Nayarit (the Náayeri King) along with feathers, shell, and cotton. In addition, they also traveled to the Mesa del Nayar to ask for the favor of rain and participated in *mitote* rites in the sierra (Arias de Saavedra 1990 [1673]:305).

In my estimation, this evidence indicates that, despite the long interval of time and the transformations that have occurred since the incursion of European culture, regional history is best viewed on a long-term scale. By observing the permanence of certain cultural practices among Indigenous groups of the Gran Nayar, it is possible to draw upon some analogies for interpretations of the past. First, social relations during the prehispanic era likely did not occur only between populations inhabiting the coast and valleys, but also likely involved the inhabitants of the sierra since the rugged geography did not represent any barrier to developing commercial, political, and religious relationships. In this sense, it is feasible that the exchange between residents of the coastal plain and the Guadiana Valley occurred due to a real need for objects and raw materials and because the people of both regions had similar conceptions about what was valuable. However, these links likely involved an exchange of ideas and perhaps even a similar shared cosmogony. My perspective is that both regions impacted each other in that things, people, and ideas moved from the coast to the valley and back, as well as to the sierra—perhaps as a point of cosmological and commercial union.

By comparing data from the archaeology, historical sources, and ethnological record, I propose that while exchange systems may have been a function of satisfying the need for unavailable products from one side of the sierra to the other, these linkages may be inseparable from other social relationships such as kinship or the establishment of political and/or military strategies. This conclusion is based on the fact that the agents involved shared a similar cosmogony, which in turn established a related conceptualization of the valuation of things. With this assessment, I do not mean to say that groups in the *altiplano*, the sierra, and the coast had a single identity or that it was a single culture, but that they had similar ideas about the world they experienced, the limits of the cosmos, the origin of the universe, the annual ritual cycle, and the conception that there are human and non-human beings, among other elements that are represented in the archaeological record.

The potential routes between the coast and *altiplano* that Kelley (2000) identified as branches of the Aztatlán Mercantile System, in addition to being a function of a commercial exchange, could relate to cosmogonic routes oriented from east to west. This proposed route may have followed the path both the sun and the dead would have traveled, where the west (and the sea) was their final resting place. However, this route also would have extended from west to east such that a pilgrimage to the place where the sun rises in the east would help to bring moisture and fertility to the dry lands of the *altiplano*, much as is known for Indigenous groups of the Gran Nayar today (Vidal Aldana and Gómez Ambríz 2017). During the prehispanic era, the Sierra Madre—rather than being a barrier between the coast and the valley—may have been a point of union which allowed for the circulation of objects, ideas, and people both in the direction of the coastal plain and vice versa.

Conclusion

With this study, two objectives were achieved: on the one hand, we find that coastal influence extended to the western valleys of Durango (especially in the Guadiana Valley). This presence developed throughout the entire Chalchihuites occupation sequence and was mainly associated with southern Sinaloa and northern Nayarit. On the other hand, we have managed to make some small advances on tracing the origin of "foreign" ceramics, now having the decorated vessels made both on the coastal plain and the highlands (Vidal Aldana 2017). By combining both results, I propose that the designs of the vessels located in Durango could be local interpretations of those produced on the Pacific coast. Thus, it is necessary to expand the analysis of petrographic samples to determine the mineralogical origin of more objects. In addition, we must expand iconographic analyses of coastal vessels to determine the similarities and differences in pottery production, such as the reproduction of certain symbols during specific periods, following the proposal of Gómez Ambríz (2018). Furthermore, it is imperative to conduct archaeological research in the intermontane valleys of Sinaloa, an area which until now remains practically unexplored (Grave et al. 2015; Grave et al. 2016; Vidal Aldana 2018) but has great potential for data from this region to broaden perspectives on Chalchihuites-Aztatlán connections.

Finally, returning to the question that gave rise to this work: Was there an Aztatlán colony in the western valleys of Durango? I consider that ceramics by themselves are insufficient evidence to answer in the affirmative. Instead, the presence and/or production of objects beyond the sierra shows us that the prehispanic inhabitants of both the coast and the valley knew and experienced a shared world, which was linked with people from near and distant regions. More studies are needed that consider other materials and interdisciplinary research which would provide a more fine-grained perspective on the ways in which, since AD 600, the inhabitants of the coastal plain, the sierra, and the *altiplano* maintained constant contact.

Notes

1. This ceramic type was named Lolandis by Kelley and Kelley (1971).
2. In their text, Kelley and Winters (1960) stated that the chronologies of the coast and the *altiplano* are contemporaneous, although the greatest interaction occurred mainly during the expansion of the Aztatlán complex between AD 700–1100.
3. In my opinion, after observing the image of the cylindrical ceramic stamp, the piece has a greater affinity with objects from private collections in the Culiacán valley.
4. This piece was originally recorded by Gámez (2004) in the Río Acaponeta delta in Nayarit.
5. In my opinion, this type is similar to Middle Chametla Polychrome.
6. Due to space constraints, I have limited the Chalchihuites-Aztatlán interpretive models to three. However, the works of Vidal Aldana (2011) and Gómez Ambríz (2018) can be reviewed for more detail on the study area.
7. For a more detailed and current study of Mesoamerican World-Systems, please consult the work of Jiménez (2018).
8. In this case, the repatriated materials from the Southern Illinois University project were analyzed while the rest of the ceramics analyzed were recovered at sites by the *Proyecto de Investigaciones Arqueológicas del Área Centro Oeste de Durango* (PIACOD).
9. See Vidal Aldana (2011) for details on the methodology, description of thin sections, and discussion of results on the mineralogical origin of the ceramics.
10. Based on Ohnersorgen's (2007) study of Aztatlán ceramics from Nayarit, it is plausible that potters obtained clays from both local and foreign sources and when preparing the clay mixed them with temper brought from other places.
11. This corresponds with the results obtained by Reitzel Rivera (2012) in the case of ceramics from northern Nayarit.
12. In the historical sources there is mention of trade routes that extended from the coast to the mountains:

The Totorames sold fish and shrimp, dried and salted, to the mountain and coastal towns, and the trade reached Durango [...] In addition to agricultural products (corn, beans, chili, and various fruits)—highly valued by the sierra towns—they exchanged textile products (clothing, blankets, fabrics), shells, snails, pearls, as well as diverse objects of gold, silver, and copper [my translation] (Álvarez et al. 2005:66).

In the same way, people were noted to walk from the mountains to the highlands. For example, the Náayeri (Cora) were said to "go to the Súchil Valley in Poana and other tasks in this Kingdom to work at the harvest time [my translation]" (del Barrio 1990 [1604]:290). It is also mentioned that "there were many Ladino baptized people among these who, as I have said, enter and leave the land of Guadiana [my translation]" (del Barrio 1990 [1604]:265).

CHAPTER 8

Interaction and Integration on the Northern Aztatlán Frontier in Sinaloa

John P. Carpenter and Guadalupe Sánchez

The region of Culiacán, Sinaloa, represents the maximum northern expansion of the Aztatlán archaeological tradition of western Mexico, with characteristic traits that include polychrome vessels with depictions of Mesoamerican deities, clay pipes, modeled spindle whorls, and other diagnostic material culture. The archaeological record suggests that there is continuity of settlements between Aztatlán societies and the early historic-period Tahue that inhabited the Culiacán valley during the sixteenth century. The Tahue are the southernmost group of the Cahita linguistic family. Cahitan-speaking groups spread from the coastal plain and *serrana* of northern Sinaloa and southern Sonora (including Mayos and Yaquis) to the Opata territory in the parallel valleys of central and northeast Sonora. Based on archaeological and ethnographic data, we propose that dissimilar communities such as Paquimé (Chihuahua) and Culiacán (central Sinaloa) could reflect the opposite nodes of a single tenuous linguistic continuum. This situation would have permitted the movement and exchange of products, ideas, and information between societies in western and northwest Mexico and the southwestern United States. Herein we explore the variety of social-political and economic effects of Tahue cultural continuity and the relationship with other Cahita groups that facilitated social interactions and the transmission of objects and ideas along the coastal plain and *serrana baja* in northwest Mexico during the prehispanic era (Figures I.1, 8.1).

The Aztatlán Complex in Sinaloa

The earliest evidence for occupation amid the mangrove lagoons in southern Sinaloa and Nayarit is represented by maritime hunter-fisher-gatherers who exploited mollusks, birds, and sea mammals beginning between approximately 2000 and 1500 BC. Scott and Foster (2000) suggest that cultigens such as melon, squash, and maize, along with agave, were cultivated in the Teacapan estuary by 1750 BC. Foster and Scott (2017:Table II) list the three corrected radiocarbon determinations from the mound, including sample S.I. 1540 as 3235±110 years (with a one Sigma range of 1755–1355 BC); sample S.I. 1541 as 3265±75 years (with a one Sigma range of 1788–1488 BC); and sample S.I. 1542 as 3845±85 years (with a one Sigma range of 2640–2090 BC). However, Foster and Scott's recalibration does not apparently account for the differential absorption of carbon by marine shell. Following Stuiver and Braziunas (1993), the one Sigma range for sample S.I. 1540 is 1247–922 BC; sample S.I. 1541 provides a one Sigma range of 1240–1009 BC; and sample S.I. 1542 yielded a one Sigma range of 1938–1719 BC. Averaging the three radiocarbon values results in a one Sigma range of 1611–1495 BC.

These results place the Cerro el Calón mound slightly later than previously reported, although, if the dates hold, it would still be among the oldest pyramidal constructions yet known in Mexico. Recently, Alfonso Grave Tirado of the Instituto Nacional de Antropología e Historia Centro Sinaloa has begun investigations anew at El Calón, and a date obtained from this work indicates that the site had a long occupation that extended until the Aztatlán period (Grave Tirado 2012b, Chapter 6, this volume). The relationship of the early Marismas people to populations of the Matanchén complex in Nayarit is uncertain, although both regions reflect relatively similar maritime adaptations that Mountjoy (1974b:117) compares to the historic-period Seri of the central coast of Sonora. However, the San Blas complex is apparently entirely absent from Sinaloa, and the Teacapan region was apparently abandoned ca. 1100 BC. In southern Sinaloa, the initial appearance of a ceramic tradition around AD 250 follows a presumed hiatus in occupation of some 1,300 years and postdates the appearance of pottery in coastal Nayarit by approximately 1,000 years.

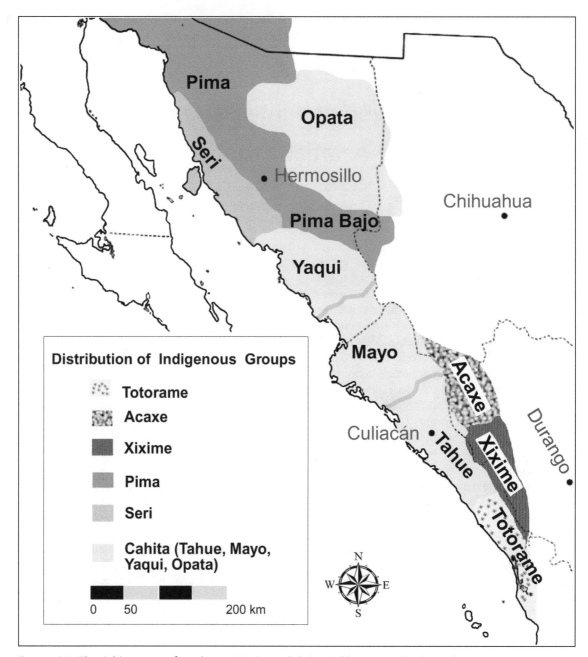

FIGURE 8.1. The Cahita group of northwest Mexico and their neighbors. Drawing by authors.

The archaeological evidence for the Aztatlán complex in Sinaloa is mostly limited to ceramic descriptions and burial data. The earliest ceramics, found at Chametla and in the Marismas Nacionales, reflect a fully developed pottery tradition with plain wares, Red-on-buff, and elaborate polychrome types. The entire Chametla ceramic series is clearly related to corresponding types at Amapa (Grosscup 1976). Grosscup (1976:267–272) argues for the long-term in situ development of local ceramic traditions that he, in turn, relates to broader ceramic developments throughout west Mexico. Settlement patterns closely reflect that observed during the sixteenth-century Guzmán *entrada*, with communities lining the floodplains of the principal rivers and estuaries. The limited site descriptions suggest a *ranchería* pattern of dispersed households. The only evidence for internal site structure comes from the Culiacán region where the distribution of either trash mounds or house mounds seemingly indicates defined plaza spaces or individual residential compounds (Kelly 1945a).

Evidence for domestic architecture is relegated to the plastered cobble pavement reported by Cabrero (1989) in Culiacán, and the few postholes encountered by Kelly (1945a) at the nearby Las Lomitas site. Again, this likely indicates the construction of reed and thatch houses such as those described by the Spaniards at contact. The El Calón mound in the Marismas Nacionales, the small, truncated pyramid and the ballcourts reported by Sauer and Brand and Grave, and the El Ombligo mound represent the only ceremonial features thus far identified. Additionally, small low mounds identified as either house or trash mounds are found between Culiacán and Nayarit. However, no significantly large sites that can be identified as central places have been reported (Vidal Aldana 2018). Subsistence data are equally limited. In addition to the early cultigens noted in the Marismas Nacionales, maize and squash were recovered from Culiacán (Kelly 1945a:156). Residue found within pipe bowls at Guasave may indicate the cultivation of tobacco (Ekholm 1942:85). Spindle whorls appear in the late Middle Chametla phase and become ubiquitous during the following Aztatlán Red-rimmed phase and are undoubtedly associated with the cultivation of cotton. Gathered resources are largely restricted to several species of molluscs. Both fish and fly eggs were found as funerary offerings at Guasave (Ekholm 1942:117).

Within Sinaloa, the normative Aztatlán mortuary practice was to place the disarticulated remains of the deceased within large plainware funerary *ollas*, although primary extended inhumations, flexed burials, and secondary bundle burials also occur. Although *olla* burials occur in the initial levels at Chametla, the data suggest that they follow an earlier horizon characterized by extended inhumations at both Culiacán and Guasave and were never common practice in the Teacapan estuary sites. The two historic-period *olla* burials recovered from Kelly's excavations at Aguaruto (Hulse 1945:198) demonstrate continuity of this practice among the Tahue. The regional variability noted by Sauer and Brand (1932) appears to be based largely upon chronological differences between the Chametla and Culiacán areas.

An overreliance upon widely dispersed regional perspectives has resulted in several disparate chronological schemes, which can be attributed to both variability in local developmental sequences and in the use of widely varying dating methods. Except for several radiocarbon dates from the Marismas Nacionales, ceramic cross-dating and obsidian hydration have figured most prominently in establishing the chronology for coastal northwest Mexico. Chronological estimates for Aztatlán materials range anywhere from AD 600 to 1400 (Ekholm 1942, 1947; Foster 1995; Grosscup 1976; Kelley and Foster 1992; Kelley and Winters 1960; Meighan 1971; Meighan, ed. 1976).

Another problem arising from these investigations is that no unanimous concept of "Aztatlán" has emerged; this term has been variously employed to describe a geographical region (Sauer and Brand 1932), a ceramic horizon (Ekholm 1940, 1942; Grosscup 1976; Kelly 1938, 1945a), a cultural complex (Ekholm 1942; Sauer and Brand 1932), a time period (Kelley and Winters 1960), and a mercantile system (Kelley 1986; Kelley and Foster 1992; Publ 1985, 1990). This situation prompted Grosscup (1976:249) to suggest that the concept of an "Aztatlán complex" should either be redefined or discontinued as an unwieldy and ill-defined concept.

As originally defined by Sauer and Brand (1932), the Aztatlán complex referred to both a geographical region corresponding to the contact-period *provincias* of Aztatlán and Culiacán and the predominant archaeological assemblages found there. Kelly (1938:19, 36) initially applied the term "Aztatlán" to pottery types having a red-banded rim with "a white band bearing sharply and neatly incised geometric motifs," although she subsequently expanded the term as a "complex" which included the Aztatlán ware, Red-rim decorated ware, Black-on-buff, and Cocoyolitos Polychrome. As Grosscup (1976:248) notes, Kelly is essentially defining a ceramic phase. Several scholars, including Ekholm (1942: 52–55), followed Kelly in assigning stylistically similar ceramics to an Aztatlán complex. Eventually, Kelley (1980; Kelley and Foster 1992) and others (Di Peso 1979; Publ 1985, 1990) added a host of traits to the complex, including copper implements, spindle whorls, elbow and stemmed smoking pipes, cylinder stamps, clay masks, and cranial deformation. The presumed core area of the Aztatlán complex extends along the coast from Guasave in the north to approximately Bahía de Banderas (Puerto Vallarta) in Jalisco, with Aztatlán-derived trade goods and/or stylistically similar traits found further inland ranging from south-central Durango to Lake Chapala on the Jalisco-Michoacán border.

Whatever interpretation of Aztatlán is employed, it is unanimously accepted as the northernmost extension of Mesoamerican society that penetrated the region of northwestern Mexico. The stimulus for this northward advance has been variously attributed to migration (Ekholm 1940, 1942; Gill 1971; Weigand 1982); climatic amelioration which extended the northern range of *temporal* farming (Braniff 1975; Wolf 1959); and/or the development of long-distance exchange systems modeled after Aztec *pochteca*, which incorporated elements of Wallerstein's (1974) World-Systems model (Braniff 1992; Di Peso et al. 1974; Kelley 1995; Kelley and Foster 1992; Pailes and Whitecotton 1979; Publ 1985, 1990; Wilcox 1986b; Wilcox et al. 2008). The archaeological evidence, however, does not support large-scale migration of populations from central Mexico, such as that proposed by Ekholm (1942). Subsequent work has both demonstrated that Mixteca-Puebla traits are widespread throughout Postclassic Mexico and failed to produce tangible evidence for significant population movement in the intervening areas. Moreover, as Grosscup (1976:250) notes, the "gradual development" of the Aztatlán ceramic tradition can be seen in the Lolandis phase at Chametla and the equivalent Tuxpan phase at Amapa and can no longer be attributed to diffusion from the Basin of Mexico. Recent work in the Culiacán Valley by Vidal (2018) also shows a long Aztatlán ceramic tradition that began at least by AD 400.

Although environmental changes may have influenced agricultural productivity and settlement patterns on a microregional level, there is presently no evidence to suggest that fluctuating climate affected settlement patterns at the regional scale. Along the coastal plain from Amapa to the Río Yaqui, site distributions and ethnohistoric data suggest that agricultural production was primarily linked to floodplain farming dependent upon fluvial processes, although temporal farming also was practiced in southern Sinaloa and Nayarit. In the more arid interior highlands from southern Zacatecas to the Durango-Chihuahua border, the spatial and temporal distribution of Loma San Gabriel sites and historic O'dam (Tepehuan) communities demonstrates that this region was continuously occupied by sedentary agriculturalists from approximately 100 BC onward.

Most recently, interpretations have centered on the concept of an Aztatlán mercantile system in attempts to interpret the Aztatlán complex, explain the northwestern expansion of Mesoamerican society, and provide a model for interaction and integration between Mesoamerica and the southwestern United States. According to this interpretation, the dispersed resources of the U.S. Southwest and northern Mexico were ultimately connected via a long chain of gateway communities (e.g., trading centers or *entrepots*) with the Mixteca-Puebla center of Cholula, located in the southeastern corner of the Basin of Mexico (Kelley 1995; Kelley and Foster 1992; Publ 1985, 1990).

The Aztatlán mercantile system is characterized in terms of early (AD 900 to 1200) and late (AD 1200 to 1500) periods. The widespread distribution of Aztatlán ceramics in the highlands of Durango, Zacatecas, and Jalisco and south along the Pacific coast during the early period is attributed to the formation of long-distance exchange networks organized by *pochteca*-like mobile merchants, or *trocadores*, from the Aztatlán region of southern Sinaloa, perhaps at Chametla (Kelley 1995; Kelley and Foster 1992). These early Aztatlán *trocadores* are believed to have established trade centers, or nascent gateway communities, throughout much of west and northwestern Mexico, including Guasave, with the interaction sphere eventually reaching as far north as Paquimé (Chihuahua), Wind Mountain and Chaco Canyon (New Mexico), and the Hohokam communities of the Salt-Gila Basin in Arizona (Kelley 1995; Kelley and Foster 1992).

In addition to pottery, other items including marine shell, pearls, dried fish, smoked shrimp, salt, obsidian, and agricultural produce have been suggested as the principal Aztatlán goods which were exchanged for minerals, precious rocks, dried buffalo meat and hides, prickly pear fruits (*tunas*), and agave and sotol products (Kelley 1995; Kelley and Foster 1992:11; Mountjoy 1995; Publ 1985:48, 1990:223–226). An integral aspect of this model is the argument that the institutionalization of trade both led to the development of increasingly complex sociopolitical organization in the core (Aztatlán) area and ultimately produced elites in the peripheral communities (Kelley and Foster 1992:18; Publ 1985:180, 1990:232–234). According to Kelley (1980, 1983), this system most certainly required "some degree of state involvement."

The most elaborately furnished burial at Guasave (Feature 29)—an adult male of large stature interred with more than 2,000 shell beads, 87 copper crotals, 19 shell bracelets, 18 pottery vessels, two trophy skulls, and a bone dagger—has been identified as a *pochteca* (Frisbie 1978:222; Kelley 1995:108–109). Kelley (1995) suggested that the El Ombligo mound was initially constructed as a monumental tomb for this individual. The current dating of the Aztatlán mercantile system suggests it was operating until the beginning of the sixteenth century. Publ (1985, 1990) proposed that the trade goods observed by the early Spanish explorers represented the last manifestation of the interaction sphere. However, the northern limits of Mesoamerican society encountered by the Spanish are placed at Culiacán (Kelly 1945a). This retraction of the Mesoamerican frontier from Guasave to Culiacán is attributed to the incursion of Cahitan-speaking peoples who were thought to have begun descending from the Sierra Madre sometime around AD 1200 (Braniff 1975, 1992; Kelly 1945a:160; Wilcox 1986b). Kelly summarized this position some 50 years ago:

> Certain it is that this rich Guasave culture cannot be attributed to the peoples who held this area at the time of the conquest. Clearly, there was a retraction of high culture in preconquest times and a subsequent occupation by the seminomadic Cáhita. It may be suggested that, in Culiacán terms, this demise of high culture in the north occurred during Early II and before the development of Early I (1945a:160).

As previously noted, this interpretation is contradicted by linguistic data suggesting that the Cahita may have occupied the coastal plain by the beginning of the

Christian era. More critically, this interpretation ignores the fact that the presumably "Mesoamerican" Tahue who occupied the Culiacán province at the moment of Spanish contact were also a Cahitan-speaking people.

The ceramic-period archaeology of Sinaloa is represented by at least two major complexes. The Huatabampo tradition, extending along the coastal plain from approximately Culiacán north to the Río Yaqui (Carpenter et al. 2023) region of south-central Sonora, appears to have arisen from the San Pedro phase of the Cochise Archaic tradition shortly before the beginning of the Christian era (Álvarez Palma 1990). San Pedro-phase assemblages are tentatively identified in a widespread distribution along both flanks of the Sierra Madre Occidental from southern Durango north into southern Arizona and southwestern New Mexico, and presumably reflect Late Archaic maize horticulturalists who gave rise to several other traditions, including the Río Sonora, Loma San Gabriel, Trincheras, Mogollon, and Hohokam. The Serrana tradition and, perhaps, the Tacuichamona tradition appear to share a particularly close affinity with the Huatabampo tradition, and may reflect little more than regional *serrana* and lowland variants. The "Rasped ware" sites found along the central coast near Culiacán may also reflect a related tradition. Although no protohistoric period Huatabampo sites have yet been identified, continuity with the historic Cahita of the coastal plain can be suggested.

The Aztatlán complex refers to a distinctive set of material traits characterized primarily by Red-on-buff and polychrome ceramics, stemmed smoking pipes, ceramic masks, modeled spindle whorls, and copper objects, which have a maximum distribution along the coastal plain between approximately Puerto Vallarta and Mochicahui, on the Río Fuerte. The Aztatlán ceramic tradition appears to have developed in the region spanning the Sinaloa-Nayarit border around AD 200 and can be linked to the broader west Mexican ceramic traditions found throughout Nayarit, Jalisco, western Michoacán, and Colima.

The widespread distribution of these traits coupled with a high degree of variability in other cultural traits such as architecture, settlement patterns, and mortuary behavior suggests that the Aztatlán complex does not reflect a single uniform cultural group, but more likely represents an artistic horizon style and, perhaps, an interaction sphere. Due to the limited extent of archaeological investigations carried out in Sinaloa, previous reconstructions of prehispanic sociopolitical organization have relied primarily upon the interpretation of documentary relations from the Spanish *entrada*. Spanish terms such as *señorío*, *reino*, *provincias*, *naciones*, or *cacicazgo* have been variously interpreted as autonomous villages, chiefdoms, paramount chiefdoms, provinces, city states, statelets, states, and kingdoms in describing levels of sociopolitical complexity on the northern Mexican coastal plain on the eve of Spanish contact (Beals 1932:117; Meighan 1971:795; Publ 1985:181–182, 1990:235–236; Riley 1987; Sauer 1935:9). These interpretations have been projected into the prehispanic past, with most scholars arguing for the existence of a state level of organization for the Aztatlán complex (e.g., Kelley 1980, 1983; Meighan 1971; Publ 1985, 1990; Sauer 1935).

However, current examination of the ethnohistoric data and the archaeological evidence calls into question the inference of a state level of organization among contact period populations on the coastal plain, suggesting that both the Aztatlán and the Huatabampo regions reflect the historical pattern of *ranchería* settlements scattered along the principal rivers between the Sierra Madre and the Sea of Cortés. The ballcourt reported by Sauer and Brand near Copala and another recently identified by Grave along the Río Presidio to the southeast of Mazatlán represent the only known ceremonial architecture dating to the ceramic period in Sinaloa. Without more tangible archaeological evidence, a state level of organization cannot presently be supported for the prehispanic populations of Sinaloa.

INTERACTION AND INTEGRATION IN NORTHERN SINALOA

In contemplating the nature of cultural interaction and integration on the Aztatlán frontier in northern Sinaloa, we offer brief summaries of the results of our investigations of the El Ombligo (Carpenter 1996, 2008) and Mochicahui funerary mound assemblages (Carpenter et al. 2010; Carpenter et al. 2011) associated with the Huatabampo archaeological tradition as well as the La Viuda/Rincón de Buyubampo habitation complex affiliated with the Serrana (formerly known as the southern branch of Río Sonora) archaeological tradition (Figure 8.2; Carpenter and Sánchez 2007; Carpenter et al. 2006).

El Ombligo

The El Ombligo funerary mound assemblage (Guasave site) has traditionally served to mark the northern terminus of the Postclassic-period (AD 900 to Contact) Mesoamerican/west Mexican expansion along the North Mexican Coastal Plain. The site consisted of a low mound measuring approximately 1.5 m high and 30 m in diameter and was situated approximately 100 m west of an abandoned meander of the Río Sinaloa, some 6 km to the southwest of the town of Guasave. Excavation over the course of three field seasons between 1938 and 1940 indicated that the mound was a formal cemetery, with the remains of 196 individuals reflecting

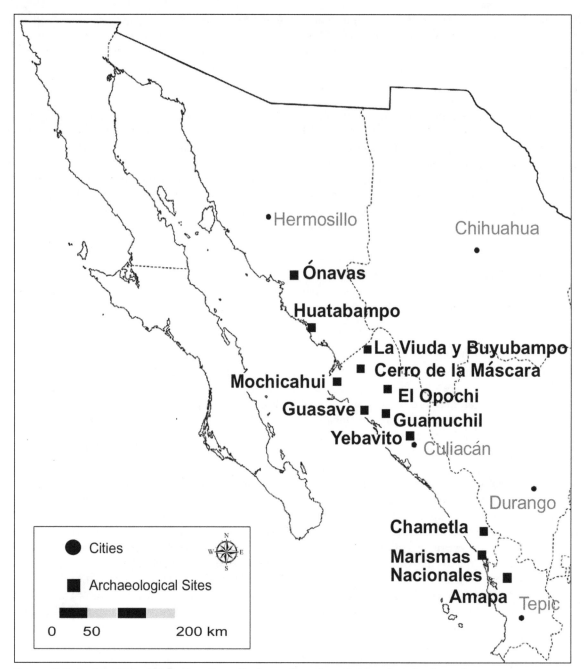

FIGURE 8.2. Archaeological sites of northern Sinaloa and southern Sonora. Drawing by authors.

a varied mortuary program (Ekholm 1939, 1940, 1942). The mortuary practices included extended inhumations with heads oriented to the north, south, and west; secondary bundle burials of disarticulated remains; and secondary interment in large funerary *ollas*. Tabular-erect cranial deformation was prevalent, and several cases of tooth filing and staining also were observed. Funerary offerings associated with these graves revealed an elaborate material culture, with several pottery types including red wares, Red-on-buff, finely incised wares, several types of highly detailed polychrome pottery, alabaster vases, copper implements, shell ornaments, pyrite and turquoise jewelry, paint-cloisonné gourd vessels, ceramic masks, clay smoking pipes, modeled spindle whorls, a cylinder stamp, prismatic obsidian blades, cotton textiles, bone daggers, human trophy skulls, and food remains (Ekholm 1942:120).

Considering variability in mortuary treatment, depth of interment, orientation, and grave lots, in conjunction with 10 new radiocarbon dates, these data indicate two chronological components reflecting a much greater temporal span than previously recognized (Carpenter 1996). The earliest Huatabampo period occupation is dated from approximately AD 700/800 to AD 1100/1150, with the subsequent Guasave period placed between approximately AD 1100/1150 and AD 1350/1400.

Sometime around AD 1000, sophisticated polychrome vessels, clay masks, and smoking pipes associated with the Aztatlán complex were either locally produced or imported from nearby Aztatlán neighbors. These objects are apparently restricted to funerary contexts and likely functioned within an ideological/ritual realm. There are relatively few, if any, tangible indications of an actual Aztatlán occupation at Guasave.

Although there are marked differences between the Huatabampo and Guasave periods, continuity of occupation is demonstrated by both the mortuary program and the material culture. In general, the Guasave-period burials reflect variations on practices established in the Huatabampo period. The most notable difference between periods is the appearance of secondary burials in *ollas* during the terminal portion of the Guasave period. However, these burials, along with the other Aztatlán components, do not reflect the long-reaching expansion of Mesoamerican/west Mexican societies into the northern frontier, but traits adopted from neighboring communities on the North Mexican Coastal Plain of Sinaloa. The Aztatlán component at El Ombligo appears to be strongly associated with the ideological realm, with little evidence for either political or economic integration on a macroregional scale. However, the manipulation of symbolically or ideologically important objects may have served both political and economic ends for high-status individuals and may also have promoted regional interaction within the Sinaloan coastal plain.

Mochicahui

Mochicahui is located in the lower Río Fuerte Valley some 10 km upriver from modern-day Los Mochis and, in the sixteenth century, was described by the Spaniards as the principal pueblo of the Zuaque—the most powerful of the groups occupying the valley. At least three funerary mounds have been documented here. In 1988, Talavera and Manzanilla (1991) recovered 15 burials from the small Los Bajos funerary mound in Mochicahui. The existence of an additional funerary mound in Mochicahui was documented in 2008. Unfortunately, this component (named the Leyva funerary mound) was thoroughly looted in the late 1970s, producing an estimated 40 to 50 burials along with approximately 120 ceramic vessels, some of which are curated in the museum collections of the Universidad Autónoma Indigenista de México. This assemblage includes Huatabampo/Guasave red wares, Guasave Red-on-buff, Guasave Polychrome, and Aztatlán Red-on-buff as well as the northernmost documented occurrence of Aztatlán Polychrome vessels (Figure 8.3). A third (Borboa) funerary mound was discovered in November 2009, and subsequent salvage excavations recovered three burials. A partially reconstructible Guasave Polychrome vessel with painted motifs resembling Aztatlán painted vessels was found associated with a child burial (Figure 8.4; Carpenter et al. 2010; Carpenter et al. 2011). Along with El Ombligo, these represent all of the funerary mounds yet documented in Sinaloa. It is likely that El Opochi (Santos 2004), located on the Río Sinaloa in the vicinity of Sinaloa de Leyva, presented what most probably was an unrecognized mound, and there is an unconfirmed report of an additional funerary mound in the vicinity of Guamúchil.

At both the Leyva and Borboa mounds, funerary practices included placing a large mollusc shell beneath the head as a "pillow," and placing a small shell in the mouth. Tabular-erect cranial deformation is evident among the burial population (Talavera 2005), and dental modification was reported by the looter of the Leyva mound (Carpenter et al. 2010; Carpenter et al. 2011). As yet, no urn burials have been documented in the Mochicahui assemblages, and the funerary offerings are much less elaborate in comparison with the El Ombligo assemblage. Geographical distribution and the predominance of local materials suggest these features can best be considered as an attribute of the Huatabampo tradition (Figure 8.5; Carpenter and Sánchez 2011). Additionally, presumably non-funerary platform mounds have been documented at the La Playa de Ocoroni site which have been incorporated into contemporary Yoreme (Mayo) rituals.

La Viuda/Rincón de Buyubampo

Lastly, recent excavations at the adjacent Serrana tradition sites of La Viuda and Rincón de Buyubampo, located in the Janalicahui Valley 5 km south of the Sonoran border, indicate that this habitation complex was heavily populated and reflect a continuous occupation from approximately AD 700 to 1700. The ceramic assemblage at La Viuda and Buyubampo reveals the intersection of several ceramic traditions from Sinaloa and southern Sonora; the chronological scheme of the ceramic types is tentative, and absolute dates will be necessary in the future to determine the chronology. The Batacosa/Cuchijaqui ceramic group from the lower Serrana is the most abundant with 48 percent ($n = 6,124$), followed by the Huatabampo/Guasave group from the coast with 37 percent ($n = 4,682$); the corrugated Serrana types of Los Camotes/San Bernardo have a representation of 9 percent ($n = 1,143$), and the Aztatlán group from Culiacán are represented by 6 percent ($n = 780$) as indicated in Table 8.1.

Artifacts recovered from both sites indicate that they participated in the Aztatlán long-distance exchange system and that the production of marine shell

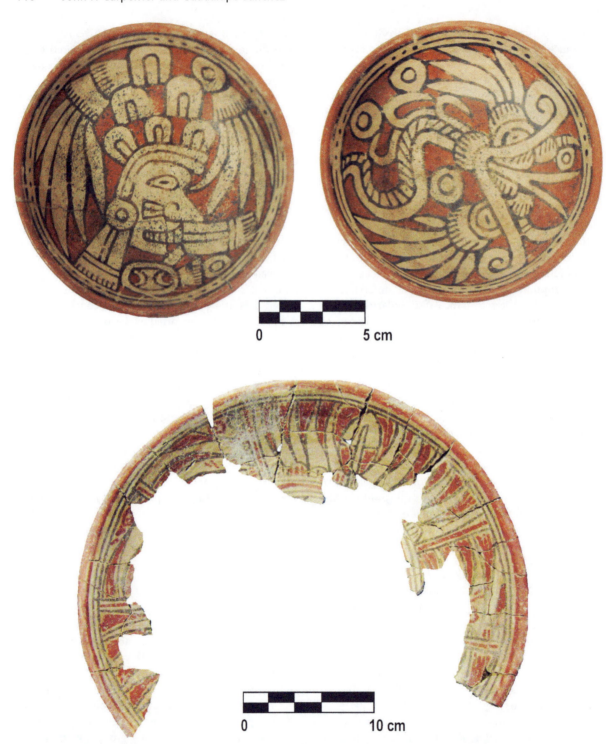

FIGURE 8.3. Aztatlán Polychrome (top row) and Guasave Polychrome plate (bottom) from Mochicahui, Sinaloa. Photos by authors.

ornaments was an important activity. At approximately AD 1200, the population shifted around 700 m from La Viuda to Rincón de Buyubampo where large multiroom domestic units were constructed atop trash-filled house mounds—an attribute previously undocumented within Sinaloa; although, in the vicinity of Culiacán, Isabel Kelly (1945a) reported low trash-filled mounds associated with postholes, presumably reflecting the remains of houses of perishable materials.

At Rincón de Buyubampo, evidence of interaction with the Aztatlán tradition is indicated by a type 1C1a copper bell, prismatic obsidian blade fragments, a cylindrical ceramic stamp, Aztatlán spindle whorls, and Navolato Polychrome and Tuxpan Red-on-orange

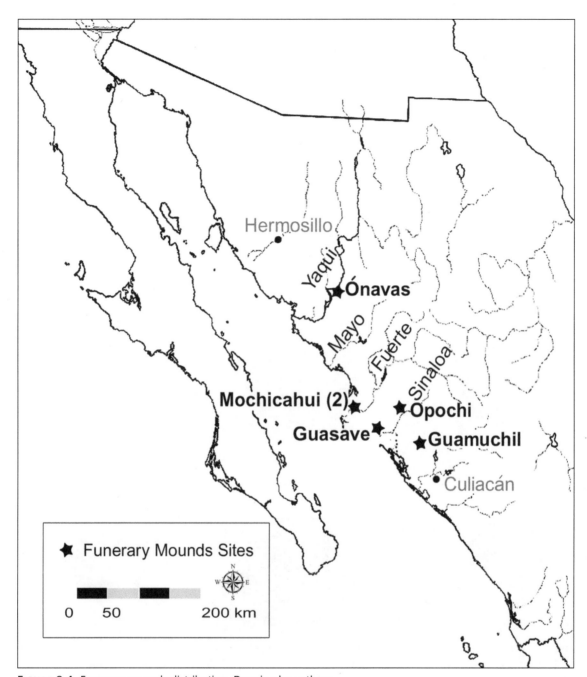

FIGURE 8.4. Funerary mounds distribution. Drawing by authors.

pottery (Figure 8.6; Carpenter et al. 2006). Additional intrusive ceramics include several sherds of Guasave Red-on-buff, Arivechi Red-on-brown, and a Babícora Polychrome—the latter representing the only documented occurrence of Chihuahuan polychromes within Sinaloa. Evidence of shell ornament production also is abundant at many of the sites documented in this region; analysis of the marine shell ornament production revealed that their manufacture was at the domestic level (Rodríguez Obregón 2017).

Our research in the Sinaloa-Sonora border region suggests that, from Mochicahui, the regional exchange route followed the Río Fuerte upstream to the vicinity of modern-day El Fuerte, Sinaloa, where we have identified the existence of two alternate routes between the Río Fuerte Valley and the vicinity of Alamos, Sonora; one route following the confluence of the Río Cuchujaqui (Arroyo Alamos) and another route following the Arroyo Janalacahui (La Viuda and Buyubampo sites), located approximately 20 km to the northeast. These alternate routes may be associated with competitive control of the local exchange routes between the Tehueco (Río Cuchujaqui) and Sinaloa (Arroyo Janalacahui). Notably, both routes were recognized as *caminos reales*

FIGURE 8.5. Foreign ceramics in Buyubampo and La Viuda, Sinaloa. (*a–b*) Culiacán-Aztatlán. (*c*) Babícora Polychrome. (*d–f*) Guasave Red-on-buff. (*g–h*) Aztatlán modeled spindle whorls. (*i*) Cylinder stamp. Photos by authors.

connecting the mining towns of El Fuerte, Sinaloa, and Alamos, Sonora, during the eighteenth century. Considering that Cabeza de Vaca and companions finally encountered their fellow Spaniards in the vicinity of Sinaloa de Leyva suggests that they passed along one of these two routes. This, in turn, leads us to suspect that this same route was utilized in 1539 by Marcos de Niza (having been guided by Esteban, who had accompanied Cabeza de Vaca), Francisco Vasquez de Coronado in 1540, and by the expedition of Francisco Ibarra in 1564, which perhaps explains the reason for their eventual arrival at Paquimé in the Casas Grandes region. We note, however, the absence of marine shell or other exotic items further upstream (east) along the Río Fuerte from this juncture. Additionally, research carried out by Enrique Chacón (2010) in the adjacent region in Chihuahua seemingly confirms our observations.

Discussion

Survey and excavation fieldwork carried out in northern Sinaloa indicates that Aztatlán ceramics from the Culiacán area were present in low quantities in many of the sites we have investigated. In the cases of El Ombligo, Mochicahui, and Rincón de Buyubampo, the

TABLE 8.1. Ceramic types from La Viuda and Buyubampo, Sinaloa.

Ceramic types	Tentative Chronology	Region	La Viuda Site	Buyubampo Site	Total
Venadito	200 BC–AD 200	Cueva de la Colmena and southern Sonora (Pailes 1972)	7	0	7
Huatabampo	200 BC–AD 900	Mochomoncobe and Guasave (Álvarez 1990; Carpenter 1996)	674	70	744
Batacosa	AD 200–1200	Serrana baja (Pailes 1972)	2,572	1,257	3,829
Cuchujaqui	AD 800–1600	Serrana baja (Pailes 1972)	2,189	106	2,295
Los Camotes/San Bernardo	AD 800–1600	Serrana alta (Pailes 1972)	178	13	191
Techobampo	AD 800–1600	Serrana alta (Pailes 1972)	39	68	107
Piedras Verdes	AD 800–1600	Serrana alta (Pailes 1972)	603	242	845
Guasave	AD 1100–1600	Guasave (Carpenter 1996)	3,117	821	3,938
Culiacán-Aztatlán	AD 800–1600	Culiacán (Kelly 1945a)	570	210	780
Total			9,949	2,787	12,736

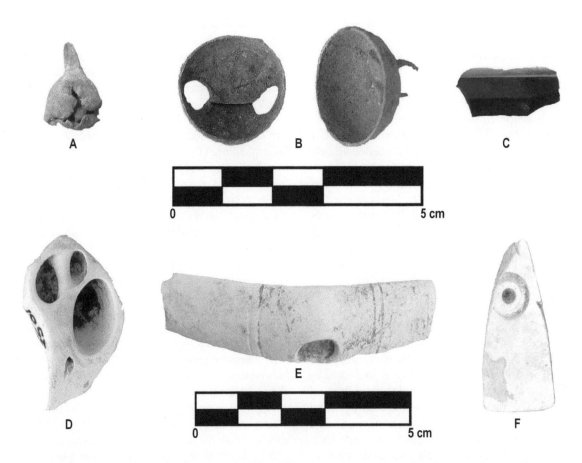

FIGURE 8.6. Objects from Buyubampo and La Viuda. (*a–b*) Copper bells. (*c*) Obsidian prismatic blade. (*d–f*) Shell ornaments. Photos by authors.

acquisition of nonlocal items more closely resembles a prestige-goods economy (see Frankenstein and Rowlands 1978; McGuire 1987) and can be considered as a consequential, and not causal, factor in the intensification of Indigenous social relations.

While the Aztatlán materials documented at El Ombligo could perhaps be interpreted as evidence for possible socio-ideological integration (Carpenter 1996), the data do not support the presence of a significant foreign population or evidence of politico-economic dominion. At present, there is no evidence to suggest that any of the late-prehispanic communities north of the Río Mocorito were politically integrated with their adjacent Aztatlán neighbors.

As an alternative to core-periphery models based on politico-economic exploitation, we suggest that interaction and integration were largely predicated by the flow of information and materials between sedentary agriculturalists who occupied the coastal plain and adjacent foothills between southern Sinaloa and the Arizona border. This model suggests that these prehistoric peoples were members of the Cahitan language group, which included the Tahue, Comanito, Mocorito, Mayo, Yaqui, and Opata (incorporating Eudeve, Jova, and Teguima groups).

David Wilcox (1986b, 2000; Wilcox et al. 2008) previously proposed the existence of a linguistic continuum that would have facilitated the transmission of information and goods between west Mexico and the U.S. Southwest. However, as an alternative to a supposed Tepiman continuum, the North Mexican Coastal Plain and the adjacent flanks of the Sierra Madre Occidental are described as a spatially, environmentally, and culturally intermediate area where the prehispanic Cahitan-speaking groups formed a continuous linguistic link extending between southern Sinaloa and the Arizona border. Importantly, this perspective turns attention from the imperial role of complex Mesoamerican polities to the localized selection and adaptation of both material and ideological traits. This scenario also suggests that the presumed withdrawal of the Mesoamerican frontier during the fourteenth century was neither linked to regional abandonment predicated by shifting ethnic boundaries nor linked to the collapse of political-economic systems. Instead, continuity of occupation by Cahita-speaking peoples in northern Sinaloa indicates the declining participation in the overt ideological and iconographic symbols associated with their linguistic kin in the Culiacán region.

Sixteenth-century Spanish chroniclers identified at least 20 groups occupying the coastal plain, foothills, and sierra of northwestern Mexico that are today recognized as Cahitan speakers (Miller 1983a, 1983b; Moctezuma 1991). Cahitan comprises one of the major linguistic subdivisions of the Southern (or Sonoran) branch of Uto-Aztecan (Miller 1983a, 1983b; Moctezuma 1991). The Cahitan-speaking groups of the coastal plain and adjacent foothills have traditionally been considered to represent late arrivals that descended from the Sierra Madre Occidental, displacing presumably Tepiman-speaking peoples (Beals 1932:145; Braniff 1992:1:217; Sauer 1935; Wilcox 1986b). However, this interpretation seems to have been based solely upon geographical appearances (Miller 1983b:333). In considering the linguistic data, Miller and others (1983a, 1983b; Shaul 2014) suggest that the Cahitans may have been established on the coastal plain near the beginning of the Christian era. Furthermore, archaeological evidence substantiates cultural continuity between the Huatabampo tradition and the various Cahitan groups (including the Guasave, Ocoroni, Zuaque) of the coastal plain, as well as the related Serrana tradition with both the Tehueco and Sinaloa groups of Cahitan speakers. Our research indicates that both the Huatabampo and Serrana archaeological traditions likely share a common origin within a Venadito Brown ceramic horizon; we have also proposed that initial differences between these traditions may be ascribed to differential adaptations to coastal and foothill environments (Carpenter and Vicente López 2009). Additionally, we note that the Serrana archaeological tradition was initially referred to as the Southern or Alamos branch of the Río Sonora culture (Pailes 1972, 1976). Cultural continuity is strongly suggested by the geographical distribution of the Río Sonora complex and the historic period Opatan groups (Carpenter 2015).

The Cahitan region to the north of the Río Mocorito represents an extensive area where sedentary agriculturalists share closest affinities with the archaeological communities of the southwestern United States but who also, during various centuries, lived "face-to-face" with traditions related to broader developments in west Mexico/Mesoamerica (Beals 1944:252). These various Cahitan groups reflect a cultural diversity that cannot be adequately explained by reference to mainstream developments in the heartlands of the U.S. Southwest or Mesoamerica. Instead, much as Ralph Beals (1944) proclaimed almost 70 years ago, this region can be better understood as a complex web of ecological factors and reciprocal relations between social groups which involved a wide range of interaction and varying degrees of integration at the regional and interregional scales.

Both archaeological and ethnohistorical data indicate that northwest Mexico was not a vast cultural netherworld separating the southwestern United States from the complex societies of Mesoamerica. Instead, it appears that by no later than AD 250 there were sedentary farming peoples occupying the North Mexican

Coastal Plain and adjacent foothills, forming a continuous link from southern Sinaloa to the Arizona border. On the basis of both linguistic and archaeological data, we have proposed that these people likely were the biocultural ancestors of the Cahitan-speaking populations encountered by the Spanish in the first half of the sixteenth century. At the southern end of this spectrum are groups identified as fully Mesoamerican, such as the Tahue, who appear to be the contact-period descendants of the late-prehistoric Aztatlán complex. The Opata, historically the northernmost Cahitan-speaking peoples, also have been identified with both the Río Sonora and Casas Grandes traditions (Braniff 1992; Dirst 1979). Recent research in the heart of the *Opatería* in the Sahuaripa region of Sonora suggests that this area was actively involved in both long-distance and regional exchange systems. Objects of west Mexican origin include a shell pectoral of *Pinctada mazatlanica* while regional, or transverse, exchange is represented by turquoise and marine shell, including *Glycymeris, Pecten, Chama,* and *Olivella,* from the Sea of Cortés. Obsidian and Ramos and Carretas Polychromes and Madera Black-on-red originate in Chihuahua.

The Cahitan-speaking groups occupied a region both spatially and environmentally intermediate between tropical Mesoamerica and the arid U.S. Southwest. The archaeological data, though limited, similarly suggest a culturally intermediate position. In this perspective, such seemingly disparate communities as Culiacán and Paquimé may have been at opposite ends of a single, attenuated linguistic spectrum. While some polities may have held a vested interest in the acquisition of goods, the actual exchange mechanism can be explained without relying upon models based upon politico-economic exploitation. Instead of concentrating on the distribution of a few isolated traits, future research will prove more fruitful if we turn attention to the full range of social, political, economic, and ideological behaviors represented in the archaeological record (Carpenter et al. 2023). Only then will we be able to assess the true nature of Mesoamerican and U.S. Southwestern interaction.

CHAPTER 9

Selective Influence of West Mexico Cultural Traditions in the Ónavas Valley, Sonora, Mexico

Cristina García Moreno, James T. Watson, and Danielle Phelps

The archaeological site of El Cementerio, dated between the Middle and Late Sonoran Ceramic Period (ca. AD 900–1600), is located in the Ónavas Valley of southeast Sonora, Mexico, on the rich alluvial floodplain of the middle Río Yaqui (Figures I.1, 9.1). The site consists of a 132 m² low earthen mound rising just under 2 m above the floodplain, plus at least one other smaller area with similar characteristics and other areas with individual burials. Intensive work over the past six years included 20 test units, a trench bisecting the western portion of the site, and a large horizontal exploration unit (Unit 4, 76 m²), but still only managed to explore 37 percent of the site, or about 1.1 ha. The sum of results obtained to date attests to an almost entirely local cultural tradition.

Indications of connections with west Mexican cultures, particularly in Sinaloa, come from the presence of nonlocal jewelry made from marine shell and/or turquoise and cranial and dental modification (Figure 9.2).

Many archaeologists have proposed that dynamic connections long existed between the U.S. Southwest (southwest United States/northwest Mexico) and other culture areas throughout much of the prehispanic sequence, and none more direct than between Paquimé (Casas Grandes) and Mesoamerica (Mathien and McGuire 1986; Wilcox et al. 2008). Arguments of interconnections were heavily influenced in the late 1970s by Wallerstein's (1974, 1979) World-Systems Theory. Archaeologists working in the region began to see elements of architecture and prestige goods as indicators of extraregional spheres of interaction through participation in long-distance trade networks (Punzo and Villalpando 2015).

In this context, J. Charles Kelley (1986) introduced the concept of the Aztatlán Mercantile System to explain the presence of Mesoamerican objects at Paquimé and across the U.S. Southwest. Under this model, Kelley posited that Guasave, a large site located on the coastal plain in Sinaloa, was a regional trade center along a chain of numerous similar sites connecting Paquimé and the U.S. Southwest to the Mixteca-Puebla area (Ekholm 2008). Following Kelley (2000), Mountjoy (2000) suggested the Aztatlán tradition represents a Mesoamerican expansion that spread to the west coast. Under this perspective, and without evidence to the contrary, a large part of Sonora would have been situated outside of this west Mexico–Paquimé route. An exception to this exclusion was proposed by Carpenter and colleagues (Carpenter 2014; Carpenter and Sánchez 2016) for an area that includes the Río Cuchujaqui, Río Janalacahui, and Río Sahuaripa located in southeastern Sonora.

Another theoretical model, developed by Nelson (1981), sought to explain the long-distance prestige-goods economy between these regions as based on consumption by elites to gain status and/or power (McGuire 1980; McGuire and Howard 1987), although the groups in power were not necessarily all directly connected to each other. For example, elites in one area might exchange prestige goods with neighboring groups in power, thus using the objects as symbols of ostentation to validate their authority (Punzo and Villalpando 2015:188). In this model, the evidence that exists for exchange between the U.S. Southwest and west Mexico is well established (see McGuire 1980:28–32).

Several scholars have considered the Río Yaqui as a natural corridor for the movement of prestige goods between the coast and Paquimé (Bradley 1999, 2000; Di Peso 1974; Wilcox et al. 2008). However, the archaeological evidence obtained to date from three sites, including El Cementerio, does not support this assumption. Most of the material culture recovered from the site is indicative of local investments and minimal interaction with prestige goods. Yet the presence of a

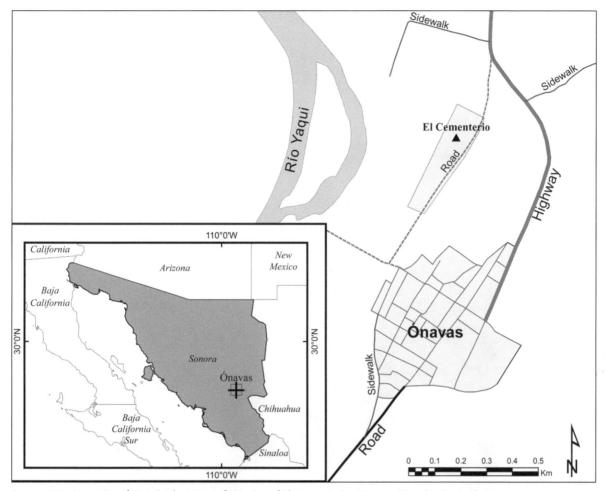

FIGURE 9.1. Map identifying the location of the site of El Cementerio, Sonora. Drawing by author.

mortuary mound containing burials with a few exotic goods and biocultural traits illustrates some level of connectivity or influence from west Mexican archaeological traditions between AD 900 and 1600. In this work, we describe the results of the excavations at El Cementerio and their bearing on the questions of the relationship between local economies along the Río Yaqui and regional and macroregional interactions.

El Cementerio

Material Culture

Intensive investigations at El Cementerio took place between 2011 and 2015 as part of the *Proyecto Arqueológico Sur de Sonora* (Archaeological Project of Southern Sonora, or PASS), in which the primary goal was to search for evidence of prehispanic material connections between Mesoamerica and the U.S. Southwest (García Moreno 2008). The project documented 130 features, including 109 mortuary features (108 inhumations containing the remains of 114 individuals and one secondary cremation), eight middens, three hearths, two postholes, and one in situ reconstructable ceramic vessel (García Moreno 2014). Seven AMS radiocarbon dates from human bone have dated the site between approximately cal AD 897 (95 percent probability) and 1635 (95 percent probability; Calibrated at 2σ with the program OxCal 4.2; Watson and García 2016:225). The early dates from El Cementerio coincide with the social consolidation of the Aztatlán tradition and its maximum extension north to the Río Mocorito (Carpenter and Sánchez 2014; Carpenter and Vicente López 2009). These dates also coincide with the abandonment of several sites on the coastal plain along the Río Mayo and Río Fuerte and a proposed northern migration of Huatabampo groups from Sinaloa (Álvarez Palma 2007). The late date from the site roughly corresponds to the arrival of Europeans in the area around AD 1600 (Guzmán 1615).

A total of 50,700 ceramic sherds were recovered from excavation units in El Cementerio. The majority of ceramics are plainwares (92 percent), most of which are apparently locally produced red- or brown-slipped monochromes—a pottery tradition shared across much of southern Sonora (Álvarez Palma 1990; Pailes 1972).

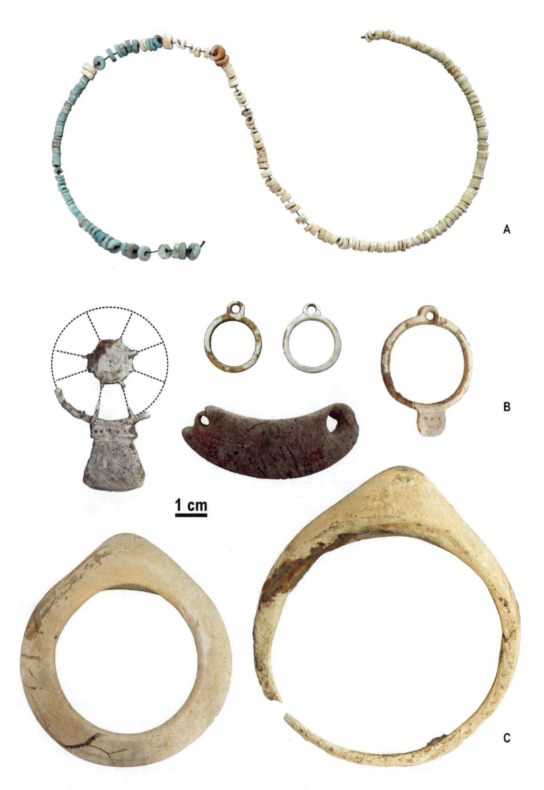

FIGURE 9.2. Artifacts associated with human burials in El Cementerio, Sonora. (*a*) Turquoise and shell-bead necklace. (*b*) Different types of shell earrings and pendants. (*c*) Two types of shell bracelets. Photos by Cristina García Moreno.

A small percentage of the assemblage (7 percent) is decorated variants of those local ceramics (Purple-on-brown; Purple-on-red; Polychrome, and others). The least-represented ceramics (0.3 percent) are foreign wares, including Huatabampo (Red and Brown) and Guasave (Red-on-brown and Red). In addition, we have a small number of sherds similar to Casas Grandes Ramos and Babícora types. The most common vessel forms recovered from the site are jars (39 percent), followed closely by *tecomates* (33 percent) and bowls (28 percent). Interior shell scraping similar to ceramics from the coast is observable on numerous sherds. In addition, a number of the sherds in the sample were worked (0.7 percent), mostly into disk or square form (with or without central perforation).

Nearly 36,761 flaked-stone artifacts were recovered from excavation units within the site, the clear majority of which is debitage (94 percent). Unifacial tools (3 percent), cores (2 percent), bifaces (0.6 percent), and core tools (0.3 percent) comprised most of the remainder of the sample. Ten projectile points made of black obsidian, chert, and jasper of different colors were recovered from excavations. The points are small (1.3–2.7 cm) and triangular, most of them with a basal notch, with serrated or nonserrated margins, and one (the only basal and side-notched) was encountered while digging a burial of an older male. Most of the flaked-stone artifacts were manufactured on cobble stones obtained from the Río Yaqui, although the geological origin is located further upstream. The proximity of the river as a supplier of this raw material leads us to consider them as local raw materials (Valdovinos Pérez and García Moreno 2017). The raw material mostly consists of lithics of igneous origin, including andesite (37 percent), basalt (24 percent), dacite (13 percent), and rhyolite (9 percent). Obsidian represents the smallest percent of materials (0.07 percent). Nearly all of the flaked stone artifacts were recovered from trash deposited as part of the construction of the mound.

Shell is the next most common material ($n = 3,276$) recovered from excavations at the site; 88 percent of which is artifacts. Thirty-seven percent of the shell sample consists of gastropods, including 15 genera (19 species). Only a few of these originate from local freshwater/terrestrial environments (*Succinea* sp. and *Polygyridae* family), whereas the majority are marine species including *Theodoxus luteofasciatus*, *Conus regularis*, and *Olivella* sp. Twelve percent of the sample are bivalves of 15 genera (17 species). Only one of these genera originates from riverine environments (*Nephronaia* sp.); the remaining materials are coastal marine species (Panamica Malocological Province). The most common bivalve species are *Chama echinata*, the black clam (*Chione fluctifraga*), Pacific Mother of Pearl (*Pinctada mazatlanica*), bittersweet clams (*Glycymeris gigantea*), and the giant clam (*Laevicardium elatum*), for example (Figures 9.2b–9.2c).

All of the shell artifacts were finished jewelry (pectorals, pendants, bracelets, earrings, and beads). In addition, all of the species identified are from the Pacific Ocean and in a few cases, such as *Spondylus princeps*, *Pinctada mazatlanica*, and *Glycymeris gigantea*—because they live in a subtidal habitat—it was necessary to have diving knowledge to obtain them. At this point of the investigation, it is difficult to know whether the area's inhabitants were responsible for collecting the material or if they obtained it by exchange with near-shore groups (García Moreno 2013a:417–437). However, the absence of manufacturing waste or pieces in progress suggests the ornaments arrived to Ónavas as complete items, probably as the result of trade with coastal groups. Although the nearest coast to the site is Guaymas (130 km to the southwest), it is more likely that these materials come from the northern coast of Sinaloa (Grimstead et al. 2013) and up the Río Yaqui.

Ground stone artifacts ($n = 147$) from the site are the least common artifact class but include polishing tools (39 percent), grinding stones (31 percent; including hand-stones, base-stones, pestles, and mortars), cutting/scraping tools (4 percent), and game pieces (2 percent). The vast majority of this material came from the three trash middens encountered in the site (Features 4, 59, 60). The exception is the 130 pieces of ground stone jewelry made of turquoise (García Moreno and Melgar Tísoc 2021) recovered from the burials of infants and children, the vast majority as bracelet beads. They were mostly encountered strung around the right wrist (sometimes together with shell beads), and occasionally as pendants strung around the neck (Figure 9.2a).

Mortuary Sample

The mortuary sample from El Cementerio consists of 110 features representing 114 individuals. Burials were recovered throughout the 2 m depth of the mound and across the site (Figure 9.3). Few burials appear to be placed in direct association with each other, but there is clear evidence of burials intruding on previous interments.

Most of the burials at El Cementerio are primary inhumations (84.3 percent), although six possible secondary inhumation burials and one secondary cremation in an urn have been documented at the site. The majority of individuals (63.1 percent) were placed in an extended position on their backs (supine), with a few individuals placed in prone positions (7.9 percent), or on their side (9.6 percent). Over half were placed with the central axis (pelvis to head) oriented to the

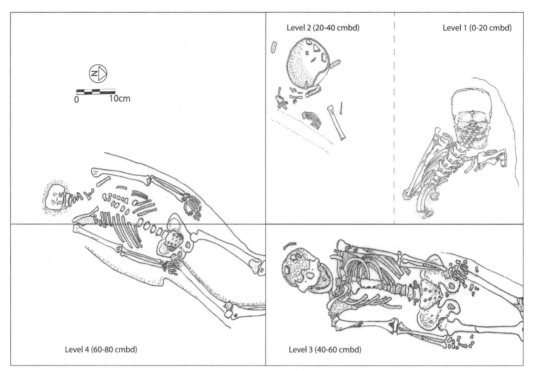

FIGURE 9.3. Burial intrusion and superposition within the burial mound at El Cementerio. Drawing by authors. Photograph of Figure 9.3 is available in the Supplemental Digital Material: https://collections.lib.utah.edu/ark:/87278/s6kb90sf.

TABLE 9.1. Frequency of associated funerary objects in sample, El Cementerio, Sonora.

	Fetal/Infant (0–3)	Child (3–12)	Adolescent (12–20)	Young Adult (20–35)	Middle Adult (35–45)	Old Adult (45+)	%
Juvenile	7/24	12/30					35.0
Male			1/4	4/13	3/12	2/4	30.0
Female			1/4	6/16	1/7	0/1	29.0
%	29.2	40.0	25.0	34.5	21.1	40.0	

east (53.3 percent), with fewer oriented to the west (16.5 percent), south (9.56 percent), and north (3.5 percent). Body position, placement, and orientation vary similarly across all age groups and between sexes across the site, as well as throughout its depth.

Half (51 percent) of the mortuary features contained associated funerary objects, which consisted largely of shell jewelry (Table 9.1). Other funerary objects included several pieces of jewelry made from turquoise (bracelets, necklaces, and pendants), a tortoise carapace, a bone pin, a utilitarian grinding stone, a small plain ware urn, a globular red ware vessel, several large sherds (from a sizable plain ware vessel), and a chert projectile point. Similar proportions of objects were observed across age groups and between males and females. One adolescent was among the few individuals buried with several objects. These include the only ceramic vessel associated with an inhumation, a shell (*Pinctada mazatlanica*) pectoral incised in the form of a frog or toad figure, a shell (*Theodoxus luteofasciatus*) pendant, and 31 small shell beads (*Conus regularis*) from an anklet.

Nearly half of the skeletal sample consists of infants and children (46.8 percent), with relatively even proportions of males (31.3 percent) and females (26 percent) among adolescents and adults (Figure 9.4). The median age at death was sometime during the third decade of life (20–35 years old), and very few adults survived into older adulthood (>45 years old). Stature estimates from six adults ranged between 158.9 cm and 173.5 cm (Auerbach and Ruff 2010), which is slightly shorter but within the range observed in earlier populations from northern Sonora and southern Arizona (Watson and Stoll 2013).

Skeletal lesions (where observable) are largely limited to degenerative disease associated with older

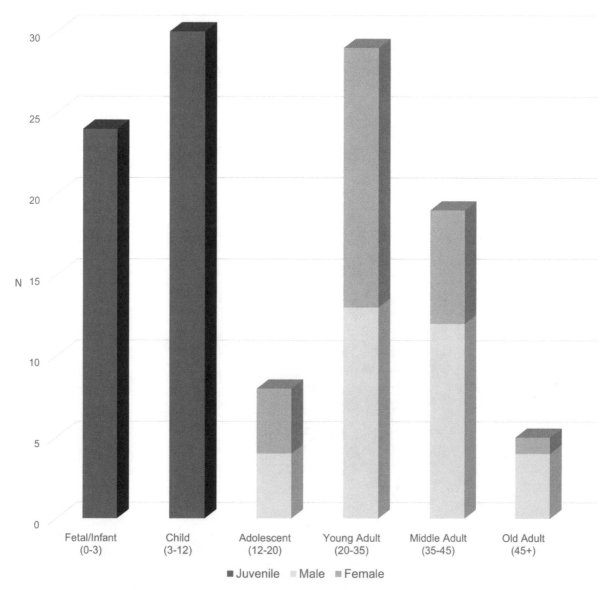

FIGURE 9.4. Bar graph displaying the age and sex distribution of the El Cementerio skeletal sample. Drawing by author.

age, including 18 individuals with bone spurs (osteophytes) on the lower vertebral column, and three cases in the neck. Other skeletal lesions observed include two individuals with ankylosing spondylitis (severe arthritic reaction and vertebral fusion), four individuals with periosteal or bone infections (osteomyelitis), 10 individuals exhibiting porotic hyperostosis or a thickened diploë (active lesions were mostly observed in juveniles), one case of cranial synostosis, and six individuals with healed fractures. Several of these healed fractures are likely representative of violent trauma. Two adult males exhibit healed blunt-force trauma to the cranium and an additional adult male has a healed parry fracture of the left ulna.

Several individuals exhibit very poor oral health, including numerous caries or extensive tooth loss and/or severe periodontal resorption. The two oldest individuals in the sample (40–50 years of age) lost the majority of their teeth. A number of individuals (21.9 percent) had (minimally) one tooth with a cavity, and similar proportions of individuals had lost at least one tooth prior to death (25 percent) or exhibited at least one enamel defect (28.1 percent), which indicates generalized systemic stress during early development.

The most conspicuous characteristics of the mortuary sample from El Cementerio are marked cranial and dental modification (Table 9.2). Among sufficiently preserved crania (n = 62), nearly all of the individuals exhibit a pronounced elongated form of tabular oblique cranial modification (96.8 percent) that was relatively evenly distributed between males and females (Figures 9.5a–9.5b). Neumann (1942) notes that this type requires the simultaneous application of hard surface pressure on both the anterior (frontal flattened ~45°)

158   Cristina García Moreno, James T. Watson, and Danielle Phelps

TABLE 9.2. Distribution of cranial and dental modification in sample, El Cementerio, Sonora.

	Cranial Modification	Dental Modification
Juvenile	26	1
Male	20	9
Female	14	5
	60 (52%)	15 (13%)

and posterior (occipital flattened between ~90° and ~120°) aspect of the cranium. Cranial modification was affected among different cultures for a variety of reasons, including as a mark of beauty or to visually identify ethnicity or class ranking (Dingwall 1931).

Dental modification—the cutting, drilling, grinding, encrusting, or staining of teeth—was recorded on 14 adult individuals and one child (31.9 percent of preserved anterior teeth) from the site (see Table 9.2).

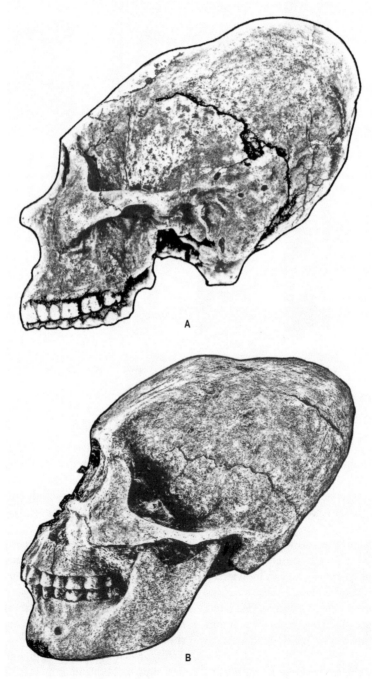

FIGURE 9.5. Examples of tabular oblique cranial modification from El Cementerio. Drawings by authors. Photographs of Figure 9.5a and 9.5b are available in the Supplemental Digital Material: https://collections.lib.utah.edu/ark:/87278/s6kb90sf.

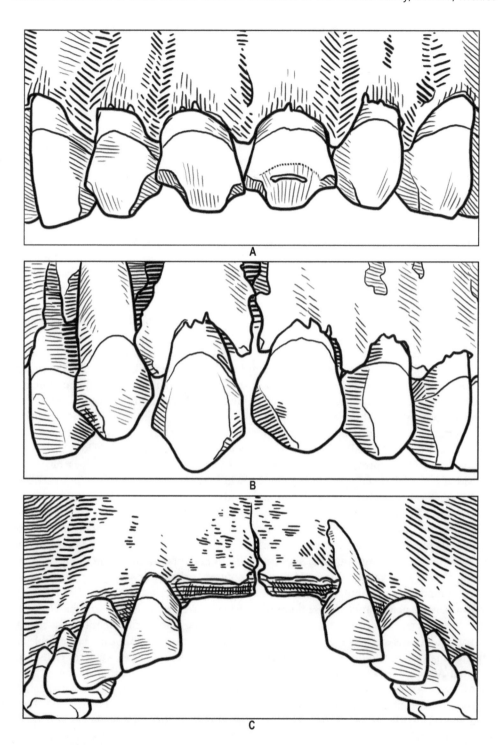

FIGURE 9.6. Illustrations demonstrating the forms of dental modification observed in the El Cementerio skeletal sample: (*a*) Type C-2 as defined by Romero (1958). (*b*) Type C-5 as defined by Romero (1958). (*c*) Dental ablation (intentional removal) of the central maxillary incisors. Drawings by Caitlin McPherson.

Nine males and three females exhibit filing of the corners of all four upper incisors and often the mesial canines (Figures 9.6a–9.6b). The forms of filing observed at El Cementerio fall into Romero's (1958, 1970) Types C-2 or C-5. In addition, two females exhibit dental ablation—the intentional removal of teeth—of the upper central incisors (Figure 9.6c). Dental modification has an equally expansive temporal and global distribution as cranial modification (Milner and Larsen 1991) and similar implications, often cited as a mark of beauty or to display ethnic or social identity (Scott and Turner II 1997).

Analysis of Burial Spatial Distribution

We conducted a series of spatial analyses in ArcMap and ArcGIS using burial locations within El Cementerio to test distributions and the potential for vertical and/or horizontal associations in placement within the mound. These tests were conducted at two scales, examining burial distribution first within the site ($n = 115$) then focusing on the more intensively excavated Unit 4 ($n = 69$), with the primary motivation of identifying if individuals (1) were intentionally concentrated at specific locations (or at particular levels), or (2) were interred randomly throughout the site.

One of the principal lingering questions about the mound at El Cementerio is whether it was intentionally constructed as a burial mound (either in incremental stages or as a one-time event) or grew in an accretional manner, resulting from contiguous occupation and the steady deposition of cultural debris. The weak, generalized, and disturbed stratigraphy observed throughout the site's depth appears to result more from internal sediment dynamics than from clear cultural depositional events. Therefore, if the mound was constructed intentionally for interment of the deceased then we might expect burials to be more evenly distributed across the mound horizontally but exhibit concentrations by depth (vertically) and/or display some internal groupings by cultural (or biological) characteristics. For example, if status was expressed in associated artifacts, individuals of similar status might be more closely placed to each other. However, if the mound was principally a locus of occupation, then we might expect burials to be concentrated in specific areas horizontally—perhaps as individuals were interred within structures as observed at contemporaneous sites on the bluffs lining the Ónavas Valley (García Moreno 2013b)—but more randomly distributed vertically as numerous individuals are placed under house floors at variable depths.

Burial distribution in the site was examined using a series of spatial analyses including Average Nearest Neighbor, Spatial Autocorrelation, Cluster Analysis, and Outlier Analysis. As stated above, burial distribution was first tested throughout the entire site, then within Unit 4 specifically. Potential correlations between location and biocultural attributes within Unit 4 were additionally tested.

Methods

The Average Nearest Neighbor tool in ArcGIS calculates the distance between the center of each feature and its nearest neighbor's center. The distances are then averaged, and if the calculated average distance is less than the average for a hypothetical random distribution, then the distribution of features is considered clustered. If the average distance is bigger than the hypothetical one, then the features are considered dispersed (ESRI 2013). Spatial Autocorrelation (Global Moran's I) shows the similarity between observations as a function of the distance between them. The spatial autocorrelation equation evaluates whether the data points are dispersed, random, or clustered (ESRI 2013). Cluster and Outlier Analyses utilize the Anselin Local Moran's I equation to identify spatial clusters of features with high or low values and the outliers within the sample group (ESRI 2013). The results of these tests are transformed into a new shapefile, which is added as a new layer to the map in ArcGIS.

Results

The results for the statistical spatial analyses are presented in Table 9.3. The Average Nearest Neighbor test indicates that the dispersed pattern of 115 inhumations found throughout the entire site of El Cementerio has a less than 1 percent likelihood of being random chance. Similarly, the first Spatial Autocorrelation test identifies that when the input field is Z (depth in cm), there is a less than 1 percent likelihood that the clustered pattern is a result of random chance. The same analysis conducted with the input field of X (Easting) reveals a less than 5 percent likelihood that the clustered pattern observed is the result of a random chance. Similar results are found when the input field is Y (Northing). However, although these results suggest burials are clustered within the site, this appears to be an artifact of the size and distribution of excavation units.

In addition to the above tests, we performed spatial autocorrelation analyses on individual attributes for the burials found in Unit 4 including age, sex, cranial modification, dental modification, body orientation, burial context (primary or secondary), and associated funerary objects. Burials were coded as either "1" (present/female/juvenile) or "2" (absent/male/adult) to perform these tests. The results identified no clustering of any specific attribute within Unit 4 (see Table 9.3).

Cluster and Outlier Analyses (Anselin Local Moran's I) based on Z (depth from the surface datum) for the entire site identified two statistically significant clusters of inhumations (Figure 9.7a). There is a concentration of high-high values (Features 68 and 69) and a concentration of 18 low-low values (Features 6–9, 42, 44, 72–73, 78–79, 85–89, 95, 101, 102). There are also eight features which are spatial outliers with high-low values (Features 37, 108, 112–113, 116, 118, 120–121). The high-low value indicates that these high values are surrounded by lower values for the input field. The results from these analyses identified 11 features which are clustered together within Unit 4 (Features 6–9, 16, 32, 35, 40, 42, 44, 111), and five features (Features 37, 108, 113, 118, 120) which are statistically significant as outliers (Figure 9.7b).

TABLE 9.3. Results of spatial analyses, El Cementerio, Sonora.

Test	z-score	p-value	Pattern
Average Nearest Neighbor			
Input: All Inhumations	167,196.583	<0.001[a]	Dispersed
Spatial Autocorrelation: All Inhumations			
Input: Z (depth)	5.467	<0.001[a]	Clustered
Input: X (Easting)	2.095	0.036[a]	Clustered
Input: Y (Northing)	20.308	<0.001[a]	Clustered
Spatial Autocorrelation: Attributes for Unit 4			
Input: Age	0.461	0.644	Random
Input: Sex	0.898	0.368	Random
Input: Cranial Deformation	-0.638	0.523	Random
Input: Orientation	1.173	0.24	Random
Input: Tooth Modification	0.305	0.76	Random
Input: Primary or Secondary Burial	1.259	0.207	Random
Input: Associated Funerary Objects	1.589	0.111	Random

[a] Denotes significance at the 0.05 level.

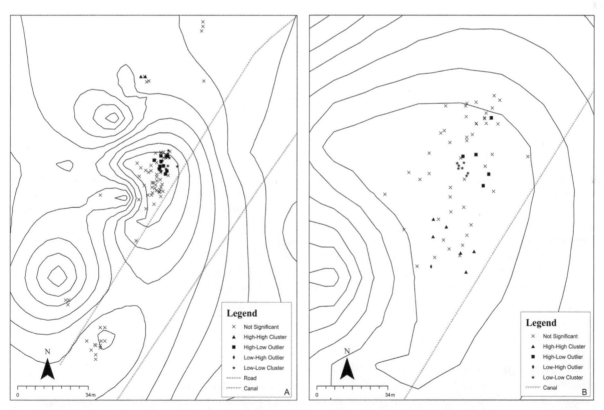

FIGURE 9.7. Cluster and outlier analysis (Local Moran's I) (*a*) Spatial Statistic for 102 inhumations throughout El Cementerio. (*b*) Spatial Statistic for the inhumations located in Unidad 4 at El Cementerio. Drawings by authors.

Interpretations

Application of the Average Nearest Neighbor to the entire site revealed that the 115 inhumations are clustered in a few areas. The results of the Spatial Autocorrelation analyses refine these conclusions by identifying that the burials cluster vertically (Z) as well as horizontally (X and Y). However, the horizontal clustering observed is likely skewed by the differential in size and depth of the excavation units across the site. The Cluster and Outlier analyses further demonstrate that the burials are clustered based on the highest and lowest values of Z (depth in cm). These high-high and low-low clusters may reflect the level of occupation surfaces on the mound. In contrast, the outliers may represent those burials that intruded on previous inhumations. Based on these results, the inhumations are clustered vertically within the site and most likely correlate with surface occupation levels of the site and with the accretional development of the mound.

The statistical spatial analyses for individual attributes associated with burials from Unit 4 indicate a random pattern. The occupants of El Cementerio apparently did not inter individuals together based on any of the attributes tested. Therefore, based on the results of these analyses, if burials are clustered vertically but not horizontally or by attributes, then it appears that the mound may have been constructed intentionally for the interment of the deceased. In addition, the presence of two vertical clusters may correspond to two distinct episodes of major incremental construction contributing to the height of the mound.

Discussion

The vast majority of material culture recovered from El Cementerio is suggestive of local cultural development with some evidence for nonlocal contact and influence. However, these few nonlocal signatures have been identified as significant markers of prestige goods exchanged between west Mexico and the U.S. Southwest. The 3.1 million pieces of worked and unworked marine shell recovered from Paquimé (Di Peso 1974) come from the coast of west Mexico (Rakita and Cruz 2015:71). The quantity indicates that it was a very important economic material for the population. Much of the material apparently arrived as finished products (McGuire et al. 1999:145) from both west Mexico and other sites in the region such as the Cerro de Trincheras (Rakita and Cruz 2015). There is still debate as to whether shell arrived to Paquimé as jewelry or was subsequently manufactured locally (Bradley 1999; Whalen 2013) and what the true significance was for the society and their connections to the coast (Whalen 2013:636). At El Cementerio, 77 percent of the total artifacts/ornaments is associated with burials; the remainder was encountered in unit fill.

The other significant evidence for prestige goods at El Cementerio, turquoise—which also appears at Paquimé—demonstrates that the site's inhabitants were consumers of this material (Rakita and Cruz 2015). Although its provenance is debated (Weigand 2008; Weigand and Harbottle 1993), the fact remains that significant quantities of turquoise were taken to Paquimé but little was used as personal ornament as evident in the lack of recovery from burial contexts (Di Peso 1974). This provides a contrast to its use at El Cementerio, where 87 percent ($n = 130$) of the turquoise pieces were recovered as personal adornment in burials, mostly those of children.

Although the Río Yaqui has been a proposed trade route between west Mexico and Paquimé, with El Cementerio situated along that route, there appear to be significant differences in the nature of consumption of these prestige goods. Therefore, at least in the Ónavas Valley, there is little archaeological evidence for trade connections to/from Paquimé. In fact, it appears very clear that any trade or regular contact occurred to the south and west with groups along the Pacific coast and in northern Sinaloa.

The Postclassic regional center at Guasave is a very plausible center of trade and influence that could have had a direct or ancillary impact on the residents along the middle and lower Río Yaqui. Part of the complex at Guasave is a mortuary mound, producing over 100 individuals that included extended primary inhumations and secondary bundle burials in pits and in large plainware urns (Carpenter 1996). Associated funerary objects were generally elaborate, including several pottery types (such as highly detailed polychrome pottery), copper bells, shell jewelry, pyrite and turquoise jewelry, pseudo-cloisonné gourd vessels, cotton textiles, ceramic masks, clay smoking pipes, modeled spindle whorls, prismatic obsidian blades, bone daggers, and human trophy skulls (Carpenter 1996:163). Several individuals exhibit fronto-lambdoidal cranial modification and dental modification similar to that observed at El Cementerio (notched incisors and canines). Some elements of body placement (inhumed and extended) are common at both Guasave and El Cementerio, but much of the quantity and elaborate types of associated funerary objects found at Guasave are lacking from El Cementerio.

Carpenter (1996:349, 353) suggests that the mortuary patterns at Guasave reflect traits adopted from neighboring communities in northern Sinaloa and were the result of the manipulation of symbolically important materials for high-status individuals. This scenario reflects a down-the-line spread of symbolism and ideology that likely extended to a limited degree up the Río Yaqui to the smaller-scale center at Ónavas. The residents of El Cementerio likely were manipulating identity (and that of their children) by embodying the symbolism associated with richer communities to the south to serve sociopolitical means.

The possibility also exists that the residents interred at El Cementerio were migrants from the coast (or other points in west Mexico). This would certainly explain the presence of cranial and dental modification at the site. However, the nearly complete lack of nonlocal ceramics, the almost absent evidence of local manufacture of shell jewelry, the lack of bundle/urn burials and elaborate grave goods (especially pottery), and the presence of infants with modified crania supports a local origin for this group. Most of the evidence points to a group largely invested in the local economy—and perhaps control—as head of the Ónavas Valley settlement system.

The near ubiquitous practice of an elongated form of cranial deformation and the presence of dental modification in several individuals from El Cementerio indicate a measurable degree of influence from larger cultural traditions to the south. Neither of these biocultural characteristics appear linked to wealth in funerary objects. Rather, there appears to be a discernable difference in how identity is expressed in this population between material and biocultural attributes, such as cultural behaviors inscribed on the biological organism (see García Moreno et al. 2021). Since the inhabitants do not appear to have been active participants in a macroregional prestige-goods economy, then manipulating (visual) symbols of identity associated with groups in control of greater capital (social, political, economic, etc.) would provide some level of political control within the community, the Ónavas Valley settlement system, or perhaps within the Middle Río Yaqui region.

Dedicated investments in longstanding local material traditions suggest that it is unlikely that coastal groups, imperialistic mercantile elites, or individuals/groups from west Mexico or Mesoamerica founded or integrated into the regional center at Ónavas. Instead, direct interactions with coastal groups—evidenced by the presence of marine shell and a few ceramics—could have facilitated the adoption of biocultural traits that would allow the manipulation of identity connected to more influential groups along the west Mexican coast and support the manipulation of status and wealth within the Ónavas Valley.

Conclusion

Archaeological work at the burial mound of El Cementerio, located in southeast Sonora, Mexico, identified a deep commitment in local cultural traditions exhibiting selective influence from contemporaneous traditions in west Mexico. With very few exceptions, most of the material culture was produced locally and in local styles. This includes, but is not limited to, locally produced red- or brown-slipped monochrome pottery, lithics flaked from cobbles in the Río Yaqui, ground stone from geological sources in the Ónavas Valley, and local animal species. Nonlocal material includes shell from the Pacific coast, a few obsidian flakes, and turquoise. However, a comparison of the quantity and use of these objects to contemporaneous sites at the opposing ends of the Río Yaqui reveals considerable differences.

Mortuary patterns appear similarly representative of local practices, although the use of nonlocal funerary objects may be indicative of connections or influence from larger communities located along the coast. The same influence is proposed for the presence of artificial cranial and dental modification observed in much of the mortuary sample. But it appears that there is no significant internal patterning to burial placement or grouping (i.e., individuals with modification or funerary objects, etc.). In contrast, the identification of levels of interment in the mound may be suggestive of the incremental construction of the mound in at least two discrete episodes.

Most of the material culture reflects local manufacture and evolution; however, the presence of marine shell and turquoise jewelry associated with some burials and the incorporation of biocultural practices of cranial and dental modification suggest a link to populations further south along the west Mexican coast between northern Sinaloa as far south as the Amapa region and the Marismas Nacionales area of Nayarit. Although the population of El Cementerio evolved within a local archaeological tradition, we consider the site to represent an example of the broader sociocultural changes associated with the Aztatlán horizon by AD 900 in west Mexico. We also suggest that this population was actively managing their identity in response to these macroregional influences by selectively adopting limited aspects of southern material culture practices including modification of their skulls and teeth.

PART III

Technologies, Economies, and Trade in the Aztatlán Region and Beyond

CHAPTER 10

Obsidian Usage and Trade in Postclassic West Mexico

Daniel E. Pierce

Given the emphasis on trade within the Aztatlán system, understanding the distribution of specific material culture items can facilitate a multi-scalar assessment of Aztatlán culture. Traders in west Mexico exchanged shell (Mills and Ferguson 2008), copper (Pendergast 1962b), pottery (Kelley 2000), and cloth (Mathiowetz 2020a) far from their western Mexican homeland. Obsidian, however, was perhaps one of the most significant trade items within this vast exchange network. This conclusion is insinuated by not only the ubiquity of obsidian at all west Mexican sites, but also by the great distances it traveled through trade (Darling 1993; Pierce 2017a, 2017b; Weigand 1989). The following discussion focuses on this exchange network through an exploration of Aztatlán obsidian usage at four major Postclassic centers located on the coastal plain of Nayarit: San Felipe Aztatán, Coamiles, Chacalilla, and Amapa (Figures I.1–I.2). In so doing, this research illustrates the ways in which obsidian was differentially utilized across space and through time for the duration of the Aztatlán tradition.

Obsidian in the Aztatlán Region

Obsidian analysis is a particularly lucrative avenue for studying the Aztatlán system given its abundance and the relative ease with which its source can be identified. Although obsidian is readily available throughout the region, we know it has been traded extensively. Rather than relying on the single most proximal source, multiple sources were typically utilized. However, trade does not appear to be driven by demand for useful blades alone. Alternatively, it may have been an accessory byproduct of the trade of other items throughout the Aztatlán region (Drennan et al. 1990), a vehicle for establishing and maintaining external connections, and/or a means for elevating oneself socially through spending power and conspicuous consumption (Pierce 2017a).

Obsidian was an important part of social, economic, and political structures throughout much of precolumbian Mesoamerica. At major Mesoamerican centers such as Teotihuacan and elsewhere (Aoyama 2015; Charlton 1978; Clark 1979; Pierce 2017a; Ponomarenko 2004; Santley 1984), the significant role obsidian played in the structuring of Mesoamerican society is unquestionable. One key benefit of the exportation of this functional yet socially significant glass lay in the prestigious exotic items received from distant locales in return (Drennan et al. 1990). Yet just as important as the material items being exchanged were the interpersonal relationships created through these economic and social negotiations. Furthermore, the relationships extended beyond mercantile interaction alone and could also be exploited for the stratification of society as dictated and perpetuated by differential access to resources and exotic goods within a population (Aoyama 2015; Levine 2015b; Pierce 2017a; Rebnegger 2010).

West Mexico features one of the largest and most diverse concentrations of quality obsidian sources of any region in the world. In the past, no single source was utilized exclusively, although some obsidian sources have been more intensively exploited while others were all but neglected entirely. Most research regarding obsidian usage in west Mexico has focused on the areas of northwestern Jalisco and Durango (Darling 1993; Darling and Hayashida 1995; Tenorio et al. 2015; Trombold et al. 1993; Weigand 1989). However, recent research has begun to focus on the relationship between sources and distribution of obsidian artifacts within the Aztatlán core along the coastal plain (Garduño Ambriz and Pierce 2022; Pierce 2015a, 2017a, 2017b, 2022), providing new insight into coastal-highland interaction.

Here, obsidian was the most common lithic material used for the production of flaked stone artifacts, including the ubiquitous prismatic blades. Given their straight parallel edges, extreme sharpness, and the efficient manner in which they can be produced, prismatic blades were of unmatched utility and are found

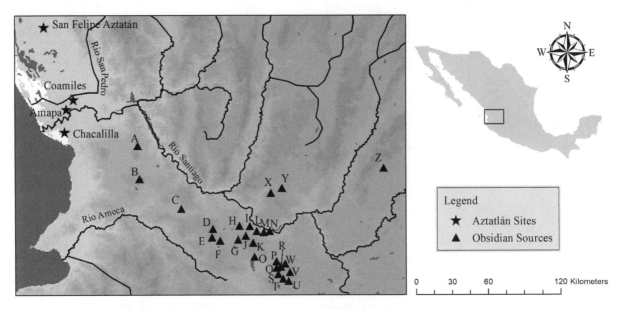

A	Volcán las Navajas	N	La Pila
B	San Leonel	O	La Mora/ Teuchitlán
C	Ixtlán del Río	P	Huaxtla
D	Llano Grande	Q	Boquillas
E	Osotero	R	La Primavera
F	Hacienda de Guadalupe	S	San Juan de los Arcos
G	San Juanito de Escobedo	T	Ahuisculco
H	La Quemada	U	Navajas
I	Cinco Minas/ Magdalena	V	Ixtépete
J	La Joya	W	San Isidro
K	La Providencia	X	La Lobera
L	Santa Teresa	Y	Huitzila
M	Tequila	Z	Nochistlán

FIGURE 10.1. Location of Aztatlán sites and known obsidian sources mentioned in the text. Sierra de Pachuca source not shown. Drawing by author.

in abundance at west Mexican sites of all sizes. Glascock and colleagues (2010) have commented on the relative quality of the various west Mexican obsidian sources, and while several sources produce obsidian of poor quality, 13 of the 26 identified sources have been categorized as "excellent."

This abundance of obsidian sources in the region provided Aztatlán sites with access to an assortment of high-quality obsidians (Figure 10.1). With so many quality sources available, the trade of obsidian may not have focused solely upon knappability and quality. Rather, it also may have been the intention to create trade networks for the acquisition of reciprocal items and/or establishing cooperative relationships between sites (Kelley 2000; Pierce 2017a). As has been observed worldwide ethnographically, superfluous economic exchange can develop as an expression of socioeconomic superiority by flaunting interpersonal relationships with powerful trading partners (Aoyama 2015; Boone 2000; Clark 1986; Neff 2014; Pierce 2017a; Plourde 2008; Quinn 2015; Weiner 1992). As one's status increases, access to more costly and diverse resources may also increase (Boone 2000). Consequently, we can at times use the material record and distribution of resources therein as expressions of past social stratification. For this reason, provenance studies of obsidian and other goods can provide for a better understanding of the broader patterns of social structure in past societies.

Analytical Methods

Most obsidian artifacts included in this study are permanently curated at the Museo Regional de Nayarit in Tepic, with others at the University of California, Los Angeles. Analyses were completed in Nayarit as well as at the University of Missouri Research Reactor (MURR). Numerous contextual and morphological attributes were recorded for each artifact, including: (1) temporal and spatial provenience, and (2) morphological traits such as weight, length, width, cortex coverage, and morphological type. Overall, these variables are among the "minimal set of attributes" typically recorded for lithic assemblages (Odell 2004). In all cases, data collection strategies were designed to allow for a statistical approach aimed at detecting group level differences among excavation units as opposed to attempting to focus on the technological or functional significance of individual artifacts.

Various taxonomic methods have been used to classify Mesoamerican lithic artifacts (Andrefsky 2005; Clark 1985; Clark and Bryant 1997; Railey and Gonzáles 2015; Santley et al. 1986). For this study, I used the comparatively broad and generally replicable technological categories of (1) complete or fragmented prismatic blades, (2) flakes, including byproducts related to polyhedral core preparation, prismatic blade or formal tool production, and angular shatter, and (3) non-prismatic formal tools (i.e., projectile points, scrapers, and worked or notched blades). This abbreviated classification system does not differentiate between classes of debitage, but does measure the relative frequency of prismatic blades, formal and expedient tools, and production debris.

Per the provenance postulate (Weigand et al. 1977), items such as obsidian from the same source will be more compositionally similar than items from differing sources. The determination of provenance therefore requires the comparison of compositional data from both artifacts and reference samples collected at the source. To gather the necessary compositional data for the reference samples as well artifacts from San Felipe Aztatán, Coamiles, and Amapa, a Bruker Tracer IIISD pXRF spectrometer was used. This allowed for rapid and reliable data collection with no damage to any of over 6,000 artifacts. The elements measured include but are not limited to Rubidium (Rb), Strontium (Sr), Ytterbium (Y), Zircon (Zr), Iron (Fe), and Niobium (Nb). To determine artifact provenance, comparisons were made between the proportions of elements (ppm) for each artifact and the compositional makeup of source samples currently curated at MURR from 26 obsidian sources in western Mexico and the well-known Sierra de Pachuca source in central Mexico. These comparisons were completed primarily through visual inspection of bivariate plots but also utilized principal component analyses and multivariate Mahalanobis distance calculations using GAUSS 8.0 software.

THE OBSIDIAN DISTRIBUTION

Throughout much of Mesoamerica, obsidian was the most common lithic material used. At Chacalilla, for example, over 99 percent of the chipped stone artifacts were produced from obsidian (Ohnersorgen 2007). Likewise, at San Felipe Aztatán, 1,501 of the 1,562 (96 percent) lithic artifacts collected were obsidian. While polyhedral cores have been recovered from multiple Aztatlán sites, few cores have been recovered relative to the abundant blades. There are multiple possible explanations for this discrepancy. It may be that blade production was rare at these sites and finished blades instead were imported along with exhausted cores as valuable goods unto themselves. It is also possible that the sampling strategies at these limited excavations simply failed to locate production workshops within the sites. A third scenario is that obsidian was at times acquired as prepared cores and/or blanks and then further reduced to exhaustion on site. Future studies may elucidate the disparity between cores and the abundance of blades more conclusively, but the present investigation remains informative of general obsidian acquisition and consumption patterns.

San Felipe Aztatán

The site of San Felipe Aztatán is located in part of a larger physiographic province extending from San Blas on the central Nayarit coast northward approximately 200 km to Mazatlán in southern Sinaloa (Garduño Ambriz 2007:37; Scott and Foster 2000). This area includes multiple biomes that are rich in land, freshwater, and marine resources. Notably, large waterways connected the area to many important locations and resources further inland and have facilitated transportation, trade, and communication between the coastal plain and the highlands of western Jalisco from antiquity through the historic era (Cárdenas 1996, 1999; Kelley 2000; Sánchez and Marmolejo 1990; Tenorio et al. 2015).

First documented by Sauer and Brand (1932), San Felipe Aztatán may represent the remains of the ethnohistorically documented capital town of the Aztatlán province (Anguiano 1992; see Garduño Ambriz, this volume; Figures 5.1–5.4). This large site features at least 110 structures and mounds (Zepeda and Fajardo 1999), including the largest mound in the entire region at over 9 m in height (Garduño Ambriz 2007; Garduño Ambriz and Gámez Eternod 2005; Pérez et al. 2000). The majority of the occupation at San Felipe Aztatán appears to be from the Cerritos (AD 900–1100) and Ixquintla/Taste-Mazatlán phases (AD 1100–1350). Ceramics dating back to at least the Late Formative, or 300 BC–AD 200/250 (Garduño Ambriz and Gámez Eternod 2005), are apparent at deeper strata as well. A small amount of Late Postclassic (AD 1250–1521) artifacts has been recorded (Ohnersorgen et al. 2012), indicting a long occupational history. In recent decades, mechanical earth-moving activities as well as the scavenging of stones and fill for the construction of modern structures have dramatically impacted the site (Gámez Eternod and Garduño Ambriz 2003; Garduño Ambriz and Gámez Eternod 2005). Therefore, the site's features were likely larger and more numerous in the past.

Excavations were conducted by the Instituto Nacional de Antropología e Historia (INAH) in 2002 in four noncontiguous areas: (1) Frente Calle Morelos,

(2) Frente Calle Hidalgo, (3) Plataforma Adosado Sur, and (4) Plataforma Oeste. Excavation areas were selected nonrandomly based on the threat of modern destruction and the likelihood of intact subsurface cultural deposits. Levels for each unit were defined using natural stratigraphic breaks, obvious changes in material culture, or divided into arbitrary 10–20 cm on a case-by-case basis. While superposition facilitates relative dating, in most cases the identification of temporally diagnostic ceramics also allowed for dating of strata for site-wide comparisons to address diachronic patterns.

A total of 1,501 obsidian artifacts were analyzed from San Felipe Aztatán. From the geochemical data produced from this sample, seven distinct sources were identified. The most proximal source is Volcán las Navajas, which contributes 29 percent of the total assemblage; La Joya comprises 34 percent; Ixtlán del Río contributes 23 percent; and Sierra de Pachuca comprises 12 percent of the assemblage. The remaining lithics originated from either San Juan de los Arcos, Boquillas, Navajas, or were left unassigned to a discrete source. The Llano Grande source was also identified in a subsequent analysis of 18 polyhedral cores found on site.

Overall, multiple sources (Ixtlán del Río, La Joya, and Sierra de Pachuca) are present primarily as prismatic blades. However, artifacts from Volcán las Navajas are almost entirely (98.6 percent) found in the form of generalized reduction debitage. These results indicate a positive correlation between the distance to a source and the proportion of prismatic blades identified from that source. Thus, it appears that more distant sources were likely either imported as finished blades or as fully prepared cores in most cases. This pattern is further apparent with the analysis of a cache of 18 exhausted polyhedral cores discovered by a local farmer on site after excavations. These cores originated at La Joya ($n = 15$), Ixtlán del Río ($n = 1$), and Llano Grande ($n = 2$). In all analyses, no cores were observed from Volcán las Navajas (Pierce 2016), despite its proximity. While the distance to the other sources would make direct procurement of these obsidians highly unlikely, the diversity of sources utilized makes institutional procurement strategies such as corporate or political control equally doubtful. This type of control includes a sponsoring agent, agency, or institutional body which collects the materials and redistributes them to the craftsmen who use them (Hirth 2008). If there was specific institutional control of obsidian, one would expect a single source to dominate the assemblage. Thus, the material record supports an indirect procurement model for obsidian acquisition at San Felipe Aztatán (see Hirth 2008).

In the deepest strata, corresponding with Chinesco (AD 0–200) and Gavilán (AD 200–500) phase sherds, it is apparent that Volcán las Navajas obsidian is most common. Ixtlán del Río and/or La Joya obsidians have rarely been identified here. During the Amapa phase (AD 500–750), there was a proportionate increase in La Joya and Ixtlán del Río obsidian artifacts as compared to those from Volcán las Navajas. It is also from within these strata that the great majority of the exotic Sierra de Pachuca artifacts have been identified. Of the total amount of Pachuca obsidian ($n = 128$) recovered, 67.7 percent dates to the Amapa phase while only 22.7 percent dates to the Cerritos phase. The remaining 9.6 percent was collected from strata not temporally identifiable through crossdating alone, but likely date to the Classic period based upon superposition. These data indicate that the extensive trade networks which typify the Aztatlán tradition may have developed their roots centuries prior to the Postclassic period during the Amapa phase. However, the spatially limited nature of the Pachuca artifacts within the site precludes our full understanding of the pervasiveness of this extensive trade during the Classic period. Nonetheless, though there was a general increase in frequency for La Joya as well as Ixtlán del Río artifacts (primarily blades) over time, there indeed remained a consistent usage of Volcán las Navajas obsidian for local consumption through generalized reduction.

Considering the spatial patterning of obsidian usage, the various sources appear to be unevenly distributed throughout the site. Namely, there are proportionally more artifacts from certain sources in some areas of the site. For example, as alluded to earlier, 126 of the 128 Pachuca artifacts were found at the Calle Hidalgo excavation area. If this assemblage represents household debris as suggested by Garduño Ambriz and Gámez Eternod (2005), variation in obsidian concentrations may then reflect differential household access to certain obsidian sources based upon their expendable resources. On the other hand, if procurement was institutionalized as in corporate or political control, we would expect sources to be more evenly distributed (Hirth 2008). In this regard, it appears that all households did in fact have a varying degree of access to tools and/or cores from La Joya and Ixtlán del Río, while the local Volcán las Navajas source was widely available for unskilled generalized reduction. Meanwhile, a more limited set of individuals at the site had access to the imported prismatic blades from the more sociopolitically significant Sierra de Pachuca source.

Coamiles

Like San Felipe Aztatán, Coamiles is located near the agriculturally productive farmland of northern coastal Nayarit (Figure 10.2). There, the site extends from the alluvial lowlands and onto the terraced slopes of the nearby Cerro de Coamiles. Approximately 60 km northwest of Tepic, Coamiles benefited from abun-

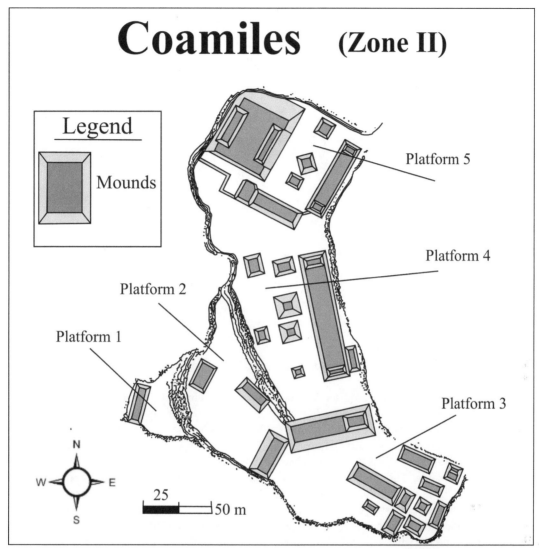

FIGURE 10.2. Site map of Coamiles (Zone II). Drawing by author after Duverger and Levine (1993:Figure 9).

dant floral and faunal resources as well as productive farmlands nourished by periodic flooding. Equally beneficial, the position of Coamiles between the Río San Pedro Mezquital to the north and the Río Grande de Santiago to the south may have even facilitated the control of the flow of population and goods across the coastal plain. As such, Coamiles was likely a key point along the critical Aztatlán trade routes to the northwest (Garduño Ambriz 2006, 2013a; Garduño Ambriz and Pierce 2022).

When it was first noted by the École des hautes études en sciences sociales (EHESS/Paris) during surveys in the 1980s, Coamiles was described as largely undisturbed by modern development. In these EHESS surveys, an assortment of vessels and ceramic sherds were collected for the purpose of determining a seriation-based chronology to be compared to sequences in other areas. Many of these vessels are elaborately embellished in symbolic designs and at times even contain anthropomorphic forms in the Mixteca-Puebla style (Garduño Ambriz 2013a).

Although Coamiles was occupied from at least the Gavilán (AD 250–500) through Ixcuintla phases (AD 1100–1350), the greatest amount of construction occurred during the Aztatlán horizon in the Cerritos and Ixcuintla phases, or AD 900–1350 (Duverger and Levine 1993). Regarding the architecture and organization of the site, Duverger and Levine (1993) described Coamiles in some detail in the decade following the EHESS surveys. Overall, architecture here appears to have been formally planned with four general areas. Zone I is located at the base of the hill and is comprised of the southern complex and four main sets of petroglyphs ($n = 149$). These elements, along with two large rectangular mounds, likely represent the main access point to the ceremonial center. Zone II, on the other hand, consists of a terraced area upon the steep slopes of the cerro and contains the main portion of the site's

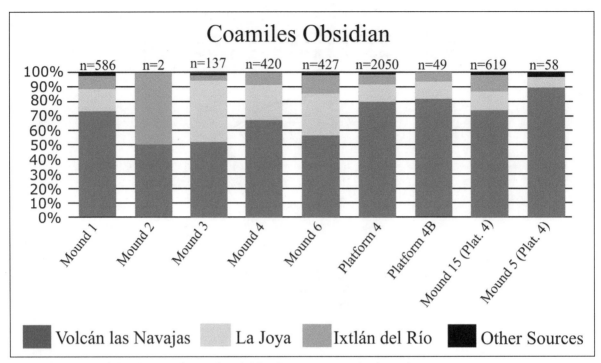

FIGURE 10.3. Spatial distribution of Coamiles obsidian by source. Drawing by author.

architecture. Zone III is another terraced section located on the southern slopes of the hill and was likely a common residential area, based upon the high density of utilitarian artifacts observed during surficial surveys (Garduño Ambriz 2006). Finally, Zone IV covers the lower elevation floodplains. Though traces are still visible in diminished form, most of the above-ground features in this zone have been destroyed by mechanical leveling and modern agriculture activity. Despite the destruction here and elsewhere at Coamiles, more recent surveys and excavations have identified several additional stone structures still in good states of preservation throughout the site as well as a wealth of artifacts (Garduño Ambriz 2006, 2013a; Garduño Ambriz and Pierce 2022).

The obsidian assemblage analyzed here is a product of the 2005–2009 excavations conducted under the auspices of the Centro Instituto Nacional de Antropología e Historia, Nayarit. These excavations were primarily focused on the distribution of ceramics for the purposes of determining the timing of various construction events and occupational histories at the site (Garduño Ambriz 2013a). However, these excavations also yielded thousands of nonceramic artifacts now available for study. Among the obsidian collections considered here, the Coamiles collection is the largest.

From Coamiles, the majority of the 4,925 obsidian artifacts originated at the most proximal source, Volcán las Navajas. Seven other sources have also been identified. Approximately 99 percent of the total number of obsidian artifacts originated from one of three sources, Volcán las Navajas (n = 3,486; 70.8 percent), Ixtlán del Río (n = 452; 9.2 percent), or La Joya (n = 910; 18.5 percent). Unlike at San Felipe Aztatán, no obsidian from the Sierra de Pachuca source has been identified here. Use patterns are nonetheless similar. At Coamiles, Volcán las Navajas appears to be primarily utilized for generalized reduction, while the other prominent sources were more likely introduced as finished tools. Most artifacts from Ixtlán del Río and La Joya are prismatic blades, yet few (only 2.4 percent) of the artifacts from Volcán las Navajas are of this form. This small proportion is in stark contrast to the distribution of La Joya lithics, for example, in which 91.5 percent are found in the form of blades.

Similar temporal patterns can also be observed as those described for San Felipe Aztatán, notwithstanding the complete absence of Sierra de Pachuca obsidian here. Over time, there was a proportionate increase in the number of prismatic blades and obsidian artifacts from more distant sources (La Joya and Ixtlán del Río), particularly during the Early/Middle Postclassic period. Volcán las Navajas, on the other hand, remained the dominant source for generalized reduction throughout the entirety of the stratigraphic sequence.

Patterning in the spatial distribution of sources at Coamiles is less clear (Figure 10.3), though statistical analysis does suggest a possible nonrandom distribution. For example, some excavation areas contain a higher percentage of La Joya obsidian as compared to Volcán las Navajas despite the site-wide ubiquity of the source. However, these results may also be affected by sample size. Excavation areas with larger sample sizes are quite consistent in their distribution of sources. Consequentially, it remains possible that spatial patterning may be coincidental. Further excavations with more robust sampling site-wide may better clarify these synchronic usage patterns.

Generally, when considered in aggregate, the above-described results lend themselves to the conclusion of importation of prismatic blades rather than local production at Coamiles, with temporal patterns similar to those observed elsewhere. The relatively uniform distribution of obsidian in both blade and non-blade form also suggests generally equal access to multiple sources.

Chacalilla

Of the major Aztatlán regional centers in the core zone, Chacalilla is the southernmost. It is located approximately 10 km north of the modern coastal city of San Blas, Nayarit, and features archaeological remains across much of a 2.4 km² hilltop. Another resource rich area, it is located near the Río Zauta as well as the southern extension of the Marismas Nacionales which provide periodically inundated and fertile lowland fields ideal for agriculture. Chacalilla was first identified by Mountjoy (1970) with subsequent surveys and mapping by Guevara (1981) and Ohnersorgen (2004, 2007). These efforts identified dozens of mounds and features, primarily at the site's ceremonial center. This area consists of three open plazas, a series of mounds of up to 4.5 m in height, sunken patio compounds, and an I-shaped ballcourt. Artifacts recovered from the site include large quantities of obsidian, pottery, copper, Mazapan-style figurines, shell, and bone (Ohnersorgen 2004, 2007). Although the precise occupation chronology is still unknown, Chacalilla seems to have peaked with the Aztatlán tradition as strata associated with the Early and Middle Postclassic are the most artifact rich (Ohnersorgen 2007). A large portion of the ancient city is located immediately to the east of the ceremonial center and sits beneath the modern *ejido* community, frustrating a full understanding of the site's extent.

Between 2004 and 2008, Michael Ohnersorgen orchestrated a large-scale survey project at Chacalilla in which the entire site was surveyed through pedestrian transects. During this survey, his team identified 253 distinct features including 63 mounds, 153 rock alignments, 26 artifact concentrations, and 12 petroglyphs (Ohnersorgen 2007). The abundance of features and tens of thousands of artifacts recovered during surveys are a testament to a large precolumbian population at Chacalilla. Furthermore, there are clear differences in architecture across the site that indicate socioeconomic inequality and presumed complexity (Ohnersorgen 2007).

Of the four sites discussed here, Chacalilla is the only site in which the provenance analysis of obsidian was not fully reliant upon archaeometric methods. Since Ohnersorgen's (2004, 2007) surveys, all artifacts have been reinterred and are thus no longer available for further study. We must therefore rely upon the survey reports for our understanding of obsidian trade and usage at Chacalilla. To these ends, Ohnersorgen used a combination of visual and geochemical sourcing (XRF and NAA) to determine the origin of 3,867 obsidian artifacts (Ohnersorgen et al. 2012). Though not ideal, other studies have shown the efficacy of visual sourcing in west Mexico (Pierce 2015), and Ohnersorgen himself tested the validity of his method with great accuracy (Ohnersorgen et al. 2012). Overall, he found that Volcán las Navajas, Ixtlán del Río, and La Joya were again the most common sources observed. Of the total 3,867 artifacts analyzed from Chacalilla, 1,287 (33.28 percent) of them likely originated at Volcán las Navajas. The other two most common sources, La Joya (49.06 percent) and Ixtlán del Río (16.01 percent), were again most often found in the form of prismatic blade fragments (92.3 percent and 68.01 percent, respectively). On the contrary, Volcán las Navajas obsidian is more frequently recovered in the form of miscellaneous debitage and production debris (61.38 percent), with only 35.82 percent being prismatic blade fragments (Ohnersorgen et al. 2012). Analyses also indicate minimal amounts of rarer sources such as La Pila and Santa Teresa (Ohnersorgen 2007).

At Chacalilla, it is not possible to assess diachronic patterning due to the assemblage being a product of surface collection alone. However, we can still consider the significance of a spatial distribution by identifying which areas of the site are more or less likely to feature obsidian from particular sources. As noted earlier, a large area in the center of the site just to the west of the modern community has been identified as the ceremonial center. Yet, the location of the modern community precludes our full understanding of the ceremonial center's extent. Beyond this area, the site radiates to the east, west, and south. To determine spatial patterning, the site has been divided into four zones: ceremonial center, south, east, and west (Figure 10.4).

Considering these four groups, some statistically significant patterning of obsidian consumption is apparent. More specifically, the southern portion of the site is characterized by an abundance of Volcán las Navajas obsidian while far fewer lithics from La Joya and Ixtlán

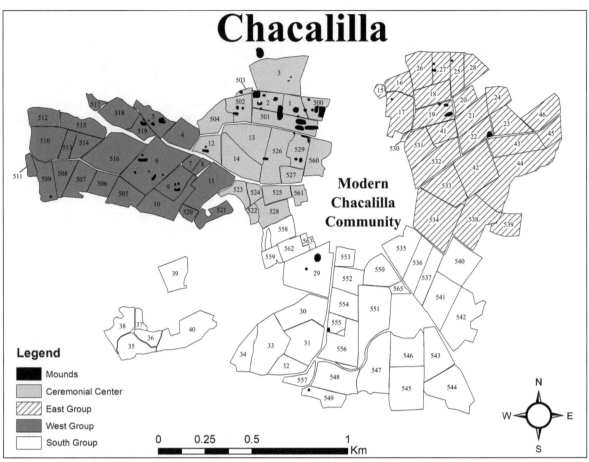

FIGURE 10.4. Site map of Chacalilla divided into four zones. Drawing by author after Ohnersorgen (2007:Figures 3.1–3.3).

del Río were recovered. In fact, here 72.5 percent of the obsidian originated from Volcán las Navajas whereas obsidian from this source comprises only 30 percent of the lithics in the ceremonial center, 32.7 percent in the west, and 27.8 percent in the east. Conversely, La Joya obsidian totaled only 12.6 percent of the southern assemblage while comprising 50–55 percent in the other areas of the site. Clearly, there is greater access to more costly distant sources in areas that were likely of higher importance and/or status. While it is possible that an uneven sampling strategy may have obscured the true spatial distribution of sources, the patterns observed are nonetheless statistically significant.

As can be expected given the abundance of La Joya and Ixtlán del Río artifacts, the majority of the lithics recovered in the ceremonial center, east, and west are prismatic blades. Conversely, in the south where Volcán las Navajas obsidian dominates, prismatic blades comprise only 15.6 percent of the obsidian collected. The preponderance of Volcán las Navajas debitage in the south may indicate universal access to a proximal source for unskilled household production. But given that a notably higher proportion of Volcán las Navajas obsidian (38 percent) is in the form of blades when compared to other coastal sites, it is also possible that prismatic blades and tools were produced in the south at a yet unidentified production area.

Amapa

Undoubtedly, Amapa is the most well-known and thoroughly excavated of the Aztatlán sites (see Figure 13.5). Located approximately 5 km from the Río Grande de Santiago and 19 km from the Pacific coast, Amapa sits on the resource-rich and fertile floodplain. While the true boundaries of the site are unknown, features including mounds have been recorded continuously from the site center all the way to the coast. To the north, however, the site's extent is limited by a large silted-in channel of the Río Grande de Santiago. Like the previously discussed sites, multiple concentrations of mounds of various sizes and orientations were located at Amapa's center, many of which are now destroyed.

The lack of evidence of long-term occupation prior to 2,000 years ago suggests that an important environmental shift may have taken place at that time promoting settlement in newly fertile areas (Meighan, ed. 1976). From this point onward, the area has remained consistently occupied. Amapa began as a relatively small but growing village on the riverbank consisting only of wattle and daub houses (Meighan, ed. 1976). There is no indication of architecture at Amapa during the Classic period Gavilán and Amapa phases. Nevertheless, as the population increased during the Postclassic, many mounds and features were constructed across the site, signaling an increasing level of social organization and complexity. Though the catalyst for it remains unclear, widespread population decline at Amapa and in the surrounding area eventually occurred during the Late Postclassic directly preceding the Spanish *entrada* (Grosscup 1964).

In 1959, Clement Meighan of the University of California, Los Angeles undertook a large-scale excavation project at Amapa that resulted in an edited volume and multiple doctoral dissertations by his students. These excavations provided a wealth of knowledge as Amapa remains the most well-studied Aztatlán site to date. In total, Meighan noted six main mound groups, all of which were sampled to a varying degree. Within these groups, a wide array of features was reported, including mounds and numerous examples of stone architecture, large ponds, and depressions of unknown utility (Meighan, ed. 1976). Likely constructed in singular events, these features were typically organized around open plazas and may have served both residential and public purposes.

Two cemeteries containing many burials, mortuary offerings, and caches of artifacts were also identified. Across all contexts, ceramic objects recovered during Meighan's excavations include pottery, beads, whistles, ear spools, spindle whorls, pipes, and over 50 flat Mazapan-style (Type A) figurines (Meighan, ed. 1976). Primarily dating to the Cerritos phase, copper artifacts such as tweezers, fish hooks, and jewelry were also found in relative abundance. Most notably, 99 copper bells were recovered, primarily in burial lots.

As at most Mesoamerican sites, lithics are found in abundance at Amapa. Groundstone artifacts such as manos and metates are common, but flaked tools are particularly ubiquitous. Chalcedony, chert, and obsidian were all commonly noted materials during excavations (Meighan, ed. 1976). However, in keeping with archaeological practice at the time (Levine 2015b), debitage as well as blades were neither routinely collected nor recorded by Meighan's team (see Coe 1959:18 for a common contemporaneous perspective of the limited information available through lithic analysis). As a result, the Amapa collection ($n = 347$) primarily consists of formal tools (Meighan, ed. 1976). We are therefore limited as to what information we can glean regarding obsidian usage at Amapa. Nonetheless, an analysis of a sample ($n = 164$) of these formal tools found that nearly the entire sample came from either Volcán las Navajas, Ixtlán del Río, or La Joya. Each of these three sources represents approximately one-third of the sample. But, due to the clearly biased collection strategy and the near complete absence of debitage and prismatic blades in the collection, little more can be learned regarding overall source usage based upon this sample alone.

A total of 17 polyhedral cores that are curated at the Amapa Municipal Museum ($n = 11$) and the Sentispac Municipal Museum ($n = 6$) were also analyzed to determine the sources utilized for prismatic blade production at Amapa. These cores were donated to the museums by local individuals, and therefore their specific spatial and temporal context within Amapa is unclear. Like the Meighan collection, these cores do not allow for detailed analysis of temporal or spatial patterns in obsidian usage. But they do permit an evaluation of which sources were accessible and utilized for various tasks even if only in a general sense.

Geochemical analyses confirm the disproportionate preference for La Joya blades as 13 of 17 of these cores derive from this source (Pierce 2015b, 2015c). Moreover, five of the Sentispec cores come from La Joya with a sixth more likely from Huitzila (Pierce 2015b). For the Amapa Municipal Museum sample, over 70 percent ($n = 8$) of the cores originate from La Joya with two from La Mora/Teuchitlán and one from San Isidro (Pierce 2015c). These results suggest a similar preference for La Joya blades as was observed at the other coastal centers.

During the excavation of two wells in 2013, a small lithic assemblage including debitage, blades, and tools was also collected from Amapa ($n = 459$). Although the analysis of this collection cannot contribute to an understanding of broad site-wide synchronic and diachronic patterns, this sample does likewise contribute towards generalizations about which sources were utilized and in what ways. Analyses reveal that the most common sources are again La Joya, Ixtlán del Río, and Volcán las Navajas. These three sources collectively represent over 96 percent of the entire assemblage from the wells. La Mora/Teuchitlán and Sierra de Pachuca together comprise another 2.4 percent of the assemblage, though the significance of the existence of Pachuca obsidian here is unknown due to the limited sampling.

Prismatic blades make up the majority of the artifacts from Ixtlán del Río (89.8 percent) and La Joya (94.2 percent) when considering only the wells. However, the usage pattern diverges from the other coastal sites with Volcán las Navajas. With this sample, blades constitute 75 percent of all artifacts from this source. The small sample size of 40 total artifacts from Volcán las Navajas here does nonetheless justify some reservation in concluding that blade production from this source was common. The aforementioned analysis of polyhedral cores from Amapa and elsewhere may suggest otherwise in this regard. Without doubt, further excavations with the collection of obsidian on a site-wide scale at Amapa is warranted for clarification.

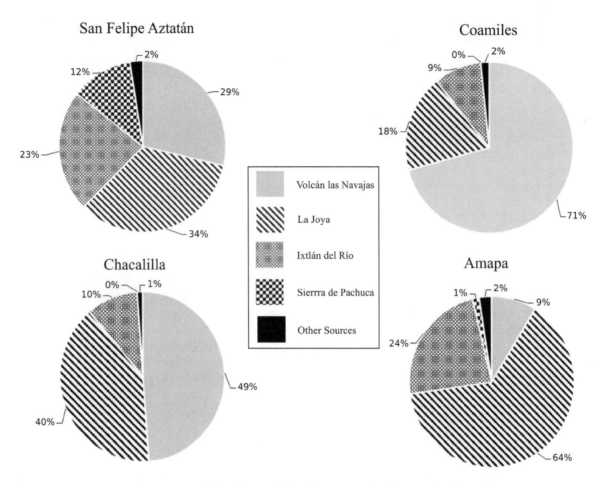

FIGURE 10.5. Overall distribution of obsidian sources by site. Drawing by author.

Overall, although the total Amapa assemblage is limited, much can yet be learned from these results. Three sources—Volcán las Navajas, La Joya, and Ixtlán del Río—comprise the vast majority of the obsidian here. Like elsewhere, it seems that certain sources were preferred for blade production either by local knappers or itinerant craftsmen. Most of the cores originated at La Joya and the majority of the La Joya artifacts recovered from the well excavations were in fact blades. Therefore, it appears that La Joya was the preferred source for blade production or import. Spatial or temporal patterns of obsidian usage at Amapa have yet to be identified, but this is largely a result of limited sampling.

Discussion and Conclusion

On the coastal plain, obsidian was certainly an important commodity beyond its functional attributes and was a major part of far-reaching trade networks. Although other quality sources were abundant in west Mexico, the same three sources (Volcán las Navajas, La Joya, and Ixtlán del Río) comprise the majority of the obsidian at all four Aztatlán sites analyzed (Figure 10.5). Usage trends are also similar among sites. Overall, Volcán las Navajas obsidian was primarily utilized for generalized reduction, while few prismatic blades or formal tools have been recovered from this source at any Aztatlán site. Volcán las Navajas obsidian was commonly reduced at all four sites and was likely a resource that could be universally acquired by all (Figure 10.6). Regardless of temporal or cultural context, there are no Aztatlán sites at which Volcán las Navajas prismatic blades have been identified in any abundance despite its proximity, excellent quality, and knappability (Pierce 2016).

Conversely, the La Joya source tends to have been universally preferred for prismatic blade production as evidenced by the high proportion of blades. While it is possible that La Joya obsidian was largely imported in a reduced or finished form, some La Joya blades were likely also created on site as evident based upon the frequency of cores and occasional late-stage reduction debris (Pierce 2017b). Evidence of on-site production in the form of polyhedral cores has been identified at Amapa and San Felipe Aztatán. However, production locales at other sites may remain unidentified due to limited sampling.

The Ixtlán del Río source was also widely used for prismatic blades, although only a few core fragments have been observed. Yet, the use of this source differs

FIGURE 10.6. Obsidian source at Volcán las Navajas in the central highlands of Nayarit. (*a*) Southern slope of the Volcán las Navajas, Nayarit, located to the east of Tepic. View to the north. (*b*) Dense deposits of obsidian debitage found on the ground surface of the southern slope of the Volcán las Navajas, Nayarit. Debitage relates to the first stages of reduction at this quarry site. Photos by Mauricio Garduño Ambriz.

from that of La Joya in other key ways. For example, there is a greater proportion of formal tools and general reduction debitage from this source than from La Joya. While a higher proportion of formal tools is found from Ixtlán del Río than any other source, they are still relatively few in number. It is therefore more likely that Ixtlán del Río obsidian commonly entered the sites as finished blades and as core blanks to be reduced at the household level, rather than the local reduction from unworked cobbles. This hypothesis accounts for not only the more frequent debitage and formal tools, but also the paucity of cortical flakes (Pierce 2017b).

Notably, a significant amount of Sierra de Pachuca obsidian has been identified at San Felipe Aztatán. Here it is found almost exclusively in the form of prismatic blades and primarily in Classic period contexts (Pierce 2015a). This discovery indicates at least some long-distance exchange with the Basin of Mexico just prior to the development of the Aztatlán tradition. Consequently, given the great sociopolitical and cosmological significance of the Sierra de Pachuca source (Aoyama 2015; Levine 2015a; Pierce 2017a; Townsend 1992), this valuable and exotic obsidian may have played a critical role in the development of sociopolitical structures at this key moment in west Mexican prehistory (Pierce 2017a).

Spatial and temporal patterns are not directly comparable between all sites due to differing collection strategies. However, a few region-wide generalities can be discerned based upon the information that is available. The explanatory power of diachronic usage patterns is based upon superposition and typological crossdating. Using these, similar ordinal patterns can be observed at multiple sites. For instance, there seems to be a trend of consistent use of Volcán las Navajas obsidian throughout the entire chronology of these sites. Over time, more distant sources were increasingly used. As populations grew in the early and middle Postclassic, the proportion of blades from more distant sources likewise increased.

Spatial patterns, on the other hand, do differ between sites. Coamiles has limited variation in obsidian usage from one portion of the site to the next. San Felipe Aztatán appears rather evenly distributed as well, notwithstanding the temporally and spatially limited distribution of Sierra de Pachuca obsidian (Pierce 2015a). At Chacalilla, however, we see distinction in the southern portion of the site where a much greater amount of Volcán las Navajas reduction debris was recovered. This area also has far fewer prismatic blades and obsidian from La Joya, and Ixtlán del Río is comparatively rarer here when compared to other areas of the site. Clearly, Volcán las Navajas, La Joya, and Ixtlán del Río were just three of many sources accessible to Aztatlán people. But, region-wide, they were all almost exclusively used in similar ways. We are therefore left with the question: why were these three specific sources used in the ways that they were?

The Law of Monotonic Decrement (Renfrew 1977) dictates that as distance to a source increases, its frequency at a site should decrease. Volcán las Navajas is not only the closest source (Pierce 2016), but it is also located along the most likely land-based trade route (Ekholm 1942; Pierce 2017b). As such, one would expect this source to comprise the overwhelming majority of the obsidian assemblages at coastal sites. However, multiple sources of similar quality and abundance (Glascock et al. 2010) were used. Therefore, some social determinant likely offset the additional acquisition cost. The Sierra de Pachuca obsidian found at San Felipe Aztatán, for example, would have been far more costly and more difficult to obtain given the distance. Likewise, La Joya obsidian, originating in the Jalisco highlands, would have been more costly to acquire than a local source. Conversely, obsidian from Volcán las Navajas would have been much easier to acquire directly. This lower acquisition cost and the ease with which Volcán las Navajas obsidian could be obtained is further demonstrated by its temporal and spatial ubiquity at all sites.

Generally, this most proximal source was used indiscriminately throughout each site, for the duration of the sites' occupational history, and for less-skilled tool manufacture. To the contrary, the more distant and presumably more costly sources were crafted into blades and were utilized with increasing frequency as the Aztatlán tradition gained regional prominence. This cultural expansion coincided with increasing social complexity thereby inextricably linking the obsidian trade to broader Aztatlán developments. Furthermore, the limited distribution of distant sources such as La Joya and particularly Sierra de Pachuca suggests unequal access to some sources based upon acquisition costs. This pattern indicates that specific obsidian sources and/or prismatic blades may have been considered a luxury item, and their presence may be indicative of status differences.

One possible explanation for the differential use of obsidians is based in socioeconomics. Perhaps obsidians were valued differently based upon rarity, distance, and sociopolitical significance. In this sense, obsidian could have played an integral role not only in the development of the Aztatlán trade networks, but may have also helped contribute to the sociopolitical complexity necessary for the creation of the large regional centers. Elsewhere, it has been suggested (Pierce 2012, 2017a, 2017b) that obsidian usage patterns are related to social status at San Felipe Aztatán. Yet, as the distribution of obsidians and trends in their usage are largely similar from one coastal center to another, it is possible that obsidian played a similar role at each site.

Based on these analyses, it is apparent that obsidian was very important on the coastal plain not only during the Postclassic period, but long before the Aztatlán florescence. Particular sources likely held both symbolic and value-based meanings related to social status for those who could acquire them. The individuals and craftspeople who made and used obsidian tools would have likely been aware of the sources that they were using, their value, and their appropriate use (Pierce 2017a). Obsidian in precolumbian west Mexico, therefore, was far more than a simple raw material; it was imbued with cultural meaning and value beyond its functional qualities alone.

Acknowledgments

I would like to thank the following people for assisting in this research: Michael Mathiowetz, Todd VanPool, Michael Ohnersorgen, and Jeff Ferguson. I also would like to give special thanks to Mauricio Garduño Ambriz of the Centro Instituto Nacional de Antropología e Historia, Nayarit, for providing artifacts, data, and assistance in all stages of this work. This work has been partially funded through MURR National Science Foundation grant BCS-1460436.

CHAPTER 11

A Spatial and Temporal Comparative Analysis of Metal Objects from Michoacán to the Greater Southwest

José Luis Punzo Díaz and Lissandra González

In characterizing the forms of interaction existing between west Mexico and the U.S. Southwest and northern Mexico, we center our analyses on the disparate regions at the extremes of an extensive network of interchange. Herein we analyze the presence of metal objects, especially bells, in a region considered to be the origin of production where we can establish a clear developmental sequence in techniques for manufacturing metals, particularly in Michoacán. Thereafter, we draw further comparisons with metal objects from northern Mexico, in the region of Paquimé and the Casas Grandes culture, as well as the Puebloan region of the southwestern United States (Figures I.1–I.2, I.10).

THE SAMPLE AND DATA COLLECTION

Studies conducted by the *Proyecto Arqueología y Paisaje del Área Centro Sur de Michoacán* (Punzo Díaz et al. 2014; Punzo Díaz et al. 2015) from 2013 until the present primarily have focused on metallurgy in west Mexico, but analyses also include metal items in northern Mexico. This research is based on the analysis of more than 1,800 metallic objects corresponding to the state of Michoacán, including 385 bells housed in various collections. The total includes objects in the *bodegas* of the Museo Regional de Michoacán, in the collection of the Museo del Estado de Michoacán, in community museums at Tepalcatepec, Apatzingán, Coahuayana, Cojumatlán, Ciudad Hidalgo, Huetamo, Lázaro Cárdenas, Uruapán, Tacambaro, and Jiquilpán, and examples found during recent excavations conducted in Huetamo, Michoacán. On the other hand, the sample of copper bells from northern Mexico and the Casas Grandes region in Chihuahua is composed of 195 bells, the majority of which were recovered by Di Peso and colleagues (1974) in their excavations at Paquimé, along with those metal items located and published over the last few decades by past and ongoing archaeological projects in the area.

CHRONOLOGIES AND REGIONAL CONTEXTS

In a series of studies, Dorothy Hosler (1986, 1988a, 1988b, 1994a, 1994b, 1997, 1998, 2005a, 2009) and a number of other scholars over the past century have amply demonstrated that the technology of metalworking likely originated in South America from the two major traditions that existed there (Anawalt 1992; Arsandaux and Rivet 1921; Clement 1932; Easby 1962; Edwards 1969; Kelly 1980; Lathrap 1973; Meggers 1975; Meighan 1969; Meighan and Nicholson 1989; Mountjoy 1969; Pendergast 1962a, 1962b; Pollard 1987; Schöndube 1980b; Schroeder 1966, and others). The Peruvian tradition is distinguished by cold-hammered works with the production of beautiful objects made of sheet metal, especially gold. The Colombian tradition was noted for the use of the lost-wax casting technique to produce intricate animal shapes and richly dressed figures. Hosler (1988a:215, 1994b:91) proposed an area in Ecuador as the most probable point of origin for the transmission of this technological knowledge from western South America to Mexico, via Pacific-coastal trade as early as AD 600. Thereafter, metallurgical processes and products were adapted and transformed to meet local needs (Hosler 1986, 1988b).

The development of metallurgy in Mesoamerica has been divided by Hosler (1994b:46) into two general periods based on artifact composition and design characteristics (Figure 11.1). The first period dates to AD 600–1200/1300, and includes copper bells, needles, open rings, awls, and tweezers. Sites where Period 1 materials were identified are generally located near the Pacific coast during the Aztatlán expansion (that

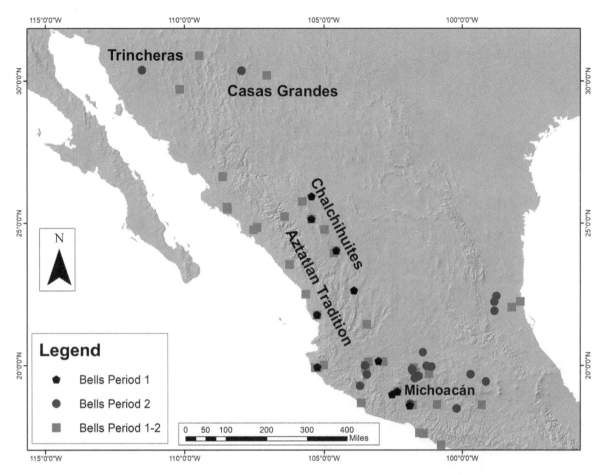

FIGURE 11.1. Regional map of bell distribution in Tarascan and southeastern Aztatlán regions. Drawing by author.

is, from AD 900–1300), although ongoing archaeological projects have found bells of this period in much of west Mexico. A fragment of sheet metal from the site of Tomatlán in coastal southern Jalisco appears to be among the earliest objects—dated around AD 600 (Mountjoy and Torres 1985). However, two bells dating between AD 600–750 were found inland at Cerro del Huistle, a site considered to be part of the Chalchihuites tradition on the border between Jalisco and Zacatecas (Hers 1989). It is important to mention that the archaeological contexts associated with metal at both sites are currently questioned and may date later in time. In addition, material from Period 1 has been found at the sites of Amapa, Coamiles, and Peñitas (Nayarit); Tizapán el Alto (Jalisco); Cojumatlán and Huandacareo (Michoacán), where there is a possible transitional bell between Periods 1 and 2; and La Villita and the Infiernillo area on the Michoacán-Guerrero border. After careful review of available collections, as well as recent findings, we can add to this period pieces from other sites including Guasave, Culiacán, and Juantillos in Sinaloa; the Tintoque site in Nayarit where traces of metal object production were found; La Ferrería, Cañón del Molino, and Navacoyán in Durango; and Teúl de González Ortega in Zacatecas (see Beltrán Medina 2019; Grave Tirado 2019; Punzo Díaz 2019). It appears that metallurgy moved inland from the coast and up the Lerma-Santiago river system, the Río Balsas, and the Lake Chapala basins (Hosler 1994b:49).

In general, pure copper compositions were the primary material used during this period even though other ore minerals were present in the region. Alloys were not developed until a few centuries later (Hosler 1994b:51). The production techniques used during Period 1 were lost-wax casting, open-mold casting, cold work, and annealing (Hosler 2005b:87). An important issue to consider is that although copper objects appear in Jalisco and Nayarit as early as AD 600, the adoption of copper metallurgy does not appear to have become a regional phenomenon until AD 800–900 (Hosler 1988b; Vargas 1994) and in association with the Aztatlán expansion between AD 900 and 1300, an important topic discussed in more detail below.

The second period ranges between AD 1200/1300 until the arrival of the Spaniards. During this era the production and diversity of metal bells increased with

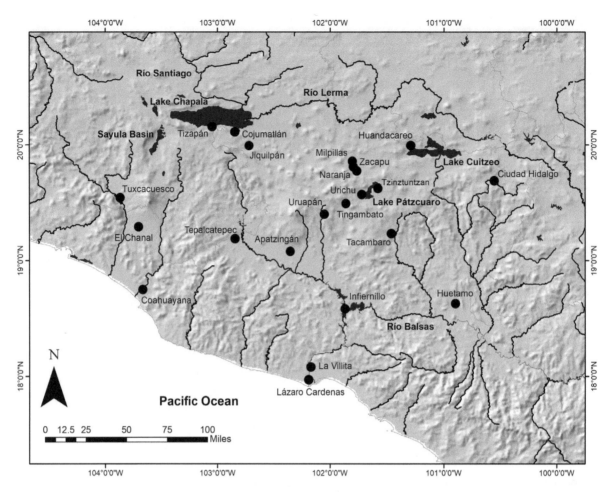

FIGURE 11.2. Archaeological sites within the broader Tarascan and southeastern Aztatlán regions. Drawing by author.

technological advances in the use, design, and experimentation in manufacturing objects. A variety of different metallic alloys were used, including the following: copper-tin bronze and copper-arsenic bronze, alloys of copper-silver, copper-gold, as well as some ternary alloys of copper-arsenic-tin and copper-silver-gold, and other alloys in Jalisco, Colima, northwest Guerrero, the southern parts of the state of Mexico, and Michoacán (Hosler 1994b:127). However, Period 1 copper artifact forms and the use of pure copper did not disappear during Period 2; the types of objects simply expanded with the use of alloys, including tweezers, needles, rings, cutting tools, and thin-walled simulated wirework bells. The use of alloys also permitted a range of colors in the final products as color and design of metal objects became important among west Mexican societies (Hosler 1986:95).

The greatest technological complex during Period 2 appears to be associated almost completely with the rise and consolidation of the Tarascan *señorío* in central Michoacán, including at the main centers of Tzintzuntzan and Urichu in the Pátzcuaro Basin, at Huandacareo in the Cuitzeo Basin, and at Milpillas near Zacapu (Figure 11.2; Cabrera 1988; Grinberg 1989; Hosler 1986; Macías Goytia 1989; Rubín de la Borbolla 1944). The beginning of Period 2 occurred during the middle of the Late Uricho phase in the Lake Pátzcuaro zone, and it was during this era when the Pátzcuaro Basin experienced a population increase which can be visible amidst major changes in architectonic patterns. During the ensuing Tariácuri phase between AD 1350–1522, the capital cities of the Tarascan *señorío* developed. Pátzcuaro first rose to primacy, followed by Ihuatzio, and then Tzintzuntzan, which expanded across a broad portion of west Mexico from the mid-fifteenth century to the Spanish conquest. Similar developments occurred outside of the Tarascan cultural sphere at Apatzingán, Michoacán; along the Río Balsas at the Infiernillo site and La Villita in coastal Guerrero; in the Sayula Basin in Jalisco; at El Chanal in Colima; and at Calixtlahuaca in the Valley of Toluca (Brush 1962; Hosler 1986; Kelly 1980).

In northern Mexico and the Greater U.S. Southwest, the earliest dated appearance of copper objects is around AD 900 at Sacaton-phase Hohokam sites (Sprague and Signori 1963; Vargas 1994:32). This is considerably earlier than the appearance of the majority of smelted copper artifacts in the Casas Grandes region during the Medio Period between AD 1200–1450 (Whalen and Minnis 2001). The beginning of Period 2 at AD 1200/1300 occurs around the same time as the end of the Viejo Period in the Casas Grandes region during which only a pair of small copper objects has been identified (Di Peso et al. 1974; Kelley 2017).

It is fundamental to consider that during the era ranging from AD 600–1300, significant changes occurred in the northern regions of Mesoamerica, including the rise of two very important cultural traditions: the Chalchihuites culture in the highlands and later the Aztatlán culture on the coast of west Mexico (Punzo Díaz 2019). Further north, more than 600 metal objects were recovered during the excavations of Paquimé by Di Peso and colleagues (1974), and today most Casas Grandes scholars agree there are no signs of possible metal manufacturing in the site or region (Figure 11.3a). The most widely accepted hypothesis is that these metal objects arrived in the north from west Mexico (Vargas 1994). Nevertheless, it is important to note there are some elements at Paquimé that may lead us to rethink the possibility that minor metal production occurred at this city. For example, there are copper nuggets worked into pendants, copper ore and sprue, and other unique objects found at Paquimé (Figure 11.3b; Di Peso 1974:7:502–504).

Unlike the majority of sites in west Mexico, most of the metal objects at Paquimé do not come from mortuary contexts, a factor which leads us to believe that control over the possession of these objects was strongly exerted by local elites. Across the Greater U.S. Southwest outside of the Casas Grandes region, metal objects are present in the Salado region of Arizona and in the Mimbres region. However, during this period more metal objects were recovered at Paquimé than the sum of all those found in the Greater U.S. Southwest, which gives us a picture of the undeniable importance of Paquimé as the major consumer of these goods (Vargas 1994:67).

For the era prior to the emergence of the Aztatlán tradition, there are two important points to note. First, it appears that the entry of metal objects to the most important sites in the southern part of Michoacán did not occur until near the end of Period 1 around AD 1200. As noted earlier, Period 2 (between AD 1300 and the Spanish invasion) was the era of greatest metallurgical development associated with the consolidation of the Tarascan *señório*. Our ongoing project is tasked with conducting archaeological research in the area that lies between Lake Pátzcuaro and the *tierra caliente* region of Michoacán, including the most important site of Tinganio or Tingambato in the Balcones region halfway between the Tarascan plateau and the Balsas-Tepalcatepec depression (the *tierra caliente* of Michoacán and Guerrero)—an area where early sites including La Villita and Infiernillo are situated.

Tingambato was the most important site in that region and likely was relevant in the exchange between coastal and plateau settlements as is clearly attested by the rich and important offerings recovered from tombs, including abundant shell objects indicative of the flow of material and people from the Pacific coast. We have preliminary evidence that the occupation of Tingambato began around AD 50 (corresponding to the Loma Alta phase) and ended probably around AD 800. However, although metal objects were present on the coast of Michoacán by then, no metal object has been recovered at Tingambato or in other sites that we believe to be of this same temporal period. We conclude that it is likely that metallurgy did not occur in this region of Michoacán until after AD 1000, the beginning of the early stages of the formation of the Tarascan *señório*.

The second key issue to address is the area of influence of the Chalchihuites culture. First, it is important to recall the bell reported at the site of Cerro del Huistle and dating to AD 650–750. From our perspective, this timing is very difficult to understand in the sense that in the rest of the Chalchihuites territory, especially in the northern region, copper objects have not been reported from the Alta Vista phase at the site of Alta Vista in Zacatecas or the Ayala phase in Durango. This leads us to believe that Cerro del Huistle was involved in another interaction network, possibly with the central regions of Jalisco and/or the coast of Jalisco or Nayarit where metal objects of this time period have been located, but this proposal also has some problems with the timeframe. Here it is worth recalling the important find of seashells at Cerro del Huistle. Between AD 600 and 800, the bonds which became essential between groups in southern Sinaloa and inland groups in the Durango highlands began to appear, especially in the Guadiana Valley via the Sierra Madre Occidental during the Tierra del Padre and Gavilán phases on the coast and the Ayala phase in Durango.

Taking into account regional archaeology, Hosler's Period 1, assuming it represents the development of metallurgy, can be associated with Aztatlán social dynamics from AD 900–1200/1300, except as noted in the region of Michoacán-Guerrero. Here it appears that metal objects became integrated into a wide distribution network of objects from AD 900 to around AD 1100. During this time period, various ceramic types with shared stylistic affinities occurred from Cojumatlán in Michoacán to Guasave in Sinaloa, including the use of geometric patterns such as step-frets (*xicalcoliuhqui*) arranged in horizontal and concentric bands as well as artistic representations of deities such as Ehecatl, Xipe Totec, and Tlaloc. These developments are part of what has been called the "Mesoamericanization" of the west,

FIGURE 11.3. Copper objects from Paquimé, Chihuahua. (*a*) Copper bells (crotals) including a turtle effigy bell. Digital image of Amerind color slide number B/13G-4 showing copper objects recovered from the Joint Casas Grandes Project. Courtesy of The Amerind Foundation, Inc., Dragoon, Arizona. (*b*) Copper nuggets, ore, and sprue. Digital image of Amerind color slide number B/13E-8 showing copper objects recovered from the Joint Casas Grandes Project. Courtesy of The Amerind Foundation, Inc., Dragoon, Arizona.

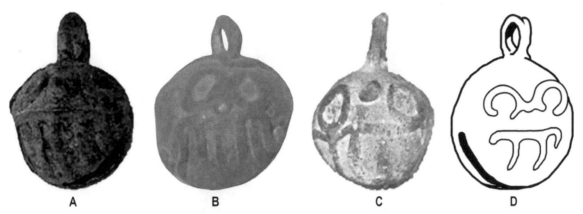

FIGURE 11.4. Tlaloc bell types in west Mexico (see Pendergast 1962b). (*a*) Type Ia5-a, Tepalcatepec, Michoacán. Private collection. Photo by author. (*b*) Type Ia5-a, Cañón del Molino, Durango. Museo de Arqueología Ganot-Peschard. Photo by Michael Mathiowetz. (*c*) Type Ia5-a, Cerro de Trincheras, Sonora. Photo by Elisa Villalpando Canchola. (*d*) Type ICIa, Paquimé, Chihuahua (after Di Peso et al. 1974). Photos authorized by Instituto Nacional de Antropología e Historia.

purportedly with a strong Toltec component. However, it seems to us that this designation should be carefully reconsidered after the integration of more archaeological data.

After AD 1100, the designs of this stylistic unity changed and with it emerged new figurative or narrative styles on vessel bodies. This shift includes codex-style representations with clear Mesoamerican iconography closely linked to the Mixteca-Puebla style, or Postclassic International Style, which was, in turn, linked to the hegemonic center of Cholula, a producer of these knowledge systems. At this point, the Aztatlán tradition reached its northernmost extent at Guasave and other sites in northern Sinaloa, marking the greatest expansion of Period 1 metal objects. For this reason, we emphasize that it is important to distinguish between what occurred before AD 900 and what transpired between this date and AD 1300 with advancements in heightened cultural connections to the north to the distant city of Paquimé and beyond to the southwestern United States.

Finally, one key issue to note is that studies of metal objects often have focused exclusively on bells made with the lost-wax technique, including classification systems which today are an important tool for establishing types and chronologies. However, there are many other objects composed of different metals and diverse alloys, the study of which can lead to broader perspectives as outlined below.

Analysis of the Sample
Bells

In the present study, we follow the classification system proposed by Pendergast (1962a, 1962b) and provide a more complete and updated assessment with consideration of metal bells from the Greater U.S. Southwest, northern Mexico, and west Mexico. The sample of 385 analyzed bells from Michoacán includes examples from Period 1 to Period 2. The majority of analyzed bells was produced using the lost-wax technique and are comprised of copper, gold, silver, and diverse alloys. Bell examples include a variety of forms, sizes, and designs, including spherical, globular, ovoid, and conical forms; zoomorphic forms; smoothed walls or horizontal lines; decorations with vertical zigzag lines; and simple forms without decorations. Sizes range from small bells at 2 cm to large bells from 8 to 10 cm. Individual bells, or those in sets of three or four, sometimes were welded to a small metal pot or pins and sometimes hung using suspension hoops (Punzo Díaz et al. 2014:148). In our analysis of Michoacán bells, we found 26 different types, which demonstrates a great diversity of stylistic differentiation. These bells can be attributed to 13 sites where we can establish the provenance, while the rest are in private collections, community museums, and *bodegas* of regional museums—all of which provide us with a general sense of regional developments and distribution.

Our analysis first emphasizes the abundance of the types IA1a-I ($n = 72$) and IA2a ($n = 69$), variants of globular bells which have a wide distribution and were used between AD 900–1500 (Pendergast 1962b:526). These types of globular bells are represented by a total of five different subtypes. It is important to note within this group the presence of the IA5a type, generally known as "Tlaloc bells" because wirework designs on the bells form the face of a known rain deity (Figure 11.4). Apparently, there were various centers of production and distribution of these kinds of bells across west Mexico. Examples in Michoacán include *tierra caliente* sites such as Apatzingán or Tepalcatepec ($n = 5$) as well as coastal sites including Coahuayana. The broad distribution of these bell forms includes

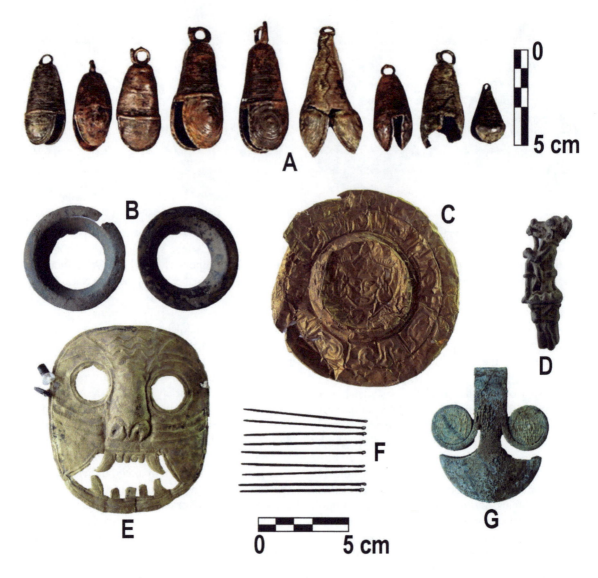

FIGURE 11.5. Diverse metal objects in west Mexico. (*a*) Type ID copper bells in Michoacán, Museo Regional Michoacano. (*b*) Earspools, Museo del Estado de Michoacán. (*c*) Discs, Museo del Estado de Michoacán. (*d*) Zoomorph, Museo del Estado de Michoacán. (*e*) Mask, Museo del Estado de Michoacán. (*f*) Needles, Museo Regional Michoacano. (*g*) Tweezer, Museo del Estado de Michoacán. Photos by author. Photos authorized by Instituto Nacional de Antropología e Historia.

the sites of Tuxcacuesco (Jalisco), Amapa (Nayarit), Paquimé (Chihuahua), Trincheras (Sonora), and Black Falls Ruin, or Wupatki (northern Arizona); this type of bell was used between AD 950–1450 (Di Peso et al. 1974; Pendergast 1962a, 1962b; Punzo Díaz 2019; Punzo and Villalpando 2015; Vargas 1995). The conical Type IC is represented in all of the identified samples, although in very low numbers. Type ID bells are well-represented in the analyzed sample (Figure 11.5a). This bell form is an extended conical type, and is associated with the shift from Period 1 to Period 2, or after AD 1200, especially in Michoacán.

Some of the types have a surface made with false wirework onto which was added a zigzag design; they are associated with late Tarascan contexts such as those found at Tzintzuntzan. The most well-represented type with these characteristics is Type ID5a ($n = 135$), the great majority of which unfortunately are unprovenienced. Our analysis only identified the bells at sites within the regions of Huetamo and Ciudad Hidalgo, outside of the nuclear Tarascan area, but with a strong presence among elite groups on the border of the Tarascan *señorío*.

Shifting to another regional locus, Charles Di Peso and colleagues (1974) reported 115 bells from excavations at Paquimé in Chihuahua, which corresponds to 16 percent of the metal items recovered. To these samples, we can add another 80 bells for a total of 195 bells. It is important to emphasize that most of the bells found by Di Peso at Paquimé were in a unique context. Bells recovered in Room 9C-8 were wrapped in a bag and possibly hung from the beams of the ceiling. Here they found two tied clusters of seven bells and one more example of six bells, all of Type IIE1a. In addition, other examples include a necklace composed of 55 bells of Type IA1a, one Type ID1a, and another Type IIB1a in addition to other adornments, the sum of which totals 78 bells in the contexts of Room 9C-8. Of the sample that comes from the Casas Grandes region, we should first emphasize the abundance of globular bells of Type IA1a-I. This single type ($n = 120$) constitutes 61 percent of the total. On the other hand, IA5a bells (Tlaloc type) are present in Paquimé, and as mentioned earlier these are present in northern Arizona (Vargas 1995) at the Black Falls Ruin (Wupatki) site which had an occupation between AD 1100–1250, or prior to the Casas Grandes Medio Period and Paquimé.

Recently in Trincheras, Sonora, four Type IA5a copper bells were recovered with one more collected from the surface, all reported in contexts with ceramics associated with Paquimé (Punzo and Villalpando 2015). Bells in the form of a turtle, catalogued by Pendergast (1962b) as Type IE2, are another item found both in Paquimé and Michoacán. These objects are present at the sites of Naranja and Tzintzuntzan in Michoacán, while one example comes from an unidentified site in the state of Guerrero. Much like in the sample from Michoacán, the conical Type IC are those that have greater variability in subtypes, nevertheless retaining a very low presence in number. We emphasize the near absence of Type ID bells of extended conical form as there are only two without precise contexts in the collection of the Arizona State Museum.

Rings

Aside from bells, metal objects during Period 1, such as rings with a circular cross section and rectangular section, also were manufactured with the cold-working technique. It is important to note that contrary to the earlier-noted point about the number of rings, around 70 percent of the objects that we have analyzed so far in collections from Michoacán correspond to this kind of object. In many cases, artisans took advantage of the flat sections of rings to make what are essentially linear forms of fret-work decorations by incising the object while cold. It is worth noting that the diameter and thickness of the rings is very consistent, showing a high degree of standardization in the manufacturing process. Aside from bells, metal objects made with cold-working techniques also were recovered in Durango, including circular rings ($n = 23$), although none of the rectangular-section type were reported. These are present at La Ferrería, Cañón del Molino, and Canelas and Loma Pelona in Zape, unlike in Michoacán where there are very few in comparison (Punzo Díaz 2019).

Awls

Awls are not very abundant but have been reported for Amapa (Nayarit), Tomatlán (Jalisco), and Infiernillo (Michoacán). While we cannot associate these with any period at the moment, we can highlight both the tip or bi-tip of these examples as well as the existence of round, square, and mixed sections. Although bells, rings, and awls have been mentioned as only some of the objects that comprise the Period 1 assemblages, there are others we wish to mention which, based upon dates linked to sites or objects themselves, may comprise part of the metal object assemblages of this time—especially in association with the Aztatlán expansion in northwest Mexico.

Earspools

Metal earspools have been reported for sites occupied during Periods 1 and 2, including Hervideros (Durango) and Guasave (Sinaloa). Likewise, metal earspools are present at Topia in the Durango sierra and one example is housed at the Museo Nacional de Antropología in the hall for the state of Jalisco. Furthermore, historical sources mention solid circular earspools in the Tarascan territory; examples have been found in museum collections in Michoacán (Figure 11.5b).

Discs

Discs are very rare and are associated more closely with Period 2; examples of plain discs occur in various parts of Michoacán, including a gold disc with a rich design belonging to the collection of the Museo del Estado de Michoacán (Figure 11.5c). Copper discs very similar to those of Michoacán were found in La Ferrería (Durango) with decorated ones found as far north as Paquimé (Di Peso et al. 1974; Punzo Díaz 2019).

Chains

At Cañón del Molino and La Ferrería in Durango, controlled excavations and looting revealed the presence of links strung together to form short metal chains which terminate in a folded U-shaped piece with the edges folded outward (Punzo Díaz 2019).

Plates

At Cañón del Molino in Durango, another unusual object recovered is a flat metal plate with a perforation in the top, perhaps used as a pendant. On one face is a series of horizontal, parallel decorations placed in an undulating line pattern and delimited on the other side by a series of crossed lines in vertical form (Punzo Díaz 2019).

Zoomorphs

Small, zoomorphic metal objects occur in various collections. The metal objects in the form of turtles stand out for their distribution, although there are mainly representations of other animals, such as coyotes or frogs in the Michoacán collections (Figure 11.5d). In Durango at Cañón del Molino, one small turtle is known while another turtle was reported at Santa Ana Zape—apparently very different from those found in Michoacán (Lumholtz 1902)—along with examples in Colima and at Paquimé that are identified as Type IE2. Another example is known at the Pavón site in Guerrero, while others from northern Veracruz were made by the false-wire technique. On a broader scale, small turtles with a smooth body were reported at Paquimé ($n = 1$) with another specimen in the Museo Regional in Morelia, Michoacán (Di Peso et al. 1974; Punzo Díaz 2019).

Masks

An outstanding, recently republished archaeological piece (Hers 2013:Figure 27) located in the Fowler Museum of the University of California, Los Angeles is a ceramic sculpture adorned with gold foil derived from Amapa or the immediate vicinity, although its original context unfortunately remains a mystery. As is well known, the Amapa region contains abundant traces of metal objects recovered from the excavation of prehispanic cemeteries. The Amapa site is considered to be significant for the production of Period 1 artifacts. The anthropomorphic sculpture in question—wearing a conical hat and situated atop an elaborately decorated base—is believed to be a representation of Xipe Totec. Xipe Totec is a figure who in some portrayals appears dressed in a human skin, as evident in the hands that appear to hang from the deity's wrists. While we cannot definitively associate this deity with our broader study, it is notable that the gold foil adorning the figure's face was applied using an exceptional technique. In Mesoamerica, Xipe Totec is associated with metalsmiths, and it cannot be denied that there are important similarities with South American pieces.

Metal masks are not common in west Mexico, but we are aware of two unprovenienced examples which may come from Michoacán. The first example is a copper mask with slightly closed eyes and open mouth and marked lips. This piece bears a headdress or band at the top of the head and braided rectangles descending lengthwise from the headdress to the end of the mask through the eyes. The second is of gold foil measuring about 10 cm; gold foils are atypical in Mesoamerican prehispanic art but more closely related to South American artistic canons. This artifact represents a character with open eyes and mouth with upper teeth (evidently two large fangs) and lower teeth badly damaged but situated apart from one another in a similar manner. The various lines which ornament the face and nose appear to signify feline characteristics (Figure 11.5e). Unfortunately, we do not know the contexts nor the periods with which these masks are associated. Another unique mask is a small one now held by the Smithsonian Institution in Washington, DC, which depicts a parrot or a macaw, probably found in the area of Paquimé.

Needles

Needles were perhaps the most abundant utilitarian metal objects in prehispanic west Mexico (Figure 11.5f). The manner of manufacturing the hole of the needle through a perforation is a distinctive signature of Period 1 (Hosler 1994b:77). Perforated needles have been recovered from sites such as Tizapán el Alto, Cojumatlán, Infiernillo, and Amapa. The second type is a loop-eye needle made with a flattened end folded back onto itself. It is noteworthy that these are by far the most abundant type in the collections analyzed in Michoacán, and there also are examples of these from Amapa. One important characteristic we observed was the consistency of the needles, both in size and thickness of these objects. However, with regard to perforated needles proposed for Period 1, only one example was found at Paquimé in Medio Period-contexts much later in time (Punzo Díaz 2019).

Tweezers

Finally, and without pretending to exhaust the discussion of all objects, we note the existence of tweezers—purportedly used for depilation—which are present from AD 900–1450 (Figure 11.5g). These objects were recovered at Amapa (Nayarit) and Tomatlán (Jalisco) and are of a reduced size, measuring only a few centimeters in length by one centimeter in width, and without any decoration. In the Michoacán collections, the vast majority of the analyzed tweezers were attached on one side to fragments of textiles while the provenience of these items sometimes involved burial contexts, such as at Huandacareo or Tzintzuntzan. During Period 2, the Petamuti—the major priest of the Tarascan *señorío*—hung tweezers around his neck as the main symbol of religious power. These tweezers have a very special coil decoration on its sides. It is noteworthy that there are reports of these kinds of tweezers to the west in the Sayula Basin of Jalisco. To the north and in the Greater U.S. Southwest, there are no reported examples of these objects—a factor which indicates the symbolic importance of tweezers in the Tarascan tradition.

Interaction Models

Much has been written on the various forms of interchange that may have characterized the economic and social networks of Paquimé, particularly as they relate to materials of presumed Mesoamerican origin recovered in diverse contexts at the site. We consider the "prestige goods economy" as the most suitable model to explain interaction between societies of the Greater U.S. Southwest and northern Mexico and those of west Mexico. With regard to copper bells, the "prestige goods economy" is one in which spheres of social interaction include the restricted means by which goods serving as indicators of superior status are exchanged between groups of elites (Nelson 1981), possibly through "middlemen" groups within these networks.

We contend that metal objects had a wholly unique ritual function in different sites and regions in which the color and sound that they produced were sacred symbols of those objects. We may consider these objects as possessing significant "agency" (see Ingold 2000) where these objects were extensions of people, forming a "personality" for actors in which the objects themselves participated in social life. These objects indicated a degree of distinction, a social status, and were participants in events of great importance. For these reasons, we do not believe that networks of exchange which moved these objects were indiscriminate, but instead were linked directly to elites and possibly obtained through intermediaries for long-distance exchanges that were present but are now scarcely visible in the archaeological record.

This research allows us to consider the idea that Pacific-coastal corridors were the means by which this interaction occurred between societies in the Greater U.S. Southwest and west Mexico. From this work, we propose that metallurgy during Period 1 (at least by the beginning of Period 2) influenced this corridor of interaction and linked together distant regions from Michoacán to the Greater U.S. Southwest, especially the Hohokam area of Arizona, through the movement of prestige goods.

Furthermore, this study concludes that at the moment of consolidation of the Tarascan *señorío*, metal items (and other objects such as ceramics) were concentrated in the Tarascan area of influence, but the types of bells consumed in the most important Tarascan cities such as Tzintzuntzan are not present in northern Mexico, including at Paquimé. Thus, we may determine that the Tarascan *señorío* was largely isolated from the broader distribution corridors of metal objects and instead produced and consumed its own objects with different forms than those in other areas. This phenomenon can be understood not only through the examination of metal objects, but in all of the Tarascan *señoríos* only a few elements tie in clearly with items found in the great cities of Lake Pátzcuaro. These items include prestige goods which were consumed by local elites—probably Tarascans leaders or lords allied with them—including objects such as earspools, pipes, lip plugs, and metal objects that were symbols of Tarascan power. Unfortunately, we do not have a solid chronological sequence since many of the analyzed bells have no archaeological context. However, it appears that the Michoacán territories sharing the most artifact types with those in the Greater U.S. Southwest are those outside of the main region of influence of the Tarascan *señorío*, especially the ones in the *tierra caliente* near the Río Balsas and Río Tepalcatepec, which probably date before the Tarascan conquests of this region during the middle of the fifteenth century.

Conclusion

If this story were to conclude following the temporal parameters established by these two periods, we would hardly be able to understand the presence of so many metal objects further north of west Mexico. One of the items mentioned repeatedly in models of the "Mesoamericanization" of the northern regions is the presence of metal objects, especially at Paquimé. Di Peso and colleagues (1974) noted that all of the hundreds of copper objects, except two which were located at Paquimé, were found in contexts defined today as the Medio Period (AD 1200–1450), which belongs to Period 2. Scholars today have ruled out the idea that Paquimé was a production locale of metal objects as was generally believed a few decades ago. Instead, it has been demonstrated that most metal objects from Paquimé have counterparts in different sites of western Mexico, particularly metal items at Amapa in Nayarit.

However, for the moment we will only concentrate on the Type 1C1a bells of Di Peso's classification and Type 1A5a from Amapa. These bell forms, called the "Tlaloc type," are found at sites with a clear late Aztatlán presence, including at Amapa (Nayarit), Cañón del Molino (Durango), Tuxcacuesco (Jalisco), and Apatzingán (Michoacán), the latter of which is outside the traditional Aztatlán area. This type of bell is also reported far to the north at the Black Falls Ruin site (Wupatki) in Arizona, as well as at the Trincheras site in Sonora where several examples of this bell type were recovered. Prior discussions of Tlaloc bells incorrectly noted Black Falls Ruin and Wupatki as separate sites (Punzo Díaz 2019; Punzo Díaz and Villalpando 2015).

Other important bells traded to the far north are the turtle-shaped form classified at Paquimé as Type IIIA1 (Di Peso et al. 1974). Identical bells of this form have been found at Naranja and Tzintzuntzan, both important Tarascan sites in Michoacán. This factor necessarily should lead us to reconsider the role of the Tarascan *señorío* in the exchange of objects to the northern regions during the Middle and Late Postclassic.

In conclusion, we contend that it is essential for scholars to reconsider the era of metallurgy in Mexico not only in light of the two major periods proposed by Hosler, but also in light of new data derived from fieldwork across the region over the past few decades. For Period 1, we conclude that there should be an initial phase (Phase 1a) from AD 600–900, or before the Aztatlán expansion. During this era, interaction networks were focused exclusively on the coastal areas of Michoacán and Jalisco with little penetration inland—except in the case of Michoacán along the Río Balsas basin—without reaching sites in the highlands such as Tingambato or the lake basins of Jalisco along the northern tributaries of the Río Grande de Santiago where early absolute dates have been established (Punzo Díaz 2019). A proposed final phase of Period 1, called Phase 1b, should extend between AD 900–1300 in full association with the Aztatlán tradition. This network includes the U.S. Southwest, northern Mexico, and the Chalchihuites region and overlaps somewhat with the beginning of Period 2, which would enable us to explain the presence of metal bells at Paquimé and elsewhere in the southwestern United States (Punzo Díaz 2019). In sum, future discoveries will provide opportunities to review more carefully the relations between the Greater U.S. Southwest and west Mexico during these periods in order to continue refining models on the historical dynamics of metal objects.

PART IV

Aztatlán Religion, Ritual Practice, and Worldview

The Archaeological Past and Continuities in the Ethnographic Present

CHAPTER 12

Funerary Practices during the Epiclassic and Postclassic

La Pitayera, Nayarit

José Carlos Beltrán Medina, María de Lourdes González Barajas,
Jorge Arturo Talavera González, and Juan Jorge Morales Monroy

The Jala-Vallarta archaeological project began in 2012 in response to the construction of a highway that crosscut an area rich in archaeological remains. The main objectives of the project consisted of the location, registration, protection, and study of the archaeological sites along this route. The presence of prehispanic settlements was evident from the beginning, and within the first 10 km we located eight large archaeological sites and an historical site with an aqueduct, which is an indication of the density and richness of human occupation. Among these is the large megalithic site of Ahuacatlán and its cemetery, called La Pitayera (Gonzáles Barajas and Beltrán Medina 2013).

This site is distributed over 80 ha at the foot of the southern slope of the Volcán Ceboruco. On the west side of the site is La Pitayera, a cemetery where among other things we found a complex cluster of stone funerary cists directly associated with human burials and Aztatlán material culture that is the focus of this chapter. The broader cemetery zone is of great importance for its archaeological depositions from different temporal periods within the same ritual space. Shaft and chamber tombs coexisted with vaulted stone tombs (*tumbas con bóveda de mampostería*), stone cists, direct burials, cremations, and funerary urns, which together indicate the cemetery's extended lifespan.

We identified intact funerary contexts with material from the end of the Epiclassic and the Early Postclassic (AD 900–1250) periods without precedent in the regional archaeology. This group of burials indicates complex funerary processes where the bodies were first incinerated in a funeral pyre, and then their remains, bones, and ashes were deposited inside ceramic urns, which were later deposited inside stone cists in an elaborate funerary process including double funerals (Morales Monroy 2012).

At the site, 11 cists with 22 human burials were detected along with 389 different artifacts consisting of shell, stone and bone jewelry, prismatic obsidian blades, Mazapan figurines, copper bells, a small textile remnant, incised and engraved spindle whorls, tripod vessels with rattle feet, axes, and ground stone tools. Some of these materials are diagnostic of the Aztatlán cultural tradition (AD 900–1350), which indicates the presence of exotic and high-value products derived from engagement with this ideological and mercantile network. Features that define the Aztatlán complex also were present, such as architecture, metallurgy, flexed burial styles and cremations, incense burners (*incensarios* or braziers) including the frying-pan style (*sahumadores*), and some Aztatlán sherds (Figure 12.1). The data obtained in the field indicate that the site and its cemetery are associated with a catastrophic Plinian eruption of the Volcán Ceboruco which occurred 1,100 years ago (Sieron and Siebe 2008).

Antecedents

Archaeological investigations in the region began in 1946 with E. W. Gifford of the University of California, who located 16 archaeological sites in the Ahuacatlán, Jala, and Ixtlán Valleys. As a result, from the collection of surface materials, Gifford (1950) established a cultural sequence for the zone composed of three cultural complexes: Early Ixtlán, dated between the Archaic period and up to AD 600; Middle Ixtlán, dated between AD 600 and AD 1100; and Late Ixtlán, dating from AD 1100 to AD 1530 (see Grosscup 1976:246, 263).

Other significant works in the region have been carried out in the city of Tepic, Nayarit, where materials were excavated of a then-unknown cultural tradition, called the Mololoa culture, after the river that crosses the Matatipac valley where it is found. The materials

FIGURE 12.1. Overview of the cemetery and cists at La Pitayera, Nayarit (view to the south). Note unexcavated Mound 7 beneath tree and Volcán Ceboruco at left in background. Photo by authors.

recovered came from funerary contexts with collective cremation burials deposited in anthropomorphic urns of Mololoa-type ceramics and in globular pots. An altar of stones with a sharp knife-like basalt piece situated as a stela and measuring 84 cm in height was reported as the main element (Beltrán Medina 2001b). Mololoa urns are a direct antecedent of the urns at La Pitayera.

In the Jala-Ahuacatlán area, few recent studies have been conducted except for the notable work of Gabriela Zepeda in 1994 during the construction of the Guadalajara-Tepic highway, as well as her work in registering petroglyphs for the Atlas Arqueológico de Nayarit project (Zepeda García-Moreno and Lazarini 1994). Archaeological work in Ahuacatlán began in 2012 with the construction of the Jala-Vallarta highway (González Barajas and Beltrán Medina 2013).

Volcán Ceboruco and the Pochotero Dome

The Ahuacatlán site and the Volcán Ceboruco are located in the western portion of the Transverse Neovolcanic Axis in the southern high plateau of Nayarit. It is a region of geographic transition in which three important physiographic provinces converge: the Neovolcanic Axis, the Sierra Madre Occidental, and the northeastern limit of the Sierra Madre del Sur. The Volcán Ceboruco, located at 2,164 m above sea level, was formed of andesite-dacite during the late Quaternary, and it is the most active volcano in western Mexico after Volcán de Colima. Its eruptions have marked periods of occupation and abandonment of the region for many years.

Of all the eruptions of Volcán Ceboruco, the one that stands out was the catastrophic Jala Plinial eruption between AD 990 and 1020 (Sieron and Siebe 2008:248). This eruption generated highly destructive pyroclastic flows, devastating an area of 560 km² mainly towards the east-northeast of the volcano where the materials reached beyond the Río Grande de Santiago, depositing a distinctive layer of pumice (*jal*), ash, and andesite pieces. Later rains contributed to the formation of large alluvia and debris flows. Afterwards, six other eruptive events were recorded which included several flows of lava and ash exhalations—the majority of which occurred in the following 400 years before the arrival of the Spaniards in the area (Sieron and Siebe 2008). Chronological dating was obtained by these researchers.

The archaeological work documented the stratigraphy of the site with clear evidence of the eruptions; since then, the area was covered by a layer of pumice produced by the Plinian eruption, and several layers of ash. This, in turn, was covered by a thick black sandy layer formed by the continuous accumulation of ash disseminated by the volcano through the present day. The deposits of the Jala eruption, in addition to serving as a clear chronological marker at the site, represent an event that had a profound impact on the lives of the inhabitants of the region. This period of intense volcanic activity greatly impacted settlement patterns and the cultural development of the region. However, archaeological evidence indicates that some of the burials found in the area of the cists are associated with the reuse of the site's cemetery in the years after the Plinian eruption.

Other volcanic elements of relatively recent geological age are found near the site, and of special interest is the formation of the gray obsidian dome called Pochotero dated to 2,355 ± 110 years ago, which is located on the eastern slope of Volcán Ceboruco (Sieron and Siebe 2008:248). The macroscopic observations of the obsidian artifacts from the site coincide with the characteristics of the obsidian recovered at the Pochotero dome, since it was a source of raw material that was exploited at least since the Classic period.

The Site of Ahuacatlán and La Pitayera

La Pitayera is a cemetery at the great site of Ahuacatlán, which has clear roots in the Shaft Tomb tradition (200 BC–AD 600) and evidence of occupation during the Epiclassic, the Postclassic Aztatlán era, and through the Spanish conquest period. It is a large and complex site formed by four groups, although there also exist minor archaeological remains in other immediate areas. The registered groups are the following:

Group A: Ahuacatlán

Group A is a ceremonial, housing, and administrative area, measuring about 25 ha and located on the far east side of the site atop a difficult-to-access promontory which is well protected by a depression and rocky walls of more than 10 m in height. It has watchtowers and because of its defensive nature, it looks like a fortress.

This group has two large access points; the western access rises 25 m to a large platform on which are three plazas arranged with mounds at different levels through which you must move to enter the upper part. The southern access point possesses a broad, open entrance that joins Group C and includes an alley carved into the rock. The upper part is formed by platforms supporting various architectural groups that connect with each other through alleys following a semicircular pattern, much like Guachimontones. There are large plazas, mounds, and complex architectural groups linked by walkways.

An elongated alley, measuring 100 m in length in the shape of a Latin "I"—possibly a field for the ballgame—was constructed in Group A, with mounds and elongated structures on both sides. In the highest mound of the ballcourt (8 m) was found a figurine head of an old man, probably Huehuetéotl, the god of fire who was related to the volcano, and another similar figurine was found in the lower part of the site; both items were discovered on the surface. In this group, we only detected two flexed burials, one of which contained a metal ring.

Group B: Ceremonial Center

Group B is a ceremonial area of about 17 ha located in the middle part of the site, 20–30 m below Group A. It contains an architectural complex of six small plazas and a dozen mounds, including rectangular, square, and circular structures, that one must pass in order to access the previous group. Several large plazas with pyramidal mounds up to 10 m tall can be found arranged in a semicircular manner in the southern portion of the group, along with large rectangular structures. At its western end, there is a stone quarry and workshops that were in full production when the site was abandoned.

Group C: La Coyotera

Group C, a residential area called La Coyotera, is located in the southeastern part of the site atop a promontory and is separated from Group A by a ravine. Group C features include housing complexes, plazas, mounds, burials, and alleys of smaller size but greater density.

Group D: La Pitayera Cemetery

The Group D area is a necropolis spanning more than 25 ha of large plazas, mounds, architectural foundations, alleys, and rectangular and circular structures associated with rituals of the dead. The cemetery was used for more than a thousand years and has at least seven burial areas (Flores Montes de Oca 2015; González Barajas and Beltrán Medina 2013; Morales 2012; Talavera and Gelover 2016).

The main area of the cemetery is located on a large platform made up of three bodies of different height, which supports an architectural complex composed of nine plazas surrounded by 22 mounds along with altars and small rocky promontories that are found in its nuclear area. The main plaza measures 9 ha and is surrounded by mounds, small lithic altars, large monoliths, promontories, a rock in the shape of a stela, and a stone measuring 1.5 m carved as a receptacle for water in the form of a marine shell. At the center of the plaza, we discovered a group of 11 funerary cists with 22 burials along with 6 cists on the ground surface that functioned as altars accompanied by various offerings, including Aztatlán materials. On the north side of the central plaza and in front of the cists is positioned a rectangular structure of great importance (Mound 7), particularly as it represents a very complete example of Aztatlán architecture coexisting with several architectural features belonging to the Shaft Tomb tradition.

In the northeast corner of the central plaza is a retaining wall measuring scarcely 60 cm high and 25 m long, which delimits and levels the plaza on this side and serves to divert a small stream into a similarly small channel outside of the platform. An arroyo passes through the east and south side of the cemetery, surrounding the funerary platform through the lower part of the site and dividing the site into two sections: east and west. To the west of the central plaza, in the lower part, there is a slightly sloped retaining wall made of large stones, measuring 23 m in length, 3 m in height, and 1.80 m in width. It is an important example of prehispanic architecture in the region. In the lower part of this wall lay Plaza 5 and an elongated mound, which extends over a modified terrace that takes advantage of the slope of the land, forming an architectural complex around three plazas surrounded by mounds. On the south side of the site, 75 m from the group of cist burials noted above, is located the Callejón de las Ánimas, a narrow and elongated corridor measuring 250 m by 20 m wide where we documented 24 shaft and chamber tombs, three masonry vault graves, and two direct burials. These were found in addition to mounds, low altars, and other architectural elements on the surface associated with the tombs. On the lower terrace were found the remains of four other direct burials that had been destroyed.

In the northeastern sector of the site and east of Mounds 5 and 6, the site continues about 40 m into the Ceboruco foothills. There is a large retaining wall measuring 80 m long and 1.80 high, housing terraces, an access corridor, and some looted shaft tombs. It was possible to detect surface alignments of stone around terraces and elongated spaces.

Funerary Architecture: The Burial Cists and Mound 7

At the center of the cemetery, at a depth of 80 cm, an occupation surface used for funeral events was located above the deposits of the Jala Plinial eruption. On this floor were found concentrations of fragments of ceramic jars, bowls, tripods, and cups as well as blades, scrapers, axes, hammerstones, and burnt remains of animal bone. These items indicate that banquets likely were held with ceremonial food and drinks in honor of the deceased who were buried in this locale. On this same floor were constructed six surface cist markers from 60 to 80 cm on each side and up to 40 to 60 cm in height raised above the surface and apparently functioned as altars and reference points for the cists and burials deposited below (Figures 12.1–12.2). There were red pigment markings on the floor in a rectangular shape, which indicated the location of the cist. In effect, 11 funerary cists were found 1 m below the surface. Inside each was deposited a pot with cremated human remains and some offerings. Nine other inhumations were found outside of these cists, including 4 direct flexed burials, 3 ollas with cremated bones inside, and 2 secondary cremated burials with Toltec-style material.

The word "cist" comes from the Greek terms for "basket" or "chest." These lithic funerary monuments were small boxes (60–70 cm per side and 70 cm in height), formed by four or more stones joined with clay and sealed with one to three stones or slabs. At the bottom of the cist, there was a mixture of earth with ashes and small pumice stones. One variant was comprised of mud walls and a slab covering. In all cases, offerings associated with the construction of the cists were located either inside, on the sides, or below the walls, including Aztatlán materials (Figures 12.2–12.3). A date obtained from Cist 1 corresponds with AD 885–995 (Beta-434018).

Mound 7

Excavated in 2014, Mound 7 is a good example of Aztatlán rectangular architecture found on the site and exhibits at least two construction stages: one corresponding with the Aztatlán period (partly contemporary with the cists), and the other stage belonging to the Late Postclassic period. The Aztatlán structure described in this work is directly associated with the cists (Figure 12.4, this volume; Mathiowetz 2015). There are two architectural bodies that comprise the structure: the main building and the platform with three frontal inner stairs. The main building is an elongated rectangle with supporting interior walls projecting forward at both ends thereby forming a southward-facing open area with long banquettes situated inside along the structure walls. In the central interior, two square bases were identified—remnants of tall stone columns that supported a large roof with the open-faced structure facing towards the main plaza. Within the central area of the building, there is a double votive cist, which contained two interior spaces apparently used to hold a lit fire. At the back of the building, to the north of the double cists, a small rectangular room with a door between the banquettes can be accessed by climbing two steps.

On the southward-facing front of the structure,

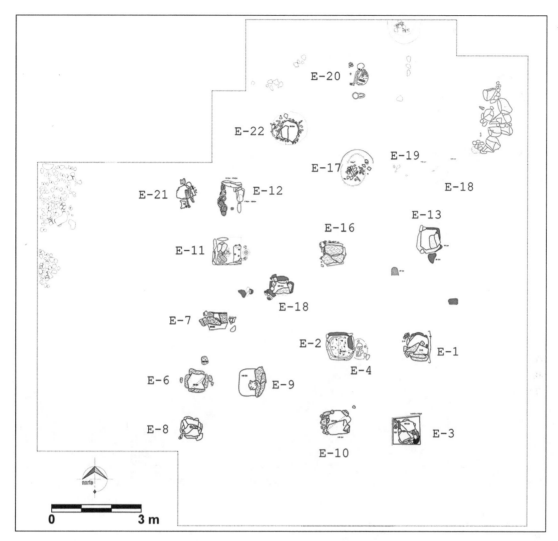

FIGURE 12.2. Plan view of cist groups in La Pitayera cemetery, Nayarit. Drawing by authors.

a central access staircase was constructed into the platform that supports the building and is divided in the middle by a banquette. Two other narrow staircases are situated on each side of the frontal face, with three steps penetrating into the building platform. Four fire pits were found on the floor lined up on either side of each column (Mathiowetz 2015). Two calibrated dates from Mound 7 correspond to AD 1270 (Beta-434017) and AD 1445 (Beta-434016) in association with the first and second construction stages. As a complement to this building, there are two lithic altars located to the north and east that pertain to the Shaft Tomb tradition, as well as an Aztatlán-style masonry altar located to the southeast of the main building. Excavations in 2012 at the lithic altar on the north side of the structure recovered Shaft Tomb ceramics. There may be an earlier Shaft Tomb component or structure located beneath Structure 7, but that remains to be confirmed with excavation.

ARCHAEOLOGICAL MATERIALS

During the archaeological excavations, a collection of artifacts of different materials was recovered. Among them, some diagnostic items of the Aztatlán era stand out. In total, 338 artifacts were deposited as offerings and 14 urns were recovered with a diverse distribution of cist markers, cists, urns, and offerings in each funerary context (Table 12.1).

Ceramics

The ceremonial monochrome ceramics in the form of *ollas*, tripod bowls, plates, and cups are widely predominant, although there are also frying-pan *incensarios*, braziers, spindle whorls, and solid figurines. The 14 urns in the cemetery are notable and were used as receptacles for the deposition of cremated bones within. These are globular jars for domestic use—generally measuring between 11 and 20 cm in height, which were

FIGURE 12.3. Set of cists as viewed from outside: (*a*) E-1 and (*b*) E-13, and inside: (*c*) E-16 and (*d*) E-18. La Pitayera, Nayarit. Photos by authors.

reused as a funerary urn. These are short-necked and brown or orange monochrome, although there is a tripod *olla* with small supports and only one pot with geometric decoration in Black and White-on-red. All of the urns had a bowl, a plate, a worked circular sherd (*tejo*), or a fragment of the skull placed upside down as a cover.

Fourteen tripod *molcajetes* recovered, which are complete or intentionally broken in three pieces, are orange-colored with rattle-footed supports. Rounded edges and incised backgrounds with geometric designs are common. Also, three semispheric bowls were recovered. Other items include a frying-pan censer and two other censers, one of which is globular with an everted rim, two supports, and a long handle. This vessel has an openwork body with incised decoration along with molding on the lower part of the body. It is orange-colored with nine perforations in the body, a bowl measuring 16 cm in diameter, and a hollow cylindrical handle. This frying-pan *incensario* and the censer with globular rattle supports are similar to those reported at the Amapa site (Meighan 1976:424).

There are other orange vases, three monochrome cups, three vessels, and two large bottles with a handle—one of them in the form of a turkey. We also recovered a small *olla* with double handle on the rim, a miniature brown *olla* measuring 5 cm in height, a flat-bottom plate and divergent walls, as well as *comales* with handles associated with the altar surface level. Fragments of globular braziers with short necks and conical decoration in the form of pochote (ceiba) thorns are among the identified material as well.

Figurines

Other important materials associated with the burials are five Mazapan-style mold-made figurines, measuring up to 14, 16, and 19 cm in height with three representing older women. The other two represent women with juvenile characteristics. They have a bilobed headdress with fret designs, bands on the forehead, earspools, and dental mutilation. They wear a blouse and long skirt, a belt, and bracelets. All have their hands placed on their bellies and one has a necklace with a circular breastplate on the chest. There are traces of red pigment on

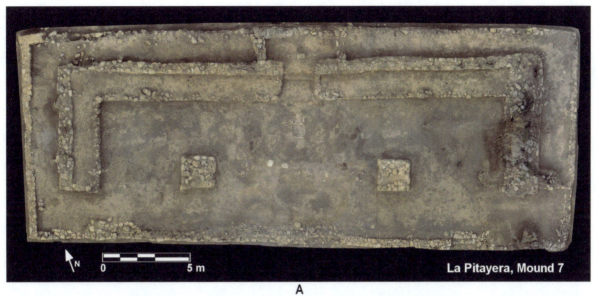

FIGURE 12.4. La Pitayera, Nayarit. (*a*) Plan view of exposed architectural components of main structure at Mound 7, La Pitayera, Nayarit. Illustration based on composite photos by Esteban Mirón Marván. (*b*) View to the southwest of valley with main structure at Mound 7 and cemetery, La Pitayera, Nayarit. Photo by Michael Mathiowetz.

TABLE 12.1. Burial and offering data from cemetery at La Pitayera, Nayarit.

Cists and burials		1	2	3	4	5	6	7	8	9	10	11	12	13	14	15	16	17	18	19	20	21	22	TOTAL
Type of burial	Primary										1		1								1	1		4
	Secondary (cremation)	1	1	1	1	1	1	1	1	1		1		1	1	1	1	1	1	1			1	18
Location of the burial	Surface stone cist marker	1											1		1	1	1				1			6
	Funerary stone cist	1	1	1	1		1	1	1			1		1	1	1	1		1				1	11
	Surface mud cist marker													1										1
	Slabs		1			2				3	2										3	1	1	15
	Pits		1							1								1		1				4
Total	Total	3	3	2	1	3	2	2	2	5	3	3	1	3	3	3	2	2	2	2	5	2	3	59
Body position	Flexed right lateral decubitus										1		1			1						1		4
Sex											?		M								M	F		
Type of burial	Urns (funerary globular jars)		1	1	1	1	1	1	1		1			2	1	1	1		1				1	13
Distribution of offerings outside of cists	tripod bowls (molcajete)			1						1							1	1						4
	Annular-base bowl (molcajete)														1									1
	Bowl															1								1
	Vessel censer								1															1
	Frying-pan censer																				1			1
	Obsidian flake	1																						1
	Grinding stone								1				1											2
	Stone axe								1															1
	Kaolinite figurine	1																						1
	Bone awl	1																						1
Distribution of offerings inside cist	pedestal-base goblets						1														1			2
	Bowls												2											2
	Plate												1											1
	Tripod bowls (molcajete)	1					1				1	1	2								1	1	1	9
	Jars with handle	1															1							2
	Ollas (pot)												2											2
	Vessel censer																				1			1
	Mazapan figurines			1							2											2		5
	Anthropo-zoomorphic figurines											1											1	2

Category	Item	C1	C2	C3	C4	C5	C6	C7	C8	C9	C10	C11	C12	C13	C14	C15	C16	C17	C18	C19	C20	Total
	Zoomorphic figurine	1																				1
	Zoomorphic pendant													1								1
	Spindle whorls	1		2		1						2	2	17		2						27
	Engraved disc bead (earspool)													1								1
	Obsidian prismatic blades	5		1					1													7
	Obsidian projectile points								1								1					2
	Shell beads													30	2					3		35
	Shell trapezoidal pendants			2								2	4			28						36
	Shell zoomorphic pendants													1								1
	Gastropod beads	56		20												86		4				166
	Pinctada mazatlanica plates													2								2
	Copper bells													4				4				8
	Copper circular object													1								1
	Stone bead					1																1
	Stone earspools	1							1			1	1		2		1					7
	Basalt lacquer												1									1
	Kaolinite			1								1										1
	Bone awl											1										1
	Bone awl	1		1	2									3								7
	Zoomorphic bone figurine														1							1
	Deer antler							1													1
	Armadillo bone/shell																		1			1
Subtotal		68	2	30	5	1	1	1	7	1	7	6	10	63	12	118	5	9	5	7	2	362
Presence of other materials	Red pigment outside the cists	1	1	1	1	1		1				1				1	1					11
	Charcoal	1	1					1					1	1	1	1	1	1				8
	Kaolinite			1									1	1								3
	Clay			1									1			1	1					3
	Pumice				1										1							2
Subtotal		2	2	1	1	1		2				1	2	1	2	4	2	1				27
Grand total		70	4	31	5	1	1	1	8	1	9	6	12	64	13	120	9	10	5	7	2	389

FIGURE 12.5. Mazapan figurines with remnants of red pigment recovered in situ at La Pitayera, Nayarit. Photo by authors.

two of the figurines and another with traces of white, black, and blue paint. These are distinctive chronological and cultural markers from the Aztatlán Tolteca era during the Early Postclassic period (AD 900–1250). In west Mexico, these Mazapan figurines are associated with Aztatlán sites (Figure 12.5).

The excavated material includes a pair of fantastic and very peculiar figurines measuring 7 cm tall and made with a mixed modeling and molding technique. These figurines stand upright and have a lizard-tailed humanoid torso. The head is triangular in shape with earspools and dental mutilation. Thus, while it has a humanoid aspect, they also have a crocodilian-like tail. The hands are placed on the belly, and they have a perforation at the level of the solar plexus.

There are also two modeled zoomorphic figurines. One is a feline measuring 7 cm while the other is a coiled-snake pendant measuring 5 cm. The eyes and nose of the latter—which seems to be a coral snake (*Micrurinae*)—are made with incisions, the mouth was made with a groove, and the body has incised transverse lines and a perforation in order to be hung.

Copper

Four copper bells (crotals) and a small copper disc were recovered in Cist 13. Four other bells, each over 3 cm in length, were found below the urn of Cist 18 (Figure 12.3d). According to Hosler's classification (2005b:160), the bells belong to Period I and correspond to Type 1a and Type 11a.

Spindle Whorls

We recovered 27 spindle whorls (2 to 4 cm) in the cists and along the sides, most of which are biconical in form. They have incised, engraved, and ribbed decoration, with geometric and cruciform motifs made with circles and parallel lines as well as stepped frets and *chalchihuites* symbols. The spindle whorls are brown-colored, although some have red slip and one exhibits a white band on the middle part of the body. One type of spindle whorl is similar to that reported in Amapa (Meighan 1976:369): biconical, red-slipped with an incised design made with a point enclosed by two circles.

LITHICS

The most outstanding worked lithic artifacts are nine prismatic blades. Four of them are made of local gray obsidian apparently from the Pochotero volcano, which is located on the eastern slope of Ceboruco and very close to the site. The other five are green obsidian blades that probably come from the Volcán las Navajas source near Tepic (see Pierce, this volume). These blades from Cist 1, measuring between 3 and 12 cm, are of great interest since they twisted due to their exposure to fire during the incineration and cremation of Burial 1, which dates to AD 885–995 (Beta-434018). Two projectile points and two scrapers of gray obsidian were also found during the excavation of the cists.

Other artifacts include seven earspools made of white or brownish-yellow stone, most of which have evidence of exposure to fire. Four have an engraved design of a flower with four petals while the other three have designs based on lines and circles. The groundstone artifacts recovered include two basalt manos, a fragment of a grooved axe, and three figurines, one of which is in the form of a frog.

Many burials had offerings made of small fragments of kaolinite, including a broken zoomorphic figurine measuring 27 cm in length with the four broken pieces placed around the outside of Cist 1. Also, most of the burials contained at least one or several large pumice stones of bluish, gray, white, or reddish color measuring from 2 to 40 cm in diameter. Finally, it is important to note the use of fine, thin slabs and stones in direct association with burials. The slabs were placed lying down on top of or next to the burial. The largest flagstone, 70 cm long and only 3 cm thick, was broken into two parts and placed at an angle of 45 degrees just above one of the flexed burials.

Shells

There are 244 artifacts made from shells and snails, all bearing evidence of exposure to fire. The most abundant are 166 pieces coming mainly from the univalve Olividae. Some snails have a cut spiral, others a circular hole in the body, and others have a cut and perforation for suspension. Second in abundance are 36 bivalve beads measuring 1.5 cm long by 1.6 cm wide, trapezoidal in shape, with a small extension on the upper end so that each bead can be laterally set. These same types of pieces have been related to the Late Classic and Early Postclassic in northern Michoacán (Pereira 1999:141).

Next, there are 35 small disc-shaped or wheel-shaped beads made from bivalves and measuring 0.5 cm in diameter. In addition, three pendants or earrings measuring 0.9 cm in length were recovered, as were two mother-of-pearl earrings measuring 1.6 cm. Finally, we registered two beautiful oval or teardrop-shaped pieces manufactured of a bivalve *Pinctada mazatlanica*, measuring 2.2 and 2.3 cm in length, respectively. This type of inlay has been found in funerary masks or pendants in other contexts in Mesoamerica.

Bone

Several worked bones were identified, including a zoomorphic figurine (3.6 cm) representing a snake with incised features and nine bone punches/awls, the longest measuring nearly 8.5 cm. A long, thin awl for drilling bears a point on one end and incisions on the other. In addition, several armadillo bones (*Novencinctus*) were associated with one of the flexed burials while a deer jaw fragment and two antler fragments were found in association with cist burials.

Textile

Inside the urn of Burial 3, a small fragment of burned textile was recovered.

THE BODIES AND THE OSTEOLOGICAL REMAINS

A total of 22 burials and 17 stone and mud cists were found: six were located on the prehispanic ground surface (−0.80 m) as altars and the other 11 cists were below the altars and extended a meter below the surface with cremations inside and outside the cists (Figure 12.2). Each burial consisted of one or several individuals; all of the cists were deposited in a small area measuring 12 m by 13 m on each side in a complex funerary process. There is clear evidence of remnants of adobe (*bajareque*).

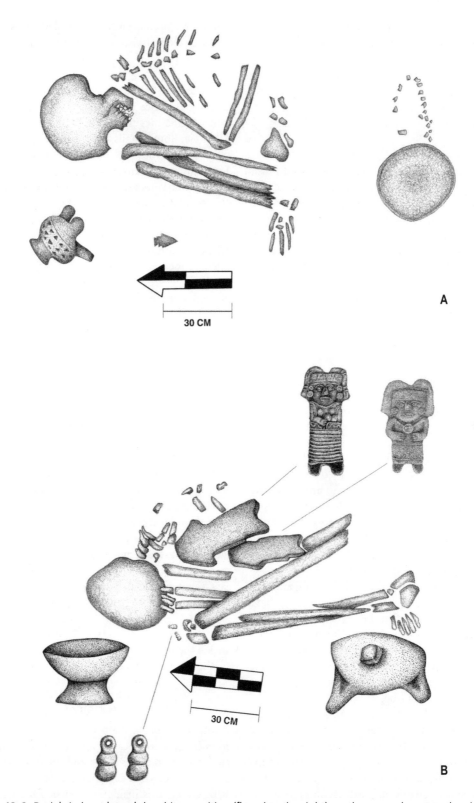

FIGURE 12.6. Burials in bent lateral decubitus position (flexed to the right) on the ground next to the cist. (*a*) Burial 20. (*b*) Burial 21. La Pitayera, Nayarit. Drawings by Oliver Fernández Sotolongo. Photographs of Figures 12.6a and 12.6b are available in the Supplemental Digital Material: https://collections.lib.utah.edu/ark:/87278/s6kb90sf.

Inside each cist, there was a vessel containing cremated remains. Several cists included additional vessels, each covered with a plate and holding cremated remains, placed outside of the structure. Two cremated secondary burials were placed directly on the floor of a cist in association with a thin slab. In total, 13 funerary ceramic urns were located, 10 of which were inside the cists with the other three outside. A single direct cremation also was located, without a vessel, deposited post-cremation inside a stone cist. Offerings were placed facing the cardinal directions, with a particular emphasis on the northwest corner, toward the volcano. The offerings also were placed along the outer walls.

In addition to the cremations, four inhumations were interred in the deeper portions of the funerary deposit, alongside the cist burials. These were found in a bent lateral decubitus position flexed to the right and next to very thin stone slabs (Figure 12.6). The body was placed at the bottom of a pit in a flexed position, with the head facing north or south and the offerings placed near the head, feet, and back. In two flexed burials, the offerings were placed towards the west with stones. The other two had very thin slabs on top of the body and another stone covering the grave pit. In addition, Burial 12 had an altar-cist on the surface of the ground marking the event.

The inhumations are of special importance because they contained Aztatlán materials such as a brazier and a long-handled frying-pan censer (*incensario*), Mazapan figurines, tripod bowls, incised spindle whorls, shell and stone pendants, and projectile points. Since they were found at the same or slightly greater depth than the cists (because they were interred on or below the subsurface floor cists), it is likely that they predate or were contemporary with the cists.

The archaeological work conducted within the group of cists revealed the presence of a complex burial process of double funerals, which makes evident the existence of elaborate death rituals led by body management specialists. The data suggest the existence of several stages during the handling of the corpse and the cremated remains until its final deposit, and it is very likely that the funeral ceremonies lasted several days.

Once the individual died, they were prepared for a complex funerary ritual of mourning and a vigil for the body. The funeral ceremony reached its most dramatic point with the cremation of the body on an open funeral pyre. Once the fire consumed the remains, they were carefully collected, deposited inside a ceramic *olla*, and covered with a plate.

Afterwards, the *olla* was deposited in the cist through an elaborate ritual which consisted of making a base of bones (that could not be incinerated) at the bottom of the cist and placing the long bones on the north and south side. Then the urn containing one or more cremated individuals was placed within, the urn was surrounded by more incinerated bones, and finally a fragment of the skull was placed on the lid. During this process, the offerings were placed inside the cist; most were burned and broken intentionally. Sometimes the interior of the cist was filled with a fine earth and ashes while others were left without being filled. Finally, the cist was sealed at the top with slabs and clay and painted red. Once the offerings were placed, the whole ensemble was covered by earth up to the ground surface where the location of the tomb was marked with red pigment, or a surface cist marker was raised, or a flagstone was placed marking the center of the burial. There is evidence of large banquets conducted around these funeral elements and also of burnt ceramic vessel remains.

Many of the artifacts were purposely broken into three parts or burned, suggesting that they were probably next to the body while burning on the funeral pyre. Along with all of the burial types and in all of the funeral deposits, one or several examples of pumice of different sizes inside the cists, excluding one measuring 40 cm in diameter found outside, were found as a symbolic offering. These have a clear allusion to fire and to the catastrophic Plinian eruption of Ceboruco.

The Micro-excavation and Bioarchaeological Analysis

Thus far, we have conducted a study of nine individuals from inside six urns from cist burials: four young female adults, two male adults, one unborn, and some bones representing two infants. These included indirect, secondary, and collective burials, and represent at least four stages in the treatment of the body (Talavera and Gelover 2016).

There is evidence that eight individuals were incinerated when the bodies still had soft tissue. Only the young female adult of Cist 6 was cremated in a dry state, that is, already defleshed. Each individual was cremated individually on an open-air funeral pyre at differential temperatures of 250° to 900° Celsius. This temperature range is inferred by the heterogeneity in the coloration of the bone elements (Talavera and Gelover 2016). Only the young female adult contained in Cist and Burial 1 may have been cremated in an oven (*horno*), a conclusion inferred by the homogeneity in the white coloration of the bones and in the torsion that is evident as well as by the fracture pattern of the bones. In this burial, there are five green obsidian blades that were bent and twisted by the fire without reaching the point of fracture.

Thanks to the micro-excavation process inside the urns, it was possible to establish that there was a special treatment and accommodation of the bone remains inside the vessel. The bones were clean, without the remains of ash or coal. This evidence indicates that there was a careful collection of the bones from the pyre in order to clean and place them inside the urns.

The reconstruction of the skeletons allowed us to obtain significant data. The skull of a young adult aged 18–20 and one of a male adult aged 36–50 exhibited intentional cephalic molding of the Tabular erect bilobed type, the most frequent in Mesoamerica. One notable feature of cephalic morphology in Mesoamerican peoples is the artificial modification of the skull, which has been evident since the Preclassic (see Carpenter and Sánchez and García Moreno et al., this volume).

Several paleopathological alterations related to health conditions also were detected. There are six cases of adult and infant individuals with traces of porotic hyperostosis in the skull, as well as periostitis in long bones of the lower extremities. These are indicators of nutritional deficiencies or general stress within the community, despite the fact that they likely belonged to a privileged class. The population probably faced adverse conditions at the site while surrounded by a hostile environment recovering from the devastation left by the eruptions.

Conclusion: Ahuacatlán in Its Regional Context

The cists of Ahuacatlán provide valuable information on the customs and funeral rites developed during the late Epiclassic and Postclassic periods, which stand out for being unique in the region since there are no similar developments in Nayarit or west Mexico. The cists were found in the center of a main-plaza cemetery, as if it were part of an event of great relevance. These burials were located in front of the important Mound 7, apparently associated with a cult of the dead.

The recovered data indicate that, after the Shaft Tomb and Epiclassic era, a stone-cist tradition developed during the end of the Epiclassic and the transition to the Early Postclassic. During this time, the new Aztatlán cultural tradition appeared and coexisted with local traditions until the Early Postclassic period while expanding its territorial extent via social and technological bases.

In Mesoamerica, Native conceptions of the world intersect with ritual practices (see Galinier 1997), including funerary rites. The use of formal urns in Nayarit, whether in stone or in large anthropomorphic ceramic cylinders, has its antecedents in the Mololoa culture where there is a funerary pattern of cremations contained in ceramic urns associated with lithic altars (Beltrán Medina 2001b). Cremation seems to be an act of purification of matter achieved through fire, related to the worship of the god of fire and the Ceboruco volcano. The presence of shell beads, copper rattles, figurines, and other materials suggests exchanges with other peoples.

The site revealed the importance of knowing the history of Ceboruco's volcanic activity and the surrounding monogenetic domes as a basis for cultural interpretations and regional comparisons. Active volcanoes have always imposed their conditions and appear to have influenced the beliefs and social practices of the inhabitants of this region. The sequence of occupation at the site is linked with the volcanic activity.

The major eruptive event of Ceboruco marked a break in the occupation sequence, thereby generating a gap between the Middle Ixtlán and Late Ixtlán periods. Another monogenetic eruptive event of great importance involved the formation of the Pochotero obsidian dome. This source of gray obsidian, located a short distance from Ahuacatlán and other volcanic resources, played an important role in the development of the local lithic industry. Apparently, this is one of the sources of obsidian used on the site from the time of the shaft tombs and Postclassic period.

The existence of volcanic products is probably one of the reasons for the interaction networks of Ahuacatlán. The presence of exogenous materials demonstrates the existence of exchanges with other geographic regions. Gray obsidian, pigments, and lapidary products were exchanged for shell jewelry, green obsidian, prismatic blades, cotton, copper bells, and Mazapan figurines. This activity was framed within the new ideological and cultural concepts at the time.

CHAPTER 13

A World within the World

Portraiture Effigy Bowls and Cargo Systems in Mitote Cycles of the Aztatlán Tradition

Michael D. Mathiowetz

One concern in the study of far west Mexico is the history of prehispanic sociopolitical and religious institutions and their relation to descendant Indigenous ritual practices, landscape use, and territoriality. The Gran Nayar region encompasses parts of Nayarit, Jalisco, Durango, and Zacatecas, today occupied by Náayeri (Cora), Wixárika (Huichol), O'dam (Tepehuan), and Náhuat (Mexicaneros) whose maize-agricultural *mitote* ritualism shares a common structure (Neurath 2000: 86). Recent research expanding on the work of early ethnologists (Lumholtz 1900, 1902; Preuss 1911, 1912; Zingg 1938) can provide insight into prehispanic social formations. Questions remain on the antiquity of *mitotes* in the Aztatlán region (Grave Tirado 2010b; Grave Tirado and Samaniega Altamirano 2012). Herein, I assess Gran Nayar *mitote* ritualism and cargo systems to discern key tenets of Aztatlán ideology, ritualism, and sociopolitical organization in relation to historic practices (Figures I.1–I.2). I contend that core-zone Aztatlán cargo systems involved portraiture bowls, which may have inspired the development of Classic Mimbres (AD 1000–1130) bowl traditions in southern New Mexico (Figure 13.1).

Prehispanic and Historic *Mitotes* in the Gran Nayar

Mitotes are night-long ceremonies involving round dances in plazas that mark critical moments during the rainy and dry season maize-agricultural cycle, including preparation of the field, sowing of seeds, the harvest, and rituals tied to ancestry, human life-cycle events, and gender (Coyle 2001; Guzmán Vázquez 2002; Neurath 2005b; Zingg 1938). Cargo systems among the Wixárika, Náayeri, and O'dam involve ranch-based *mitotes* operating in conjunction with village-level cargo-system *mitotes* (Coyle 2001:35; Fikes 1985; Hinton 1964; Neurath 2000; Reyes Valdez 2006; Téllez Lozano 2014). Náayeri rainy-season *mitotes* relate to stages of maize agriculture while dry-season *mitotes* relate to equivalent stages in the human life cycle (Guzmán Vázquez 2002) during which deceased ancestors return as rain clouds (Lumholtz 1902:1:523), much like Puebloan katsina ritualism (Mathiowetz 2011:376–383). Náayeri *mitote* ceremonies held in plazas are fertility rites in which ancestors return as rain to observe and participate in the seasonal solar and maize-agricultural cycles that bind living participants and their ancestors within a vast sacred landscape. Sixteenth- and seventeenth-century documents note the practice of *mitotes* (Coyle 2001:76–86; McCarty and Matson 1975) despite Spanish missionization (Coyle 2001:75–78). Ultimately, Catholic ceremonialism in mission communities replaced the region-wide preconquest Náayeri chiefdom with community-level political-religious authorities (Coyle 2001:75–76; Neurath 2000).

Three deities (among others) are notable in Gran Nayar and Aztatlán *mitotes*: (1) the sun, (2) Venus as Morning and Evening Star, and (3) the feathered serpent. As their ethnological and archaeological attributes are characterized elsewhere (Mathiowetz 2011, 2018, 2019a, 2019b, 2020a; Mathiowetz et al. 2015), below I outline the nature and geographical scope of *mitotes* and cargo systems linked to these three gods and trace their historical origin in the Aztatlán world.

The Sun, Venus, and Horned and Feathered Serpents within Contemporary Mitote *Ritualism in the Gran Nayar*

In the 1530s, the solar deity Piltzintli (also called Teopiltzintli or Xochipilli) was a major god associated with the east and dawn in the Totorame region (the former Aztatlán core zone) of northern Nayarit and southern Sinaloa who was revered by ethnic groups across highland Nayarit, northern Jalisco, southern Zacatecas, and southern Durango (Mathiowetz 2011, 2018, 2019a,

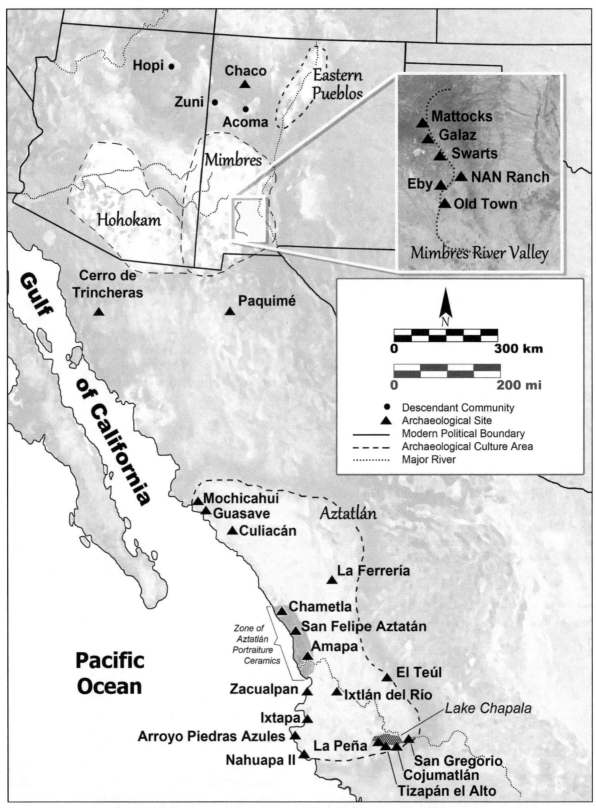

FIGURE 13.1. Map of the Aztatlán region and the broader southwestern United States and northwest Mexico in relation to the location of figurative (portraiture) bowl traditions. Drawing by Will Russell.

2019b; Scott 2017). Worship of Piltzintli was centered at the Mesa del Nayar (Mesa del Tonati) and focused on a lineage of oracular mummies of deceased Náayeri "sun kings" (or Tonati) linked to the seasons as the personification or earthly intermediary of this deity (Figure 13.2a). The term "Tonati" also suggests an affiliation with the highland Mexican sun god Tonatiuh.

The transit of the Piltzintli sun across the sky and through the underworld during the daily and annual solar cycle is linked to the seasonal and maize-agricultural *mitote* cycles and a "day sun/male/hunting" and "night sun/female/agriculture" complementary duality. The Franciscan friar Antonio Arias de Saavedra in 1673 described *mitote* dances at the Mesa del Nayar:

> Their worst vices are dancing and drunkenness, and they believe that when they are thus engaged they are banishing poverty. They ask for many things during their dances, all of them temporal. They ask their Piltzintli for a long life to spend in pleasure and gluttony (in McCarty and Matson 1975:207).

After the conquest of the Náayeri in 1722, the eighteenth and nineteenth centuries saw missionaries implement Christian ceremonies in towns dedicated to saints and civil-religious offices, although Náayeri continued their *mitote* practices in secret. Early historic accounts describe peyote and liquor consumption, first-fruits rites with offerings to the sun god, maize blessings, plaza dances, cognatic or maize-bundle descent systems, community or *ranchería* maize-bundle group elders, the use of bow-drums, and tear-filled displays by participants—all of which relate to *mitote* rites. Indigenous revivalism in 1767 sought to reestablish *mitotes* and the office of "sun king" at the Mesa del Nayar (Coyle 2001:76–86; Meyer 1989). While the Spaniards did not eliminate *mitotes* that are central to Indigenous sociopolitical and religious organization today, they suppressed the centralized preconquest practice of human sacrifice to the Náayeri sun god Piltzintli at the Mesa del Nayar that are evident today as animal sacrifices.

Piltzintli/Xochipilli solar ritualism concentrated in the Aztatlán coastal core zone is traceable to the Early Postclassic period (Mathiowetz 2011, 2018, 2019a, 2019b, 2020a, 2022). White stone effigy vessels in the form of Piltzintli/Xochipilli, for example, were recovered at Siqueros, Sinaloa, near Mazatlán (Mathiowetz 2011:Figures 6.1a–6.1b). At Chacalilla, Nayarit, a burial-mound complex dated to AD 850/900–1350+ contained decapitated human crania. This mortuary complex, excavated in 2008, was interpreted as an observatory to chart the annual solar and agricultural cycle in relation to the solstices and equinoxes, revered ancestors, and a Flower World domain—all linked to a form of Aztatlán *mitote* ritualism (Ohnersorgen et al. 2010a, 2010b).[1] Similar solar mound complexes—akin to rudimentary Maya E-groups (see Freidel et al. 2017)—are reported nearby at Amapa, Las Ánimas, and Las Tinajas (Garduño Ambriz 2022; Mathiowetz 2011:444–445). In north-coastal Nayarit, solar discs in petroglyphs and ceramics and portrayals of solar deities on ceramics are evident (Figures 13.2b–13.2e). On ceramics, solar-related Aztatlán figures at times wear a butterfly brow piece like that of Late Postclassic Aztec and Mixtec sun gods and other deities and elites, including Maya deities, a device related to the jade Jester God diadem worn by the Early Postclassic Tonatiuh at Chichén Itzá and Classic Maya kings (Figures 13.2d–13.2i; see Taube 2010:149–150, Figure 3).

Venus is a culture hero revered by various names among multiple ethnic groups—particularly in his Morning Star aspect—including the Náayeri (e.g., Cuanamoa, Xurave, Ha'atsíkan, Taha, Tonarikan, or San Miguel); Wixárika (e.g., Xurawe Temai, Tamatsi Parietsika, or Tamáts Pálike Tamoyéke); O'dam (e.g., Txidiúkam or Ixcaichoing) and Tepecan; and Náhuat (e.g., Piltonte), which indicates pan-regional Venus ritualism (Mathiowetz et al. 2015; Neurath 2005b). The Náayeri Morning Star (Cuanamoa) and Evening Star (Ceutarit or Sautari) duality was noted by the Jesuit padre José Ortega in the 1720s (Neurath 2005b:78). The Morning Star is identified with the east/dawn, and he: (1) created the milpa, (2) created the important ceremonies and rituals (e.g., the first *mitotes*), (3) first received the sacred songs, (4) is related to maize agriculture, war/hunting, and ancestors as rain, and (5) has an arrow as his "face" (Mathiowetz 2011:349–357; Mathiowetz et al. 2015; Neurath 2005b). The morning and evening aspects of Venus and the sun interrelate with the forces of the dry season (day/light/above/male) and the rainy season (night/darkness/below/female) that foster growth and fertility (Mathiowetz 2011:349–353; Mathiowetz et al. 2015; Neurath 2005b; Solar Valverde 2019) such that "the destiny of the Sun follows the same logic of Venus" (Figure 13.3; Neurath 2005b:87).

The feathered serpent is a major deity linked to rain, breath/wind, vegetal growth, Venus, and the sun. For Wixárika, the female deity Tatei Nia'ariwame or Na'arihuame ("Mother East-Water" or "Goddess of the First Rains") is akin to Quetzalcoatl as a feathered cloud/rain-serpent deity (*haiku*) of the east. Linked to breath, she initiates the monsoon rainy season in June (Neurath 2005b:90–92, fn. 29). This deity's serpentine form is embodied in the line of *peyotero* cargo holders (a composite group of ancestor-deities including Morning Star) who return with and as beneficient rain during the Hikuli Neixa (Peyote Dance) following the observation of the birth of the sun in Wirikuta in San

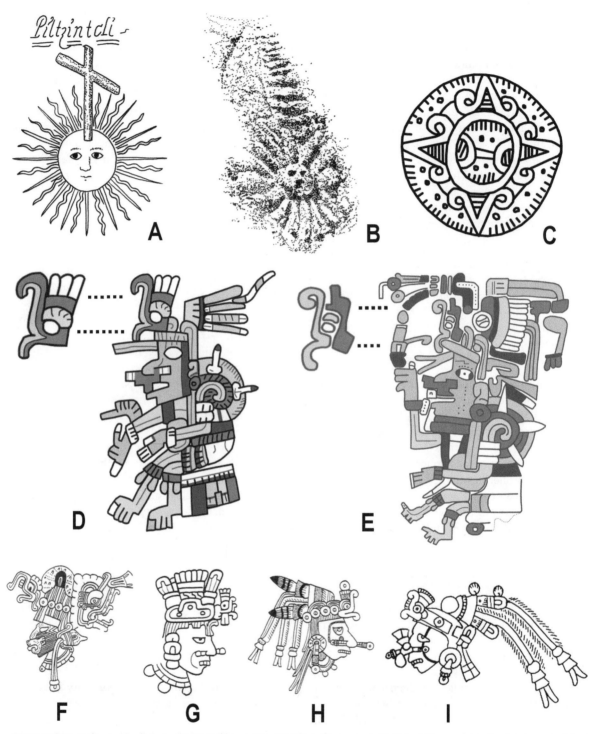

FIGURE 13.2. Solar symbolism in the Aztatlán region. (*a*) Piltzintli sun god. Detail of Cora solar calendar in report by Fray Antonio Arias de Saavedra, 1673 (after Estampa 25, Archivo General de Indias, Ministerio de Educación, Cultura y Deporte, Spain). (*b*) Petroglyph of sun on *imúmui* (solar ladder) at Pila de los Monos, east of Acaponeta, Nayarit (after Furst and Scott 1975:Figure 2). (*c*) Solar disc with "A"-shaped rays. Detail of Santiago Engraved (AD 1350+) double jar, Amapa, Nayarit (after Meighan, ed. 1976:Plate 162). (*d*) Solar ancestor-god (perhaps Piltzintli/Xochipilli) wearing butterfly brow piece. Detail of Iguanas Polychrome (AD 1100–1350+) codex-style jar. Catalog number M.2000.86, Los Angeles County Museum of Art (after photo by author). (*e*) Solar ancestor-god wearing butterfly brow piece. Detail of Iguanas Polychrome (AD 1100–1350+) codex-style jar (after Von Winning 1977:Figure 2). (*f*) Figure wearing butterfly brow piece, Santa Rita, Belize (Drawing by Karl Taube). (*g*) Maya goddess wearing butterfly brow piece, Tulum, Quintana Roo (Drawing by Karl Taube). (*h*) Sun god Tonatiuh wearing butterfly brow piece, *Codex Borgia* p. 70 (Drawing by Karl Taube). (*i*) Mixtec sun god One Death wearing butterfly brow piece, *Codex Nuttall* p. 79 (Drawing by Karl Taube). Drawings by author unless indicated otherwise.

FIGURE 13.3. Venus as Morning Star and god bowls. (*a*) Detail of Botadero Incised (AD 850/900–1100) jar exterior, Nayarit. Note stellar eyes, flint knives, and speech/song scroll. Museo Regional de Nayarit, Tepic. Author's illustration. (*b*) Detail of Botadero Incised (AD 850/900–1100) jar exterior, Nayarit. Note stellar eyes, flint knives, and speech/song scroll. Museo Regional de Nayarit, Tepic. Author's illustration. (*c*) Cerritos Polychrome (AD 850/900–1100) annular-based bowl, Las Varas area, Nayarit. Note stellar eyes and flint knives. Museo Regional de Nayarit, Tepic. (*d*) Ixcuintla Polychrome (AD 1100–1350+) annular-based bowl, Amapa, Nayarit. Note stellar eyes and darts. Catalog number 246-1782, Fowler Museum Archaeology Curation Facility, University of California, Los Angeles, and Instituto Nacional de Antropología e Historia. Photo by author. (*e*) Tizapán White-on-red (AD 1100–1250) tripod bowl, La Peña, Nayarit. Note dart at nose and crossed bones. Photo by author, courtesy of Susana Ramírez Urrea (see Ramírez and Cárdenas 2006:Figure 79). (*f*) Venus-affiliated crossed bones. Probable Sentispac Red-on-buff (AD 1100–1350+) annular bowl, Peñitas, Nayarit. Catalog number 184-9, Fowler Museum Archaeology Curation Facility, University of California, Los Angeles, and Instituto Nacional de Antropología e Historia. Photo by author.

Luis Potosí (Lumholtz 1900:13; Neurath 2005b:90–92). Neurath (2005b:90–92) likened the return of the feathered serpent deity and the dissemination of seeds to the descent of the Morning Star deity to earth to teach people the *mitotes*. The feathered serpent is reportedly present among the Náayeri (Jáuregui 2002), while Náhuat (Mexicanero) rites include a feathered serpent embodied by a line of dancers carrying bows (linking them to the Morning Star as archer) headed by a man wearing an elaborate plumed and mirrored headdress (see Mathiowetz 2011:367).

Like the sun and Venus, the Wixárika feathered serpent has dual aspects affiliated with the east/above/Wirikuta and the west/underworld/sea. The western serpent (Tatei Kiewimuka) is linked to Evening Star/Evening Sun and *kieri* while the eastern feathered serpent (Tatei Nia'ariwame) is linked to Morning Star/Day Sun and peyote, a duality reported in the 1670s (Figure 13.4; Magriña 2001; Mathiowetz 2011:365–369; Neurath 2005b:91; Zingg 1938:338–342). In Wixárika accounts, the sun established the rainy season and regulates the directional Rain Mothers (five principal goddesses) who reside on the landscape. The sun and principal Rain Mother Nia'ariwame (the feathered serpent) work together to release the ancestral rains to water the maize fields (Fikes 2011:126–131; Lumholtz 1900:13–14).

Some Rain Mothers—who are associated with snakes—relate in some ways with horned serpents. On the shield of Father Sun, the Rain Mother Tatei Kiewimuka ("Mother West Water") was portrayed as a serpent with backward recurving horns that also are feathers (Lumholtz 1900:120). Smoke clouds produced by burning first travel to terrestrial springs or pools (the residence of the Rain Mothers) where they become plumed rain serpents that fly through the air as falling or flowing water during the rainy season (Lumholtz 1900:20). Wixárika horned, plumed, and winged or flying rain serpents (*haiku*) resemble Tepecan (southern Tepehuan) horned serpents (*chanes, chaneque,* or *o'oikam*) who inhabit springs and streams and guard the resident ancestral cloud spirits (Mason 1912b; see Beekman 2003:312–313). For Náayeri, horned water serpents are called *chacanes* (Hinton 1972:36). J. Alden Mason described Tepecan *chanes* as follows:

> The *chanes* are malevolent water-serpents which inhabit the springs and streams. They are horned and of many colors. They always travel in pairs, male and female, and love to stretch themselves through the clouds in rainy weather, head in one spring and tail in another, visiting. In this form they appear as rainbows. They are called the "winds of the water". The *chanes* are vicious and will sting those who have not placated them […] When a man decides to build a house and make his home on a new site it is necessary for him to placate the *chanes* of the spring whence he draws his water supply (Mason 1918:126).

The Tepecan *chanes* have a close connection to the austere Venus as Morning Star yet bear malevolent attributes that must be placated through offerings (Mason 1918:125–129; 1981:65–66). Water-dwelling *chaneque* were reported in 1652 in the Tecuexe region of east-central Jalisco (Paso y Troncoso 1946 [1652:17–18]; see Beekman 2003:312). One deep arroyo (called Arroyo el Chan) located 13 km northwest of Etzatlán, Jalisco, leads into the Laguna Magdalena (Beekman 2003:313), formerly a major Aztatlán political, economic, and ritual hub (Weigand 2013).

The homes of beneficent or destructive feathered and horned serpents appear to relate to terrestrial springs and pools where the ancestral rain spirits reside. Aztatlán cargo landscape ritualism may have involved people traveling to waterholes and springs to placate the rain-bearing serpent and ancestral rain-spirit inhabitants as evident in water sources where rock art is found, such as at Alta Vista and Pila de los Monos in central and northern Nayarit, respectively (Mathiowetz 2023, 2025b). As plumed and flying rain serpents sometimes are coiled (Lumholtz 1900:54), spirals common in coastal Aztatlán rock art may signify rain serpents who reside at their homes. Wixárika who desire to become *mara'akame* (singers) must travel to San Blas, Nayarit, to find the locales where the mother goddesses emerged, places which are marked by coiled water serpents (*haiku*) pecked in stone (Knab 2004:151). Around San Blas, spiral petroglyphs are abundant (Figures 3.12–3.13; Ohnersorgen 2007:27, Figures 3.12–3.13), including some with snake-like heads (Mountjoy 1970:113–114, Figures 77, 80, 1974a, 1987b). The relation between horned water serpents (*chanes*), the feathered serpent, and Morning Star suggests a set of related ideas with a post-AD 850/900 origin. Thus, ethnological and ethnohistorical records indicate that Venus, horned and feathered serpents, and the sun have key roles in Gran Nayar *mitote* and landscape ritualism that are traceable in the Aztatlán archaeological record. In turn, Aztatlán horned rain-serpent ritualism may have inspired ritualism in the Mimbres, Jornada, Casas Grandes, and Puebloan regions where horned water serpents appeared after AD 1000 in ceramics and rock art and in post-AD 1300 kiva murals when Aztatlán socioeconomic and ideological networks expanded to these northern regions (see Phillips Jr. et al. 2006; Schaafsma 2001; Schaafsma and Taube 2006; Taube 2001; for water serpents of the Yuman region, see Field 2018).

FIGURE 13.4. The feathered serpent, wind god Ehecatl, and god bowls. (*a*) Feathered serpent. Detail of ceramic cylinder stamp, Ixtlán del Río, Nayarit (after Gifford 1950:Figure 19m). (*b*) Feathered serpent. Note tab-like feathers. Detail of Tuxpan Engraved (AD 900–1100) bowl exterior bottom, Nayarit (after Stern 1977:Figure 2). (*c*) Feathered serpent. Note eye scroll, open maw, and bifid tongue. Detail of Ixcuintla Polychrome (AD 1100–1350+) bowl interior, Amapa, Nayarit. Catalog number 246-3041, Fowler Museum Archaeology Curation Facility, University of California, Los Angeles, and Instituto Nacional de Antropología e Historia (after photo by author). (*d*) Feathered serpent. Note eye scroll, open maw, and bifid tongue. Botadero Black-on-buff bowl interior (AD 850/900–1100), Boca de Chila, Nayarit. Fowler Museum Archaeology Curation Facility, University of California, Los Angeles, and Instituto Nacional de Antropología e Historia. Photo by author. (*e*) Cross-cut conch shell. Sentispac Red-on-buff bowl (AD 850/900–1100), El Pirul, Nayarit. Museo Regional de Nayarit and Instituto Nacional de Antropología e Historia. Photo by author. (*f*) Cross-cut conch shell. Tuxpan Red-on-orange bowl (AD 850/900–1100), Coamiles, Nayarit. Museo Regional de Nayarit and Instituto Nacional de Antropología e Historia. Photo by Mauricio Garduño Ambriz. (*g*) Cross-cut conch shell. Cojumatlán Polychrome engraved (AD 850–1100) tripod bowl, Tizapán el Alto, Jalisco. Archival photo, Fowler Museum Archaeology Curation Facility, University of California, Los Angeles, and Instituto Nacional de Antropología e Historia. (*h*) Wind god Ehecatl. Detail of Iguanas Polychrome (AD 1100–1350+) jar. Catalog number M.2000.86, Los Angeles County Museum of Art (after photo by author). (*i*) Wind god Ehecatl. Detail of Iguanas Polychrome (AD 1100–1350+) jar. Catalog number M.2000.86, Los Angeles County Museum of Art (after photo by author). (*j*) Wind god Ehecatl. Detail on Xipe Totec effigy vessel. Catalog number X73.273, Fowler Museum, University of California, Los Angeles (after photo by author). Drawings by author.

A World Within the World: Cargo Systems and Bowl Bearers in *Mitotes* of the Gran Nayar

Indigenous cargo systems (or civil-religious hierarchies) in Mesoamerica have long been a focus of study, with speculation on their possible prehispanic roots (Bunzel 1959; Cancian 1965; Carrasco 1961; Chance and Taylor 1985; Chick 2002; De Walt 1975; Ekern 2011; Flores-Marcial 2015; Haviland 1966; Mathews 1985; Parsons 1936; Price 1974; Romero Melgarejo 2018; Rus and Wasserstrom 1980; Tax 1937; Vogt 1964, 1969; Vogt and Cancian 1970; Wolf 1957, 1959). Cargo-related Wixárika *mitotes* include gourd bowls (*Lagenaria siceraria*) with interior designs of gods, people, animals, and entities fashioned from beads, coins, cotton, maize seeds, yarn, and wax (Kindl 2000, 2003; Preuss 1911, 1912; Seler 1992; Taube 2009; Zingg 1938:632–635). Wixárika gourd bowls, called *jícaras* (*xicallis*) or *xukurite*, include two types: (1) effigy bowls and (2) votive bowls. Effigy bowls are decorated with designs related to a particular deity while votive bowls bear images related to people and their plants and animals (Kindl 2000; Lumholtz 1900:209). Náayeri gods and Catholic saints are worshiped together and, like Wixárika bowls, "each one of them has its pagan representation in a votive bowl called a '*tecomate*'" (Hinton 1972:38). Náayeri bowls are a model of the universe and *mitote* dance patio and relate to 12 principal community elders who are the ancestor gods and first humans (see Figure 14.6; Guzmán 2002; Neurath 2000:86; Preuss 1911, 1912), much like bowls of the first Wixárika ancestor gods. Gourd bowls among the Tepecan/Tepehuan of Azqueltán, Jalisco (Mason 1981:67–68), parallel Wixárika bowls (Fikes 1985:82–83).

Deities and mythological scenes are depicted in Wixárika effigy bowls while votive bowls are offered to deified ancestors as prayers for good harvests, luck in hunting, and health (Kindl 2000:39). The Sun first established Wixárika bowl-bearer cargo offices, and in the "Sun Myth" he ordered "keepers of the votive bowls" to attend to his commands (Zingg 1938:16, 188). Bowls are rain-making devices that attract clouds to fill the bowls with water, which links them to maize growth (Zingg 1938:634–635). This concept resembles the ancestral katsina rain spirits as personified water-filled bowls/jars that are evident in the Puebloan region after AD 1300 (Mathiowetz 2011:818–821; see Schaafsma 2002). Effigy bowls are like "mothers" or "wombs" from which ancestral deities are born (Taube 2009), hence the depiction of deities and related designs in the interior. Since every object in the world is said to contain the world, bowls are microcosms (Kindl 2000:57)—a world within the world. Effigy bowls are used in four places: (1) in *tukipa* ceremonial centers (the dwelling places of the oldest deities), (2) in *xiriki* (smaller shrines/god houses linked to ancestors in a kin group), (3) in the house of the governor and town church in the community center, and (4) at pilgrimage sites on the sacred landscape. Votive bowls are used by individuals to offer prayers at sacred sites in individual or collective ceremonies (Kindl 2000:39).

Wixárika cargo initiates engage in ritual purification and self-deprivation as the ideal of austerity (Neurath 2000:94–95). Initiates embody the original first community of their own ancestors wherein they themselves are deities who live at (and are) the sacred spots on the landscape and in the temples and shrines at ceremonial centers (Kindl 2000). Ceremonial centers are the original communities of first ancestors from which derive all other household units (*ranchos*) as people moved to found new communities. Membership in religious hierarchies requires one to travel to the original ancestral political-ceremonial center to become the ancestors. At the *tukipa* center, cargo holders take the names of and embody deified ancestors and live in their respective god house (*xiriki*) for five-year terms, taking charge of sacred gourd bowls that are wrapped in cloth and curated within their *xiriki* (Kindl 2000, 2003).

The Wixárika cargo-holder hierarchy is designated through dreams by a Council of Elders called *kawiterutsixi* (Kindl 2000:45). Cargos are typically held by young male adults, but older males, females of different ages, children, and toddlers also may hold cargos. While women fulfill the cargo of female deities, males take the cargo of either male or female deities (Johannes Neurath, personal communication 2020). Cargo offices generally consist of a husband and wife team. After five-year terms, the new cargo holder (or spouse) reproduces their predecessor's bowl (Kindl 2000:41; Neurath 2000), the same bowl can be used for years (Fikes 1985:131), or the old bowl is buried (Kindl 2000:56). Deceased Wixárika *mara'akate* (singers) can be interred with one or multiple effigy *jícaras*, but cargo bowls can be inherited by cargo successors or consanguineal descendants (Kindl 2003:144)—all practices with archaeological implications.

Typically, there is one cargo holder per gourd bowl due to the difficulty of cargo obligations, and in each political center there are a limited range of cargo holders. In the *tuki* at Tateikie (San Andres Cohamiata) there were 30 bowl bearers (Kindl 2000:41); in the *tuki* in Keuruwit+a in Tuapurie (Santa Catarina) there were 26 gourd bowls (Johannes Neurath, personal communication 2020); and in the *tuki* of Mukuxetá in Wautia (San Sebastián Teponahuaxtlán) there were 20 bowl bearers (Kindl 2000:45). Bowls are used by cargo holders in ceremonies and community-wide events where the initiates assume the identity of those gods and beings in various forms. They enact their part in mythohistorical events where bowl designs are mnemonic devices to remember mythological narratives of deities, help to make mental maps of places on the sacred landscape, and are mediums of communication (Kindl 2000: 49–51). Designs do not "represent" beings; instead, the bowls themselves are the embodiment of deities who inhabit the temples and god houses (Kindl 2000:46). Effigy bowls today are used as ancestor-deity cargos in *mitote* rites to enact mythohistorical events and narratives, rites that may have originated in Aztatlán cargos.

Bowl Bearers and Cargo Systems in the Aztatlán Region

Portrait-style animals, humans, and gods in bowl interiors appeared after AD 850/900 in a concentrated area roughly between Mazatlán, Sinaloa, and San Blas, Nayarit. More disparate examples occur at sites along the southern Nayarit and northern Jalisco coast, at highland sites around Lake Chapala in Jalisco and far western Michoacán, and in far northern coastal Sinaloa although they are apparently absent in Durango and rare in Zacatecas (Figures 13.3c–13.3f, 13.4c–13.4g, 13.6a–13.6e, 13.6g–13.6h).

The Distribution of Aztatlán Portraiture Vessels

Prior to AD 850/900, portrait-style vessel traditions are rare in west Mexico except for limited examples in Epiclassic Chalchihuites pseudo-cloisonné pedestal cups in Zacatecas (Alta Vista, La Quemada, and El Teúl) generally dating between AD 650/750–850 and Súchil and Amaro ceramics in Durango. However, the themes identified do not reflect the sun (Piltzintli), Venus, and feathered serpent ritualism discussed herein since these deities apparently did not exist in far west Mexico before AD 850/900. To my knowledge, Rodríguez Zariñán (2009) was the first to propose that some Epiclassic west Mexican vessels were akin to contemporary Gran Nayar cargo bowls, characterizing the portrayal of full-figured birds holding a serpent within the interior of pseudo-cloisonné cups as an antecedent to the solar Wixárika goddess Tatei Wierika Wimari ("Our Mother Young Eagle"). However, no other deities have been identified in these cups, and portrayals of the celestial eagle goddess are yet to be identified in Postclassic Aztatlán art or material culture.

In the Aztatlán core zone, portraiture vessels are unknown from Chinesco (AD 0–250), Gavilán (AD 250–500), or Amapa-phase (AD 500–750) ceramics until the Cerritos (AD 850/900–1100) and Ixcuintla phases (AD 1100–1350+). These Postclassic portraiture vessels vary in size and form, including simple bowls (roughly 10 to 20 cm in diameter) to annular bowls/plates. Around 700 whole or restorable vessels were recovered at Amapa (Meighan 1976:128), mostly from two Group E cemeteries (Figures 13.5–13.6). Offerings in the 45 identified grave lots ranged from one to 10 ceramic vessels per grave lot, with 16 burials containing more than five vessels (Meighan 1976:130–131). The cemeteries spanned both the Cerritos and Ixcuintla phases but were used more intensively during the latter phase (Meighan 1976:131).

The type, style, and designs of 662 vessels were analyzed by Betty Bell (1960:225), who believed them to be the product of specialists rather than part-time craftspersons. Most were apparently unused and interred as burial offerings (Bell 1960:225); however, modern use-wear analysis is deserved. Various bichrome and polychrome vessels bear central interior images of anthropomorphs, birds, turtles, coatimundi, rabbits, canids, crocodiles, butterflies, composite creatures, and other beings (see Bell 1960:149, Figures 20–52), with some icons on the exterior bottom (e.g., Meighan, ed. 1976:Plates 139a, 139d).

Cerritos-phase (AD 850/900–1100) vessels with central interior icons at Amapa include Botadero Black-on-buff (Meighan, ed. 1976:Plates 9m–9n, 127k), Mangos Polychrome (Meighan, ed. 1976:Plate 157a, 157c–157e, 158a–158b, 158d, 159a, 159c), and Tuxpan Red-on-orange (Meighan, ed. 1976:Plate 168c). Ixcuintla-phase (AD 1100–1350+) examples include Ixcuintla Polychrome (Meighan, ed. 1976:Plates 140d, 141c-d, 143a-b, 144a-b, 145a-d, 146a-c, 153b) and Iguanas Polychrome, the latter of which crosscuts both the Cerritos and Ixcuintla phases. One Santiago Red-on-orange portraiture bowl was recovered (Meighan, ed. 1976:Plate 171c), but the chronology of this type is unclear. One bowl with a central incised zoomorphic portrait was excavated by Michael Ohnersorgen (personal observation 2008) at nearby Chacalilla, and two bowls from Coamiles include a cut-conch shell and possible feathered serpent (see Favarel-Garrigues 1995:Figures 25, 32). Bowl interiors at Peñitas include animal and anthropomorphic portrayals (personal observation 2009; Von Winning 1956:Figures 5t, 6r). In northern Nayarit at San Felipe Aztatán, a Cerritos-phase "hybrid" annular-base bowl with exterior Cerritos Polychrome and interior Tuxpan Red-on-orange designs bears the portrait of a human face in profile in the interior (Mauricio Garduño Ambriz, personal communication 2021).

Along the southern Nayarit coast, sherds from Boca de Chila include central interior depictions of an opossum and a human (personal observation 2016). At one site near Monteón, some bowl fragments contain central interior animal designs (personal observation 2016). Near Banderas Bay, a polychrome bowl with the portrait of a male hunter/warrior holding an *atlatl* and darts was reported at Arroyo Piedras Azules, Jalisco (Figure 1.6e; Mountjoy et al. 2020:Figure 4.4b), which

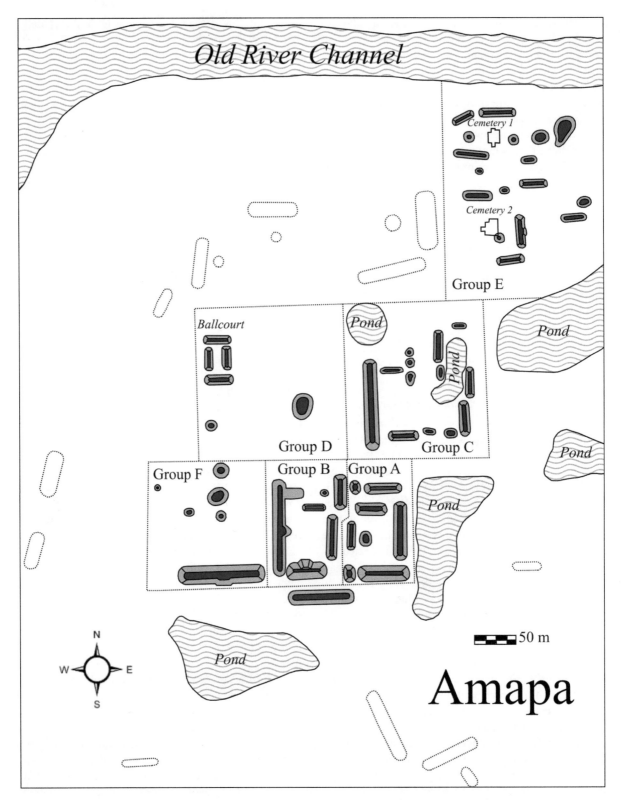

FIGURE 13.5. Site map of Amapa, Nayarit. Drawing by Daniel Pierce after Meighan (1976:Map 2).

FIGURE 13.6. Aztatlán portraiture vessels. (*a*) Rabbit. Tuxpan Red-on-orange (AD 850/900–1100) bowl, Amapa, Nayarit. Archival photo, Catalog number 246-3039. (*b*) Composite rabbit-like figure, Amapa, Nayarit. Note tail, wing, and bifid tongue. Mangos Polychrome (AD 850/900–1100) bowl. Catalog number 246-3886. Photo by author. (*c*) Bird (Ibis?). Mangos Polychrome (AD 850/900–1100) bowl, Amapa, Nayarit. Catalog number 246-3045. Photo by author. (*d*) Canine. Mangos Polychrome (AD 850/900–1100) bowl, Amapa, Nayarit. Archival photo, Catalog number 246-1914. (*e*) Turtle. Ixcuintla Polychrome (AD 1100–1350+) quadrupedal bowl. Archival photo, Catalog number 246-2159. (*f*) Human. Ixcuintla Polychrome (AD 1100–1350+) bowl exterior bottom, Amapa, Nayarit. Archival photo, Catalog number 246-1884. (*g*) Coatimundi(?). Ixcuintla Polychrome (AD 1100–1350+) annular bowl, Amapa, Nayarit. Archival photo, Catalog number 246-2578. (*h*) Bird. Iguanas Polychrome, late variant (AD 1100–1350+) annular bowl, Amapa, Nayarit. Catalog number 246-2109. All photos in Fowler Museum archives unless indicated otherwise. Fowler Museum Archaeology Curation Facility, University of California, Los Angeles, and Instituto Nacional de Antropología e Historia.

may relate to dry-season cargo holders. At Nahuapa II, in coastal Jalisco, a Red-on-buff sherd dated around AD 1200 (Joseph Mountjoy, personal communication 2022) depicts the partial limbs and body of an animal on the central interior while a second animal may be present within another bowl (see Figure 1.3, bottom row [third from left] and center row [second from left]). In Sinaloa, portrait-style bowls were not reported at Chametla or Culiacán (Kelly 1938, 1945a), although some bowls at Guasave include central depictions of human faces, a skeletal Venus deity, flint knives, and a bird descending through tri-lobed flowers (Ekholm 1942:Figures 4a, 4g–4i, 5a, 6c, 6e, 9b, 10e–10f). Two portraiture bowls from Mochicahui include a human with feathered headdress and a split-view feathered serpent, believed to date around AD 1300 (see Carpenter and Sánchez, Figure 8.3, this volume).

In highland Jalisco around Lake Chapala, Cojumatlán Polychrome incised bowls (AD 850–1100) at La Peña include a central interior human figure (Ramírez and Cárdenas 2006:Figure 73, Photo 198b). At Tizapán el Alto, portraiture bowls include interior depictions of canids and other unidentified icons (Meighan and Foote 1968:Figure 26, Plates 10a, 10c–10d, 12a, 15b–15c, 16c, 17d). In addition, Cojumatlán Polychrome incised/engraved bowls from San Gregorio, Michoacán, depict central canids and a raptorial bird (Meighan and Foote 1968:Figures 29–30, Plates 10b, 29–30). In sum, the greatest diversity and concentration of portraiture bowls occur in the core zone of the broader Amapa region of Nayarit with limited examples from surrounding regions. Much like for Wixárika today, effigy-style bowls in Aztatlán sites may have also been made from gourds, less likely to preserve in the archaeological record.

Aztatlán "God Bowls" as Religious Cargos

The portrayal of deities and related icons on the central interior of Aztatlán vessels likely marks these as cargo "god bowls." For Wixárika, ceramic *jícaras* are "more authentic" and often were manufactured in the past (Kindl 2003:64; Lumholtz 1900:164). *Jícaras* are "drinking-gourds offered to the gods, who, so to speak, drink in the prayers of the people" (Lumholtz 1900:161), which may have been the case for Aztatlán "god bowls." Wixárika bowls are often smeared with sacrificial animal-blood offerings, which may relate to the abundant depictions of sacrificial flint knives (often tipped with blood) in Aztatlán ceramics as noted by many scholars (Bojórquez Diego 2009:81–89; Ekholm 1942; Mathiowetz 2011; Mathiowetz et al. 2015; Solar Valverde 2019). Knife imagery may relate to prehispanic solar-related human sacrifices involving blood-filled bowls like that observed during the early-historic period at the Mesa del Nayar, much like animal blood-filled bowls today (see Kindl 2003:109–110; Mathiowetz 2011:357–364; McCarty and Matson 1975; Solar Valverde 2019). Aside from animal and human portraits in Aztatlán bowl interiors, two deities and their related icons are prominent: Venus and the feathered serpent.

The Venus War God as Morning/Evening Star and God Bowls

New Venus ceremonialism and symbolism appeared in the same coastal area as Piltzintli/Xochipilli ritualism after AD 850/900 in the form of skeletal deities ornamented with stars and flint knives or arrows, often in association with crossed bones (Mathiowetz 2011; Mathiowetz et al. 2008, 2015; but see Solar Valverde 2019).[2] Following Neurath's (2005b) ethnological observations, I (Mathiowetz 2011:349–353) proposed that the complementary aspects of Venus (Morning Star/Evening Star) and the Piltzintli/Xochipilli solar deity (Day Sun/Night Sun) existed in Aztatlán cosmology. The skeletal beings in Aztatlán art are identified as a stellar Venus deity with Morning and Evening Star attributes, an analogue of the highland Mexican skeletal Venus war god Tlahuizcalpantecuhtli (Figures 13.3a–13.3f; Mathiowetz 2011, 2025a; Mathiowetz et al. 2015). Material culture from many sites along the Pacific-coastal core zone (between the Nayarit/Sinaloa border south to Matanchen Bay) bear depictions of this skeletal deity or related crossed-bone symbolism, the precise region where ritualism of the eastern solar deity Piltzintli/Xochipilli and the eastern feathered serpent flourished. Spare examples of the deity range as far north as Guasave, Sinaloa (Mathiowetz et al. 2015:Figure 13), and to the south near Banderas Bay, Jalisco, at Arroyo Piedras Azules (see Mountjoy, this volume, Figures 1.6h–1.6i). Recently, crossed-bone icons were found to occur on a Sentispac Red-on-buff (AD 850/900–1100) pyriform tripod jar recovered in Mazatlán (Santos 2022)—a vessel form linked to cacao that may further link Venus to cacao ritualism, the sun, and dawn (see Mathiowetz 2019a, 2025b).

Aztatlán scholars often attribute skeletal figures and crossed-bone icons to the death god Mictlantecuhtli despite the lack of a major death god among Gran Nayar descendants. Laura Solar Valverde (2019, 2023) contested our interpretation of some Aztatlán skeletal beings as a visage of Morning Star, instead broadly interpreting them as "death gods" linked to the underworld, west, and sacrifice. She contends that in ancient Mesoamerican thought, west Mexico since the Shaft Tomb era was perceived across Mesoamerica as a "symbolic necropolis" or "land of the dead." In her view, these skeletal figures are a general class of beings that are part of a "cult of the dead" (Solar Valverde 2023:802). However, despite the prominence placed on Venus as Morning Star as a major culture hero in the Gran Nayar among multiple ethnic groups, it is notable that Solar Valverde has not identified any Morning Star deity in Aztatlán iconography. While considering a possible affiliation with Venus as we first proposed for these star-marked beings, she concluded that an Evening Star association would be more plausible since examples are most common at Pacific-coastal core-zone sites, the rationale being that the humid coast (i.e., west) is linked to death and the underworld. Following this logic, depictions of the revered Morning Star should be prominent in the eastern Aztatlán region; however, this is not the case. Only rare examples of this being are known from the Lake Chapala-region sites; one carved stone with a portrait of this deity with a dart projecting from the nose (a possible Venus *tepari*) was reported at El Teúl (Zacatecas); and no depictions of this being are reported at La Ferrería (Durango).

In my view, it is implausible that prehispanic Aztatlán societies along the Pacific coastal lowlands (e.g., Amapa) were organized around a death/underworld cult while societies in highland Zacatecas (e.g., El Teúl) were associated with the dawning sun in some sort of complementary ideological relationship based on geographical location. Historical documents indicate that the lowlands in Nayarit are largely situated within ancestral Wixárika and Náayeri territory while the sites of El Teúl and Cerro de las Ventanas are within the ancestral Caxcan region (Figure I.3a; Mathiowetz 2023a). Worldview and ritual practices during the Aztatlán era surely were not subdivided into complementary relations between ethnic groups just as they are not partitioned among descendant groups today. Rather, ethnic groups in different regions that comprised the Aztatlán tradition likely retained their own holistic ritual traditions anchored at particular sites that defined their sacred landscape. For core zone people, their ideology encompassed *both* Morning and Evening Star ritualism. Jill Furst (1982) noted that the obsession with skeletal imagery in Mesoamerican art as a sole indicator of death and gore is a Western construct. Mixtec skeletal beings often are the antithesis of death gods and instead are life-sustaining figures of generation and fertility, the idea being that bones remaining after flesh decays are like "seeds" for the generation of life (Furst 1982). While death and the underworld surely were facets of complementary oppositions in Aztatlán cosmology with nocturnal beings related to this realm represented in certain iconographic contexts (see Mathiowetz 2025a), symbolism in the coastal core zone often emphasized revered and austere deities of day, light, east, and the above (among others in the pantheon).

In our analyses (Mathiowetz 2011; Mathiowetz et al. 2015:28), we emphasized Neurath's (2005b) observation that Venus has dual but complementary aspects linked to maize agriculture. We stressed the need to distinguish these dualities in Aztatlán symbolism. Solar Valverde (2019, 2023:802, fn. 2) omits this point in her critiques and inaccurately characterizes our interpretation, claiming that we asserted that "all" of these skeletal beings represent Venus as Morning Star. In fact, we noted that while Venus as Morning Star today is revered as the creator of *mitotes* and recipient of the first *mitote* songs, Venus as Evening Star is associated with the nocturnal forces of chaos, disorder, and the wildness of youthful "sin" and fertility associated with the wet season—attributes that are antithetical to the ethics and aspirations of cargo holders (also see Mathiowetz 2025a). For example, each Wixárika *tukipa* center has a founding ancestor as tutelary deity. The *tukipa* at San Andres Cohamiata is associated with the ancestor-deity Venus as Morning Star (Kindl 2003:90), a fact that exemplifies the preeminence of the morning/eastern aspect of this deity. Venus as Morning Star is most closely valued by community members, cargo initiates, and elders in the social-political hierarchy as a supreme cultural ideal where self-sacrifice, austerity, and ritual-knowledge acquisition during the Morning Star-affiliated dry season place elders in closer proximity to the deified ancestors (Neurath 2005b).

In contrast, the Wixárika Evening Star does not even have a name, and there exist no cargos or god houses of this deity (Johannes Neurath, personal communication 2020)—factors that likely extended to Aztatlán Venus cargos and god houses. Likewise, the Náayeri Evening Star named Sautari plays a comparatively less esteemed though important role as one of a group of nocturnal stellar beings of chaos called *xumuabikari* who are linked to darkness, the wild *monte*, and the underworld as sources of unbridled fertility (Mathiowetz 2011:391–412; Mathiowetz et al. 2015; Neurath 2005b). These stellar beings terrorize communities as highly sexualized, blackened, stripe-painted, drunken, and disheveled stellar clowns who are emblematic of improper behavior. During Semana Santa, these Evening Star forces of chaos attack the sun only to be defeated at daybreak. The *xumuabikari* are comparable to the highland Mexican skeletal and stellar *tzitzimime* whose leader is the Venus god Tlahuizcalpantecuhtli (Mathiowetz et al. 2015). Evening Star-related *xumuabikari* have been identified in coastal core-zone ceramics with diagnostic features (apart from stellar attributes), the same region where Morning Star symbolism is evident (Mathiowetz 2025a). Beings related to Venus as Evening Star appear in other material culture contexts with traits that seem particular to this deity and related figures, such as blackened skin, curly hair that is typical of nocturnal stellar beings, and/or *anahuatl* shell disks (Mathiowetz 2024). The Aztatlán antecedents for the Náayeri *xumuabikari* may have served as an intellectual inspiration for Puebloan Koshare clowns, a stellar-associated aspect of the Sun Youth deity (Mathiowetz 2012). We may presume that Morning Star and Evening Star aspects are inherent in portrayals of the Venus deity first depicted in the Aztatlán region after AD 850/900. Given the logic of contemporary Indigenous perspectives of Venus, while the less heroic Evening Star surely was a complementary antithesis to the austere Morning Star, this chaotic side likely was not the aspect emphasized in Venus symbolism of prehispanic cargos, god bowls, or god-house stones (*teparite*) in the Aztatlán region.

For these reasons, the Morning Star aspect of Venus is likely the figure portrayed as a central icon in bowls in the broader Aztatlán core region beginning in the Cerritos phase (AD 850/900), including one Cerritos Polychrome purportedly from Las Varas, Nayarit (Figure 13.3c; Mathiowetz et al. 2015:Portfolio 6). At Amapa, this deity is portrayed in the interior of an Ixcuintla Polychrome (AD 1100–1350) annular bowl (Figure 13.3d; Meighan, ed. 1976:Plate 143a). Venus-affiliated crossed-bones icons occur as a central motif in two bowls at Peñitas (Figure 13.3f), perhaps a shorthand icon for this being. Two Venus examples from a burial mound at Guasave in northern Sinaloa (ca. AD 1300) include one full-figured, feathered, skeletal Venus deity in the central interior of a polychrome bowl (Ekholm 1942:Figure 4a, 6i; Mathiowetz et al. 2015:Figures 12h, 13, Portfolio 8). At La Peña in highland Jalisco, a skeletal Venus figure with crossed bones occurs within one Tizapán White-on-red tripod bowl dated to AD 1050/1100–1300/1350 during the Tizapán phase (Figure 13.3e; Ramírez and Cárdenas 2006:Figure 75b). A similar skeletal figure is depicted in the interior of a Tizapán-phase Tizapán Polychrome incised tripod vessel from a private collection in Atoyac, Jalisco (Ganot Rodríguez and Peschard Fernández 1997:Figure 158), which may have come from nearby La Peña (Susana Ramírez Urrea, personal communication 2020).

Rain-bringing Feathered Serpents and God Bowls

Feathered serpents first appear in Aztatlán art after AD 850/900 in ceramic vessel interior and exterior designs (and rare textile stamps) primarily in the coastal core zone (Figures 13.4a–13.4d). Along the Nayarit coast, full-figured feathered serpents occur on the central exterior bottom of Cerritos and Ixcuintla-phase bowls (AD 850/900–1350+) and as a primary icon on Santiago Engraved (Santiago phase, AD 1350+) vessel exteriors (Mathiowetz 2011:Figures 6.10c–6.10f). Portrait-style feathered serpents occur in Mangos Polychrome (AD 850/900–1100) and Ixcuintla Polychrome (AD 1100–1350+) bowl interiors at Amapa (Figure 13.4c). One Iguanas Polychrome bowl interior from Peñitas bears an apparent feathered serpent with bifid tongue (Mathiowetz 2011:Figure 6.9b) and one bowl interior at Coamiles contains a feathered serpent-like design (see Favarel-Garrigues 1995:Figure 32). A Botadero Black-on-buff (AD 850/900–1350+) bowl sherd from Boca de Chila, Nayarit, also depicts a feathered serpent (Figure 13.4d). One split-view feathered serpent design within a bowl interior was reported far to the north at Mochicahui, Sinaloa (see Figure 8.3 [top right], Carpenter and Sánchez, this volume).

Cross-cut conch shells on vessel interiors are an aspect of Aztatlán feathered-serpent worship with the conch "wind jewel" (*ehecailacacozcatl*) of Quetzalcoatl symbolizing wind and rain (Figures 13.4e–13.4g; Bojórquez Diego 2009:71–72; Ekholm 1942:55; Mathiowetz 2011:369–370). Cut-conch symbols occur in the central interior of at least seven bowls at Amapa, including Botadero Red-on-white, Mangos Polychrome, Iguanas Polychrome, and Ixcuintla Polychrome (Meighan, ed. 1976:Plates 127k, 146a, 157e, 163a), which spans the Cerritos and Ixcuintla phases (AD 850/900–1350+). Cerritos-phase examples of cut-conch designs occur in a Tuxpan Red-on-orange bowl at Coamiles and in Sentispac Red-on-buff bowls at El Pirul and Chicoche/El Quemado on the Nayarit coast and at Siqueros in southern Sinaloa. One example occurs on a post-AD 1300 Aztatlán polychrome bowl at Guasave in far northern Sinaloa (Bojórquez Diego 2009:71–72, Figure 10; Ekholm 1942:Figure 4h). Near Lake Chapala, cut-conch designs occur at Tizapán el Alto within two Cojumatlán Polychrome engraved tripod bowls (Figure 13.4g; Bojórquez Diego 2009:Figure 10; Meighan and Foote 1968:Plates 11a, 15b), an Early Postclassic type (see Ramírez and Cárdenas 2006:331, 346–348). At La Peña, a cross-cut conch is portrayed in the interior of one Cojumatlán-phase (AD 850–1100) Citala Polychrome incised tripod bowl (Ramírez and Cárdenas 2006:348, Figure 74). Around Chapala, only bowls at La Peña have explicit Venus (skeletal figure and crossbones) and Quetzalcoatl-related (cut-conch) symbolism while Tizapán el Alto only has the latter. I am unaware of feathered serpents, cut-conch, or Venus icons in material culture from Durango (e.g., La Ferrería), although one cut-conch in a vessel interior is known from El Teúl, Zacatecas.

Cut-conch "god bowls" linked to Quetzalcoatl may be Aztatlán antecedents to bowls for the Wixárika Rain Mother Tatei Nia'ariwame—the "Goddess of the First Rain" who is the eastern rain-bringing feathered cloud serpent—or for the related wind god. For Wixárika, the brother of this feathered serpent goddess is the wind god Tamatsi Eaka Teiwari (whose name recalls the wind god Ehecatl), and the cargo-holder of this deity uses a conch-shell trumpet (Neurath 2000:91, 2005b:90–92). In Mesoamerica, the duck-billed wind god Ehecatl (the Mixtec "Nine Wind") is a creator deity and avatar of the feathered serpent Quetzalcoatl (Taube 2018). At least two Aztatlán vessels bear portrayals of Ehecatl. Four full-figured Ehecatl images occur in different scenes within a narrative sequence on one Iguanas Polychrome (AD 1100–1350+) codex-style vessel from north-coastal Nayarit or southern Sinaloa (Figures 13.4h–13.4i, this volume; Pohl 2012b). Ehecatl's face is portrayed twice in profile on a Xipe Totec effigy vessel attributed to the Amapa region in central-coastal Nayarit (Figure 13.4j). These Aztatlán Ehecatl figures may be prehispanic antecedents to the conch trumpet-related Wixárika wind god Tamatsi Eaka Tewari, the brother of the rain-bringing feathered serpent deity of the east who is the analogue of Quetzalcoatl. Thus, the feathered serpent and cross-cut conch "wind jewel" god bowls and related cargo rites in the Aztatlán region date Ehecatl-Quetzalcoatl wind and rain ritualism to after AD 850/900, which may have been the ultimate intellectual source for feathered serpent/conch ritualism in the Casas Grandes and Puebloan regions after AD 1200/1300 (Mathiowetz 2011; see Mills and Ferguson 2008; Schaafsma 2001; Taube 2001).

Aztatlán portraiture bowls with links to the sun, Venus, and feathered serpent may have comprised an integral part of *mitotes and* cargo systems that integrated paramount political centers and smaller communities, much like cargos of *jicareros* in Wixárika political center (*tukipa*) and *ranchería* ritualism. Cargo holders who cared for god bowls probably became those gods, perhaps using bowls in rituals as mnemonic devices in the retelling and enacting of mythohistorical events that created the world anew. Not all Aztatlán subregions have portraiture bowls, although some centers may have used gourd *jícaras* or even effigy vessels (e.g., Tlaloc effigies) rather than ceramic bowls for cargos (see Mathiowetz 2019a:Figure 6a). The diverse animals depicted in portraiture bowls may have various meanings, including as animal alter egos or companions of a particular ancestor-god or perhaps animals "awoken" by the Sun during the course of the annual seasonal cycle. These bowls may be (1) votive bowls for offerings or "prayers" to particular animals on the landscape in relation to the behaviors, meteorological phenomena, or ecology linked to each creature, or (2) cargo effigy bowls wherein bowl bearers took on the role of the animal depicted and reenacted their role in mythohistorical narratives, including accounts of how the world came to be. For example, Wixárika create wood and sotol-fiber animal effigies including rabbits that are dedicated to the sun (Zingg 1938:659–662), perhaps due to the principal role of the rabbit in naming the new sun (Lumholtz 1900:11). In this regard, Aztatlán effigy bowls with rabbit portraits may be solar cargo effigy bowls or votive bowls used for offerings related to the sun (Figure 13.6a–13.6b). Among the only other Early Postclassic societies with such an explicitly intertwined Sun (Tonatiuh or Xochipilli), feathered serpent (Quetzalcoatl), Venus (Tlahuizcalpantecuhtli), and cargo-related Flower World tradition were Tula and Chichén Itzá (Mathiowetz 2011, 2023a), though portraiture bowls are absent.

Aztatlán effigy god bowls may have been used during landscape ritualism (Mathiowetz 2025b). For example, the cave and rock art site of Cantil de las Ánimas (Garduño Ambriz 2013c)—located along the Río Grande de Santiago near Cerro Picachos (Figure I.2)—contains petroglyphs of the skeletal Venus deity and female genitalia (symbols of fertility) and may have been a "home" of the Venus god. Cerro Picachos was reported by José Antonio Bugarín in 1768–1769 to have an important *mitote* patio dedicated to Venus as Morning Star (Guzmán Vázquez 2002:19). While a town called Picachos is located northeast of Acaponeta (Craumassel 2013:71), Guzmán Vázquez (2002) specified that Bugarín's Cerro Picachos is located south of Náayeri territory (i.e., near Cantil de las Ánimas). Treks to dwellings of gods at natural features are integral for Wixárika cargos and define the sacred landscape through ritual acts (Kindl 2000:46–49). As there are no Wixárika Evening Star cargos, Aztatlán visitors to this rock art may have been Morning Star cargo holders.

Carved Stone *Tepari* in the Aztatlán Region

Wixárika god houses (*xiriki*) include large circular or quadrangular stones (*tepari*) made of solidified volcanic ash and carved with geometric and/or naturalistic designs that are affiliated with particular deities and their relation to the world (Lumholtz 1900:24–59, 133; Zingg 1938:601–602, 604–606). The sun first instructed Wixárika on how to create *tepari* (Zingg 1938:194), which are "shields" (*nierikate*) set atop ceremonial pits, placed inside caves or temples, used as bases upon which sculptures or statues of deities stand, or embedded in the upper walls above the entrances of *xiriki* (Figure 13.7). A *tepari*, when placed atop temples, "symbolizes the presence of the gods," and these are renewed during temple renovations (Lumholtz 1900:60). *Teparite* also may be buried in a family's field (MacLean 2012:39). In the Aztatlán world, stones modified into circular or quadrangular forms were carved with abstract, geometric, or naturalistic designs, including portraits of

FIGURE 13.7. Aztatlán and Wixárika cargo-system material culture. The presence of Aztatlán "god bowls" and *tepari*—both linked to "god house" ritualism—strongly suggests the existence of a prehispanic core-zone cargo system that directly predates the historic-period Wixárika cargo system. (*a*) Venus "god bowl" linked to probable Morning Star cargo, Cerritos Polychrome (AD 850/900–1100), Las Varas area, Nayarit. Museo Regional de Nayarit, Tepic. Photo by Mauricio Garduño Ambriz. (*b*) Probable Aztatlán circular stone *tepari* linked to Venus as Morning Star cargo and "god house." Unknown provenience, Nayarit. Catalog number HM5607, William P. Palmer III Collection, Hudson Museum, University of Maine. (*c*) Wixárika family standing in front of "god house" (*xiriki*). Note circular stone *tepari* embedded in the upper wall of the front of the god house, Tuapurie (Santa Catarina Cuexcomatitlán), Jalisco. Photo by Johannes Neurath.

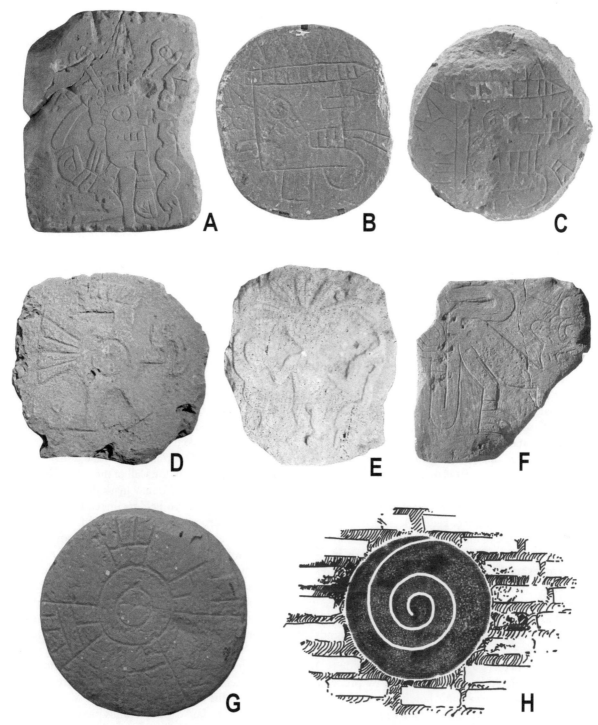

FIGURE 13.8. Aztatlán carved-stone *teparite* probably used in god houses. (*a*) Venus deity. Amapa, Nayarit. Fowler Museum Archaeology Curation Facility, University of California, Los Angeles, and Instituto Nacional de Antropología e Historia. Photo by author. (*b*) Venus deity. Museo Comunitario de Compostela, Nayarit. Unknown provenience, Nayarit. Instituto Nacional de Antropología e Historia, Nayarit. Photo by author. (*c*) Venus deity. Unknown provenience, Nayarit. Catalog number HM5607, William P. Palmer III Collection, Hudson Museum, University of Maine. (*d*) Bird. Unknown provenience, Nayarit. Museo Regional de Nayarit and Instituto Nacional de Antropología e Historia, Nayarit. Photo by Mauricio Garduño Ambriz. (*e*) Human with possible lightning. Museo Regional de Nayarit, Tepic. Unknown provenience, Nayarit. Archival photo, Fowler Museum Archaeology Curation Facility, University of California, Los Angeles, and Instituto Nacional de Antropología e Historia. (*f*) Feline (puma or jaguar?). Amapa, Nayarit. Archival photo, Fowler Museum Archaeology Curation Facility, University of California, Los Angeles, and Instituto Nacional de Antropología e Historia (*g*) Quadripartite design. Museo Comunitario de Compostela. Unknown provenience, Nayarit. Instituto Nacional de Antropología e Historia, Nayarit. Photo by author. (*h*) Spiral-shaped stone embedded in wall of primary circular structure, or "Temple of Quetzalcoatl," Ixtlán del Río, Nayarit (after Gifford 1950:Figure 3b). Drawing by author.

deities such as the Venus war god (Figures 13.7b, 13.8). Carved stones in this form are unknown in far west Mexico prior to AD 850/900, including at Epiclassic sites such as Alta Vista and La Quemada and Late Formative to Classic Teuchitlán sites, which indicates that Aztatlán ritualism did not evolve from Epiclassic antecedents as Solar Valverde (2023) implies.

A group of 10 shaped stones (mostly quadrangular) with engraving, low-relief carvings, and drilled pits was found overlying one cemetery in Group E at Amapa (Meighan 1976:43–45; Meighan, ed. 1976:Plates 14–20). Two others were recovered from the ballcourt wall in Group D, and one was found in Group B (Meighan 1976:43). All appear to have been robbed from an earlier structure. The finer relief-carved stones include the Venus deity with stellar eyes and darts emanating from the head (Figure 13.8a), a spotless feline (Figure 13.8f), and other unidentified partly effaced creatures and geometric designs. The feline, which Meighan (1976:44) considered to be a jaguar, may symbolize Venus in his dual form as either a jaguar or puma (see Neurath 2005b:84)—the "sons of the Tonati" (Guzmán Vázquez 2002:144)—perhaps most likely the Morning Star-affiliated puma. Alternatively, it may be one of the directional cargo-holding 'awatamete, who are hunters with feline avatars or alter egos (see Neurath 2000:94). Linear drill-pitted designs on an oblong stone found at Amapa (Meighan, ed. 1976:Plate 20) resemble the pitted "star chart" constellation designs reported by Carl Lumholtz on the *tepari* of the sky goddess Tatei Wierika Wimari (Neurath 2005b:80, Figure 1).

In the Museo Comunitario de Compostela, a circular carved stone with the Venus deity is nearly identical to an example in the Hudson Museum (Figures 13.8b–13.8c), both of which may be Venus *tepari*. The Museo Regional de Nayarit has multiple unprovenienced examples of birds carved in relief on roughly discoidal stones (Figure 13.8d), one of which stands upon or clasps a serpent. An unprovenienced discoidal carved stone depicts a full-figured human (deity?) wearing a feathered headdress, flanked by probable lightning bolts or serpents, and holding a round object (Figure 13.8e). One discoidal example with two central concentric circles and four radial elements exists in the Museo Comunitario de Compostela (Figure 13.8g). One rectangular carved stone bearing an animal with tail is known at the Jardín Museo in Zacualpan in central coastal Nayarit, presumably from the area (personal observation, 2018). *Tepari* are used in the vicinity today in the *xiriki* of the sea goddess Tatei Haramara at Haramaratsie near San Blas, only 30 km south of Amapa (Liffman 2011:223, fn. 5). At Ixtlán del Río, a red-colored quadrangular volcanic slab with a geometric design was found at the base of the main circular structure and was originally situated in the outer wall (see Figure I.4a; Gifford 1950:193–195, Figures 3a–3b). A discoidal stone with spiral-shaped design (Figure 13.8h) was embedded in the wall of the circular structure (Gifford 1950:193)—commonly considered to be a wind temple of Quetzalcoatl. This stone may mark the structure as a "god house" amidst palace compounds at this major highland-lowland cultural crossroads (see Mathiowetz 2019a:298–299).

Decorated *teparite* were collected in the early 1900s by Konrad Theodor Preuss, including one depicting the serpent *haiku* (cloud/rain serpent) in the form of a spiral and associated with the goddess of fish Tatei Uteanaka (Neurath, ed. 2007:8; see Guzmán Vázquez 2002: Figure 81; Zingg 1938:195) who first taught the Wixárika to make gourd cargo bowls (Guzmán Vázquez 2002). Tatei Uteanaka is the Corn Mother linked to green corn (where fish are a multivalent symbol of green corn). On her effigy, she wears upon her back a depiction of the eastern plumed/feathered serpent, or *haiku* (Lumholtz 1900:52–56), an analogue of Quetzalcoatl. Spirals occur on Wixárika *teparite*, on the painted faces of *peyotero* cargo holders, in choreography of *mitote* dances, and on *jícaras*, masks, and statues, among other contexts (Kindl 2003:182–183, Figure 79). In Mesoamerica, spirals are often linked to wind/rain and relate to the feathered serpent Quetzalcoatl (Taube 2001). Thus, the *tepari* with spiral in the wall of the central circular structure at Ixtlán del Río may mark this as a place of ancestor gods and cargo holders linked to wind, rain, the feathered serpent, and bountiful corn.

Around Lake Chapala, rectangular volcanic stones (*tezontle*) were found within the walls and banquettes of structures in Group A at the Sayula Basin site of La Peña. Various fragments ($n = 12$) were carved with geometric designs, possible zoomorphs, and anthropomorphs (Reveles 2006:382–383). Designs on quadrangular carved stones from a collection in Teocuitatlán de Corona—reportedly from La Peña—include a rabbit with flower and a human with sharply pointed nose and feathered headdress (see Reveles 2006:Figure 80) that may relate to the dart-nosed Venus deity.

These Aztatlán carved stones may be prehispanic forms of *tepari* used in god houses or related structures where initiates may have resided to fulfill cargo obligations of deities (such as Morning Star) while becoming an ancestor deity. Animal portrayals in Aztatlán *teparite* may relate to creatures linked to particular deities. Notably, there are no Wixárika god houses or cargos for the Evening Star aspect of Venus, only the Morning Star (Johnanes Neurath, personal communication 2020). This ethnographic fact supports the identification of Venus in his Morning Star aspect both in prehispanic Aztatlán cargo god bowls and *teparite* rather than as a depiction of the Evening Star aspect of Venus (see Solar Valverde 2019). Together, these objects point to the existence of an Aztatlán core-zone cargo system involving god bowls and god houses (Figures 13.1, 13.7a–13.7b). Additional evidence of cargo systems can be found in the portrayal of coastal Aztatlán cargo holders with gold-disk mirror pectorals in this same region along with evidence of cargo behaviors such as cacao consumption during feasts and probable cacao depositional practices during landscape ritualism (Mathiowetz 2023a, 2025b). Quadrangular-shaped foundations atop earthen mounds at some coastal-plain sites may have been structures that functioned as god houses. This collective evidence for a cargo system implies that Aztatlán cargo holders probably engaged in travel to Wirikuta, a central part of Wixárika cargo ritualism today.

IMPLICATIONS FOR MESOAMERICA AND SW/NW INTERACTION: MODELING THE AZTATLÁN-HUASTECA NETWORK

Aztatlán cargo holders who in all likelihood acquired peyote annually at Wirikuta in San Luis Potosí would have been situated near the decentralized polities of the northern Huasteca (see Faust and Richter 2015). This hypothesized cross-continental network between Aztatlán and Huastec polities (the "Aztatlán-Huasteca Network") may explain why west Mexican metallurgy appears in the Huasteca (Hosler and Stresser-Pean 1992) along with material-culture parallels (see Solar Valverde, this volume). In addition, Aztatlán cargo holders may have been the agents of scarlet macaw acquisition from the Huasteca for distribution to societies in the U.S. Southwest and northwest Mexico (SW/NW) (Figures I.9, I.10; Mathiowetz 2023a, 2023b, 2025b). Scarlet macaw bones were recovered in Late Postclassic contexts at Vista Hermosa, Tamaulipas (see Manin and Lefèvre 2017:14–16, 47), only 200+ km from Wirikuta. This model of an "Aztatlán-Huasteca Network" provides an alternate to the model of Mimbres-Huasteca relations. Gilman and colleagues (2014, 2019) propose that Mimbres people traveled to the Huasteca via the Río Grande to obtain scarlet macaws (see George et al. 2018), returning with knowledge of the Maya Popol Vuh. The proposed Río Grande to Gulf Coast route is attractive to some because the distance to the Huasteca is shorter than a Pacific-coastal route to acquire scarlet macaws around the Isthmus of Tehuantepec (Schwartz et al. 2022:328). However, with increasing evidence that the Aztatlán core zone was an important locale in connection with the SW/NW, Aztatlán cargo holders may have had a key role in Mesoamerica and SW/NW interactions. Aztatlán cargo-bowl traditions may have inspired the development of Mimbres portraiture bowls beginning with Style II (AD 880/950–1020/1050) and most prominently the Style III (AD 1000–1130) bowls (see Brody 2004).

The demise of the proposed "Aztatlan-Huasteca Network" may relate to increasing Aztec expansion to the Gulf Coast and the later tributary demands of Moctezuma Ilhuicamina, who ruled from AD 1440–1469 (Ruvalcaba Mercado 2015:199), which may have cut off Aztatlán cargo holders' access to scarlet macaws. Curtailed access to these birds may have consequently contributed to the collapse of scarlet macaw-centered ritualism of the Casas Grandes culture at Paquimé in Chihuahua around AD 1450 (Mathiowetz 2018). In addition, Tarascan expansion to the Pacific coast during the fifteenth century (e.g., to the port of Zacatula) may have severed Aztatlán connectivity to the southeast (Kelley 2000:152–153; Pohl and Mathiowetz 2022).

CONCLUSION

Herein I propose that *mitotes* and cargo systems in the Aztatlán region appeared after AD 850/900 along with new Feathered Serpent, Venus, Piltzintli/Xochipilli, and solar Flower World ritualism (see Mathiowetz and Turner 2021) as part of a "Birth of the Sun" narrative linked to the Wixárika peyote pilgrimage. Wixárika oral traditions describe the sacking of the Epiclassic site of La Quemada by cargo holders due to interference in the pilgrimage (Weigand 1975). Thus, Aztatlán cargo systems may have existed by AD 850+ when archaeological evidence indicates that La Quemada was sacked and burned (see López-Delgado et al. 2019). There is little evidence for cargos, *mitotes*, and landscape ritualism focused on these deities and Flower Worlds in west Mexico during the Classic and Epiclassic, which suggests a political-religious disjunction rather than an evolutionary continuum (see Grave Tirado, this volume; Solar Valverde 2023). While Grave Tirado (2010b) compares *xirikis* (god houses) to ritualism between AD 500–700 in southern Sinaloa, the portraiture cargo bowls, *teparite*, and deities linked to *mitotes* are not evident at this date.

Much like at Wixárika *tukipa* centers today, Aztatlán community-level *mitotes* at paramount centers such as Amapa may have been intertwined with kinship-based *mitotes* at smaller sites wherein cargo initiates returned to centers (the original "rancho of the gods") for community rites. Familial connections between outlying small communities and paramount centers may be traceable in ancient DNA studies, which could help to define prehispanic territorial provinces. Some Aztatlán centers in the core zone may have had an austere solar "priest-king" or *cacique* who served as a living Piltzintli sun god (Mathiowetz 2019b) and/or a Council of Elders who as living gods "dreamed" the role of cargos for community members. For example, a council of ancestor-gods seated in *uweni* (*icpalli*) god chairs, as portrayed around the neck of one codex-style vessel (Figure I.7a, I.7b) from northern Nayarit, may have presided over various rites depicted on the body of codex vessels, such as baptism or heart sacrifice (Garduño Ambriz 2013b; Pohl 2012b; Von Winning 1977).

Aztatlán bowls used in cargo systems and feasting contexts as mnemonic or storytelling devices for the enactment of mythohistorical narratives may find parallels further afield in other portraiture-bowl traditions in Mesoamerica and Lower Central America. For example, Classic Maya bowls, plates, and vases often depict palace scenes, creation events, animals, and deities such as the maize god (e.g., Doyle 2016; Taube 1985:Figure 5). Gulf Coast portraiture bowls include Epiclassic Cerro Montoso examples in the Tuxtla region (Veracruz) along with Postclassic examples at Isla de Sacrificios (Nuttall 1910). Postclassic Nahua-Mixteca palace-feasting networks in southern Mexico also involved drinking vessels and portraiture bowls that revolve around a solar and Xochipilli theme, such as Cholula Polychromes (see McCafferty 2001; Pohl 2004; Rojas Martínez Gracida 2008a). Further south, Lower Central American portraiture bowls occur in Nicaragua, Greater Nicoya (Costa Rica), and Gran Coclé in Panama (Lothrop 1926, 1942). Aztatlán portraiture cargo bowls may reflect new Flower World ritualism hybridized with highland or southern Mesoamerican (e.g., Cholula Polychrome) and/or Lower Central American bowl traditions.

To the far north, the Mimbres "picture bowl" tradition developed during an era of social-religious reorganization. Interaction routes between coastal Aztatlán sites and Mimbres villages may have followed routes (e.g., the Sahuaripa corridor) that later linked Paquimé to west Mexico (see Carpenter and Sánchez 2022). Such distant connectivity may help to explain Mimbres genetic relations to Wixárika and Náayeri (Snow et al. 2011), their importation of copper bells, the adoption of horned water-serpent ritualism, the acquisition of scarlet macaws (from the Huasteca by Aztatlán cargo holders?), and the adaptation of Aztatlán bowl traditions, among others. Since Mimbres bowls portray flora and fauna from local ecosystems, a form of cargo landscape ritualism linked to a Mimbres Flower World may have been adapted to the geography, plants, animals, and seasonal cycles of southern New Mexico.

In sum, analyses of Aztatlán religious and sociopolitical organization benefit from comparative "Big Picture" assessments of cultural dynamics among societies in adjoining regions of the U.S. Southwest, north and west Mexico, Mesoamerica, and beyond. Sites like Amapa that exhibit evidence of cargo systems evidently relate to historical processes of Wixárika and Náayeri ethnogenesis and can factor into claims of Indigenous historical territoriality in the face of continued land encroachment by corporations and the Mexican state (see Coyle 2000; Liffman 2011; Neurath 2022).

Notes

1. A statement of clarification is required regarding the excavation and interpretation of the Chacalilla solar observatory. The 2008 field research at this burial-mound complex by Michael Ohnersorgen and colleagues (2010a, 2010b) resulted in detailed excavation data and an unpublished manuscript with illustrations, photos, and original insights that were presented at the 2010 Society for American Archaeology meetings. These data and text were published in their entirety without proper permission nor academic attribution to the rightful authors by Lourdes Couoh Hernández and Arturo Talavera González (2017), who were unaffiliated with the 2008 field research and excavation. An unpublished text written in 2009 by Michael Mathiowetz detailed the significance of the Chacalilla solar mound complex in relation to Wixárika and Náayeri ethnohistoric and ethnographic data on Piltzintli/Xochipilli worship, the annual solar and maize-agricultural cycle, Flower World, and the crystallized souls of Wixárika ancestors (*urukáme*). This text and associated images were improperly published verbatim and uncredited on pages 145–150 of the Couoh Hernández and Talavera González (2017) article.

2. Our identification of skeletal beings in Aztatlán art in relation to Venus (including stellar skybands with flint knives and extruding eyeballs) was formulated during our participation in a "Codices of Ancient Mexico" seminar by Karl A. Taube held in Fall 2006 at the University of California, Riverside, and presented publicly in March 2008 at the 73rd Annual Meeting of the Society for American Archaeology (Coltman et al. 2008). Aztatlán examples of these skeletal stellar figures first drew my attention in 2005 when I initiated my dissertation research program to systematically document Aztatlán iconography in field and museum research. Our research and conclusions on stellar attributes in Aztatlán iconography were developed independently of Laura Solar Valverde (2007, 2019, 2023).

CHAPTER 14

The Flowering World of the Gran Nayar

An Ethnographic Approach for Conceptualizing Political Legitimacy in the Aztatlán World

Philip E. Coyle

In the mountainous Sierra Madre pine forests of Santa Teresa, one of the principal ancestral villages of the Náayeri (Cora) people of the Gran Nayar region of Mexico, winters bring biting cold (Figure 14.1). As the last light of day faded on such a winter evening and most people in the town and surrounding ranches leaned closer to their hearths, a group of town elders assembled and began their walk up the slope of the town's foremost mountain, called "Our Grandfather" (Tayaxuri). They would spend five of the coldest nights of the year fasting and praying around a ceremonial fire at the "Upper Patio," the hidden circular plaza where the ritual traditions of these elders have been practiced continuously for at least the past 500 years.

These men are the *ancianos* of the town, the living representatives of the deceased ancestors who continue to manifest themselves as the seasonal rains and as intermediaries to more distant ancestral deities. As they sat on low rocks around the fire, most smoked unfiltered cigarettes, the senior pair among them puffing on native *makuchi* tobacco out of special clay pipes nearly identical to those excavated from the Aztatlán towns that flourished about 1,000 years ago on the coastal plain just below these mountains (e.g., Ekholm 1942; Meighan, ed. 1976). From the circular plaza on that high mountain peak, the jagged horizon of the chain of mountains to the east was clearly visible, with particular high points marking the sunrise locations of the summer and winter solstices.

In 1994, the year I joined the elders for parts of this ceremony, the night I spent staying awake with them at the fire seemed to go on forever. While I shivered in a sleeping bag leaning against a tree, I could see the stringy muscles of the old men's bare legs in the fire light. As they talked quietly and concentrated on their smoking, I struggled to fight off sleepiness. Finally, the bitterly cold darkness gave way to the first hint of light on that distant horizon. The stars and constellations began to fade as the men rose to their feet. "Don't sleep now, gringo," one man said to me, "you've almost made it." At that moment, a miracle happened. The planet Venus as the morning star rose in the early morning light, transecting the arch of fresh flowers tied to the ritual *tepextle* altar on the eastern edge of the plaza (Figure 14.2). The men stood together facing the altar and the cosmic spectacle beyond, smoking and praying hushed poems handed down to them from the ancients in their Náayeri language. As the morning star reached the apogee of the flowered arch, the sun's edge breached the horizon beyond, and so the altar's aligned platform where gourd bowls with ritual offerings lay waiting. The sun's rays extended over the land, shining on the rugged canyons and mountains and filling the flower arch with brilliant white light. The morning star seemed to disappear into this flowery brightness, as the sun followed its path and ascended through the arch and into the sky.

On the last night of the five nights of fasting and prayer, Náayeri people began to arrive from near and far carrying finely decorated hand-woven bags full of food and ritual objects and building smaller fires around the patio to prepare for the night to come. This was the culmination of the fasting vigils of the previous nights. It is the "Fiesta de la Rueda," or "Wheel Festival," perhaps the most important and unifying ceremony of Santa Teresa's extensive and symbolically complex ceremonial year. It is named for the large pole which serves as the axis for a series of white, cloth-covered "wheels," each an image of a Náayeri world (*cháanaka*) (Figures 14.3–14.4). This ceremony, undertaken shortly after the traditional authorities for the year were selected by the same group of elders, is a kind of symbolic recreation of the history of Náayeri existence in that town and region even as it is also a political statement about the fundamental legitimacy of these elders and their ancestors

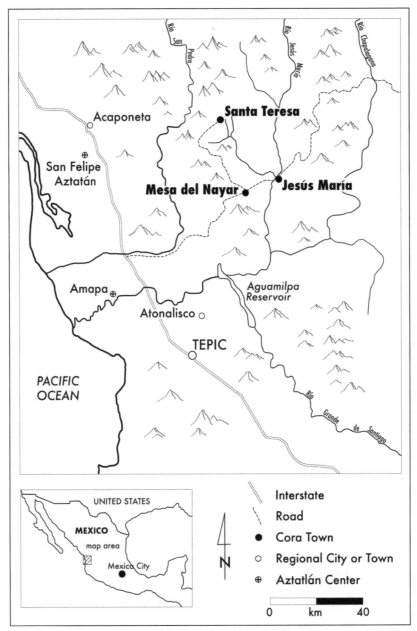

FIGURE 14.1. Regional map of the Gran Nayar region with archaeological sites and towns discussed in text. Drawing by author.

before them. It is part of a yearly (and multiyear) ceremonial cycle that reaches back to the preconquest chiefdoms of the coastal plain and probably even to those of the earlier Aztatlán period (see Mathiowetz, this volume). They are practiced not only in Santa Teresa, but by contemporary Indigenous people throughout the mountainous Gran Nayar region that lies directly upriver from the archaeologically rich Pacific coast. Understanding something of these ceremonial cycles not only helps us to appreciate the cosmological vision of the Náayeri and other native people of the Gran Nayar region, but these also shed light on the cosmology and politics of those archaeologically and ethnohistorically known groups that are the subject of this volume.

Jane Hill's (1992) article "The Flower World of Old Uto-Aztecan" gave renewed momentum to comparative studies among ancient and contemporary Uto-Aztecan-speaking societies both in Mesoamerica and the U.S. Southwest (Hays-Gilpin and Hill 1999; James 2000; Merrill 1996; Wilcox et al. 2008). In particular, Mathiowetz (2011, this volume) focuses extensively on links to the Flower World religious complex that continues to be reproduced among Indigenous peoples in northwestern Mexico and the southwestern United

FIGURE 14.2. Undecorated *tepextle* altar at Santa Teresa's Cerro de los Mitotes. Photo by author.

States including the prehispanic Pueblo, Casas Grandes (Paquimé), and Aztatlán cultures. This kind of "upstreaming" is methodologically sound; despite the devastating consequences of conquest and colonization for Indigenous peoples of the region, major patterns of culture have remained stable over long periods producing repeated cultural uniformities (see Axtell 1979). My own previous work used this technique to explain the acceptance of Catholic-derived symbols into the fundamentally Mesoamerican ceremonial cycle of Náayeri people during the colonial period (Coyle 1998). Indeed, historical connections between the coastal Aztatlán area and the Gran Nayar have long been recognized, and ethnohistoric data shows that, in particular, Cora—or Náayeri as they refer to themselves in their own language—are likely the descendants of the chiefdoms destroyed by Nuño de Guzmán—particularly at Sentispac and the salt-producing town of San Felipe Aztatán (Figure I.2, this volume; Magriñá 2002:128, 132).

Sauer and Brand (1932) point to many of these connections between preconquest chiefdoms and contemporary Náayeri people in the original work that identified the archaeological Aztatlán culture. They cite the 1565 account of Pantecatl, "the son of the cacique of Acaponeta, [who] witnessed the Conquest, and wrote a memorial of his observations and of the ancestral traditions" (Sauer and Brand 1932:42). This account tells of the flight of people associated with the towns around Acaponeta into the sierra in order to avoid destruction by the Nahuatl-speaking allies of the Spanish conquistador. They also mention linguistic connections between preconquest chiefdoms and the Cora-speakers of the highlands as well as an economic reliance on the kind of slash-and-burn *coamil* farming still practiced by many Náayeri people today (Sauer and Brand 1932:52, 57). In addition, archaeologists have noted trade connections, presumably including trade in salt, from the coastal plains through the Gran Nayar and to chiefdoms located on the eastern slopes of the Sierra Madre during the Aztatlán period (Kelley 2000; Mountjoy 2000:102–103).

The small and isolated contemporary Náayeri villages of the Gran Nayar region may seem like pale and distant reflections of the preconquest Mesoamerican cities and trade hubs that once connected the coastal plain with the sierra beyond, but I argue here that from a ritual and cosmological perspective they are likely

FIGURE 14.3. Undecorated *cháanaka* pole in Santa Teresa's church. Photo by author.

to have much in common. As among the Kachin of Myanmar so famously described by Leach (1954), these Mesoamerican Indigenous societies have gone through periods of consolidation and dispersion; or "centripetal" and "centrifugal" organization, as Eric Wolf (1959) called it. Indeed, the dialectical cosmology of the Indigenous people of this region recognizes and accepts such oscillating social changes within a kind of Mesoamerican *longue durée* historiography, which they see as having clear roots in preconquest Mesoamerica (Coyle 2001; see Blanton et al. 1996). If we take this cosmological historiography seriously, as I think we should, then recent research in the Gran Nayar can also offer new insights on the complex interplay of cosmology and ritual that has long been tied up with the legitimation of Indigenous political leaders in the region. It can help us to understand more clearly how, as Mathiowetz (2011:310) puts it, "restricted elite access to ritual knowledge" in the Aztatlán world may have been important "in the legitimization and justification of elite political and socioreligious positions." The Indigenous people of the contemporary Gran Nayar region, then, continue ceremonial traditions that are far more than the "faint traces of aboriginal life" that Sauer and Brand (1932:62) long ago imagined might exist there.

Three areas of recent ethnographic research in the Gran Nayar shed light on the connection of cosmology and ritual to the legitimation of political authorities

FIGURE 14.4. An appearance of the *cháanaka* wheel in Santa Teresa, Nayarit, Mexico. Photo by Frine Castillo Badillo.

in this Mesoamerican region: (1) The perpetuation of synecdochical and hierarchical symbolic relationships that position political authorities as occupying a "central" and "higher" cosmological and ritual position than other "peripheral" and "lower" people, (2) the use of sacrifice and visionary shamanism, through a hunting metaphor, which positions political authorities as mediators between living people and the deceased ancestors through whom regenerative power flows, and (3) the evocation of alternative ontologies, or realms of being, by political authorities which again positions them at a key life-channeling point between the living and the dead.

Synecdoche and Hierarchy

The articles in the special issue of the *Journal of the Southwest* dedicated to research in the Gran Nayar focused on the powerful symbolic relationships that organize cultural understandings of the Náayeri and Wixárika people's place in the universe (see Coyle and Liffman 2000). The widely recognized "god's eye" pattern, referred to by the term *námiche* by the Náayeri people I knew in Santa Teresa, presents the universe as a nested series of crossed circles that can refer equally to the most distant earthly horizons; to the smaller crossed circles of particular ancestral territories, village boundaries, and ceremonial plazas; or even small

FIGURE 14.5. A Cora *watsiku* ceremonial offering, which demonstrates the *námiche* pattern. Photo by author.

gourd bowls (Figure 14.5). It is a dualistically oriented, synecdochically embedded, and hierarchically organized worldview reproduced through ceremonial cycles carried out continuously in the Indigenous communities of the region since long before the Spanish conquest.

Johannes Neurath (2000) discussed these relationships in his article of that special issue and in a series of other important publications on Wixárika (Huichol) ceremonialism and worldview (e.g., Neurath 2002, 2003). He showed that the spatial organization of *tukipa* ceremonial centers of particular Wixárika communities, such as Tuapurie (Santa Catarina), delineates connections between sacred buildings within the ceremonial center and radiating sets of more and more distant sacred sites on the landscape. These ultimately tie points in the ceremonial centers with the most expansive limits of the Wixárika territory, a space that includes at least 90,000 km² of land extending from the peyote desert of Wirikuta in San Luis Potosí to the coast in Nayarit and from the highest mountain in Durango to Lake Chapala in Jalisco (Liffman and Coyle 2000). Liffman (2000) connects this discussion of the synecdochical embeddedness of *námiche*-shaped ceremonial centers (within the similarly patterned territory beyond) with the Wixárika concept of *nanayeri* or "rootedness," through which household-level ceremonial patios are seen to be more recently flowering "gourdvines" within an ancient "plant" that extends back in time to the larger *tukipa* ceremonial centers and further still to the origins of the world at distant territorial horizon points.

My own work (Coyle 2001) shows how similarly embedded synecdochical, part-for-whole relationships organize household and village-level ceremonialism among the Náayeri, a characteristic also documented by Valdovinos (2002) and Alcocer (2003) in the Náayeri community of Jesús María. Guzmán Vázquez (2000) again identifies these embedded part-for-whole god's eye symbolic relationships within particular Náayeri *mitote* ceremonial patios—such as the one where the Festival of the Wheel is held in Santa Teresa—which are also connected to outlying sacred springs from where special water is brought before the beginnings of particular *mitote* ceremonies, all of which replicate this symbolic pattern (Coyle 2000). Kindl (2000) shows how even the small gourd bowls—which are used to make offerings or represent particular traditional officeholders among the Wixárika—replicate this pattern.

Crucially, as Magriñá (2002:258) and others (Jáuregui 2000) point out, this god's eye pattern is seen as a "dualized hierarchy," in which the eastern point of the pattern is represented as "higher" than its opposed point on the west. This east-west duality is reflected in a constant celestial and terrestrial motion throughout the day and year, and so represents a dynamic cosmic struggle (Bonfiglioli et al. 2006:23) that even gender and family relationships among people embody. Castillo (2014:78), for example, shows how these relationships are represented as extending into the very bodies of Náayeri people, who must be "put together" (*compuesto*) through ritual exchanges and ceremonies beginning in the first years of their lives. She (Castillo 2014:78) notes:

> This is made possible through social relationships, the exchange of offerings, bonds with the saints, patterns of the *mitote* ceremonies and their incorporation in those ceremonies, always with consideration for the parental ties that together construct the body.

Her research reminds us that the *námiche* pattern should not be seen as only a symbolic trope, but also as a cultural theory of human health and well-being. For Náayeri people, the ceremonial reproduction of this synecdochical and hierarchical symbolic worldview is inextricably linked to a life-pattern of ceremonial positionings and initiations through which Náayeri people—and particularly the "highest" and "centermost" ceremonial elders—keep sickness "tamped down" (*tapado*), as one Tereseña put it to me. Thus, the health of all Náayeri people is seen as depending on the well-ordered but dynamic arrangement of the synecdochical and hierarchical *námiche* ceremonial pattern both outward and inward.

At the time of the Spanish conquest of the Gran Nayar region, the focus of this pattern was on Indigenous governing authorities with ancient ties to prehispanic coastal chiefdoms who were considered to be descendants of the sun king (Castillo 2014:15; Magriñá 2002:15; Mathiowetz 2019b). Today, that singular position of supreme authority among the Indigenous peoples of the Gran Nayar region is vacant. As Lira Larios (2018) points out, among the Wixárika, the annual round of ceremonialism actively denies any clear and stable position for a central authority, and so undermines any tendency for *cacicazgo*, which is encouraged by the contemporary Mexican state. In the preconquest Gran Nayar, and so presumably in the ancient chiefdoms of the coastal plain, this now-empty or only "ephemeral" position was filled by veritable "sun kings" whose ceremonial positioning within sacred landscapes and ritual spaces made their actions crucially important for the well-being of all the peoples associated with their ceremonial centers. Their position at the highest and centermost point in an extensive *námiche*-patterned ritual landscape would have focused attention on their actions as the vital dynamo at the heart of that ceremonially enacted world.

Sacrifice and Shamanism

Recent ethnography makes very clear the key role of ceremonial elders in the Indigenous societies of the Gran Nayar region. As living ancestors, they are seen as occupying the high ground between the worlds of sickness-prone living people and those of the immortal deceased ancestors (Jáuregui et al. 2003). Their role is to open and maintain careful connection between these two worlds—and so a benevolent organization of hierarchically organized but dynamic vital forces—through sacrifice. Deer-hunting is a key trope in the practice of these sacrifices, and this hunt is ritually depicted in similar ways among the Indigenous people of the Gran Nayar region.

In contemporary Indigenous deer dances of the region, hunter and deer are depicted as meeting at, and intertwining to form, a world tree. This world tree is presented as opening a sunrise connection from the ritual spaces of people onto an eastern "flower world" (Coyle 2008). Deer, the original food of the most ancient ancestors of the living Indigenous people of the region, are thought to stand in both realms. Because of their timeless vision far beyond the narrow limits of human eyesight, no hunter could ever hope to capture or kill a deer without divine aid. This aid is sought through the fasting and bodily self-sacrifice of the living ceremonial elders who as a group deny themselves food, water, salt, sleep, sex, and other bodily needs for days and nights at a time in order to open up and concentrate a special kind of piercingly meditative "thought" that extends upward and eastward—as if ascending a staircase—into the world of the deer. Through their thoughts, which can only be focused through this kind of agonizing self-sacrifice, the ceremonial elders convince the deer to pity the hunter, and so all living humans, and give itself freely (Neurath 2008).

The hunt, then, is far from the ritualized man versus animal masculine combat that is so familiar in Mexican popular culture where men are seen as dominating and subduing a feminized nature (see Dundes 1997). Instead, in these deer hunts, the intertwined world tree comprised of the hunter (representing living people) and the deer (representing the ancestral world) shows the ambivalence and mutual transformation that sacrifice initiates. Through their austere fasts and focused thought, the *ancianos* produce what has been called a magical creative force (Neurath 2001, 2005a). This world-tree flow of magical energy, constituted through a mysterious blending and separating of oppositions, is seen as the source of all health and fertility (and

FIGURE 14.6. Gourd bowl at a Cicada Ceremony near Santa Teresa, Nayarit (May 2016). Photo by author.

potential dangers). It is ultimately the role of traditional authorities like the ceremonial elders to address and continue this seasonal and life span-oriented set of connections through their sacrificial thoughts.

Neurath (2005b:94) discusses this theme of ambivalence and transformation in his work on the Venus-related ritual and myth of the Wixárika people. He pointed out that the dualistic astronomical characteristic of the planet Venus, which appears as either the morning or evening star, creates "various kinds of ambivalent ritual contexts [...] of simultaneous antagonism and identification." Indeed, the morning star is itself seen as an imbricated hunter/deer ancestral deity among the Indigenous people of the Gran Nayar, a role that ancient political leaders would have themselves embodied.

For Neurath, the ambivalent transformations implicit in the self-sacrifice of the deer to the hunter is also crucial in apprehending two distinct, but intertwined, forms of ritual exchange. The first is the reciprocal, back-and-forth ritual gift-giving of normal people, and the second and "higher" is the "free gift" that is the domain of the self-sacrificing deer as well as the exalted and semidivine political authorities whose sacrificial fasting and "thinking" make that primordial gift possible. The two forms of gift-giving, which are "ritually condensed" (Neurath 2013:48) in a tension that replicates the "higher" (eastern, morning star) and "lower" (western, evening star) aspects of the ceremonially produced cosmology, are additionally represented by ceremonial arrows and gourd bowls, respectively. Ceremonial arrows represent the deer's self-sacrifice, and so the special, visionary power of ceremonial elders. Gourd bowls, with their offerings of sacred corn and chia, represent the earth and the exchange of food (Figure 14.6). These objects help to create a "hierarchized synthesis that reunites antagonistic aspects of existence," and puts the eternal sources of fertility within the control of ancestral deities and so their living, semidivine representatives who stand above the chaotic give-and-take of humanity (Neurath 2008:270; see Mathiowetz, this volume). The deer's "free gift," however, is itself dependent on the self-sacrifices of ceremonial elders, whose thought travels beyond human time and space. The ritual pilgrimages undertaken by the Indigenous people of the Gran Nayar region, most famously the Wixárika peyote pilgrimage to the desert of Wirikuta, are themselves a ritual reenactment of these primordial thoughts (Gutiérrez del Ángel 2002). Neurath (2008:268) describes it as follows:

> Walking the routes of the god's first journey from the sea to the sunrise, the pilgrims seek to achieve the visionary experiences of their grandparent/ancestors, to renew the first moments of creation, and, in a way, to convert themselves into their own ancestors.

The thought of the ceremonial elders that allows the "free gift" of the deer's self-sacrifice is a kind of world-creating, cosmogonic act. As Neurath (2005a:601) explains, "it is through ritual that the world is always created anew; and one might say that if the world were not created in ritual any longer, it would not have ever existed."

Neurath is also very clear in seeing possible continuities between the contemporary sacrificial "thought" of ceremonial elders and those of preconquest times. In chiefdoms along the coastal plain, this type of sacrificial thinking, and sacrifices themselves, likely would have been associated with the chiefdom's morning-star leader as part of an ancient warrior cult (Neurath 2008:270). Although the Mesoamerican-related sacrificial religion that existed in the Gran Nayar region until the Spanish conquest of the sierra in 1722 has today been "democratized," and is no longer "focused on the sanctuary of one royal family of 'suns' who were seen as the principal source of fertility," social hierarchy and the sacrificial thought that sustains it have not entirely disappeared (Neurath 2008:271).

ALTERNATIVE ONTOLOGIES

The symbolically dense and profound sacrificial symbolism of the Indigenous peoples of the Gran Nayar region opens onto a third area of recent research: an interest in the alternative ontologies that sacrifices create and connect. The term *ontology* refers to distinct cultural theories of being and existence. In recent years, scholars of the Indigenous peoples of the Amazon have drawn attention to the ways that plants, animals, ceremonial objects, and other "things" may themselves be thought of as active beings, alive in their own ways. As beings of an alternative ontology, these plants, animals, and objects may then have distinct perspectives—thus the term *perspectivism* for this area of research—that are not congruent with those of human beings (Vivieros de Castro 1998). Indeed, these plants, animals, and objects may be far more alike than they are different from their own perspectives. At the same time, humans may seem less like a unique species than one of many similar beings, those comprised of "meat," for example, and so may be thought of as "prey" by the alternative beings that humans may glimpse through the in-between character of those intermediary plants, animals, and ceremonial objects (Vivieros de Castro 1996).

In the Gran Nayar, the material existence of the alternative ontologies in this world is accessed through the concentrated "thought" of ceremonial elders. This thought may be something like the kind of focused but flowing concentration experienced by musicians everywhere, and indeed bow-drum music and singing are seen among the Náayeri as a kind of pure thought (see Basso 1985). Benciolini (2014:313) provides translations of Náayeri bow-songs that speak of ancestral deities "thinking" the world at places like Santa Teresa's sacred lake. She also points out that the most respected traditional authorities are referred to in the Náayeri language as "the Thinkers," and that for the Náayeri "thinking is a very important activity. It deals with creative acts that concretize themselves in the world and have consequences for it" (Benciolini 2014:311). For example, to make a ritual patio "implies, in the first place, to think it" (Benciolini 2014:258).

Pure thought solidifies into ritual objects, like the gourd bowls and ceremonial arrows discussed by Neurath, which are sung and thought as much as they are physically made. As Neurath (2015:61) puts it, "Initiates transform into their own ancestors and, at the same time, into the objects of their visions: peyote, deer, rain, and the sun." For Neurath, this means that Wixárika art and ritual should be seen as part of a series of ontological shifts that characterize the ongoing ritual movement of particular ceremonies as a kind of ontological syncopation. During rituals, participants dynamically assume the perspectives of different ceremonial objects, which are this-world manifestations of distinct perspectives onto the eternal, but ritually reproduced, ancestral world. Masks are direct expressions of these shifting ontological perspectives. Neurath (2005c) points out that masks are not worn as disguises or as representations of deities, but that in wearing them a person *becomes* that "god," and so embodies their being and perspective.

For Valdovinos (2010:246), the connection between alternative existences reflects a kind of "multi-empathy" in which "the subject experiences distinct relations during the course of ritual action." In other words, during Náayeri *mitote* ceremonies, a multiplicatively empathetic condensed relationship between the normally distinct perspectives of gods and humans emerges, particularly through the ritual use of songs and a ritual object referred to as the *cháanaka*, or "world," an object analogous to the pole that is the focus of Santa Teresa's Wheel Festival. The songs refer to Ha'atsikan, the morning star-related culture hero who—despite the warnings of his mother—kills a deer. As it dies the deer is revealed to be his own elder brother. The key point here is that the deer's two-sidedness is represented as its key feature: the fundamental ambivalence that opens the possibility for multiple empathetic perspectives of what would normally be distinct modes of existence. "Ha'atsikan," she writes, "always appears as an anthropomorphic deer-person, as hunter and captive, as divinity and human being" (Valdovinos 2010:250). Similarly, the *cháanaka*, as described by Valdovinos, is a woven ritual object made by the year's incoming traditional authorities that is meant to represent the Náayeri world as a whole in a "deer-like," multiempathic way. The object—like the one made for the Wheel Festival in Santa Teresa—is made by people, but it is meant to be seen by Tayau, the principal Náayeri divinity, "so that he will watch over and care for all who live within the space illustrated by the design" (Valdovinos 2010:215). As she puts it, "this multiempathic object cannot be explained without taking into account the simultaneous presence of different forms of experiencing that space" (Valdovinos 2010:215).

From this ontological perspective, many kinds of sacred objects stand in a kind of two-way mirror or Janus-faced position between distinct ontologies. Even humans, who briefly embody and share the perspectives of those objects in ritual, may thus be seen as sacred, or *delicado* (Gutiérrez del Ángel 2000). The ontological turn in recent research in the Gran Nayar also helps us to understand the connections of particular living bodies to the sacrifice-enacted ritual territory of each community. Just as ritual thought may condense into useful ceremonial objects, so may it turn out badly as well. A misplaced thought, or the presence of a bad-thinking stranger, or even the selfish and conniving thoughts of an insider with evil intent may cause dangerous objects to condense. These objects are believed to lodge in the bodies of living people and can cause them to sicken. Without the aid of a curing shaman, who specializes in clear and sacrificial visionary thought, people may be killed by such objects. To avoid negative outcomes, the ceremonial elders of each community direct the annual and life-span cycles of ceremonies in such a way as to maintain a beneficial flow of "magical creative force." They do this by addressing themselves to, and through, all of the distinct and well-ordered ritual objects that clear "thought" recreates in the world of living people.

Benciolini (2014:17), for example, points out how, for the Náayeri, flowers and the ceremonial use of the progression of distinct flowers through the year serve to maintain an ongoing connection between distinct ontological realms. She argues that they are articulating elements connecting the worlds of living people with the ancestors. That connection is based on the perceived need to maintain an active channel of vitality linking distinct ontological realms, and so allows living people to remain healthy and resilient. As she puts it, this magical force "can now be conceptualized as the regenerative capacity of things and of the world, the same as is seen more strikingly in the case of flowers" (Benciolini 2014:81). Although the decoration of ceremonial objects, spaces, and indeed entire towns with gathered flowers is a key element for maintaining the connection, Benciolini (2014:107) additionally points out that the flowers are just one set of instruments joining and renewing distinct realms. All of them are discrete manifestations of song-like meditative "thought" through which ritual specialists in harmony with still-active deceased ancestors imagine, and so create, particular objects and spaces. Indeed, flowers themselves are referred to as "thoughts of the ancestors" (Benciolini 2014:311). Thus, Benciolini sees the connection between the people of the Gran Nayar and their ancestors not as a simple rhetorical act of referring to a given alternate reality, a flowery world that eternally exists somewhere—like heaven—but rather as the ongoing cosmogonic creation of a flowering world. Once "thought," and so concretized and enacted, this flowering world becomes a joined sacred space where the agency and willingness of humans, ritual objects (like flowers), and deities manifest a renewed magical life-force (Benciolini 2014:326).

Conclusion

Recent ethnographic research clearly shows that the ceremonies of the contemporary Indigenous people of the Gran Nayar region form a coherent and consistent cosmology in which the political authority of ceremonial elders is directly connected to the ongoing cultivation of ontologically generated life forces in a sacred landscape through sacrifice. This research, in addition to helping us understand and appreciate the symbolic complexity and philosophical sophistication of these people and their ceremonial systems, of which Santa Teresa's Wheel Festival is one key part, also has implications for understanding political legitimacy in the preconquest chiefdoms of the coastal plain.

Mathiowetz (2011:42) touches on many of these themes in his work on the Flower World complex in the Aztatlán world, which he sees as symbolically associated with the young, dawning sun at the eastern sunrise, a place of "light, fertility, warmth and moisture, rebirth, and spiritual power." In particular, the present discussion helps to shed light on what Mathiowetz (2011:55) refers to as "Flower Road," the "celestial floral pathway of the sun, gods, and ancestors." For Aztatlán people, the pathway likely would have been constituted through dynamic ceremonial cycles that cosmogonically recreated the "road" of ontological connection through the "thoughts" of the priest-kings themselves. Indeed, those priest-kings likely would have embodied the young solar deity Piltzintli (Xochipilli) whose appearance as or in relation to the morning star would have implied the dynamic "cosmic battle" that the directional shifts of the strange, oscillating star also reflect (see Mathiowetz 2011, 2019b).

Aztatlán priest-kings along with their ceremonial retinue may well have stood at important political-religious centers amidst architectural complexes with astronomical orientations pointed to sunrise and sacred directions, which would have been seen as the ritual object-like instantiation of the surrounding hierarchically organized and synechdochically embedded ritual landscape (see Mathiowetz, this volume). Animal and human sacrificial practices—such as one human sacrifice depicted on an Aztatlán vessel from northern Nayarit (see Garduño Ambriz 2013b, this volume)— may have been understood as a material manifestation of the focused road-making "thoughts" of the priest-king himself. It seems likely to have extended the hunting metaphor, at times, to actual war with other chiefdoms. These sacrifices would have been seen as the key source of renewed life-energy for the people associated with the architectural complexes. The body of the priest-king as the young solar deity would have stood as a "composed" living organization of world-tree life-force in ongoing contact with the ancestral deities whose original "thoughts" brought humanity into existence, even as the rituals at these sites would have cosmogonically renewed those deities through the manipulation of ritual objects by the priest-king himself. The *námiche* pattern of the Gran Nayar—and its implications for understanding ritual landscape, sacrifice, and ontology—has deep roots in the region and would have been a powerful organizing force in the preconquest chiefdoms that once existed there.

PART V

Concluding Thoughts and New Directions

CHAPTER 15

Discussion

The Three Transitions of Aztatlán

Christopher S. Beekman

Aztatlán has received much fresh attention in the past decade, including a recently published edited volume (Solar Valverde and Nelson 2019) and two synthetic volumes on research in the Marismas Nacionales (Foster, ed. 2017; Grave Tirado 2012d). Aztatlán plays a prominent role in the World-Systems model of Jiménez (2018, 2020) and the ritual-economic model by Mathiowetz (2011, 2019a, 2019b; Mathiowetz et al. 2015). The present volume emphasizes the wider interactions with neighboring regions and brings the visual record of gods and ritual practices into a closer dialogue with the archaeological evidence.

I come to this discussion as an outsider to Aztatlán research. Joseph Mountjoy in his chapter has provided a very effective summary of the history of investigations, and the editors have already reviewed the authors' contributions at the beginning of the volume. I will therefore focus my discussion on issues that I find particularly relevant—such as the ongoing debates and the distant connections to other regions. I put a broader frame around Mountjoy's chapter, address certain terminological issues, and then group some current debates and interpretations into three major transitions. In line with Coyle's contribution, I will refer below to the Cora and Huichol as the Náayeri and Wixárika, respectively.

WHY DID SAUER AND BRAND GO SOUTH ANYWAY?

In his chapter, Joseph Mountjoy rightly identifies the 1930 survey by Carl Sauer and Donald Brand (1932) as the zero point for Aztatlán archaeological research, though there is a deeper backstory that should be acknowledged. The first illustrated publication of archaeological materials from western Mexico to my knowledge is a collection of Aztatlán artifacts published in the *Anales del Museo Mexicano* (Figure 15.1). Miguel Retes (1845) illustrated recognizable ceramics, figurines, and spindle whorls collected near Santiago Ixcuintla in coastal Nayarit. For Retes and later writers, these artifacts were comparable to those from central Mexico and recalled the Native accounts of the late preconquest migrations into central Mexico from the northwest. Retes's report referred to the "infinite number of monuments [...] that are found almost without interruption all along the river's right bank, but principally on the hills and locations that by their elevation are sheltered from the flooding of the river."[1] He attributed them to the wanderings of the Aztecs, or alternately to refugees from defeat by the Spaniards:

> And once [the Aztecs] had conquered the towns of Anahuac, they maintained their relationships with these remote lands; and at the fall of Cuauhtemoc and the Mexican Empire, various Mexican tribes fled to the frontier and to the nearby hills to weep at the loss of their freedom (Retes 1845:4).[2]

Towards the end of the century, a less sentimental author (Chavero 1887:460–463) proposed that Aztlán, the mythical Aztec homeland, was in central-coastal Nayarit near San Felipe Aztatán, the head town of the contact-period polity described by Mauricio Garduño Ambriz in his contribution to this volume. The island town of Mexcaltitan, located just 50 km to the south, was pinpointed by Chavero as the original Aztlán. Despite the thin basis for the claim, it was later accepted by Jiménez Moreno (Heyden 1994:10, fn. 9), and President López Portillo supported the identification. Political and economic promotion led to widespread popular acceptance (Jáuregui 2004; Weigand 1994).

Chavero's proposal must have helped shape the work of the International School of Archaeology and Ethnology of Mexico (1910–1920), which was founded on the model of the foreign schools throughout the eastern Mediterranean world. Under the sequential directorships of distinguished scholars such as Eduard Seler, students and faculty engaged in projects across

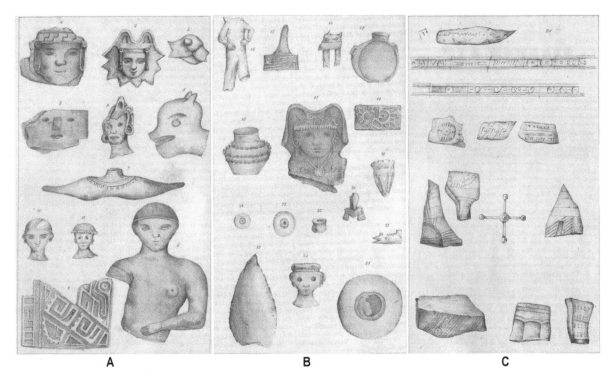

FIGURE 15.1. Three illustrations of artifacts found in Santiago Ixcuintla in the Territory of Tepic, present day Nayarit (Retes 1845). The pieces illustrated are largely from the Early Postclassic, including ceramic, Types A (Mazapan), H, and L figurines, animal figurines, stamps, and spindle whorls comparable to those from nearby Amapa (compare with Meighan, ed. 1976:Plates 28, 30, 31, 46, 60, 72, 82, 83).

central and western Mexico. From their own list of priorities (Chavez 1913:4–7; Seler 1911), it appears that these researchers sought to understand the pivotal role of Nahua speakers by tracing Aztec history back into the northwestern part of the country. Manuel Gamio (1910, 1922) established the sequence of Archaic, Teotihuacan, and Aztec cultures in the Basin of Mexico; Alfred Tozzer (1921) excavated at Santiago Ahuitzotla; and George Engerrand reported evidence of parallel Archaic cultures in Colima (MacCurdy 1914:695). Franz Boas studied remnants of the Nahuatl language at El Teúl and the Nahuatl enclave down the coast at Huatulco, Oaxaca (Boas 1913, 1917; McVicker 2005:153). J. Alden Mason addressed acculturation among the Tepecanos of northern Jalisco (Mason 1912a, 1912b, 1914, 1916, 1918).

The International School soon declined without synthesizing this research, but other contributors emerged. Mexican archaeologists noticed ceramics in distant Sinaloa with designs reminiscent of late central Mexico (Toro 1925). While older American institutions such as the Carnegie Institute, Tulane, and Harvard directed their efforts towards the Maya area, west-coast scholars from the University of California, Berkeley (e.g., Donald Brand, Isabel Kelly, Carl Sauer) and later the University of California, Los Angeles (Ralph Beals, George Brainerd, Clement Meighan, Henry Nicholson) pursued the study of the Pacific coast from Sonora down to Guerrero. As Mountjoy notes, UCLA began its research program partly instigated by Hasso von Winning's (1956) publication of looted objects from coastal Nayarit donated to the Southwest Museum of Los Angeles. The resulting Amapa project greatly advanced Aztatlán research and is cited across many of the chapters. It also holds an ethically awkward legacy. It was one of the first archaeological projects to receive National Science Foundation funding but was also financially supported by Hollywood talent agent and precolombian art collector Phil Berg and others (Los Angeles Times 1959; Murphy 1959; Thomas 1953). Project director Clement Meighan even brought along a group of collectors from southern California to participate in the fieldwork (Meighan, ed. 1976:3). The large scale of the Amapa excavations was possible because of this double dipping into two worlds and illustrates their mutual entanglement in the 1950s and 1960s.

This brief background illustrates several points. Western Mexico was once seen as part of an integrated solution to research questions of importance to other parts of Mesoamerica. Some of the greatest anthropologists of the time took a wide perspective and pursued combined ethnographic, archaeological, linguistic, and ethnohistoric studies that linked the central and western states. Carl Sauer and Donald Brand's expedition down the Pacific coast thus followed research that saw northwest Mexico as the origin of the better-known central Mexican cultures. But following the Mexican Revolution and the Cristero Revolt (associating the northwest with violence and instability) and the establishment of a centralized federal government, convictions about the dominance of central Mexico had solidified into a new paradigm. By the time Gordon Ekholm (1942) wrote in the 1940s, the arrow of influence had reversed direction. Investigators assumed that central Mexican "core" polities held priority and must have been the source of these complex western developments, even though no new chronological data had surfaced to alter interpretations. West Mexico was, however, well on its way to being marginalized from Mesoamerica, with concrete implications for research in the area (Beekman 2024).

These proposed links to central Mexico explain the assumptions that investigators have held about languages spoken on the Pacific coast. Certainly, the Caxcan language of highland Jalisco and Zacatecas indicates continuity with central Mexican Nahuatl, and Carl Sauer (1948) wrote about the widespread use of Nahuatl in sixteenth-century Colima (see a more current discussion of the linguistic landscape in Dakin 2017). But were languages closely related to Nahuatl spoken along the Pacific Coast of Nayarit and Sinaloa where most of the Aztatlán polities emerged? Certainly, many researchers regularly use Nahuatl names for deities so that they can draw upon the fuller documentation from central Mexico. I suggest several reasons why we should take greater care with the use of Nahuatl when speaking about Aztatlán religion. First, existing records point to rather more distant members of the broader Southern Uto-Aztecan language family along the coast. Second, using Nahuatl names as a default or even as a simple shorthand implies that the language was spoken here, and implies that external relationships were solely to central Mexico. Grave Tirado (Chapter 6) and Carpenter and Sánchez (Chapter 8) refer to linguistic evidence for a complex mosaic of languages throughout the Aztatlán zone, while Pohl (2012b:95–98) has identified one figure from an Aztatlán vessel as a *ñuhu*, a being best known from the Mixteca. Third, and as Mathiowetz notes in his chapter (Chapter 13), even Southern Uto-Aztecan speakers had their own variations on the deities documented from central Mexico, and they may not correspond in all respects. In Mesoamerican ontology, deities or other supernatural figures are conceptually and iconographically composite beings whose attributes vary across contexts and ethnolinguistic groups (Coyle, Chapter 14; Faugère and Beekman 2020). I draw attention to the way this problem was handled in the Maya region, where researchers initially assigned more neutral designations (e.g., "God K") to recurring figures in the artwork, even when they certainly suggested affinities to known central Mexican deities. These labels were then superseded as hieroglyphic inscriptions were deciphered, and local terms became available.

ADVANCES AND CLARIFICATIONS OF BASIC DEFINITIONS

Many of the authors note that the term Aztatlán has been used in different ways hindering communication, and there is unfortunately no shortage of comparable examples in Mesoamerica. Terms like Capacha, Teotihuacanoid, Mexicanized Maya, and many others have been used as vague labels for material culture to avoid providing detail on specific ceramic types, defined chronological phases, or individual sites that would sharpen the comparison. It is useful to remind ourselves periodically that terms like Aztatlán are synthetic labels that can only be applied after description has taken place ("ceramic type X from phase X indicates participation in the Aztatlán network"), but they are not appropriate at the descriptive stage ("we found Aztatlán ceramics").

Early twentieth-century definitions of Aztatlán by Sauer, Brand, and Ekholm, among others, narrowly emphasized ceramic iconography. Such a definition tends to focus research on ideological connections, on portable visual media likely used in small-scale rituals, and hence on performative ritual practices shared among some sector of the population. Mauricio Garduño Ambríz is one of the few who deliberately incorporated architecture into his definition of Aztatlán and is cited at length by Mountjoy in his chapter (Chapter 1). Solar Valverde and colleagues (2019) recently characterized Aztatlán as a network of polities interlinked by shared high-status goods. They define this network to include Apatzingán in Michoacán, El Chanal in Colima, and El Teúl in northern Jalisco, based on the mutual occurrence of ancillary materials such as pipes, shell, spindle whorls, and metal artifacts. But of course, all these items were used across much of Early Postclassic Mesoamerica, while spindle whorls are not so much "traits" speaking to cultural practices as pan-Mesoamerican evidence for cloth production. Susana Ramírez Urrea proposes another Aztatlán sphere around Autlán based on Autlán Polychrome ceramics (Chapter 4). Autlán Polychrome (and its cousin Chanal Polychrome at El Chanal) seems distinct in its iconographic content and the reason for its inclusion in the Aztatlán system should be more specifically defined. All of this is meant to say that Aztatlán may be more effectively demarcated by something other than the mere trade in high-status goods. Chapters by Mathiowetz, Pohl, and Vidal Aldana (Chapters 13, 3, and 7, respectively) indicate that the exchange of specific beliefs and knowledge was at least as important for defining the Aztatlán network, setting it off from neighboring communities like El Chanal that prioritized other relationships.

Contributors to this volume also sharpen our understanding of Aztatlán chronology, or at least the debates about it. John Carpenter and Guadalupe Sánchez note in their chapter (Chapter 8) how the dates attributed to Aztatlán contexts show an overly broad range from AD 600–1400, or perhaps even later given that San Felipe Aztatán is potentially the contact-era site encountered by Nuño Beltrán de Guzmán. The chronological debate seems less about substantive differences and more about the presentation. Some contributors continue to use uncalibrated radiocarbon dates and cite estimated ranges from older publications (especially Meighan, ed. [1976] on Amapa) rather than assessing the calibrated date ranges afresh. In addition, authors who argue for an autochthonous development of Aztatlán may include the preceding phase(s) in the ranges they present. While absolute calibrated dates would certainly make discussion easier, common ground can still be found by using phase names and avoiding vague terms like "Early Postclassic" or "Aztatlán" as chronological indicators since they are used differently by different investigators. Without implying either a local or intrusive origin, the editors (seconded by Mountjoy, Chapter 1) frame the Aztatlán network as beginning AD 850/900 and continuing until AD 1350/1450, all dates in calendar years. These five or six centuries are in most places divisible into two or even three phases. The editors adopt the two-part chronological division into Early (Acaponeta) Aztatlán and Late (Guasave) Aztatlán originally proposed by Kelley and Winters (1960), and this provides a useful tool to frame the three transitions of Aztatlán—that is, the perceived emergence, transformation, and decline of the network.

The First Transition: Early (Acaponeta) Aztatlán— Gradual or Sudden, Local or Foreign

The most fundamental and consequential topic currently under debate is whether the Aztatlán network after AD 850/900 emerged locally or whether it was brought about through external contacts. For instance, Grave Tirado argues for continuity in settlement patterns and ceramic iconography at Chametla in Sinaloa (Chapter 6, see also Grave Tirado 2012d), while Ramírez Urrea (Chapter 4) sees the iconography as clearly intrusive into the Sayula Basin of Jalisco, where it overran the earlier Sayula-phase substrate. The dichotomy of autochthonous vs. intrusive is addressed by the contributors largely through an assessment of continuity vs. discontinuity and gradual vs. rapid change for demography and settlement, material culture, and ceramic forms and iconography. The debate is comparable to that over the affiliations of Paquimé in Chihuahua, whose biological and cultural relationships to the south, west, east, and north have all come under intense scrutiny (Lekson 1999; Mathiowetz et al. 2015; Minnis and Whalen 2015; Morales-Arce et al. 2017; Pailes 2017:381–393; Seltzer-Rogers 2021; Watson and García 2016; Whalen and Minnis 2003, to name a few).

Any assessment of Aztatlán's origins is complicated by the evidence for environmental disruption from AD 500–1000. There is widespread evidence for drought across the Neo-volcanic Axis from highland Nayarit to central Mexico, peaking around AD 800 (Metcalfe et al. 2015). This drought likely impacted agriculture in parts of the interior, disrupting trade routes and potentially pushing people towards the higher-precipitation regimes of the highlands or Pacific Coast (Beekman 2019). A more acute problem would have been the volcanic eruption that left a thick tephra layer in southern Nayarit, as noted by Beltrán Medina and colleagues at Ahuacatlán (Chapter 12). Edward Gifford (1950:185, 188–190) observed this layer and noted that it separated his Early Ixtlán and Middle Ixtlán phases (hence falling between AD 500–900). At one location, Gifford (1950:190) added that the pumice overlies a thick layer of reddish-brown earth, echoed later by Zepeda's (1994: 58–59) statement that a reddish clay layer also separated her Early and Middle Ixtlán-phase materials in the same area. The tephra layer is most likely the Plinian Jala eruption of the Volcán Ceboruco, though I know of no tephrachronological analysis that confirms this. That eruption is dated by multiple combined radiocarbon dates to AD 990–1020 (Sieron and Siebe 2008:246, Table 1). This seems quite late given that the Early Ixtlán phase should have ended circa AD 500 and yet materials typical of the period AD 500–900 in the general region are not reported by either Gifford or Zepeda. More in keeping with the archaeological evidence would be an AD 500 eruption followed by a period of depopulation and recovery around AD 900. Flood events are also involved. Project members proposed an abandonment of Amapa or even the entire coastal plain between the Amapa and Cerritos phases (or approximately AD 750–950) based on a decline in sherd frequency and a gap in obsidian hydration dates (Grosscup 1964:7, 209–213, Figure 43; Meighan, ed. 1976:58, Figure 5). In addition, Foster and Scott (2017:55) noted a gap in the archaeological record in the Marismas Nacionales between the Late Estero and Early Conchera phases, or AD 700–1000. Foster (2017a:16) cites geological evidence suggesting inundation during this period. It seems apparent that disruption to the subsistence base and subsequent demographic shifts were very much a part of the lead-up to Aztatlán.

It is no surprise then that the emergence of Early (Acaponeta) Aztatlán around AD 850/900 was accompanied by rapid population growth along the Pacific coast, whether due to growth and recovery from earlier disruptions or to the influx of migrants from elsewhere. While several of the major Aztatlán communities had earlier occupations, such as at San Felipe Aztatán, the only reported evidence for ceremonial structures and a prior political or religious center is presented in Grave Tirado's discussion of Chametla (Chapter 6). Even there however, new institutions were introduced with early Aztatlán. Ballcourts had been very common prior to AD 500 at highland centers of the Teuchitlán culture but became vanishingly rare across western Mexico over the period AD 500–850/900. Their reintroduction at Aztatlán sites such as Amapa, Chametla, Copala, Mazatlán, Chacalilla, Ixtapa, Arroyo Seco, El Walamo, and Isla del Macho (mentioned by various contributors) is thus especially interesting. The rubber ballgame is convincingly associated with the mediation of internal competition within the Teuchitlán communities, so did it play a similar role in addressing social conflict as people of various origins aggregated into the Early Aztatlán centers (as suggested by the diversity of mortuary data that Beltrán Medina and colleagues document for La Pitayera in Chapter 12)? This could imply that the ballcourts were most relevant in Early Aztatlán, but less so in Late Aztatlán. Or was the ballgame an integral part of Aztatlán ceremonialism and conflict management over the entire span of the network? Simply glossing the ballcourts as an Aztatlán "trait" does not help to address social and theoretical questions, and we need more precision.

Several changes in material culture are associated with the emergence of Aztatlán coastal centers. While different features are emphasized by different authors, Aztatlán in the minds of most is fundamentally associated with the spread of copper artifacts and the Postclassic Religious Style (Smith and Heath-Smith 1980: 18–31), or PRS (also Postclassic International Style). Dorothy Hosler (1994b) established that copper metallurgy was introduced into western Mexico from South America. She identified an early stage from AD 600–900 when artifacts were very few and found across a limited area of coastal Nayarit and slightly inland. Some of the authors here express caution about these earliest cases, and I agree that these deserve review. However, one example that is not widely known is that of a copper bead from a Comala-phase shaft tomb in Colima (Zavaleta Lucido and Flores Ramírez 2016:67, n. 1). This pushes back the earliest known occurrence of copper metallurgy in Mesoamerica. But it also highlights yet again that people in western Mexico (and the Maya region) made casual use of copper prior to AD 900.

This example suggests how we might move past the current debate over Aztatlán's origins. Current approaches that seek to define Aztatlán can rely too much on the presence/absence of traits rather than how they were used. Copper metallurgy is not a defining feature of Aztatlán. What changed is the way in which copper became a new medium for the expression of specific ideological concepts linking participating elites (Pohl's cultural capital). After AD 900, coastal people strategically chose to make use of existing copper metallurgy to make a much wider array of visually distinctive objects (Punzo Díaz and González, Chapter 11). The materials are the means, not the end. Similarly, public architecture was not entirely new, but people strategically chose to construct architectural spaces with solar orientations appropriate to public performance. People strategically chose to combine some existing pottery decoration with many new designs and forms with foreign origins. People strategically chose to maintain existing long-distance trade relationships with the people who supplied them with obsidian (Pierce, Chapter 10). This more agency-based approach also leaves more room for how, as Ramírez Urrea notes (Chapter 4), each polity and its supporting economy tailored their participation within the wider network.

Whether researchers consider Aztatlán to have been intrusive or not hinges on the dating of related ceramics elsewhere, but this requires a review. Smith and Heath-Smith (1980; see also Kelley 1986) associated the Postclassic Religious Style (PRS) with Early (Acaponeta) Aztatlán ceramics in western Mexico, Aztec I (Culhuacan) ceramics in the southern Basin of Mexico and Cholula, and Middle Polychrome ceramics in the Gran Nicoya region of Nicaragua and the Guanacaste peninsula in Costa Rica. In their review, Aztatlán and Guanacaste were the earliest occurrences of the PRS. This led Smith and Heath-Smith to suggest that the PRS began earlier in the "peripheries" than in central Mexico. Multiple contributors to this volume repeat this point and add that pyriform vessels with horizontal design bands seem to link Aztatlán more with the Central American ceramics than with central Mexico (although the decorative colors remind me more of the Cholula sequence and pyriform vessels also occur at Cholula [Noguera 1954:72, 74]).

Our understanding of these three key regions presents a different picture today and needs to be more thoroughly integrated into the discussion rather than citing old reviews. Ceramics bearing the PRS in Nicaragua and Guanacaste emerge rapidly around AD 800 with the Sapoá phase and with ties to contemporary types further to the north, such as Isla de Sacrificios White-on-cream (McCafferty 2015, 2019; McCafferty and Dennett 2016; McCafferty and Steinbrenner 2005). The calibrated radiocarbon intercepts for Aztec I ceramics from the southern Basin of Mexico now stretch from AD 900–1250 (Crider 2011:409–410; Overholtzer 2014), while parallel types from Cholula such as Cocoyotla Black-on-natural (also known as Xicotenco Black-on-orange) are less well pinned-down by absolute dates but appear to cover the same range (Lind et al. 2002; McCafferty 1996, 2001:Table 2.1). Similar elaborations of PRS iconography thus begin from AD 800/900 in all three of the regions that have been cited as early adopters. Within the vagaries of radiocarbon dating, no region shows priority.

Some argue that individual designs were used earlier in parts of western Mexico. Alfonso Grave Tirado (Chapter 6; see also Vidal 2018) notes the early occurrence of specific designs at Chametla, and I (Beekman 1996, 2019) have argued that step frets and many other designs in the Epiclassic western Mexican highlands were isolated elements that contributed to Aztatlán iconography. Chronologically, these features correspond to the use of similar designs in Coyotlatelco pottery in central Mexico (Rattray 1966), which were elaborated into Aztec I ceramics. In Nicaragua, the new complex appears more suddenly at the Bagaces/Sapoá transition circa AD 800 (McCafferty 2019; McCafferty and Dennett 2013:199). So, two of the three regions seen as participants in the Postclassic Religious Style show a similar trend in which isolated and difficult to interpret designs were present in the latter part of the Classic period, followed by their rapid consolidation into more complex arrangements circa AD 850/900, while portraits or narratives of recognizable deities emerged still later. There seems to be little secure evidence for chronological priority among the three geographically distinct regions, suggesting that they did indeed form a network in which changes spread quickly among their members.

The editors posit that Early (Acaponeta) Aztatlán was more aligned with developments at Tula circa AD 850/900 (see also Jiménez 2018, 2020), and that Late (Guasave) Aztatlán shifted towards Mixteca-Puebla following Tula's collapse (more on this below). The association with Tula is evidenced by the occurrence of Mazapan figurines across a wide swath of inland western Mexico (Forest et al. 2020:Figure 3), Pachuca obsidian, Plumbate and its imitators in Michoacán (Jadot et al. 2019:Figure 1), and related sculpture and architecture at places like El Cerrito in Querétaro and El Teúl in Zacatecas (Crespo 1991). Tula's involvement in the western highlands along the Río Lerma appears compelling and surely linked to Caxcan-speaking polities, but hard to interpret by the time it reaches Lake Chapala and the Aztatlán communities of the coast. This is because the material evidence dwindles to Mazapan figurines (which Solar Valverde sees as more akin to those of El Salvador [Bruhns and Amaroli 2006] than those of Tula) and the rare occurrence of Plumbate ceramics, which could be coming up the coast directly from the manufacturing area in Chiapas and without having any connection to Tula at all. These are certainly useful chronological markers but do not obviously indicate a political or even economic network associated with Tula. Laura Solar Valverde (Chapter 2) and José Luis Punzo Díaz and Lissandra González (Chapter 11) note how general sumptuary goods (e.g., metal, turquoise) are sometimes associated with Tula when they surely circulated in their own independent networks.

There are of course other datasets to consider. Mathiowetz points to iconographic evidence for the sun, Venus, and the feathered serpent in southern Aztatlán sites in parallel with evidence from Tula and Chichén Itzá (Chapter 13). I do not want to be dismissive of those contacts, but I also find them harder to pin down to Tula as a political entity, or to religious concepts derived from Tula. Other centers that participated in competitive or cooperative relationships with Tula, such as Cholula, need to be part of this conversation. Indeed, the importance of the sun and deliberately contrasting imagery of light and darkness (noted by Mathiowetz in Aztatlán ceramics) both occur in Cholula polychromes (Hernández Sánchez 2008; Rojas Martínez 2008b), which as noted below date earlier than currently appreciated.

There is also limited consideration here of events at Tula itself. The Early Tollan phase focused on Ucareo obsidian and ceramics with western affinities but shifted significantly towards the east in the Late Tollan phase (ca. AD 1050 or so), with a predominance of Pachuca obsidian and Gulf Coast-inspired ceramics (Healan 2012:69, 87; Mastache et al. 2002:43, 71–72). Thus, attributing Pachuca obsidian (which is specific to Epiclassic and Early Postclassic Aztatlán according to Pierce, Chapter 10) to long-distance interaction with Tula is awkward when Tula itself did not emphasize that source until around AD 1050 and collapsed just a century later (Healan et al. 2021). We would expect participation in a Tula obsidian network during Early Aztatlán to be marked by the importation of Ucareo obsidian.

Furthermore, the decorated ceramics on the coast, which seem so central to the definition of an Aztatlán network of elites, show little similarity to any Tollan-phase materials at Tula, but they are comparable to the Middle and Late Tlachihualtepetl phases at Cholula (or the alternate Aquiahuac phase proposed in Lind et al. 2002). I am thinking specifically of Cocoyotla Black-on-natural Incised (McCafferty 2001:Figures 4.25c, 4.25d, 4.26), Ocotlan Red Rim and its variants (McCafferty 2001:Figures 4.35–4.42), and San Pedro Polished Red (McCafferty 2001:Figures 4.43b–h). Cuaxiloa Matte (McCafferty 2001:Figures 4.29–4.33) and Torre Polychrome (McCafferty 2001:Figures 4.45–4.54) may be somewhat later (Tecama phase in Lind et al. 2002) but are also reminiscent of Early Aztatlán design layouts at Cojumatlán and Amapa. Additionally, in their discussion of metallurgical parallels during Early Aztatlán, Punzo Díaz and González find more reason to refer to Cholula than Tula (Chapter 11).

This contrast between Tula and Cholula sources is not limited to the western Mexican coast over the tenth and eleventh centuries. Within the contemporaneous Basin of Mexico, the northwestern valleys gravitated towards Tula and its suite of material culture while the southeastern valleys were oriented towards Cholula, with interesting exceptions that highlight how participation was a matter of choice (Brumfiel 2005). Centers elsewhere in Mesoamerica also seem to have chosen between Tula and Cholula networks. Distinct enclaves of central Mexican migrants to El Salvador and Nicaragua drew alternately upon Early Tollan-phase Tula (Fowler 2019) or contemporary Cholula (McCafferty and Steinbrenner 2005) for inspiration in ceramics, architecture, and religious figures. Whether the choices being made reflected the linguistic affiliation of the migrants (Nahuatl vs. Otomanguean) or disinterested participation in rival economic/political systems, the contrast was often stark. The Early Aztatlán centers of Nayarit and Sinaloa may have been less picky. Aztatlán vessel iconography better expresses a connection to Cholula's extended ritual network. The prevalence of pyriform vessels in Early Aztatlán suggests that the Cholula network may have been accessed via maritime connections to the Isthmus of Tehuantepec or further south. Mazapan figurines suggest a separate and qualitatively different network, one that remains hard to interpret because of the figurines' often domestic associations (but see Solar Valverde et al. 2011).

The material culture of El Chanal in Colima may help to further illuminate these contrasting long-distance relationships. Connections between El Chanal and Michoacán, Tula, and/or El Salvador are suggested by ceramics, including food preparation techniques (Olay Barrientos 2004:523–532), and the numerous ceramic effigies of the Flayed God (Fowler 1989; Nicholson 1989; Scott 1993) rather than Flower World themes. Von Winning (1984) links male ceramic effigies from El Chanal that are seated on *equipales* to central Mexican costume elements of Mixcoatl. Links further down the Pacific coast are also supported by gold jewelry with iconographic ties to Monte Albán (Kelly 1985). Thus, while El Chanal and the Aztatlán communities were often in contact with similar regions (central Mexico or Central America), they interacted with different communities, participated in different networks, and ultimately used very different forms of material culture.

Current Models of Early Aztatlán Society

Setting aside these questions of origins and affiliations, the contributors to this volume have much to say about the internal economic, sociopolitical, and ideological organization of Aztatlán centers. One issue in need of attention is that the evidence for cultural patterns and processes is rarely distinguished by whether it describes Early versus Late Aztatlán. Either there is little change over time, or there has been less attention to this issue. My comments therefore are largely about Aztatlán as a whole, and I keep them relatively brief when compared to those on the transitions.

The economy, including both production and exchange, has tended to garner the most attention. Mountjoy (Chapter 1) has argued persuasively for many years that different Aztatlán centers engaged in specialized production of metalwork, ceramics, cacao, shellwork, salt, and marine and estuary resources. This appears to be broadly accepted, and some researchers such as Garduño Ambriz (Chapter 5) believe that elites controlled production. The economic specialization has always implied regional-scale trade, especially along the Pacific-coastal plain or via maritime transport. While some goods surely followed terrestrial roads along the coastal plain, this remains poorly documented. Sea travel seems securely implicated in trade or contacts with Oaxaca and Central America, but maritime themes seem strangely absent from the iconography. It is true that some highland groups today see the ocean as the place of their ancestors (Reyes Valdez and Zavala 2019), but these beliefs may owe their genesis to post-Aztatlán movements away from the coast. Were Aztatlán centers consumers of long-distance goods, but not travelers themselves, as implied by Cristina García Moreno and colleagues at El Cementerio (Chapter 9)? The absence of axe-monies, a medium of exchange peculiar to Postclassic centers in central and southern Mexico (Cullen Cobb et al. 2022; Hosler et al. 1990), would also seem to suggest a difference in how Aztatlán centers participated in trade. Aztatlán towns are generally located some distance inland and along rivers. In some instances, this may be due to a shifting shoreline, but towns may have relied upon smaller communities directly on the coast to handle the coastal trade, a common pattern along the Pacific coast. More research has been devoted to trade from the coast into the highlands (in the chapters by Cinthya Vidal Aldana and Daniel Pierce), especially the northern route into Durango, or the southern route through central Jalisco to Lake Chapala.

Models for exchange have come a long way since the older *pochteca* or World-Systems models that sought to link Mesoamerica with the U.S. Southwest and northwest Mexico. Carpenter and Sánchez (Chapter 8) review past proposals, and a prestige-goods model currently predominates (as illustrated in the chapters by Punzo Díaz and González and Solar Valverde). Our models for exchange have been theoretically limited, however. Although elite-centered models have been proposed over the years, the variability in the distribution of trade goods even within a single settlement (as seen in the Pierce chapter) suggests to me that households or lineages may be more relevant units of analysis, with each developing its own trading partners. We might have better success with models that look more like the Kula ring rather than capitalism-derived models of cores, peripheries, and professional merchants, or rulers who combined economic and political power.

Coyle's chapter reminds us that our detailed analyses of material life (subsistence, goods, etc.) dramatically outpace the serious consideration of ritual and symbolism. Fortunately, more culturally sensitive models are now being proposed. Chapters by Mathiowetz, Pierce, Pohl, and Vidal Aldana note that some goods may have been exchanged to maintain social and political relationships, while the goods themselves were of secondary importance. Once again, they are the means, not the end. I was especially interested in Vidal Aldana's ethnography-inspired proposal (Chapter 7) that the exchange of some goods may also transmit the qualities of its region of origin. This is consistent with Mesoamerican concepts of Tlalocan, Tamoanchan, and Flower World, such that a goal of exchange with tropical lowland zones was to obtain goods that would materially instantiate their conception of paradise. I am reminded of the work of Emma Britton (2018) at Paquimé in Chihuahua who found that even ceramic temper may carry cosmological associations.

Aztatlán political activity has been a lower priority than economics, but given what we know about Mesoamerican systems of authority, we should not assume that all polities had a stereotypical priest-king. Michael Mathiowetz has developed a complex and far-reaching model over multiple publications in which the ritual authority of Aztatlán elites was intertwined with goods (cacao, cotton, ceramic vessels) that materialized Flower World concepts and referenced the god Xochipilli (Piltzintli). His chapter in this volume examines the iconographically complex ceramic bowls, which he compares to the gourd cargo bowls used by modern religious practitioners in the Gran Nayar. He sees them as a ritual technology used during the various yearly *mitotes* and tied up with the ritual authority of something like a council of elders. This echoes Coyle's comments about leadership among the historic Náayeri, who had not only lineage elders but also the Sun King on the Mesa del Nayar, who embodied a more centralized hierarchy of authority (Chapter 14). Grave Tirado (Chapter 6) draws upon the Sun King as an analogy for Aztatlán leadership and suggests that researchers need to address the various kinds of power that may have been cultivated by these rulers. I very much agree with his insistence on recognizing multiple forms of power, which could also be phrased as the strategies pursued by elites as they established and legitimized their positions. Coyle (Chapter 14) references additional ethnographic research that contrasts this Náayeri pattern of a centralized ruler, with the Wixárika pattern in which the advancement of one individual or family over the others was deliberately suppressed. His discussion resonates strongly with my understanding of the Late Formative and Classic period Teuchitlán culture, which corresponds better to the Wixárika tendency to avoid centralized authority. However, I see little evidence for the continuation of elements of Teuchitlán ritualism during the Epiclassic period that separates its collapse from the rise of Aztatlán unless it retreated to the remote mountains along the border of Jalisco and Nayarit.

This brings us to the very broad topic of religious beliefs in society as well as their role in defining politics. The model that Mathiowetz has been developing is a sweeping interpretation of Aztatlán that identifies important points of contact with Tula and Chichén Itzá on the one hand and with Paquimé on the other. I will be interested to see how he addresses some of the diversity emerging within Aztatlán research. For instance, Ramírez Urrea (Chapter 4) defines three iconographic styles within Aztatlán that she seems to relate to political entities, and I would like to know whether their iconographic or narrative content differs or whether these better reflect artistic technologies of practice. Beltrán Medina and colleagues (Chapter 12) identify a striking array of burial procedures at La Pitayera that probably index distinct views towards the afterlife. Solar Valverde (Chapter 2) notes that other communities participating in the elaborate ritualism of the Postclassic Religious Style supported a variety of different political systems, ranging from the marriage alliances among the Mixtec, the rotating offices of Cholula, or the centralized rulership described ethnohistorically for Tula. Do the conceptual themes and interpretations of Flower World across the Postclassic vary in concert with the local political system, or were these more distant concepts that did not bear upon the nitty-gritty details of who held power?

One dataset that could help with all the economic,

political, and religious questions is that of settlement and architecture. Regional settlement patterns are important evidence to clarify subsistence adaptations and the distribution of production activities, but there seem to be few examples of phase-by-phase maps of changing settlement distribution. Ramírez Urrea (Chapter 4) proposes a model in which high-value goods are being produced at one level within the local hierarchy and consumed at another, highlighting the need for high-resolution full-coverage survey mapping everything from major centers down to isolated farmsteads. Carpenter and Sánchez (Chapter 8) and García Moreno and colleagues (Chapter 9) describe a distinct pattern in northern Sinaloa and southern Sonora, respectively, where isolated burial mounds were used by a dispersed residential population, suggesting a very different relationship between elites and non-elites. I presume that the absence of regional maps is due to the widespread damage to the archaeological record thanks to coastal development projects (Grave Tirado 2019), but Mountjoy, for example, has published survey maps that could be separated into phases to produce a more dynamic view of settlement change. We also appear to lack estimates of population for centers, polities, or regions. Demographic data are necessary to calculate agricultural production or assess urbanism, and even approximate estimates of settlement populations would go a long way towards improving communication with non-Aztatlán archaeologists and with one another.

Settlement layout and architectural morphology have been critical elsewhere in Mesoamerica for the reconstruction of elements of cosmology. Public architecture is an important dataset to examine for references to worldview, to understand the design of ritual performance space, and to recognize the restricted or open nature of ritual. A more consistent approach to describing and analyzing Aztatlán architectural spaces is an important next step for evaluating political variability across this vast region. For example, Garduño Ambríz and Grave Tirado (Chapters 5 and 6, respectively) identify solar (especially solstitial) orientations in the public architecture, which parallel Mathiowetz's reconstruction of beliefs associated with a solar-affiliated deity. It also recalls the toponym of Tonatiuh Yuetzyan, possibly in Sinaloa, as depicted on page 73 of the *Lienzo de Tlaxcala* (Chavero, ed. 1979 [1892]). But both Garduño Ambriz and Grave Tirado also refer to variability in the architecture, and regional differences that may indicate that different polities or regions held different interpretations of Flower World, or weighted components of the concept differently. I would especially like to know why the Aztatlán centers of Ixtlán del Río and Cojumatlán (both on the route inland from the coast to Lake Chapala) instead built columned structures or large platforms, respectively. This variability in the spaces where public ritual was performed and elites were housed is not marginal to discussions of ideology, but central to them.

The Second Transition: Transformation and Late (Guasave) Aztatlán

The timing and causes of the second transition of Aztatlán are less clear than the first, and interpretations continue to be intertwined with the view that central Mexican sequences were their source. Kelley and Winters (1960) recognized an early "Acaponeta" and later "Guasave" Aztatlán, which stands today. But the original article unfortunately embellished this transition as a shift from a "Toltec" to a "Mixteca-Puebla" affiliation (Kelley and Winters 1960:558, 560), which plays a role in interpretations in this volume. Jiménez (2018:133–187) turns Kelley's earlier comparisons into a macroeconomic model and sees the fall of Tula (which Jiménez dates to AD 1150–1200) as removing an important node linking central Mexico to the west. Pohl also sees Tula's fall as a catalyst for a shift in ties towards Cholula and Oaxaca. Early Postclassic markers such as Mazapan figurines and Plumbate ceramics, and Pachuca obsidian from central Mexico, all disappear or decline in Late (Guasave) Aztatlán.

I noted earlier that Tula's engagement with Aztatlán polities is less clear-cut than this model suggests, and that Cholula may have been closely implicated from the emergence of Early Aztatlán. Kelley does not appear to have meant his published statements to indicate a Toltec (as in Tula) political or cultural affiliation, but only a temporal one (and we see once again the problem with multivalent labels). At the time, Aztec I ceramics (his point of comparison) were recognized as contemporary with "Full Toltec" (the term for Early and Late Tollan phases at that time). Kelley's (1986) later publication muddied the water considerably, as he then incorrectly shifted Aztec I to the Middle Postclassic period but repeated his characterization that Aztatlán was divided into "Toltec" and "Mixteca-Puebla" phases (Kelley 1986:84–86). As noted in the previous section, Kelley was right about the chronology the first time, and he could have better characterized the comparisons between Aztatlán and central Mexico without ethnic labels. Today we could rephrase his intended comparison as follows: the transition from Early to Late Aztatlán shows temporal and iconographic parallels with the transition from Culhuacan Black-on-orange (and its parallel and related types at Early Postclassic Cholula) to the more elaborated iconography of the Late Postclassic Religious Style. This leaves much less room for Tula's involvement on the Pacific coast.

There has been considerable discussion of mapping the transition to Late Aztatlán using ceramic changes. John Pohl (Chapter 3, see also Pohl 2012b) attributes the occurrence of a more codex-style narrative format on pottery to a Cholula origin (based on estimated dates there at AD 1250), which was then adopted throughout the Mixteca and ultimately up the coast. Garduño Ambriz, Grave Tirado, and Ramírez Urrea dispute this in their chapters and see codex-style pottery originating in the Aztatlán region by AD 1100. Resolving the issue to everyone's satisfaction would require greater specificity as to dating, context, and illustration of examples. For instance, I notice that the term codex style is used in McCafferty's (2001) monograph on Cholula ceramics in reference to portrayals of deity heads alone, whereas Pohl appears to refer to full-figure narratives. Rojas Martínez and Hernández Sánchez (2019) refer to both middle and late Cholula polychromes (AD 1150–1550) as codex style. This is not the first time that terms and definitions associated with the Mixteca-Puebla concept have lacked clarity, and these older and unresolved debates continue to haunt the Aztatlán region.

What seems more demonstrable during Late Aztatlán is the expansion of the Aztatlán network of elite performative ritual up and down the coast and changing patterns of exchange. Mountjoy points to highly decorated Aztatlán ceramics at Arroyo Piedras Azules on the coast of Jalisco in the early thirteenth century (Mountjoy et al. 2020). Carpenter and Sánchez present evidence confirming an AD 1100/1150 date for the more elaborate ceramics at Guasave, in the far north of Sinaloa. In their view, the occurrence of Late Aztatlán ceramics in the burial mound at El Ombligo (I would like to know the origin of that name!) shows few ties to either economics or politics, and more likely indicates the local adoption of religious ideas from the south. The work of García Moreno and colleagues at El Cementerio (Chapter 9) provides a very useful characterization of the activities in the Ónavas Valley, suggesting that Guasave inspired secondary emulation by smaller centers that engaged with a wider array of partners. Pierce describes a widening circle of obsidian sources exploited by Aztatlán polities, but also indicates that the long-distance trade in Pachuca obsidian declined from its Epiclassic and Early Aztatlán peak. This suggests declining interest or access to the obsidian even as local awareness of trends in high-end central Mexican ceramics continued much as before. Punzo Díaz and González (Chapter 11) document a narrowing of production of some types of metal artifacts within the state of Michoacán as manufacture was increasingly dominated by the emerging Tarascan state. What remains very curious to me given the arguments for Aztatlán trade is the continuing absence of copper or copper alloy axe-monies, the medium of exchange in widespread use among the small polities described by Pohl for Oaxaca and Puebla.

The Third Transition: Decline of Aztatlán

Aztatlán's "end" also serves to highlight differing interpretations. By the fourteenth or fifteenth centuries, the characteristic features of the Aztatlán communities were disappearing. Mountjoy (Chapter 1) sees Aztatlán sites undergoing a decrease in population and trade, but particularly a diminished use of the Postclassic Religious Style. He proposes climate change as a potential reason, citing evidence from Mesa Verde, Colorado. One problem is that broader northwest Mexico and southwestern United States experienced climatic trends opposite of those in this area of Mesoamerica (e.g., Méndez and Magaña 2010). More pertinent paleoclimatic records from within the western Mexican highlands instead tend to show a period of recovery from the droughts of the Epiclassic and Early Postclassic (Metcalfe et al. 2015). For these reasons, we really need climate proxies from within the Pacific-coastal zone, preferably integrated with archaeological settlement-pattern survey, to assess the role for drought in the Late Postclassic.

Another cause worthy of investigation is the rise of the Tarascan Empire in Michoacán as a kind of bulwark or barrier to continued interaction with central Mexico. The empire's extent at the time of the Spanish conquest would have allowed it to block traffic along the Río Lerma and Río Balsas, the major waterways linking the central highlands with the western coast. Punzo Díaz and González (Chapter 11) showed how particular types of metal products were being increasingly produced and consumed within the territory of the Tarascan state by the Middle Postclassic. While this was not a blockade (the Tarascans traded with the Aztecs after all [Pollard and Vogel 1994]), this could have introduced a serious discontinuity into metallurgical traditions within the region. Of course, it appears that much of the contact between Aztatlán polities and southern Mexico, Central America, and even central Mexico took place via the coast. An emergent Tarascan state would not have been able to block that trade until after its conquest of Zacatula, practically on the eve of the Spanish arrival.

In a more agent-centered perspective, Carpenter and Sánchez (Chapter 8) suggest that people ceased to participate in the Aztatlán network's most distinctive component, the performative rituals underpinning the entire system, including the vessels used in cargo rituals as described by Mathiowetz in Chapter 13 (the argument reminds me of Houston et al. 2003). These authors, along with Grave Tirado and Garduño Ambríz (Chapters 6 and 5, respectively), emphasize continuity between Late Aztatlán settlement patterns and those documented by the early Spanish conquerors. It may be the case that we have not yet identified the very latest Aztatlán centers, since the absence of the highly decorated ceramics would have left these sites less easily recognizable and less likely to be excavated and dated. In this view, it is the ceremonialism that faded away or became less archaeologically visible along the coast but continued in less-hierarchical form among highland groups (the source of most religious analogies for coastal communities as in the chapters by Mathiowetz, Solar Valverde, and Vidal Aldana).

This brings us to the final issue of the descendant populations of Aztatlán today. Many contributors to this volume propose that the Náayeri, Wixárika, Totorame, and Tahue were and are among the historic heirs of Aztatlán and that their practices and beliefs provide analogies to interpret the ancient past. I observe that these groups pertain to different branches of the Southern Uto-Aztecan language family. Indeed, the branch that is conspicuously absent is that of Nahuatl, which I suggest was represented at El Chanal in Colima and El Teúl in the Caxcan zone (Sauer 1948; Yáñez Rosales 2001). As noted earlier, these two sites participated in some trade with the Aztatlán towns but were not participants in the ritual cargo system of Aztatlán proper (as defined by Mathiowetz) that shows so many ties to Cholula. El Teúl and El Chanal also had more connections with Tula than the Aztatlán centers did in the form of sculpture and images of the Flayed God, respectively. There are therefore some curious parallels between linguistic affiliation and long-distance patterns of interaction that require serious investigation in the future.

Coyle's chapter potentially provides the reader with a final definition of Aztatlán. While the Náayeri people today share many subsistence practices and a common subaltern status with other groups in the modern Mexican state, this does not define their sense of community identity. They see themselves as formed or assembled as a group through ritual exchanges, ceremonies, and sacrifices that reinforce their commitment to one another and to their gods (see also Monaghan 1995). When we ask why Aztatlán transformed, faded away, or disappeared, these are the final bonds that must be addressed and understood.

Conclusion

The contributors to this volume show us that Aztatlán is beginning to take shape as a coherent research topic, and a body of specialists has emerged. Debates over the origin, transformation, and decline of the Aztatlán network demonstrate the health and maturity of the field. Aztatlán communities covered a huge territory in northwestern Mexico and provide the best evidence to date for a bridge between Mesoamerica and the U.S. Southwest. The problem with networks is that they can be extended transitively to the ends of the earth, and there needs to be equal consideration given to how Aztatlán was *not* just like its neighbors, or how Aztatlán varied from community to community. It will also be important to scrutinize older claims more closely, such as those about chronology, mercantilism, and long-distance comparisons that are often no longer consistent with current data. In the future, I expect fewer empirical summaries and more problem-oriented studies that develop specific proposals. But most importantly, I hope that the researchers represented here and in other publications will continue to openly debate the major issues and engage with one another's findings.

Acknowledgments

I would like to express my thanks to John Pohl and Michael Mathiowetz for the invitation to participate in the volume and for their responses to my inquiries. Many long and complicated emails with Michael Mathiowetz have helped to clarify, if not always convince, on various issues with Aztatlán. My thanks to Catalina Barrientos Pérez, Marion Forest, John Hoopes, Geoffrey McCafferty, Rebecca Mendelsohn, Patricia Plunket, and Gabriela Uruñuela, who clarified issues from other regions. Thanks go to Megan O'Neil for the newspaper articles on funding for the Amapa project.

Notes

1. "infinidad de monumentos […] que se encuentran casi sin interrupción en toda la orilla derecho del rio, pero principalmente en las lomas y puntos que por su elevación están al abrigo de las inundaciones del rio."
2. "[…] que una vez que conquistaron a los pueblos del Anahuac, mantuvieron sus relaciones con estos países remotos; que a la caída de Guatimozinc y del imperio mexicano, varias tribus mexicanas huyeron a estos bordes y a las sierras inmediatas a llorar la perdida de su libertad."

References

Acosta, Jorge R.
1940   Exploraciones en Tula, Hidalgo. *Revista Mexicana de Estudios Antropológicos* 4:172–194.

Acuña, René
1988   *Relaciones Geográficas del Siglo XVI: Nueva Galicia.* Universidad Nacional Autónoma de México, Mexico City.

Adams, E. Charles, and Andrew I. Duff (editors)
2004   *The Protohistoric Pueblo World, A.D. 1275–1600.* University of Arizona Press, Tucson.

Akins, Nancy J.
2003   The Burials of Pueblo Bonito. In *Pueblo Bonito: Center of the Chacoan World*, edited by Jill E. Neitzel, pp. 94–106. Smithsonian Institution Press, Washington, DC.

Alarcón, Gerardo, and Guillermo Ahuja
2015   The Materials of Tamtoc: A Preliminary Evaluation. In *The Huasteca: Culture, History, and Interregional Exchange*, edited by Katherine A. Faust and Kim N. Richter, pp. 37–58. University of Oklahoma Press, Norman.

Alcocer, Paulina
2003   El Mitote Parental de la Chicharra (*Metineita Tsik+ri*) en Chuisete'e. In *Flechadores de Estrellas: Nuevas Aportaciones a la Etnología de Coras y Huicholes*, edited by Jesús Jáuregui and Johannes Neurath, pp. 181–206. Instituto Nacional de Antropología e Historia and Universidad de Guadalajara, Guadalajara, Mexico.

Altschul, Jeffrey H., Keith W. Kintigh, Terry H. Klein, William H. Doelle, Kelley A. Hays-Gilpin, Sarah A. Herr, Timothy A. Kohler, et al.
2017   Fostering Synthesis in Archaeology to Advance Science and Benefit Society. *Proceedings of the National Academy of Sciences of the United States of America* 114(42):10999–11002.

Álvarez Palma, Ana M.
1990   Huatabampo: Consideraciones sobre una Comunidad Agrícola Prehispánica en el Sur de Sonora. *Noroeste de México* 9:9–93.

2007   Reinterpretando Huatabampo. In *Memoria del Seminario de Arqueología del Norte de México*, edited by Cristina García Moreno and Elisa Villalpando, pp. 99–114. Centro Instituto Nacional de Antropología e Historia, Sonora, and El Consejo Nacional para la Cultura y las Artes, Hermosillo, Sonora, Mexico.

Álvarez Palma, Ana M., Luis A. Grave Tirado and Rubén Manzanilla (editors)
2005   *Historia General de Sinaloa, Época Prehispánica*, José Gaxiola López and Carlos Zazueta Manjarrez, general editors. El Colegio de Sinaloa, Culiacán, Mexico.

Amaroli, Paúl E., and Karen O. Bruhns
2013   450 Years Too Soon: Mixteca-Puebla Style Polychrome Ceramics in El Salvador. *Anales del Instituto de Investigaciones Estéticas* 35(103):231–249.

Anawalt, Patricia R.
1992   Ancient Cultural Contacts between Ecuador, West Mexico, and the American Southwest: Clothing Similarities. *Latin American Antiquity* 3(2):114–129.

Andrefsky, William, Jr.
2005   *Lithics: Macroscopic Approaches to Analysis*, 2nd ed. Cambridge Manuals in Archaeology Series, Cambridge University Press, New York.

Anguiano, Marina
1992   *Nayarit: Costa y Altiplanicie en el Momento del Contacto.* Universidad Nacional Autónoma de México, Mexico City.

Anyon, Roger, and Steven A. LeBlanc
1984   *The Galaz Ruin: A Prehistoric Mimbres Village in Southwestern New Mexico.* Maxwell Museum of Anthropology and University of New Mexico Press, Albuquerque.

Aoyama, Kazuo
2015   Symbolic and Ritual Dimensions of Exchange, Production, Use, and Deposition of Ancient Maya Obsidian Artifacts. In *Obsidian Reflections: Symbolic Dimensions of Obsidian in Mesoamerica*, edited by Marc N. Levine and David M. Carballo, pp. 127–158. University Press of Colorado, Boulder.

Arias de Saavedra, Antonio
1990   [1673] Información Rendida en el Siglo XVII por el P. Antonio Arias de Saavedra acerca del Estado de la Sierra de Nayarit y sobre Culto Idolátrico, Gobierno y Costumbres Primitivas de los Coras. In *Los Albores de un Nuevo Mundo: Siglos XVI y XVII. Colección de Documentos para la Historia de Nayarit I*, edited by Thomas Calvo, pp. 284–309. Universidad de Guadalajara and Centro de Estudios Mexicanos y Centroamericanos, Mexico City.

Arsandaux, Henri, and Paul Rivet
1921   Contribution á l'étude de la Métallurgie Mexicaine. *Journal de la Société des Américanistes de Paris* 13:261–280.

Ashmore, Wendy, and A. Bernard Knapp (editors)
1999   *Archaeologies of Landscape: Contemporary Perspectives.* Blackwell, Malden, MA.

Auerbach, Benjamin M., and Christopher B. Ruff
2010   Stature Estimation Formulae for Indigenous North American Populations. *American Journal of Physical Anthropology* 141(2):190–207.

Axtell, James
1979   Ethnohistory: An Historian's Viewpoint. *Ethnohistory* 26(1):1–13.

Barba, Luis, José Luis Ruvalcaba, and Niklas Schulze
2004   *Análisis de Cuatro Objetos de Metal Procedentes de Nayarit*. Informe Técnico. Archivo del Laboratorio de Prospección Arqueológica. Instituto de Investigaciones Antropológicas, Universidad Nacional Autónoma de México, Mexico City.

Bartholomew, Doris
1980   Otomanguean Influence on Pochutla Aztec. *International Journal of American Linguistics* 46(2):106–116.

Basso, Ellen B.
1985   *A Musical View of the Universe: Kalapalo Myth and Ritual Performance*. University of Pennsylvania Press, Philadelphia.

Beals, Ralph
1932   *The Comparative Ethnology of Northwestern Mexico Before 1750*. Ibero-Americana 2. University of California Press, Berkeley.
1944   Relations Between Mesoamerica and the Southwest. In *El Norte de México y el Sur de Estados Unidos: Tercera Reunión de Mesa Redonda sobre Problemas Antropológicas de México y Centro América*, pp. 245–252. Sociedad Mexicana de Antropología, Mexico City.

Beekman, Christopher S.
1996   El Complejo El Grillo del Centro de Jalisco: Una Revisión de su Cronología y Significado. In *Las Cuencas del Occidente de México: Época Prehispánica*, edited by Eduardo Williams and Phil C. Weigand, pp. 247–291. El Colegio de Michoacán, Zamora.
2003   Agricultural Pole Rituals and Rulership in Late Formative Central Jalisco. *Ancient Mesoamerica* 14(2):299–318.
2019   El Grillo: The Reestablishment of Community and Identity in Far Western Mexico. In *Migrations in Late Mesoamerica*, edited by Christopher S. Beekman, pp. 109–147. University Press of Florida, Gainesville.
2024   Branding West Mexico: The Role of Collectors and Dealers in Reshaping the Archaeological Discourse. In *Collecting Mexican Art before 1940*, edited by Andrew D. Turner and Megan E. O'Neil, pp. 279–298. Getty Research Institute, Los Angeles.

Beekman, Christopher S., Justin Jennings, and Michael D. Mathiowetz
2025   Structure and History in the Americas, 600–1350 CE: Closed and Interconnected. In *Entangled Isolation: Connectivity and Diversity in Medieval Worlds*, edited by Daniel König and Jürgen Osterhammel. History of the World series, Jürgen Osterhammel and Akira Iriye, general editors. Harvard University Press and C. H. Beck, Cambridge, UK, and Munich.

Beekman, Christopher S., and Colin McEwan (editors)
2022   *Waves of Influence: Pacific Maritime Networks Connecting Mexico, Central America, and Northwestern South America*. Dumbarton Oaks Research Library and Collection, Washington, DC.

Bell, Betty B.
1960   Analysis of Ceramic Style: A West Mexican Collection. PhD dissertation, Department of Anthropology, University of California, Los Angeles.
1971   Archaeology of Nayarit, Jalisco, and Colima. In *Archaeology of Northern Mesoamerica*, edited by Gordon F. Ekholm and Ignacio Bernal, pp. 694–752. Handbook of Middle American Indians, Vol. 11, Robert Wauchope, general editor, University of Texas Press, Austin.

Beltrán Medina, José C.
1997   *Informe Técnico del Proyecto Punta de Mita. Primera Temporada*. Archivo Técnico, Consejo de Arqueología, Instituto Nacional de Antropología e Historia, Mexico City.
2001a *La Explotación de la Costa del Pacífico en el Occidente de Mesoamérica y los Contactos con Sudamérica y con Otras Regiones Culturales*. Cuadernos del Seminario Nayarit: Región y Sociedad. Universidad Autónoma de Nayarit, Instituto Nacional de Antropología e Historia, Nayarit, Tepic.
2001b La Cultura Mololoa. *Arqueología Mexicana* 8(47):64–67.
2019   Aspectos Diversos de la Ocupación Aztatlán en Punta Mita, Bahía de Banderas, Nayarit. In *Aztatlán: Interacción y Cambio Social en el Occidente de México ca. 850–1350 d.C.*, edited by Laura Solar Valverde and Ben A. Nelson, pp. 39–59. El Colegio de Michoacán, Zamora, and Arizona State University, Tempe.

Benciolini, Maria
2014   Iridiscencia de un Mundo Florido: Estudio sobre Relacionalidad y Ritual Cora. PhD dissertation, Universidad Nacional Autónoma de México, Mexico City.

Berdan, Frances F., and Patricia R. Anawalt
1997   *The Essential Codex Mendoza*. University of California Press, Berkeley.

Berlin, Heinrich
1947   *Fragmentos Desconocidos del Códice de Yanhuitlán y otras Investigaciones Mixtecas*. Antigua Librería Robredo de J. Porrúa, Mexico City, Mexico.

Bernardini, Wesley
2005   *Hopi Oral Tradition and the Archaeology of Identity*. University of Arizona Press, Tucson.

Bernardini, Wesley, Stewart B. Koyiyumptewa, Gregson Schachner, and Leigh Kuwanwisiwma (editors)
2021   *Becoming Hopi: A History*. University of Arizona Press, Tucson.

Berrojalbiz Cenigaonaindia, Fernando
2012   *Paisajes y fronteras del Durango prehispánico*. Instituto de Investigaciones Estéticas, Instituto de Investigaciones Antropológicas, Universidad Nacional Autónoma de México, Mexico City.

Blanton, Richard E., Gary M. Feinman, Stephen A. Kowaleski, and Peter N. Peregrine.
1996 A Dual-Processual Theory for the Evolution of Mesoamerican Civilization. *Current Anthropology* 37(1):1–14.

Blomster, Jeffrey P. (editor)
2008 *After Monte Albán: Transformation and Negotiation in Oaxaca, Mexico*. University Press of Colorado, Boulder.

Boas, Franz
1913 Archaeological Investigations in the Valley of Mexico by the International School, 1911–1912. *Proceedings of the Eighteenth International Congress of Americanists*, pp. 176–179. London.
1917 El Dialecto Mexicano de Pochutla, Oaxaca. *International Journal of American Linguistics* 1(1):9–44.

Bojórquez Diego, Victoria L.
2009 El Complejo Ritual Aztatlán del Occidente. Interacción e Innovación durante el Posclásico Temprano. Bachelor's thesis, Escuela Nacional de Antropología e Historia, Mexico City.

Bonfiglioli, Carlo, Arturo Gutiérrez, and María Eugenia Olavarría (editors)
2006 *Las Vías del Noroeste I: Una Macroregión Indígena Americana*. Universidad Nacional Autónoma de México, Mexico City.

Boone, Elizabeth H., and Michael E. Smith
2003 Postclassic International Styles and Symbol Sets. In *The Postclassic Mesoamerican World*, edited by Michael E. Smith and Frances F. Berdan, pp. 186–193. University of Utah Press, Salt Lake City.

Boone, James L.
2000 Status Signaling, Social Power, and Lineage Survival. In *Hierarchies in Action: Cui Bono?*, edited by Michael W. Diehl, pp. 84–110. Occasional Papers No. 27, Center for Archaeological Investigation, Southern Illinois University, Carbondale.

Borck, Lewis, and Jeffrey J. Clark
2021 Dispersing Power: The Contentious, Egalitarian Politics of the Salado Phenomenon in the Hohokam Region of the U.S. Southwest. In *Power from Below in Premodern Societies: The Dynamics of Political Complexity in the Archaeological Record*, edited by T. L. Thurston and Manuel Fernández-Götz, pp. 247–271. Cambridge University Press, Cambridge, UK.

Bordaz, Jacques
1964 Pre-Columbian Ceramic Kilns at Peñitas, a Post-Classic Site in Coastal Nayarit, Mexico. PhD dissertation. Department of Anthropology, Columbia University, New York.

Bourdieu, Pierre
1986 The Forms of Capital. In *Handbook of Theory and Research for the Sociology of Education*, edited by John G. Richardson, pp. 241–258. Greenwood Press, New York.

Boyce, Ian M.
2015 Situating Copper Bells in Prehispanic Southwestern Societies: An Analysis of the Spatial, Temporal, and Contextual Distributions. Master's thesis, Department of Anthropology, Trent University, Peterborough, Ontario.

Boyd, Carolyn E.
2016 *The White Shaman Mural: An Enduring Creation Narrative in the Rock Art of the Lower Pecos*. University of Texas Press, Austin.

Bradley, Ronna J.
1999 Shell Exchange within the Southwest: The Casas Grandes Interaction Sphere. In *The Casas Grandes World*, edited by Curtis F. Schaafsma and Carroll L. Riley, pp. 213–228. University of Utah Press, Salt Lake City.
2000 Networks of Shell Ornament Exchange: A Critical Assessment of Prestige Economies in the North American Southwest. In *The Archaeology of Regional Interaction: Religion, Warfare, & Exchange across the American Southwest & Beyond*, edited by Michelle Hegmon, pp. 167–187. University Press of Colorado, Boulder.

Brand, Donald D.
1971 Notes on the Geography and Archaeology of Zape, Durango. In *The North Mexican Frontier: Readings in Archaeology, Ethnohistory, and Ethnology*, edited by Basil C. Hedrick, J. Charles Kelley, and Carroll L. Riley, pp. 21–49. Southern Illinois University Press, Carbondale.

Braniff Cornejo, Beatriz
1975 The West Mexican Tradition and the Southwestern United States. *Kiva* 41(2):215–222.
1989 *Arqueomoluscos de Sonora, Noroeste y Occidente de Mesoamérica*. Cuadernos de Trabajo 9. Escuela Nacional de Antropología e Historia, Mexico City, Mexico.
1992 *La Frontera Protohistórica Pima-Opata en Sonora, México: Proposiciones Arqueológicas Preliminares*, Vols. 1–3. Colección Científica, Serie Arqueología. Instituto Nacional de Antropología e Historia, Mexico City.

Britton, Emma L.
2018 The Mineralogical and Chemical Variability of Casas Grandes Polychromes throughout the International Four Corners. PhD dissertation, Department of Anthropology, University of California, Santa Cruz.

Brody, J. J.
2004 *Mimbres Painted Pottery*, revised edition. School of American Research Press, New Mexico.

Bruhns, Karen O., and Paul E. Amaroli
2006 Mazapan Style Figurines in El Salvador. *La Tinaja* 17(1–2):11–15.

Brumfiel, Elizabeth M.
2005 Opting in and Opting out: Tula, Cholula and Xaltocan. In *Settlement, Subsistence, and Social Complexity: Essays Honoring the Legacy of Jeffrey R. Parsons*, edited by Richard E. Blanton, pp. 63–88. Cotsen Institute of Archaeology Press, University of California, Los Angeles.

Brush, Charles F.
1962   Pre-Columbian Alloy Objects from Guerrero, Mexico. *Science* 138:1336–1337.

Bunzel, Ruth
1959   *Chichicastenango: A Guatemalan Village*. University of Washington Press, Seattle.

Byland, Bruce E., and John M. D. Pohl
1994   *In the Realm of 8 Deer: The Archaeology of the Mixtec Codices*. University of Oklahoma Press, Norman.

Cabeza de Vaca, Alvar Nuñez
1993   *Adventures in the Unknown Interior of America*. Translated and edited by Cyclone Covey. University of New Mexico Press, Albuquerque.

Cabrera C., Rubén
1988   Nuevos Resultados de Tzintzuntzan, Michoacán, en su Décima Temporada de Excavaciones. In *Primera Reunión sobre las Sociedades Prehispánicas en el Centro Occidente de México*, pp. 193–218. Instituto Nacional de Antropología e Historia, Mexico City.

Cabrero, Maria T.
1989   Rescate Arqueológico en Culiacán, Sinaloa. *Antropológicas* 3:39–65.

Camacho Ibarra, Fidel
2011   El Camino de Flores: Ritual y Conflicto en La Semana Santa Mayo. Bachelor's thesis, Escuela Nacional de Antropología e Historia, Mexico City.

Campbell, Lyle, and Ronald W. Langacker
1978   Proto-Aztecan vowels: Part 1. *International Journal of American Linguistics* 44(2):85–102.

Cancian, Frank
1965   *Economics and Prestige in a Maya Community: The Religious Cargo System in Zinacantan*. Stanford University Press, CA.

Canetti, Elias
1983   *Masa y poder*. Translation by Horts Vogel. Alianza Editorial, Muchnik, Madrid.

Carballal, Margarita, Ma. Antonieta Moguel Cos, and Estéfana J. Padilla y Yedra
1994   Informe del Rescate Puente Teófilo Noris, Plazuela Rosales, Desarrollo Urbano Tres Ríos, Culiacán, Sinaloa. Archivo Técnico de la Coordinación Nacional de Arqueología, Instituto Nacional de Antropología e Historia, Mexico City.

Cárdenas García, Efraín
1996   La tradición arquitectónica de los patios hundidos en la vertiente del Lerma medio. In *Las Cuencas del Occidente de México: Época Prehispánica*, edited by Eduardo Williams and Phil C. Weigand, pp. 157–183. El Colegio de Michoacán, Zamora.
1999   *El Bajío en el Clásico*. El Colegio de Michoacán, Zamora.

Carpenter, John P.
1996   El Ombligo en la Labor: Differentiation, Interaction and Integration in Prehispanic Sinaloa, Mexico. PhD dissertation, Department of Anthropology, University of Arizona, Tucson.
2008   El Conjunto Mortuorio de El Ombligo: Su Análisis e Interpretación. In *Excavaciones en Guasave, Sinaloa, México*. Reprinted. Los Once Ríos. Siglo XXI Editores, El Colegio de Sinaloa, Instituto Nacional de Antropología e Historia, Mexico, pp. 149–181. Originally published 1942. Anthropological Papers of the American Museum of Natural History, Vol. 38, Pt. 2. The American Museum of Natural History, New York.
2014   The Prehispanic Occupation of the Río Fuerte Valley, Sinaloa. In *Building Transnational Archaeologies/Construyendo Arqueologías Transnacionales*, edited by Elisa Villalpando and Randall H. McGuire, pp. 37–52, Arizona State Museum Archaeological Series No. 209, Arizona State Museum, University of Arizona, Tucson.
2015   The Proyecto Arqueológico Río Sahuaripa: Interaction, Integration and Cultural Dynamics in the Sonoran Serranía. Paper presented at the 80th Annual Meetings of the Society for American Archaeology, San Francisco.

Carpenter, John, and Matthew Pailes (editors)
2022   *Borderlands Histories: Ethnographic Observations and Archaeological Interpretations*. University of Utah Press, Salt Lake City.

Carpenter, John, and Guadalupe Sánchez
2007   Nuevos Hallazgos Arqueológicos en La Región del Valle del Río Fuerte, Norte de Sinaloa. *Diario de Campo* 93:18–29.
2011   Burial Practices in Viejo Cinaloa. Paper presented at the 76th Annual Meeting of the Society for American Archaeology, Sacramento, California.
2014   Continuidad Cultural en la Periferia Sur del Noroeste/Suroeste: El Periodo Protohistórico en el Sur de Sonora y el Norte de Sinaloa. In *Building Transnational Archaeologies/Construyendo Arqueologías Transnacionales*, edited by Elisa Villalpando and Randall H. McGuire, pp. 111–132, Arizona State Museum Archaeological Series No. 209, Arizona State Museum, University of Arizona, Tucson.
2016   The Sahuaripa Valley. *Archaeology Southwest* 30(3):13–14.
2022   Archaeology and Ethnohistory of the Northwestern Slope of the Sierra Madre Occidental. In *Borderlands Histories: Ethnographic Observations and Archaeological Interpretations*, edited by John P. Carpenter and Matthew Pailes, pp. 25–49. University of Utah Press, Salt Lake City.

Carpenter, John, and Guadalupe Sánchez (editors)
1997   *Prehistory of the Borderlands: Recent Research in the Archaeology of Northern Mexico and the Southern Southwest*. Arizona State Museum Archaeological Series 186, Arizona State Museum, University of Arizona, Tucson.

Carpenter, John, Guadalupe Sánchez, and Haydee Chávez
2006   *Informe Final del Proyecto Salvamento Arqueológico Álamo Dorado de la Minera Corner Bay S.A. de C.V.* Archivo Técnico de la Coordinación Nacional de Arqueología, Instituto Nacional de Antropología e Historia, Mexico City.

Carpenter, John, Guadalupe Sánchez, Patricia O. Hernández Espinoza, Claudia E. León-Romero, Andrew R. Krug, Alejandra Abrego-Rivas, M. Steven Shackley, Jeffrey Ferguson, and Matthew Pailes
2021 Recent Research in the Sahuaripa Region of Sonora, Mexico. *Kiva* 87(4):461–485.

Carpenter, John, Guadalupe Sánchez, Lizete Mercado, Alejandra Abrego, Ismael Sánchez, and Victor Hugo García
2011 *Informe Técnico Final CONACyT del Proyecto Arqueológico Norte de Sinaloa: Rutas de Intercambio (2008-2011)*. Archivo Técnico de la Coordinación Nacional de Arqueología, Instituto Nacional de Antropología e Historia, Mexico City.

Carpenter, John, Guadalupe Sánchez, Ismael Sánchez, Alejandra Abrego, Victor Hugo García, and Daniela Rodríguez
2010 *Proyecto Arqueológico Norte de Sinaloa: Rutas de Intercambio, Investigaciones en Mochicahui, Sinaloa. Informe Técnico de la Temporada 2009*. Archivo Técnico de la Coordinación Nacional de Arqueología, Instituto Nacional de Antropología e Historia, Mexico City.

Carpenter, John P., Guadalupe Sánchez, Rommel Tapia-Carrasco, Andrew R. Krug, Edson Cupa, Dakota Larrick, Carlos Eduardo Hernández, Robin R. Singleton, and Matthew C. Pailes
2023 In Search of a Borderland: Material Culture Patterns on the Southern Limits of the North American Southwest. *Journal of Field Archaeology*. DOI:10.1080/00934690.2023.2258715

Carpenter, John, and Julio C. Vicente López
2009 Fronteras Compartidas: La Conformación Social en el Norte de Sinaloa y Sur de Sonora durante el Periodo Cerámico (200 d.C.–1532 d.C.). *Espaciotiempo* 3:82–96.

Carrasco, Davíd, and Scott Sessions
2007 *Cave, City, and Eagle's Nest: An Interpretive Journey through the Mapa de Cuauhtinchan No. 2*. University of New Mexico Press, Albuquerque.

Carrasco, Pedro
1961 The Civil-Religious Hierarchy in Mesoamerican Communities: Pre-Spanish Background and Colonial Development. *American Anthropologist* 63(3):483–497.

Caseldine, Christopher R.
2020 A Reevaluation of Mesoamerica in the Southwest through the Examination of Hohokam and Northwest Mexican Relationships South of the Lower Salt River, Central Arizona. *Journal of Arizona Archaeology* 7(2):200–215.

Caso, Alfonso
1938 *Thirteen Masterpieces of Mexican Archaeology*. Editoriales Cultura y Polis, Mexico City.

Castañeda, Quetzil E., and Christopher N. Matthews (editors)
2008 *Ethnographic Archaeologies: Reflections on Stakeholders and Archaeological Practices*. AltaMira, Lanham, MD.

Castillo Badillo, Frine
2014 Nahué'ra'a: El Concepto de Cuerpo entre los Coras de Santa Teresa del Nayar. Bachelor's thesis. Universidad Nacional Autónoma de México, Mexico City.

Castillo Badillo, Frine, and Philip E. Coyle
2021 The Holy Week of Puáaxku jitsé in Santa Teresa. In *Seasons of Ceremonies: Rites and Rituals in Guatemala and Mexico*, edited by William Frej, pp. 162–195. Museum of New Mexico Press, Santa Fe.

Chacón, Enrique
2010 Una Historia de la Cultura Tubar y los Tubares: Las Barrancas de la Sierra Tarahumara. Bachelor's thesis, Escuela Nacional de Antropología e Historia, Mexico City.

Chance, John K., and William B. Taylor
1985 Cofradías and Cargos: An Historical Perspective on the Mesoamerican Civil-Religious Hierarchy. *American Ethnologist* 12(1):1–26.

Charlton, Thomas H.
1978 Teotihuacan, Tepeapulco, and Obsidian Exploitation. *Science* 200:1227–1236.

Chase-Dunn, Christopher, and Thomas D. Hall
1997 *Rise and Demise: Comparing World-Systems*. New Perspectives in Sociology. Westview Press, Boulder.

Chavero, Alfredo
1887 *México a Través de los Siglos, Tomo Primero, Historia Antigua y de la Conquista*. Dirección General de D. Vicente Riva Palacio. Espasa y Compañia, Barcelona.

Chavero, Alfredo (editor)
1979 [1892] *El Lienzo de Tlaxcala*. Editorial Innovación, Mexico City.

Chávez, Ezequiel A.
1913 *Informe del Presidente de la Junta Directiva. Escuela Internacional de Arqueología y Etnología Americanas Año Escolar de 1911 a 1912*. Müller Hermanos, Mexico City.

Chick, Garry
2002 Cultural and Behavioral Consonance in a Tlaxcalan Festival System. *Field Methods* 14(1):26–45.

Chinchilla Mazariegos, Oswaldo
2023 South Meets North: Cotzumalhuapa and the Origins of Flower World Representations at Chichen Itza. In *When East Meets West: Chichen Itza, Tula, and the Postclassic Mesoamerican World*, Vols. 1–2, edited by Travis W. Stanton, Karl A. Taube, Jeremy D. Coltman, and Nelda I. Marengo Camacho, pp. 149–165. British Archaeological Reports S3134. BAR Publishing, London.

Claessen, Henri J. M.
1979 *Antropología Política: Estudio de las Comunidades Políticas (Una Investigación Panorámica)*. Estudio Preliminar y Notas de Rolando Tamayo y Salmorán. Translation by Guillermo F. Margadant. Universidad Nacional Autónoma de México, Mexico.

Clark, Grahame
1986 *Symbols of Excellence.* Cambridge University Press, Cambridge.

Clark, John E.
1979 A Specialized Obsidian Quarry at Otumba, Mexico: Implications for the Study of Mesoamerican Obsidian Technology and Trade. *Lithic Technology* 8(3):46–49.
1985 Platforms, Bits, Punches, and Vises: A Potpourri of Mesoamerican Blade Technology. *Lithic Technology* 14(1):1–15.

Clark, John E., and Douglas D. Bryant
1997 A Technological Typology of Prismatic Blades and Debitage from Ojo de Agua, Chiapas, Mexico. *Ancient Mesoamerica* 8(1):111–136.

Clement, André
1932 Note Sur la Dureté des Haches Précolombiennes de l'Équateur et du Mexique. *Journal de la Société des Américanistes,* n.s. 24(1):85–91.

Cobb, Kim Cullen, Christopher S. Beekman, Emily Kaplan, and Thomas Lam
2022 The Craft and Use of Axe-Monies in Mesoamerica. In *Waves of Influence: Pacific Maritime Networks Connecting Mexico, Central America, and Northwestern South America,* edited by Christopher S. Beekman and Colin McEwan, pp. 347–415. Dumbarton Oaks Research Library and Collection, Washington, DC.

Coe, Michael D.
1965 Archaeological Synthesis of Southern Veracruz and Tabasco. In *Archaeology of Southern Mesoamerica,* edited by Gordon Ekholm and Ignacio Bernal, pp. 679–715. Handbook of Middle American Indians, Vol. 11, Robert Wauchope, general editor, University of Texas Press, Austin.

Coe, William R.
1959 *Piedras Negras Archaeology: Artifacts, Caches, and Burials.* University Museum, University of Pennsylvania Monographs, Philadelphia.

Coltman, Jeremy
2020 Nahua Sorcery and the Classic Maya Antecedents of the Macuiltonaleque. In *Sorcery in Mesoamerica,* edited by Jeremy D. Coltman and John M. D. Pohl, pp. 306–329. University Press of Colorado, Louisville.
2021 City of the Sun: Early Postclassic Chichen Itza (900–1150 CE) and the Legacy of Solar Ideology in Late Postclassic Yucatan and Central Mexico. PhD dissertation, Department of Anthropology, University of California, Riverside.
2023 The Flower World of Chichen Itza. In *When East Meets West: Chichen Itza, Tula, and the Postclassic Mesoamerican World,* Vols. 1–2, edited by Travis W. Stanton, Karl A. Taube, Jeremy D. Coltman, and Nelda I. Marengo Camacho, pp. 167–201. British Archaeological Reports S3134. BAR Publishing, London.

Coltman, Jeremy D., Guilhem Olivier, and Gerard van Bussel
2020 An Effigy of Tezcatlipoca from the Bilimek Collection in Vienna. *Ancient Mesoamerica* 31(2):343–359.

Coltman, Jeremy, Karl Taube, Michael Mathiowetz, and Polly Schaafsma
2008 The Darts of Dawn: The Tlahuizcalpantecuhtli Venus Complex in the Iconography of Mesoamerica and the American Southwest. Paper presented at the 73rd Annual Meeting of the Society for American Archaeology, Vancouver, Canada.

Colwell-Chanthaphonh, Chip, and T. J. Ferguson (editors)
2008 *Collaboration in Archaeological Practice: Engaging Descendant Communities.* AltaMira, Lanham, MD.

Couoh Hernández, Lourdes R., and Jorge A. Talavera González
2017 Los Cráneos Decapitados de Chacalilla, Nayarit (900–1350 d.C.): Análisis de Colágeno Residual para Conocer el Orden de su Depósito Funerario y sus Implicaciones Bioarqueológicas. *Arqueología* 52:137–153.

Coyle, Philip E.
1998 The Customs of Our Ancestors: Cora Religious Conversion and Millennialism, 2000–1722. *Ethnohistory* 45(3):509–542.
2000 "To Join the Waters": Indexing Metonymies of Territoriality in Cora Ritual. *Journal of the Southwest* 42(1):119–128.
2001 *Náyari History, Politics, and Violence: From Flowers to Ash.* University of Arizona Press, Tucson.
2008 La Cacería de Venado de los Uto-nahuas Centrales. In *Por los Caminos del Maíz: Mito y Ritual en la Periferia Septentrional de Mesoamérica,* edited by Johannes Neurath, pp. 294–335. Fondo de Cultura Económica and Consejo Nacional para la Cultura y las Artes, Mexico City.

Coyle, Philip E., and Paul M. Liffman (editors)
2000 Ritual and Historical Territoriality of the Náyari and Wixárika Peoples. *Journal of the Southwest* 42(1). The Southwest Center, University of Arizona, Tucson.

Craumassel, Chantal
2013 El sistema de cargos en San Bernardino de Milpillas Chico, Durango. *Culturales,* epoca II 1(1):69–106.

Crespo, Ana M.
1991 El Recinto Ceremonial de El Cerrito. In *Querétaro Prehispánico,* edited by Ana M. Crespo and Rosa Brambila, pp. 163–223. Instituto Nacional de Antropología e Historia, Mexico City.

Crider, Destiny L.
2011 Epiclassic and Early Postclassic Interaction in Central Mexico as Evidenced by Decorated Pottery. PhD dissertation, School of Human Evolution and Social Change, Arizona State University, Tempe.

Crown, Patricia L.
1994 *Ceramics & Ideology: Salado Polychrome Pottery.* University of New Mexico Press, Albuquerque.
2016 Just Macaws: A Review for the U.S. Southwest/Mexican Northwest. *Kiva* 82(4):331–363.

Crown, Patricia L. (editor)
2020 *The House of the Cylinder Jars: Room 28 in Pueblo Bonito, Chaco Canyon.* University of New Mexico Press, Albuquerque.

Crown, Patricia L., and W. Jeffrey Hurst
2009 Evidence of Cacao Use in the Prehispanic American Southwest. *Proceedings of the National Academy*

of Sciences of the United States of America 106: 2110–2113.

Cruz Antillón, Rafael, and Timothy D. Maxwell (editors)
2018 *La Cultura Casas Grandes*. Secretaria de Cultura de Chihuahua, Instituto Nacional de Antropología e Historia, and Gobierno del Estado de Chihuahua, Chihuahua.

Cushing, Frank H.
1883 My Adventures in Zuni. *Century Magazine* 25: 500–511.

Dakin, Karen
2017 Western and Central Nahua Dialects: Possible Influences from Contact with Cora and Huichol. In *Language Contact and Change in Mesoamerica and Beyond*, edited by Karen Dakin, Claudia Parodi, and Natalie Operstein, pp. 264–300. John Benjamins Publishing, Philadelphia, PA.

Darling, J. Andrew
1993 Notes on Obsidian Sources of the Southern Sierra Madre Occidental. *Ancient Mesoamerica* 4(2): 245–253.

Darling, J. Andrew, and Frances M. Hayashida
1995 Compositional Analysis of the Huitzila and La Lobera Obsidian Sources in the Southern Sierra-Madre Occidental, Mexico. *Journal of Radioanalytical and Nuclear Chemistry* 196(2):245–254.

Davies, Nigel
1977 *The Toltecs Until the Fall of Tula*. Civilization of the American Indian Series. University of Oklahoma Press, Norman.

Dean, Jeffrey S. (editor)
2000 *Salado*. Amerind Foundation, Dragoon, AZ, and University of New Mexico Press, Albuquerque.

Dean, Jeffrey S., and John C. Ravesloot
1993 The Chronology of Cultural Interaction in the Gran Chichimeca. In *Culture and Contact: Charles C. Di Peso's Gran Chichimeca*, edited by Anne I. Woosley and John C. Ravesloot, pp. 83–103. Amerind Foundation, Dragoon, AZ, and University of New Mexico Press, Albuquerque, NM.

del Barrio, Francisco
1990 [1604] Relación de Cosas Sucedidas en las Serranías de Choras y Tepehuanes e de las Costumbres y Ritos destas Naciones y de la Disposición y Sitios de sus Tierras. In *Los Albores de un Nuevo Mundo: Siglos XVI y XVII. Colección de Documentos para la Historia de Nayarit I*, edited by Thomas Calvo, pp. 256–273. Universidad de Guadalajara and Centro de Estudios Mexicanos y Centroamericanos, Mexico City.

de los Ríos, Magdalena
2004 *Reporte Técnico del Fechamiento de una Muestra de Carbón (INAH-2108) Procedente de la Localidad de San Felipe Aztatán, Nayarit*. Laboratorio de Radiocarbono, Archivo Técnico, Subdirección de Laboratorios y Apoyo Académico del Instituto Nacional de Antropología e Historia, Mexico City.

DeMarrais, Elizabeth, Luis J. Castillo, and Timothy Earle
2002 Ideology, Materialization, and Power Strategies. In *Bronze Age Economies: The Beginnings of Political Economies*, edited by Timothy Earle, pp. 348–385. Westview Press, Cambridge, MA.

de Sahagún, Bernardino
1950–1982 *Florentine Codex: General History of the Things of New Spain*. Vols. 1–12. Translated from the Aztec into English by Arthur J. O. Anderson and Charles E. Dibble. School of American Research, Santa Fe, NM, and University of Utah Press, Salt Lake City.

De Walt, Billie R.
1975 Changes in the Cargo Systems of Mesoamerica. *Anthropological Quarterly* 48(2):87–105.

Diehl, Richard A.
1993 The Toltec Horizon in Mesoamerica: New Perspectives on an Old Issue. In *Latin American Horizons*, edited by Don S. Rice, pp. 263–294. Dumbarton Oaks Research Library and Collection, Washington, DC.

Diguet, M. León
1903 Contribution a l'ethnographie Précolombienne du Mexique: le Chimalhuacan et ses Populations avant la Conquête Espagnole. *Journal Société des Américanistes de Paris*, n.s. 1(1):1–57.

Dingwall, Erik J.
1931 *Artificial Cranial Deformation: A Contribution to the Study of Ethnic Mutilations*. John Bale, Sons & Danielsson, London, UK.

Di Peso, Charles C.
1974 *Casas Grandes: A Fallen Trading Center of the Gran Chichimeca*. Vols. 1–3. Northland Press, Flagstaff, AZ.
1979 Prehistory: Southern Periphery. In *Southwest*, edited by Alfonso Ortiz, pp. 152–161. Handbook of North American Indians, Vol. 9, William C. Sturtevant, general editor. Government Printing Office, Smithsonian Institution, Washington, DC.

Di Peso, Charles C., John B. Rinaldo, and Gloria Fenner
1974 *Casas Grandes: A Fallen Trading Center of the Gran Chichimeca*, Vols. 4–8. Northland Press, Flagstaff, AZ.

Dirst, Victoria A.
1979 A Prehistoric Frontier in Sonora. PhD dissertation, Department of Anthropology, University of Arizona, Tucson.

Domenici, Davide, and Laura Laurencich Minelli
2014 Domingo de Betanzos' Gifts to Pope Clement VII in 1532–1533: Tracking the Early History of some Mexican Objects and Codices in Italy. *Estudios de Cultura Náhuatl* 47:169–209.

Dongoske, Kurt E., Mark Aldenderfer, and Karen Doebner (editors)
2000 *Working Together: Native Americans & Archaeologists*. Society for American Archaeology, Washington, DC.

Doyel, David E.
2022 Further Remembrances of David Wilcox: Itinerant Scholar and Archaeologist Extraordinaire. *Kiva* 73(2):10–12.

Doyle, James A.
2016 Creation Narratives on Ancient Maya Codex-Style Ceramics in the Metropolitan Museum. *Metropolitan Museum Journal* 51:42–63.

Doyle, James, John W. Hoopes, and David Mora-Marín
2021 Shining Stones and Brilliant Regalia: Connections

between Classic Mesoamerica and Central America and Colombia. In *Pre-Columbian Central America, Colombia, and Ecuador: Toward an Integrated Approach*, edited by Colin McEwan and John W. Hoopes, pp. 89–99. Dumbarton Oaks Research Library and Collection, Washington, DC.

Drennan, Robert D., Philip T. Fitzgibbons, and Heinz Dehn
1990 Imports and Exports in Classic Mesoamerican Political Economy: The Tehuacán Valley and the Teotihuacan Obsidian Industry. In *Research in Economic Anthropology*, Vol. 12, edited by Barry L. Isaac, pp. 177–199. JAI Press, Greenwich, CT.

Duff, Andrew I.
2002 *Western Pueblo Identities: Regional Interaction, Migration, and Transformation*. University of Arizona Press, Tucson.

Dundes, Alan
1997 *From Game to War and Other Psychoanalytic Essays on Folklore*. University of Kentucky Press, Lexington.

Duverger, Christian
1998 Coamiles, Nayarit: Hacia una Periodización. *Antropología e Historia del Occidente de México*. Tomo I:609–628. Memorias de la XXIV Mesa Redonda de la Sociedad Mexicana de Antropología. Universidad Nacional Autónoma de México, Mexico City.

Duverger, Christian, and Daniel Levine
1993 *Informe Relativo a la Exploración Arqueológica del Sitio de Coamiles, Municipio de Tuxpan, Estado de Nayarit*. Technical Report, Archivo Técnico de la Sección de Arqueología, Centro Instituto Nacional de Antropología e Historia, Nayarit, Tepic.

Duverger, Christian, Daniel Levine, Claude Ney, Pierre Guibert, Max Schvoerer, and W.G. Mook
1993 Approche chronologique du site de Coamiles, Nayarit (Mexique). Datations par Thermoluminescence et par Carbone 14. *Journal de la Société des Américanistes* 79:105–139.

Duwe, Samuel
2020 *Tewa Worlds: An Archaeological History of Being and Becoming in the Pueblo Southwest*. University of Arizona Press, Tucson.

Duwe, Samuel, and Robert W. Preucel (editors)
2019 *The Continuous Path: Pueblo Movement and the Archaeology of Becoming*. Amerind Studies in Anthropology. University of Arizona Press, Tucson.

Earle, Timothy K.
1997 *How Chiefs Come to Power: The Political Economy in Prehistory*. Stanford University Press, Stanford.
2002 *Bronze Age Economics: The Beginnings of Political Economies*. Westview Press, Boulder.

Easby, Dudley T., Jr.
1962 Two "South American" Metal Techniques Found Recently in Western Mexico. *American Antiquity* 28(1):19–24.

Edwards, Clinton R.
1969 Possibilities of Pre-Columbian Maritime Contacts among New World Civilizations. In *Pre-Columbian Contact within Nuclear America*, edited by J. Charles Kelley and Carroll L. Riley, pp. 3–10. Mesoamerican Studies 4, University Museum Research Record. Southern Illinois University Press, Carbondale.

Ekern, Stener
2011 The Production of Autonomy: Leadership and Community in Mayan Guatemala. *Journal of Latin American Studies* 43(1):93–119.

Ekholm, Gordon F.
1939 Results of an Archaeological Survey of Sonora and Northern Sinaloa. *Revista Mexicana de Antropología* 3(1):7–11.
1940 The Archaeology of Northern and Western Mexico. In *The Maya and Their Neighbors*, edited by Clarence L. Hay, Ralph Linton, Samuel K. Lothrop, Harry L. Shapiro, and George C. Vaillant, pp. 307–320. D. Appleton-Century, New York.
1942 *Excavations at Guasave, Sinaloa, Mexico*. Anthropological Papers of the American Museum of Natural History, Vol. 38, Pt. 2. American Museum of Natural History, New York.
1944 *Excavations at Tampico and Panuco in the Huasteca, Mexico*. Anthropological Papers of the American Museum of Natural History, Vol. 38, Pt. 5. American Museum of Natural History, New York.
1947 Recent Archaeological Work in Sonora and Northern Sinaloa. *Proceedings of the Twenty-seventh International Congress of Americanists, 1939*, pp. 69–73. Mexico City.
2008 *Excavaciones en Guasave, Sinaloa*. Reprinted. Los Once Ríos. Siglo XXI Editores, El Colegio de Sinaloa, Instituto Nacional de Antropología e Historia, Mexico. Originally published 1942. Anthropological Papers of the American Museum of Natural History, Vol. 38, Pt. 2. American Museum of Natural History, New York.

Eliade, Mircea
1994 *Imágenes y Símbolos*. Translation by Carmen Castro. Obras Maestras del Pensamiento Contemporáneo 85. Planeta-Agostini, Barcelona.

Englehardt, Joshua D., Verenice Y. Heredia Espinoza, and Christopher S. Beekman (editors).
2020 *Ancient West Mexicos: Time, Space, and Diversity*. University Press of Florida, Gainesville.

ESRI
2013 ArcGIS 10.1 Resource Center. Electronic document, http://resources.arcgis.com/en/help/main/10.1/index.html, accessed February 11, 2024.

Evans, Susan T.
2008 *Ancient Mexico & Central America: Archaeology and Culture History*, second edition. Thames & Hudson, London.

Evers, Larry, and Felipe S. Molina
1987 *Yaqui Deer Songs/Maso Bwikam*. Sun Tracks and University of Arizona Press, Tucson.

Fahmel Beyer, Bernd
1988 *Mesoamérica Toltecas: Sus Cerámicas de Comercio Principales*. Universidad Nacional Autónoma de México, Mexico City.

Fargher, Lane F., Richard E. Blanton, and Verenice Y. Heredia Espinoza
2010   Egalitarian Ideology and Political Power in Prehispanic Central Mexico: The Case of Tlaxcallan. *Latin American Antiquity* 21(3):227–251.

Fargher, Lane F., Richard E. Blanton, Verenice Y. Heredia Espinoza, John Millhauser, Nezahualcoyotl Xiuhtecutli, and Lisa Overholtzer
2011   Tlaxcallan: The Archaeology of an Ancient Republic in the New World. *Antiquity* 85(327):172–186.

Faugère, Brigitte, and Christopher S. Beekman
2020   Gods, Ancestors, and Human Beings. In *Anthropomorphic Representations in Highland Mexico: Gods, Ancestors, and Human Beings*, edited by Brigitte Faugère and Christopher S. Beekman, pp. 3–28. University Press of Colorado, Louisville.

Faust, Katherine A., and Kim N. Richter (editors)
2015   *The Huasteca: Culture, History, and Interregional Exchange.* University of Oklahoma Press, Norman.

Favarel-Garrigues, Isabelle
1995   La Céramique de Coamiles (Nayarit, Mexique) Typologie, Chronologie. PhD dissertation, École des Hautes Études en Sciences Sociales, Paris.

Ferguson, T. J.
2007   Zuni Traditional History and Cultural Geography. In *Zuni Origins: Toward a New Synthesis of Southwestern Archaeology*, edited by David A. Gregory and David R. Wilcox, pp. 377–403. University of Arizona Press, Tucson.

Ferguson, T. J., and Chip Colwell-Chanthaphonh
2006   *History is in the Land: Multivocal Tribal Traditions in Arizona's San Pedro Valley.* University of Arizona Press, Tucson.

Field, Margaret
2018   Sacred Water and Water-dwelling Serpents: What can Yuman Oral Tradition Tell Us about Yuman Prehistory? *Journal of the Southwest* 60(1):2–25.

Fikes, Jay C.
1985   Huichol Indian Identity and Adaptation. PhD dissertation, Department of Anthropology, University of Michigan, Ann Arbor.
1993   *Carlos Castaneda, Academic Opportunism and the Psychedelic Sixties.* Millenia Press, Victoria, British Columbia.
2011   *Unknown Huichol: Shamans and Immortals, Allies Against Chaos.* AltaMira, Lanham, MD.

Fish, Suzanne K., and Paul R. Fish (editors)
2007   *The Hohokam Millennium.* School for Advanced Research Press, Santa Fe.

Flannery, Kent V., and Joyce Marcus
1983   *The Cloud People: Divergent Evolution of the Zapotec and Mixtec Civilizations.* Academic Press, New York.

Flores-Marcial, Xochitl M.
2015   A History of Guelaguetza in Zapotec Communities of the Central Valleys of Oaxaca, 16th Century to Present. PhD dissertation, Department of History, University of California, Los Angeles.

Flores Montes de Oca, Berenice
2015   *Análisis de Dos Incrustaciones de Contexto Funerario de La Pitayera, Ahuacatlán, Nayarit.* Archivo Técnico de la Dirección de Salvamento Arqueológico, Instituto Nacional de Antropología e Historia, Mexico City.

Forest, Marion, Elsa Jadot, and Juliette Testard
2020   Mazapan-style Figurines at El Palacio and Their Significance for Early Postclassic Regional Interactions in Northern Michoacán. *Ancient Mesoamerica* 31(3):431–450.

Foster, Michael S.
1986a   The Mesoamerican Connection: A View from the South. In *Ripples in the Chichimec Sea: New Considerations of Southwestern-Mesoamerican Interactions*, edited by Frances J. Mathien and Randall H. McGuire, pp. 55–69. Southern Illinois University Press, Carbondale.
1986b   The Weicker Site: A Loma San Gabriel Hamlet in Durango, Mexico. *Journal of Field Archaeology* 13(1):7–19.
1995   The Chalchihuites Chronological Sequences: A View from the West Coast of Mexico. In *Arqueología del Norte y del Occidente de México: Homenaje al Doctor J. Charles Kelley*, edited by Barbro Dahlgren and Ma. Dolores Soto de Arechavaleta, pp. 67–92. Universidad Nacional Autónoma de México, Mexico City.
1999   The Aztatlán Tradition of West and Northwest Mexico and Casas Grandes: Speculations on the Medio Period Florescence. In *The Casas Grandes World*, edited by Curtis F. Schaafsma and Carroll L. Riley, pp. 149–163. University of Utah Press, Salt Lake City.
2000   The Archaeology of Durango. In *Greater Mesoamerica: The Archaeology of West and Northwest Mexico*, edited by Michael S. Foster and Shirley Gorenstein, pp. 197–219. University of Utah Press, Salt Lake City.
2017a   Physical Setting. In *The Archaeology, Ethnohistory, and Environment of the Marismas Nacionales: The Prehistoric Pacific Littoral of Sinaloa and Nayarit, Mexico*, edited by Michael S. Foster, pp. 10–37. University of Utah Press, Salt Lake City.
2017b   Ceramics. In *The Archaeology, Ethnohistory, and Environment of the Marismas Nacionales: The Prehistoric Pacific Littoral of Sinaloa and Nayarit, Mexico*, edited by Michael S. Foster, pp. 143–207. University of Utah Press, Salt Lake City.

Foster, Michael S. (editor)
2017   *The Archaeology, Ethnohistory, and Environment of the Marismas Nacionales: The Prehistoric Pacific Littoral of Sinaloa and Nayarit, Mexico.* University of Utah Press, Salt Lake City.

Foster, Michael S., and Shirley Gorenstein (editors)
2000   *Greater Mesoamerica: The Archaeology of West and Northwest Mexico.* University of Utah Press, Salt Lake City.

Foster, Michael S., and Stuart D. Scott
2017   Chronology. In *The Archaeology, Ethnohistory, and Environment of the Marismas Nacionales: The

Prehistoric Pacific Littoral of Sinaloa and Nayarit, Mexico, edited by Michael S. Foster, pp. 52–69. University of Utah Press, Salt Lake City.

Foster, Michael S., and Phil C. Weigand (editors)
1985   *The Archaeology of West and Northwest Mesoamerica*. Westview Press, Boulder.

Fowler, William R.
1989   *The Cultural Evolution of Ancient Nahua Civilizations: The Pipil-Nicarao of Central America*. University of Oklahoma Press, Norman.
2019   The Pipil Migrations in Mesoamerica: History, Identity, and Politics. In *Migrations in Late Mesoamerica*, edited by Christopher S. Beekman, pp. 285–326. University Press of Florida, Gainesville.

Fowles, Severin M.
2010   The Southwest School of Landscape Archaeology. *Annual Review of Anthropology* 39:453–468.
2013   *An Archaeology of Doings: Secularism and the Study of Pueblo Religion*. School for Advanced Research Press, Santa Fe.

Fowles, Severin, and Barbara J. Mills
2017   On History in Southwest Archaeology. In *The Oxford Handbook of Southwest Archaeology*, edited by Barbara J. Mills and Severin Fowles, pp. 3–71. Oxford University Press, New York.

Frankenstein, Susan, and Michael J. Rowlands
1978   The Internal Structure and Regional Context of Early Iron Age Society in Southwestern Germany. *Bulletin of the Institute of Archaeology* 15:73–112.

Freidel, David A., Arlen F. Chase, Anne S. Dowd, and Jerry Murdock (editors)
2017   *Maya E Groups: Calendars, Astronomy, and Urbanism in the Early Lowlands*. University Press of Florida, Gainesville.

Friedman, Jonathan
1998   *System, Structure, and Contradiction: The Evolution of Asiatic Social Formations*. AltaMira, Walnut Creek, CA.

Frisbie, Theodore R.
1978   High Status Burials in the Greater Southwest: An Interpretive Synthesis. In *Across the Chichimec Sea: Papers in Honor of J. Charles Kelley*, edited by Carroll L. Riley and Basil C. Hedrick, pp. 202–227. Southern Illinois University Press, Carbondale.

Furst, Jill L.
1978   *Codex Vindobonensis Mexicanus I: A Commentary*. Institute for Mesoamerican Studies No. 4. State University of New York at Albany, Albany.
1982   Skeletonization in Mixtec Art: A Re-evaluation. In *The Art and Iconography of Late Post-Classic Central Mexico*, edited by Elizabeth H. Boone, pp. 207–225. Dumbarton Oaks Research Library and Collection, Washington, DC.

Furst, Peter T.
1972   *Flesh of the Gods: The Ritual Use of Hallucinogens*. Praeger, New York.

Furst, Peter T., and Stuart D. Scott
1975   La Escalera del Padre Sol: Un Paralelo Etnográfico-Arqueológico desde El Occidente de Mexico. *Boletín* 12:13–20.

Galinier, Jacques
1997   *The World Below: Body and Cosmos in Otomí Indian Ritual*. University Press of Colorado, Boulder.

Gálvez, Héctor
1967a   *Informe de Trabajo de la Delegación de Monumentos Prehispánicos en Nayarit y Sinaloa*. Archivo Técnico de la Coordinación Nacional de Arqueología, Instituto Nacional de Antropología e Historia, Mexico City.
1967b   *Informe de Actividades de la Zona del Noroeste durante los Meses de Mayo, Junio y Julio*. Archivo Técnico de la Coordinación Nacional de Arqueología, Instituto Nacional de Antropología e Historia, Mexico City.
1968   *Informe Preliminar de los Trabajos Realizados en el Área Arqueológica de Culiacán, Sinaloa, Sitio Ejido Los Mezcales*. Archivo Técnico de la Coordinación Nacional de Arqueología, Instituto Nacional de Antropología e Historia, Mexico City.

Gámez Eternod, Lorena
2004   Sucesión Cultural Prehispánica en la Llanura Deltaica del Río Acaponeta (Nayarit). Master's thesis. Escuela Nacional de Antropología e Historia, Mexico City.

Gámez Eternod, Lorena, and Mauricio Garduño Ambriz
1997   La Destrucción del Patrimonio Arqueológico en el Sector Noroccidental de Nayarit. *UNIR* 14:10–17. Revista de la Universidad Autónoma de Nayarit, Tepic.
2001   Salvamento Arqueológico en la Planicie Costera del Sur de Sinaloa. *Memoria del Primer Congreso de Cronistas de Sinaloa*, pp. 15–24. Dirección de Investigación y Fomento de Cultura Regional de Sinaloa, Culiacán.
2003   *Rescate Arqueológico CECYTEN, Plantel 06 San Felipe Aztatán, Municipio de Tecuala (Nayarit)*. Reporte Técnico de los Trabajos de Sondeo/Análisis de Materiales Arqueológicos. Technical report, Archivo Técnico de la Sección de Arqueología, Centro Instituto Nacional de Antropología e Historia, Nayarit, Tepic.

Gamio, Manuel
1910   Los Monumentos Arqueológicos de las Inmediaciones de Chalchihuites, Zacatecas. Estudio Arqueológico. In *Anales del Museo Nacional de Arqueología, Historia, y Etnografía*, Época 3, Tomo 2, pp. 467–492. Museo Nacional de México, Mexico City.
1922   *La Población del Valle de Teotihuacán: El Medio en que se ha Desarrollado; Su Evolución Étnica y Social; Iniciativas para Procurar su Mejoramiento*. Dirección de Talleres Gráficos, Secretaría de Educación Pública, Mexico City.

Ganot Rodríguez, Jaime, and Alejandro A. Peschard Fernández
1995   The Archaeological Site of El Cañón del Molino, Durango, México. In *The Gran Chichimeca: Essays*

on the Archaeology and Ethnohistory of Northern Mesoamerica, edited by Jonathan E. Reyman, pp. 146–178. Avebury, Aldershot, UK.
1997 Aztatlán: Apuntes para la Historia y Arqueología de Durango. Gobierno del Estado de Durango and Secretaría de Educación, Cultura y Deporte, Durango, Mexico.

García Moreno, Cristina
2008 Interacciones Southwest/Noroeste y Mesoamérica. Proyecto Arqueológico Sur de Sonora. Proyecto Presentado al Consejo de Arqueología. Archivo Técnico, Instituto Nacional de Antropología e Historia, Mexico City.
2013a Informe de la Sexta Temporada. Interacciones Southwest/Noroeste y Mesoamérica, Proyecto Arqueológico Sur de Sonora. Archivo Técnico, Instituto Nacional de Antropología e Historia, Mexico City.
2013b Interacciones Culturales en el Valle de Ónavas. Paper presented at the Primer Congreso Internacional Carl Lumholtz, Creel, Chihuahua, Mexico.
2014 Cultural Interactions in Ónavas Valley, Sonora, México. Paper presented at the 79th Annual Meeting of the Society for American Archaeology, Austin, TX.

García Moreno, Cristina, Patricia O. Hernández Espinoza, and James T. Watson
2021 Childhood and Identity Acquisition in the Late Prehispanic Ónavas Valley, Sonora, Mexico. *Childhood in the Past* 14(1):38–54.

García Moreno, Cristina, and Emiliano Melgar Tísoc
2021 La Turquesa del Valle de Ónavas. *Noroeste de México* 4(11–40).

García Zaldúa, Johan S.
2007 Arqueometalurgia del Occidente de México: La Cuenca de Sayula, Jalisco. Como punto de Conjunción de Tradiciones Metalúrgicas Precolombinas. Bachelor's thesis, Universidad Autónoma de Guadalajara, Guadalajara, Mexico.
2016 Nuevos Conocimientos sobre la Metalurgia Antigua del Occidente de México: Filiación Cultural y Cronología en la Cuenca de Sayula, Jalisco. *Latin American Antiquity* 27(2):184–206.

Garduño Ambriz, Mauricio
2005 Salvamento Arqueológico en el Ejido Valle de la Urraca, Municipio de Acaponeta (Nayarit). Propuesta de Trabajo y Presupuesto. Archivo Técnico de la Sección de Arqueología, Centro Instituto Nacional de Antropología e Historia, Nayarit, Tepic.
2006 Investigaciónes Arqueológicas en el Cerro de Coamiles, Nayarit. Reporte Técnico Final de la Primera Temporada de Campo 2005. Technical report, Archivo Técnico, Centro Instituto Nacional de Antropología e Historia, Nayarit, Tepic.
2007 Arqueología de Rescate en la Cuenca Inferior del Río Acaponeta. *Diario de Campo: Boletín Interno de los Investigadores del Area de Antropología* 92:36–52. El Consejo Nacional para la Cultura y las Artes and Instituto Nacional de Antropología e Historia, Mexico City.
2008 Investigaciones Arqueológicas en el Cerro de Coamiles, Nayarit. Reporte Técnico Final/Temporada de Campo 2007. Technical report, Archivo Técnico de la Sección de Arqueología, Centro Instituto Nacional de Antropología e Historia, Nayarit, Tepic.
2009 Descubren Observatorio Astronómico en Coamiles. *Arqueología Mexicana* 17(98):12.
2012a Sobre la "Tradición Aztatlán," de John Pohl. *Arqueología Mexicana* (19)117:6–7.
2012b Cerro de Coamiles, Nayarit: Un Sitio Emblemático Aztatlán del Septentrión Costero Mesoamericano. *Diario de Campo (Nueva Epoca): Boletín Interno de los Investigadores del Area de Antropología* 10:24–32. Coordinación Nacional de Antropología and Instituto Nacional de Antropología e Historia, Mexico City.
2013a Análisis de Materiales de Excavación del Proyecto Arqueológico Coamiles (2005-2010). Reporte Técnico del Análisis Ceramica/ Temporadas 2007 y 2008. Technical report, Archivo Técnico, Centro Instituto Nacional de Antropología e Historia, Nayarit, Tepic.
2013b Excepcional Vasija Estilo Códice Aztatlán. *Arqueología Mexicana* 21(122):10.
2013c Localizan Petrograbado Vinculado a la Red Aztatlán. *Arqueologia Mexicana* 19(120):10.
2014 San Felipe Aztatán: Nuevos Datos sobre la Iconografia del Complejo Cultural Aztatlán (850/900–1350 d.C.) de las Tierras Bajas Noroccidentales de Nayarit. Paper presented at the 79th Annual Meeting of the Society for American Archaeology, Austin, TX.
2015 San Felipe Aztatán: Arqueología de Rescate en la Zona Nuclear Costera Aztatlán. *Revista Occidente del Museo Nacional de Antropología* (June):1–19.
2016 Análisis Iconográfico Preliminar de una Vasija Estilo Códice Aztatlán Procedente de la Cuenca Inferior del Río Acaponeta, Nayarit. Manuscript in possession of author.
2019 Cerro de Coamiles, Nayarit: Arquitectura y Simbolismo de un Centro Ceremonial Aztatlán. In *Aztatlán: Interacción y Cambio Social en el Occidente de México ca. 850–1350 d.C.*, edited by Laura Solar Valverde and Ben A. Nelson, pp. 89–114. El Colegio de Michoacán, Zamora, and Arizona State University, Tempe.
2022 Nuevos Datos sobre la ocupación Aztatlán en las Tierras Bajas Noroccidentales de Nayarit. *Arqueología Mexicana* 177:11.

Garduño Ambriz, Mauricio, and Lorena Gámez Eternod
2005 Programa Emergente de Rescate Arqueológico en San Felipe Aztatán, Municipio de Tecuala (Nayarit). Informe Técnico Final/Trabajos de Sondeo Arqueológico. Technical report, Archivo Técnico de la Sección de Arqueología, Centro Instituto Nacional de Antropología e Historia, Nayarit, Tepic.

Garduño Ambriz, Mauricio, Lorena Gámez, and Manuel Pérez
2000 Salvamento Arqueológico en la Franja Costera Noroccidental de Nayarit. *UNIR: Revista de la Universidad Autónoma de Nayarit* 23–24:4–12.

Garduño Ambriz, Mauricio, and Daniel Pierce
2022 Trade, Production, and Cultural Integration at Cerro de Coamiles, Nayarit. *Journal of Archaeological Science: Reports* 43:103480.

Garduño Ambriz, Mauricio, and Miguel Angel Vázquez del Mercado
2005 Investigaciones Arqueológicas en el Cerro de Coamiles, Nayarit. *Boletín Diario de Campo* 81:65–75. Coordinación Nacional de Antropología, Instituto Nacional de Antropología e Historia, Mexico.

George, Richard J., Stephen Plog, Adam S. Watson, Kari L. Schmidt, Brendan J. Culleton, Thomas K. Harper, Patricia A. Gilman, et al.
2018 Archaeogenomic Evidence from the Southwestern US Points to a pre-Hispanic Scarlet Macaw Breeding Colony. *Proceedings of the National Academy of Sciences of the United States of America* 115(35): 8740–8745.

Gifford, E. W.
1950 *Surface Archaeology of Ixtlan del Rio, Nayarit.* University of California Publications in American Archaeology and Ethnology 43(2):183–302. University of California Press, Berkeley.

Gill, George W.
1971 The Prehistoric Inhabitants of Northern Coastal Nayarit: Skeletal Analysis and Description of Burials. PhD dissertation, Department of Anthropology, University of Kansas, Lawrence.
1974 Toltec-Period Burial Customs within the Marismas Nacionales of Western Mexico. In *The Archaeology of West Mexico*, edited by Betty B. Bell, pp. 83–105. Sociedad de Estudios Avanzados del Occidente de México, Ajijic, Mexico.

Gillespie, Susan D.
2011 Toltecs, Tula, and Chichén Itzá: The Development of an Archaeological Myth. In *Twin Tollans: Chichén Itzá, Tula, and the Epiclassic to Early Postclassic Mesoamerican World*, revised edition, edited by Jeff K. Kowalski and Cynthia Kristan-Graham, pp. 61–92. Dumbarton Oaks Research Library and Collection, Washington, DC.

Gilman, Patricia A., and Steven A. LeBlanc
2017 *Mimbres Life and Society: The Mattocks Site of Southwestern New Mexico.* University of Arizona Press, Tucson.

Gilman, Patricia A., Marc Thompson, and Kristina C. Wyckoff.
2014 Ritual Change and the Distant: Mesoamerican Iconography, Scarlet Macaws, and Great Kivas in the Mimbres Region of Southwestern New Mexico. *American Antiquity* 79(1):90–107.
2019 The Diffusion of Scarlet Macaws and Mesoamerican Motifs into the Mimbres Region. In *Interaction and Connectivity in the Greater Southwest*, edited by Karen G. Harry and Barbara J. Roth, pp. 82–114. University Press of Colorado, Louisville.

Glascock, Michael D.
2007 *X-Ray Fluorescence Analysis of Obsidian Artifacts from Chacalilla, Nayarit.* Archaeometry Laboratory/Research Reactor Center. University of Missouri, Columbia.

Glascock, Michael D., Phil C. Weiland, Rodrigo Esparza López, Michael A. Ohnersorgen, Mauricio Garduño Ambriz, Joseph B. Mountjoy, and J. Andrew Darling
2010 Geochemical Characterization of Obsidian Sources in Western Mexico: The Sources of Jalisco, Nayarit, and Zacatecas. In *Crossing the Straights: Prehistoric Obsidian Source Exploitation Along the Pacific Rim*, edited by Yaroslav V. Kuzmin and Michael D. Glascock, pp. 201–217. British Archaeological Reports International Series S2152, Archaeopress, Oxford, UK.

Glassow, Michael A.
1967 The Ceramics of Huistla, a West Mexican Site in the Municipality of Etzatlán, Jalisco. *American Antiquity* 32(1):64–83.

Glowacki, Donna M.
2015 *Living and Leaving: A Social History of Regional Depopulation in Thirteenth-Century Mesa Verde.* University of Arizona Press, Tucson.

Glowacki, Donna M., and Scott Van Keuren (editors)
2011 *Religious Transformation in the Late Pre-Hispanic Pueblo World.* Amerind Studies in Archaeology. University of Arizona Press, Tucson.

Gómez Ambríz, Emmanuel A.
2013 La Iconografía Cerámica Chalchihuiteña: Análisis Iconográfico de las Imágenes Centrales en Espiral. Bachelor's thesis, Escuela Nacional de Antropología e Historia, Mexico City.
2018 En Busca del Sentido: La Arqueosemiótica en la Discusión del Problema Aztatlán. Análisis Semiótico de Vasos Trípodes Policromos de Sinaloa y Durango. Master's thesis, Escuela Nacional de Antropología e Historia, Mexico City.

Gómez Ambríz, Emmanuel Alejandro, and Cinthya I. Vidal Aldana
2014 Vasijas y Barro, Pipas y Humo: Objetos Cerámicos e Ideología en el Sur de Sinaloa. In *De Mazatlán a Las Labradas: Historia y Arqueología*, edited by Gilberto López Castillo, Luis Alfonso Grave Tirado, and Víctor Joel Santos Ramírez, pp. 195–216. H. Ayuntamiento de Mazatlán and Centro Instituto Nacional de Antropología e Historia, Sinaloa, Culiacán.

González Barajas, María de Lourdes, and José Carlos Beltrán Medina
2007 Arqueología de la Bahía de Banderas. In *El Occidente de México: Perspectivas Multidisciplinarias*, edited by Rosa H. Yáñez Rosales, pp. 312–324. Universidad de Guadalajara, Guadalajara, Mexico.
2010 Materiales del Formativo y del Clásico Temprano en la Costa Sur de Nayarit. In *El Sistema Fluvial Lerma-Santiago durante el Formativo Terminal y el Clásico Temprano: Precisiones cronológicas y dinámicas culturales*, edited by Laura Solar Valverde, pp. 109–130. Colección Científica 565, Serie Arqueología. Instituto Nacional de Antropología e Historia, Mexico City.
2013 *Informe. Reporte del Reconocimiento de Superficie. Reporte de la Excavación de las Cistas del Sitio La*

Pitayera. Catálogo de los Objetos Arqueológicos. Primera Temporada 2012. Archivo Técnico de la Coordinación Nacional de Arqueología, Instituto Nacional de Antropología e Historia, Mexico City.

Grave Tirado, Luis A.

2000 *Informe Proyecto Arqueológico de Salvamento Carretera San Blas-Mazatlán, Tramo Sinaloa. Subtramos Mazatlán, El Rosario y Escuinapa, Límites entre Sinaloa y Nayarit.* Archivo Técnico de la Coordinación Nacional de Arqueología, Instituto Nacional de Antropología e Historia, Mexico City.

2003 La Región Fundada en la Tradición: El Norte de Nayarit y el Sur de Sinaloa, una Región a lo Largo del Tiempo. Master's thesis, Instituto de Investigaciones Filológicas, Universidad Nacional Autónoma de México, Mexico City.

2010a El Calón, un Espacio Sagrado en las Marismas del Sur de Sinaloa. *Estudios Mesoamericanos* 8:19–39.

2010b Evidencias de a los Culto Ancestros en el Sur de Sinaloa. Excavaciones Arqueológicas en San Miguel La Atarjea, Escuinapa, Sinaloa. *Arqueología* 45:101–119.

2011 *La Violencia Domesticada: La Guerra, el Sacrificio Humano y las Fiestas en Mesoamérica.* Editorial Académica Española, Saarbrücken, Germany.

2012a Sobre la "Tradición Aztatlán," de John Pohl. *Arqueología Mexicana* 19(117):6.

2012b *Informe de la Segunda Temporada del Proyecto Marismas del Sur de Sinaloa.* Archivo Técnico de la Coordinación Nacional de Arqueología, Instituto Nacional de Antropología e Historia, Mexico City.

2012c Aproximaciones a la Fiesta del Mar de las Cabras. In *Trópico de Cáncer: Estudios de Historia y Arqueología Sobre el Sur de Sinaloa,* edited by Luis A. Grave Tirado, Víctor J. Santos Ramírez, and Gilberto López Castillo, pp. 153–167. Instituto Nacional de Antropología e Historia, Sinaloa, and Consejo Estatal de Ciencia y Tecnología-Sinaloa, Culiacán, Sinaloa, Mexico.

2012d *"…Y Hay Tantas Ciénagas que no se Podía Andar": El Sur de Sinaloa y el Norte de Nayarit, una Región a lo Largo del Tiempo.* Instituto Nacional de Antropología e Historia, Mexico City.

2017 Patrón de Asentamientos Prehispánicos en la Cuenca Baja del Río Baluarte, Sinaloa. *Arqueología* 54:7–27.

2018a *Ideología y Poder en el México Prehispánico: De los Mayas a los Mayos de Sinaloa.* Colección Arqueología, Serie Fundamentos. Instituto Nacional de Antropología e Historia, Mexico City.

2018b Intensificación Productiva e Ideología en las Marismas de Escuinapa, Sinaloa: Patrón de Asentamiento Prehispánico y Fuentes Etnohistóricas. *Americae* 3:79–98.

2019a Patrón de Asentamiento Prehispánico y Complejidad Social en el Sur de Sinaloa. In *Aztatlán: Interacción y Cambio Social en el Occidente de México ca. 850–1350 d.C.,* edited by Laura Solar Valverde and Ben A. Nelson, pp. 115–148. El Colegio de Michoacán, Zamora, and Arizona State University, Tempe.

2019b Una Historia de la Arqueología de Sinaloa. Manuscript in possession of author.

2020 Un Largo Transepto entre la Sierra y el Mar: Proyecto Arqueológico de Salvamento Gasoducto El Oro-Mazatlán. *Ventana Arqueológica* 1:84–108.

2021 Los Frijoles: Una Provincia Perdida en la Cuenca Baja del Río Quelite, Sinaloa. *Cuicuilco: Revista de Ciencias Antropológicas* 82:125–148.

Grave Tirado, Luis A., Emmanuel Gómez Ambriz, Óscar López, Víctor Ortega, and Cinthya Vidal Aldana

2015 *Informe Primera Etapa (Reconocimiento de Superficie), Proyecto Arqueológico de Salvamento Gasoducto-El Oro-Mazatlán.* Archivo Técnico de la Coordinación Nacional de Arqueología, Instituto Nacional de Antropología e Historia, Mexico City.

Grave Tirado, Luis A., Emmanuel Gómez Ambriz, Cinthya Vidal Aldana, Óscar López, Óscar Peña, and Manuel Ramírez

2016 *Informe de la Segunda Etapa (Reconocimiento de Variantes y Excavación) Proyecto Arqueológico de Salvamento Gasoducto El Oro-Mazatlán, Tomo II. Análisis de Materiales.* Archivo Técnico de la Coordinación Nacional de Arqueología, Instituto Nacional de Antropología e Historia, Mexico City.

Grave Tirado, Luis A., and Angélica C. Nava Burgueño

2012 Juana Gómez: Investigaciones Arqueológicas de Salvamento en la Periferia de Escuinapa. In *Trópico de Cáncer: Estudios de Historia y arqueología Sobre el Sur de Sinaloa,* edited by Luis A. Grave Tirado, Víctor J. Santos Ramírez, and Gilberto López Castillo, pp. 119–136. Instituto Nacional de Antropología e Historia, Sinaloa, and Consejo Estatal de Ciencia y Tecnología-Sinaloa, Culiacán, Sinaloa, Mexico.

Grave Tirado, Luis A., and Víctor Ortega León

2020 Límites Difusos, Dinámicas Intensas: Sinaloa Llegada de los Españoles. *Anales de Antropología* 54(2):7–18.

Grave Tirado, Luis A., and Francisco J. Samaniega Altamirano

2012 Un Patio de Mitote de la Sierra del Nayar como Referente Etnoarqueológico para el Sur de Sinaloa. Paper presented at the Coloquio de Antropología e Historia del Noroccidente de México 2012, Mexico City.

2013 La Gráfica Rupestre del Gran Nayar y la Cerámica Aztatlán: Manifestaciones de una Misma Tradición Cultural. In *American Indian Rock Art* 40, edited by Peggy Whitehead and Mavis Greer, pp. 749–764. International Federation of Rock Art Organizations 2013 Proceedings. American Rock Art Research Association, Glendale, AZ.

Gregory, David A., and David R. Wilcox (editors)

2007 *Zuni Origins: Toward a New Synthesis of Southwestern Archaeology.* University of Arizona Press, Tucson.

Grimstead, Deanna, Matthew Pailes, Katherine Dungan, David Dettman, Natalia Martínez Tagüeña, and Amy Clark

2013 Identifying the Origin of Southwestern Shell: A Geochemical Application to Mogollon Rim Archaeomolluscs. *American Antiquity* 78(4):640–661.

Grinberg, Dora M.
1989   Tecnologías Metalúrgicas Tarascas. *Ciencia y Desarrollo* 15(89):37–52.

Grosscup, Gordon L.
1961   A Sequence of Figurines from West Mexico. *American Antiquity* 26(3):390–406.
1964   The Ceramics of West Mexico. PhD dissertation. Department of Anthropology, University of California, Los Angeles.
1976   The Ceramic Sequence at Amapa. In *The Archaeology of Amapa, Nayarit*, edited by Clement W. Meighan, pp. 207–272. Monumenta Archaeologica, Vol. 2. Institute of Archaeology, University of California Press, Los Angeles.

Gruner, Erina P.
2019   Ritual Assemblages and Ritual Economies: The Role of Chacoan and Post-Chacoan Sodalities in Exotic Exchange Networks, A.D. 875–1300. PhD dissertation, Department of Anthropology, State University of New York, Binghamton University.

Guevara López, Germán
1981   *Reporte de la Zona Arqueológica de Chacalilla, Municipio de San Blas, Nayarit.* Cuadernos de los Centros Regionales: Occidente No. 1, Instituto Nacional de Antropología e Historia, Mexico City.

Gutiérrez del Ángel, Arturo
2000   Blood in Huichol Ritual. *Journal of the Southwest* 42(1):111–118.
2002   *La Peregrinación a Wirikuta: El Gran Rito de Paso de los Huicholes.* Colección Etnografía de los Pueblos Indígenas de México, Serie Estudios Monográficos. Instituto Nacional de Antropología e Historia and Universidad de Guadalajara, Guadalajara, Mexico.

Guzmán, Diego
1615   Carta del padre Diego Guzmán al padre provincial de septiembre de mil seiscientos veinte y nueve. In *Historia 15. Memorias para la historia de la provincia de Sinaloa.* Archivo General de la Nación, Mexico City.

Guzmán, Fabiola
2004   *Análisis Arqueoictiológico de los Peces Recuperados en San Felipe Aztatán (Huachotita), Municipio de Tecuala, Nayarit.* Laboratorio de Arqueozoología. Archivo Técnico, Subdirección de Laboratorios y Apoyo Académico. Instituto Nacional de Antropología e Historia, Mexico City.

Guzmán Vázquez, Adriana
2000   Mitote and the Cora Universe. *Journal of the Southwest* 42 (1):61–80.
2002   *Mitote y Universo Cora.* Colección Etnografía de los Pueblos Indígenas de México, Serie Estudios Monográficos. Instituto Nacional de Antropología e Historia and Universidad de Guadalajara, Guadalajara, Mexico.

Gyarmati, János, Boglárka Maróti, Zsolt Kasztovszky, Boglárka Döncző, Zita Szikszai, László E. Aradi, Judith Mihály, Gerald Koch, and Veronika Szilágyi
2022   Hidden Behind the Mask: An Authentication Study on the Aztec Mask of the Museum of Ethnography, Budapest, Hungary. *Forensic Science International* 333(111236):1–11.

Hansen, Mogens H. (editor)
2000   *A Comparative Study of Thirty City-State Cultures: An Investigation Conducted by the Copenhagen Polis Center.* Royal Danish Academy of Sciences and Letters, Copenhagen.

Harbottle, Garman, and Phil C. Weigand
1992   Turquoise in Pre-Columbian America. *Scientific American* 266(2):78–85.

Haury, Emil W.
1976   *The Hohokam: Desert Farmers & Craftsmen: Snaketown, 1964–1965.* University of Arizona Press, Tucson.

Haviland, William A.
1966   Social Integration and the Classic Maya. *American Antiquity* 31(5):625–631.

Hays-Gilpin, Kelley A., Sarah A. Herr, and Patrick D. Lyons (editors)
2021   *Engaged Archaeology in the Southwestern United States and Northwestern Mexico.* University Press of Colorado, Louisville.

Hays-Gilpin, Kelley, and Jane H. Hill
1999   The Flower World in Material Culture: An Iconographic Complex in the Southwest and Mesoamerica. *Journal of Anthropological Research* 55(1):1–37.

Hays-Gilpin, Kelley, and Polly Schaafsma (editors)
2010   *Painting the Cosmos: Metaphor and Worldview in Images from the Southwest Pueblos and Mexico.* Museum of Northern Arizona Bulletin No. 67. Museum of Northern Arizona, Flagstaff.

Healan, Dan M.
2012   The Archaeology of Tula, Hidalgo, Mexico. *Journal of Archaeological Research* 20(1):53–115.

Healan, Dan M., Robert H. Cobean, and Robert T. Bowsher
2021   Revised Chronology and Settlement History of Tula and the Tula Region. *Ancient Mesoamerica* 32(1): 165–186.

Hegmon, Michelle (editor)
2000   *The Archaeology of Regional Interaction: Religion, Warfare, & Exchange Across the American Southwest & Beyond.* University Press of Colorado, Boulder.

Heitman, Carrie C., and Stephen Plog (editors)
2015   *Chaco Revisited: New Research on the Prehistory of Chaco Canyon, New Mexico.* Amerind Studies in Anthropology. University of Arizona Press, Tucson.

Helms, Mary W.
1979   *Ancient Panama: Chiefs in Search of Power.* University of Texas Press, Austin.
1993   *Craft and the Kingly Ideal: Art, Trade, and Power.* University of Texas Press, Austin.

Hermann Lejarazu, Manuel
2011   La Serpiente de Fuego en la Iconografía Mesoamericana. *Arqueología Mexicana* 19(109):67–70.

Hernández Díaz, Verónica
2013   Las Formas del Arte en el Antiguo Occidente. In *Miradas Renovadas al Occidente Indígena de México*, edited by Marie-Areti Hers, pp. 21–77. Universidad Nacional Autónoma de México-Instituto de

Investigaciones Estéticas, Instituto Nacional de Antropología e Historia, and Centro de Estudios Mexicanos y Centroamericanos, Mexico City.

Hernández Sánchez, Gilda
2008 Vasijas de Luz y de Oscuridad: La Cerámica Tipo Códice del Estilo Mixteca-Puebla. *Itinerarios* 8:113–127.

Hers, Marie-Areti
1989 *Los Toltecas en Tierras Chichimecas.* Cuadernos del Historia del Arte 35. Instituto de Investigaciones Estéticas and Universidad Nacional Autónoma de Mexico, Mexico City.
1996 Durango y Sinaloa: Estado Actual de la Cronología de la Ocupación Mesoamericana. Paper presented at the Seminario Cronología Historiográfica del Occidente, Centro de Estudios Antropológicos del Occidente, Nogueras, Comala, Colima.
2013 Aztatlán y los Lazos con el Centro de México. In *Miradas Renovadas al Occidente Indígena de México*, edited by Marie-Areti Hers, pp. 273–311. Universidad Nacional Autónoma de México, Instituto de Investigaciones Históricas, Instituto Nacional de Antropología e Historia, and Centro de Estudios Mexicanos y Centroamericanos, Mexico City.

Hers, Marie-Areti (editor)
2013 *Miradas Renovadas al Occidente Indígena de México.* Universidad Nacional Autónoma de México, Instituto de Investigaciones Históricas, Instituto Nacional de Antropología e Historia, and Centro de Estudios Mexicanos y Centroamericanos, Mexico City.

Hers, Marie-Areti, José L. Mirafuentes, María de los Dolores Soto, and Miguel Vallebueno (editors)
2000 *Nómadas y Sedentarios en el Norte de México: Homenaje a Beatriz Braniff.* Universidad Nacional Autónoma de México, Instituto de Investigaciones Antropológicas, Instituto de Investigaciones Estéticas, and Instituto de Investigaciones Históricas, Mexico City.

Heyden, Doris (editor)
1994 *The History of the Indies of New Spain by Fray Diego Durán.* University of Oklahoma Press, Norman.

Hill, Jane H.
1992 The Flower World of Old Uto-Aztecan. *Journal of Anthropological Research* 48(2):117–144.

Hill, J. Brett
2018 *From Huhugam to Hohokam: Heritage and Archaeology in the American Southwest.* Lexington Books, Lanham, MD.

Hill, Matthew E., and Lauren W. Ritterbush (editors)
2022 *People in a Sea of Grass: Archaeology's Changing Perspective on Indigenous Plains Communities.* University of Utah Press, Salt Lake City.

Hinton, Thomas B.
1964 The Cora Village: A Civil Religious Hierarchy in Northern Mexico. In *Culture Change and Stability: Essays in Memory of Olive Ruth Barker and George C. Barker Jr.*, edited by Ralph L. Beals, pp. 44–62. University of California Press, Los Angeles.
1972 Un Análisis del Sincretismo Religioso entre los Coras de Nayarit. In *Coras, Huicholes, y Tepehuanes*, edited by Thomas B. Hinton, pp. 33–41. Instituto Nacional Indigenista, Mexico City, Mexico.

Hirth, Kenneth G.
2008 The Economy of Supply: Modeling Obsidian Procurement and Craft Provisioning at a Central Mexican Urban Center. *Latin American Antiquity* 19(4):435–457.

Hopkins, Maren P.
2012 A Storied Land: *Tiyo* and the Epic Journey Down the Colorado River. Master's thesis, School of Anthropology, University of Arizona, Tucson.

Hopkins, Maren P., Leigh Kuwanwisiwma, Stewart B. Koyiyumptewa, and Wesley Bernardini
2021 Hopi Perspectives on History. In *Becoming Hopi: A History*, edited by Wesley Bernardini, Stewart B. Koyiyumptewa, Gregson Schachner, and Leigh Kuwanwisiwma, pp. 15–26. University of Arizona Press, Tucson.

Hosler, Dorothy
1986 The Origins, Technology, and Social Construction of Ancient West Mexican Metallurgy. PhD dissertation, Department of Anthropology, University of California, Santa Barbara.
1988a Ancient West Mexican Metallurgy: A Technological Chronology. *Journal of Field Archaeology* 15:191–217.
1988b Ancient West Mexican Metallurgy: South and Central American Origins and West Mexican Transformations. *American Anthropologist* 90:832–855.
1994a Arqueología y Metalurgia en el Occidente de México. El Bronce Mesoamericano: Orígenes, Desarrollo y Difusión. In *Transformaciones Mayores en el Occidente de México*, edited by Ricardo Ávila, pp. 115–125. Colección Fundamentos, Universidad de Guadalajara, Guadalajara, Mexico.
1994b *The Sounds and Colors of Power: The Sacred Metallurgical Technology of Ancient West Mexico.* MIT Press, Cambridge, MA.
1997 Los Orígenes Andinos de la Metalurgia del Occidente de México. *Boletín Museo de Oro* 42:3–25.
1998 Artefactos de Cobre en el Periodo Posclásico Tardío Mesoamericano: Yacimientos Minerales, Regiones Productivas y Uso. In *El Occidente de México: Arqueología, Historia y Medio Ambiente: Perspectivas Regionales*, edited by Ricardo Ávila, Jean P. Emphoux, Luis G. Gastélum, Susana Ramírez, Otto Schöndube, and Francisco Valdez, pp. 319–330. Actas del IV Coloquio de Internacional de Occidente 1996. Instituto Francés de Investigación Científica para el Desarrollo y la Cooperación and Universidad de Guadalajara, Guadalajara, Mexico.
2005a Excavaciones en el Sitio de Fundición de Cobre de El Manchón, Guerrero, México. Foundation for the Advancement of Mesoamerican Studies, Inc. Electronic document, www.famsi.org/reports/01058es/01058es Hosler01.pdf, accessed August 12, 2020.
2005b *Los Sonidos y Colores del Poder: La Tecnología Metalúrgica Sagrada del Occidente de México.* El Colegio Mexiquense, Zinacantepec.

2009 West Mexican Metallurgy: Revisited and Revised. *Journal of World Prehistory* 22(3):185–212.

Hosler, Dorothy, Heather Lechtman, and Olaf Holm
1990 *Axe-monies and Their Relatives.* Studies in Pre-Columbian Art and Archaeology, No. 30. Dumbarton Oaks Research Library and Collection, Washington, DC.

Hosler, Dorothy, and Guy Stresser-Péan
1992 The Huastec Region: A Second Locus for the Production of Bronze Alloys in Ancient Mesoamerica. *Science* 257(5074):1215–1220.

Houston, Stephen, Héctor Escobedo, Mark Child, Charles Golden, and René Muñoz
2003 The Moral Community: Maya Settlement Transformation at Piedras Negras, Guatemala. In *The Social Construction of Ancient Cities*, edited by Monica Smith, pp. 212–253. Smithsonian Institution Press, Washington, DC.

Houston, Stephen D., and Karl A. Taube
2000 An Archaeology of the Senses: Perceptions and Cultural Expression in Ancient Mesoamerica. *Cambridge Archaeological Journal* 10(02):261–294.

Hu, Di
2013 Approaches to the Archaeology of Ethnogenesis: Past and Emergent Perspectives. *Journal of Archaeological Research* 21:371–402.

Hull, Sharon, Mostafa Fayek, Frances J. Mathien, and Heidi Roberts
2014 Turquoise Trade of the Ancestral Puebloan: Chaco and Beyond. *Journal of Archaeological Science* 45:187–195.

Hull, Sharon, Mostafa Fayek, Frances J. Mathien, Phillip Shelley, and Kathy R. Durand
2008 A New Approach to Determining the Geological Provenance of Turquoise Artifacts Using Hydrogen and Copper Stable Isotopes. *Journal of Archaeological Science* 35(5):1355–1369.

Hull, Sharon, Timothy D. Maxwell, Mostafa Fayek, and Rafael Cruz Antillón
2013 Chasing Beauty: Evidence for Southwestern U.S. Turquoise in Mexico. Paper presented at the 78th Annual Meeting of the Society for American Archaeology, Honolulu.

Hulse, Frederick S.
1945 Appendix III: Skeletal Material. In *Excavations at Culiacán, Sinaloa*, by Isabel Kelly, pp. 187–198. Ibero-Americana 25. University of California Press, Berkeley.

Ingold, Tim
2000 *The Perception of the Environment: Essays on Livelihood, Dwelling and Skill.* Routledge, London.

Jadot, Elsa, Gregory Pereira, Hector Neff, and Michael D. Glascock
2019 All that Glitters is not Plumbate: Diffusion and Imitation of Plumbate Pottery during the Early Postclassic Period (AD 900–1200) at the Malpaís of Zacapu, Michoacán, Mexico. *Latin American Antiquity* 30(2):318–332.

James, Susan E.
2000 Some Aspects of the Aztec Religion in the Hopi Kachina Cult. *Journal of the Southwest* 42(4):897–926.

Jardel, Enrique
1994 Diversidad Ecológica y Transformaciones del Paisaje en el Occidente de México. In *Transformaciones Mayores en el Occidente de México*, edited by Ricardo Avila Palafox, pp. 13–39. Departamento de Estudios del Hombre. Universidad de Guadalajara, Guadalajara, Mexico.

Jáuregui, Jesús
2000 La Judea de los Coras: Un Drama Astral de Primavera. México en Movimiento. In *La Religion Popular,* edited by Hermans Hub, Dick Papousek, and Catherine Raffi-Béroud, pp. 28–53. Centro de Estudios Mexicanos, Groningen, Netherlands.
2002 La Serpiente Emplumada entre los Cora y Huicholes. *Arqueología Mexicana* 9(53):64–69.
2004 Mexcaltitán-Aztlán: Un Nuevo Mito. *Arqueología Mexicana* 12 (67):56–61.
2005 Las Pachitas en La Mesa del Nayar (Yaujque'e). *Dimensión Antropológica* 34:23–66.

Jáuregui, Jesús (editor)
1993 *Música y Danzas del Gran Nayar.* Centro de Estudios Mexicanos y Centroamericanos and Instituto Nacional Indigenista, Mexico City.

Jáuregui, Jesús, Paulina Alcocer, Philip E. Coyle, Arturo Gutiérrez, Adriana Guzmán, Laura Magriñá, Johannes Neurath, and Margarita Valdovinos
2003 La Autoridad de los Antepasados: Un Sistema de Organización Social de Tradición Aborigen entre los Coras y Huicholes. In *La Comunidad sin Límite,* Vol. 3, edited by Saúl Millán and Julieta Valle, pp. 115–216. Instituto Nacional de Antropología e Historia, Mexico City.

Jáuregui, Jesús, and Laura Magriñá
2013 Turí Tuchieve ("ya los esperamos"): La Despedida de un Chamán Cora. In *Los Sueños y los Días: Chamanismo y Nahualismo en el México Actual, Vol. 1. Pueblos del Noroeste*, edited by Miguel Ángel Bartolomé and Alicia M. Barabas, pp. 181–219. Instituto Nacional de Antropología e Historia, Mexico City.

Jáuregui, Jesús, and Johannes Neurath (editors)
1998 *Fiesta, Literatura y Magia en el Nayarit: Ensayos Sobre Coras, Huicholes y Mexicaneros de Konrad Theodor Preuss.* Centro Estudios Mexicanos y Centroamericanos and Instituto Nacional Indigenista, Mexico City.
2003 *Flechadores de Estrellas: Nuevas Aportaciones Etnológicas sobre Coras y Huicholes.* Colección Etnografía de los Pueblos Indígenas de México, Serie Estudios Monográficos. Instituto Nacional de Antropología e Historia and Universidad de Guadalajara, Guadalajara, Mexico.

Jiménez, Peter F.
2014 Aztatlán: Inroads on Its Encroachment. Paper presented at the 79th Annual Meeting of the Society for American Archaeology, Austin.

2018   Orienting West Mexico: The Mesoamerican World System 200–1200 CE. PhD dissertation, Department of Historical Studies, University of Gothenburg, Gothenburg, Sweden.

2020   *The Mesoamerican World System, 200–1200 CE: A Comparative Approach Analysis of West Mexico.* Cambridge University Press, Cambridge, UK.

Jiménez, Peter, and Laura Solar Valverde

2008   La Red Aztatlán y sus Vínculos con otras Redes. Paper presented at the Primer Seminario-Taller Regional de Arqueología Aztatlán, Instituto Nacional de Antropología e Historia and Museo Regional de Guadalajara, Guadalajara, Jalisco.

2012   Aztatlán Tierra Adentro: Observaciones sobre la Naturaleza de los Vínculos entre la Llanura Costera del Pacífico y las Tierras Altas del Occidente. Paper presented at the Segunda Mesa Redonda sobre Arqueología Aztatlán, Instituto Nacional de Antropología e Historia and Museo Regional de Guadalajara, Guadalajara, Jalisco.

Johnson, Matthew

2000   *Teoría Arqueológica: Una Introducción.* Editorial Ariel, Barcelona.

Jordan, Keith

2023   Of Plumbate and Paradise: A Hypothesis for the Appeal and Distribution of Fancy Tohil Plumbate Ceramics. In *When East Meets West: Chichen Itza, Tula, and the Postclassic Mesoamerican World*, Vols. 1–2, edited by Travis W. Stanton, Karl A. Taube, Jeremy D. Coltman, and Nelda I. Marengo Camacho, pp. 127–148. British Archaeological Reports S3134. BAR Publishing, London.

Joyce, Arthur A.

2010   *Mixtecs, Zapotecs, and Chatinos: Ancient Peoples of Southern Mexico.* Wiley-Blackwell, Malden, MA.

Joyce, Arthur A., Andrew G. Workinger, Byron Hamann, Peter Kroefges, Maxine Oland, Stacie M. King

2004   Lord 8 Deer "Jaguar Claw" and the Land of the Sky: The Archaeology and History of Tututepec. *Latin American Antiquity* 15(3):273–297.

Kelley, Jane H.

2017   How Paquimé Went from Trading Center to Shrine. In *Not So Far from Paquimé: Essays on the Archaeology of Chihuahua, Mexico*, edited by Jane H. Kelley and David A. Phillips Jr., pp. 176–192. University of Utah Press, Salt Lake City.

Kelley, Jane H., and David A. Phillips Jr. (editors)

2017   *Not So Far from Paquimé: Essays on the Archaeology of Chihuahua, Mexico.* University of Utah Press, Salt Lake City.

Kelley, J. Charles

1953   Reconnaissance and Excavation in Durango and Southern Chihuahua, Mexico. *Yearbook of the American Philosophical Society*, pp. 172–176. American Philosophical Society, Philadelphia.

1954a   *Juego de Tarjetas de Exploraciones en el Sitio Schroeder Durango, Vol I.* Archive of Southern Illinois University, Carbondale. Archivo Técnico de la Coordinación Nacional de Arqueología, Instituto Nacional de Antropología e Historia, Mexico City.

1954b   *Juego de Tarjetas de Exploraciones en el Sitio Schroeder Durango, Vol II.* Archive of Southern Illinois University, Carbondale. Archivo Técnico de la Coordinación Nacional de Arqueología, Instituto Nacional de Antropología e Historia, Mexico City.

1956   *Graphic Survey of Work at the Schroeder Site (LCAJ1-1) Durango, Mexico 1954–1956.* Archive of Southern Illinois University, Carbondale. Archivo Técnico de la Dirección de Monumentos Prehispánicos del Instituto Nacional de Antropología e Historia, Durango.

1980   Discussion of Papers by Plog, Doyel and Riley. In *Current Issues in Hohokam Prehistory: Proceedings of a Symposium*, edited by David Doyel and Fred Plog, pp. 49–71. Anthropological Research Papers No. 23, Arizona State University, Tempe.

1985   The Chronology of the Chalchihuites Culture. In *The Archaeology of West and Northwest Mesoamerica*, edited by Michael S. Foster and Phil C. Weigand, pp. 269–287. Westview Press, Boulder.

1986   The Mobile Merchants of Molino. In *Ripples in the Chichimec Sea: New Considerations of Southwestern-Mesoamerican Interactions*, edited by Frances J. Mathien and Randall H. McGuire, pp. 81–104. Southern Illinois University Press, Carbondale.

1990   The Early Post-Classic in Northern Zacatecas and Durango: IX to XII Centuries. In *Mesoamérica y Norte de México, Siglos IX–XII*, edited by Federica Sodi Miranda, pp. 487–519. Sociedad Mexicana de Antropología, Instituto Nacional de Antropología e Historia, Mexico City.

1995   Trade Goods, Traders and Status in Northwestern Greater Mesoamerica. In *The Gran Chichimeca: Essays on the Archaeology and Ethnohistory of Northern Mesoamerica*, edited by Jonathan E. Reyman, pp. 102–145. Avebury, Aldershot, United Kingdom.

2000   The Aztatlán Mercantile System: Mobile Traders and the Northwestward Expansion of Mesoamerican Civilization. In *Greater Mesoamerica: The Archaeology of West and Northwest Mexico*, edited by Michael S. Foster and Shirley Gorenstein, pp. 137–154. University of Utah Press, Salt Lake City.

Kelley, J. Charles, and Michael S. Foster

1992   Aztatlán: Of Red-Rims, Polychromes, Mobile Traders, and Speculations on the Prehistory of West and Northwest Mexico. Paper presented at the Center for Indigenous Studies' Round-table on New World Prehistory: Cultural Dynamics of Precolumbian West and Northwest Mesoamerica, Phoenix, Arizona.

Kelley, J. Charles, and Ellen Abbott Kelley

1971   *An Introduction to the Ceramics of the Chalchihuites Culture of Zacatecas and Durango, Mexico, Pt. 1: The Decorated Wares.* Mesoamerican Studies 5. Research Records of the University Museum, Southern Illinois University, Carbondale.

Kelley, J. Charles, and Howard D. Winters
1960 A Revision of the Archaeological Sequence in Sinaloa, Mexico. *American Antiquity* 25(4):547–561.

Kelly, Isabel T.
1938 *Excavations at Chametla, Sinaloa*. Ibero-Americana 14. University of California Press, Berkeley.
1941 The Relationship between Tula and Sinaloa. *Revista Mexicana de Estudios Antropológicos* 5(2–3):199–207.
1944 West Mexico and the Hohokam. In *El Norte de México y el Sur de Estados Unidos*. Tercera Reunión de Mesa Redonda sobre Problemas Antropológicos de México y Centro América, pp. 206–222. Sociedad Mexicana de Antropologia, Mexico City.
c. 1944 A Surface Survey at the Sayula-Zacoalco Basins of Jalisco (1941–1944). Manuscript on file in the archive of the Sayula Basin Archaeological Project.
1945a *Excavations at Culiacán, Sinaloa*. Ibero-Americana 25. University of California Press, Berkeley.
1945b *The Archaeology of the Autlán-Tuxcacuesco Area of Jalisco, I: The Autlán Zone*. Ibero-Americana 26. University of California Press, Berkeley.
1948 Ceramic Provinces of Northwest Mexico. In *El Occidente de México. Cuarta Reunión de la Mesa Redonda sobre Problemas Antropológicos de México y Centro América*, pp. 55–71. Sociedad Mexicana de Antropología, Mexico City.
1980 *Ceramic Sequence in Colima: Capacha, an Early Phase*. Anthropological Papers of the University of Arizona, No. 37. University of Arizona Press, Tucson.
1985 Some Gold and Silver Artifacts from Colima. In *The Archaeology of West and Northwest Mesoamerica*, edited by Michael S. Foster and Phil C. Weigand, pp. 153–179. Westview Press, Boulder.

Kennett, Douglas J., Stephen Plog, Richard J. George, Brendan J. Culleton, Adam S. Watson, Pontus Skoglund, Nadin Rohland, et al.
2017 Archaeogenomic Evidence Reveals Prehistoric Matrilineal Dynasty. *Nature Communications* 8:14115.

Kindl, Olivia
2000 The Huichol Gourd Bowl as a Microcosm. *Journal of the Southwest* 42(1):37–60.
2003 *La Jícara Huichola: Un Microcosmos Mesoamericano*. Colección Etnografía de los Pueblos Indígenas de México, Serie Estudios Monograficos. Instituto Nacional de Antropologia e Historia and Universidad de Guadalajara, Guadalajara, Mexico.

King, J. C. H., Max Carocci, Caroline Cartwright, Colin McEwan, and Rebecca Stacey (editors)
2012 *Turquoise in Mexico and North America: Science, Conservation, Culture, and Collections*. Archetype, London.

Kirchhoff, Paul
1961 Se Puede Localizar Aztlan? *Anuario de Historia* 1:59–73.

Knab, Timothy J.
1980 When Is a Language Really Dead: The Case of Pochutec. *International Journal of American Linguistics* 46(3):230–233.
1983 En Qué Lengua Hablaban Los Tepalcates Teotihuacanos? (No Era Nahuatl). *Revista Mexicana de Estudios Antropológicos* 29(1):145–158.
2004 *Mad Jesus: The Final Testament of a Huichol Messiah from Northwest Mexico*. University of New Mexico Press, Albuquerque.

Knab, Timothy J., and John M. D. Pohl
2019 Round and Round We Go: Cholula, Rotating Power Structures, Social Stability, and Trade in Mesoamerica. In *Interregional Interaction in Ancient Mesoamerica*, edited by Joshua D. Englehardt and Michael D. Carrasco, pp. 292–312. University Press of Colorado, Louisville.

Kohler, Timothy A., Mark D. Varien, and Aaron Wright (editors)
2010 *Leaving Mesa Verde: Peril and Change in the Thirteenth-Century Southwest*. Amerind Studies in Archaeology. University of Arizona Press, Tucson.

Kowalski, Jeff K., and Cynthia Kristan-Graham (editors)
2011 *Twin Tollans: Chichén Itza, Tula, and the Epiclassic to Early Postclassic Mesoamerican World*, revised edition. Dumbarton Oaks Research Library and Collection, Washington, DC.

Kristiansen, Kristian
2006 Cosmology, Economy and Long-Term Change in the Bronze Age of Northern Europe. In *Ecology and Economy in Stone Age and Bronze Age Scania*, edited by Karl-Göran Sjögren, pp. 170–193. Skånska spår-arkeologi längs Västkustbanan Series. National Heritage Board, Stockholm.
2010 Decentralized Complexity: The Case of Bronze Age Northern Europe. In *Pathways to Power: New Perspectives on the Emergence of Social Inequality*, edited by T. Douglas Price and Gary M. Feinman, pp. 169–192. Springer, New York.

Kristiansen, Kristian, and Thomas B. Larsson
2005 *The Rise of Bronze Age Society: Travels, Transmissions and Transformations*. Cambridge University Press, Cambridge, UK.

Kuwanwisiwma, Leigh J., T. J. Ferguson, and Chip Colwell (editors)
2018 *Footprints of Hopi History: Hopihiniwtiput Kukveni'at*. University of Arizona Press, Tucson.

Lathrap, Donald W.
1973 The Antiquity and Importance of Long-distance Trade Relationships in the Moist Tropics of Pre-Columbian South America. *World Archaeology* 5(2):170–186.

Leach, Edmund
1954 *Political Systems of Highland Burma: A Study of Kachin Social Structure*. Harvard University Press, Cambridge, MA.
1973 *Political Systems of Highland Burma: A Study of Kachin Social Structure*. London School of Economics Monographs on Social Anthropology 44. Bloomsbury Academic, London, UK.

Leal Carretero, Silvia
1992 *Xurawe o la Ruta de los Muertos: Mito Huichol en Tres Actos*. Centro de Investigación de Lenguas

Indígenas, Universidad de Guadalajara, Guadalajara, Mexico.

Lekson, Stephen H.
1999 *The Chaco Meridian: Centers of Political Power in the Ancient Southwest*. Alta Mira Press, Walnut Creek, CA.
2008 *A History of the Ancient Southwest*. School for Advanced Research, Santa Fe.
2011 Historiography and Archaeological Theory at Bigger Scales. In *Movement, Connectivity, and Landscape Change in the Ancient Southwest*, edited by Margaret C. Nelson and Colleen Strawhacker, pp. 457–466. University Press of Colorado, Boulder.
2015 *The Chaco Meridian: One Thousand Years of Political and Religious Power in the Ancient Southwest*. Rowman & Littlefield, Lanham, MD.
2018 *A Study of Southwestern Archaeology*. University of Utah Press, Salt Lake City.

Lekson, Stephen H. (editor)
2006 *The Archaeology of Chaco Canyon: An Eleventh-Century Pueblo Regional Center*. School of American Research Press, Santa Fe, NM.

Lekson, Stephen H., and Peter N. Peregrine
2004 A Continental Perspective for North American Archaeology. *The SAA Archaeological Record* 4(1):15–19.

Lenski, Gerhard E.
1966 *Power and Privilege: A Theory of Social Stratification*. McGraw-Hill, New York.

Levine, Marc N.
2015a Obsidian Obsessed? Examining Patterns of Chipped-Stone Procurement at Late Postclassic Tututepec, Oaxaca. In *Obsidian Reflections: Symbolic Dimensions of Obsidian in Mesoamerica*, edited by Marc N. Levine and David M. Carballo, pp. 159–191. University Press of Colorado, Boulder.
2015b Reflections on Obsidian Studies in Mesoamerica: Past, Present, and Future. In *Obsidian Reflections: Symbolic Dimensions of Obsidian in Mesoamerica*, edited by Marc N. Levine and David M. Carballo, pp. 3–41. University Press of Colorado, Boulder.
2019 Ceramic Molds for Mixtec Gold: A New Lost-Wax Casting Technique from Prehispanic Mexico. *Journal of Archaeological Method and Theory* 26(2):423–456.
2020 La Orfebrería Mixteca: Nueva Evidencia de Tututepec sobre la Producción Metalúrgica en el Postclásico Tardío. In *Patrimonio Cultural de Oaxaca: Investigaciones Recientes*, edited by Joel O. Vázquez Herrera and Patricia Martínez Lira, pp. 571–608. Centro Instituto Nacional de Antropología e Historia, Oaxaca, Mexico.

Levine, Morton H.
1958 *An Area Co-Tradition for Mesoamerica*. Kroeber Anthropological Society Papers No. 18, Berkeley.

Liffman, Paul M.
2000 Gourdvines, Fires, and Wixárika Territoriality. *Journal of the Southwest* 42(1):129–166.
2011 *Huichol Territory and the Mexican Nation: Indigenous Ritual, Land Conflict, and Sovereignty Claims*. University of Arizona Press, Tucson.

Liffman, Paul M., and Philip E. Coyle
2000 Introduction: Ritual and Historical Territoriality of the Cora (Náyari) and Huichol (Wixárika) Peoples. *Journal of the Southwest* 42(1):1–11.

Lind, Michael D.
1994 Cholula and Mixteca Polychromes: Two Mixteca-Puebla Regional Sub-styles. In *Mixteca-Puebla: Discoveries and Research in Mesoamerican Art and Archaeology*, edited by H. B. Nicholson and Eloise Quiñones Keber, pp. 79–100. Labyrinthos, Culver City, CA.

Lind, Michael D., Catalina Barrientos, Charles Caskey, Chris Turner, Geoffrey McCafferty, Carmen Martinez, Martha Orea, and Alicia Herrera
2002 La Cerámica Polícroma de Cholula. Manuscript in possession of author.

Linné, Sigvald
1934 *Archaeological Researches at Teotihuacan, Mexico*. Ethnographical Museum of Sweden, New Series No. 1. Oxford University Press, London.

Liot, Catherine
1998 Les Salines Préhispaniques du Bassin de Sayula (Ouest du Mexique): Mileu et Techniques. PhD dissertation, L'Université de Paris I Panthéon-Sorbonne, Paris.
2000 *Les Salines Prehispaniques du Bassin de Sayula (Occident du Mexique): Milieu et Techniques*. British Archaeological Reports International Series 849. Archaeopress, Oxford, UK.

Liot, Catherine, Susana Ramírez, Javier Reveles, and Carmen Melgarejo
2007 Producción, Distribución y Relaciones Interregionales en la Cuenca de Sayula del 500–1100 d.C. In *Dinámicas Culturales, entre el Occidente, el Centro-norte y la Cuenca de México, del Preclásico al Epiclásico*, edited by Brigitte Faugère, pp. 165–200. El Colegio de Michoacán, Zamora, and Centro de Estudios Mexicanos y Centroamericanos, Mexico City.

Liot, Catherine, Susana Ramírez, Javier Reveles, and Otto Schöndube
2006 Discusión General: Transformaciones Socioculturales y Tecnológicas en La Peña. In *Transformaciones Socioculturales y Tecnológicas en el Sitio La Peña, Cuenca de Sayula, Jalisco*, edited by Catherine Liot, Susana Ramírez, Javier Reveles, and Otto Schöndube, pp. 407–432. Universidad de Guadalajara and Instituto Nacional de Antropología e Historia, Guadalajara.

Liot, Catherine, Susana Ramírez, Javier Reveles, and Otto Schöndube (editors)
2006 *Transformaciones Socioculturales y Tecnológicas en el Sitio de La Peña, Cuenca de Sayula, Jalisco*. Universidad de Guadalajara and Instituto Nacional de Antropología e Historia, Guadalajara.

Liot, Catherine, and Javier Reveles
2006 Área de Excavación V: Plaza Oeste. In *Transformaciones Socioculturales y Tecnológicas en el Sitio La Peña, Cuenca de Sayula, Jalisco*, edited by Catherine

Liot, Susana Ramírez, Javier Reveles, and Otto Schöndube, pp. 225–237. Universidad de Guadalajara and Instituto Nacional de Antropología e Historia, Guadalajara.

Liot, Catherine, Javier Reveles, and Rosario Acosta
2006   Área de Excavación VI: Plaza Oeste, Inhumaciones del Postclásico Medio y Rituales Asociados. In *Transformaciones Socioculturales y Tecnológicas en el Sitio La Peña, Cuenca de Sayula, Jalisco*, edited by Catherine Liot, Susana Ramírez, Javier Reveles, and Otto Schöndube, pp. 239–264. Universidad de Guadalajara and Instituto Nacional de Antropología e Historia, Guadalajara.

Lister, Robert H.
1947   Archaeology of the Middle Río Balsas Basin, Mexico. *American Antiquity* 13(1):67–78.
1949   *Excavations at Cojumatlan, Michoacan, Mexico*. Publications in Anthropology 5. University of New Mexico Press, Albuquerque.
1971   Archaeological Synthesis of Guerrero. In *Archaeology of Northern Mesoamerica*, Pt. 2, edited by Gordon F. Ekholm and Ignacio Bernal, pp. 619–631. Handbook of Middle American Indians, Vol. 11, Robert Wauchope, general editor, University of Texas Press, Austin.

López Austin, Alfredo, and Leonardo López Luján
2009   *Monte Sagrado-Templo Mayor: El Cerro y la Pirámide en la Tradición Religiosa Mesoamericana*. Instituto Nacional de Antropología e Historia and Universidad Nacional Autónoma de México-Instituto de Investigaciones Antropológicas, Mexico City.

López-Delgado, Verónica, Avto Goguitchaichvili, Carlos Torreblanca, Rubén Cejudo, Peter Jiménez, Juan Morales, and Ana María Soler
2019   La Quemada: Decline and Abandonment in Two Stages on the Classic Period Northern Frontier of Mesoamerica. *Journal of Archaeological Science: Reports* 24:574–581.

Los Angeles Times
1959   "Archeologist's Show Covers 4,500 years." *Los Angeles Times*, January 8, 1959, B1. With photo. ProQuest Historical Newspapers, accessed April 25, 2022.

Lothrop, Samuel K.
1926   *Pottery of Costa Rica and Nicaragua*. Vols. 1–2. Contributions from the Museum of the American Indian, No. 8, Heye Foundation, New York.
1942   *Coclé, an Archaeological Study of Panama: Part II, Pottery of the Sitio Conte and Other Archaeologial Sites*. Memoirs of the Peabody Museum of Archaeology and Ethnology, Vol. 8, Harvard University, Cambridge.
1979   [1926] *Cerámica de Costa Rica y Nicaragua*. Fondo Cultural Banco de América, Managua, Nicaragua.

Luhman, Niklas
1995   *Poder*. Translation by Luz Mónica Talbot. Universidad Iberoamericana, Anthropos, Barcelona, Sp.

Lumholtz, Carl
1900   *Symbolism of the Huichol*. American Museum of Natural History, New York.
1902   *Unknown Mexico*, Vols. 1–2. Charles Scribner's Sons, New York.

MacCurdy, George G.
1914   Anthropology and Ethnology. In *The American Year Book: A Record of Events and Progress 1913*, edited by Francis G. Wickware, pp. 691–699. D. Appleton and Company, New York.

Macías Goytia, Angelina
1989   La Cuenca de Cuitzeo. In *Historia General de Michoacán*, Vol. 1, edited by Enrique Florescano, pp. 171–190. Gobierno del Estado de Michoacán, Morelia, Mexico.

MacLean, Hope
2012   *The Shaman's Mirror: Visionary Art of the Huichol*. University of Texas Press, Austin.

Magriñá, Laura
2001   El Peyote (Hikuri) y el Kieri (Tapat): Las Culebras de Agua del Valle de Matatipac. *Antropología: Boletin Oficial del Instituto Nacional de Antropología e Historia* 64:41–50.
2002   *Los Cora entre 1531 y 1722*. Instituto Nacional de Antropología e Historia and Universidad de Guadalajara, Guadalajara, Mexico City.

Malkin, Irad
2011   *A Small Greek World: Networks in the Ancient Mediterranean*. Oxford University Press, Oxford, UK.

Manin, Aurelie
2015   Informe Preliminar de los Restos de Fauna del Proyecto Cuenca de Sayula, Jalisco. Manuscript on file in the archive of the Sayula Basin Archaeological Project.

Manin, Aurélie, and Christine Lefèvre
2017   Utilización material y simbólica de los animales en Vista Hermosa. In *Vista Hermosa: Nobles, Artesanos, y Mercaderes en los Confines del Mundo Huasteco. Estudio Arqueológico de un Sitio Posclásico Tardío del Municipio de Nuevo Morelos, Tamaulipas, México, Volumen III: El Arte y la Vida en la Huasteca Posclásica*, edited by Claude Stresser-Péan, pp. 9–50. Secretaría de Cultura, Instituto Nacional de Antropología e Historia, and Museo Nacional de Antropología, Mexico City.

Manrique, Jimena
2004   *Informe Arqueozoológico de los Materiales de CECYTEN (Plantel 06) y San Felipe Aztatán (Huachotita), Municipio de Tecuala, Nayarit*. Archivo Técnico de la Sección de Arqueología, Centro Instituto Nacional de Antropología e Historia, Nayarit, Tepic.

Manzanilla, Rubén López, and Jorge A. Talavera González
1988   *Informe de los Trabajos de Salvamento e Investigación Arqueológica en la Población de Mochicahui, Municipio del Fuerte, Estado de Sinaloa, México*. Technical report, Dirección de Antropología Física, Departamento de Salvamento Arqueológico, Instituto

Nacional de Antropología e Historia, Mexico City, Mexico.

Marcus, Joyce
1983 A Synthesis of the Cultural Evolution of the Zapotec and Mixtec. In *The Cloud People: Divergent Evolution of the Zapotec and Mixtec Civilizations*, edited by Kent V. Flannery and Joyce Marcus, pp. 355–360. Academic Press, New York.

Mas, Elodie
2015 A Parure en Coquille à Sayula, Occident du Mexique: Approche techno-stylistique et rôle dans la dynamique socioculturelle entre 450 et 1000 apr. J.-C. Vols. 1–2. PhD dissertation, L'Université de Paris I Panthéon-Sorbonne, Paris.

Mason, J. Alden
1912a The Fiesta of the Pinole at Azqueltán. *The Museum Journal of the University of Pennsylvania* 3:44–50.
1912b The Tepehuan Indians of Azqueltán. *Proceedings of the Eighteenth International Congress of Americanists*, pp. 344–351. Harrison and Sons, London, UK.
1914 Folk-Tales of the Tepecanos. *The Journal of American Folklore* 27(104):148–210.
1916 Tepecano, a Piman Language of Western Mexico. *Annals of the New York Academy of Sciences* 25:309–416.
1918 Tepecano Prayers. *International Journal of American Linguistics* 1(2):91–153.
1971 Late Archaeological Sites in Durango, Mexico, from Chalchihuites to Zape. In *The North Mexican Frontier*, edited by Basil C. Hedrick, J. Charles Kelley, and Carroll L. Riley, pp. 130–143. Southern Illinois University Press, Carbondale.
1981 The Ceremonialism of the Tepecan Indians of Azqueltán, Jalisco. In *Themes of Indigenous Acculturation in Northwest Mexico*, edited by Thomas B. Hinton and Phil C. Weigand, pp. 62–76. Anthropological Papers of the University of Arizona 38. University of Arizona Press, Tucson.

Mastache, Alba G., Robert H. Cobean, and Dan M. Healan
2002 *Ancient Tollan: Tula and the Toltec Heartland*. University Press of Colorado, Boulder.

Mathews, Holly F.
1985 "We are Mayodormo": A Reinterpretation of Women's Roles in the Mexican Cargo System. *American Ethnologist* 12(2):285–301.

Mathien, Frances J., and Randall H. McGuire (editors)
1986 *Ripples in the Chichimec Sea: New Considerations of Southwestern-Mesoamerican Interactions*. Southern Illinois University Press, Carbondale.

Mathiowetz, Michael D.
2011 The Diurnal Path of the Sun: Ideology and Interregional Interaction in Ancient Northwest Mesoamerica and the American Southwest. PhD dissertation, Department of Anthropology, University of California, Riverside.
2012 Life as it Should Not Be: Clowns in the Casas Grandes World. Paper presented at the 17th Biennial Mogollon Conference, Silver City, NM.
2015 *Final Report on the Excavation of Mound 7 and Mound 8 at the Site of La Pitayera in Ahuacatlán, Nayarit. Proyecto Arqueológico Autopista Jala-Compostela*. Archivo Técnico de la Sección de Arqueología, Centro Instituto Nacional de Antropología e Historia, Nayarit, Tepic.
2018 The Sun Youth of the Casas Grandes Culture, Chihuahua, Mexico (A.D. 1200–1450). *Kiva: Journal of Southwestern Anthropology and History* 84(3):367–390.
2019a A History of Cacao in West Mexico: Implications for Mesoamerica and U.S. Southwest Connections. *Journal of Archaeological Research* 27(3):287–333.
2019b El Hijo de Dios que está en el Sol: Autoridad Política y Personificación del Dios Sol en el Antiguo Noroccidente de México. In *Aztatlán: Interacción y Cambio Social en el Occidente de México ca. 850–1350 d.C.*, edited by Laura Solar Valverde and Ben A. Nelson, pp. 287–312. El Colegio de Michoacán, Zamora, and Arizona State University, Tempe.
2020a Weaving our Life: The Economy and Ideology of Cotton in Postclassic West Mexico. In *Ancient West Mexicos: Time, Space, and Diversity*, edited by Joshua D. Englehardt, Verenice Y. Heredia Espinoza, and Christopher S. Beekman, pp. 302–348. University Press of Florida, Gainesville.
2020b Classic Mimbres Art, Innovation or Inspiration? Representational and Portraiture Traditions on Aztatlán Ceramics in West Mexico (AD 850/900–1350+). Poster presented at the Seventeenth Biennial Southwest Symposium Archaeological Conference, Tempe, AZ.
2021a Life in Bloom: The Casas Grandes Flower World and Its Antecedents in Northwest Mesoamerica, Northern Mexico, and the American Southwest. In *Flower Worlds: Religion, Aesthetics, and Ideology in Mesoamerica and the American Southwest*, edited by Michael D. Mathiowetz and Andrew D. Turner, pp. 174–200. Amerind Seminars in Anthropology. University of Arizona Press, Tucson.
2021b Beyond Maize, Beans, and Squash: Pinpointing the Source and Nature of Mesoamerican Influence on U.S. Southwest/Northwest Mexican Dynamics after the Origin of Agriculture. Presentation for Crow Canyon Archaeological Center, Online Resource: https://www.youtube.com/watch?v=oMRpdodBQdo, accessed July 26, 2022.
2021c Mimbres, the View from West Mexico: Aztatlán Cargo Systems and Figurative Bowl Traditions and Their Influence on Classic Mimbres Ceramics, Worldview, and Social Change in Southwestern New Mexico. Presentation for Crow Canyon Archaeological Center, Online Resource: https://www.youtube.com/watch?v=SsUwsqaLKOo, accessed July 26, 2022.
2022 "The Dance of the Sprouting Corn": Casas Grandes Maize Ceremonialism and the Transformation of the Puebloan World. In *Borderlands Histories:*

Ethnographic Observations and Archaeological Interpretations, edited by John Carpenter and Matthew Pailes, pp. 159–192. University of Utah Press, Salt Lake City.

2023a Journey to Dawn: Gold-Disk Pectorals and Divine Solar Authority in Postclassic Mesoamerica, West Mexico, and the Lower Central American Connection. In *When East Meets West: Chichen Itza, Tula, and the Postclassic Mesoamerican World*, edited by Travis W. Stanton, Jeremy Coltman, Karl A. Taube, and Nelda I. Marengo Camacho, pp. 85–126. British Archaeological Reports, London, UK.

2023b "The Road Not Taken": Assessing the Evidence for Gulf Coast Huastec and West Mexican Aztatlán Routes of Connectivity with the U.S. Southwest/Northwest Mexico. Paper presented at the 18th Biennial Southwest Symposium Archaeological Conference, Santa Fe, NM.

2023c "Nuestros Pequeños Raspadores Floridos": Los Raspadores Musicales Dentados y La Materialización del *Sea Ánia* (Mundo Flor) Yoeme. *Arqueología Mexicana* 30(181):34–42.

2025a Los Hijos del Tonati: Costumbre Náayeri y los Aspectos Diurno y Nocturno de Venus y el Sol en el Occidente Prehispánico de México. In *Presencia Náayeri. Historia y Antropología de un Pueblo*, edited by Adriana Guzmán, Regina Lira, and Rodrigo Parra Gutiérrez. Universidad Autónoma de Nayarit, Tepic.

2025b "The Sun Father Carried with Him the Chocolate": Ethnological Insights on Cacao Use, Landscape Ritualism, and Interregional Interaction in the Gran Nayar and Aztatlán Regions of West Mexico. In *Fuimos Cacaoteros: Historia y Antropología del Cacao en América*, Edith Ortiz Díaz and Verónica Velásquez, eds. Universidad Nacional Autónoma de Mexico, Mexico City.

Mathiowetz, Michael, Polly Schaafsma, Jeremy Coltman, and Karl Taube

2015 The Darts of Dawn: The Tlahuizcalpantecuhtli Venus Complex in the Iconography of Mesoamerica and the American Southwest. *Journal of the Southwest* 57(1):1–102.

Mathiowetz, Michael D., and Andrew D. Turner (editors)

2021 *Flower Worlds: Religion, Aesthetics, and Ideology in Mesoamerica and the American Southwest*. Amerind Seminars in Anthropology. University of Arizona Press, Tucson.

McCafferty, Geoffrey G.

1994 The Mixteca-Puebla Stylistic Tradition at Early Postclassic Cholula. In *Mixteca-Puebla: Discoveries and Research in Mesoamerican Art and Archaeology*, edited by H. B. Nicholson and Eloise Quiñones Keber, pp. 53–77. Labyrinthos, Culver City, CA.

1996 The Ceramics and Chronology of Cholula, Mexico. *Ancient Mesoamerica* 7:299–323.

2001 *Ceramics of Postclassic Cholula, Mexico: Typology and Seriation of Pottery from the UA-1 Domestic Compound*. Cotsen Institute of Archaeology, Monograph 43, University of California, Los Angeles.

2015 The Mexican Legacy in Nicaragua, or Problems when Data Behave Badly. *Archeological Papers of the American Anthropological Association* 25:110–118.

2019 Mixteca-Puebla Style Ceramics from Early Postclassic Pacific Nicaragua. *Mexicon* 41(3):77–83.

McCafferty, Geoffrey G., and Carrie L. Dennett

2013 Ethnogenesis and Hybridity in Proto-Historic Nicaragua. *Archaeological Review from Cambridge* 28(1):191–215.

2016 El Horizonte Cerámico de Engobe Blanco del Postclásico Temprano de México y Centro América. In *Arqueología de Nicaragua: Memorias de Mi Museo y Vos*, edited by Nora Zambrano Lacayo and Geoffrey G. McCafferty, pp. 316–329. Museo de Arqueología Precolombina Mi Museo, Granada, Nicaragua.

McCafferty, Geoffrey G., and Larry Steinbrenner

2005 The Meaning of the Mixteca-Puebla Stylistic Tradition: The View from Nicaragua. In *Art for Archaeology's Sake: Material Culture and Style across the Disciplines*, edited by Andrea Waters-Rist, Christine Cluney, Calla McNamee, and Larry Steinbrenner, pp. 282–292. Proceedings of the Thirty-third Annual Chacmool Conference, Archaeological Association of the University of Calgary, Calgary, Canada.

McCarty, Kieran, and Dan S. Matson

1975 Franciscan Report on the Indians of Nayarit, 1673. *Ethnohistory* 22(3):192–221.

McEwan, Colin, and John W. Hoopes (editors)

2021 *Pre-Columbian Central America, Colombia, and Ecuador: Toward an Integrated Approach*. Dumbarton Oaks Research Library and Collection, Washington, DC.

McEwan, Colin, Andrew Middleton, Caroline Cartwright, and Rebecca Stacey

2006 *Turquoise Mosaics from Mexico*. Duke University Press, Durham, NC.

McGregor, John C.

1943 Burial of an Early American Magician. *Proceedings of the American Philosophical Society* 86(2):270–298.

McGuire, Randall H.

1980 The Mesoamerican Connection in the Southwest. *Kiva* 46(1–2):3–38.

1987 The Greater Southwest as Periphery of Mesoamerica. In *Centre and Periphery: Comparative Studies in Archaeology*, edited by Timothy C. Champion, pp. 40–66. Unwin Hyman, London.

1996 Book review of *The Gran Chichimeca: Essays on the Archaeology and Ethnohistory of Northern Mesoamerica*, edited by Jonathan E. Reyman, Avebury Press. *American Anthropologist*, n.s. 98(2):433–434.

2011 Pueblo Religion and the Mesoamerican Connection. In *Religious Transformation in the Late Pre-Hispanic*

Pueblo World, edited by Donna M. Glowacki and Scott Van Keuren, pp. 23–49. Amerind Studies in Archaeology. University of Arizona Press, Tucson.

McGuire Randall H., and Ann V. Howard
1987 The Structure and Organization of Hohokam Shell Exchange. *Kiva* 52(2):113–146.

McGuire, Randall H., and Elisa Villalpando
2007 The Hohokam and Mesoamerica. In *The Hohokam Millennium*, edited by Suzanne K. Fish and Paul R. Fish, pp. 57–64. School for Advanced Research Press, Santa Fe.

McGuire, Randall H., and Elisa Villalpando (editors)
2012 *Excavations at Cerro de Trincheras, Sonora, Mexico*, Vols. 1–2. Arizona State Museum Archaeological Series 204, Arizona State Museum, University of Arizona, Tucson.

McGuire, Randall H., Elisa Villalpando, Victoria D. Vargas, and Emiliano Gallaga Murrieta
1999 Cerro de Trincheras and the Casas Grandes World. In *The Casas Grandes World*, edited by Curtis F. Schaafsma and Carroll L. Riley, pp. 134–146. University of Utah Press, Salt Lake City.

McVicker, Mary F.
2005 *Adela Breton: A Victorian Artist Amid Mexico's Ruins*. University of New Mexico Press, Albuquerque.

Medellín Zenil, Alfonso
1955 *Exploraciones en la Isla de Sacrificios*. Informe. Gobierno del Estado de Veracruz, Xalapa. Dirreción General de Educación, Departamento de Antropología, Mexico City.

Meggers, Betty J.
1975 The Transpacific Origin of Mesoamerican Civilization: A Preliminary Review of the Evidence and Its Theoretical Implications. *American Anthropologist* 77(1):1–27.

Meighan, Clement W.
1969 Cultural Similarities between Western Mexico and Andean Regions. In *Pre-Columbian Contact Within Nuclear America*, edited by J. Charles Kelley and Carroll L. Riley, pp. 11–25. Mesoamerican Studies 4, Research Records of the University Museum. Southern Illinois University Press, Carbondale.
1971 Archaeology of Sinaloa. In *Archaeology of Northern Mesoamerica*, Pt. 2, edited by Gordon F. Ekholm and Ignacio Bernal, pp. 754–767. Handbook of Middle American Indians, Vol. 11, Robert Wauchope, general editor, University of Texas Press, Austin.
1976 The Archaeology of Amapa, Nayarit. In *The Archaeology of Amapa, Nayarit*, edited by Clement W. Meighan, pp. 1–205. Monumenta Archaeologica, Vol. 2. Institute of Archaeology, University of California, Los Angeles.

Meighan, Clement W. (editor)
1976 *The Archaeology of Amapa, Nayarit*. Monumenta Archaeologica, Vol. 2. Institute of Archaeology, University of California, Los Angeles.

Meighan, Clement W., and Leonard J. Foote
1968 *Excavations at Tizapán el Alto, Jalisco*. Latin American Studies, Vol. 11. University of California, Los Angeles.

Meighan, Clement W., and H. B. Nicholson
1989 The Ceramic Mortuary Offerings of Prehistoric West Mexico: An Archaeological Perspective. In *Sculpture of Ancient West Mexico: Nayarit, Jalisco, and Colima. A Catalogue of the Proctor Stafford Collection at the Los Angeles County Museum of Art*, pp. 29–67. Los Angeles County Museum of Art, Los Angeles, and University of New Mexico Press, Albuquerque.

Méndez, Matías, and Victor Magaña
2010 Regional Aspects of Prolonged Meteorological Droughts over Mexico and Central America. *Journal of Climate* 23:1175–1188.

Mendoza, Rubén G.
2022 The Turquoise Corridor: Mesoamerica Prestige Technologies and Social Complexity in the Greater Southwest. In *Trade Before Civilization: Long Distance Exchange and the Rise of Social Complexity*, edited by Johan Ling, Richard Chacon, and Kristian Kristiansen, pp. 251–285. Cambridge University Press, Cambridge, UK.

Merrill, William L.
1996 Uto-Aztecan Religions and Cosmologies: Reflections on a Research Project in Response to Armin W. Geertz. *Method & Theory in the Study of Religion* 8(1):65–73.

Meskell, Lynn
2002 The Intersections of Identity and Politics in Archaeology. *Annual Review of Anthropology* 31:279–301.

Metcalfe, Sarah E., John A. Barron, and Sarah J. Davies
2015 The Holocene History of the North American Monsoon: "Known Knowns" and "Known Unknowns" in Understanding Its Spatial and Temporal Complexity. *Quaternary Science Reviews* 120:1–27.

Meyer, Jean
1989 *El Gran Nayar*. Colección de Documentos para la Historia de Nayarit III. Universidad de Guadalajara and Centro de Estudios Mexicanos y Centroamericanos, Mexico City, Mexico.

Miller, Myles R.
2018 A Millennium of Identity Formation and Maintenance in the Jornada Mogollon Region. In *Life Beyond the Boundaries: Constructing Identity in Edge Regions of the North American Southwest*, edited by Karen G. Harry and Sarah A. Herr, pp. 239–272. University Press of Colorado, Louisville.

Miller, Wick R.
1983a Uto-Aztecan Languages. In *Southwest*, edited by Alfonso Ortiz, pp. 113–124. Handbook of North American Indians, Vol. 10, William C. Sturtevant, general editor. Government Printing Office, Smithsonian Institution, Washington, DC.
1983b A Note on Extinct Languages of Northwest Mexico of Supposed Uto-Aztecan Affiliation. *International Journal of American Linguistics* 49(3):328–335.

Mills, Barbara J. (editor)
2004   *Identity, Feasting, and the Archaeology of the Greater Southwest.* University Press of Colorado, Boulder.

Mills, Barbara J., Jeffrey J. Clark, Matthew A. Peeples, W. R. Haas Jr., John M. Roberts Jr., J. Brett Hill, Deborah L. Huntley, et al.
2013   Transformation of Social Networks in the Late Pre-Hispanic US Southwest. *Proceedings of the National Academy of Sciences of the United States of America* 110(15):5785–5790.

Mills, Barbara J., and T. J. Ferguson
2008   Animate Objects: Shell Trumpets and Ritual Networks in the Greater Southwest. *Journal of Archaeological Method and Theory* 15:338–361.

Milner, George R., and Clark S. Larsen
1991   Teeth as Artifacts of Human Behavior: Intentional Mutilation and Accidental Modification. In *Advances in Dental Anthropology*, edited by Marc A. Kelley and Clark S. Larsen, pp. 357–378. Wiley-Liss, New York.

Minnis, Paul E., and Michael E. Whalen (editors)
2015   *Ancient Paquimé and the Casas Grandes World.* Amerind Studies in Anthropology. University of Arizona Press, Tucson.

Moctezuma Zamarrón, José L.
1991   Las Lenguas Indígenas del Noroeste de México: Pasado y Presente. In *El Noroeste de México, sus Culturas Étnicas: Seminario de Etnografía "Fernando Camara Barbachano,"* edited by Donaciano Gutiérrez and Josefina Gutiérrez Tripp, pp. 125–136. Instituto Nacional de Antropología e Historia, Mexico City.

Molina, Felipe S., and David Delgado Shorter
2021   "The Living Beautiful Part of Our Present World": The Yoeme *Sea Ania* (Flower World). In *Flower Worlds: Religion, Aesthetics, and Ideology in Mesoamerica and the American Southwest*, edited by Michael D. Mathiowetz and Andrew D. Turner, pp. 70–86. Amerind Seminars in Anthropology. University of Arizona Press, Tucson.

Monaghan, John
1995   *The Covenants with Earth and Rain: Exchange, Sacrifice, and Revelation in Mixtec Sociality.* University of Oklahoma Press, Norman.

Montgomery, Lindsay M.
2015   Yndios Bárbaros: Nomadic Archaeologies of Northern New Mexico. PhD dissertation, Department of Anthropology, Stanford University, Stanford, CA.

Morales Monroy, Juan Jorge
2012   *Informe: Reporte de la excavación de las cistas funerarias del cementerio de Ahuacatlán. Primera Temporada 2012.* Archivo Técnico de la Sección de Arqueología, Centro Instituto Nacional de Antropología e Historia, Nayarit, Tepic.

Morales-Arce, Ana Y., Meradeth H. Snow, Jane H. Kelley, and M. Anne Katzenberg
2017   Ancient Mitochondrial DNA and Ancestry of Paquimé Inhabitants, Casas Grandes (A.D. 1200–1450). *American Journal of Physical Anthropology* 163(3):616–626.

Morris, Nathaniel
2020   *Soldiers, Saints, and Shamans: Indigenous Communities and the Revolutionary State in Mexico's Gran Nayar, 1910–1940.* University of Arizona Press, Tucson.

Morrison, Kenneth M.
1992   Sharing the Flower: A Non-Supernaturalistic Theory of Grace. *Religion* 22:207–219.

Mountjoy, Joseph B.
1969   On the Origin of West Mexican Metallurgy. In *Pre-Columbian Contact Within Nuclear America*, edited by J. Charles Kelley and Carroll L. Riley, pp. 26–42. Mesoamerican Studies 4, Research Records of the University Museum. Southern Illinois University Press, Carbondale.

1970   Prehispanic Culture History and Cultural Contact on the Southern Coast of Nayarit, Mexico. PhD dissertation, Department of Anthropology, Southern Illinois University, Carbondale.

1974a   Some Hypotheses Regarding the Petroglyphs of West Mexico. *Mesoamerican Studies*, No. 9. Research Records of the University Museum. Southern Illinois University, Carbondale.

1974b   San Blas Complex Ecology. In *The Archaeology of West Mexico*, edited by Betty B. Bell, pp. 106–119. Sociedad de Estudios Avanzados del Occidente de México, Ajijic, Jalisco, Mexico.

1982   *El Proyecto Tomatlán de Salvamento Arqueológico: Fondo Etnohistórico y Arqueológico, Desarrollo del Proyecto, Estudios de la Superficie.* Colección Científica Arqueología, No. 122. Instituto Nacional de Antropología e Historia, Mexico City.

1983   Investigaciones Arqueológicas en la Cuenca del Río Tomatlán, Jalisco: 1975–1977. *Pantoc* 5:21–50. Universidad Autónoma de Guadalajara, Guadalajara, Mexico.

1987a   *El Proyecto Tomatlán de Salvamento Arqueológico: El Arte Rupestre.* Colección Científica Arqueología, No. 163, Instituto Nacional de Antropología e Historia, Mexico City.

1987b   Antiquity, Interpretation, and Stylistic Evolution of Petroglyphs in West Mexico. *American Antiquity* 52(1):161–174.

1990   El Desarrollo de la Cultura Aztatlán Visto desde su Frontera Suroeste. In *Mesoamérica y Norte de México: Siglo XI–XII*, Vol. 2, edited by Federica Sodi Miranda, pp. 541–564. Instituto Nacional de Antropología e Historia, Museo Nacional de Antropología, Mexico City.

1991   West Mexican Stelae from Jalisco and Nayarit. *Ancient Mesoamerica* 2:21–33.

1993   El Pasado Prehispánico del Municipio de Puerto Vallarta. In *Una Aproximación a Puerto Vallarta*, edited by Jaime Olveda, pp. 23–40. El Colegio de Jalisco, Zapopan.

1995   Some Important Resources for Prehispanic Cultures on the Coast of West Mexico. In *The Gran Chichimeca: Essays on the Archaeology and Ethnohistory of Northern Mesoamerica*, edited by Jonathan E. Reyman, pp. 61–87. Avebury, Aldershot, UK.

2000 Prehispanic Cultural Development along the Southern Coast of West Mexico. In *Greater Mesoamerica: The Archaeology of West and Northwest Mexico*, edited by Michael S. Foster and Shirley Gorenstein, pp. 81–106. University of Utah Press, Salt Lake City.

2001a El Misterio del Mictlantecuhtli. *Arqueología* 24: 115–128. Instituto Nacional de Antropología e Historia, Mexico City.

2001b Aztatlán Complex. In *Archaeology of Ancient Mexico and Central America: An Encyclopedia*, edited by Susan T. Evans and David L. Webster, pp. 57–59. Garland, New York.

2005 Algunos Patollis Abreviados Encontrados entre los Petrograbados de Jalisco. In *Los Petrograbados del Norte de México*, edited by Victor Joel Santos Ramírez and Ramón Viñas Valverdú, pp. 180–184. Centro Instituto Nacional de Antropología e Historia, Sinaloa, and Actualidades Arqueológicas, Mexico City.

2008 *Arqueología de la Zona Costera de Jalisco y del Municipio de Villa Purificación. Miscelánea Histórica de Villa Purificación: Testimonios del 475 Aniversario de su Fundación*, edited by Aristarco Regalado Pinedo and Juan Sánchez Vázquez, pp. 21–39. Ayuntamiento Constitucional de Villa Purificación, Mexico.

2018 *Los Petroglifos del Valle de Mascota, Jalisco: Descripción, Análisis e Interpretación*. Universidad de Guadalajara, Guadalajara, Mexico.

2019 *Proyecto Tomatlán de Salvamento Arqueológico. Fondo Etnohistórico y Arqueológico. Desarrollo del Proyecto. Estudios de la Superficie.* Segunda edición, actualizada y expandida. Universidad de Guadalajara, Guadalajara, Mexico.

Mountjoy, Joseph B., Fabio G. Cupul-Magaña, Rafael García de Quevedo-Machain, and Martha L. López Mestas Camberos

2020 The Early Postclassic Aztatlán Colonization of the Pacific Coast of Jalisco. In *Ancient West Mexicos: Time, Space, and Diversity*, edited by Joshua D. Englehardt, Verenice Y. Heredia Espinoza, and Christopher S. Beekman, pp. 131–158. University Press of Florida, Gainesville.

Mountjoy, Joseph, Rafael García de Quevedo-Machain, Karla G. Ríos-González, and Fabio G. Cupul-Magaña

2022 *Arroyo Piedras Azules y la Colonización Aztatlán de la Costa de Jalisco en el Posclásico Temprano*. Universidad de Guadalajara and Centro Universitario de la Costa, Puerto Vallarta, Jalisco, Mexico.

Mountjoy, Joseph B., and Otto Schöndube Baumbach

2014 *Investigaciones Arqueológicas en la Zona Costera de Jalisco*. Technical report. Archivo Técnico de la Coordinación Nacional de Arqueología, Instituto Nacional de Antropología e Historia, Mexico City.

Mountjoy, Joseph B., Tammy C. Smith, Ryun Papson, Debbie Guida, John Pleasants, Chris Witmore, and Cheryl Cross

2003 *Arqueología del Municipio de Puerto Vallarta*. Electronic document, https://archaeology.uncg.edu/Vallarta/, accessed August 12, 2020.

Mountjoy, Joseph B., and Luis Torres M.

1985 The Production and Use of Prehispanic Metal Artifacts in the Central Coastal Area of Jalisco, Mexico. In *The Archaeology of West and Northwest Mesoamerica*, edited by Michael S. Foster and Phil C. Weigand, pp. 133–152. Westview Press, Boulder, CO.

Murguía Hernández, Ana I.

2011 El Tiempo y la Arqueología del Noroeste Durangueño. Bachelor's thesis, Universidad Autónoma de Zacatecas Francisco García Salinas, Unidad Académica de Antropología, Zacatecas.

Murphy, Bill

1959 Relics Tell of Ancient Mexican Civilization: UCLA Anthropologist Finds New Facts on Tribes Once Living in Guadalajara Area. *Los Angeles Times*, August 9, 1959, 19. With photo. ProQuest Historical Newspapers.

Myerhoff, Barbara G.

1974 *Peyote Hunt: The Sacred Journey of the Huichol Indians*. Cornell University Press, Ithaca.

Neff, Hector

2014 Pots as Signals: Explaining the Enigma of Long-distance Ceramic Exchange. In *Craft and Science: International Perspectives on Archeological Ceramics*, edited by Marcos Martinón-Torres, pp. 1–11. University College of London Qatar Series in Archaeology and Cultural Heritage, Vol. 1. Bloomsbury Qatar Foundation, Doha, Qatar.

Negrín da Silva, Diana

2018 "It is loved, and it is defended": Critical Solidarity Across Race and Place. *Antipode* 50(4):1016–1036.

Nelson, Ben A.

2004 Current and Future Directions in Northwest Mexican Archaeology. In *Surveying the Archaeology of Northwest Mexico*, edited by Gillian E. Newell and Emiliano Gallaga, pp. 289–296. University of Utah Press, Salt Lake City.

2006 Mesoamerican Objects and Symbols in Chaco Canyon Contexts. In *The Archaeology of Chaco Canyon: An Eleventh-Century Pueblo Regional Center*, edited by Stephen H. Lekson, pp. 339–371. School of American Research Press, Santa Fe.

Nelson, Ben A., Paul R. Fish, and Suzanne K. Fish

2017 Mesoamerican Connections. In *The Oxford Handbook of Southwest Archaeology*, edited by Barbara J. Mills and Severin Fowles, pp. 461–479. Oxford University Press, New York.

Nelson, Ben A., and Paul E. Minnis

2018 Connectivity of Social Change in Mimbres and Points South. In *New Perspectives on Mimbres Archaeology: Three Millennia of Human Occupation in the North American Southwest*, edited by Barbara J. Roth, Patricia A. Gilman, and Roger Anyon, pp. 232–247. University of Arizona Press, Tucson.

Nelson, Ben A., Elisa Villalpando Canchola, Jose L. Punzo Díaz, and Paul E. Minnis

2015 Prehispanic Northwest and Adjacent West Mexico, 1200 B.C.–A.D. 1400: An Inter-Regional Perspective. *Kiva* 81(1–2):31–61.

Nelson, Margaret C., and Michelle Hegmon (editors)

2010 *Mimbres Lives and Landscapes*. School for Advanced Research Press, Santa Fe.

Nelson, Margaret C., and Colleen Strawhacker (editors)
2011   *Movement, Connectivity, and Landscape Change in the Ancient Southwest*. University Press of Colorado, Boulder.

Nelson, Richard
1981   The Role of a Puchteca System in Hohokam Exchange. PhD dissertation, Department of Anthropology, New York University, New York.

Neumann, George K.
1942   Types of Artificial Cranial Deformation in the Eastern United States. *American Antiquity* 7(3): 306–310.

Neurath, Johannes
2000   *Tukipa* Ceremonial Centers in the Community of Tuapurie (Santa Catarina Cuexcomatitlán): Cargo Systems, Landscape, and Cosmovision. *Journal of the Southwest* 42(1):81–110.
2001   El Cerro del Amanecer y el Culto Solar Huichol. In *La Montaña en el Paisaje Ritual*, edited by Johanna Broda, Stanislaw Iwaniszewski, and Arturo Montero, pp. 475–488. Universidad Autónoma de Puebla and Instituto de Ciencias Sociales y Humanidades/Universidad Nacional Autónoma de Mexico/Instituto Nacional de Antropología e Historia, Mexico City.
2002   *Las Fiestas de la Casa Grande: Procesos Rituales, Cosmovisión y Estructura Social en una Comunidad Huichola*. Colección Etnografía en el Nuevo Milenio, Serie Estudios Monográficos. In stituto Nacional de Antropología e Historia and Universidad de Guadalajara, Guadalajara, Mexico.
2003   Cosmovisión y Sexualidad en la Fiesta *Namawita Neixa* de Keuruwit+a. In *Flechadores de Estrellas: Nuevas Aportaciones a la Etnología de Coras y Huicholes*, edited by Jesús Jáuregui and Johannes Neurath, pp. 207–220. Instituto Nacional de Antropología e Historia and Universidad de Guadalajara, Mexico City.
2005a   Cosmogonic Myths, Ritual Groups, and Initiation: Toward a New Comparative Ethnology of the Gran Nayar and the Southwest of the U.S. *Journal of the Southwest* 47(4):571–614.
2005b   The Ambivalent Character of Xurawe: Venus-Related Ritual and Mythology among West Mexican Indians. *Archeoastronomy* 19:74–102.
2005c   Máscaras Enmascaradas: Indígenas, Mestizos y Dioses Indígenas Mestizos. *Relaciones* 26(101): 21–50.
2008   Cacería Ritual y Sacrificios Huicholes: Entre Depredación y Alianza, Intercambio e Identificación. *Journal de la Société des Américanistes* 94(1):251–283.
2013   *La Vida de las Imágenes: Arte Huichol*. Artes de México and El Consejo Nacional de la Cultura y las Artes, Mexico City.
2015   Shifting Ontologies in Huichol Ritual and Art. *Anthropology and Humanism* 40(1):58–71.
2021   Becoming Peyote, or the Flowers of Wirikuta. In *Flower Worlds: Religion, Aesthetics, and Ideology in Mesoamerica and the American Southwest*, edited by Michael D. Mathiowetz and Andrew D. Turner, pp. 52–69. Amerind Seminars in Anthropology. University of Arizona Press, Tucson.
2022   Wixárika Polytheism as Ecology. *Oscillations: Non-Standard Experiments in Anthropology, the Social Sciences, and Cosmology*, pp. 1–26. Online Resource: https://oscillations.one/Assets/Neurath+2022.pdf, accessed July 26, 2022.

Neurath, Johannes (editor)
2007   Arte Antiguo Cora y Huichol: La Colleción de Konrad T. Preuss. *Artes de México* 85. Artes de México, Mexico City.

Neurath, Johannes, Paulina Alcocer, Philip E. Coyle, Arturo Gutiérrez, Jesús Jáuregui, and Héctor Medina
2003   Los que Caminan en el Amanecer: Territorialidad, Peregrinaciones y Santuarios en el Gran Nayar. In *Diálogos con el Territorio: Simbolizaciones sobre el Espacio en las Culturas Indígenas de México*, Vol. 3, pp. 39–123. Alicia M. Barabas, general editor. Instituto Nacional de Antropología e Historia, Mexico City.

Nicholson, H. B.
1982   The Mixteca-Puebla Concept Revisited. In *The Art and Archaeology of Late Post-Classic Central Mexico*, edited by Elizabeth H. Boone, pp. 227–254. Dumbarton Oaks Research Library and Collection, Washington, DC.
1989   The Cult of Xipe Totec in Pre-Hispanic West Mexico. In *Homenaje a Isabel Kelly*, edited by Yólotl González, pp. 109–119. Instituto Nacional de Antropología e Historia, Serie Arqueología, Mexico City.
2001   Mixteca-Puebla Style. In *The Oxford Encyclopedia of Mesoamerican Cultures: The Civilizations of Mexico and Central America*, Vol. 2, edited by Davíd Carrasco, pp. 329–330. Oxford University Press, New York.

Nicholson, H. B., and Eloise Quiñones Keber
1994   Introduction. In *Mixteca-Puebla: Discoveries and Research in Mesoamerican Art and Archaeology*, edited by H. B. Nicholson and Eloise Quiñones Keber, pp. vii–xv. Labyrinthos, Culver City, CA.

Noguera, Eduardo
1954   *La Cerámica Arqueológica de Cholula*. Editorial Guarania, Mexico City.

Nuttall, Zelia
1910   The Island of Sacrificios. *American Anthropologist* 12(2):257–295.

Ocampo, Daisy
2019   Spiritual Geographies of Indigenous Sovereignty: Connections of Caxcan with Tlachialoyantepec and Chemehuevi with Mamapukaib. PhD dissertation, Department of History, University of California, Riverside.

Odell, George H.
2004   *Lithic Analysis*. Kluwer Academic and Plenum, New York.

Ohnersorgen, Michael A.
2004   Informe Técnico Final de Proyecto "Investigaciónes Arqueológica Preliminar de Chacalilla, Nayarit, México, Temporada 2003." Archivo Técnico de la

Sección de Arqueología, Centro Instituto Nacional de Antropología e Historia, Nayarit, Tepic.

2007 *La Organización Socio-económica y la Interacción Regional de un Centro Aztatlán: Investigaciones Arqueológicos en Chacalilla, Nayarit. Informe Técnico Parcial, Temporada de 2005*. Archivo Técnico de la Sección de Arqueología, Centro Instituto Nacional de Antropología e Historia, Nayarit, Tepic.

2019 Aspectos Económicos de la Tradición Aztatlán: Producción Artesanal, Intercambio e Interacción en la Costa Central de Nayarit. In *Aztatlán: Interacción y Cambio Social en el Occidente de México ca. 850–1350 d.C.*, edited by Laura Solar Valverde and Ben A. Nelson, pp. 61–88. El Colegio de Michoacán, Zamora, and Arizona State University, Tempe.

Ohnersorgen, Michael A., Michael D. Glascock, Joseph B. Mountjoy, and Mauricio Garduño Ambriz

2012 Chemical Analysis of Obsidian Artifacts from the West Coast of Mexico: Implications for Regional and Interregional Economic Organization. Manuscript on file in the Department of Anthropology, University of Missouri, Saint Louis.

Ohnersorgen, Michael A., Michael D. Mathiowetz, Mauricio Garduño Ambriz, and Enrique Soruco Saenz

2010a Solar Ceremonialism and Human Sacrifice: The Aztatlán Tradition at Chacalilla, Nayarit. Manuscript in possession of authors.

2010b Solar Ceremonialism and Human Sacrifice: The Aztatlán Tradition at Chacalilla, Nayarit. Paper presented at the 75th Annual Meeting of the Society for American Archaeology, Saint Louis, MO.

Olay Barrientos, María de los Ángeles

2004 *El Chanal, Colima: Lugar que Habitan los Custodios del Agua*. Universidad de Colima and Instituto Nacional de Antropología e Historia, Mexico City.

2006 *Volcán de Fuego, Cuna del Agua, Morada del Viento: Desarrollo Social y Procesos de Cambio en el Valle de Colima, Mexico. Una Propuesta de Interpretación*, Vol. II. Instituto Nacional de Antropología e Historia, El Consejo Nacional para la Cultura y las Artes, and El Colegio de Michoacán, Mexico City.

Ortega Léon, Víctor, and Luis A. Grave Tirado

2019 "Por Tierras no Sabidas y tan Estrañas": Geografía Protohistórica de la Costa Noroccidental del Pacífico: La Ruta de Guzmán. Colección Scientia/Científica, Serie Ensamblaje. Secretaría de Cultura, Instituto Nacional de Antropología e Historia, Escuela de Antropología e Historia del Norte de México, Mexico City.

Ortman, Scott G.

2012 *Winds from the North: Tewa Origins and Historical Anthropology*. University of Utah Press, Salt Lake City.

Oseguera, Andrés, Ricardo Pacheco Bribiesca, Eduardo Saucedo, and Antonio Reyes Valdez

2015 De la Ambivalencia al Tabú: Las Transformaciones del Concepto de Persona en el Noroeste de México. In *Cosmovisiones y Mitologías Indígenas II*, edited by Catherine Good Eshelman and Marina Alonso Bolaños, pp. 97–174. Instituto Nacional de Antropología e Historia, Mexico City.

Overholtzer, Lisa

2014 A New Bayesian Chronology for Postclassic and Colonial Occupation at Xaltocan, Mexico. *Radiocarbon* 56(3):1077–1092.

Pagden, Anthony (editor)

1986 *Hernán Cortés: Letters from Mexico*. Yale University Press, New Haven, CT.

Pailes, Matthew

2017 Northwest Mexico: The Prehistory of Sonora, Chihuahua, and Neighboring Areas. *Journal of Archaeological Research* 25(4):373–420.

Pailes, Matthew C., and Michael T. Searcy

2022 *Hinterlands to Cities: The Archaeology of Northwest Mexico and Its Vecinos*. Society for American Archaeology Press, Washington, DC.

Pailes, Richard A.

1972 An Archaeological Reconnaissance of Southern Sonora and Reconsideration of the Río Sonora Culture. PhD dissertation, Department of Anthropology, Southern Illinois University, Carbondale.

1976 Recientes Investigaciones Arqueológicas en el Sur de Sonora. In *Sonora: Antropología del Desierto*, edited by Beatriz Braniff and Richard Felger, pp. 137–156. Colección Científica 27. Instituto Nacional de Antropología e Historia, Mexico City.

Pailes, Richard A., and Joseph W. Whitecotton

1979 The Greater Southwest and Mesoamerican World System: An Exploratory Model of Frontier Relationships. In *The Frontier: Comparative Studies*, Vol. 2, edited by William W. Savage Jr. and Steven I. Thompson, pp. 105–121. University of Oklahoma Press, Norman.

Parsons, Elsie Clews

1936 *Mitla: Town of Souls*. University of Chicago, Chicago.

Parsons, Lee A.

1969 *Bilbao, Guatemala: An Archaeological Study of the Pacific Coast Cotzumalhuapa Region*, Vol. 2. Publications in Anthropology 12, Milwaukee Public Museum, Milwaukee, WI.

1978 The Peripheral Coastal Lowlands and the Middle Classic Period. In *Middle Classic Mesoamerica: A.D. 400–700*, edited by Esther Pasztory, pp. 25–34. Columbia University Press, New York.

Paso y Troncoso, Francisco

1946 [1652] *Relaciones Geográficas del Siglo XVIII* [sic] *San Pedro Teocaltiche*. Biblioteca Aportación Histórico. Editor Vargas Rea, Mexico City.

Pasztory, Esther

1978 Historical Synthesis of the Middle Classic Period. In *Middle Classic Mesoamerica: A.D. 400–700*, edited by Esther Pasztory, pp. 3–22. Columbia University Press, New York.

Patel, Shankari

2012 Journey to the East: Pilgrimage, Politics, and Gender in Postclassic Mexico. PhD dissertation, Department of Anthropology, University of California, Riverside.

Peeples, Matthew A.
2018 Connected Communities: Networks, Identity, and Social Change in the Ancient Cibola World. University of Arizona Press, Tucson.

Pendergast, David M.
1962a Metal Artifacts from Amapa, Nayarit, Mexico. American Antiquity 27(3):370–379.
1962b Metal Artifacts in Prehispanic Mesoamerica. American Antiquity 27(4):520–545.

Peregrine, Peter N., and Stephen H. Lekson
2006 Southeast, Southwest, Mexico: Continental Perspectives on Mississippian Politics. In Leadership and Polity in Mississippian Society, edited by Brain M. Butler and Paul D. Welch, pp. 351–364. Southern Illinois University Press, Carbondale.

Pereira, Gregory
1999 Potrero Guadalupe: Anthropologie funéraire d´une Communauté pré-Tarasque du Nord du Michoacán, Mexique. Monographs in American Archaeology 5. British Archaeological Reports International Series 816, Archaeopress, Oxford, UK.

Pérez, Manuel, Lorena Gámez, and Mauricio Garduño
2000 Proyecto de Salvamento Arqueológico "Autopista Entronque San Blas-Mazatlán, Tramo Nayarit." Informe Técnico. Trabajos de Reconocimiento de Superficie y Excavación (julio-noviembre de 1998). Dirección de Salvamento Arqueológico, Centro Instituto Nacional de Antropología e Historia, Nayarit, Tepic.

Pérez de Ribas, Andrés
1999 [1645] History of the Triumphs of Our Holy Faith amongst the Most Barbarous and Fierce Peoples of the New World. Translated by Daniel T. Reff, Maureen Ahern, and Richard K. Danford. University of Arizona Press, Tucson.

Phillips Jr., David A.
2002 Mesoamerican-Southwestern Relationships: An Intellectual History. In Culture and Environment in the American Southwest: Essays in Honor of Robert C. Euler, edited by David A. Phillips Jr. and John A. Ware, pp. 177–195. SWCA Environmental Consultants, Phoenix, AZ.

Phillips, Jr., David A., Christine S. VanPool, and Todd L. VanPool
2006 The Horned Serpent Tradition in the North American Southwest. In Religion in the Prehispanic Southwest, edited by Christine S. VanPool, Todd L. VanPool, and David A. Phillips Jr., pp. 17–29. AltaMira, Lanham, MD.

Pierce, Daniel E.
2012 Obsidian Source Frequencies as a Social Attribute at San Felipe Aztatán, Mexico. Master's thesis. Department of Anthropology, University of Missouri, Columbia.
2015a Visual and Geochemical Analyses of Obsidian Source Use at San Felipe Aztatán, Mexico. Journal of Anthropological Archaeology 40:266–279.
2015b Portable X-ray Fluorescence Analysis of Obsidian Polyhedral Cores Curated at the Museum of Sentispac. Technical report on file, University of Missouri Research Reactor, University of Missouri, Columbia.
2015c Portable X-ray Fluorescence Analysis of Obsidian Polyhedral Cores Curated at the Municipal Museum of Amapa. Technical report on file, University of Missouri Research Reactor, University of Missouri, Columbia.
2016 Volcán las Navajas: The Chemical Characterization and Usage of a West Mexican Obsidian Source in the Aztatlán Tradition. Journal of Archaeological Science: Reports 6:603–609.
2017a Finding Class in the Glass: Obsidian Source as a Costly Signal. Journal of Anthropological Archaeology 48:217–232.
2017b Obsidian Source Distribution and Mercantile Hierarchies in Postclassic Aztatlán, West Mexico. PhD dissertation, Department of Anthropology, University of Missouri, Columbia.
2022 A Regional Assessment of Obsidian Use in the Postclassic Aztatlán Tradition. Ancient Mesoamerica 33(2):383–402.

Plog, Stephen
1993 Changing Perspectives on North and Middle American Exchange Systems. In The American Southwest and Mesoamerica: Systems of Prehistoric Exchange, edited by Jonathon E. Ericson and Timothy G. Baugh, pp. 285–292. Plenum Press, New York.

Plog, Stephen, Christopher W. Schwartz, and Patricia Gilman
2022 Birds of the Sun: The Many Dimensions of Macaws and Other Parrots in the Lives of the Pre-Hispanic People of the U.S. Southwest and Mexican Northwest. In Birds of the Sun: Macaws and People in the U.S. Southwest and Mexican Northwest, edited by Christopher W. Schwartz, Stephen Plog, and Patricia A. Gilman, pp. 3–28. Amerind Studies in Anthropology. University of Arizona Press, Tucson.

Plourde, Aimée M.
2008 The Origins of Prestige Goods as Honest Signals of Skill and Knowledge. Human Nature 19(4):374–388.

Plunket Nagoda, Patricia, and Gabriela Uruñuela Ladrón de Guevara
2018 Cholula. Fondo de Cultura Económica and El Colegio de México, Mexico City.

Pohl, John M. D.
1994 The Politics of Symbolism in the Mixtec Codices. Vanderbilt University Publications in Anthropology, No. 46. Vanderbilt University, Nashville.
1999 The Lintel Paintings of Mitla and the Function of the Mitla Palaces. In Mesoamerican Architecture as a Cultural Symbol, edited by Jeffrey K. Kowalski, pp. 176–197. Oxford University Press, Oxford.
2001 Chichimecatlalli: Strategies for Cultural and Commercial Exchange between Mexico and the American Southwest, 1100–1521. In The Road to Aztlan: Art from a Mythic Homeland, edited by Virginia M. Fields and Victor Zamudio Taylor, pp. 86–101. Los Angeles County Museum of Art, Los Angeles.
2003a Creation Stories, Hero Cults, and Alliance Building: Postclassic Confederacies of Central and Southern Mexico from A.D. 1150–1458. In The Postclassic Mesoamerican World, edited by Michael E. Smith

and Frances F. Berdan, pp. 61–66. University of Utah Press, Salt Lake City.

2003b Ritual Ideology and Commerce in the Southern Mexican Highlands. In *The Postclassic Mesoamerican World*, edited by Michael E. Smith and Frances F. Berdan, pp. 172–177. University of Utah Press, Salt Lake City.

2003c Ritual and Iconographic Variability In Mixteca Puebla Polychrome Pottery. In *The Postclassic Mesoamerican World*, edited by Michael E. Smith and Frances F. Berdan, pp. 201–206. University of Utah Press, Salt Lake City.

2003d Royal Marriage and Confederacy Building among the Eastern Nahuas, Mixtecs, and Zapotecs. In *The Postclassic Mesoamerican World*, edited by Michael E. Smith and Frances F. Berdan, pp. 243–248. University of Utah Press, Salt Lake City.

2004 Nahua Drinking Bowl with an Image of Xochiquetzal. *Record of the Art Museum, Princeton University* 63:41–45.

2007 *Narrative Mixtec Ceramics of Ancient Mexico*. Cuadernos No. 10. Princeton University Program in Latin American Studies, Princeton.

2008 History on a Mixtec Vase. *Journal of the Gilcrease Museum* 15(2):52–64.

2009 Introduction. In *Lord Eight Wind of Suchixtlan and the Heroes of Ancient Oaxaca: Reading History in the Codex Zouche-Nuttall* by Robert L. Williams, pp. 1–26. University of Texas Press, Austin.

2012a La Tradición Aztatlán de Nayarit-Jalisco y el Estilo Nahua-Mixteca de Cholula. *Arqueología Mexicana* 20(115):60–65.

2012b The Odyssey of the Plumed Serpent. In *Children of the Plumed Serpent: The Legacy of Quetzalcoatl in Ancient Mexico*, edited by Virginia M. Fields, John M. D. Pohl, and Victoria I. Lyall, pp. 94–107. Los Angeles County Museum of Art, Los Angeles.

2015 *Armies of Castile and Aragon 1370–1516*. Osprey Press, Oxford.

2016a Transnational Tales: A Millennium of Indigenous Cultural Interaction between the United States and Mexico. In *The Forked Juniper: Critical Perspectives on Rudolfo Anaya*, edited by Roberto Cantú, pp. 253–288. University of Oklahoma Press, Norman.

2016b Dramatic Performance and the Theater of the State: The Cults of Divus Triumphator, Parthenope, and Quetzalcoatl. In *Altera Roma: Art and Empire from Mérida to Mexico*, edited by John M. D. Pohl and Claire L. Lyons, pp. 127–146. Cotsen Institute of Archaeology Press, Los Angeles.

2017 The Nahua-Mixteca International Style and the Confederacies of Southern Mexico. In *On the Mount of Intertwined Serpents: The Pictorial Power, Rule, and Land on Lienzo Seler II*, edited by Viola König, pp. 121–130. Staatliche Museen zu Berlin–Preussischer Kulturbesitz, Berlin, Ger.

2021 The Flower World of Cholula. In *Flower Worlds: Religion, Aesthetics, and Ideology in Mesoamerica and the American Southwest*, edited by Michael D. Mathiowetz and Andrew D. Turner, pp. 222–242. Amerind Studies in Anthropology. University of Arizona Press, Tucson.

Pohl, John M. D., and Bruce E. Byland
1990 Mixtec Landscape Perception and Settlement Patterns. *Ancient Mesoamerica* 1(1):113–131.

Pohl, John M. D., and Michael D. Lind
2024 A Postclassic Cholula Plate Painted with a Classic Maya Glyph. Manuscript in author's possession.

Pohl, John M. D., and Michael D. Mathiowetz
2022 Our Mother the Sea: The Pacific Coastal Exchange Network of Postclassic Mexico. In *Waves of Influence: Pacific Maritime Networks Connecting Mexico, Central America, and Northwestern South America*, edited by Christopher S. Beekman and Colin McEwan, pp. 167–201. Dumbarton Oaks Research Library and Collection, Washington, DC.

Pollard, Helen P.
1987 The Political Economy of Prehispanic Tarascan Metallurgy. *American Antiquity* 52(4):741–752.

2000 Tarascan External Relationships. In *Greater Mesoamerica: The Archaeology of West and Northwest Mexico*, edited by Michael S. Foster and Shirley Gorenstein, pp. 71–80. University of Utah Press, Salt Lake City.

Pollard, Helen P., and Thomas A. Vogel
1994 Implicaciones Políticas y Económicas del Intercambio de Obsidiana dentro del Estado Tarasco. In *Arqueología del Occidente de México: Nuevas Aportaciones*, edited by Eduardo Williams and Robert Novella, pp. 159–182. El Colegio de Michoacán, Zamora.

Ponomarenko, Alyson L.
2004 The Pachuca Obsidian Source, Hidalgo, Mexico: A Geoarchaeological Perspective. *Geoarchaeology: An International Journal* 19(1):71–91.

Powell, Wayne, Michael Frachetti, Cemal Pulak, H. Arthur Bankoff, Gojko Barjamovic, Michael Johnson, Ryan Mathur, Vincent C. Pigott, Michael Price, and K. Aslihan Yener
2022 Tin from Uluburun Shipwreck Shows Small-Scale Commodity Exchange Fueled Continental Tin Supply Across Late Bronze Age Eurasia. *Science Advances* 8(48):eabq3766.

Powell-Martí, Valli S., and Patricia A. Gilman (editors)
2006 *Mimbres Society*. University of Arizona Press, Tucson.

Preuss, Konrad T.
1911 Die Opferblutschale der alten Mexikaner erläutert nach Angaben der Cora-Indianer. *Zeitschrift für Ethnologie* 43:293–308.

1912 *Die Nayarit-Expedition. Textaufnahmen und Beobachtungen unter mexikanischen Indianern 1. Die Religion der Cora-Indianer*. Druck and Verlag von B. G. Teubner, Leipzig, Ger.

1998a El Mito del Diluvio entre los Coras y Tribus Emparentadas. In *Fiesta, Literatura y Magia en el Nayarit: Ensayos sobre Coras, Huicholes y Mexicaneros de Konrad Theodor Preuss*, edited by Jesús Jaúregui and Johannes Neurath. Instituto Nacional Indigenista and Centro de Estudios Mexicanos y Centroamericanos, Mexico City.

1998b Acerca del Carácter de los Mitos y Cantos Huicholes que he Registrado. In *Fiesta, Literatura y Magia en el Nayarit: Ensayos sobre Coras, Huicholes y Mexicaneros de Konrad Theodor Preuss*, edited by Jesús Jaúregui and Johannes Neurath, pp. 369–383. Instituto Nacional Indigenista and Centro de Estudios Mexicanos y Centroamericanos, Mexico City.

1998c Una Visita a los Mexicaneros de la Sierra Madre Occidental. In *Fiesta, Literatura y Magia en el Nayarit: Ensayos sobre Coras, Huicholes y Mexicaneros de Konrad Theodor Preuss*, edited by Jesús Jaúregui and Johannes Neurath, pp. 201–212. Instituto Nacional Indigenista and Centro de Estudios Mexicanos y Centroamericanos, Mexico City.

Price, Barbara J.

1974 The Burden of the Cargo: Ethnographic Models and Archaeological Inferences. In *Mesoamerican Archaeology: New Approaches*, edited by Norman Hammond, pp. 445–467. University of Texas Press, Austin.

Publ, Helmut

1985 Prehispanic Exchange Networks and the Development of Social Complexity in Western Mexico: The Aztatlán Interaction Sphere. PhD dissertation, Department of Anthropology, Southern Illinois University, Carbondale.

1990 Interaction Spheres, Merchants, and Trade in Prehispanic West Mexico. *Research in Economic Archaeology* 12:201–242.

Punzo Díaz, José L.

2013 Los Moradores de las Casas en Acantilado de Durango. Rememorando el Mundo de la Vida de los Grupos Serranos en el Siglo XVII. PhD dissertation, Escuela Nacional de Antropología e Historia, Mexico City.

2014 La Población Chalchihuiteña del Valle de Guadiana. In *Historia de Durango, Vol. 1*, edited by José Luis Punzo Díaz and Marie-Areti Hers, pp. 191–206. Instituto de Investigaciones Históricas de la Universidad Juárez del Estado de Durango, Mexico.

2019 La Metalurgía y las Relaciones entre el Altiplano y la Costa: Vistas desde la Cultura Chalchihuites en Durango. In *Aztatlán: Interacción y Cambio Social en el Occidente de México ca. 850–1350 d.C.*, edited by Laura Solar Valverde and Ben A. Nelson, pp. 221–236. El Colegio de Michoacán, Zamora, and Arizona State University, Tempe.

Punzo Díaz, José L., Mijaely Castañón Suárez, Lissandra González González, and Cesar Valentin Hernández

2015 Proyecto Arqueología y Paisaje del Área Centro Sur de Michoacán. Informe Técnico Parcial Temporada 2015. Archivo Técnico de la Sección de Arqueología, Centro Instituto Nacional de Antropología e Historia, Michoacán, Morelia.

Punzo Díaz, José L., Emmanuel A. Gómez Ambríz, Cinthya I. Vidal Aldana, and Cindy Sandoval Mora

2011 Informe Técnico de la Temporada 2011 "Proyecto de Investigaciones Arqueologicas del Area Centro Oeste del Estado de Durango." Archivo Técnico de la Coordinación Nacional de Arqueología, Instituto Nacional de Antropología e Historia, Mexico City.

Punzo Díaz, José L., Lissandra González González, and José F. Avalos Mora

2014 Proyecto Arqueología y Paisaje del Área Centro Sur de Michoacán. Informe Técnico Parcial Temporada 2014. Archivo Técnico de la Sección de Arqueología, Centro Instituto Nacional de Antropología e Historia, Michoacán, Morelia.

Punzo Díaz, José L., and Cindy Sandoval Mora

2012 Analisis Material Arqueologico del Rescate en Sitio de Las Humedades. Informe Técnico, Archivo Técnico de la Coordinación Nacional de Arqueología, Instituto Nacional de Antropología e Historia, Mexico City.

Punzo Díaz, José L., Cindy Sandoval Mora, Israel Andrade González, and Rosa M. Ortiz Barrera

2012 Informe Sitio de Las Humedades "Rescate arqueológico en Sitio Las Humedades Durango, Dgo." Archivo Técnico de la Coordinación Nacional de Arqueología, Instituto Nacional de Antropología e Historia, Mexico City.

Punzo Díaz, José L., Julio C. Vicente López, and Ana I. Murguía Hernández

2017 Presencia Aztatlán en Sitios Chalchihuites del Valle de Guadiana, Durango. *Arqueología* 53:54–69.

Punzo Díaz, José L., and M. Elisa Villalpando

2015 Paquimé: A Revision of Its Relationships to the South and West. In *Ancient Paquimé and the Casas Grandes World*, edited by Paul E. Minnis and Michael E. Whalen, pp. 172–191. Amerind Studies in Anthropology. University of Arizona Press, Tucson.

Quinn, Colin P.

2015 Signals in Stone: Exploring the Role of Social Information Exchange, Conspicuous Consumption, and Costly Signaling Theory in Lithic Analysis. In *Lithic Technological Systems and Evolutionary Theory*, edited by Nathan Goodale and William Andrefsky Jr., pp. 198–222. Cambridge University Press, New York.

Railey, Jim A., and Eric J. Gonzáles

2015 The Problems with Flake Types and the Case for Attribute Analysis of Debitage Assemblages. In *Works in Stone: Contemporary Perspectives on Lithic Analysis*, edited by Michael J. Shott, pp. 11–32. University of Utah Press, Salt Lake City.

Rakita, Gordon F.M., and Rafael Cruz

2015 Organization of Production at Paquimé. In *Ancient Paquimé and the Casas Grandes World*, edited by Paul E. Minnis and Michael E. Whalen, pp. 58–82. Amerind Studies in Anthropology. University of Arizona Press, Tucson.

Ramírez, Susana, Victoria Bojórquez, and Catherine Liot

2006 Área de Excavación II: Plaza Oeste/Plataforma Norte. In *Transformaciones Socioculturales y Tecnológicas en el Sitio La Peña, Cuenca de Sayula, Jalisco*, edited by Catherine Liot, Susana Ramírez, Javier Reveles, and Otto Schöndube, pp. 99–124.

Universidad de Guadalajara and Instituto Nacional de Antropología e Historia, Guadalajara.

Ramírez, Susana, and Cinthya Cárdenas
2006 Análisis de la Cerámica del Postclásico. In *Transformaciones Socioculturales y Tecnológicas en el sitio La Peña, Cuenca de Sayula, Jalisco,* edited by Catherine Liot, Susana Ramírez, Javier Reveles, and Otto Schöndube, pp. 307–372. Universidad de Guadalajara and Instituto Nacional de Antropología e Historia, Guadalajara.

Ramírez, Susana, Catherine Liot, and Otto Schöndube
2006 Introducción. In *Transformaciones Socioculturales y Tecnológicas en el Sitio La Peña, Cuenca de Sayula, Jalisco*, edited by Catherine Liot, Susana Ramírez, Javier Reveles, and Otto Schöndube, pp. 13–26. Universidad de Guadalajara and Instituto Nacional de Antropología e Historia, Guadalajara.

Ramírez Urrea, Susana
1996 La Cerámica de la Fase Amacueca en la Cuenca de Sayula, Jalisco. *Estudios del Hombre* 3:81–126.
2003 The Aztatlán Horizon in Western and Northwestern Mexico: Problems, Iconography, and Relationships. Paper presented at The Dimensions of the Mixtec-Puebla Style, 10th Mixtec Gateway, Las Vegas, NV.
2005 El Papel Interregional de la Cuenca de Sayula, Jalisco en el Epiclásico y Posclásico Temprano: Observaciones Preliminares. In *IV Coloquio Pedro Bosch Gimpera, el Occidente y Centro de México*, edited by Ernesto Vargas Pacheco, pp. 151–198. Instituto de Investigaciones Antropológicas, Universidad Nacional Autónoma de México, Mexico City.
2006a Relaciones Interregionales en la Tradición Aztatlán (Postclásico Temprano y Medio). In *Transformaciones Socioculturales y Tecnológicas en el Sitio de La Peña, Cuenca de Sayula, Jalisco*, edited by Catherine Liot, Susana Ramírez, Javier Reveles, and Otto Schöndube, pp. 435–443. Universidad de Guadalajara and Instituto Nacional de Antropología e Historia, Guadalajara.
2006b Área de Excavación IV: Plaza Este/Plataforma Norte. In *Transformaciones Socioculturales y Tecnológicas en el Sitio La Peña, Cuenca de Sayula, Jalisco*, edited by Catherine Liot, Susana Ramírez, Javier Reveles, and Otto Schöndube, pp. 163–224. Universidad de Guadalajara and Instituto Nacional de Antropología e Historia, Guadalajara.
2011 The Anthropomorphic Representation in the Aztatlán Tradition (AD 850–1300), Western Mexico: An Approach. Paper presented at the 76th Annual Meeting of the Society for American Archaeology, Sacramento, CA.
2016 Organización Sociopolítica en la Tradicion Aztatlán en el Occidente de México durante el Postclásico Temprano y Medio (900–1350 d.C.): El Caso de La Cuenca de Sayula, un estudio de caso. PhD dissertation, Escuela Nacional de Antropología e Historia, Mexico City.
2018 Formas y Estilos en la Cerámica de la Tradición Aztatlán (Occidente de México) (850–1350 dC): Elementos de Cohesión y de Identidad Cultural durante el Postclásico Temprano y Medio. In *Cerámica en México: El Universo Técnico, Social y Cognitivo del Alfarero Prehispánico*, edited by Annick Daneels and Chloé Pomedio, pp. 65–88. Instituto de Investigaciones Antropológicas de la Universidad Nacional Autónoma de México, Mexico City.
2019 Dinámica Sociocultural en la Cuenca de Sayula (Jalisco) durante el Postclásico Temprano y Medio: La Tradición Aztatlán, la Fase Sayula Tardía y la Fase Amacueca Temprana. In *Aztatlán: Interacción y Cambio Social en el Occidente de México ca. 850–1350 d.C.*, edited by Laura Solar Valverde and Ben A. Nelson, pp. 169–198. El Colegio de Michoacán, Zamora, and Arizona State University, Tempe.

Ramírez Urrea, Susana, Catherine Liot, Javier Reveles, Otto Schöndube, Cinthya Cárdenas, Franca Mata, Carmen Melgarejo, Leonardo Santoya, and Victoria Bojórquez
2005 La Peña: Un Sitio de Transición entre el Epiclásico y Posclásico Temprano en la Cuenca de Sayula, Jalisco. In *El Antiguo Occidente de México: Nuevas Perspectivas sobre el Pasado Prehispánico*, edited by Eduardo Williams, Phil C. Weigand, Lorenza López Mestas, and David C. Grove, pp. 305–330. El Colegio de Michoacán, Zamora.

Ramírez Urrea, Susana, Javier Reveles, Luis Gómez Gastelum, Otto Schöndube, and Carlos Santos
2000 *Rescate Arqueológico del Sitio de La Peña, Citala, Municipio de Teocuitatlán de Corona, Jalisco.* Informe Técnico, Consejo de Arqueología del Istituto Nacional de Antropología e Historia. Universidad de Guadalajara and Instituto Nacional de Antropología e Historia, Guadalajara, Jalisco.

Rangel Guzmán, Efraín
2008 El Mito del Camino de los Muertos en la Cosmovisión Tepehuana. *Transición* 36:39–62.

Rattray, Evelyn
1966 An Archaeological and Stylistic Study of Coyotlatelco Pottery. *Mesoamerican Notes* 7–8:87–211.

Rebnegger, Karin J.
2010 Obsidian Production and Changing Consumption in the Lake Pátzcuaro Basin, Michoacán, Mexico. *Ancient Mesoamerica* 21(1):79–89.

Reitzel Rivera, Hannah
2012 La Cerámica Aztatlán de la Costa de Nayarit: Investigaciones Preliminares sobre Fabricación. Paper presented at the Segunda Mesa sobre Arqueología Aztatlán, Guadalajara.

Renfrew, Colin
1977 Alternative Models for Exchange and Spatial Distribution. In *Exchange Systems in Prehistory*, edited by Timothy K. Earle and Jonathon E. Ericson, pp. 71–90. Academic Press, New York.

Renfrew, Colin, and John F. Cherry (editors)
1986 *Peer Polity Interaction and Socio-Political Change.* Cambridge University Press, Cambridge.

Retes, Miguel
1845 Apuntes de un Viage: Santiago Ixcuintla (Departamento de Jalisco). *Museo Mexicano* Época 2:1–6.

Reveles, Javier
2006 Análisis Preliminar de los Materiales Líticos. In *Transformaciones Socioculturales y Tecnológicas en el sitio La Peña, Cuenca de Sayula, Jalisco*, edited by Catherine Liot, Susana Ramírez, Javier Reveles, and Otto Schöndube, pp. 373–393. Universidad de Guadalajara and Instituto Nacional de Antropología e Historia, Guadalajara.
2021 Producción de los Artefactos Líticos en la Cuenca de Sayula, Jalisco. Master's thesis, Faculty of Philosophy and Letters, Universidad Nacional Autónoma de Mexico, Mexico City.

Reyes Valdez, Antonio
2006 *Los que están Benditos: El Mitote Comunal de los Tepehuanes de Santa María de Ocotán*. Instituto Nacional de Antropología e Historia, Mexico City.
2013 Soñar para Curar: Las Imágenes Oníricas en el Chamanismo Tepehuán. In *Los Sueños y los Días: Chamanismo y Nahualismo en el México Actual, Vol. 1, Pueblos del Noroeste*, edited by Miguel Ángel Bartolomé and Alicia M. Barabas, pp. 245–266. Instituto Nacional de Antropología e Historia, Mexico City.

Reyes Valdez, Antonio, and Bridget M. Zavala
2019 Por el Camino de los Muertos: Nuevas Interpretaciones acerca de los Materiales Costeños en los Sitios Chalchihuites de Durango. In *Aztatlán: Interacción y Cambio Social en el Occidente de México ca. 850–1350 d.C.*, edited by Laura Solar Valverde and Ben A. Nelson, pp. 237–250. El Colegio de Michoacán, Zamora, and Arizona State University, Tempe.

Reyman, Jonathan E.
1995 Pala'tkwabi: Red Land of the South. In *The Gran Chichimeca: Essays on the Archaeology and Ethnohistory of Northern Mesoamerica*, edited by Jonathan E. Reyman, pp. 320–335. Avebury, Aldershot, UK.

Reyman, Jonathan E. (editor)
1995 *The Gran Chichimeca: Essays on the Archaeology and Ethnohistory of Northern Mesoamerica*. Avebury, Aldershot, UK.

Riley, Carroll L.
1987 *The Frontier People: The Greater Southwest in the Protohistoric Period*. University of New Mexico Press, Albuquerque.
2005 *Becoming Aztlan: Mesoamerican Influence in the Greater Southwest, AD 1200–1500*. University of Utah Press, Salt Lake City.

Robertson, Roland
1992 *Globalization: Social Theory and Global Culture*. Sage, London.

Rocek, Thomas R., and Nancy A. Kenmotsu (editors)
2018 *Late Prehistoric Hunter-Gatherers and Farmers of the Jornada Mogollon*. University Press of Colorado, Louisville.

Rodríguez Obregón, Daniela
2017 Los Objetos de Concha en el Norte de Sinaloa. Bachelor's thesis, Escuela Nacional de Antropología e Historia, Mexico City.

Rodríguez Zariñán, Nora
2009 El Conjunto Iconográfico Águila-Rombo-Serpiente en Chalchihuites, Zacatecas: Un Acercamiento a través de la Analogía *Wixarika* (Huichola). Bachelor's thesis, Escuela Nacional de Antropología e Historia, Mexico City.

Rojas Martínez Gracida, Araceli
2008a Los Entretenedores en los Polícromos del Tipo Albina de Cholula: Una Propuesta Inconográfica. *Arqueología* 39:77–92.
2008b La Iconografía e Iconología Relacionada con el Sol en Polícromos de Cholula. *Arqueología* 37:140–154.

Rojas Martínez Gracida, Araceli, and Gilda Hernández Sánchez
2019 Writing and Ritual: The Transformation to Mixteca-Puebla Ceramics of Cholula. *Americae: European Journal of Americanist Archaeology* 4:47–70.

Romano, Arturo
1965 *Estudio Morfológico de la Deformación Craneana en Tamuín, S.L.P. y en la Isla del Ídolo, Ver*. Serie Investigaciones 10. Instituto Nacional de Antropología e Historia, Mexico City.

Romero, Javier
1958 *Mutilaciones Dentarias Prehispánicas de México y América en General*. Instituto Nacional de Antropología e Historia, Mexico City.
1970 Dental Mutilation, Trephination, and Cranial Deformation. In *Physical Anthropology*, edited by T. D. Stewart, pp. 50–67. The Handbook of Middle American Indians, Vol. 9, Robert Wauchope, general editor. University of Texas Press, Austin.

Romero Melgarejo, Osvaldo A.
2018 El Sistema de Cargos en una Comunidad Nahua de la Región del Volcán la Malinche, Tlaxcala. *Convergencia Revista de Ciencias Sociales* 15:115–130.

Roth, Barbara J., Patricia A. Gilman, and Roger Anyon (editors)
2018 *New Perspectives on Mimbres Archaeology: Three Millennia of Human Occupation in the North American Southwest*. University of Arizona Press, Tucson.

Roudometof, Victor
2016 *Glocalization: A Critical Introduction*. Routledge, London.

Rounds, J.
1978 The Role of the Tecuhtli in Ancient Aztec Society. *Ethnohistory* 24(4):343–361.

Rubín de la Borbolla, Daniel F.
1944 Orfebrería Tarasca. *Cuadernos Americanos* 3(3):127–138.

Runciman, W. G.
2000 *The Social Animal*. University of Michigan Press, Ann Arbor.

Rus, Jan, and Robert Wasserstrom
1980 Civil-Religious Hierarchies in Central Chiapas: A Critical Perspective. *American Ethnologist* 7:466–478.

Ruvalcaba Mercado, Jesús
2015 Linguistic Diversity, Cultural Unity, and the Question of Maize and Religion in the History of the Huasteca. In *The Huasteca: Culture, History, and Interregional Exchange*, edited by Katherine A.

Faust and Kim N. Richter, pp. 195–213. University of Oklahoma Press, Norman.

Salmón, Enrique
1999 Sharing Breath with Our Relatives: Rarámuri Plant Knowledge, Lexicon, and Cognition. PhD dissertation, Department of Anthropology, Arizona State University, Tempe.

Sánchez Correa, Sergio A., and Emma G. Marmolejo Morales
1990 Algunas apreciaciones sobre el Clásico en el Bajío central, Guanajuato. In *La Época Clásica: Nuevos Hallazgos, Nuevas Ideas*, edited by Amalia Cardos de Méndez, pp. 267–278. Instituto Nacional de Antropología e Historia, Mexico City.

Sánchez Olmedo, José G.
1980 *Etnografía de la Sierra Madre Occidental: Tepehuanes y Mexicaneros*. Instituto Nacional de Antropología e Historia, Mexico City.

Sandstrom, Alan R.
1992 *Corn Is Our Blood: Culture and Ethnic Identity in a Contemporary Aztec Indian Village*. University of Oklahoma Press, Norman.

Santley, Robert S.
1984 Obsidian Exchange, Economic Stratification, and the Evolution of Complex Society in the Basin of Mexico. In *Trade and Exchange in Early Mesoamerica*, edited by Kenneth G. Hirth, pp. 43–86. University of New Mexico Press, Albuquerque.

Santley, Robert S., Janet M. Kerley, and Ronald R. Kneebone
1986 Obsidian Working, Long-Distance Exchange, and the Politico-Economic Organization of Early States in Central Mexico. In *Research in Economic Anthropology, Supplement 2. Economic Aspects of Prehispanic Highland Mexico*, edited by Barry L. Isaac, pp. 101–132. JAI Press, Greenwich.

Santos, Victor J.
2004 *Informe del rescate arqueológico realizado en el sitio de "El Opochi," Sinaloa*. Archivo Técnico de la Coordinación Nacional de Arqueología, Instituto Nacional de Antropología e Historia, Mexico City.
2022 Descubren Nuevo Sitio Arqueológico de la Cultura Aztatlán en la Zona Urbana del Puerto de Mazatlán, Sinaloa. Boletín No. 241, Secretaría de Cultura, Instituto Nacional de Antropología e Historia, Mexico City.

Santoyo Alonso, Leonardo
2012 *Agua que Vuelve: La Tecnología Hidráulica Prehispánica en la Cuenca de Sayula, Jalisco*. Universidad Autónoma de Zacatecas, Zacatecas.

Sauer, Carl O.
1935 *Aboriginal Population of Northwestern Mexico*. Ibero-Americana 10. University of California Press, Berkeley.
1948 *Colima of New Spain in the Sixteenth Century*. Ibero-Americana 29. University of California Press, Berkeley.

Sauer, Carl O., and Donald D. Brand
1932 *Aztatlán: Prehistoric Mexican Frontier on the Pacific Coast*. Ibero-Americana 1. University of California Press, Berkeley.

Scarborough, Vernon L., and David R. Wilcox (editors)
1991 *The Mesoamerican Ballgame*. University of Arizona Press, Tucson.

Schaafsma, Curtis F., and Carroll L. Riley (editors)
1999 *The Casas Grandes World*. University of Utah Press, Salt Lake City.

Schaafsma, Polly
1999 Tlalocs, Kachinas, Sacred Bundles, and Related Symbolism in the Southwest and Mesoamerica. In *The Casas Grandes World*, edited by Curtis F. Schaafsma and Carroll L. Riley, pp. 164–192. University of Utah Press, Salt Lake City.
2000 *Warrior, Shield, and Star: Imagery and Ideology of Pueblo Warfare*. Western Edge Press, Santa Fe.
2001 Quetzalcoatl and the Horned and Feathered Serpent of the Southwest. In *The Road to Aztlan: Art from a Mythic Homeland*, edited by Virginia M. Fields and Victor Zamudio-Taylor, pp. 138–149. Los Angeles County Museum of Art, Los Angeles.
2002 Pottery Metaphors in Pueblo and Jornada Mogollon Rock Art. In *Rock Art and Cultural Processes*, edited by Solveig A. Turpin, pp. 51–66. Special Publication 3, Rock Art Foundation, San Antonio, TX.

Schaafsma, Polly (editor)
2000 *Kachinas in the Pueblo World*. University of Utah Press, Salt Lake City.

Schaafsma, Polly, and Karl A. Taube
2006 Bringing the Rain: An Ideology of Rain Making in the Pueblo Southwest and Mesoamerica. In *A Pre-Columbian World*, edited by Jeffrey Quilter and Mary Miller, pp. 231–285. Dumbarton Oaks Research Library and Collection, Washington, DC.

Schafer, Harry J.
2003 *Mimbres Archaeology at the NAN Ranch Ruin*. University of New Mexico Press, Albuquerque.

Scheffer, Marten, Egbert H. van Nes, Darcy Bird, R. Kyle Bocinsky, and Timothy A. Kohler
2021 Loss of Resilience Preceded Transformations of pre-Hispanic Pueblo Societies. *Proceedings of the National Academy of Sciences of the United States of America* 118(18):e2024397118.

Schele, Linda, and Jeffrey H. Miller
1983 *The Mirror, the Rabbit, and the Bundle: Accession Expressions from the Classic Maya Inscriptions*. Studies in Pre-Columbian Art and Archaeology 25. Dumbarton Oaks Research Library and Collection, Washington, DC.

Schmidt, Peter J.
1998 Chichén Itzá: Los Contactos con el Centro de México y la Transición al Periodo Posclásico. In *Los Mayas*, edited by Peter Schmidt, Mercedes de la Garza, and Enrique Nalda, pp. 427–449. El Consejo Nacional para la Cultura y las Artes and Instituto Nacional de Antropología e Historia, Mexico City.

Schöndube, Otto, Jean Pierre Emphoux, Francisco Valdez, Jean Guffroy, Ricardo Avila, Rosario Acosta, and Andres Noyola
1994 *Proyecto Arqueológico Cuenca de Sayula. Segundo Informe Técnico al Consejo de Arqueología del*

Instituto Nacional de Antropología e Historia. Archivo Técnico, Instituto Nacional de Antropología e Historia, Guadalajara.

Schöndube, Otto, Jean Pierre Emphoux, Francisco Valdez, Jean Guffroy, Ricardo Avila, Rosario Acosta, Susana Ramírez Urrea, and Luis Gómez Gastelum

1996 *Proyecto Arqueológico Cuenca de Sayula. Tercer Informe Técnico al Consejo de Arqueología del Instituto Nacional de Antropología e Historia.* Archivo Técnico, Instituto Nacional de Antropología e Historia, Guadalajara.

Schöndube B., Otto

1974 Deidades Prehispanicas en el Area de Tamazula-Tuxpan-Zapotlan en el Estado de Jalisco. In *The Archaeology of West Mexico*, edited by Betty Bell, pp. 168–181. Sociedad de Estudios Avanzados del Occidente de México, Ajijic, Jalisco, Mexico.

1980a Época Prehispánica. In *Historia de Jalisco, desde Tiempos Prehistóricos hasta Fines del Siglo XVII*, edited by José María Muriá, pp. 113–257. Gobierno de Jalisco, Secretaría General, Universidad de Guadalajara, Guadalajara, Mexico.

1980b La Nueva Tradicion. In *Historia de Jalisco*, Vol. 1, pp. 213–258. Gobierno del Estado de Jalisco, Unidad Editorial, Guadalajara, Mexico.

Schroeder, Albert H.

1966 Pattern Diffusion from Mexico into the Southwest after A.D. 600. *American Antiquity* 31(5):683–704.

Schwartz, Christopher W., Stephen Plog, and Patricia A. Gilman

2022 Exploring Variation in the Frequency and Context of Macaws and Parrots in the U.S. Southwest and Mexican Northwest. In *Birds of the Sun: Macaws and People in the U.S. Southwest and Mexican Northwest*, edited by Christopher W. Schwartz, Stephen Plog, and Patricia A. Gilman, pp. 321–346. Amerind Studies in Anthropology. University of Arizona Press, Tucson.

Schwartz, Christopher W., Stephen Plog, and Patricia A. Gilman (editors)

2022 *Birds of the Sun: Macaws and People in the U.S. Southwest and Mexican Northwest*. University of Arizona Press, Tucson.

Schwindt, Dylan M., R. Kyle Bocinsky, Scott G. Ortman, Donna M. Glowacki, Mark D. Varien, and Timothy A. Kohler

2016 The Social Consequences of Climate Change in the Central Mesa Verde Region. *American Antiquity* 81(1):74–96.

Scott, George R., and Christy G. Turner II

1997 *The Anthropology of Modern Human Teeth: Dental Morphology and Its Variation in Recent Human Populations*. Cambridge University Press, Cambridge, UK.

Scott, Patricia K.

2017 The Marismas Nacionales: A Historical View of the Conquest and Early Postconquest Periods. In *The Archaeology, Ethnohistory, and Environment of the Marismas Nacionales: The Prehistoric Pacific Littoral of Sinaloa and Nayarit, Mexico*, edited by Michael S. Foster, pp. 366–403. University of Utah Press, Salt Lake City.

Scott, Stuart D.

1974 Un Templo en el Estuario: Hallazgos Prehistóricos en las Marismas de Sinaloa y Nayarit. *Notas Antropológicas* 1(3):1–12.

1985 Core Versus Marginal Mesoamerica: A Coastal West Mexican Perspective. In *The Archaeology of West and Northwest Mesoamerica*, edited by Michael S. Foster and Phil C. Weigand. Westview Press, Boulder.

1999 The Marismas Nacionales Project, Sinaloa and Nayarit, Mexico. In *Pacific Latin America in Prehistory: The Evolution of Archaic and Formative Cultures*, edited by Michael Blake, pp. 13–24. Washington State University Press, Pullman.

Scott, Stuart D., and Michael S. Foster

2000 The Prehistory of Mexico's Northwest Coast: A View from the Marismas Nacionales of Sinaloa and Nayarit. In *Greater Mesoamerica: The Archaeology of West and Northwest Mexico*, edited by Michael S. Foster and Shirley Gorenstein, pp. 107–135. University of Utah Press, Salt Lake City.

Scott, Sue

1993 *Teotihuacan Mazapan Figurines and the Xipe Totec Statue: A Link Between the Basin of Mexico and the Valley of Oaxaca*. Vanderbilt University Publications in Anthropology, No. 44. Nashville, TN.

Searcy, Michael T., and Richard K. Talbot

2015 Late Fremont Cultural Identities and Borderland Processes. In *Late Holocene Research on Foragers and Farmers in the Desert Southwest*, edited by Barbara J. Roth and Maxine E. McBrinn, pp. 234–264. University of Utah Press, Salt Lake City.

Secretaría de Programación y Presupuesto

1981 *Síntesis Geográfica de Nayarit*. Coordinación General de los Servicios Nacionales de Estadística, Geografía e Informática, Mexico City, Mexico.

Seler, Eduard

1911 The Basis and Object of Archeological Research in Mexico and Adjoining Countries. *Science* 33(846):397–402.

1992 Quauhxicalli, the Mexican Vessel for Sacrificial Blood. In *Collected Works in Mesoamerican Linguistics and Archaeology*, Vol. 3, edited by Frank E. Comparato, pp. 79–83. Labyrinthos, Culver City, CA.

Seltzer-Rogers, Thatcher A.

2021 Ancestral Relations and Late Prehispanic Dynamics Between the Mimbres and Casas Grandes Cultures of the American Southwest/Mexican Northwest Region. *Journal of Anthropological Archaeology* 64:101371.

Shafer, Harry J.

2012 Classic Mimbres Social Field and Drinking Buddies: What DNA Evidence and Large Pots May Tell Us about Mimbres Ceremonies and Feasts. Paper presented at the 17th Biennial Mogollon Archaeology Conference, Silver City, NM.

Sharp, Rosemary

1978 Architecture as Interelite Communication in Preconquest Oaxaca, Veracruz, and Yucatán. In *Middle*

Classic Mesoamerica: A.D. 400–700, edited by Esther Pasztory, pp. 158–171. Columbia University Press, New York.

Shaul, David L.
2014 *A Prehistory of Western North America: The Impact of Uto-Aztecan Languages.* University of New Mexico Press, Albuquerque.

Sieron, Katrin, and Claus Siebe
2008 Revised Stratigraphy and Eruption Rates of Ceboruco Stratovolcano and Surrounding Monogenetic Vents (Nayarit, Mexico) from Historical Documents and New Radiocarbon Dates. *Journal of Volcanology and Geothermal Research* 176(2):241–264.

Smith, Erin M., and Mikael Fauvelle
2015 Regional Interactions between California and the Southwest: The Western Edge of the North American Continental System. *American Anthropologist* 117(4):710–721.

Smith, Michael E., and Frances F. Berdan
2003 Postclassic Mesoamerica. In *The Postclassic Mesoamerican World*, edited by Michael E. Smith and Frances F. Berdan, pp. 3–13. University of Utah Press, Salt Lake City.

Smith, Michael E., and Frances F. Berdan (editors)
2003 *The Postclassic Mesoamerican World.* University of Utah Press, Salt Lake City.

Smith, Michael E., and Cynthia M. Heath-Smith
1980 Waves of Influence in Postclassic Mesoamerica? A Critique of the Mixteca-Puebla Concept. *Anthropology* 4(2):15–50.

Snead, James E.
2008 *Ancestral Landscapes of the Pueblo World.* University of Arizona Press, Tucson.

Snow, Meradeth H., Harry Shafer, and David G. Smith
2011 The Relationship of the Mimbres to Other Southwestern and Mexican Populations. *Journal of Archaeological Science* 38(11):3122–3133.

Sociedad Mexicana de Antropología
1941 *Revista Mexicana de Estudios Antropológicos* 5(2–3).

Solar Valverde, Laura
2002 Interacción Interregional en Mesoamérica: Una Aproximación a la Dinámica del Epiclásico. Bachelor's thesis, Escuela Nacional de Antropología e Historia, Mexico City.
2007 Analogías entre el Ceremonialismo Prehispánico del Noroccidente y los Grupos Actuales del Gran Nayar. Paper presented at the Simposio Antropología e Historia del Occidente de México, 2007. Homenaje a John Lilly, Instituto Nacional de Antropología e Historia and Museo Zacatecano, Zacatecas, Mexico.
2011 El Sur de Zacatecas y sus Vínculos con la Red Aztatlán. Paper presented at the Primera Mesa Redonda de Arqueología Aztatlán, Instituto Nacional de Antropología e Historia and Museo Regional de Nayarit, Tepic, Nayarit.
2019 Muerte y Sacrificio Ritual en la Iconografía Postclásica de la Llanura Costera del Pacífico. In *Aztatlán: Interacción y Cambio Social en el Occidente de México ca. 850–1350 d.C.*, edited by Laura Solar Valverde and Ben A. Nelson, pp. 251–286. El Colegio de Michoacán, Zamora, and Arizona State University, Tempe.
2023 The Epiclassic and Early Postclassic Mesoamerican Weave: Multiregional Warp, Ideological Weft. In *When East Meets West: Chichen Itza, Tula, and the Postclassic Mesoamerican World*, edited by Travis W. Stanton, Karl A. Taube, Jeremy D. Coltman, and Nelda I. Marengo Camacho, pp. 793–826. British Archaeological Reports, London, UK.

Solar Valverde, Laura, and Peter Jiménez Betts
2008 *El Cerro del Teúl: Desarrollo histórico y contexto regional de un centro ceremonial de la caxcana. Proyecto de investigación, primera temporada.* Manuscript on file, Archivo Técnico de Arqueología del Instituto Nacional de Antropología e Historia, Mexico City.

Solar Valverde, Laura, Laura Magriñá, and Lourdes González
2011 Las Figurillas Mazapa y las Malinches de los Coras. *Arqueología Mexicana* 18(108):66–71.

Solar Valverde, Laura, Luis Martínez Méndez, and Peter Jiménez Betts.
2021 La Red Aztatlán Tierra Adentro (Sur de Zacatecas). Webposio de Arqueología del Occidente de México en el Posclásico Temprano. Online Resource: https://www.youtube.com/watch?v=Cg2O--CjhtY, accessed January 15, 2023.

Solar Valverde, Laura, and Ben A. Nelson (editors)
2019 *Aztatlán: Interacción y Cambio Social en el Occidente de México ca. 850–1350 d.C.* El Colegio de Michoacán, Zamora, and Arizona State University, Tempe.

Solar Valverde, Laura, Ben A. Nelson, and Michael A. Ohnersorgen
2019 Aztatlán: Una Red de Interacción en el Occidente de México. In *Aztatlán: Interacción y Cambio Social en el Occidente de México ca. 850–1350 d.C.*, edited by Laura Solar Valverde and Ben A. Nelson, pp. 1–38. El Colegio de Michoacán, Zamora, and Arizona State University, Tempe.

Spence, Michael
1978 A Cultural Sequence from the Sierra Madre of Durango, Mexico. In *Across the Chichimec Sea: Papers in Honor of J. Charles Kelley*, edited by Carroll L. Riley and Basil C. Hedrick, pp. 165–189. Southern Illinois University Press, Carbondale.

Spielmann, Katherine A. (editor)
1991 *Farmers, Hunters, and Colonists: Interaction between the Southwest and the Southern Plains.* University of Arizona Press, Tucson.

Spores, Ronald
1972 *An Archaeological Settlement Survey of the Nochixtlan Valley, Oaxaca.* Vanderbilt University Publications in Anthropology, No. 1. Vanderbilt University, Nashville.
1993 Tututepec: A Postclassic-period Mixtec Conquest State. *Ancient Mesoamerica* 4(1):167–174.

Sprague, Roderick, and Aldo Signori
1963 Inventory of Prehistoric Southwestern Copper Bells. *Kiva* 28(4):1–20.

Stanton, Travis W., Karl A. Taube, and Jeremy D. Coltman
2023 Social Mobility in the City of the Sun: The Legacy of Chichen Itza at the Turn of the Postclassic Period. In *When East Meets West: Chichen Itza, Tula, and the Postclassic Mesoamerican World*, Vols. 1–2, edited by Travis W. Stanton, Karl A. Taube, Jeremy D. Coltman, and Nelda I. Marengo Camacho, pp. 3–30. British Archaeological Reports S3134. BAR Publishing, London.

Stanton, Travis W., Karl A. Taube, Jeremy D. Coltman, and Nelda I. Marengo Camacho (editors)
2023 *When East Meets West: Chichen Itza, Tula, and the Postclassic Mesoamerican World*, Vols. 1–2. British Archaeological Reports S3134. BAR Publishing, London.

Steinbrenner, Larry, Alexander Geurds, Geoffrey G. McCafferty, and Silvia Salgado (editors)
2021 *The Archaeology of Greater Nicoya: Two Decades of Research in Nicaragua and Costa Rica*. University Press of Colorado, Louisville.

Stern, Jean
1977 A Carved Spindle Whorl from Nayarit. In *Pre-Columbian Art History: Selected Readings*, edited by Alana Cordy-Collins and Jean Stern, pp. 135–144. Peck Publications, Palo Alto, CA.

Stuiver, Minze, and Thomas F. Braziunas
1993 Modeling Atmospheric 14C Influences and 14C Ages of Marine Samples to 10,000 B.C. *Radiocarbon* 35(1):137–189.

Sweetman, Rosemary
1974 Prehistoric Pottery from Coastal Sinaloa and Nayarit, Mexico. In *The Archaeology of West Mexico*, edited by Betty Bell, pp. 68–82. Sociedad de Estudios Avanzados del Occidente de México, Ajijic, Jalisco, Mexico.

Swidler, Nina, Kurt E. Dongoske, Roger Anyon, and Alan S. Downer (editors)
1997 *Native Americans and Archaeologists: Stepping Stones to Common Ground*. AltaMira Press, Walnut Grove, CA.

Talavera, Jorge A.
2005 Usos y Costumbres Funerarios. In *Historia General de Sinaloa Época Prehispánica*, edited by José Gaxiola López and Carlos Zazueta Manjarrez, pp. 91–116. Colegio de Sinaloa, Sinaloa, Mexico.

Talavera, Jorge A., and Nancy Gelover
2016 *Informe de Campo de los Trabajos de Exploración de Cistas Funerarias Localizadas en el Sitio La Pitayera, Ahuacatlán, Nayarit. Proyecto Autopista Jala-Compostela*. Archivo Técnico de la Sección de Arqueología, Centro Instituto Nacional de Antropología e Historia, Nayarit, Tepic.

Talavera, Jorge A., and Ruben Manzanilla Lopez
1991 Proyecto de Investigación y Salvamento Arqueológico en Mochicahui, Sinaloa. *Antropología* 34:22–27.

Taube, Karl A.
1985 The Classic Maya Maize God: A Reappraisal. In *Fifth Palenque Roundtable, 1983*, edited by Merle Greene Robertson, pp. 171–181. Pre-Columbian Art Research Institute, San Francisco.
2000 Lightning Celts and Corn Fetishes: The Formative Olmec and the Development of Maize Symbolism in Mesoamerica and the American Southwest. In *Olmec Art and Archaeology in Mesoamerica*, edited by John E. Clark and Mary E. Pye, pp. 297–337. Yale University Press, New Haven, CT.
2001 The Breath of Life: The Symbolism of Wind in Mesoamerica and the American Southwest. In *The Road to Aztlan: Art from a Mythic Homeland*, edited by Virginia M. Fields and Victor Zamudio-Taylor, pp. 102–123. Los Angeles County Museum of Art, Los Angeles.
2009 The Womb of the World: The Cuauhxicalli and Other Offering Bowls of Ancient and Contemporary Mesoamerica. In *Maya Archaeology 1*, edited by Charles Golden, Stephen Houston, and Joel Skidmore, pp. 86–106. Precolumbia Mesoweb Press, San Francisco.
2010 At Dawn's Edge: Tulúm, Santa Rita, and Floral Symbolism in the International Style of Late Postclassic Mesoamerica. In *Astronomer's Scribes and Priests: Intellectual Interchange Between the Northern Maya Lowlands and Highland Mexico in the Late Postclassic Period*, edited by Gabrielle Vail and Christine Hernández, pp. 145–191. Dumbarton Oaks Research Library and Collection, Washington, DC.
2016 Through a Glass, Brightly: Recent Investigations Concerning Mirrors and Scrying in Ancient and Contemporary Mesoamerica. In *Manufactured Light: Mirrors in the Mesoamerican Realm*, edited by Emiliano Gallaga M. and Marc G. Blainey, pp. 285–314. University of Colorado Press, Niwot.
2018 Orígenes y Simbolismo de la Deidad del Viento en Mesoamérica. *Arqueología Mexicana* 26(152):34–39.

Tax, Sol
1937 The Municipios of the Midwestern Highlands of Guatemala. *American Anthropologist* 39(3):423–444.

Téllez Lozano, Víctor M.
2014 Acercamiento al Estudio de los Sistemas de Cargos entre las Comunidades Huicholas de Jalisco y Nayarit, México. *Diálogo Andino* 43:17–40.

Tello, Fray Antonio
1968 [ca. 1650] *Crónica miscelánea de la sancta provincia de Xalisco, libro segundo*, Vols. 1–2. Gobierno del Estado de Jalisco and Instituto Jalisciense de Antropología e Historia, Guadalajara.

Tenorio, Dolores, Melania Jiménez Reyes, Juan R. Esparza López, Thomas F. Calligaro, and Luis A. Grave Tirado
2015 The Obsidian of Southern Sinaloa: New Evidence of Aztatlán Networks through PIXE. *Journal of Archaeological Science: Reports* 4:106–110.

Thibodeau, Alyson M., David J. Killick, Saul L. Hedquist, John T. Chesley, and Joaquin Ruíz
2015 Isotopic Evidence for the Provenance of Turquoise in the Southwestern United States. *The Geological Society of America Bulletin* 127(11–12):1617–1631.

Thibodeau, Alyson M., Leonardo López Luján, David J. Killick, Frances F. Berdan, and Joaquin Ruiz
2018 Was Aztec and Mixtec Turquoise Mined in the

American Southwest? *Science Advances* 4(6): eaas9370.

Thomas, Bob.
1953 "He's One Man Who Quit Hollywood". *Daytona Beach Morning Journal*. May 12, 1953. https://news.google.com/newspapers?nid=1873&dat=19590512&id=_48tAAAAIBAJ&sjid=7MkEAAAAIBAJ&pg=749,1972411&hl=en, accessed April 25, 2022.

Thompson, J. Eric S.
1953 Relaciones entre Veracruz y la Región Maya. *Revista Mexicana de Estudios Antropológicos* 13(2–3): 447–454.

Toro, Alfonso
1925 Una Nueva Zona Arqueológica en Sinaloa. *Anales del Museo Nacional de Arqueología, Historia, e Etnografía*, Época 5a, Tomo 3(1):56–58.

Tosa, Paul, Matthew J. Liebmann, T. J. Ferguson, and John R. Welch
2019 Movement Encased in Tradition and Stone: Hemish Migration, Land Use, and Identity. In *The Continuous Path: Pueblo Movement and the Archaeology of Becoming*, edited by Samuel Duwe and Robert W. Preucel, pp. 60–77. University of Arizona Press, Tucson.

Townsend, Richard F.
1992 *The Aztecs*. Thames and Hudson, London.

Tozzer, Alfred M.
1921 *Excavation of a Site at Santiago Ahuitzotla, D.F. Mexico*. Smithsonian Institution Bureau of Ethnology, Bulletin 74. Government Printing Office, Smithsonian Institution, Washington, DC.

Trombold, Charles D., James F. Luhr, Toshiaki Hasenaka, and Michael D. Glascock
1993 Chemical Characteristics of Obsidian from Archaeological Sites in Western Mexico and the Tequila Source Area: Implications for Regional and Pan-Regional Interaction within the Northern Mesoamerican Periphery. *Ancient Mesoamerica* 4:255–270.

Turner, Andrew D.
2016 Cultures at the Crossroads: Art, Religion, and Interregional Interaction in Central Mexico, AD 600–900. PhD dissertation, Department of Anthropology, University of California, Riverside.
2019 The Murals of Cacaxtla: Monumental Art as Evidence of Migration. In *Migrations in Late Mesoamerica*, edited by Christopher S. Beekman, pp. 205–240. University Press of Florida, Gainesville.

Turner, Andrew D., and Michael D. Mathiowetz
2021 Introduction. Flower Worlds: A Synthesis and Critical History. In *Flower Worlds: Religion, Aesthetics, and Ideology in Mesoamerica and the American Southwest*, edited by Michael D. Mathiowetz and Andrew D. Turner, pp. 3–32. Amerind Seminars in Anthropology. University of Arizona Press, Tucson.

Tuross, Noreen
2017 Strontium Sourcing of Human Remains from Tomb 7 at Monte Alban. Manuscript in author's possesion.

Valdez, Francisco, Otto Schöndube, and Jean P. Emphoux (editors)
2005 *Arqueología de la Cuenca de Sayula*. Universidad de Guadalajara and Institut de Recherche pour le Développement, Guadalajara.

Valdovinos, Margarita
2002 Los Cargos del Pueblo de Jesús María (Chuísete'e): Una Réplica de la Cosmovisión Cora. Bachelor's thesis, Escuela Nacional de Antropología e Historia, Mexico City.
2010 Acción y "Multiempatía" en el Estudio de las Imágenes Rituales. In *Las Artes del Ritual: Nuevas Propuestas para la Antropología del Arte desde el Occidente de México*, edited by Elizabeth Araiza, pp. 245–265. El Colegio de Michoacán, Zamora, Mexico.

Valdovinos Pérez, Víctor, and Cristina García Moreno
2017 Sobre Cantos de Río: La Industria Lítica en el Valle de Ónavas, Sureste de Sonora. *Arqueología* 52:47–75.

Van Akkeren, Ruud
2000 *Place of the Lord's Daughter: Rab'inal, Its History, Its Dance-Drama*. Research School CNWS and School of Asian, African, and Amerindian Studies, Leiden, Netherlands.

Van Dyke, Ruth M., and Carrie C. Heitman (editors)
2021 *The Greater Chaco Landscape: Ancestors, Scholarship, and Advocacy*. University Press of Colorado, Louisville.

VanPool, Christine S., and Todd L. VanPool
2007 *Signs of the Casas Grandes Shamans*. University of Utah Press, Salt Lake City.

VanPool, Todd, Christine VanPool, Gordon F. M. Rakita, and Robert D. Leonard
2008 Birds, Bells, and Shells: The Long Reach of the Aztatlán Trading Tradition. In *Touching the Past: Ritual, Religion, and Trade of Casas Grandes*, edited by Glenna Nielsen-Grimm and Paul Stavast, pp. 5–14. Popular Series 5, Museum of Peoples and Culture, Provo.

Vargas, Victoria D.
1994 Copper Bell Trade Patterns in the Prehistoric Greater American Southwest. Master's thesis, Department of Anthropology, University of Oklahoma, Norman.
1995 *Copper Bell Trade Patterns in the Prehispanic U.S. Southwest and Northwest Mexico*. Arizona State Museum Archeological Series 187. Arizona State Museum, University of Arizona, Tucson.
2001 Mesoamerican Copper Bells in the Pre-Hispanic Southwestern United States and Northwestern Mexico. In *The Road to Aztlan: Art from a Mythic Homeland*, edited by Virginia M. Fields and Victor Zamudio Taylor, pp. 196–211. Los Angeles County Museum of Art, Los Angeles.

Vicente López, Julio C.
2004 *Informe del Rescate Arqueológico Realizado en el Sitio La Colorada, Municipios de Culiacán y Navolato, Sinaloa*. Archivo Técnico de la Sección de Arqueología, Instituto Nacional de Antropología e Historia, Sinaloa, Culiacán.
2005 *Informe del Rescate Arqueológico en El Palmar. Sindicatura El Dorado, Culiacán, Sinaloa*. Archivo Técnico de la Sección de Arqueología, Instituto Nacional de Antropología e Historia, Sinaloa, Culiacán.

Vidal Aldana, Cinthya I.
2011   El Intercambio en el Noroccidente Prehispánico: La Relación entre la Rama Guadiana de la Tradición Arqueológica Chalchihuites y la Tradición Aztatlán, entre el 600–1300 d.C. Bachelor's thesis, Escuela Nacional de Antropología e Historia, Mexico City.
2017   De la Lámina Delgada al Agente Humano: Una Revisión de la Interacción Aztatlán-Chalchihuites. *Arqueología* 54:60–74.
2018   Vivir entre los Tres Ríos: Arqueología de Paisaje en el Valle de Culiacán. Master's thesis, Instituto de Investigaciones Filológicas, Universidad Nacional Autónoma de México, Mexico City.

Vidal Aldana, Cinthya I., and Emmanuel A. Gómez Ambríz
2017   Siguiendo el Camino del Sol: Pensamientos Cosmogónicos Compartidos entre la Costa Sinaloense y el Valle de Guadiana. *Arqueología* 54:28–42.

Villalpando, Elisa, and Randall H. McGuire
2017   Sonoran Pre-Hispanic Traditions. In *The Oxford Handbook of Southwest Archaeology*, edited by Barbara J. Mills and Severin Fowles, pp. 381–395. Oxford University Press, New York.

Villalpando, Elisa, and Randall H. McGuire (editors)
2014   *Building Transnational Archaeologies/Construyendo Arqueologías Transnacionales*. Arizona State Museum Archaeological Series 209, Arizona State Museum, University of Arizona, Tucson.

Villanueva, Gerardo
2004   *Informe Malacológico sobre el Material Arqueozoológico Recuperado en San Felipe Aztatán (Municipio de Tecuala, Nayarit)*. Sección de Biología, Area de Malacología. Archivo Técnico, Dirección de Salvamento Arqueológico. Instituto Nacional de Antropología e Historia, Mexico City.

Vogt, Evon Z.
1964   Ancient Maya and Contemporary Tzotzil Cosmology: A Comment on Some Methodological Problems. *American Antiquity* 30(2):192–195.
1969   *Zinacantan: A Maya Community in the Highlands of Chiapas*. Harvard University Press, Cambridge, MA.

Vogt, Evon Z., and Frank Cancian
1970   Social Integration and the Classic Maya: Some Problems in Haviland's Argument. *American Antiquity* 35(1):101–102.

Von Winning, Hasso
1956   Offerings from a Burial Mound in Coastal Nayarit. *Masterkey* 30:157–170.
1977   Rituals Depicted on Polychrome Ceramics from Nayarit. In *Pre-Columbian Art History: Selected Readings*, edited by Alana Cordy-Collins and Jean Stern, pp. 121–134. Peek Publications, Palo Alto, CA.
1984   Der westmexikanische *equipal*-Stuhl. Ein ethnologish-archäologischer Vergleich. *Indiana* 9:175–187.
1996   *Arte Prehispánico del Occidente de México*, edited by Phil C. Weigand and Eduardo Williams. El Colegio de Michoacán and Secretaría de Cultura de Jalisco, Zamora.

Wallace, Henry D.
2014   Ritual Transformation and Cultural Revitalization: Explaining Hohokam in pre-A.D. 1000 Southeastern Arizona. In *Between Mimbres and Hohokam: Exploring the Archaeology and History of Southeastern Arizona and Southwestern New Mexico*, edited by Henry D. Wallace, pp. 433–499. Archaeology Southwest, Anthropological Papers No. 52, Tucson.

Wallace, Henry D. (editor)
2014   *Between Mimbres and Hohokam: Exploring the Archaeology and History of Southeastern Arizona and Southwestern New Mexico*. Archaeology Southwest, Anthropological Papers No. 52, Tucson.

Wallerstein, Immanuel
1974   *The Modern World System I: Capitalist Agriculture and the Origins of the European World-Economy in the Sixteenth Century*. Academic Press, New York.
1979   *The Modern World System II: Mercantilism and the Consolidation of the European World-Economy, 1600–1750*. Academic Press, New York.

Ware, John A.
2014   *A Pueblo Social History: Kinship, Sodality, and Community in the Northern Southwest*. School for Advanced Research Press, Santa Fe.

Washburn, Dorothy K., William N. Washburn, and Petia A. Shipkova
2011   The Prehistoric Drug Trade: Widespread Consumption of Cacao in Ancestral Pueblo and Hohokam Communities in the American Southwest. *Journal of Archaeological Science* 38(7):1634–1640.

Watson, Adam, Stephen Plog, Brendan J. Culleton, Patricia A. Gilman, Steven A. LeBlanc, Peter M. Whiteley, Santiago Claramunt, and Douglas J. Kennett.
2015   Early Procurement of Scarlet Macaws and the Emergence of Social Complexity in Chaco Canyon, NM. *Proceedings of the National Academy of Sciences of the United States of America* 112:8238–8243.

Watson, James T., and Cristina García
2016   Postclassic Expansion of Mesoamerican Biocultural Characteristics into Sonora, Mexico. *Journal of Field Archaeology* 41(2):222–235.

Watson, James T., and Marijke Stoll
2013   Gendered Logistic Mobility among the Earliest Farmers in the Sonoran Desert. *Latin American Antiquity* 24(4):433–450.

Webb, Malcolm C.
1978   The Significance of the "Epiclassic" Period in Mesoamerican Prehistory. In *Cultural Continuity in Mesoamerica*, edited by David L. Browman, pp. 155–178. Mouton, The Hague.

Weber, Max
1977   *Estructuras de Poder*. Translation by Rufino Arar. Editorial La Pléyade, Buenos Aires.

Webster, Laurie D., and Maxine E. McBrinn (editors)
2008   *Archaeology Without Borders: Contact, Commerce, and Change in the U.S. Southwest and Northwestern Mexico*. University Press of Colorado, Boulder.

Weigand, Phil C.
1975   Possible References to La Quemada in Huichol Mythology. *Ethnohistory* 22(1):15–20.
1982   Mining and Mineral Trade in Prehispanic Zacatecas.

In *Mining and Mineral Techniques in Ancient Mesoamerica*, edited by Phil C. Weigand and Gretchen Gwynne, pp. 82–134. *Anthropology* 6. Department of Anthropology, State University of New York, Stony Brook.

1989 The Obsidian Mining Complex at La Joya, Jalisco. In *La Obsidiana en Mesoamérica*, edited by Margarita Gaxiola González and John E. Clark, pp. 205–211. Colección Científica, Serie Arqueológica, No. 176, Instituto Nacional de Antropología e Historia, Mexico City.

1993 *Evolución de una Civilización Prehispánica: Arqueología de Jalisco, Nayarit y Zacatecas*. El Colegio de Michoacán, Zamora, Mexico.

1994 *Rerum Novarum*: El Mito de Mexcaltitán como Aztlán. In *Arqueología del Occidente de México*, edited by Eduardo Williams and Robert Novella, pp. 363–381. El Colegio de Michoacán, Zamora.

2008 Turquoise: Formal Economic Interrelationships between Mesoamerica and the North American Southwest. In *Archaeology without Borders: Contact, Commerce and Change in the U.S. Southwest and Northwestern Mexico*, edited by Laurie D. Webster and Maxine E. McBrinn, with Eduardo Gamboa Carrera, pp. 343–353. University Press of Colorado, Boulder.

2013 Archaeology and Ethnohistory of Etzatlán and Its Region. In *Correspondence Analysis and West Mexico Archaeology: Ceramics from the Long-Glasgow Collection*, edited by C. Roger Nance, Jan de Leeuw, Phil C. Weigand, Kathleen Prado, and David S. Verity, pp. 17–66. University of New Mexico Press, Albuquerque.

Weigand, Phil C., Christopher S. Beekman, and Rodrigo Esparza

2008 *La Tradición Teuchitlán*. El Colegio de Michoacán, Zamora, and Secretaria de Cultura del Gobierno del Estado de Jalisco, Guadalajara.

Weigand, Phil C., and Acelia García de Weigand

2001 A Macroeconomic Study of the Relationships between the Ancient Cultures of the American Southwest and Mesoamerica. In *The Road to Aztlan: Art from a Mythic Homeland*, edited by Virginia M. Fields and Victor Zamudio Taylor, pp. 184–195. Los Angeles County Museum of Art, Los Angeles.

Weigand, Phil C., and Garmon Harbottle

1993 The Role of Turquoise in the Ancient Mesoamerican Trade Structure. In *The American Southwest and Mesoamerica: Systems of Prehistoric Exchange*, edited by Jonathon E. Erickson and Timothy G. Baugh, pp. 159–178. Plenum Press, New York.

Weigand, Phil C., Garman Harbottle, and Edward V. Sayre

1977 Turquoise Sources and Source Analysis: Mesoamerica and the Southwestern U.S.A. In *Exchange Systems in Prehistory*, edited by Timothy K. Earle and Jonathon E. Ericson, pp. 15–34. Academic Press, New York.

Weik, T. M.

2014 The Archaeology of Ethnogenesis. *Annual Review of Anthropology* 43:291–305.

Weiner, Annette B.

1992 *Inalienable Possessions: The Paradox of Keeping-While-Giving*. University of California Press, Berkeley.

Weiner, Robert S.

2015 A Sensory Approach to Exotica, Ritual Practice, and Cosmology at Chaco Canyon. *Kiva* 81(3–4):220–246.

Whalen, Michael E.

2013 Wealth, Status, Ritual, and Marine Shell at Casas Grandes, Chihuahua, Mexico. *American Antiquity* 78:624–639.

Whalen, Michael E., and Paul E. Minnis

2001 *Casas Grandes and Its Hinterland: Prehistoric Regional Organization in Northwest Mexico*. University of Arizona Press, Tucson.

2003 The Local and the Distant in the Origin of Casas Grandes, Chihuahua, Mexico. *American Antiquity* 68(2):314–332.

2009 *The Neighbors of Casas Grandes: Excavating Medio Period Communities of Northwest Chihuahua, Mexico*. University of Arizona Press, Tucson.

Whiteley, Peter M. (editor)

2018 *Puebloan Societies: Homology and Heterogeneity in Time and Space*. School for Advanced Research Press, Santa Fe.

Wilcox, David R.

1986a A Historical Analysis of the Problem of Southwestern-Mesoamerican Connections. In *Ripples in the Chichimec Sea: New Considerations of Southwestern-Mesoamerican Interactions*, edited by Frances J. Mathien and Randall H. McGuire, pp. 9–44. Southern Illinois University Press, Carbondale.

1986b The Tepiman Connection: A Model of Mesoamerican-Southwestern Interaction. In *Ripples in the Chichimec Sea: New Considerations of Southwestern-Mesoamerican Interactions*, edited by Frances J. Mathien and Randall H. McGuire, pp. 135–154. Southern Illinois University Press, Carbondale.

1991 The Mesoamerican Ballgame in the American Southwest. In *The Mesoamerican Ballgame*, edited by Vernon L. Scarborough and David R. Wilcox, pp. 101–125. University of Arizona Press, Tucson.

2000 El Nexo Tepiman: Un Modelo de Interacción entre Mesoamérica y el Suroeste Norteamericana. *Relaciones, Estudios de Historia y Sociedad* 21(82):59–84. El Colegio de Michoacán, Zamora, Michoacán, Mexico.

Wilcox, David R., and Charles Sternberg

1983 *Hohokam Ballcourts and their Interpretation*. Arizona State Museum Archaeological Series No. 160. University of Arizona, Tucson.

Wilcox, David R., Phil C. Weigand, J. Scott Wood, and Jerry B. Howard

2008 Ancient Cultural Interplay of the American Southwest in the Mexican Northwest. *Journal of the Southwest* 50(2):103–206.

Wilkerson, Jeffrey K.

2001 Gulf Lowlands. In *Archaeology of Ancient Mexico and Central America: An Encyclopedia*, edited by

Susan T. Evans and David L. Webster, pp. 324–334. Garland, New York.

Willey, Gordon R., and Phillip Phillips
2001   *Method and Theory in American Archaeology.* University of Alabama Press, Tuscaloosa.

Willey, Gordon R., and Jeremy A. Sabloff
1993   *A History of American Archaeology*, 3rd edition. W. H. Freeman and Company, New York.

Williams, Eduardo
2020   *Ancient West Mexico in the Mesoamerican Ecumene.* Archaeopress, Oxford, UK.

Williams, Eduardo, Phil C. Weigand, Lorenza López Mestas, and David C. Grove (editors)
2005   *El Antiguo Occidente de México: Nuevas Perspectivas sobre el Pasado Prehispánico.* El Colegio de Michoacán, Zamora.

Wiseman, Regge N.
2019   *Pruning the Jornada Branch Mogollon: Changing Perspectives—Prehistory of Southeastern New Mexico.* Secord Books, Albuquerque.

Wolf, Eric R.
1957   Closed Corporate Communities in Mesoamerica and Java. *Southwestern Journal of Anthropology* 13(1):1–18.
1959   *Sons of the Shaking Earth: The People of Mexico and Guatemala—Their Land, History, and Culture.* University of Chicago Press, Chicago.

Wolynec, Renata B., Terry Block, Andrew Anderson, and Betty Davis
1968   Juana Gómez. In *Archaeological Reconnaissance and Excavations in the Marismas Nacionales, Sinaloa and Nayarit, Mexico. West Mexican Prehistory*, edited by Stuart D. Scott, Pt. 2:12–21. Mimeograph, Department of Anthropology, State University of New York, Buffalo.

Woosley, Anne I., and John C. Ravesloot (editors)
1993   *Culture and Contact: Charles C. Di Peso's Gran Chichimeca.* Amerind Foundation, Dragoon, AZ, and University of New Mexico Press, Albuquerque.

Wren, Linnea, Cynthia Kristan-Graham, Travis Nygard, and Kaylee Spencer (editors)
2017   *Landscapes of the Itza: Archaeology and Art History of Chichen Itza and Neighboring Sites.* University Press of Florida, Gainesville.

Wright, Aaron M.
2014   *Religion on the Rocks: Hohokam Rock Art, Ritual Practice, and Social Transformation.* University of Utah Press, Salt Lake City.
2021   The Iconography of Connectivity between the Hohokam World and Its Southern Neighbors. *Journal of Archaeological Research* 30:117–167.

Xelhuantzi, Susana
2003   *Informe sobre el Análisis de Restos Orgánicos Procedentes de San Felipe Aztatán, Municipio de Tecuala, Nayarit. Laboratorio de Paleobotánica.* Archivo Técnico, Subdirección de Laboratorios y Apoyo Académico. Instituto Nacional de Antropología e Historia, Mexico City.

Yáñez Rosales, Rosa H.
2001   *Rostro, Palabra y Memoria Indígenas: El Occidente de México: 1524–1816.* Centro de Investigaciones y Estudios Superiores en Antropología Social, Mexico City.

Young, M. J.
2000   The Interconnection Between Western Puebloan and Mesoamerican Ideology/Cosmology. In *Kachinas in the Pueblo World*, edited by Polly Schaafsma, pp. 107–120. University of Utah Press, Salt Lake City.

Zavala Moynahan, Bridget, and Ana I. Murguía Hernández
2013   *Proyecto Arqueológico Sextín "Temporada de Campo 2010."* Archivo Técnico de la Coordinación Nacional de Arqueología, Instituto Nacional de Antropología e Historia, Mexico City.

Zavaleta Lucido, Marcus T., and Rosa M. Flores Ramírez
2016   The Shaft Tombs of Parcelas 12, 19, and 25 and Their Inhabitants: Funerary Considerations on Recent Archaeological Finds in Colima. In *Shaft Tombs and Figures in West Mexican Society: A Reassessment*, edited by Christopher S. Beekman and Robert B. Pickering, pp. 55–71. Gilcrease Ancient Americas Series, Gilcrease Museum, Tulsa, OK.

Zborover, Danny, and Peter C. Kroefges (editors)
2015   *Bridging the Gaps: Integrating Archaeology and History in Oaxaca, Mexico.* University Press of Colorado, Boulder.

Zeitlin, Judith F.
1993   The Politics of Classic-Period Ritual Interaction: Iconography of the Ballgame Cult in Coastal Oaxaca. *Ancient Mesoamerica* 4(1):121–140.

Zepeda García-Moreno, Gabriela
1994   *Ixtlán: Ciudad del Viento.* Instituto Nacional de Antropología e Historia, Nayarit, and Grupo ICA, Tepic.

Zepeda García-Moreno, Gabriela, and Noé Fajardo
1999   *Puntos Básicos para Elaborar el Anteproyecto de Declaratoria de la Zona Arqueológica de Huachotita, Municipio de Tecuala. Expediente Técnico. Proyecto INAH-Procede (5ª Etapa).* Archivo Técnico de la Sección de Arqueología, Centro Instituto Nacional de Antropología e Historia, Nayarit, Tepic.

Zepeda García-Moreno, Gabriela, and Carlos Lazarini
1994   *Proyecto Rescate Arqueológico Autopista Ixtlán-Tepic. Resultados de la Segunda Etapa de Excavación: Área de Panteones, Tomo II.* Archivo Técnico de la Sección de Arqueología, Centro Instituto Nacional de Antropología e Historia, Nayarit, Tepic.

Zingg, Robert M.
1938   *The Huichols: Primitive Artists.* G. E. Stechert, New York.
2004   *Huichol Mythology*, edited by Jay C. Fikes, Phil C. Weigand, and Acelia García de Weigand. University of Arizona Press, Tucson.

Žižek, Slavoj
2003   Introducción: El Espectro de la Ideología. Translation by Marianna Podetti. In *Ideología, un Mapa de la Cuestión*, edited by Slavoj Zizek, pp. 7–42. Fondo de Cultura Económica, Siglo XXI, Buenos Aires, Ar.

Contributors

CHRISTOPHER S. BEEKMAN is professor of anthropology at the University of Colorado Denver.

JOSÉ CARLOS BELTRÁN MEDINA is professor of scientific research at the Centro Instituto Nacional de Antropología e Historia in Nayarit, Mexico.

JOHN P. CARPENTER is research professor at the Centro Instituto Nacional de Antropología e Historia in Sonora, Mexico.

PHILIP E. (TED) COYLE is professor of anthropology and sociology at Western Carolina University in Cullowhee, North Carolina.

CRISTINA GARCÍA MORENO is a full-time researcher at the Centro Instituto Nacional de Antropología e Historia in Sonora, Mexico.

MAURICIO GARDUÑO AMBRIZ is an investigator at the Centro Instituto Nacional de Antropología e Historia in Nayarit, Mexico.

LISSANDRA GONZÁLEZ is an archaeologist at the Centro Instituto Nacional de Antropología e Historia in Michoacán, Mexico.

MARÍA DE LOURDES GONZÁLEZ BARAJAS is an archaeologist at the Centro Instituto Nacional de Antropología e Historia in Nayarit, Mexico.

LUIS ALFONSO GRAVE TIRADO is a member of the Sistema Nacional de Investigadores (SNI) and an investigator in the Centro Instituto Nacional de Antropología e Historia and the Museo Arqueológico de Mazatlán in Sinaloa, Mexico.

MICHAEL D. MATHIOWETZ is a research specialist at the Getty Research Institute in Los Angeles, California.

JUAN JORGE MORALES MONROY is a collaborator and archaeologist at the Instituto Vallartense de Cultura in Puerto Vallarta, Jalisco, Mexico.

JOSEPH B. MOUNTJOY is research professor at the Universidad de Guadalajara Centro Universitario de la Costa in Puerto Vallarta, Jalisco, Mexico.

DANIELLE PHELPS is a grant writer for the Jewish Family & Children's Services in southern Arizona.

DANIEL E. PIERCE is a research archaeologist in the Bernice S. Warren Center for Archaeological Research at Missouri State University in Springfield.

JOHN M. D. POHL is adjunct professor of art history at the University of California Los Angeles and lecturer in anthropology at California State University Los Angeles.

JOSÉ LUIS PUNZO DÍAZ is a Level 1 member of the Sistema Nacional de Investigadores (SNI) and a researcher in archaeology for the Centro Instituto Nacional de Antropología e Historia in Michoacán, Mexico.

SUSANA RAMÍREZ URREA is Director of the Laboratory of Archaeology "Otto Schöndube Baumbach" and associate professor in the Departmento de Estudios Mesoamericanos y Mexicanos at the Universidad de Guadalajara, in Guadalajara, Jalisco, Mexico.

GUADALUPE SÁNCHEZ is a research associate at the Centro Instituto Nacional de Antropología e Historia in Sonora, Mexico.

LAURA SOLAR VALVERDE is a full-time researcher at the Centro Instituto Nacional de Antropología e Historia in Zacatecas, Mexico.

JORGE ARTURO TALAVERA GONZÁLEZ is professor of scientific research in the Department of Physical Anthropology of the Instituto Nacional de Antropología e Historia and Coordinator of the Bioarchaeology Section in the Department of Salvage Archaeology of the Instituto Nacional de Antropología e Historia in Mexico City.

CINTHYA ISABEL VIDAL ALDANA is a PhD candidate in the Doctorado de Estudios Mesoamericanos program at the Universidad Nacional Autónoma de México and an associate archaeologist at the Centro Instituto Nacional de Antropología e Historia in Durango, Mexico.

JAMES T. WATSON is Associate Director and Curator of Bioarchaeology at the Arizona State Museum and Professor of Anthropology (School of Anthropology) at the University of Arizona.

Index

Page numbers in *italics* indicate figures.
Page numbers in *italics* followed by *m* indicate maps.
Page numbers in *italics* followed by *t* indicate tables.

Abbeville, Sanson d': *America Septentrional*, 41
Acaponeta division, of Aztatlán Complex, 44, 244–47
agriculture: as Aztatlán Complex link, 17; and climate, 244; construction for, 50; and environmental changes, 141–42; increase in practice of, 116; landscape affected by, 97, 99; nobility controlling, 24, 28; present-day, 229; rituals for, 35, 51, 109–10, 207, 209; sedentary, 150–51; success of, 99
Ahuacatlán site, 193–94, 195, 206, 244
Alcocer, Paulina, 232
Alta Vista (Zacatecas), and Alta Vista phase, 58, 183, 212, 215, 224
Amapa Municipal Museum, 175
Amapa phase, 103, 109, 170
Amapa site, *216m*; about, 174–76, 242; artifacts of, 44–45, 188, 189, *213*, 215, *217*, 223, 224, 244; and Aztatlán occupation, 44–46, 54, 108; and cosmology, 220
America Septentrional (Abbeville), 41
Anales del Museo Mexicano, 241
Ancestral Pueblos, 19, 73, 76, 79
animals: buried with humans, 46–47, 90; as food, 51, 109, 110; as motifs, 50, 90, 215, 218, 221, 224; sacrifice of, 23, 209, 218, 233–35
ArcGIS, 160
Archaeological Project of Southern Sonora. *See* PASS
architecture, *11–13*, *101*, *199*; astronomy influencing, 110; of Cerritos phase, 109; domestic, 140–41; of Early Postclassic, 50; funerary, 195–97; importance of, 243; networks influencing, 73; planning of, 171–72; political stratification indicated by, 116–17; public, 175, 245, 249; regional differences in, 87–90; residential, 29, 175; and ritualism, 80; and settlement, 248–49
ArcMap, 160
Arias de Saavedra, Antonio, 117, 209
Arroyo Piedras Azules site, 44, 47, 51, *52*, 53, 58, 215, 218, 250
artifacts, 16, 44, 47, 48, 49, 52, 66, 68, 74, 92, 93, 102, 106, 120, 127–30, 135, 146, 148, 149, 154, 184–86, 202, 211, *213*, *217*, 222, 223, 242
ash, volcanic, 194–95
Average Nearest Neighbor, 160, 162
Aztatlán (term), 41–42, 141
Aztatlán Complex, 17, 23–24, 41, 42–43, 44, 99, 139–43
Aztatlán culture: basis of, 51; ceramics in, 21, 47; complexity of, 99; decline of, 250–51; early, 247–49; expansion of, 58, 249–50; extent of, 53–54; as research topic, 251; rise of, 183; stability of, 229; transitions of, 244–51

Aztatlán-Huasteca network, 225
Aztatlán Mercantile System, 17, 126, 137, 152
Aztatlán network, 53, 61–65, *62m*, 67, 69, 94–95, 244, 250–51
Aztatlán phase, 44, 49–50, 56, 58
Aztatlán phenomenon: about, 1–3; cultural inventory of, 43; diverse approaches to, 14, 23; duration of, 54–58; historical basis for, 41–42; objects associated with, 45, 51, 53; as peripheral, 27; recent information on, 50; sites of, 46; variation within, 42–43
Aztatlán region, *10m*, *30m*, *181m*, *182m*, *208m*
Aztatlán tradition, *94m*; about, 91, 94–95; historical perspective on, 1; identification of, 76; influences on, 77, 79; intraregional interactions of, 85–86; local rituals within, 219; regional interactions of, 14, 17–21, 23, 31, 34, 83–85, 86–91; variations within, 29; views of, 27
Aztec people, 27, 34, 100, 225, 241–42, 246
Aztlán (Aztec home), 100, 241

back-shields/back mirrors, 35, 73, *74*, 75, *75*, 82
ballgames and ballcourts, v, xiii, 45, 49, 51, *52*, 53, 73, 76, 77, 80, 115, 116, 117, 119, 143, 173, 195, 224, 245
banquettes, 104, 196–97, 224
Basurero 1, 104, *105*, 108–9
beads, 43, 46, 49, 50, 104, 124, 142, 155, 156, 175, *201t*, 203, 206, 214, 245
Beals, Ralph, 150
Beekman, Christopher, 1, 24, 25
Bell, Betty, 45–46, 215
bells, metal, *181*, *185*, *186*; analysis of, 185–87; in burials, 175; and cultural interaction, 19–20; distribution of, 49, 76, 189–90; time periods of, 125, 180–82, 183
Beltrán Medina, José C., 20, 244, 245, 248
Benciolini, Maria, 235, 236
Berdan, Frances F., 95
Berg, Phil, 242
Berrojalbiz, Fernando, 125
Black Falls Ruin, 186, 187, 189. *See also* Wupatki site
blades, prismatic: about, 167–68; and Aztatlán culture, 42, 53; fire-damaged, 203, 205; importation of, 19, 170, 172–73; location of, 174; ritualistic use of, 20; sources of obsidian for, 50, 108, 169, 175–76, 178
Boas, Franz, 242
bodies, human, *158t*; dental health indicators in, 157; modification of, 157–59, *158*, *158t*, *159*, 206; position of, 155–56. *See also* burials

295

bones, animal, 46, 51, 90–91, 109, 203
bones, human, 90–91, 153
Bordaz, Jacques, 44–45
Bourdieu, Pierre, 71
bowl bearers, 214–15, 221; *See also* cargo holders; cargo systems; *jicareros*; peyote
bowls, *211*, *213*, *217*, *222*, *234*; in cargo systems, 21, 28, 207, 214–15, 218, 221, 224–27; ceramic, 28, 197–98; effigy, 214–15, 218, 221; in goods exchange, 53; gourd, 21, 214–15, 231–32, 234; portraiture, 207, 215, 218, 221, 225–26; religious use of, 132–33. *See also* god bowls
Brainerd, George, 44–45
Brand, Donald: archaeological identification by, 15, 21, 124; on archaeological sites, 101, 115, 141, 169; on Aztatlán Complex, 141; on ballcourts, 143; concepts developed by, 41–43, 99–100, 230; on connections with past, 229; influences on, 241–43
Braziunas, Thomas F., 139
Britton, Emma, 248
burials, *89*, *156*, *157t*, *161*, *161t*, *200–201t*; animals in, 46–47, 90; artifacts from, 43, 125, 142, 143–45, 175, 193, 197–98, 202–3; as data source, 20, 140; of elites, 79–80; in modified hills, 115–16; spatial analysis of, 160–62; variations in, 89–90, 141, 155–59, 193–94, 195–96, 204–6. *See also* mounds, burial

cabeceras, 14, 83, 94–95, 109. *See also* city-states; *señoríos*
Cabeza de Vaca, Alvar Nuñez, 18–19, 148
Cabrero, Maria T., 140
cacao, 34–35, 62, 82, 218, 247, 248; cultivation zones, *3m*, 15; deposition in landscape ritualism, 225; in feasting, 225; traded to the U.S. Southwest and northwest Mexico, 33, 34–35, 81
Cahita linguistic family, 139, *140m*
Cahitan-speaking groups, 17, 35, 36, 139, 140, 142–43, 150–51. *See also* Mayo people (Yoreme); Opata people; Tahue people; Yaqui people (Yoeme)
calendars, 50, 51, 91, 109–10
Cañón del Molino site, 47, 125, 181, *185*, 187–88, 189. *See also* El Cañón del Molino site
Cantil de las Ánimas site, 221
capital, cultural, 71, 73, 77, 79, 80
carbon dating. *See* radiocarbon dating
cargo holders, 209, 214, 218, 219, 221, 224–26. *See also* bowl bearers; cargo systems; *jicareros*, peyote
cargo systems, 222; about, 207, 225–26; age of, 21; and astronomy, 219–20; ceramics used in, 28, 215, 221; goods exchange in, 225; and *mitotes*, 214–15; stones used in, 224–25
Carpenter, John P.: on Aztatlán organization, 27; on burials, 162, 249; on ceramics dating, 250; on cultural interaction, 18; on dates, 244; and definitions, 23; on exchange systems, 248; on languages, 243; on rituals, 250–51; study area of, 17; on trade areas, 152
Casas Grandes site. *See* Paquimé (Casas Grandes) site
Caseta site, 86, 90–91, *92*, 94, 95, 96
Castañeda, Carlos, 21
Castillo Badillo, Frine, 233
Catholicism, 207, 214, 229

Caxcan people (Caz' Ahmo), *xiv*, *10*, 36, 219, 243, 246, 251
Ceboruco volcano. *See* Volcán Ceboruco
cemeteries, 20, 45, 90, 91, 193, *194*, 195–96, *197*, *199*, 204. *See also* burials; mounds, burial
Central America, *xiv*, 1, 15, 19, 20, 21, 24–25, 26, 32, 33, 41, 61, 63, 64, 65, 69, 73, 76, 81, 226, 247, 250. *See also* Costa Rica; Nicaragua; Panama
centralization, political, 14, 80–81. *See also* decentralization, political
Centro Instituto Nacional de Antropología e Historia, Nayarit, 172
ceramics, *16*, *44*, 47–49, *52*, *54*, *66*, 92, *102*, *106*, 120, 127–30, 132–34t, *135*, *146*, 148, *149t*, 151, 153, 210–11, *212–13*, 214, *217*, *222*. *See also* god bowls
ceramics, Aztatlán culture indicated by, 1, 139–43, 243–44, 249–51
ceramics, codex-style, 15, *16*, 23, 25, 51, 52, 53, 91, 92, 94, 95, 96, *106*, 107, 108, *120*, 185, 210, 221, 226, 250. *See also* codices
ceramics, horizon-style, 76–77, 150
ceramics, in cultural interaction, 17–18, 50, 119, 124–25, 126, 129–33, 145–47, 183, 185, 245–47
ceramics, in domestic life, 104–5
ceramics, in goods exchange, 67, 95
ceramics, in rituals, 2–3, 111, 209
ceramics, Plumbate, 24–25, 43, 50, 65, 104–5, *106*, 240, 246, 249
ceramics, polychrome: as Aztatlán style, 1, 2–3, 42, 64–65; diversity in, 129, 130–32; influences on, 21, 54, 58; status indicted by, 23–24, 28, 77; symbolism of, 24–25; variants of, 86, 91, 95
ceramics, quality of, 41, 51, 53
ceramics, timespan indicated by, 47, 91, 103, 145, 169–70
ceramics, types of: Aguaruto Exterior Incised, 129; Amapa Polychrome, 125; Amapa Red-on-buff, 125; Arivechi Red-on-brown, 147; Autlán Polychrome, 86, 91, 95, 243; Aztatlán Banded Red-on-buff, 46; Aztatlán Polychrome, 2–3, 15, 24, *44*, 46, 53, 58, 77, 79, 95, 145, 221, 243; Aztatlán Red-banded-on-buff, 49; Aztatlán Red-on-buff, 47, 144; Aztatlán ware, 42, 43, 44, 51, 53, 101, 128, 129, 141, 155; Babícora, 155; Babícora Polychrome, 147; Band-incised-buff, 46; Black and White-on-red, 198; Black-banded Engraved, 129; Black-on-buff, 42, 141; Botadero Black-on-buff, 215, 220; Botadero Incised, 91, 125, 131; Botadero Red-on-white, 220; Brown-on-cream Engraved, 125; Carretas Polychrome, 151; Cerritos Polychrome, 91, 215, 220; Cerro Izábal, 129, 131; Chametla Polychrome, 125; Chanal Polychrome, 243; Chapala Red-on-brown, 54; Chihuahuan polychromes, 147; Cholula Polychrome, 25, 226, 246, 250; Citala Polychrome, 221; Cocoyolitos Polychrome, 141; Cocoyotla Black-on-natural Incised, 246–47; Cojumatlán Polychrome, 218, 220; Cuaxiloa Matte, 247; Culhuacan Black-on-orange, 249; Culiacán Dun, 129; Culiacán Polychrome, 129; El Taste Polychrome, 129, 131; El Taste Red-on-cream, 107; El Taste Satin, 129, 131, 132; Gavilán Polychrome, 25; Guasave Red, 145, 155; Guasave Red-on-brown, 155; Guasave Red-on-buff, 131, 145, 147; Huatabampo Brown, 155; Huatabampo Red, 145, 155; Iguanas Polychrome, *16*, 107, 129, 131, 215, 220, 221; Isla de Sacrificios White-on-cream,

245–46; Ixcuintla Polychrome, 129, 215, 220; Madera Black-on-red, 151; Mangos Polychrome, 215, 220; Middle Chametla Polychrome, 129, 131; Middle Chametla Polychrome Engraved, 54, 129, 131; Navolato Polychrome, 147; Nevería, 136; Ocotlan Red Rim, 247; Orange and Black-on-natural, 125; Otinapa, 124, 133, 136; Plumbate, 24–25, 43, 65, 240, 246, 249; pseudo-cloisonné, 162, 215; Purple-on-brown, 155; Purple-on-red, 155; Ramos, 151, 155; Red-on-buff, 43, 46, 47, 54, 58, 125, 131, 140, 143, 144, 145, 147, 218, 221; Red-rimmed Decorated, 42, 44, 129, 131; Red-rimmed Utility, 54, 129; Red-rimmed Utility (*Mano colorada* type), 129; San Pedro Polished Red, 247; Santiago Engraved, 220; Santiago Red-on-orange, 215; Santiago White-on-red, 103; Sentispac Polychrome, 129; Sentispac Red-on-buff, 218, 220; Sinaloa Polychrome, 124, 131, 133, 136; Tizapán Polychrome, 220; Tizapán White-on-red, 220; Tohil Plumbate, 47, 50, 51, 104–5; Torre Polychrome, 247; Tuxpan Engraved, 91, 125, 129, 131; Tuxpan Red-on-orange, 147, 215, 220; White and Red-on-cream Engraved, 125; Xicotenco Black-on-orange, 246; Zapotlán Engraved, 55

ceramics, uses of, 49, 90–91, 197–98, 206

ceremonialism, 2, 50, 63, 86, 218, 232, 236–37

ceremonies, 22, 232, 234; about, 236–37; architecture for, 29, 49, 101, 103, 110, 116–17, 119, 143; centers for, 86, 173–74, 195, 214, 232; Christian, 209; continuance of, 227–28, 230; and elders, 233–35; evidence of, 50, 196; features for, 141; funerary, 108, 205; hierarchy of, 231–33; and ontologies, 235–36; synecdoche of, 231–33; unity from, 77. *See also mitotes* (maize festivals)

Cerritos phase, 50–51, 103–4, 110, 215, 220

Cerro de Coamiles. *See* Coamiles site

Cerro de las Cabras, 119

Cerro de las Casitas, 129

Cerro del Huistle site, 181, 183

Cerro del Muerto, 119

Cerro de los Mitotes, 229

Cerro de Teúl site. *See* El Teúl site

Cerro el Calón mound. *See* El Calón site

Cerro Picachos, 221

cháanaka (world) 227, 230–31, 235

Chacalilla site, 19, 167, 169, 173–74, *174m*, 178, 209, 215, 226, 245

Chaco Canyon, 18, *30*, 31, 32, 35, 79, 81, 142

Chacón, Enrique, 148

Chalchihuites culture, 58, 124–25, 129, 133, 137, 183

Chametla site, 42–43, *112m*, 115–17, *116m*, 131–32, 140–41, 142

Chapala Basin site. *See* Lake Chapala

Chavero, Alfredo, 241; *Lienzo de Tlaxcala*, 249

Chichén Itzá site, 73, *74*, 209, 221, 246, 248

Chimalhuacan Confederation, 42

Chinesco cultural complex, *102*, 103, 109, 170, 215

Cholula site, 24–25, 77, 80–81, 246–47, 249–50

Christianity, 21, 207, 209, 214, 229

Cicada Ceremony, 234

cists, funerary, 20, 193, *194*, 195–97, *197–98*, 203, 205, 206

city-states, 15, 24, 73, 75, 76, 79, 80–81, 82, 91, 94–95, 96. *See also cabeceras; señoríos*

Claessen, Henri, 111

Classic period, 45, 58, 83, 103

climate change, 58, 250

Cluster Analysis, 160, *161*, 162

Coamiles site, 45, 110, 170–73, *171m*, *172t*, 178, 213

coastal zones, *3m*, 12; archaeological challenges in, 97, 99–100; and Aztatlán connections, 41–42, 58, 61–65; cultural interaction in, 142–43, 150–51, 155, 162–63; habitation in, 124–26, 129–31, 133, 136–37

codices, 53, 71, *72*, 73, 74–76, *75*, *77*, *78*; *Codex Bodley*, 75, 77; *Codex Borgia*, 53, 65, 74, *210*; *Codex Colombino*, 75, 77; *Codex Mendoza*, 35; *Codex Nuttall*, 65, 71, 72, 75, 78, *210*; *Codex Selden*, 75; *Codex Vienna*, 71, 72, 74; *Florentine*, 117. *See also* ceramics, codex-style

Cojumatlán site, 43, 46, 51, 53, 85, 86, 90, 91, 181, 183, 188, 247, 249

collaboration, 36–37

colonialism, 229

colonization, 41, 50, 51, 109, 125–26

Comala culture, 34, 245

communication systems: and Aztatlán tradition, 15, 24, 85; bowls in, 214–15; and cultural interaction, 61; and goods exchange, 61, 67; networks in, 2; pictographic, 76; religious ideology in, 14

conflict, 113, 120, 245

Contreras, Eduardo, 44

copper, *184*; and Aztatlán connections, 19, 20, 27, 35, 245; artifacts, *74*, *93*, *108*, *149*, *181m*, 181–83, 184, 185, *185*, *186*, 203

Cora people, xiv, *10*, 17, 21, 22, 23, 25, 36, 138, 207, 210, 227, 229, 241, 232. *See also* Náayeri people

core-periphery models, 18, 27, 28, 150

Corona Núñez, José, 43–44

cosmology, 67, 69, 218, 227–28, 229–31, 234, 236

Costa Rica, 226, 245. *See also* Central America

Council of Elders, 214, 225–26

Couoh Hernández, Lourdes, 226

Coyle, Philip E., 23, 248, 251

cremations, 20, 107–8, 155, 193, 194, 195, 205–6

Crónica (Tello), 41–42

Crown, Patricia L., 34–35

Cueva del Maguey site, 125

Culiacán (Sinaloa), 139

Culiacán site, 17, 42–43, 44, 129, 140–43, 146, 148

Culiacán Valley, 128, 129, 131, 133, 137, 139, 142

cultural continuity, 17, 23, 36–37, 150

data, control of, 32–34

dead, and the living, 17, 231, 233–35

death, 20, 107, 136, 218–19

decentralization, political, 27–29, 36, 63, 77, 225

deer, and deer hunting, 19, 23, 50, 51, 52, 90, 99, 109, *201t*, 203, 233, 234, 235–36

de Sahagún, Bernardino, 18

Diguet, M. Leon, 41–42

Di Peso, Charles, 31, 33, 73, 76, 180, 183, 186–87, 189

drought, 244, 250

Durango (Mexico), *13*, *126m*; artifacts in, *127*, 187–88; as Aztatlán area, 47, 53–54, 58; colonization of, 124–26, 130–31, 137

Duverger, Christian, 45

East Plaza complex, 88, 90
École des hautes études en sciences sociales (EHESS), 171
effigies, 20, 25
Ehecatl (god), 43, *213*, 221. *See also* Quetzalcoatl (god)
Ehecatl-Quetzalcoatl (god), 50, *72*
Eight Deer (Lord), 52, 53, 71, *72*, 75, 75–76, 77, *78*
Ekholm, Gordon, 43, 141, 243
El Calón site, 117, *118*, 119, 139, 141
El Cañon del Molino site, 47, 49, 118, 125, 187–88. *See also* Cañón del Molino site
El Cementerio site, *153m*, *157*; about, 152–53,162–63; burials of, 156–60, *157*, *158*, *158t*, *159*, *161*, *161t*, 162; cultural interaction in, 17–18; material culture of, 153, 155
El Chanal site, 70, 92, 95, 182, 243, 244, 247, 251
elders, 214, 225–26, 227–28, 233–36
El Gachupín site, 113, 115
elites: about, 14–15, 79–80; and Aztatlán connections, 230; cultural interaction of, 24, 69, 79, 189; and economic exchanges, 77; funerary customs of, 45, 249; goods exchange of, 51, 110, 152, 248, 250; power of, 91, 94, 95, 183; production oversight of, 20, 53, 247; residences of, 23, 50; and ritual objects, 71, 74–75, 76; social organization of, 85; trade affecting, 142
El Macho site, 117
El Ombligo site, 43, 51, 54, 141, 142, 143–45, 148, 149–50, 250
El Rey Nayar (noble), 25
El Teúl site, 13, 51, 53, 215, 219, 220, 242, 243, 246, 251
El Walamo site, 115, 245
empedrados. *See* pavement
Engerrand, George, 242
Epiclassic period, 63, 103, 193, 195, 206, 215, 246
equinoxes, 50, 110, 209
Escuinapa marshlands, *114m*, 116, 117–19, *118*
ethnogenesis, 36–37
ethnolinguistic regions, *10m*
Evans, Susan Toby, 41

farming. *See* agriculture
felines, 182, 202, 223, 224
fertility, 35, 115, 136, 137, 219, 224, 233, 234, 235, 236
festivals, 21, 51, 110, 113, 119, 120, 123, 227. *See also mitotes* (maize festivals); Wheel Festival (Fiesta de la Rueda)
figurines. *See* Mazapan figurines
fish, as food, 50–51, 108–9
fishing, 110, 117
floods, 171, 244
flowers, 36, 132, 218, 227, 236. *See also* Flower World
Flower World, 35–36, 221, 225, 226, 228–29, 236–37, 248, 249. *See also* flowers
Foote, Leonard J., 46
Formative period, 14, 45, 49, 73, 103, 109, 117, 169, 224, 248
Foster, Michael, 124, 139
Four Corners region, 31–32
Four Jaguar (Lord), 71, *72*, 77
funerary objects, 156, *156t*, 162, 163
Furst, Jill, 219
Furst, Peter, 21, 34

Gálvez, Héctor, 115
Gámez Eternod, Lorena, 50, 170
Gamio, Manuel, 242
Ganot Rodríguez, Jaime, 125
García Moreno, Cristina, 17–18, 247, 249, 250
Garduño Ambriz, Mauricio: concepts developed by, 170, 243; observations by, 14–15, 50, 51, 241, 249, 250, 251; study area of, 23; work of, 45
Gavilán phase, 103, 109, 170, 171, 175, 183, 215
geochemical analyses, 175
geochemical sourcing, 173
Gifford, E. W., 43, 193, 244
Gilman, Patricia A., 225
Glascock, Michael D., 168
Glassow, Michael, 46
glocalization, 27–29
god bowls, 21, 218, 220–21, 224–25. *See also* ceramics, types of
god houses, 214, 220, 221, 222, 223, 224, 225
gold and gold alloys, 19, 20, 25, 27, 35, 46, 71, 73, 76, 91, 92, 95, 138, 180, 182, 185, *186*, 187, 188, 225, 247
gold-disk pectorals: as cargo mirrors, 225
Goldschmidt, Walter, 21
González, Lissandra, 19, 25, 246, 247, 250
González Barajas, Lourdes, 20
Gran Nayar region, 136, *228m*, 233–35; and Aztatlán connections, 23, 34, 36, 207; ceremonies of, 227–28, 236; gods of, 218–19; peoples of, 228–30; and ritualism, 212, 214–15
Grave Tirado, Luis Alfonso: archaeological identification by, 141, 143, 249; concepts developed by, 15, 28, 243, 244, 248; observations by, 246, 251; opinions of, 250; projects of, 139
Great Gambler of Chaco Canyon, 81
great houses, 28, 31, 80
Grosscup, Gordon, 45, 140, 141, 142
Guadiana Valley, 126, 129–31, *129*, *130*, 133, 136
Guasave division, of Aztatlán Complex, 44, 244, 246, 249–50
Guasave periods, 144–45
Guasave site and area (Sinaloa), 17–18, 43, 44, 47, 125, 133, 141, 142, 143–45, 152, 162, 181, 183, 185, 250; artifacts of, 43, 51, 58, 66, 124, 125, *127*, 130, 131, 144–45, 187, 218, 220, 250
Guevara López, Germán, 173
Gulf Coast, *xiv*, 21, 65, 66, 67, *68*, 225, 226, 246
Gutiérrez del Ángel, Arturo, 132
Guzmán Vázquez, Adriana, 221, 232

Ha'atsikan (hero), 209, 235–36
heart extraction, 107–8
Heath-Smith, Cynthia, 64–65, 67, 69, 245
Hernández Sánchez, Gilda, 250
Hers, Marie-Areti, 125
hierarchies, religious. *See* cargo systems
hierarchy, 14, 34, 24, 50, 86, 94, 103, 214, 219, 231–33, 235, 248, 249
Hikuli Neixa (Peyote Dance), 209, 212
Hill, Jane, 35, 228
Historia Tolteca-Chichimeca, 23, 77

Hohokam *v, xiii, 30,* 31, 32, 34, 35, 76, 79, 142, 143, 182, 189. *See also* Black Falls Ruin; Wupatki site
Hosler, Dorothy, 125, 180, 203
Huasteca people, 21, 65, 225, 226
Huatabampo tradition, 143, 144–45, 150, 153
Huehuetéotl (god), 195
Huichol people, *xiv,* 21, 23, 34, 36, 132, 207, 232, 241. *See also* Wixárika people
Huistla site, 46
human figures, *122*
hydraulic systems, 91

Iaillot, H., 41
Ibarra, Francisco, 148
INAH (Instituto Nacional de Antropología e Historia). *See* Instituto Nacional de Antropología e Historia
incense burners, 46, 50
inhumations, 141, 144–45, 155, 196, 205
Instituto Nacional de Antropología e Historia, 45, 47, 99, 109, 169–70
Isla del Macho site, *116m,* 117, 245
Isla de Sacrificios site, *66,* 67, 226
Ixcuintla phase, 45, 50, 99, 107, 109, 110, 171, 215, 220
Ixtapa site, *48,* 49, 54, 245
Ixtlán del Río site, *10m, 11, 213, 223;* about, 1, 29; archaeological excavations of, 43–44; as obsidian source, 170, 172, 173–74, 175–76, 178; significance of, 79
Ixtlán periods, 193, 206
Ixtlán phases, 244

Jala Plinial eruption, 194–95, 205
Jala-Vallarta archaeological project, 20, 193–94
Jalisco (Mexico), 53–54, 58
Jardín Museo, 224
jars, ceramic, *16*
jewelry, 17, 42, 51, 71, 73, 76, 81, 144, 152, *154,* 155, 156, 162, 163, 175, 193, 206, 247
jícaras. See bowls
jicareros, iv, 221. *See also* bowl bearers; cargo holders; cargo systems; peyote
Jiménez, Peter, 51, 53, 241, 249
Johnson, Matthew, 125
Jornada Mogollon culture, 31, 212
Journal of the Southwest, 231–32
Juana Gomez site, 117, *118*

Kelley, Jane, 32
Kelley, J. Charles: archaeological excavations by, 131, 133; concepts developed by, 24, 33, 124, 125–26, 152, 244; discoveries by, 137; investigations by, 44; observations by, 142; projects of, 141; vacillations by, 249
Kelly, Isabel, 42–43, 47, 124, 140–41, 142, 146
kilns, 45, 132
Kindl, Olivia, 132–33, 232

La Coyotera (residential area), 195
La Ferrería site, *13,* 44, 47, 53, 58, 124, 125, *127, 128,* 129–31, 133, *135,* 136, 181, 187, 219, 220

La Guásima site, 50, 103
La Joya site, 19, 45, 50, 53, 108, 170, 172–74, 175–76, 178
Lake Chapala, and Chapala Basin sites: analysis of, 14, 29, 43, 46, 53, 54, 58, 83, 141, 182, 215, 218, 219, 220, 224, 232, 246, 248, 249; comparisons with, 50, 85–86, 90–91, 94–95
Lake Pátzcuaro, 183, 189. *See also* Pátzcuaro Basin
La Limonera site, 115
La Montosa (mound), 103, 109–10
landscape ritualism, 21, 212, 221, 225, 226
La Peña site, 14, 50, 51, 53, 85–86, 87–91, *88, 89, 92, 93,* 94, 96, *211,* 218, 220, 224
La Pitayera (cemetery), 20–21, 193, *194,* 195–96, *197, 198, 199, 200–201t, 202, 204*
La Quemada, 215, 224, 225
Las Humedades site, 125, 129, 133
Las Joyas phase, 58
Las Navajas volcano. *See* Volcán las Navajas
Late Postclassic International Style, 2, 15, 20, 21, 24, 25, 26, 28, 76–77, 185
La Viuda site, 143, 145–46, *147,* 148, 149
Law of Monotonic Decrement, 178
Leach, Edmund, 230
Levine, Daniel, 45
Lienzo de Tlaxcala (Chavero), 249
Lira Larios, Regina, 233
Lister, Robert, 43
lithics, 169, 174, 175, 203, 206
living, and the dead, 17, 231, 233–35
Loma Cecyten (platform), 104
Loma de la Cruz (mound), 100, 101, *101,* 103, 104, 107, 109–10
Loma de Ramírez site, 115–16
Loma San Gabriel culture, 124, 142, 143
looting, 44, 47, 49, 70, 117, 125, 145, 187, 196, 242
Lumholtz, Carl, 21, 224

macaws, scarlet, 21, 32, 33, 34, 35, 73, 225, 226
Magriñá, Laura, 232–33
maize, 20, 21, 36, 58, 99, 104, 108, 110, 139, 141, 143, 207, 209, 212, 214, 219, 226. *See also mitotes* (maize festivals)
malacology, 108
Manzanilla, Rubén, 145
Mapa de Teozacoalco, 74
Mapas de Cuauhtinchan, 23, 77
marismas de Escuinapa. *See* Escuinapa marshlands
Marismas de Mazatlán, 113, 115
Marismas Nacionales, *3,* 46–47, 109, 133, 136, 140–41, 163, 173, 241, 244–45
Marismas people, 139
marriages, 3, 17, 18, 25, 29, 76, 77, 79, 248; bridewealth, 82; dowry, 82
Martínez, Juan: *Portulano de las Costas Occidentales,* 41
masks, in religion, 19, 43, 62, 107, 141, 143, 144, 145, 162, *186,* 188, 203, 224, 235
Mason, J. Alden, 124, 212, 242
Matanchén complex, 139
material culture, 92–93, *102, 104, 106, 222;* in cemeteries, 153, 155, 162; coastal, 124–25; local production of, 163

Mathiowetz, Michael D.: concepts developed by, 28, 230, 236–37, 241, 244, 246, 248; observations by, 21, 243; study area of, 228–29
Matus, Juan, 23
Maya culture and people, *13m*, 18, 21, 24, 26, 35, 51, 54, 64, 73–74, 209, *210*, 225, 226, 242, 243, 245
Mayo people (Yoreme), 17, 36, 145, 150. *See also* Cahitan-speaking groups
Mazapan figurines, *49*, *106*, *202*, *242*; about, 20; Aztatlán connection of, 15, 43–44, 65, 67, 76, 246, 247; in burials, 198, 202, 203; conflict revealed by, 120
McCafferty, Geoffrey, 250
McGuire, Randall, 32
Medio-period, 31, 33, 34, 183, 187, 188, 189
Meighan, Clement, 45, 46, 175, 242
Mesa del Nayar, *13*, 22, 136, 209, 218, 248
Mesoamerica, 1, *2m*, *4–9t*, *26m*, 29, 31–37, 142–43, 150–51, 152
Mesoamericanization, 183, 185, 189
metallurgy, 14, 15, 25, 53, 109, 189, 190, 193, 247, 250; beginnings of, 19–20, 76, 95; cultural interaction in, 65, 225, 245; development of, 110; time periods of, 180–83
metal objects, 19, 20, 41, 43, 46, 47, 49, 50, 51, 53, 62, 65, 68, 70, 81, 90, 95, 108, 110, *181m*, *184*, 185–89, *186*, 195, 243, 246, 250. *See also* copper; gold and gold alloys
Mexicanero people (Náhuat), *xiv*, 207, 212
Mexico, *62m*
Mexico, Central, 84, 241, 242–43, 247, 249, 250
Mexico, North, *2m*, 29, 31–35, 81, 180, 182–83, 190
Mexico, Northwest, *4–9t*, *30m*, *208m*, 250; and Aztatlán connections, 83, 141, 251; cultural interaction in, 150–51, 243; and United States southwest, 29, 31–36, 139
Mexico, West, *84m*; and Aztatlán connections, 1; cultural interaction in, 24–25, 27, 152–53, 162–63; and Mesoamerica, 242–43; obsidian in, 167–68, 179; and United States southwest, 33–35, 150–51
Michoacán (Mexico), 43, 54, 180, 182–83, 186–90, 250
Mictlantecuhtli (death god), 34, 43, 49, 50, 107–8, 218
Mimbres region, 18, 30, 34, 35, 30, 31, 73, 183, 212
Mimbres societies and traditions, 31, 207, 225, 226
mirrors, 14, 35, 73–76, *74–75*, 81, 82, 225, 236
Mitla site, 29, 73, 79
mitotes (maize festivals): about, 21, 207, 225; and Aztatlán connections, 119; and cargo system, 214–15, 219, 221; and ceremonies, 232–33, 235; and ritualism, 207, 209, 212
Mixteca-Puebla peoples: and Aztatlán connections, 41, 69, 246, 249–50; ceramic styles of, 65; influence of, 43, 119; networks of, 141–42
Mixtec people: and Aztatlán connections, 53, 250; cultural capital of, 77, 79; expansionism of, 20; influence of, 65; intermarriages with, 15; and Nahua, 25, 27–29; networks of, 73, 80; nobility of, 17; objects representative of, 71, 73–76; skeletal imagery of, 219
Mixtec-Zapotec traditions, 73–77, 79–82
Mochicahui site, 53, 143, 145, *146*, 147, 148, 218, 220
Moctezuma Ilhuicamina, 225
Mogollon culture, *xiii*, *30*, 31, 73, 143
Mololoa culture, 193–94, 206
Morales Monroy, Juan Jorge, 20

mounds, *100m*, 169, 174–75
mounds, burial, *147m*, *156*, *199*; burial distribution in, 160, 162–63; funerary customs indicated by, 43, 46–47, 143–45, 195–97; goods exchange indicated by, 17–18, 152–53; and solar observation, 209
mounds, house, 140–41, 146
mounds, platform, 45, 49, 73, 79–80
mounds, pyramidal, *11*, 100–101, 103, 115–16, 117, 139
mounds, shell, 115, 117, *118*
mounds, solar, 209, 226
Mountjoy, Joseph: archaeological identification by, 173; concepts developed by, 23, 94, 152, 247; maps of, 249; observations by, 1, 21, 139, 241, 242, 250
mummies, 17, 25, 28, 71, 76, 79, 209
MURR (University of Missouri Research Reactor), 108, 168, 169, 179
Museo Comunitario de Chametla, 120
Museo Comunitario de Compostela, 224
Museo del Estado de Michoacán, 180, 187
Museo Nacional de Antropología, 187
Museo Regional de Michoacán, 180, 188
Museo Regional de Nayarit, 168, 224
music, 63, 235
Myerhoff, Barbara, 21, 34

NAA (Neutron Activation Analysis), 50, 108, 173
Náayeri people: cargo system of, 207, 226; and centralized authority, 248; ceremonies of, 227–29; gods of, 212, 219; heritage of, 251; past connected with, 229–30; religious practices of, 209, 214; worldview of, 231–36
Nahua-Mixteca style. *See* Late Postclassic International Style
Nahua people, 2, *10*, 15, 17, 24, 25, 27–29, 71, 73, 77, 79, 80, 81, 242
Nahuatl language, 14, 26, 42, 71, 73, 79, 117, 229, 242, 243, 247, 251
námiche (pattern), 231, 232–33, *232*, 237
National Science Foundation, 46, 179, 242
Nayarit (Mexico), *13*, 22; and Aztatlán connections, 41–42, 43, 44–47, 49–51, 53–54, 58; geography of, 97, 99
Nelson, Richard, 152
Neo-Volcanic Axis, 194, 244
Neumann, George K., 157–58
Neurath, Johannes, 232, 234–35
Neutron Activation Analysis, 50, 108
Nicaragua, 226, 245, 246, 247. *See also* Central America
Nicholson, Henry B., 46
Nine Grass (Lady), 28, 75–76
Nine Wind. *See* Quetzalcoatl (god)
noble class: control by, 15, 17, 28; and cultural interaction, 25, 73, 79; and decentralization, 29; and gifts exchange, 71; and goods exchange, 19, 23–24, 27; hierarchies in, 23–24, 28; ritual objects of, 74, 76, 77; role of, 14
North Acropolis, 110: at Coamiles, 110; at San Felipe Aztatán, 50
Nuño de Guzmán, 23, 41–42, 229, 244

obsidian, 167–79; about, 19, 167–68, 176, 178–79; analysis of, 168–69; as archaeological evidence, 203, 246; control of,

44, 53; distribution of, *168m*, 169–76, *172*, *176*; importance of declining, 250; sources of, 45, 108, *177*, 195, 206; uses of, 20–21, 42–43, 50, 155
O'dam people, *xiv*, *10*, 36, 142, 207, 209. *See also* Tepehuan people
offerings, 90, *200–201t*, 205, 218, 232
Ohnersorgen, Michael, 173, 215, 226
ollas, 42, 104, 141, 198, 205
Ónavas Valley, 17, 152, 155, 160, 162, 163, 250
One Death (sun god), 71, *72*, *210*
ontologies, 21, 36, 231, 235–37, 243
Opata people, 17, 19, 36, 139, 150–51. *See also* Cahitan-speaking groups
Ortega, José, 209
Ortelius, Abraham, *Teatrum Orbis Terrarum*, 41, 69, 99
Outlier Analysis, 160, *161*, 162

Pacific Coastal Plain, 97, 124, 126, 136, 247
PAMSS (*Proyecto Arqueológico Marismas del Sur de Sinaloa*), 117
Panama: Gran Coclé, 226. *See also* Central America
Pantecatl, Francisco, 42, 229
Panzacola site, 117
Paquimé (Casas Grandes) site: about, *30*, 31, 139, 142, 148, 151, 180, 185, 225, 226, 229, 244, 248; and cultural interaction, 33–34, 81; in goods exchange, 17–18, 73, 82, 152, 162; metal products from, *74*, 76, 183, *184*, *185*, 186–90; as ritual center, 29
Particle-Induced X-ray Emission (PIXE), 108
PAS (*Proyecto Arqueológico Sextín*), 125
PASS (*Proyecto Arqueológico Sur de Sonora*), 153
Pátzcuaro Basin, 182. *See also* Lake Pátzcuaro
pavement, 44, 50, 103, 104, 140
Pendergast, David M., 185, 187
Peñitas site, 44–45, 53, 54, 181, *211*, 215, 220
Peripheral Coastal Lowlands, 63, *64m*
Peschard Fernández, Alejandro, 41, 47, 125
petroglyphs, 43, 45, 115, *121*, 171, 173, 194, 209, *210*, 212, 221. *See also* rock art
petrography, 17, 126, 129, *130*, 131, 132, 137
peyote, 23, 209, 212, 225; *peyotero*, 209, 224
Phelps, Danielle, 17
PIACOD (*Proyecto de Investigaciones Arqueológicas del Área Centro Oeste de Durango*), 125
pictographs, 14, 21, 24, 25, 28, 45, 107
Piedra del Danzante, *122*
Pierce, Daniel, 19, 20–21, 108, 248, 250
piercings, 71, 77
Piltzintli (sun god), *16*, 21, 22, 25, 34, 120, 207, 209, *210*, 218, 225, 237, 248
PIXE. *See* Particle-Induced X-ray Emission
Plain of Puebla, 28, 80
Plan de Ayala site, 129
platforms, 87–88, 90, 104, 107, 115, 117, 195–97. *See also* mounds, platform
Plog, Stephen, 32
Pochotero Dome, 195, 203, 206
Pohl, John, 2, 3, 27, 243, 244, 248, 249, 250

polyhedral cores, 169, 170, 175
population decline, 31–32, 115, 175, 244, 250
population growth: causes of, 15, 244–45; consequences of, 14, 50, 76, 116, 175, 178; evidence of, 113, 115, 182
Portulano de las Costas Occidentales (Martínez), 41
Postclassic period, *26m*; artifacts of, 195–96, 206, 215; and Flower World, 248; human organization during, 14; language groups of, 79; and Mesoamerica, 83; migration during, 141–42; phases of, 86; population during, 175; stages of, 90; trade system of, 126
Postclassic period, Early: artifacts of, ceramic, 15, 21, 24, 243; artifacts of, domestic, 103–4; artifacts of, figurine, 20, 202; artifacts of, metal, 65; artifacts of, shell, 203; artifacts of, stone, 172, 178, 246; Aztatlán expansion during, 14, 41, 206; Aztatlán role in, 83–84, 103; burials of, 107–8, 193; cosmology of, 209; government centers of, 99; and Mesoamerica, 2; networks of, 64, 69; phases of, 45, 50, 249
Postclassic period, Late: architecture of, 196; artifacts of, 24, 74–75, 169, 190, 225; and Aztatlán, 81; climate of, 250; communication style during, 25; cultural capital during, 77, 80; exchange systems of, 71; glocalization of, 28; metallurgy during, 65; networks of, 73
Postclassic period, Middle: artifacts of, 65, 103, 172, 178, 190; Aztatlán role in, 83–84; burials of, 107–8; government centers of, 99; industry of, 95; and Mesoamerica, 2; networks of, 64, 69; phases of, 249; significance of, 85–86
Postclassic Religious Style, 65, 69, 245–46, 248, 249, 250
pottery. *See* ceramics
power, 81, 111, 113, 119–20, 123
prestige goods: about, 64; and decentralization, 67; in economic networks, 64, 189; in goods exchange, 150, 152, 162; movement of, 17
Preuss, Konrad Theodor, 21, 224
priest-rulers, 116–17, 119
PROCUMA (*Proyecto de Investigación y Conservación de las Casas en Acantilado de la Cueva del Maguey de Durango*), 125
projectile points, 155
Proyecto Arqueología y Paisaje del Área Centro Sur de Michoacán, 180
Proyecto Arqueológico Marismas del Sur de Sinaloa, 117
Proyecto Arqueológico Sur de Sonora, 153
Proyecto de Investigaciones Arqueológicas del Área Centro Oeste de Durango, 125
Proyecto de Investigación y Conservación de las Casas en Acantilado de la Cueva del Maguey de Durango, 125
Proyecto INAH-Procede en Nayarit, 100–101
Puebloans, 34, 220
Pueblo Bonito site, 73, 79
pumice, 194–95, 203
Punta de Mita site, 51
Punzo Díaz, José Luis, 19, 25, 125, 246, 247, 250
Purépecha culture. *See* Tarascan culture

Quetzalcoatl (god), 34, 43, 77. *See also* Ehecatl (god); Ehecatl-Quetzalcoatl (god); serpent, feathered

radiocarbon dating, 45, 54, *55–57t*, 58, 109, 139, 144, 153, 244, 246
radiometric dating, 109
Rain Mothers, 212, 221
Ramírez Urrea, Susana, 14, 23–24, 243, 244, 245, 248–49, 250
Rancho La Loma, 115
religion, 21, 31–32, 34, 132–33, 209, 226, 248–49. *See also* cargo systems; Flower World
Retes, Miguel, 241
Rincón de Buyubampo site, 143, 145–48
Río Acaponeta, 97, 99, 101, 103, 109, 131, 132
Río Baluarte sites, 97, 113, 115–17, *122*, 131–144
Río Presidio sites, 113, 115, *120*, 143
Río Quelite sites, 113, 115, *121*
Río Yaqui, 17, 142–143, 152–53, 155, 162–63
Río Zacanta, 115
rites and rituals, 22; about, 1, 248–49, 250–51; and astronomy, 109–10; Aztatlán, 20–21, 23–24, 50, 63; and ceramics, 133, 136; continuance of, 227–28, 229–31; funerary, 107, 205–6; Mixtec, 17; natural materials associated with, 132–33; objects associated with, 3, 14–15, 71, 73–77, 79–82; ontological perspective on, 235–37; sacrificial, 107–8, 233–35; spaces for, 87–90, 117, 119. *See also* cargo systems; *mitotes* (maize festivals)
ritualism, 82; centers for, 29; economic aspects of, 28; gods associated with, 209, 218–19; in goods exchange, 2–3, 23, 34–36, 80; and hierarchies, 24, 80; landscape, 212, 221; objects associated with, 21, 25, 74–75, 209, 218–19, 221, 225–26; and sacrifice, 20. *See also* cargo systems; *mitotes* (maize festivals)
rock art, 119, 212, 221. *See also* petroglyphs
Rodríguez Zariñán, Nora, 215
Rojas Martínez Gracida, Araceli, 250
Romero, Javier, 159
royalty, 25, 75–76, 77
Runciman, W.G., 111, 113

sacrifice: animal, 209, 218; human, 53, 107–8, 120, 123, 209, 218; and rituals, 20; self, by animals, 23, 233–35
Sahuaripa (region), *30m*, 31, 151, 226
salt industry, 95, 117, 229
Sánchez, Guadalupe: on artifacts dating, 244, 250; on Aztatlán organization, 27; on burials, 249; on ceramics, 250; on cultural interaction, 18; and definitions, 23; on goods exchanges, 248; on languages, 243; on rituals, 250–51; study area of, 17
San Felipe Aztatán (Nayarit), 97, 100–101, 244
San Felipe Aztatán site, *98m*, *100m*, *101*, *105*, 229, 241; about, 97–105, 99, 109–10; archaeological description of, 103–4; artifacts from, 14–15, *102*, *104*, 104–7, *106*, 169–70, 215; and Aztatlán connections, 42, 45, 50–51, 76, 95, 245; and elites, 23–24, 28; obsidian at, 19, 108, 167–72, 176, 178
San Gregorio site, 85, 86, 90, 94, 218
San Juan de Abajo site, 11
Sauer, Carl: archaeological identification by, 15, 21, 124; on archaeological sites, 101, 115, 141, 169; and Aztatlán (term), 76; on Aztatlán Complex, 141; on ballcourts, 143; concepts developed by, 41–43, 99–100, 229–30; on connections with past, 229; influences on, 241–43
Sayula Basin sites: about, 83; analysis of, 14, 85–86; artifacts from, 54; and Aztatlán connections, 50–51, 54, 58, 63, 83–87, *87m*, 90, 91, 94–96
Sayula Complex, 86, 90, 95, 96
Sayula phase, 50, 54, 58, 86, *87*, 244
Schöndube, Otto, 83
Schroeder site. *See* La Ferrería site
Schwartz, Christopher W., 35
Scott, Stuart, 46, 117, 139
Seler, Eduard, 21, 241
señoríos, 2, 14, 27, 28, 76, 91, 99, 103, 109, 143, 182, 183, 186, 188, 189, 190. *See also cabeceras*; city-states
Sentispac Municipal Museum, 175
septic tank excavation, 50, 104–5
sequences, chronological, *4–9t*
serpent, feathered, *213*; affiliations of, 91; on ceramics, 215, 218, 220–21; as religious theme, 21, 225, 246; role of, 207, 209, 212; on stone, 224. *See also* Quetzalcoatl (god)
serpent, fire, 43, 46, 53, 73, 74, *74*, 91, 110. *See also* Xiuhcoatl (god)
serpent, horned, 207, 212, 226
serpent, turquoise, 73. *See also* Xiuhcoatl (god)
serpent, water, 212
Serrana tradition, 139, 143, 145, *149t*, 150
Shaft Tomb tradition, 83, 195, 196, 197
shamanism, 21, 23, 231, 233–35
shell (material), 155–56, 75, 86, 104, 108, 115, 117, 124, 136, 139, 142, 173, 195; exchange networks, 3, 18, 19, 20, 23, 27, 73, 81, 124, 145, 148, 151, 152, 162, 163, 167, 183, 243; jewelry, 43, 46, 49, 62, 81, 82, 90, 95, 124, 142, 144, 147, *149*, 151, *154*, 155, 156, 162, 163, 193, *201t*, 205, 206, 220; symbolism of, 46, 213, 215; trumpet, 75, 221
shell (species): *Glycymeris gigantea*, 81, 82, 151, 155; *Pinctada mazatlanica* (Mother of Pearl), 51, 104, 151, 155, 156, *201t*, 203; *Spondylus princeps*, 46, 51, 155
shellfish, 15, 116–17
Sierra de Pachuca, 169–70, 172, 175, 178
Sierra Madre Occidental, 14, 31, 63, 67, 125, 137, 143, 150, 183, 194
Sinagua culture, 79, *80*
Sinaloa (Mexico), *112m*, *114m*, *116m*, *144m*; archaeological sites in, *112m*, 117, 119, *144m*; as area of Aztatlán, 53–54, 58; ceramics of, 131–33, *148*; cultural interaction in, 124, 137; microgeographic zones in, *112m*, 113; societies in, 119–20, 123
sites, archaeological, *2m*, *3m*, *10m*, 11, 13, *26m*, *30m*, *40m*, *62m*, *64m*, *84m*, *87m*, 88, 89, *94m*, 98, *100m*, 101, *112m*, *114m*, *116m*, *118m*, 121, 122, *126m*, 135, *144m*, *147m*, *153m*, 156, *168m*, *171m*, *174m*, 177, *181m*, *182m*, 194, *197m*, 198, *199*, 204, *208m*, *216m*, *228m*
Six Monkey (Lady), 75–76
skeletons, 156–57, *157t*, 159, 218–20
Smith, Michael E., 64–65, 67, 69, 95, 245
Smithsonian Institution, 188
social complexity, 27, 113, 117, 178
social networks, *xiii*, 19, 29–32, *30m*, 189

social structures, 83, 85–86
solar deities, *16*, 21, 23, 34, 107–8, 209, *210*, 212, 214, 218, 220, 221, 233, 237. *See also* Piltzintli (sun god); Xochipilli (Flower Prince)
solar ritualism, 35, 36, 50, 105, 107, 110, 136, 207, 209, *210*, 212, 218, 225–26, 245, 249
Solar Valverde, Laura: concepts developed by, 2–3, 224, 243, 246; doubts raised by, 27, 36, 218–19; observations by, 14, 248
solstices, 119, 209
Sonora (Mexico), *144m*
Soustelle, Jacques, 45
Southwest (U.S.). *See* United States, Southwest
Spanish invaders: comparisons by, 76; native allies of, 229; and native practices, 207, 209; observations by, 81, 116; populations encountered by, 17, 36, 142–43, 150–51, 241; resistance to, 23, 36–37; routes of, 148
Spatial Autocorrelation, 160, 162
Spence, Michael, 124–25
spindle whorls, 20, 42, 43, 46, 58, 62, 65, 70, 104, 124–25, 129, 139, 141, 143–143, 147, 162, 175, 193, 197, 203, 205, 241, 243
spirals, in design, 212, 224
stelas, 45, 49, 50, 110, 194, 195
stones, 155, 193, 203, 221, 224–25
stratification, political, 113, 116–17
stratification, social, 19, 50, 77, 113, 168
stratigraphy, 90, 103, 109, 160
Stresser-Péan, Guy, 65
Stuiver, Minze, 139
Sweetman, Rosemary, 46
synecdoche, 231–33, 237

Tahue people, 17, 36, 139, 141, 143, 150, 151, 251. *See also* Cahitan-speaking groups
Talavera González, Jorge Arturo, 20, 145, 226
Tamatsi Eaka Teiwari (wind god), 220–21
Tarascan culture, 20, 29, 36, 54, *181–82m*, 182, 183, 186, 187, 188–90, 225, 250
Teatrum Orbis Terrarum (Ortelius), 41
tecuhtli/tecuhtli system, 15, 17, 28, 77–79, *78*, 80, 82
Tello, Antonio: *Crónica*, 41–42
temper, in ceramics, 131–32, 137, 248
Temple of Quetzalcoatl, *10*, *11*, 77, 223, 224
Teopiltzintli (sun god). *See* Piltzintli (sun god)
tepari/teparite (carved stones), 219, 221, 222–23, 224–25
Tepehuan people, *xiv*, 10, 21, 142, 207, 212, 214. *See also* O'dam people
tepextle altar, 227, *229*
tetecuhtin (lineage head), 14, 15, 17, 24, 80–81
Teuchitlán culture, 224, 245, 248
textiles, 25, 46, 63, 76, 88, 93, 95, 138, 193, 203, 220
tezcacuitlapilli. *See* back-shields/back mirrors
thought, intentional, 23, 233–37
Tilantongo (royal lineage), 28, 71, *72*, 75–76, 77
Tingambato (Tinganio) site, 183, 190
Tizapán el Alto site, 46, 50, 51, 53, 55, 56, 85, 86, 90, 91, 92, 94, 181, 188, 211, *213*, 218, 220
Tlahuizcalpantecuhtli (god), 21, 34, 43, 218, 219, 221

Tlaloc (*tlaloque*, rain god), 34, 35, 46, 47, 50, 51, 90, 91, 117, *121*, 183, 185, *185*, 187, 189, 221
Tollan phase, 246–47, 249
Tolteca-Chichimeca people, 2, 15, 26, 28, 29, 71, 74–75, 77, *78*, 79, 80, 81
Toltec culture: and Aztatlán connections, 15, 24–25, 202, 249; designs of, 43; in goods exchange, 79, 104–5; influence of, 69; legacy of, 42; and obsidian use, 20–21; warrior shields of, 73
Tomatlán site, 47, 181, 187, 188
Tonati (sun kings), 209, 224
topography, 27, 97, 100–101, 103
Totorame people, 136, 207, 251
Tozzer, Alfred, 242
trade routes, 3, 126, 137, 147–48, 171, 180, 189, 225, 244, 247
Transverse Neo-Volcanic Axis, 194, 244
trash, evidence from, 43, 51, 140–41, 146, 155
Trincheras culture, *30*, 162, *185*, 186, 187, 189
Tula site: artifacts of, 73; and Aztatlán, 24, 248, 249; and ceramics trade, 15, 24–25; exchange system of, 79, 246–47; nobility associated with, 76; as Toltec center, 20–21
turkey, 51, 99, 109, 110, 198,
turquoise, 15, 18, 19, 27, 43, 51, 71, 73–74, *74*, 75, 76, 77, 79–80, 82, 110, 144, 151, 152, *154*, 155, 156, 162, 163, 246
Tututepec (city-state), 15, 20, 25, 27, 28, 75, *75*, 77, 79
Tuxcueca site, 86, 91, 94
Tuxpan phase, 54, 142
Two Dog (Lord), 71, *72*
Two Rain (Lord), 77

United States, Southwest, *2m*, *4–9t*, *30m*, *208m*; and agriculture, 17; climate in, 250; cultural connections of, 34–37, 79–80, 150–51, 152, 189; identity formation in, 36; linguistic connections of, 150; and Mesoamerica, 61, 142, 228–29; metal objects found in, 182–83; political power in, 81; trade connections of, 18, 19, 27, 29–34, 225
Universidad Nacional Autónoma de México, 110
University of California, Berkeley, 242
University of California, Los Angeles, 169, 242
University of Missouri Research Reactor, 108, 168, 169. *See also* MURR
urns, funerary: about, 193–94, 197–98; and burial types, 155; changes indicated by, 20; codex-style, 107; networks indicated by, 67, 124–25; rituals indicated by, 205–6; time period indicated by, 115–16
Uto-Aztecan language family, 14, 119, 150, 228, 243, 251

Valdovinos, Margarita, 232, 235–36
VanPool, Christine, 34
VanPool, Todd, 34, 179
Venus (Evening Star), 207, 209, 212, 218–20, 221, 224–25, 234
Venus (Morning Star), 207, 209, *211*, 212, 218–20, 221, 222, 224–25, 227, 234, 235, 237
Venus (planet), 21, 227, 234
Venus (war god), 34, 221, 224
vessels, 66, 92, 106, 120, 127, *135*, 217; about, 119; and Aztatlán connections, 42–43, 45–46; codex-style, 15, 107, 225–26; funerary use of, 145, 205; in goods exchange, 15, 65,

131–33, 136, 137; portraiture, 215; rites portrayed on, 107–8; sequences indicated by, 171
Vidal Aldana, Cinthya, 17, 19, 125, 142, 244, 248
Volcán Ceboruco, 20, 193, 194–95, 196, 203, 205, 206, 244
Volcán las Navajas, *177*; artifacts from, 170, 172–73, 175–76, 203; as obsidian source, 19, 21, 45, 108, 173–74, 176, 178
Von Winning, Hasso, 44–45, 242, 247

Wallerstein, Immanuel, 141, 152
war/warfare: and Venus, 34, 218, 224, 235; nature of, 76, 113, 120, 123, 209, 237. *See also* Venus (war god)
waste sites. *See* Basurero 1
watsiku (ceremonial offering), 232
Watson, James, 17
Weber, Max, 111
Weicker Site, 124
West Plaza complex, 88–89, *89*, 90, 110
Wheel Festival (Fiesta de la Rueda), 227–28, 231, 232, 235, 236
Wilcox, David, *v*, *xiii*, *xiv*, 150
Winters, Howard, 44, 124, 244, 249
Wirikuta (sacred desert), 21, 132, 209, 212, 225, 232, 234–35
Wixárika people, 222; cargo system of, 207, 214, 218; centralized authority avoided by, 233, 248; gods of, 209, 212, 219, 220–21, 224–26; heritage of, 251; and natural materials, 132–33, 136; ritualism of, 233–35; worldview of, 231–33. *See also* Huichol people
Wolf, Eric, 230
World-Systems Theory, 27, 125–26, 137, 141, 152, 241, 248
Wupatki site, 79, 186, 187, 189. *See also* Black Falls Ruin

Xipe Totec (god), 34, 46, 50, *120*, 183, 188, *213*, 221
Xiuhcoatl (god), 43, *44*, 46, 50, 51, 53, 73, 91, 110
Xochipilli (Flower Prince), 24, 25, 28, 29, 35, 207, 221, 226, 248. *See also* Piltzintli (sun god)
Xochipilli-Piltzintli (sun god). *See* Piltzintli (sun god)
xumuabikari (stellar beings), 219–20

Yaqui people (Yoeme), 17, 21, 36, 150. *See also* Cahitan-speaking groups

Zacatecas (Mexico), 13, 58, 219
Zapotec people, 17, 29, 73, 74–75, 76, 79, 81–82
Zavala, Bridget, 125
Zepeda, Gabriela, 194, 244
Zingg, Robert, 21
zoological materials, 108–9
zoomorphs, 188, 202, 203
Zuaque people, 145, 150